HISTORY OF THE SOUTHERN RAILWAY

HISTORY
of the
SOUTHERN RAILWAY

C. F. DENDY MARSHALL
Revised by R. W. KIDNER

LONDON
IAN ALLAN LTD

First revised edition published 1963
Reprinted 1982

ISBN 0 7110 0059 X

© Ian Allan Ltd 1963

Published by Ian Allan Ltd, Shepperton, Surrey;
and printed by R. J. Acford, Chichester, Sussex

Contents

PART I

PAGE

THE EARLIEST RAILWAYS IN THE SOUTH OF ENGLAND

I	THE FIRST LINES IN SURREY	11
II	THE CANTERBURY AND WHITSTABLE RAILWAY	18
III	EARLY RAILWAYS IN THE WEST COUNTRY	26
IV	THE FIRST RAILWAY IN LONDON	30
V	THE LONDON AND CROYDON RAILWAY	38

PART II

THE LONDON AND SOUTH WESTERN RAILWAY

VI	THE LONDON AND SOUTHAMPTON RAILWAY	53
VII	THE SOUTH WESTERN DOWN TO 1849	66
VIII	THE SOUTH WESTERN IN THE 'FIFTIES	87
IX	THE SOUTH WESTERN FROM 1860 TO 1875	105
X	THE SOUTH WESTERN FROM 1876 TO 1900	124
XI	THE SOUTH WESTERN FROM 1901 TO 1922	137
XII	SOUTH WESTERN LOCOMOTIVES	158
XIII	SOUTH WESTERN STEAMER SERVICES	179
XIV	THE ISLE OF WIGHT RAILWAYS	183

PART III

THE LONDON, BRIGHTON AND SOUTH COAST RAILWAY

XV	THE LONDON AND BRIGHTON RAILWAY	193
XVI	THE LONDON, BRIGHTON AND SOUTH COAST DOWN TO 1860	207
XVII	THE LONDON, BRIGHTON AND SOUTH COAST FROM 1861 TO 1880	216
XVIII	THE LONDON, BRIGHTON AND SOUTH COAST FROM 1881 TO 1900	232
XIX	THE LONDON, BRIGHTON AND SOUTH COAST FROM 1901 TO 1922	240
XX	BRIGHTON LOCOMOTIVES DOWN TO 1869	249
XXI	BRIGHTON LOCOMOTIVES, 1870–1922	258
XXII	LONDON, BRIGHTON & SOUTH COAST RAILWAY STEAMER SERVICES	273

PART IV

THE SOUTH EASTERN AND CHATHAM RAILWAY

XXIII THE SOUTH EASTERN RAILWAY DOWN TO 1850 281
XXIV THE SOUTH EASTERN FROM 1851 TO 1875 . 294
XXV THE SOUTH EASTERN FROM 1876 TO 1898 . 308
XXVI SOUTH EASTERN LOCOMOTIVES DOWN TO 1898 316
XXVII THE LONDON, CHATHAM & DOVER RAILWAY
TO 1870 324
XXVIII THE LONDON, CHATHAM & DOVER FROM 1871
TO 1898 337
XXIX LONDON, CHATHAM & DOVER LOCOMOTIVES . 349
XXX THE SOUTH EASTERN & CHATHAM JOINT
COMMITTEE 355
XXXI SOUTH EASTERN & CHATHAM LOCOMOTIVES
1899–1922 371
XXXII SOUTH EASTERN, & CHATHAM AND DOVER
STEAMER SERVICES 375

PART V

THE SOUTHERN RAILWAY

XXXIII THE SOUTHERN UP TO 1934 . . . 391
XXXIV THE SOUTHERN FROM 1935 TO 1939 . . 422
XXXV SOUTHERN RAILWAY LOCOMOTIVES . . 427
XXXVI MANUFACTURING AND REPAIRING WORKS . 440
XXXVII THE SECOND WORLD WAR . . . 448
XXXVIII THE END OF THE SOUTHERN . . . 454
XXXIX THE SOUTHERN ELECTRICS . . . 457
XL SOUTHERN RAILWAY STEAMERS . . . 463
XLI SOUTHERN RAILWAY DOCKS AND HARBOURS . 471
XLII HOW THE SOUTHERN SERVED THE PUBLIC . 480

APPENDICES PAGE
I CHIEF ADMINISTRATORS AND OFFICIALS . 487
II DATES OF LINES OPENED 491
III DATES OF LINES CLOSED 504
IV DATES OF SERVICES ELECTRIFIED . . . 506
V OPENINGS AND CLOSINGS OF STATIONS TO 1948 509
VI STATIONS RENAMED 536
VII BIBLIOGRAPHY 544
INDEX 547

Preface to the Second Edition

WHEN Dendy Marshall's History first appeared in 1937, among the voices acclaiming its magnitude and patient scholarship were a number referring somewhat pointedly to certain errors, and over the years there was built up a tradition among railway historians that 'you can't trust Dendy Marshall'. Close examination by many experts, including H. V. Borley, M. D. Greville, and J. G. Spence, did not in fact show up more than about fifty minor errors, which in a book of 700 pages, compiled in days when historical railway research was less keenly pursued than today, does not amount to a major indictment. Moreover, the author had good reasons for trusting some of his sources which later proved fallacious – indeed one incorrect date was actually given by the South Eastern Chairman to a Company Meeting. Every effort has been made in this second edition to put these mistakes right, but preoccupation with these details must not be allowed to obscure the great value of the work of the original author.

Some of the material which was included in 1937 for policy reasons has been excluded as no longer relevant. The plans, which were a weak feature of the original edition, have been redrawn. The multitude of photographs of seals and emblems have been omitted to make way for pictures of the railways in action.

I am aware that there is a great deal of detailed history about the constituent companies now available which is not in this book. It could not be added without both destroying the character of the original text and making the work impossibly bulky. Where there might be misunderstanding, however, a considerable number of interpolations in the text and some explanatory footnotes have been added.

Dendy Marshall did not always give full dates for events. Rather than incorporate all these in the text, they are covered in a remarkably complete list of openings and closings of lines and stations which appear in the appendices.

R. W. KIDNER,

Lingfield

PART I

THE EARLIEST RAILWAYS IN THE SOUTH OF ENGLAND

I

The First Lines in Surrey

No satisfactory account has ever been written of the earliest history of railways. All those which have come down show that their first introduction was in connection with mines or quarries. As far as is known at present they seem to have originated in Germany.

We do not even know for certain when or where railways first made their appearance in this country. There is undoubted evidence that 'railes' were in use to bring coals from mines on the estates of Sir Francis Willoughby, of Wollaton Hall, Nottinghamshire, by 1597.

Not long afterwards they were adopted in the coal districts of Durham and Northumberland. R. L. Galloway, in his *History of Coal Mining in Great Britain*, states that there were none at the Newcastle collieries in 1600. Nicholas Wood (Treatise on Railroads, 1825) puts the date of their introduction in that neighbourhood as between 1602 and 1649. However that may be, it is certain, on the strength of a book called the *Life of Lord Keeper North* (first published in 1740), that they were by no means uncommon in the district by about 1676. By the time another hundred years had passed there was hardly a colliery without one. But it was not until the nineteenth century that the first railway was made south of the Thames.

In most cases the rails were of wood, sometimes with iron plates nailed on the top, although by the last quarter of the eighteenth century the use of cast iron was gradually coming in. But it was sufficiently of a novelty for the first railway in the South to call itself the 'Surrey Iron Railway'.

All the previous lines referred to above had been private ones, used for the sole benefit of the persons who laid them down. The Surrey Iron Railway opened a new era, in that it was a public railway – the first in the world. Not only so, but it was the first railway company in the world; its predecessors having all, without exception, been merely ancillary to other undertakings, and made by those engaged in the latter for their own purposes.

The project grew out of a proposal made in 1799 for a canal between Croydon and Wandsworth. This proceeding, if it had been carried out, would have involved the canalisation of the River Wandle, on which at that time so many mills and factories were situated, being dependent on it for the power they required, that it was found to be impracticable.

The demand for easier and more rapid conveyance of the products of the district to London, and coal and other necessities therefrom, was so great that an alternative was sought for, and it was decided to have a railway. Accordingly a bill was presented to Parliament in 1801, and received the Royal Assent on 21st May of that year (41 Geo. III, c. 33).

The Act recited at its opening:

Whereas the making and maintaining a railway for the passage of waggons and other carriages from or from near a place called Ram Field in the parish of Wandsworth to or near a place called Pitlake Meadow in the town of Croydon and a collateral branch from the said railway from or near Mitcham Common to or near to a place called Hack Bridge in the parish of Carshalton and the making a dock for barges and other vessels with a lock cut and other works from the said railway at or near Ram Field aforesaid into Wandsworth Creek and thereby to communicate with the river Thames in the said parish of Wandsworth, all in the County of Surrey, will be a great advantage to several considerable manufacturers established in the neighbourhood and to the inhabitants of many towns and places and of a very populous country lying on or near to the line of the said intended railway by opening a cheap and easy communication for the conveyance of coals, corn and other goods, wares and merchandize to and from the metropolis and other places.

The Act proceeded to say that the line was to be called the 'Surrey Iron Railway'. The land required was to be 20 yards in breadth, 'except in those places where it shall be judged necessary for waggons or other carriages to turn, lie or pass each other or where any warehouses, cranes or weighbeams may be erected'. Section 65 provided:

That all persons whomsoever shall have free liberty to use with horses, cattle and carriages the roads ways and passages to be made by virtue of this Act for the purpose of conveying any goods wares merchandise or other things to and from the said railway and docks basin and every part thereof without paying anything for the use of such roads ways and passages and also pass upon and use the said railway with waggons or other carriages and into and use the said dock or basin with vessels properly constructed respectively as hereinbefore mentioned and to employ the said wharfs and quays for loading and unloading such goods and other things upon payment of such rates as shall be demanded by the said company not exceeding the respective sums herein mentioned.

Section 59 covered rates which were for the use of the railway only; other charges were made for traffic 'navigated, carried or conveyed into or out of the said dock or basin'. The railway was looked upon as a kind of highway, which anyone was at liberty to use on payment of certain tolls.

The engineer was William Jessop. His name is an important one in railway history, since he may almost be said to have been the originator of the present form of wheel and rail.

When railways were first introduced into England, during the regime of wooden rails, the wheels were usually formed with flanges as at present; sometimes very exaggerated, according to modern ideas. But when the first rails made entirely of metal came in, they were cast with a vertical lip, the rims of the wheels being flat. This was thought to be an improvement, since ordinary road carts could run on them. This kind of rail was called a 'plate-rail', and the lines usually 'plate-ways'. They were found to accumulate stones and mud, and the flange was inconvenient when they had to cross on a level. It was to meet this last objection that Jessop designed a rail called the 'edge-rail', which was more or less like the modern one, and transferred the flange back to the wheels. This he did at Loughborough in 1789.

Strange to say, Jessop did not use his new system on the Surrey Iron Railway; perhaps he was prevented from doing so by people who did not want new-fangled ideas; anyhow, the old plate-rails were used, some of which have survived.

The line appears to have been double throughout. It was laid on stone blocks, many of which have been used for buildings, rockeries, kerbs, etc., in the neighbourhood. It was opened for traffic on 26th July, 1803. The first capital raised was £55,000, and the cost of construction worked out at £7,000 per mile.

Shortly after its completion a new company was formed to construct a continuation from Croydon southwards, called the 'Croydon, Merstham & Godstone Railway', with an intended branch to Reigate. This new company received its Act in 1803, and the section from Croydon to Merstham was opened to the public on 24th July, 1805. The southern end was at the Greystone Lime Works at Merstham, and that is as far as it ever got.

Returning to the original undertaking, the basin referred to in the Act, with a lock leading to the Thames, is still in existence, being situated a few yards east of the River Wandle, and is the property of the South Eastern Gas Board. Inside the inner gates is the basin, built to hold thirty or so barges for the traffic to or from the railway. The site of the railway station and dock is today known as the Railway Wharf and, while 'Ram Field' cannot be identified, there is a Ram Brewery; and, until considerable street alterations were effected and York Road was continued up to High Street and Red Lion Street swept away, there was a Ram Square.

The railway came out of the Railway Wharf and proceeded along Red Lion Street. Until the alterations just named were made, a kerb formed of the stone sleepers was in existence from the wharf gates to the Ram Brewery. The line crossed High Street and proceeded along what is now known as Buckhold Road up to the River Wandle, which was crossed by a wooden bridge. The line curved to the left and again crossed the river by a second wooden bridge, and entered Garratt Lane at the site of a blacksmith's shop near the 'Waggon and Horses' Inn – both of which landmarks have now disappeared. The east side of Garratt Lane was followed, and when the London & Southampton Railway was built the latter crossed over the Surrey Iron Railway, near where Earlsfield Station is today, by an arch of 22ft span and 15½ft high. The line was continued through Summerstown, crossed the London–Epsom highway on the level at Collier's Wood, just above Merton, and continued to Mitcham village along the present Church Road. Thence it followed the course of Ravensbury Path and Baron Walk and, after crossing the Sutton main road, followed a course to the south of the existing Mitcham Station along what is now a public thoroughfare known as Tramway Lane, part of which was used for the construction of the Croydon–Wimbledon Railway which was opened in 1855. That line struck the course of the old railway at Beddington Lane Station, and the direction taken by the Surrey Iron Railway cannot now be traced until Waddon Marsh Lane is reached near the level crossing of the Croydon–Wimbledon line over the main road to Waddon. Thence it passed near what is now the Electricity Works, and ended near the 'Gun Tavern', a little short of Croydon Parish Church.

Near the present Mitcham Junction Station the branch, 1¼ miles long, for Hackbridge and Carshalton was led away to the south. It followed what is still known as the Tramway Path, behind 'Tramway Terrace', and so by the 'Goat Inn' at Beddington Corner to Carshalton Park, which it entered at Culver's Avenue Lodge gates and crossed to the bridge over the Wandle.

The gauge of the railway was about 5ft from centre to centre of the stone sleepers and 4ft 8in between the outer faces of the rails. The rails were of the 'Outram' pattern: 3ft 2in long, 4in wide in the tread and 1in thick except for 5 or 6 inches at each end, where they were half an inch thicker. Below the outside edge was a rib or fish-belly, about 2ft long, for additional strength. The flange to guide the wheels was about 1in wide at the base and rather less at the top, and was curved, being only 1½in high at the ends and 3¾in in the middle. At level crossings the flanges were 1in high and straight throughout. The rails were laid on stone blocks 15 to 16 inches square, by 8 or 9 inches deep. Into a plughole, sunk about half-way down, an octagonal oak trenail was driven nearly to the bottom

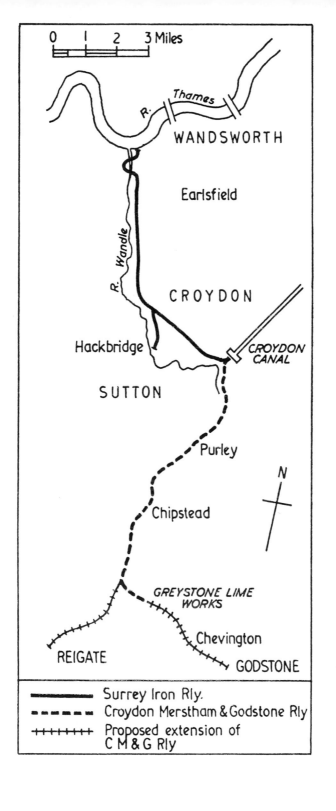

0 1 2 3 Miles

R. Thames

WANDSWORTH

Earlsfield

R. Wandle

CROYDON

Hackbridge

CROYDON CANAL

SUTTON

Purley

Chipstead

N

GREYSTONE LIME WORKS

Chevington

REIGATE

GODSTONE

—————— Surrey Iron Rly.
– – – – – Croydon Merstham & Godstone Rly
+++++++ Proposed extension of
           C M & G Rly

and sawn off even with the top of the stone. A hole was bored in the trenail into which was driven a spike that fitted notches in the ends of adjacent rails.

At crossings, where the rails converged, a portion of the ledge could be turned about a vertical hinge, so as to guide the wheels into the desired track.

The wagons were authorised to be drawn by horses, donkeys or mules.

The line, which was described by writers of the period as 'a vast and important concern', did not meet with success. It was seriously affected by the Croydon Canal from Rotherhithe, which was opened in 1809. Matters became worse, when its companion, the Croydon, Merstham & Godstone, was closed in 1838. In 1844 it was purchased by the London & South Western Railway, which company sold it to the London & Brighton company. The latter found no use for the line except where the route of the Wimbledon & Croydon intersected it, and in 1846 an Act was obtained to abandon it. The material was recovered and removed to the wharf at Wandsworth, and sold. Some of the stone sleepers were used in making banks for the dock.

The length was about 9½ miles, plus about 1¼ miles for the branch to Hackbridge. This line was looked upon by some of the more enthusiastic of its supporters as being the first link in a chain of railways to connect London with Portsmouth. In the Patent Office Library there is a pamphlet entitled *An Examination into the respective merits of the proposed Canal and the Iron Railway from London to Portsmouth,* by Robert Marshall (of Godalming), 1803. The estimate for the canal was £800,000, and for the railway, £400,000.

'The Surrey Iron Railway' is described in Tredgold's *Practical Treatise on Rail-roads and Carriages,* 1825 (2nd edition, 1835). It also attracted the attention of foreign engineers. A foreign description occurs in a small book published in Berlin in 1829: 'Railways in England. Observations made during a journey in the years 1826 and 1827, by C. von Oeynhausen and H. von Dechen'. It mentions that there were double tracks, with inclination nowhere more than 1 in 120. The first rails were without the lower strengthening rib, but became much worn. The wagons weighed about a ton; being about 5ft wide, 8ft long and 2ft deep, with cast-iron wheels 32in in diameter.

The Croydon, Merstham & Godstone Railway was also engineered by William Jessop, in company with his son Josiah. Their estimate was £52,347, but the company could only raise £45,500, and that sum was absorbed by the time they had arrived at Merstham, a distance of 8½ miles. It was not double throughout.

Site of the Croydon, Merstham & Godstone Railway at Merstham. [*Jeoffrey Spence*

Building of the London & Croydon Railway, as seen from an overbridge at New Cross. [*British Railways*

Above
The Canterbury & Whitstable
Railway from Church Street, on
the opening day, 3rd May, 1830.
[*British Railways*

Right
The Canterbury & Whitstable
locomotive *Invicta* as rebuilt and
with certain parts restored for
preservation.

[*British Railways*

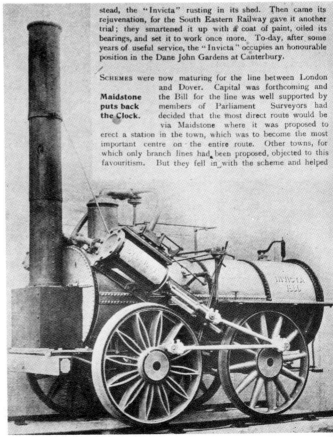

stead, the "Invicta" rusting in its shed. Then came its
rejuvenation, for the South Eastern Railway gave it another
trial; they smartened it up with a coat of paint, oiled its
bearings, and set it to work once more. To-day, after some
years of useful service, the "Invicta" occupies an honourable
position in the Dane John Gardens at Canterbury.

SCHEMES were now maturing for the line between London
and Dover. Capital was forthcoming and
Maidstone the Bill for the line was well supported by
puts back members of Parliament Surveyors had
the Clock. decided that the most direct route would be
via Maidstone where it was proposed to
erect a station in the town, which was to become the most
important centre on the entire route. Other towns, for
which only branch lines had been proposed, objected to this
favouritism. But they fell in with the scheme and helped

Its course was more or less by the side of the Brighton main road. At Smitham Bottom the line of route was cut through by the Chipstead Valley Railway. Here there is still a piece of the original embankment that carried the railway up to a bridge – since removed – over the Epsom–Coulsdon Road. On the other side of this road was another embankment. Nearing Merstham the line went into a cutting nearly a mile long and, in places, 30ft deep. On this section are three overbridges, which still stand.

An episode which occurred on the line between Croydon and Merstham is well worth mentioning. According to the *Annual Register* for 1805, there was on 24th July of that year, as a result of a wager, a test of the capacity of a horse as a means of locomotion. The animal drew with apparent ease a train of twelve wagons weighing 38 tons 4 cwts 2 qrs a distance of six miles in 1 hour 41 minutes, and brought back sixteen wagons, weighing 55 tons 6 cwts 2 qrs.

The line of the London & Brighton company was planned to pass over part of the Croydon, Merstham & Godstone Railway. The Act of 15th July, 1837, of the former company, therefore, authorised the purchase of the line. This was done by the end of 1838 and, by an Act passed 1st July, 1839, the Croydon, Merstham & Godstone Railway Company was dissolved.

II

The Canterbury and Whitstable Railway

WE have seen that the Southern Railway may claim to be the descendant of the first public railway in the world. Another of its ancestors was the first railway to convey passengers by means of a locomotive. It is true that this was eventually done by the Stockton & Darlington Railway, which was opened in 1825, but all their passenger coaches were drawn by horses until 7th September, 1833, and continued to be, on parts of the line, until 7th April, 1834.*

It was the Liverpool & Manchester Railway which was really the first of the modern kind, and which set the ball rolling, by attracting the attention of the whole civilised world to the possibilities of railways worked by locomotives. Still, it is impossible to gainsay the facts that the Canterbury & Whitstable did use a locomotive for some years, and was opened on 3rd May, 1830, whereas the Liverpool & Manchester did not make its bow to the public until 15th September of that year.

The making of the Canterbury & Whitstable line came about in consequence of the falling through of an ambitious scheme for which an Act was obtained in June, 1825, namely to make the River Stour navigable up to Canterbury, and to provide harbour accommodation at Sandwich. This undertaking was found likely to be so costly that it was abandoned without even being commenced. Meanwhile, the inhabitants of Canterbury were still longing for a better communication with the sea than was afforded by the road, and so fell back on a proposal for a railway to Whitstable, which was also on the tapis.

The suggestion for a railway emanated from William James, who originally put it forward in April, 1823, having already made a preliminary survey. He was a man whose name has not received the honour it deserves. He has, perhaps, the best claim of anyone to be called the 'Father of Railways'. At the beginning of the century he was rich and powerful, and had projected a number of railways which were in operation, mostly in connection with estates and mines in

---

* Tomlinson's *History of the North Eastern Railway*, p. 385.

18

which he was interested. About 1808 he put forward a scheme for a 'General Railroad Company' with a capital of a million pounds. In 1821 he became the first promoter of the Liverpool & Manchester Railway,* and two years later, that of the line we are now considering. Owing to his becoming financially embarrassed, and falling into ill-health, he dropped out of the railway world about this time, and so failed to share in the glory and profits which were reaped by others.

Powers for the construction of the line from Canterbury to Whitstable, and for a harbour at the latter place, were obtained in 1825, by 6 Geo. IV, c. 120, and were amended and enlarged by further Acts obtained in 1827, 1828 and 1835. Three different types of propulsion were sanctioned for the railway: locomotive power, stationary engines, and horses. A curious feature of the passage of the bill through Parliament was an unsuccessful attempt on the part of the Turnpike Commissioners of the Whitstable road to get a clause inserted to compel the railway company to compensate them, during a period of twenty years, for the loss of revenue they would sustain owing to traffic being taken away from the road.

The total capital had been originally put at £25,000, but in consequence of doubts having arisen as to whether this sum was sufficient, it was decided to refer the matter to George Stephenson for his opinion. He considered it was too low, and it was increased by £6,000. Otherwise the scheme remained as proposed by James. He had prepared the survey – which differed from the original one by being more direct – and the route; and the plan and section submitted to Parliament – still preserved in the Royal Museum at Canterbury – were signed by him.

For reasons already given, James had to withdraw from active work, and a fresh engineer had to be found, The line was handed over the George Stephenson. He delegated the work to assistants, sending first Locke, who, however, only stayed a fortnight, and then John Dixon, who superintended the whole of the construction.

The accompanying map on page 20 shows the course of the railway, an alteration permitted by an Act of 1827 being indicated by dots. It is a single line six miles long, and, as will be seen from the diagram, rises 1 in 76 for the first 264 yards, and then, for 2,860 yards, on gradients varying between 1 in 41 and 1 in 56. After 1 mile 220 yards fairly level the line falls, at 1 in 63, for 154 yards, and then, at 1 in 28 and 1 in 31, for 1,430 yards, followed by 1 mile 330 yards of level. Thence

* See *Centenary History of the Liverpool and Manchester Railway*, Dendy Marshall (1930), Ch. III. Also *The Two James's and the Two Stephensons* (1962).

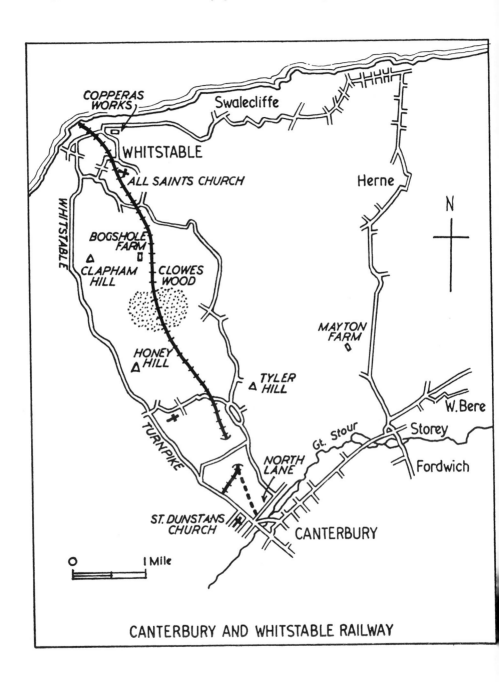

CANTERBURY AND WHITSTABLE RAILWAY

there are 1,078 yards of 1 in 57 and 1 in 50, after which the line falls gradually into Whitstable.

The top of the first bank from Canterbury is at Tyler's Hill, where there was a stationary engine of 25 h.p. to deal with that incline. At the end of the 1 mile 220 yards is Clowes Wood, where there was another 25 h.p. stationary engine to deal with trains between Tyler's Hill and Bogshole Brook, where the 1 mile 330 yards of level began. Thence to Whitstable a locomotive was at first employed. There is one tunnel, called Tyler's Hill.* It is 828 yards long, situated on the 1 in 56 gradient and its size was such that loads could not exceed a height of 9ft 3in at the side and 11ft in the middle. It may be remarked that the locomotive was not intended to work through the tunnel. (Owing to restricted clearance, when standard locomotives were used later they had to be fitted with specially short chimneys.)

No special engineering difficulties were experienced beyond a few falls of earth during the tunnelling, but the financial path was by no means smooth. A further £19,000 had to be obtained, authorised by

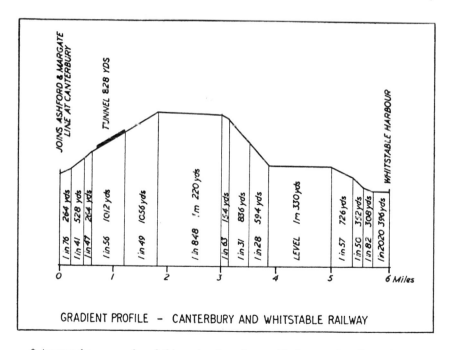

GRADIENT PROFILE - CANTERBURY AND WHITSTABLE RAILWAY

* Among the many absurd things that have been said about early railways is a statement that the tunnel was quite unnecessary, and was made merely for the sake of providing a novelty. The nature of the country is such that it was indispensible, if the line was to follow a direct course between its terminal points.

the Act of 1827, phich also permitted a more convenient entrance into Canterbury.

The opening ceremony took place on 3rd May, 1830. There were two trains, consisting altogether of twenty carriages and twelve wagons, all of which were joined into one and drawn by the locomotive *Invicta* for the last two miles into Whitstable. The assemblage of spectators was immense, all along the line. Flags were everywhere displayed, the bells of the Cathedral were rung at intervals during the day, and guns were fired to announce the departure of the train.

The *Invicta*, about which more will be said presently, was driven by Edward Fletcher, who had brought it by sea from Newcastle. He became Locomotive Superintendent of the North Eastern Railway in 1854, a post which he occupied until 1882.

With regard to the rails, there does not seem to be any record of their weight. Whishaw's *Railways of Great Britain and Ireland* (1840) says: 'The rails are of wrought iron, of light weight, and are set in chairs with three feet bearings; the chairs being spiked down to cross sleepers of oak.'

The opening proceedings closed with an elaborate dinner at the King's Head, Canterbury. The turtle, the wine and the dessert were most excellent, we are told, and the company separated at a late hour.

From Whishaw it may be gathered that the total cost was £111,000.

One disappointment was that the *Invicta* proved incapable of hauling trains up the gradients of 1 in 50 and 1 in 57, and had to be confined to the 1 mile 330 yards of level. A third stationary engine of 15 h.p. was supplied by Robert Stephenson & Co. for the inclines, in 1832.

The harbour at Whitstable was opened on 19th March, 1832; again an occasion for great local rejoicings. For about two months in this year Sunday trains were run – in the afternoon only – and were well patronised, but protests by the clergy of Canterbury led to their being taken off. In March, 1834, season tickets were issued, the first in the world.

In 1836 the Canterbury & Whitstable Steam Packet Company was formed, which ran a steamer (the *William the Fourth*) every other day between London and Whitstable; the trains being worked in connection. In 1838 the line was leased to Messrs. Nicholson and Baylis. By 1840 they became in arrears with the rent, and went bankrupt the following year. An unsuccessful attempt was made to let it again, and it was carried on by the directors. In 1844 a lease was arranged with the South Eastern Railway Company, who from that time forward worked the line, using locomotives entirely in 1846, after making some alterations and laying down heavier rails. This year saw the first dividend distribution, namely 2 per cent, which gradually increased to 5. In 1853 the line was sold to the South Eastern company, the shareholders being paid off at par.

When the South Eastern line was made from Ashford to Canterbury, it crossed the Whitstable line on the level at the latter place, so a junction was put in which allowed the Whitstable trains to use Canterbury West Station, instead of their original terminus, which, however, was not closed entirely until the beginning of the present century. Passenger traffic on the Canterbury and Whitstable line has ceased to be carried on since the end of 1930.

Canon R. B. Fellowes, in his excellent history of the line, published in 1930 – from which much of the information in this chapter has been obtained – says:

> From a financial point of view the railway was hardly a success, but it cannot be regarded as a complete failure, since all debts were ultimately paid, and the invested capital was returned intact. The railway was undoubtedly an advantage to the district, and it also played its part in helping to familiarise the public with steam traction at a time when there was much prejudice to overcome.

It now remains to describe the *Invicta*. Although, principally owing to the very steep gradients which she was set to negotiate, she turned out to be of very little use to the company, she is nevertheless an important landmark in locomotive design, being the first one ever built with outside cylinders at the leading end, an arrangement which afterwards became such a popular one. The *Invicta* was about the twentieth engine constructed by Robert Stephenson & Company, and about the seventieth railway locomotive to be built. She is said by Warren, in his *Century of Locomotive Building* (1923), to have followed the *Rocket*, which very likely was so, but was preceded by four more engines for the Liverpool & Manchester Railway in date of delivery, which was in May, 1830. The makers did not reproduce the design, as, after making a batch of engines of the general type of the *Rocket*, with the cylinders at the rear, they went to inside cylinders, in the *Planet* and her successors.

The cylinders were 10½in by 18, wheels 4ft; boiler 3ft 4in diameter and 8ft long. Like that of the *Rocket*, it was multitubular, with a heating surface of 157 square feet in the tubes and 39 in the firebox, the pressure being 40 lb. to the square inch (or possibly 50); the weight was 6¼ tons, exclusive of tender. The driver stood on a footboard halfway along the left side of the boiler, the fireman riding on the tender.

In 1838 an unsuccessful attempt was made to improve the steaming by removing the firebox and tubes, and substituting a cylindrical furnace, and three tubes only, which was obviously a retrograde step. This proceeding settled matters, and the directors advertised her for sale in September, 1839. No purchaser was forthcoming, so the engine was kept, being put under cover.

She now stands in the Dane Johns Gardens at Canterbury, having been presented to the City by the late Sir David Salomons, a director of the South Eastern Railway, who had previously purchased her.

A description of the method of working the line may be interesting.

The passing place was at Clowes Wood, up and down trains being timed to meet there. When trains were ready to start from Canterbury, for a brief period after the opening of the railway intimation was conveyed by a signal. A wooden rectangular frame on a post was erected at the south end of the tunnel mouth. Pivoted longitudinally across it at the centre was a board painted white, presumably controlled by a spring. A wire attached to the lever working the axis of the board led to the Canterbury Station. The signal frame normally showed an open space, but when a train was ready to start, the wire was pulled and the white board filled the frame. A boy was employed at the tunnel mouth to repeat the signal to the Tyler's Hill engineman, but he was so inattentive that this plan of signalling was abandoned and the staff at Canterbury Station pushed the train back a few yards with the rope attached. This caused the winding drum at Tyler's Hill to revolve, and intimated to the engineman there that the train was ready to start.

For signalling between the stationary engine houses, a drum was run up the chimney, its appearance at the top being an indication to the man at the next engine house to 'haul away'.

Thomas Cabry, who was in charge of the line during its early years, gave the following account of the working from Clowes Wood to Whitstable, before a House of Lords Committee on the Great Western Railway Bill.

The passenger carriages were first detached from the goods wagons and were allowed to descend by their own weight; sometimes as many as three carriages would descend together. Each carriage would hold sixteen passengers; the maximum speed attained in going down the inclines was thirty miles an hour, but usually the speed did not exceed twenty-four miles an hour. No difficulty was experienced in checking the speed of the carriages. They were checked by a brake on the circumference of the wheel worked by a lever. Three carriages travelling at the rate of twenty-four miles an hour down these inclines could be stopped dead in a hundred yards; the rope was not attached to the passenger carriages going down, but to goods wagons which followed the passenger carriages after a short interval and were joined up to them at the bottom of the incline. The rope was attached to the wagons for two reasons: firstly that it might be taken down in readiness for use for hauling up the next train; secondly to check the speed of the wagons, there being a slight tension on the rope. At Bogshole Brook, the *Invicta* was attached to the train, now made up of the carriages with the goods wagons attached behind, and hauled it to Whitstable, just over two miles, at a speed of about twelve miles an hour. After she had been put out of commission, horses were used for the level part of the way, until locomotive working was adopted throughout, in April, 1846.

An important part of the traffic was coal, arriving at Whitstable Harbour from the North of England. Later it went the other way; coal being sent over the line from Chislet Colliery for shipment at Whitstable!

III

Early Railways in the West Country

ABOUT the beginning of the nineteenth century, proposals were put forward for a canal between Padstow in North Cornwall, and Fowey in the south, thus to unite the Bristol and English Channels. Again James is said to have been on the spot, and to have suggested a railway instead.*

The only outcome of the scheme was a railway between Bodmin and Wadebridge. Speaking of this line, Whishaw, in the work already quoted, says:

The county of Cornwall, till of late years, was but ill supplied with the means of internal conveyance for the valuable products of its numerous mines. The minerals were either transported on the backs of mules, or in rough carts over rugged cross roads. In the principal mining districts, single lines of railway were laid down some years ago, which have hitherto been entirely worked by horses, but the opening of the Bodmin & Wadebridge Railway introduced into the county of Cornwall that splendid triumph of art, the locomotive engine, without which railways to this day could have been considered only as improved turnpike roads.

The railway was sanctioned in 1832 by 2 & 3 Will. IV, c. 47, and the main line of 7 miles was opened on 4th July, 1834; a branch 6½ miles long up the Camel Valley to Wenford Bridge, and another of 1 mile to Ruthern Bridge following on 30th September of the same year. The following is an account of the opening, from the *West Briton and Cornwall Advertiser* for 3rd October, 1834:

As soon as the different parties were arranged the procession set out in the following order: a waggon in which were the bricklayers employed in the work, with their tools, preceded the locomotive engine and tender in which sat Messrs. Hopkins, the engineers, Thomas Woollcombe Esq., and several other gentlemen. To the engine seventeen waggons and an omnibus were attached. These vehicles were tastefully fitted up, and were decorated with flags, green branches, etc. On one waggon was displayed a flag on which was neatly painted a representation of the engine and the waggons attached, with the words 'Science, Prudence and Perseverance' as a motto. The persons who had obtained tickets, and amongst whom were many ladies, took their places in the carriages, the middle one being occupied by the band [Royal Cornwall Militia in full uniform]. The arrangements were completed about twelve o'clock when the very beautiful and powerful engine was put in motion, and it proceeded drawing the long train of carriages amidst the cheers of the multitude occupying every spot that afforded a view of the road,

* *The Two James's*, p. 89. But there does not seem to be any other evidence of his activities in this direction.

26

the band playing the national anthem. By this time the weather had cleared up, and the scene defies description, a more grand or imposing sight was never, perhaps, witnessed in this county. The train moved forward at the rate of six miles an hour occasionally increasing in speed to about ten miles in the same time until arriving at Dunmeer, 5½ miles from Wadebridge, where a fresh supply of water was taken in, when the procession again moved forward; at Tresarratt another supply was obtained; and, at Wenford Bridge which is the termination of the main line being twelve miles from Wadebridge, a halt of upwards of half an hour took place in order to arrange for returning to Dunmeer, which being effected in the best style, the engine, after stopping to take in water etc. as before, ascended the Branch to Bodmin, drawing the tender, omnibus and waggons and, preceded by the workmen employed on the railway, walking two and two and reached the town at five o'clock amidst the cheers of the multitude assembled to witness the arrival. . . . We are most happy to add that not the slightest accident occurred to damp the satisfaction universally expressed by all who were present.

The capital in the first Act was £22,500 plus a loan of £8,000. A second Act (1835) permitted another loan of £5,000, total £35,500. The total cost, including two Acts of Parliament and two locomotives and other stock, came to £35,498 2s. 9d., which is at the rate of only £2,450 a mile.

The line, which was single, was fairly level for the five miles from Wadebridge to Boscarne, but the remaining portion on to Bodmin rose at 1 in 51, ending up with 1 in 40. The Ruthern branch was 1 in 158. The gauge was 4ft 8½in, the rails being of the parallel form, weighing 40 lb. per yard; supported in chairs laid on granite blocks 12in thick and 20in square, which cost 8d. each. There were eight bridges, of which three were movable for the convenience of water traffic. In 1840 there were two locomotives and two carriages, the latter built by the company.

The principal traffic was sea sand, which was conveyed inland for use as manure. Passenger traffic was very small; in 1838 only 3,274 persons were carried, the fares amounting to £88 2s. 3d. It is said that at one time the passenger carriages only ran on Saturdays; even in much later times they only went on every other day. A train of a comparatively recent date is shown in the illustration section, with the original carriages, one of which was for many years an object of interest on the concourse at Waterloo Station. The goods stock in 1840 consisted of 13 wagons for ores, etc., with wheels only 22in diameter; and 27 for sand and coal, with 3ft wheels.

Financial results were melancholy, and in 1845 the then Cornwall Railway – between Plymouth and Falmouth and now part of the Great Western – offered to buy the line, but a company, known as the Devon & Cornwall Central, which proposed to build a railway between Exeter and Falmouth in opposition to the South Devon & the Cornwall, made a more satisfactory offer, and it was accepted.

The Devon & Cornwall Central did not, however, proceed with its scheme and was left with the Bodmin & Wadebridge on its hands. The London & South Western, having the intention of invading Cornwall, came to the rescue and, in 1847, acquired the property, in spite of the fact that it was about 200 miles off! There was no parliamentary authority for the transaction; in fact it was not until 1886 that the South Western legally absorbed the line, and not until 1895 was the Bodmin & Wadebridge joined to the London & South Western, by the opening of the Delabole–Wadebridge section of the North Cornwall Railway.

In 1887 the Great Western built a branch to Bodmin, and the following year continued it to Boscarne on the Bodmin & Wadebridge; after which time they worked the part from Boscarne to Bodmin, the South Western continuing to operate the rest.

It may be remarked that this line is not shown in Bradshaw's magnificent railway map published '1st mo.', 1839.

The Ruthern Bridge branch was closed 30th December, 1933.

The centenary of the opening was celebrated – two months late – on 5th September, 1934, when a large party of visitors were received by the Wadebridge Urban District Council and the Bodmin Borough Council, and inspected the remains of the old line.

The following passage, relating to the first locomotive, appeared in the newspaper already cited, on 17th October, 1834, under the heading, 'Authentic statistics respecting the Bodmin and Wadebridge Railway':

In the summer of 1833 a considerable difference of opinion existed among the Board of Directors as to the description of the locomotive engine best adapted for this railway. They therefore deputed Dr Harry, one of their body, to examine the various locomotive engines at work in South Wales for the transport of heavy goods; and after having done so, he recommended an engine to be constructed by the Neath Abbey Iron Company, who had executed several which had answered well – his recommendation was adopted. Accordingly Mr Roger Hopkins was sent to Neath Abbey to settle the plan and specification with the Neath Abbey Iron Company and to contract for the engine. After making several alterations and amendments in the plan and specification Mr Hopkins finally closed the contract, agreeably to which the engine has been constructed at a cost of £725 including the tender. It is called the *Camel* and is mounted on 6 wheels of 3ft 9in diameter. Its weight is 11½ tons when working. The cylinders are 10½in diameter and the length of the stroke is 2ft. The working pressure of the steam is 50 lb on the square inch. The weight of goods intended to be drawn by the engine upwards on every part of the main line of railway is 50 tons each trip exclusive of the carriages and tender, and on the Bodmin branch 25 tons. The rate of travelling decided on is six miles an hour ascending, and eight miles descending. The engine has travelled at the rate of 25 miles an hour.

There were two locomotives, *Camel* and *Elephant*. Unfortunately there is no general arrangement drawing, and it is not possible to make a satisfactory reconstruction. From a sketch of the *Camel* made at the opening, however, it seems that the pistons drove the coupling rods (all six wheels were coupled) through bell-cranks, the cylinders being vertical. The *Elephant* differed in that the piston rods worked through the tops of the cylinders, which were larger, being 12in in diameter. They were connected by 'bow' connecting rods to the bell cranks.

Among detail drawings which survive are two of boilers, one with 77 vertical water-tubes; the other with 28 horizontal fire-tubes. Whether both were used on the two engines respectively or whether they were alternative designs, does not appear. These two engines were scrapped in 1864 and replaced by *Ajax* and *Atlas*, two old Jones & Potts engines, and a Fletcher & Jennings 0-4-0ST *Bodmin*. These had gone by 1893, when L.S.W.R. No. 458, a Hawthorn saddle-tank, took over. From 1895 when the track was rebuilt, standard engines worked.

In the same session (1832) as that in which the Bodmin & Wade-bridge was sanctioned, an Act was obtained for a line from Exeter to Crediton. There was, however, one great difference between the two lines in that the Crediton one was not built until later; the powers lapsed, and when the time came for a railway to be constructed, fresh powers, as will be related in due course, had to be sought.

There remains, however, the fact that such a line was proposed as long ago as 1832. It was of additional interest in that its route was to be from the basin of the Exeter Canal at St Thomas, Exeter, to 'the flour Mills at Crediton'. One reason for that added interest is that, next to the Foss Dyke in Lincolnshire – which was made by the Romans – the Exe Canal is the oldest in Great Britain, as it was in the middle of the sixteenth century – in 1563–65 – that a portion of the River Exe was canalised. Another point of interest is that had the railway been built as originally proposed, it would probably have been on the route through the city taken by the South Devon and the Bristol & Exeter. Instead, when the Crediton powers were revived in 1845, what is now the Great Western main line to the West had possession, and the new line was planned to begin by a junction with the Bristol & Exeter at Cowley Bridge, 1¼ mile north of St. David's Station.

IV

The First Railway in London

To the Southern Railway belongs the earliest London line, namely the London & Greenwich, the Act for which received the Royal Assent on the 17th May, 1833. It was not quite the first to be authorised, as the London & Birmingham had obtained theirs eleven days earlier, but was the first to come into operation.

The total length was only 3¾ miles, practically level; the line being formed from one end to the other on a viaduct of 878 arches of brick-work. At first there was only one intermediate station, at Deptford High Street, but after a few years another was made, at Spa Road – which has a claim to be called the first London station, since passenger traffic was begun on the 8th February, 1836, by running trains between that point and Deptford, a distance of about two miles. There was a lifting bridge over the river Ravensbourne, which, apart from reinforcement with wrought-iron beams, existed for over a century, practically in its original condition.

Under the original Act the capital was £400,000, but, with the assistance of seven subsequent ones, authority was obtained to raise, by shares or loans, the sum of £993,330.* The prospectus was issued in September, 1832, George Walter being the projector of the railway, and the first Secretary of the company. The original survey was by Francis Giles; Lieut.-Col. G. T. Landmann, R.E. (retired), proposed a viaduct throughout, and designed the works. On 9th June, 1835, the first recorded trial trip took place, when the engine *Royal William* ran a mile in four minutes, near Blue Anchor Road, in the presence of noblemen, directors and shareholders. Public working seems to have begun on part of the line towards the end of the year, as in November the following enlightened paragraph appeared in *John Bull*:

> Loss of life on that favourite toy from Liverpool to Manchester has always been terrific. Mr Huskisson was the first martyr; and the last splendid exhibition took place on Thursday upon the new tomfoolery to Greenwich, when 'by some accident' one of the carriages in which a party of noodles ventured themselves was thrown off the rail, but although it ran a vast number of yards no serious accident occurred. How lucky! Nobody killed the first day!

* Scrivenor's *Railways of the United Kingdom*, 1849, p. 288.

Colonel Landmann improved the occasion by congratulating the shareholders on the derailment, as it showed how safe accidents were.

On 14th December, 1836, the line was opened from London Bridge to Deptford by the Lord Mayor, with much ceremony. The proceedings more or less resembled those when the Liverpool & Manchester Railway was opened, fortunately this time without any tragic happening. Grand stands were erected. The Lord Mayor, Sheriffs, Common Council, Directors, etc., left in the first train, which, halting some distance out, was passed by four others crowded with guests. These then stopped, and the Lord Mayor's train led the way to Deptford. Church bells rang, and people crowded the housetops all the way. The Scots Guards and Coldstream bands attended at London Bridge and Deptford, and a third one went on one of the trains. According to one contemporary account, there was a band of Beefeaters on the top of the principal carriage. But perhaps this requires a grain, or so, of salt. The proceedings terminated as usual, with a dinner – at the Bridge House Tavern.

By this time J. Y. Akerman had become the Secretary, the Chairman being A. R. Dottin. In 1837 the latter was superseded by George Money. Walter, who had become Managing Director, had to resign owing to financial disputes between him and the company.

In 1838 it was announced that, owing to complaints of noise from the stone sleepers and leakage through the arches, the Deptford–Greenwich section would be laid on wood, and be made watertight with asphalt. On 24th December the line was opened throughout to Greenwich, at a temporary station.

In 1839 a Mr Shadbolt became Chairman. Mr Curtis was the 'locomotive manager'. On 5th June trains of the London & Croydon Railway began running over the Greenwich line from Corbett's Lane to London Bridge – 1¾ mile – into a station of their own, just north of the Greenwich one. The Greenwich terminus was at what was later called 'London Bridge, Low Level'. By an arrangement with the Croydon company, which will be referred to again, the Greenwich exchanged their station at London Bridge for the new one built by the former company. The toll fixed for the use of the line by the Croydon company's trains was at first 3d. per passenger. In the following year the Greenwich company obtained powers to widen their line, in view of its use by the Croydon and South Eastern companies, and were authorised to charge a toll of 4½d.

The station at Greenwich was finished in 1840, and described on all sides as 'magnificent'. It was designed by George Smith, architect to the Mercers' Company. It was taken down in 1878 when the line was extended, and re-erected farther back to serve for the new station. It contained the first 'traverser' for locomotives, moving them bodily sideways on arrival, to the unoccupied line.

In January, 1842, the Greenwich Railway reduced the first-class fares and abolished the second, thus anticipating the policy of the Midland in 1874.

The Croydon and South Eastern companies complained bitterly about the 4½d. toll which the Greenwhich continued to take. The first-named company said that it killed their traffic altogether. The Greenwhich refused to make any reduction, so the other two companies made a fresh line into London, 1¾ mile long, from just below Corbett's Lane and bearing to the left to a point adjacent to the Old Kent Road, near the 'Bricklayers' Arms' public-house; from which the new terminus took its name. It was built partly on piles, which in the early 'fifties' were replaced by embankment. The cost was £250,000.

It may be mentioned, in passing, that Vignoles, when giving evidence before the Select Committee on the North Kent lines – to be mentioned later – in 1845, said 'the making of the Bricklayers' Arms station was a matter of compulsion in driving the Greenwich people to reasonable terms'.

This branch was opened in May, 1844, and all the Croydon trains and half the South Eastern were diverted from the London Bridge terminus. The effect on the Greenwich line may be imagined. The directors offered to reduce the toll, and an elaborate agreement was drawn up, under which they were to lay an additional set of rails from Corbett's Lane, but it came to nothing; and the situation was dealt with by leasing the line to the South Eastern for 999 years, at a yearly rental of £36,000, increasing by £1,000 a year to £45,000. The South Eastern Railway accordingly took over the working on 1st January, 1845, and the arrangement continued until 1923.

The cost of the Greenwich Railway per mile was £266,322. Dividends were intermittent and low, until the lease, when they settled down to about 4½ per cent on the original capital for good. In spite of the obviously expensive character of the construction, few railways have been ushered in with such high hopes. The writer has two contemporary pamphlets on the subject of the advantages of the railway. One, published in 1833, estimated the yearly receipts at £103,550, of which £80,000 was to be profit, being at the rate of 20 per cent on the capital of £400,000, 'the whole of which, it is expected, will not be required'. One item on the credit side was £5,000 for rent of

A train on the Bodmin & Wadebridge about 1880, at Wadebridge. The vehicle next to the engine is a water-tank.   [*BTC Collection*

Two of the Bodmin & Wadebridge carriages at Waterloo carriage sidings, for preservation.
[*Locomotive Publishing Co.*

An early print of the London & Greenwich Railway crossing the Deptford marshes.   [*British Railways*

Right:
Pipes from the atmospheric railway dug out in 1933 at West Croydon.
  [*British Railways*

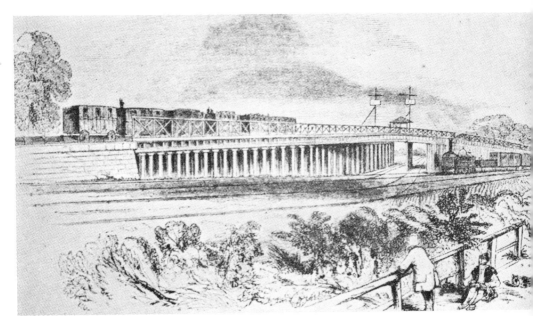

The 'flying junction' where the atmospheric line diverged from the London & Brighton, south of Jolly Sailor (now Norwood).   [*British Railways*

arches, which, it was fondly imagined, would be eagerly sought after by tenants. The other, published in 1834, is still more optimistic. Tolls for walking and driving on the strips of land at the sides of the line were to bring in £50 a day, and the rent from shops, warehouses, dwelling houses etc., were to yield £20,000 a year. The estimated expenses are reduced from £23,550 – the figure of the 1833 paper – to £20,000; and the profits increased to £116,800, or 30 per cent on the capital (still considered more than required).

As matters turned out, the line cost getting on for a million pounds; the arches failed to attract tenants; and no attempt was made to exploit the passages along the sides of the railway, which still exist, derelict, in some places.

It was tremendously patronised at first, as a kind of show, from the novelty of the thing; an aspect which the directors tried to encourage, by having bands in the early days, at London Bridge and Deptford, to play the trains in and out of the stations! The following interesting passage occurs in *Nelson's Hardy; his Life, Letters and Friends*, by A. M. Broadley and R. G. Bartelot:

Lady Hardy made up a party for a trial trip, and the journey both ways was effected in twenty minutes. None of the guests had ever travelled before in the new fashioned manner. Sir Thomas Hardy declined to go at any price, saying it was a needless risk to run, and until his death four years later, could never be persuaded to enter a railway carriage.

One would have thought that a hero of Trafalgar might have screwed up his courage to go. And he was only 67!

It should be mentioned that the London & Greenwich Railway Company preserved its identity right down to the amalgamation of 1923.

There were a number of petty accidents during the time the company worked the line, but none involving the death of a passenger.

In giving evidence before a Select Committee on Railways in March, 1841, John Entwistle, one of the directors, stated that since the opening of the Greenwich Railway 170,000 journeys had been made, conveying 6,800,000 passengers without the loss of life or limb to anyone. He said that in the cases of thick fog they had men stationed so close together that they could hear one another talk.

The locomotives are extremely interesting, but no really satisfactory description of them has come down. There were nine altogether, down to the time the South Eastern Railway took over the working. Whishaw, in the book already mentioned, *Railways of Great Britain*, which cannot by any means be trusted implicitly, gives dimensions and builders.

The following account is taken principally from *The First Railway in London*, by the late A. R. Bennett, which was published in 1912, and from which much of the history in this chapter has been gathered. The names, makers, etc., were as follows:

LOCOMOTIVES OF THE GREENWICH RAILWAY

No.	Name	Maker	Date	Cylinders	No. Wheels
1	Royal William	Tayleur & Co.	1835	Inside	4
2	Royal Adelaide	Braithwaite & Milner	1836	Outside ?	4
3	Princess Victoria	,,	,,	?	6
4	Dottin	,,	,,	Inside ?	4
5	Twells	Forrester & Co.	,,	Outside	4
6	Walter	,,	,,	,,	4
7	?	Haigh Foundry ?	1839	Inside ?	6
8	?	R. & W. Hawthorn	1840	Inside	6
9	?	R. Stephenson & Co.	1838	,,	6

A drawing has survived of No. 1. She was Tayleur's twenty-fifth engine; the cylinders being 10 by 16 inches and wheels 3ft 9in and 5ft. The boiler was 8ft long by 2ft 10in diameter; total heating surface 318.4 sq. ft. She was the first locomotive to work regularly in London.

Of the Braithwaite engines, Nos. 2, 3 and 4, so far as their form is concerned, little is known. Two were four-wheelers and one, six. One of the former, probably No. 2, was of a nearly unique design, if a sketch is to be trusted which was given in a paper read by Theodore West before the Institution of Cleveland Engineers in 1886, which had been given to him by E. A. Cowper, a well-known engineer. The cylinders were horizontal, above the trailing wheels, which they drove by means of a rocking lever and return connecting rod. Only one other example of this arrangement is known to have been built, namely an engine named *Union*, supplied by Rothwell and Hick to the Bolton & Leigh Railway in 1830, but that was still more peculiar, in having a vertical boiler.

According to the *Railway Magazine* of April, 1836, an engine then being constructed for the Greenwich Railway was formed so as to present the appearance of an ancient Roman galley. Unfortunately no illustration has come down. It would probably be the six-wheeler, No. 3.

The names given to Nos. 4, 5 and 6 may not be correctly distributed, but are in the most probable order. Twells was the deputy chairman.

The two Forrester engines were of a design of which examples had been supplied to the Dublin & Kingstown Railway and the Liverpool & Manchester, except that the Greenwich ones are said to have been tank engines. They combined outside horizontal cylinders with outside driving bearings and, owing to the necessarily wide spread of the former, were very unsteady in running. This combination was not perpetuated in Great Britain, but has been widely used on the Continent.

Bennett has made a mistake over Nos. 7 to 9. Both Whishaw and a Board of Trade Report of 1841 give 8 as Hawthorn and 9 as Stephenson.

The particulars given by Whishaw are the only ones we have of Nos. 7 and 8, the driving wheels of which were 5ft and 5ft 6in respectively. He gives the maker of No. 7 as Day, meaning, no doubt, Summers, Groves and Day, of Southampton. So far as can be ascertained, they never built locomotives, but repaired them, and sometimes acted as agents for their supply.

Messrs Stephenson supplied Bennett with an outline and some particulars of No. 9, which was their No. 191; driving wheels, 5ft; carrying 3ft 6in; boiler barrel, 8ft by 3ft 3in; five bearings on the driving axle; valve-gear, four-excentric gab motion.

The four-wheelers seem to have been all that were required for the traffic. Walter wrote in 1840: 'The six wheelers cost more to build and to work. They slip in wet weather for want of requisite adhesion, which the four-wheelers possess, from nearly the whole weight being on the driving wheels. They are also not so good for working round curves.' Also, a complaint from the *Railway Magazine* of December, 1838, speaking of the Stephenson engine, after remarking that powerful machines of 12 to 14 tons were not required, went on to say: 'No such Goliaths can be wanted. It appears highly improvident to rattle such heavy engines over the arches.' What would the writer of that paragraph say if he could have seen the engines of 100 years later going over those same arches?

Just about the time of the lease, Nos. 1, 2 and 3 were replaced by three new six-wheeled engines built by Marshall and Co., formerly Braithwaite and Milner, with 5ft driving wheels. They had been ordered by the Greenwich Railway in 1844, and were taken over by the South Eastern Railway.

There is a tradition that a rotary engine, invented by Lord Dundonald, was tried on this line, which had the unfortunate peculiarity that when the steam was turned on the casing went round instead of the rotor. But the writer has been unable to discover anything definite about the matter.

In 1836 a strange form of carriage was introduced, with the frames underhung, being only four inches above the rails; this was so that they would not overturn if derailed. The first-class carriages had three compartments and weighed 2¾ tons; the second-class had one door on each side, with seats all round the interior; while the thirds were 'stanhopes' or 'stand-ups' – that is to say, merely open trucks, without seats. In January, 1838, the entire stock of fifty-six vehicles was sold to Wright, a well-known carriage-builder of Goswell Road, London, whose business eventually developed into the Metropolitan Carriage and Wagon Company. In 1844 the underhung carriages were given up and coaches of the normal form provided.

In the early days of railways, before any regular system of fixed signals had been introduced, the traffic was regulated by policemen, who were supplied with elaborately painted batons.

A type of fixed signal was used on the Greenwich Railway from 1839. When the line was clear, a board was turned parallel with the rails. These seem to have been introduced when the Croydon trains began to use the line. At first, signalling after dark was still done by hand-lamps. The first signalbox in the world was built at Corbett's Lane, and was called the 'lighthouse', according to contemporary accounts.

The arrangements put into force when the 'lighthouse' was opened were, that when the points were set for the Greenwich line a disc, painted a reddish orange, would be turned edgeways so as not to be visible; at night a white light would be shown in all directions. When the road was made for the Croydon line the disc would be turned and exposed to view in all three directions, i.e. towards London, Greenwich, and Croydon; at night there would be a red light.

The *Railway Magazine* for July, 1839, when describing the opening of the London & Croydon Railway, said: 'At the junction is an octagonal lighthouse with powerful parabolic reflectors, from which signals by coloured lights can be given a long way off to approaching trains so as to prevent the chance of collision.'

At this point it may be remarked that when Sir Frederick Smith inspected the London & Brighton Railway in July 1841, he expressed his surprise at red – 'ordinarily the signal of danger' – being used to intimate to drivers using the line for Croydon trains that the junction was made.

The signals carried by the trains were: for the Croydon train, by day a red ball at the end of a rod held out on the right-hand side by the conductor riding on the first carriage; by night a double white light on the engine. The Greenwich trains were to be distinguished by their carrying no signal either by day or night. Both trains were to have a red light attached to the rear carriage.

For many years the Greenwich trains were peculiar in keeping to the right, instead of following the usual British rule of the road. They did not do so at first, but the change was made at a very early date.*

* Thos. Wright, however, in his *History of London* 1837, states the right-hand track was used from the commencement.

V

The London and Croydon Railway

ONE of the hopes of the projectors of the Greenwich Railway was that it would form the southern entrance to London. The first step towards the fulfilment of this aspiration – which, unlike most of the others, came true – was the opening of a railway from Croydon, at what is now known as West Croydon Station, to a junction with the Greenwich line at Corbett's Lane. It was incorporated 5th June, 1835, and opened throughout on 5th June, 1839. The length was 8¾ miles, the first three or so, i.e. from Croydon to Anerley, being laid on the bed of the Croydon Canal, which had been purchased for £40,250 for the property, and one shilling in respect of profits.

In constructing the line there was considerable trouble with the cuttings at Forest Hill and New Cross, whence 650,000 and 590,000 cubic yards respectively of material were removed; and the slopes had to be improved afterwards. That fact is mentioned here because Francis, in his *History of the English Railway*, said that the Croydon line was 'remarkable for nothing save its huge cost', a remark inspired by the expense having been £615,160 instead of the estimated £180,000.*

In a Report submitted to the fifth half-yearly meeting in March, 1838, it was stated that a contract had been entered into for the supply of 15,000 cross sleepers, adding 'With a view to the possible future expediency of widening the gauge of the rails from four feet eight inches to six or seven feet, and upon the supposition that this experiment and its accompaniments (now carrying into effect on the Great Western Railway) may turn out to be so decisive in character, and that its principles may also be applicable to all lines of railway, your Directors have contracted for the delivery of cross sleepers nine feet in length.'† The same report says that five locomotives had been ordered at a cost of £9,625. The line was laid with

---

* The figures are taken from Whishaw's *Railways of Great Britain and Ireland*, p. 283.

† At this time much discussion was going on as to the most advantageous gauge: a controversy which raged until it was laid to rest by the Gauge Commission of 1845. One newspaper spoke of the Great Western as being condemned by Holy Writ; being 'the broad way which leads to destruction'!

squat, broad-based T-rails (the T being, of course, inverted), screwed to longitudinal timbers with an intermediate layer of felt; the timbers resting on cross sleepers. The felt afterwards had to be removed, as it decayed.

The intermediate stations were New Cross (now New Cross Gate), Dartmouth Arms (Forest Hill), Sydenham, Penge, Anerley, and the Jolly Sailor (Norwood Junction). The course was fairly level, except for one formidable gradient of 1 in 100 from New Cross* up to the Dartmouth Arms, a distance of 2¾ miles. Here there had been no fewer than twenty-eight locks on the canal.

Contemporary writers were enthusiastic about the beauty of the country through which this line passed. The writer has one of the 'Mulready' covers for letters, with a time-table printed on the inside – evidently used by the company for their correspondence. There is no date on it, but it is probably 1840. Below the time-table – which shows an hourly service in the week and a half-hourly one on Sundays (except between 10 and 2) – is the following note:

DAY TICKETS. – In order to afford the Public an opportunity of viewing the beautiful Scenery upon this Line, more at leisure than the rapid transit of the Trains will now permit, the Directors have given orders that DAY TICKETS shall be issued, which will enable the holders, BY PAYING THE FARE TO CROYDON AND BACK, to stop at all or any of the stations, and proceed by any other train (IN WHICH THERE MAY BE ROOM) to or from Croydon.

An announcement to the same effect appears in Robinson's *Railway Directory* for September, 1840, to which is added:

MARQUEES &c ARE ERECTED IN THE WOOD, Close to the Anerley Station, and Parties using the Railway will be permitted to ANGLE IN THE ADJACENT CANAL, WHICH ABOUNDS IN FISH.

The station at New Cross occupied 2¾ acres of ground. There was an octagonal engine house, with a central turntable; probably the first to be made of this convenient form.

The Croydon station and depot were coextensive with the basin, wharves, etc., formerly occupied by the Canal company, and extended to nearly five acres of ground.

The line was formally opened on 1st June, 1839. Some two hundred guests took part in the ceremony, including the Lord Mayor of London, 'the Archbishop of Canterbury's lady', etc.

Two trains were provided to accommodate the party. Leaving the London Bridge station at one o'clock, the journey to Croydon occupied 31 minutes exactly, including a stop of 1¾ minutes at a

* For a short distance south of New Cross the actual gradient is 1 in 85.

station *en route*. After viewing the 'extensive' station at Croydon, which our authority states was 'excellently arranged and contained every comfort that can be desired', the guests again entrained, and journeyed to New Cross. Here they were joined by the Directors of the Brighton, South Eastern, and Greenwich Railways, who arrived in three trains. For the amusement of the company a band of music played in the octagonal engine house, and 'the effect from the reverberation of sound by the walls was truly grand'.

The whole party then went by train to Croydon, visiting the Dartmouth Arms, Jolly Sailor, and other stations on the way.

At Croydon station 'an elegant cold collation' was partaken of, followed by the speeches usual upon such occasions.

Whishaw described the trains thus:

> Each train is usually made up of two first- and two second-class carriages: the stopping and starting of the trains is well managed; and punctuality of departure and arrival are strictly attended to.
>
> We found the average weight of nine trains, taken in June, July, and December, 1839, to amount to 44,651 lb gross; the average velocity to be at the rate of 20·78 miles an hour; and the stoppages to occupy each on an average ·72 minute.

The duration of the stoppages indicate smart working, but fancy trains weighing under 20 tons gross!

There seems to have been no third class at first. The *Railway Times* for 2nd January, 1841, contains an advertisement that 'on and after the 25th inst. open third-class carriages will run between Croydon and New Cross only, stopping at the intermediate stations'; fare all the way, 8d. In the second half of 1840 the London and Croydon conveyed 256,000 passengers, the receipts from whom were £16,741 1s. 9½d. – the report does not say whether this amount is gross, or net, i.e. after deducting the tolls to the Greenwich company. The goods receipts were £1,391 15s. 9d., being principally derived from the carriage of coal and fullers' earth.

The Greenwich terminus was to have been used, but, before the line was opened, the Croydon company in 1836, obtained powers to build an independent station on the north side of the Greenwich station. In contrast to the original Greenwich terminus, the station erected by the Croydon company no longer exists, as it was swept away when the South Eastern line was extended, in 1864, to Cannon Street and Charing Cross.

Meanwhile, during the construction of the Croydon Railway, the South Eastern had been sanctioned in 1836, and the London & Brighton in 1837. Both railways were ultimately to reach London over the Croydon's metals to Corbett's Lane and thence over the

Greenwich Railway to London Bridge. The Royal Commission of 1839 on Railway Communication was alarmed at four companies' trains using the same line, and the Croydon company, in 1840, applied for powers to widen the Greenwich company's viaduct on the south side so that it would carry four lines of way; the additional lines being intended for the use of the Croydon, South Eastern, and Brighton companies. Parliament, however, decided that the widening should be done by the Greenwich company, as was related in the preceding chapter.

In consequence of the trains of the latter companies being on the south side of the Greenwich trains, and as the stations at London Bridge were exactly contrary to this, the two sets of trains would have had to cross each other's paths. It was therefore agreed in 1840 that the ownership of the stations should be exchanged, i.e. the Greenwich should take the new – the more northern – station and the Croydon take the original, Greenwich, station and the latter – apparently a very crude affair – was improved and enlarged at the expense of the three companies other than the Greenwich.

On this subject of the future station for the Croydon company the Report for the half-year ended 31st July, 1838, said:

Having frequently adverted to the advantages which the possession of an independent station in Tooley Street will ensure to this company, and to the position of it close to the centre of traffic and therefore affording greater convenience of access to the public than any other railway station in or near the metropolis, the directors will only add that under the powers conferred upon this company by their recent Act of Parliament the space for stations in possession of the Croydon Company, when added to that already in use by the Greenwich Railway, is so ample, whether united in arrangement or separate, as to afford all the accommodation to the public which can be desired.

The widening was completed in 1842 and the exchange of stations effected in 1844.

The London & Brighton company's trains commenced to run on 12th July, 1841, and the South Eastern on 26th May, 1842. As the distance their passengers had to travel over the Croydon rails was much longer than that of the Croydon over the Greenwich, the toll payable to the Croydon was made 1s. The question of tolls, particularly the $4\frac{1}{2}$d. payable to the Greenwich, was irritating to all concerned and, in order to be independent, the Croydon and South Eastern jointly obtained powers in 1843 to make a line 1 mile 52 chains long, to which reference has already been made in the previous chapter, from a point near where the Croydon line crossed the Surrey Canal to a station to be built at Bricklayers' Arms. Under the same

Act the line was to be transferred to the South Eastern, and that company opened the branch on 1st May, 1844.

It had been paid for as to one-third by the Croydon, and two-thirds by the South Eastern Railway. Before the branch was made, the Croydon directors had (in 1842) actually passed a resolution to give up running their own trains, on account of the toll to the Greenwich company, and to confine their business to taking the tolls of the Brighton and South Eastern companies.

The new terminus had the advantage of being suitable for dealing with goods traffic, as it was down on the ground level instead of being perched up on arches. It has retained its name to the present day, but since 1866 has only been used for goods and occasional excursions.

The Bricklayers' Arms branch has an important place in the history of signalling. It was here that Mr, later Sir, Charles Hutton Gregory installed a frame which contained the germ of interlocking, in 1843. He put up at the junction a shelter in which there were four levers, one each for the two signals to and from Bricklayers' Arms, and one each for the London Bridge ones. The chains for the signals were coupled to 'stirrups' in a framework and were pulled to 'clear' by the signalman putting his foot in the particular stirrup concerned and pressing it down. The stirrups fouled each other when used and thereby conflicting signals could not be lowered at the same time.

Mr Gregory appears to have carried his interlocking no further, although to extend it to the points seems so logical, that it is surprising to find that thirteen years elapsed before this was accomplished. In 1856 Saxby interlocked six pairs of points and eight semaphore arms at this junction.

In 1844 the London & Croydon company obtained powers to lay an additional line of rails, which they did on the down side. A most interesting feature of this development was the decision to work this line on the atmospheric principle; an intention which was, however, only carried out on the portion between New Cross and Croydon; the Dartmouth Arms–Croydon section being opened in the latter part of 1845, and the northward continuation to New Cross in January, 1847. The whole system was abolished in May of that year by the London, Brighton & South Coast Railway, whose property it had by then become.

In view of the fact that the nature of the atmospheric principle will probably be quite unknown to many readers, a description of this interesting episode in railway history had better be given.

About ten years after the opening of the Liverpool & Manchester Railway in 1830, which appeared to have firmly established the locomotive as the most suitable moving power for railways, this rival system was introduced, which for a time seemed quite formidable, and had many powerful advocates, among whom were Farey, Field, Brunel, Vignoles and Cubitt. The trains were drawn by a piston travelling in a tube laid between the rails, from which the air was exhausted by stationary engines. The first projectors of the principle of using atmospheric pressure for railways were George Medhurst, who wrote between 1810 and 1827; John Vallance, of Brighton, who put the whole train in a tunnel, and constructed a short experimental line in 1826; and Henry Pinkus, who had his own special method of sealing the slot in the top of the tube – which it was necessary to have, in order to connect the carriage with the piston – namely, by means of a flexible cord. A prospectus was issued in 1835 of the 'National Pneumatic Railway Association', to exploit Pinkus' patent, but it failed to materialise.

Then came Clegg and Samuda, who were very nearly successful. Under this system, a piston truck drew the carriages, the piston being kept tight by a leather packing, and connected to the train by an iron plate, which travelled through a slot in the top of the pipe. The slot was covered by a valve, formed of a strip of leather riveted between iron plates. This valve was opened by four wheels, as the piston proceeded, and closed again by a wheel on the carriage. The final sealing of the valve was done with a composition of beeswax and tallow, by means of a copper heater filled with burning charcoal, which re-melted the composition that had been broken by the lifting of the valve.

In the course of some preliminary experiments at their works at Southwark, Clegg and Samuda, with a tube 'about the diameter of a tumbler', drew thirteen people and 13 cwt of iron up an incline of 1 in 30. In June, 1840, they laid down an experimental line of about half a mile at Wormwood Scrubs, and the results raised high hopes. The steam engine, though only 16 h.p. (nominal), could propel $13\frac{1}{2}$ tons up a gradient of 1 in 115 at 20 miles an hour, and 5 tons at 45 miles an hour. These weights seem insignificant, but it must be remembered that in those days a first-class carriage only weighed about 4 tons.

In consequence of the results obtained on this experimental line the system was put into practical application between Kingstown and Dalkey, the Government granting a loan of £25,000 to the Dublin & Kingstown Railway for the purpose. This line, which was set to work in August, 1843, was single, about a mile and three-quarters long, with an average gradient of 1 in 115, and sharp curves. The tube was 15in in diameter, and the engine 100 h.p. Weights of 30 tons could be drawn up at 30 miles an hour, and 70 tons at 20 miles an hour. As much as 57½ miles an hour was attained. The railway operated from 1843 to 1855 quite satisfactorily, the chief reason for its abandonment being an extentsion to Bray, which was to be worked by locomotives, and the consequent inconvenience of having a portion in the middle of the line from Dublin to Bray on a different system.

The next atmospheric line was the one with which we are now concerned.

There were three stationary engine houses, namely at what are now Forest Hill, Norwood and Croydon. The following is an extract from one of the newspapers of the period:

Considerable apprehension has been entertained by lovers of the sweet rusticity of English landscape, lest the Stations on lines of Atmospheric Railway should destroy the picturesque character of the inland districts, by giving them the chimneyed aspect so singularly indicative of manufacturing localities. It appears, that for the purpose of blowing off the air withdrawn from the Atmospheric tubes, and discharging the surplus steam from the powerful engines to be used in effecting the exhaustion, tall chimnies, or 'stalks', as they are technically called, will be necessary at the Stations. These would, of course, be very unsightly objects, and as such are justly objected to by all persons of taste, to say nothing of the gentry who might be favoured with one or more within sight of their park walks or drawing-room windows. To get over this difficulty, it has been determined by the architects of the Croydon and Epsom line to give their chimneys an architectural character, and to relieve their baldness by the additions of proportions and decorations which have hitherto belonged almost exclusively to the bell-towers of the early Gothic churches. And, as in the opinion of the promoters of this scheme, beauty is as cheap as deformity, they have taken another step in the right direction, by a resolution to construct the station and engine houses in the style of the half-timbered manor houses of the Middle Ages.

The first section, Dartmouth Arms to Croydon, was inspected on behalf of the Government by General Pasley on 1st November, 1845, who reported that the distance of 5 miles was covered in 6¾ minutes, or at the rate of 44½ miles an hour.

Before that came about, two companies had been fighting in Parliament for powers to make a line to Epsom. One, the Epsom & South Western, wished to make a branch of 5 miles from the London & South Western main line at Kingston (now Surbiton) Station; while the Croydon & Epsom formed an 8-mile extension of the Croydon Railway through Carshalton to Epsom, to be on the atmospheric system. The latter route was 18 miles from London, as against 14 miles by the other, but, relying on the alleged superiority of the atmospheric system, its promoters offered a more frequent, and faster, service, at lower fares.

The Committee decided in favour of the Croydon line, as it passed through several large villages *en route*, which the other did not. They also feared that the four trains a day offered by the South Western company could not be exceeded without seriously incommoding the long distance traffic to and from Southampton and Gosport!

They were also attracted by the opportunity of making a more extended trial of the atmospheric system. Much evidence was given on the subject, Brunel and Cubitt being in favour, while Locke and Robert Stephenson were against. About this time, the latter had made a careful examination of the Kingstown and Dalkey line, and submitted an elaborate adverse report to the directors of the Chester & Holyhead Railway, who were considering the question of adopting the system.

So many railways were proposing to 'go atmospheric' at this time, that a Select Committee was appointed in March, 1845, to enquire into the question. Evidence was given by several of the principal engineers of the day. Brunel said that he had examined the Dalkey line, and that there did not appear to be any mechanical difficulties in the way of working the same system over a considerable length of line as was there applied to a short length, and that he had recommended it for the South Devon Railway. Vignoles was another favourable witness. He was advocating it for an extension from Dalkey to Kingstown, and for a line in Austria (neither of which recommendations was eventually adopted).

Robert Stephenson said that the Chester & Holyhead directors had abandoned the idea, in consequence of his report. He refused to admit the superiority of the atmospheric system, either on the grounds of economy or safety, but he paid it the handsome compliment of saying that the longitudinal valve was 'a complete triumph of mechanism'.

William Cubitt, the engineer of the London & Croydon, said that he was putting in the system between London and Croydon and was going to adopt it on the by then sanctioned extension from Croydon to Epsom. He added that he had recommended it for the London & Portsmouth and for the line from Croydon to Maidstone and Tonbridge and on to Ashford. He said that he had staked his reputation on its success. It was well adapted, he considered, to very hilly districts and to large passenger traffic which required to go at short intervals and very quickly. It was particularly applicable to short lines with a large number of passengers, but it was doubtful whether it was equally adaptable to a long line under the same circumstances. With experience and good management it might, though, come to that. He considered it quite feasible to use wooden rails!

Locke gave adverse evidence, followed by Bidder, on the same side, except that the latter admitted the suitability of the system where the traffic is simple, the line not very long and the trains very frequent.

The concluding paragraph of the Committee's Report was as follows:

> While your committee have thus expressed a strong opinion in favour of the general merits of the atmospheric system they feel that experience can alone determine under what circumstances of traffic or of country the preference to either system should be given.

The Forest Hill–Croydon line must have worked fairly satisfactorily, as the writer has a prospectus of the 'Dorking, Brighton & Arundel Atmospheric Railway' – capital a million pounds – which cites the Croydon line as 'having exceeded the most sanguine anticipations, and as proving that railways constructed on the atmospheric principle must eventually supersede all others'. Nevertheless it was soon abolished after the amalgamation with the Brighton Railway. In spite of the considerable number of lines projected about this time – many of which were authorised – to operate on this principle, only two more were actually made: the Paris & St. Germain Railway, which was opened in 1847, and worked till 1860; and the Exeter–Newton Abbot section of the South Devon Railway, opened in January, 1848, which was an utter failure, and had to be altered to locomotive working at the end of the year.

In the middle of 1845 the London & Croydon company was actively promoting an atmospheric line from Sydenham to Chatham, in opposition to the South Eastern (and to another proposed 'North Kent Railway', called Vignoles'). It had been originally projected by Brunel, under the name of the 'London, Chatham & Portsmouth Railway', also with the intention of working 'atmospheric'. It fell into the hands of the Croydon company, whereupon Brunel resigned, and Cubitt became the engineer. The western part was to proceed by way of the Portsmouth Atmospheric, of which more will be said in a succeeding chapter.

It appears, from a *Statement of the Directors of the Croydon Railway Company* of 1844, in the writer's collection, that it was at first proposed to work hand in hand with the South Eastern company in this matter, but that the latter broke off negotiations, and preferred to act independently, so the Croydon directors applied themselves to an opposition scheme. Two other points of interest in the pamphlet are that the Greenwich Board had also announced their intention of promoting a railway toward the north of Kent; and that discussions were on foot for the South Eastern to lease the Croydon line, which came to nothing.

On 27th July, 1846, the Croydon and Brighton companies amalgamated under the name of London, Brighton & South Coast, and 4th May, 1847, saw the last of the atmospheric system; by which time nearly half a million of money had been spent on it. An interesting fact is that, in order to allow it to cross the ordinary line, the first 'flying junction' was constructed near Norwood.

According to a Board of Trade Report of October, 1841, the Croydon Railway at that time possessed eight engines, all with six wheels. Whishaw gives a list of seven existing in 1840, and mentions another, but his details are not all correct.

LOCOMOTIVES OF THE CROYDON RAILWAY.

No.	Name	Maker	Date	Cylinders	D. Wheels
1	*Surrey*	Sharp, Roberts	1838	13 × 18 (I)	5ft 6in (2)
2	*Croydon*	G. & J. Rennie	,,	,, (O)	5ft 0in (4)
3	*Sussex*	Sharp, Roberts	,,	,, (I)	5ft 6in (2)
4	*Kent*	,,	,,	,, ,,	,, ,,
5	*London*	,,	1839	,, ,,	,, ,,
6	*Archimedes*	G. & J. Rennie	,,	,, (O)	5ft 0in (4)
7	*Hercules*	Sharp, Roberts	,,	14 × 18 (I)	,, ?
8	*Victoria*	,,	,,	13 × 18 (I)	5ft 6in (2)
	(renamed *Sydenham*)				

No illustration of the Sharp engines has come down, but they were (except No. 7) no doubt of that firm's standard design, an example of which is known from those supplied to the South Eastern Railway.

The Rennie engines were an innovation in design, having outside cylinders and leading coupled wheels, which never took root in England, but became popular for a time in Scotland, and quite a rage on the Continent. They were used as 'banking' engines up the New Cross incline.

Whishaw says that an engine named *Coryndon*, built by Chanter & Co., was added to the stock in 1840, but it is more probable that it was only tried, and not accepted. In *The Locomotives of the L.B.S.C.R.* it is said that this engine, which was unusual for the period in burning coal – fed through a hopper – was afterwards No. 79 on the South Eastern Railway, but this is extremely doubtful.

In April or May, 1842, the rolling stock of the Croydon and Dover (i.e. South Eastern) lines began to be used in common, and managed by a Joint Committee. The agreement was announced as having been entered into in a report of the South Eastern Railway dated 31st May, 1842.* In March, 1844, the Brighton company's engines came into the pool. On 31st January, 1846, the Joint Committee was abolished and, the Croydon company being on the point of dissolution, the stock was divided up between the Brighton and South Eastern companies. The engines did not all return to their original owners, and, while the South Eastern retained the Joint Committee numbers, the Brighton company altered those which fell to their share in a rather haphazard manner. The full story is a very interesting one, but extremely complicated, and the following account is the first attempt to unravel it, in print, at all events – a result for which the writer has to thank Mr A. C. W. Lowe for much valuable assistance.

LOCOMOTIVES OF THE JOINT COMMITTEE

Nos. 1 to 8 were the Croydon engines given above.

Nos. 9 to 34 were the first South Eastern Railway engines, originally 1–26 on that line, as below.

No.	Name	Makers	Date	Type	D. Wheels	Cylinders
9	Hengist	Sharp	1841	2-2-2	5ft 6in	13 by 18
10	Horsa	,,	,,	,,	,,	,,
11	Caesar	,,	1842	,,	,,	,,
12	Vortigern	,,	,,	,,	,,	,,
13	Vortimer	,,	,,	,,	,,	,,
14	Ethelbert	,,	,,	,,	,,	,,
15	Egbert	,,	,,	,,	,,	14 by 18
16	Sweyn	,,	,,	,,	,,	,,
17	Canute	,,	,,	,,	,,	,,
18	Hardicanute	,,	,,	,,	,,	13 by 18
19	Ironsides	,,	,,	,,	,,	,,
20	Harold	,,	,,	,,	,,	14 by 18
21–23	?	Bury	,,	2-2-0	,,	,,
24	Stour	,,	,,	,,	,,	,,
25	Teise	,,	,,	,,	,,	,,
26	Beult	,,	,,	0-4-0	5ft 0in	,,
27	Man of Kent	Rennie	1843	2-2-2	5ft 6in	15 by 18
28	Maid of Kent	,,	,,	,,	,,	,,
29	Escus	Sharp	,,	,,	,,	14 by 18
30	Octa	,,	,,	,,	,,	?
31	Samson	,,	,,	,,	,,	15 by 18
32	Goliath	,,	,,	,,	,,	,,
33	Cray	Bury	,,	2-2-0	,,	14 by 18
34	Rother	,,	,,	,,	,,	,,

* *Railway Times*, Vol. V, p. 586.

London & Croydon Railway design of station and pumping house.

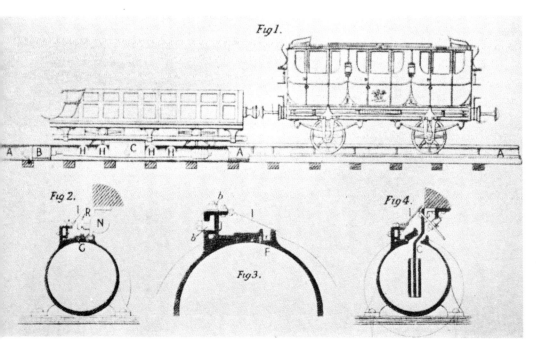

Clegg & Samuda Atmospheric System; Fig. 4 shows the longitudinal valve open, with the bar attached to the train within it.

Waterloo station and engine house in 1848. [*British Railways*

Southampton Station (up side) in the earliest days. [*BTC Collection*

Nos. 35–44 were ordered by the Joint Committee:

No.	Name	Makers	Date	Type	D. Wheels	Cylinders
35	Achilles	Sharp	1843	0-4-2	?	14 by 18
36	Shakespear	,,	,,	2-2-2	5ft 6in	,,
37	King Lear	,,	,,	,,	,,	,,
38	Gog	Bury	,,	0-4-0	4ft 6in	14 by 20
39	Magog	,,	,,	,,	,,	,,
40	Hermeuric	Sharp	,,	2-2-2	5ft 6in	14 by 18
41	Eadbald	,,	1844	,,	,,	,,
42	Ercombert	,,	,,	,,	,,	,,
43	Medway	Bury	,,	2-2-0	,,	,,
44	White Horse of Kent	?	,,	2-2-2	5ft 6in	15 by 22?

The *White Horse of Kent* was one of the earliest engines constructed under Robert Stephenson's 'long boiler' patent. The cylinders were outside; all the wheels were in front of the firebox, the driving wheels being in the middle. She figures prominently in the evidence before the Gauge Commission, from which one gathers she was a very unsteady runner at speed. When she eventually came into the hands of the South Eastern Railway they altered her to 2-4-0, with 6ft wheels. *King Lear* was also altered in this way.

Nos. 45–75 were the Brighton stock, numbered on that railway 1 to 31. They were all in order, except that No. 6 became 51; and 7, 50.

No.	Name	Makers	Date	Type	D. Wheels	Cylinders
45	Brighton	Jones	1839	2-2-2	5ft 6in	13 by 18
46	Shoreham	,,	,,	0-4-2	5ft 0in	15 by 22
47	Merstham	Sharp	,,	2-2-2	5ft 6in	14 by 18
48	Coulsdon	,,	,,	,,	,,	,,
49	?	Fairbairn	1841	,,	,,	,,
50	Eagle	Rennie	1840	,,	,,	,,
51	Venus	Sharp	1839	,,	,,	13 by 18
52	Vulture	Rennie	1840	,,	,,	14 by 18
53	Satellite	,,	1841	,,	,,	,,
54	Jupiter	Sharp	1839	,,	,,	13 by 18
55	Mars	,,	1840	,,	,,	14 by 18
56	Saturn	,,	1841	,,	,,	,,
57	Mercury	,,	,,	,,	,,	,,
58	Orion	,,	,,	,,	,,	,,
59	Sirius	,,	,,	,,	,,	,,
60	?	,,	,,	,,	,,	,,
61–66	—	Bury	,,	2-2-0	,,	,,
67–72	—	Sharp	,,	2-2-2	,,	,,
73–75	—	Fairbairn	1842	,,	,,	,,

The following were delivered to the Joint Committee:

No.	Makers	Date	Type	D. Wheels	Cylinders
76, 77	Forrester	1844	2-4-0	5ft 6in	14 by 18
78	Bury	,,	?	?	?
79	?	,,	'Sharp'	5ft 6in	13 by 18?

No.	Makers	Date	Type	D. Wheels	Cylinders
80	Bury	1884	0-4-0	5ft 0in	14 by 24
81	,,	,,	,,	?	,,
82	,,	,,	,,	4ft 6in	,,
83	,,	,,	,,	?	,,
84–89	Sharp	,,	2-2-2	5ft 6in	15 by 18
90–95	,,	1845	,,	,,	,,
96–99	Hawthorn	,,	,,	,,	,,
100	Bodmer	,,	,,	?	?
101, 102	Hick	,,	,,	5ft 6in	13 by 18
103	Sharp	1841	,,	,,	15 by 18
104–106	,,	1842	,,	,,	,,
107–112	Bury	1845	0-4-0	5ft 0in	14 by 24
113–118	Jones	,,	2-2-2	5ft 6in	15 by 22
119–122	Tayleur	,,	0-6-0	4ft 9in	15 by 24
123, 124	Bodmer	,,	2-2-2	5ft 6in	16 by 30

No names are known, except No. 82, *Woodman*.

The three Bodmer engines, Nos. 100, 123 and 124, had double pistons working opposite to one another in the same cylinder. Nos. 103–106 were bought from the Manchester & Birmingham Railway in 1845. Only 122 engines were divided up; the two which disappeared are believed to have been No. 78, which exploded, and No. 100, which was returned to the maker. The distribution between the two companies will be shown in the chapters dealing with their loco-motives.

An important development in signalling occurred on the London & Croydon Railway in 1841 or 1842, when Gregory put up the first semaphore signal to be used on a railway, at New Cross. Previously, as on the Greenwhich line, boards or discs were used. The semaphore had been invented in France by Chappe in 1791. In 1793 'telegraphy' – the word was in use before the application of electricity – by means of semaphores, was practised during the French Revolution. Some years later the Admiralty set up a complete chain of them between London and Portsmouth.

The writer has not come across any records of accidents on the London & Croydon Railway, which is rather remarkable, considering that it operated for seven years, and included only the second example in the world of a junction between railways running over the same lines (the first was that between the Liverpool and Manchester, and the Grand Junction). Moreover, it went through a district notorious for bad fogs. If one or two serious collisions had occurred, the development of railways might have been set back indefinitely.

PART II
THE LONDON AND SOUTH WESTERN RAILWAY

VI

The London and Southampton Railway

THE tribulations sustained by shipping in the passage up the English Channel during the Napoleonic Wars, together with the frequent delays caused by contrary winds and fogs, turned the minds of those interested towards the consideration of the possibilities of making a short cut to the Metropolis. The first results of the pursuit of this idea were some schemes for a ship canal from Portsmouth to London. The latest, and most ambitious one, was estimated to cost about £7,000,000. The route was investigated by Sir John Rennie, and surveyed by Francis Giles, a prominent engineer of the day, who had been responsible for a number of harbour works, river improvements, and canals. Nothing, however, came of this project.

The success of the Stockton and Darlington, and of the Liverpool & Manchester railways, suggested that the problem might be solved by making Southampton the port of arrival, and carrying the passengers and cargoes on to London by rail.

The first step towards the formation of the railway was a meeting, on 26th February, 1831, at the residence of Mr Abel Rous Dottin, one of the two members of Parliament for Southampton, afterwards the first chairman of the Greenwich Railway. The meeting led to money being subscribed for the initial expenses, the appointment of Giles as the engineer, and the issue, on 6th April, of the prospectus of the Southampton, London & Branch Railway & Dock Company, with the proposed capital of $1\frac{1}{2}$ million. Colonel George Henderson was the chairman. The branch referred to in the title was to be from Basingstoke to Bath and Bristol, and the London terminus was to be at Nine Elms, Vauxhall. As the bill for the London & Birmingham Railway was to be submitted to Parliament in the following session, it was decided to see how that fared before offering the Southampton proposals. Meanwhile, it was determined to abandon the idea of new docks, and the proposed capital was reduced to one million.

The London and Birmingham Act was passed in 1833, and in 1834 the London & Southampton Railway bill came before Parliament. It was for the main line only, as the branch to Bath and Bristol was held over. The bill received the support of the naval authorities and of shipping interests, and it became the Act 5 Will. IV, c. 88 (1834).

A bill for the Bath and Bristol branch was deposited for consideration by the Parliament of 1835. It was offered as an alternative to the proposals of the Great Western, whose bill, after passing the House of Commons, had, the previous year, been rejected by the Lords. The Southampton company proposed to leave the main line at Basingstoke, and to pass through Newbury, Hungerford, Devizes, Trowbridge – a fine string of places, and in decided contrast to those on the Great Western route – namely Bradford-on-Avon and Bath, and thence to Bristol.

The Great Western submitted their proposals again in 1835, and these were approved and the Basingstoke–Bath–Bristol effort rejected. Not only were the Southampton people defeated on that point, but the Great Western got powers to make a line from Thingley, immediately west of Chippenham, to Trowbridge; and a branch from Holt, on the new line to Bradford-on-Avon, which crossed the path of the Southampton company's proposed line from Basingstoke. It was thus, in 1835, and in the earliest days of the two companies, that there was begun the severe competition between the London & South Western and the Great Western which was to last, with occasional lulls, for many years.

In connection with the Great Western's first Act, the interesting fact may be mentioned that the London & Southampton company, quite innocently, created the first opening for the adoption of the broad gauge. It was the custom in those days for the intended gauge to be recited in the Act for a new railway. Probably by accident, the Act for making the London & Southampton failed to do so, and when Brunel, in 1835, desired that the London and Bristol bill should not mention the gauge proposed for that line, but leave it an open question, he was able to show that this had been done in the Southampton Act. The precedent thus created therefore paved the way for the adoption, for good or ill, of the broad gauge.

It cannot be said that the London & Southampton was fortunate in its first engineer. When the Liverpool & Manchester Railway was before Parliament in 1825, Giles was one of the engineering witnesses against it, particularly with respect to its crossing Chat Moss. He said:

In my judgment a railroad of this description certainly cannot be safely made over Chat Moss without going to the bottom of the Moss. It will be necessary, therefore, in making a railroad, which is to stand, to take out, along the whole line of road, the whole of the Moss to the bottom and to cut down to 33 or 34ft and afterwards to fill it up to such a height as the railroad is to be carried over the soil, with other soil mixed with a portion of the moss; and therefore, if Mr. Stephenson be right in placing the level of the railroad 15ft below* the Moss they

* He must have meant 'above'.

would not only have to cut out 34 but to build up the other 15ft and, unless that were done, I do not think that a railroad would stand. My estimate for the whole cutting and embanking over Chat Moss is £270,000 nearly, at those quantities and those prices which are decidedly correct. No engineer in his senses would go through Chat Moss if he wanted to make a railroad from Liverpool to Manchester.

As is well known, the Liverpool & Manchester was carried – and remains today – over Chat Moss. Stephenson built the line and the deepest section of solid embankment had a depth of only 20ft, instead of, as Giles anticipated, 49ft. Moreover, the total cost of executing that work was only £28,000. Those false premises of the future engineer of the London & Southampton Railway did that line no good; in fact, they prejudiced its interests, inasmuch as people who might have invested their money in the undertaking were chary of doing so. Giles was a good engineer – he designed two fine bridges at Wethcral and Corby on the Newcastle & Carlisle Railway – but probably lacked business ability. He had many difficulties to contend with on the Southampton line, and the progress was slow; consequently the shareholders in Manchester – who had furnished half the capital – remembering the Chat Moss incident – appointed a committee if investigation, resulting in Giles' resignation. The Directors thereupon appointed Joseph Locke, the engineer of the Grand Junction, to succeed him, and the new engineer entered upon his duties in 1837.

An equally great acquisition by the company was made also in the same year, namely William James Chaplin, of the carrying firm of Chaplin and Horne. Chaplin, having complete faith in the future of the railway, and believing that it meant the practical elimination of the carrier, sold the greater part of his business and invested a large portion of the proceeds in the London & Southampton Railway, thereby adding greatly to its financial standing.

As John Francis* may be considered the most intelligent and unprejudiced of the writers of that day, his views are worthy of examination. On the subject of the London & Southampton he made some lengthy remarks which are reproduced here, particularly for the sake of what he said about Chaplin and Locke. Francis observed:

When, in 1832, the London and Southampton line was presented to the notice of an intelligent public it was considered somewhat strange and singular. It was natural enough to have a trunk line between Liverpool and Manchester; it was perfectly legitimate to propose the iron way betwixt Birmingham, which supplied the world with its manufactures, and London, the temporary recipient of its produce. But Southampton was in the position of neither; it possessed no manufactures like Manchester; it was deficient in the commercial power of Liverpool;

* *History of the English Railway* (1851).

it lacked the capitalists of Birmingham; it had not the attraction of Brighton; it required no rapid communication with the capital; and when its promoters first proposed to the people of Southampton the advantages they would derive from the rail, and Sir John Easthope explained to the *savans* (*sic*) of the city the premium they would procure from its scrip, it does not appear to have met with a very enthusiastic reception. The energy of its supporters, however, carried through this portion of its difficulties, and when Lancashire, the home and haunt of railway enterprise, supported it; when the shrewd Scotch followed the example, and they of the Stock Exchange dealt in its shares, a more hopeful feeling spread throughout the body corporate.

The first estimate was between £800,000 and £900,000, and this, in the absence of that information which has since been so dearly paid for, appeared fair and feasible. It would be inconvenient to enter on the subject of its early difficulties, they were patent to all the lines, and it is sufficient to state that in July, 1834, the Act of incorporation received the royal assent. The amount authorised to be raised was £1,000,000, in 20,000 shares of £50 each, with an additional power to borrow £330,000 by loan.

A grievous error was committed, and these sums soon proved insufficient. In entering into contracts for the works, they were unhappily given in small lots to small men, at a low price, instead of being let to those who had capital and credit to lose, and upon whom full security could be placed. It was on low and unsatisfactory estimates that the bill was passed; and while the work was easy, while prices and pay remained depressed, while nothing extraordinary occurred, the work was done; but when any engineering novelty arose, the poor contractor was powerless. The smallest difficulty stayed him, the slightest danger paralysed him. He could not complete his contracts; he lacked resources to pay the penalty; the works were often stopped; the directors as often in despair. A second Act was passed in 1837, empowering an additional capital stock of £400,000, with a loan of £130,000; and in 1839, a third Act was passed for the purpose of constructing a branch to Gosport.

Previous to the Act of 1837, it was evident to all connected with the line that £500,000 more would be required, and the proprietors were startled. The calls were difficult to be procured, the shares were at a terrible discount, the prospects of the company gloomy, when the gentlemen of Lancashire, who were interested, inquired into the circumstances connected with its progress. Aware of the difficulties which had beset the paths of railways generally, they with great promptitude appointed a deputation to examine the accounts, to revise the estimates, and to report on the position of the corporation. This inquiry was satisfactory. Money to continue the works was advanced, two of the committee were appointed directors, and an entirely new system was adopted. Mr Giles resigned the engineership, the services of Mr Locke were procured, a complete plan, showing the exact position of the work, was drawn out; everything which could assist in lessening the difficulties was adopted, and a thorough revision of traffic and expenses entered into. Mr Chaplin, wisely adopting the new mode of travelling as the basis of his future proceedings, joined their ranks, and to his sagacity may be traced much of the ultimate success of this railway. He gave every information which his experience had procured; he offered every recommendation which his information could suggest, he assisted them by his counsel, and he raised them by his influence. A fresh estimate was made of the cost of the line; much unnecessary work was avoided; £1,700,000 was regarded as the probable sum it would ultimately cost; and it will afford a significant remembrance of the difficulties which yet clung to the railroad when it is said that the only way of procuring the money necessary to finish the undertaking was to raise £50 shares and sell them at £25, thus issuing them at a fearful discount.

Under the new management the new line proceeded rapidly. Able and responsible contractors were chosen; the expenditure of one year doubled that of the three preceding years, and the line opened throughout on the 11th May, 1840. So close and cautious had been Mr Chaplin's estimate of traffic, that within three months the receipts amounted to the sum proposed.

*   *   *

The cost of this line is another curiosity when compared with the estimate. The capital proposed was one million; the capital raised was two millions. The actual expenditure was £2,592,000, the land alone costing more than one-third of the entire original estimate. Thirteen thousand pounds per mile was the supposed – more than double was the real – cost.

It has been seen that Mr Locke was called upon to finish the line, and the intelligent countenance of this gentleman, for whom all the honours due to a high order of engineering have been claimed, is sufficiently familiar. The pupil of George Stephenson, his fame dates from Chat Moss, over which he assisted to form the road, and to which he owes much of his early experience. The Grand Junction from Liverpool to Birmingham was by him; the London and Southampton was under his inspection. Young and energetic, he was a valuable aid in all those parliamentary struggles between landowners and railways which have excited so much attention, and spent so much money. Since then he has raised a great reputation. He formed the magnificent viaduct and tunnel of the Manchester and Sheffield; he introduced passenger traffic into Spain, and to this gentleman has been awarded the praise of keeping his works within his estimates.

There is an easy elegance in the oratory of Mr Locke, which is agreeable to hear, and this is equalled by his choice of language. A member of the legislature,* he speaks there with much effect, worthily representing the interest to which he is allied.

Such was the man who took the place of Mr Giles at the time that Mr Chaplin gave his assistance to the London & Southampton, and to none more than Mr Chaplin was the new mode of travel important. It struck at the root of his business; it was destroying the arrangement of years; it was upsetting the combinations of a life. When, therefore, this proprietor of numerous coaches and almost innumerable horses, saw the London & Birmingham road occupied, and every other way seized on by the advocates of the locomotive; he saw also that he must take some decided course. It is not then to be wondered at that when, as already shown, that which is now known as the London & South Western was in difficulties, Mr Chaplin possessing both mind and money to aid it, assisted, instead of decrying the railway; parted with his stock in trade, became one of its directors, and entered boldly and decidedly into it. His intelligence and capital were recognised: he soon became deputy chairman; was elected in 1842 to the chair itself, and since then has maintained his position. Like other railway men, he has entered Parliament and is not undistinguished among that class which owns a Stephenson, a Glyn, a Hudson, and a Locke in our great house of legislature.

The following table, which is also taken from Francis, is interesting as showing the costs of the first four great lines, apart from those of the actual construction. The amounts are per mile.

	Law, Engineering and Direction	Parliamentary	Land and Compensation
London and Southampton	£900	£650	£4,000
London and Birmingham	£1,500	£650	£6,300
London and Brighton	£1,800	£3,000	£8,000
Great Western	£2,500	£1,000	£6,300

* He was M.P. for Honiton, 1847–1860.

The figures on the previous page show that, in comparison with the other lines, the London & Southampton may have been said to be quite economical.

In a pamphlet of 1834 entitled *The Advantages and Profits of the London & Southampton Railway analysed*, it is said that the principle on which the line was laid down was simply the avoidance of estates, the owners of which would have been likely to have offered it opposition. 'The line was therefore carried through a barren and desolate country, where the soil was so valueless, that the landowners were glad to get rid of it at any price.' The author of the pamphlet scorns the idea that 'the travellers for pleasure, the idle tourists of the Isle of Wight, or the quiet families who are coming to spend their summer at Southampton, shall all yield up the comforts of their travelling carriages and post horses, and ensconce themselves behind the smoke of a steam engine.' Evidence is quoted that the whole traffic between London and Southampton was then carried on by eight stage-coaches, four wagons per week, and one barge weekly on the Basingstoke Canal (the £100 shares of which then stood at £5). The excavations and embankments were said to be of a more stupendous nature than had ever been projected. According to this account, the line was supported by the landowners in Hampshire, who possessed the barren ground, and by people at Southampton who supposed – rightly, as it turned out – that their trade would be improved; while the Surrey landowners were against it. Its opponents observed that if Southampton possessed all the advantages as a port which were put forward, it was surprising that it had enjoyed so little commerce, compared with Bristol or Liverpool, which were so much farther from London.

The answer to that argument is that the passage up and down Southampton Water is none too easy for sailing vessels, but is ideal for steamers, and it is partly due to their coming into general use, and not only to the railway, that the prosperity of Southampton made so much progress from that time forward.

It should be put upon record that the contractor for the first fifteen miles out of London, i.e. from Wandsworth to the River Wey Navigation, was Thomas Brassey, who was said in one of Mr Locke's reports, to be 'a very able and responsible contractor'.

He afterwards entered into a ten-year contract to keep the 77 miles of line from London to Southampton in repair for the sum of £24,000 per annum. When the contract came to an end, the company found it could be done considerably cheaper.

The London terminus of the line was at Nine Elms, which according to a contemporary writer, was 'a low swampy district, occasionally overflowed by the Thames. Its osier beds, pollards, windmills and the river, give it a Dutch aspect, but the ground is fast becoming occupied with buildings, and losing its peculiar character.' The architect of the station was no less a person than William Tite, who designed the Royal Exchange.

The report for the first half year of 1837 concluded with the following observations:

It is highly worthy of remark that the circumstances of this railway having one of its termini at the water's edge in Southampton harbour and the other at a wharf on the banks of the Thames, affords every convenience which Nature and Art combined can give for such a traffic. With respect to the situation of the London terminus, as it bears upon the convenience of passengers, the following statement of the distances from the Royal Exchange and from Charing Cross of the termini of the London and Birmingham, the Great Western and the Southampton Railways will show the local merits of each:

	To Charing Cross	To the Royal Exchange
From Euston	1 mile 65 chains	3 miles 16 chains
Paddington	2 ,, 60 ,,	4 ,, 26 ,,
Nine Elms	1 ,, 77 ,,	3 ,, 9 ,,

In addition to the usual accommodation by omnibuses arrangements are being made by which the passengers will be conveyed in small steamboats and landed at any point between Vauxhall and London Bridge within a few minutes of the time of their arrival at the station. These small steamboats will be in waiting at the terminus wharf (i.e. the then Nine Elms pier) for the arrival of the different trains, and, in like manner, they will start from the various points of embarkation along the river in time to reach the station before the departure of the trains.

Mention of the termini prompts the quotation of the following remarks from the report presented to the half-yearly meeting in February, 1839:

The sum of £75,000 estimated – or rather, assumed – on that occasion (the half-yearly meeting twelve months previously) as the first cost of stations, engines, carriages, wagons and machinery, has been found entirely insufficient to provide these accommodations on such a scale as is required by the probable traffic of the railway and due attention to public convenience. The directors have deemed it prudent, and, ultimately, economical, to construct these establishments on the requisite scale at the outset, in preference to merely opening the line of railway as a road and then having to incur fresh expense in altering and adding to inadequate establishments; besides failing, until that object should be accomplished, in either giving satisfaction to the public or doing justice to the character and capability of the undertaking.

There has been no unnecessary expense in architectural designs or decorations. The objects aimed at have been utility and durability at the smallest possible cost; and although the expense will greatly exceed the estimated or assumed sum of £75,000, yet the directors have the satisfaction to inform you that they will be enabled to complete the whole undertaking without calling for any extension of capital or contemplating any further application to Parliament.

The first section to be brought into use was from Nine Elms to Woking Common, with intermediate stations at Wandsworth, Wimbledon, Kingston, Ditton Marsh, Walton and Weybridge. Wandsworth Station, which was situated at Freemasons' Bridge, was later renamed Clapham, and was closed when the present Clapham Junction station was opened on 2nd March, 1863. The original Kingston was on the west side of Ewell Road Bridge, but in response to representations from local inhabitants, the company decided in April, 1839, to provide another station on the present site. Ditton Marsh is now Esher.

It was intended to open the section in question on 1st June, 1838, but it so happened that earlier in the week there came Epsom races, including the 'Derby', and so the arrangements for the inauguration were hurried on, and the line was brought into use on 21st May.

In view of the services that were later to be rendered by the London & South Western Company to race meetings it may be noted that in *The Times* of 29th May, 1838, there appeared an advertisement to the effect that extra trains for Epsom races would be run on the Tuesday, Wednesday, Thursday, and Friday of that week 'to a point on the railway south of Kingston which is nearest to Epsom'. The result of the advertisement may be seen in the following quotation from the issue of that paper for 31st May:

It is speaking very much within bounds to say that at an early hour upwards of 5,000 persons were assembled at the gates of the Southampton Railway at Nine Elms, near Vauxhall, for the purpose of going by the railroad trains to the Kingston station and from thence by other conveyances to the race course. The steamboats which ply from London Bridge and from Hungerford were filled with passengers who made sure of getting down to Epsom by the railroad. Hundreds were fated to be disappointed. There were ten times more applicants for seats in the train vans than there were seats for their accommodation. The proprietors did what they could to meet the demands for conveyance, but they could not do what was impossible.

Shortly after the opening the secretary to the company wrote to John Herapath, the editor of the *Railway Magazine* of the period, and said that 'although there are seven stopping places between London and Woking, the engines perform their journey of 23 miles within the hour. Among the engines those made by Rennie and Company have been particularly remarkable by the simplicity and excellence of construction and the ease and rapidity with which they perform their journey, often at the rate of between 40 and 50 m.p.h.'

From the report presented to the half-yearly Meeting on 30th August, 1838, it seems that the estimated number of passengers was 2,150 per week. The actual number had, however, been 7,586 and, up to that date, the gross receipts had been £13,390, the expenditure £4,620, and the net receipts £8,770. It may be noted that the question of Sunday travel was raised by a shareholder, to which the chairman replied that they did not feel justified in shutting up the road on a Sunday and debarring the public from health, air, exercise and relaxation.

The line was extended to Shapley (Winchfield) on 24th September, 1838, and thence to Basingstoke on 10th June, 1839. The next section was from Basingstoke to Winchester, but was delayed owing to a deviation being necessary, for which powers were obtained in 1837. From Winchester to Southampton was, however, ready and it was opened on the same day as the Shapley–Basingstoke section.

In the report read at the half-yearly Meeting on 27th February, 1839, it was said as to the Basingstoke–Winchester section:

This work is all comprised in one contract with Mr Brassey, and is proceeding most satisfactorily, although the section still presents a large quantity of unfinished earthwork; but the energy which is evinced, and which is in unison with the conduct of the same contractor in former instances, affords the directors entire confidence in the completion of Mr Brassey's contract at the stipulated time, viz. the 1st of May, 1840, on which day the directors believe that the whole distance to Southampton will be opened.

Brassey kept his word, and the gap was filled when the Basingstoke–Winchester section was opened on 11th May, 1840, completing the whole distance.

There were four short tunnels: one at Litchfield, 198 yards long; two at Popham, 264 and 287 yards; and one at Wallers Ash, 495 yards.

Meanwhile, in 1839, powers were given to build a line from Bishopstoke – now Eastleigh – to 'outside the fortifications at Gosport'. As there was a strong objection in Portsmouth to that town being served by a company in whose name the rival port of Southampton was so prominent, the same Act also sanctioned the change of name to the London & South Western Railway.*

The branch to Gosport was opened on 29th November, 1841, but as Locke was nervous about the stability of the tunnel at Fareham, the line was closed four days later. It was reopened on 7th February, 1842.

The Board of Trade Report after the inspection of this line is interesting. It is dated 28th November, 1841 – and therefore before

* It may be of interest to note that another line called the 'South Western Railway' went unsuccessfully before Parliament in 1837, of which George Stephenson was the Engineer. It was to run from a junction with the London & Southampton near Basingstoke, to the Bristol & Exeter near Taunton, with a branch to Winchester.

the line was closed – and therein Sir Frederick Smith, the chief inspecting officer, said of the tunnel and its approaches:

These works pass through a soil which has baffled all calculation. In excavating, both in the cutting and tunnel, the workmen were obliged to blast a good proportion of the ground with gunpowder and yet, from exposure to wet, it has become almost semi-fluid and in the cutting there is scarcely any slope at which it would stand. At the north end of the tunnel the slopes have in consequence, lost all regularity of form and pour over the retaining walls upon the rails.

The construction of the line nearly ruined the contractor, Thomas Brassey, and it is possible to conceive that the building of railways would have had a serious setback had that misfortune followed.

As a matter of further interest it may be noted that a very important question was raised by Sir Frederick Smith in his Report, which was to take an acute form after the failure of the Tay Bridge in 1878. He observed:

I have not discovered any cause for apprehension in respect to this tunnel in my present inspection of it, but in my former report I observed that the Lords of the Council (the Board of Trade) could take no responsibility in such work as tunnels, even under ordinary and favourable circumstances, as their officials have no official knowledge of the sufficiency of the sectional strength of the sustaining arches and side walls and of the inverts, or of the quality of the work of which they are composed.

The force of this observation applies much more strongly in such a case as the present where the work has already given evidence that it is exposed to great and sudden pressure and, therefore, the whole responsibility of using this tunnel must rest with the directors of the company, for they have had the means, by frequent personal inspection and by reports of their engineer, of arriving at a full knowledge of all the circumstances connected with this work and whether, if its form has undergone any change, that change has been to such an extent as to afford any grounds of apprehension for the safety of the work.

These references to the Gosport branch suggest the mention of another incident connected therewith. The electric telegraph was first tried for railway purposes between Euston and the stationary engine-house at Camden Town in 1837; was installed between Paddington and West Drayton in July, 1839, and was used in 1840 on the London & Blackwell Railway. When the Gosport branch was opened the Admiralty wished for an electric telegraph to be installed between Gosport and Nine Elms to supersede the semaphore system from Whitehall to Portsmouth. The half-yearly meeting of the railway company on 28th March, 1844, approved of a contract being entered into with Cooke and Wheatstone, the inventors of the electric telegraph, to install and maintain it on payment of £1,500 a year. It was said that the cost would be £8,000.

When the line was first opened, policemen were more numerous than any other class of servant; they acted as signalmen and ticket collectors and, until the date of the extension to Basingstoke, were stationed along the line at regular intervals; subsequently they were taken off their beats and sent to various stations. Their uniform consisted of a swallow-tailed, chocolate-coloured coat, dark trousers, and tall hat with a leather crown.

Some interesting information is to be found in Freeling's *London & Southampton Railway Companion* (1839). Among a number of sailors who spoke to the advantages of Southampton as a port, was Sir Thomas Hardy, although, as we have seen, he was never induced to risk his neck on a railway. The Quartermaster General of the Army proved the importance of the line from a military point of view, owing to the facilities it would present for the movement of troops and stores. At the time this guide was written, the line was only open as far as Basingstoke. Six trains ran the whole way in each direction, together with three to Woking only; the fares to Basingstoke being 11s. first class, and 7s. second class – no third-class fares being given. Only the times of starting are indicated, those of arrival being left to the imagination.

A rival publication, *The London & Southampton Railway Guide*, was published the same year by Wyld. It begins with an interesting and racy account of the process of obtaining an Act for a railway. Both guides are mainly taken up with a description of the country on either side of the line. Robinson's *Railway Directory* (1840) says:

The first-class Trains will perform the journey in three hours, taking first-class passengers only, excepting that accommodation will be afforded for a limited number of servants in livery. The fare will be 20s. each passenger; the fare for servants in livery, 13s. each. These trains will not call at any Stations between London and Woking Common, but will take up and set down Passengers at all the Stations between Woking Common and Southampton.

The Mixed Trains will call at all the Stations, except the Train which leaves London at 7 o'clock a.m.; the fare from London to Southampton by these Trains will be 18s. first class; 12s. second-class.

Two goods trains ran every day each way, taking six hours.

There are some interesting details of the passengers carried during the second half of the year 1840, in a Board of Trade Return, ordered to be printed 8th March, 1841:

Class	Conveyed by	Per mile	Number
First	First Class trains	$3\frac{1}{5}$d. }	
,,	Mails and mixed	$2\frac{3}{4}$d. }	118,824
Second	,, ,,	$1\frac{3}{4}$d.	$225,181\frac{1}{2}$
Third...... ..Goods trains		$1\frac{1}{5}$d.	19,652
			$363,657\frac{1}{2}$

Receipts for that period were: Passengers, £115,016 0s. 7½d.; Horses, £1,772 6s. 3d.; Carriages, £3,220 8s. 6d.; Goods, £16,130 15s. 7½d.

As a direct result of the establishment of the railway, the Peninsular, Mediterranean, Oriental and West Indian mails were all transferred from Falmouth to Southampton on 18th September, 1843.

There was a collision at Nine Elms on 17th October, 1840, by which one passenger was killed. A train had arrived very late, and the next one came up before its time, and ran into the former, owing to a man, whose duty it was, neglecting to show a red light.

Another collision occurred at Kingston on 16th October, 1841, of a somewhat similar nature. Though much more severe in its effect on the rolling stock, there were no injuries to speak of. But it is interesting, because in the report there is a mention of what must have been one of the first proposals for 'cab-signals'. Sir Frederick Smith (the Government Inspector) said, apropos of a statement by the driver of the second train that he saw no red light:

It may, however, be doubted whether any (tail) light would have aroused the attention of the engineman Maitland or his fireman Jervis (of the mail train) who, I suspect, must have been in a state of great drowsiness, and the question naturally arises what would have been the most effective way of drawing the attention of men under such circumstances, or in foggy weather, and I am inclined to believe that the 'puppets' tried by Mr. Bury (the locomotive superintendent) on the London and Birmingham line, would best answer the required object. They are fixed to the rail at the place where it is required to attract the notice of the engine driver, fireman or guard, and, as the engine passes, it touches a lever by which a steam whistle is sounded and a red light, which is attached to the engine, is turned full on the face of the driver, so that all parties may be aroused, and the driver and fireman carry with them, in this red light, an evidence that a signal has been given to them.

It is instructive to observe in the comments that immediately follow, that, as with his successors in later years, the Board of Trade inspector saw another side to the proposal, also that it was not desirable to substitute mechanism for the human agent. Sir Frederick continued:

The only argument which occurs to me that could be urged against this plan is that delicate machinery is likely to get out of order and will not be efficient when required. The answer is that the machinery is not so delicate as to be very liable to such casualties and that, if it should fail when wanted, there is still the policeman (signalman) or other servant to make the ordinary signal. What I am anxious to see is not the removal of the present safeguard by means of human agency and the substitution of machinery, but the application of both, so that if the one should fail the other may succeed. I think the public are entitled to the security that this, or similar simple inventions, for so important an object, would afford.

The opening of the Bideford Extension Railway in 1855.

Joseph Beattie's first engine, the *Milo*.

Beattie's first tank engine, the *Tartar*.

Mazeppa, L.S.W.R. No. 53 of 1865, one of a batch of three 0-6-0 engines supplied by Beyer Peacock.

The following interesting entries appear in *A Quaker Journal* (the diary of William Lucas of Hitchin, 1804–1861; published 1934).

1838. 7th Month, 9th day.

> To Uxbridge by Great Western Railway, sad want of punctuality at starting, and when off, rate only fourteen miles an hour. How have the mighty promises of Brunel fallen.

13th day (same month and year)

> Went to the Kingston station of the Southampton railroad, saw several trains, punctuality admirable, rate above 30 miles an hour, not many passengers.

This chapter may be concluded by a quotation from *The Kentish Observer* of 28th May, 1840; which shows the attitude of the anti-railway press of the period:

> The admirers of railroad are in high glee; several new lines and branches have been opened during the week. The lovers of the convenient and picturesque may now be puffed, and rattled, and squeaked along from Nine Elms to Southampton in about three hours, without the nuisance of seeing anything of the country, or the possibility of hearing themselves speak. It is gratifying to know that coffins and stretchers are always ready at the different stations, and a new regulation is in course of completion, by which every passenger on all the lines, Eastern, Western, Midland, Birmingham, &c., &c., will be supplied with a label, to be suspended round his neck, so that when the crash comes, his bones, head, &c., may all be carefully collected, and sent home to his expectant relations and friends, according to the address on his ticket.

VII

The South Western down to 1849

THE first extension of the London & South Western Railway after the events related in the last chapter was the Guildford Junction Railway, which was from the main line at Woking to Guildford. The line was authorised under powers obtained by a private company in 1844, and its acquisition by the South Western was sanctioned in 1845 by 8 & 9 Vic., c. 185.

An item of interest in connection with the Guildford Railway was that is original owners intended that it should be laid with Prosser's patent railway, which had been demonstrated on Wimbledon Common in the summer of 1845.

Sir John Aspinall, in his Thomas Hawksley Lecture at the Institution of Mechanical Engineers on 6th November, 1925, which was entitled *Some Railway Notes, Old and New*, said of Prosser's railway:

A great many odd proposals were made in the early days of railways with regard to the rolling stock which should be used upon them, but I think the most curious was that of Mr. William Prosser, who proposed that there should be no flanges on the carrying wheels of locomotives or other rolling stock and that the vehicles should be kept upon the line by certain angular guide-wheels pressing on the top and sides of the rail. This system was said by its author, who patented it in 1844, to have been first adopted on the Guildford and Woking Railway and that the locomotive had travelled during a period of two months about 3,000 miles without requiring the slightest repair.

As a matter of fact, Prosser's idea was never used on the Guildford Railway, and it is therefore obvious that if the engine mileage quoted was run, it must have been done during the demonstration on Wimbledon Common. The London & South Western declined the proposal, and the purchase money paid to the original company included £2,000 compensation for Prosser on the cancellation of the agreement to use his scheme.

This line was arranged to be opened 1st May, 1845, but was not ready and was actually opened for traffic on 5th May.

Although the South Western authorities would have nothing to do with Prosser, his system, or something very similar, was used on the Paris, Sceaux & Limours Railway, which was opened in 1848, and was about 25 miles long, and survived until 1891.*

* *Locomotive Magazine*, Vol. VIII (1903), p. 57.

The fight over a line to Epsom, in which the South Western suffered defeat, has been dealt with in Chapter V.

There was further trouble with the London & South Western's future great competitor, the Great Western, in 1844, in connection with the provision of railway communication to the borough of Newbury by a line from Basingstoke. Nowadays it seems rather absurd that the South Western company should think of going to Newbury, as, obviously, that town was in the sphere of influence of the Great Western. As a matter of fact, when such a line was first proposed, the South Western chairman, at a special meeting of the proprietors on 30th December, 1843, said, when telling the meeting of a deputation that had waited upon him:

> In truth I thought the Newbury population would be eventually conveyed by the Great Western Railway and suspected that they – the deputation – were coquetting with us merely to enable them to make better terms with our neighbours. Hence I declined at first, somewhat abruptly I fear, to have anything to do with it.

In those days it was usually the case that the main influence in new schemes for railway communication was the connection with London. The Basingstoke and Newbury was, however, based more on its association with Southampton. Coal, for instance, would come by sea to Southampton, and on its arrival at Newbury by rail could be sold for 30s. per ton, in comparison with the then price of 40s. But the main advantage put forward was that the port of Southampton was by then being used as a mail station for India and the East.

It must be remembered, too, that, at that time, the only route to the north of England, other than through London, was by the Bristol and Gloucester, the Birmingham and Gloucester, the Birmingham and Derby, and the North Midland. The Great Western line through Reading had been brought into use between London and Bristol, and the Cheltenham & Great Western Union between Swindon and Kemble, while the extension of the last named to Gloucester was under construction. The line from Didcot to Oxford was then being completed – it was opened on 24th June, 1844 – but no extension north of Oxford had been sanctioned. What then appeared a reasonable scheme was for the proposed line to be made from Basingstoke to Newbury and, under powers subsequently to be obtained, on to Swindon and, by the line thence, to Gloucester, so forming part of a through route between Southampton and the north.

Thus, the South Western came to the 1844 session for powers to build a line between Basingstoke and Newbury. The Great Western,

at the same time, sought authority to build a line from Pangbourne
to Newbury. The latter, obviously, was mainly to cater for the
London traffic. The Great Western company complained bitterly of
its neighbour's action and, apparently, of the attitude of the Newbury
people. The chairman of that company said that the connection had
always been intended and that plans and maps were prepared in
1838 and again in 1840. With the then comparatively rapid growth
of railway communication the failure of the Great Western – after
submitting the plans in 1838 – to seek definitely for powers suggests
some indifference.

Both bills were referred, in the House of Commons to the same
committee – of five members – who unanimously passed the London
& South Western and rejected the Great Western one. When the
former bill subsequently came up for second reading it was, in spite
of the appeal of the Great Western that it should share the same fate
as their bill, passed by the House of Commons by 166 votes to 73.
In the Lords it was considered by a committee of four peers who,
after a hearing of twelve days, threw out the South Western bill on
25th June, 1844. The grounds for so doing were stated to be:

> That if a railway to Newbury be required the competing line from Pangbourne
> would afford more advantages to that town and its neighbourhood than would
> be obtained from the present bill, first as affording a more expeditious and cheap
> communication with the capital; and, secondly, as giving a communication with
> the midland and northern counties with which a more active trade has hitherto
> been carried on than that which has existed, or is likely to exist, with the south.
> Further, as regards the interests of the country at large they are of the opinion
> that the communication by railway between the north of England and the towns
> of Southampton, Portsmouth, etc., and the southern coast will be hereafter more
> usefully effected by the contemplated lines in connection with Pangbourne than
> by an extension of the Basingstoke and Newbury line to Swindon.

At the half-yearly meeting of the Great Western on 15th August,
1844, Mr Charles Russell, the chairman, announced that the junction with the main line would be at Reading instead of at Pangbourne. In view of what was said just now as to the only route from
the south to the north, other than through London, being through
Gloucester, it is significant to note that Russell added that to complete the scheme it would be necessary to obtain powers to continue
the line from Oxford to Rugby – which, by the way, was a gap of no
less than 50 miles.

The half-yearly report presented to the Great Western meeting
just mentioned not only intimated that the company would renew
its application for powers to make a line to Newbury – from Reading,
however, instead of from Pangbourne – but for a line between

Reading and Basingstoke also. This was duly done in the session of 1845, except that the Newbury proposals went on to Hungerford. The South Western, in its turn, deposited a bill for a Basingstoke and Didcot Junction Railway, and Mr Chaplin, speaking at a special meeting of the proprietors, held on 7th December, 1844, said:

We have so deposited our plans and surveys before the Board of Trade as will enable us to take all the benefits or advantages they may be pleased to confer upon us. We embrace all the leading features of the country and we have so arranged them as to take an alternative. If the Government should feel that the application on the part of the London & Birmingham to make a narrow gauge line from Rugby to Oxford and Didcot, with a view to provide a direct north and south communication by the narrow gauge all the way from Aberdeen to the south, doubtless they will grant our line (from Didcot) to Basingstoke, simply because it is the best. In that case we should not extend our western line through Newbury beyond Marlborough. But if the Government, as they may, feel that the line from Swindon to Gloucester and from Gloucester to Birmingham will be a benefit to the north and south traffic we shall carry out our line from Basingstoke, by Newbury, to Swindon and drop the Didcot branch.

The South Western were at the time also interested in a much more important scheme, which was a line from Southampton to Dorchester and Weymouth, via Redbridge, Lyndhurst, Brockenhurst, Ringwood, Wimborne and Wareham, with a branch to Poole. This proposed line was popularly called 'Castleman's Corkscrew', or 'Snake', from its sinuous character, and from the fact that the chief promoter was Mr. Castleman, a Wimborne solicitor. The South Western afterwards deserted the scheme in favour of another route, so Castleman approached the Great Western, which company agreed to construct the line, of course intending it to be broad gauge.

It is now necessary to say that, as a result of the Regulation of Railways Act, 1844, the Railway Department of the Board of Trade was strengthened under a Minute passed on 21st August, 1844. Earl Dalhousie, afterwards connected with the Government of India, was the chairman, and the other four members were: Samuel Laing – who, later, became the chairman of the Brighton; G. R. Porter, a leading authority on economics, and a founder of the Statistical Society; Captain D. O'Brien and Captain Coddington; the last-named was afterwards the general manager of the Caledonian Railway. This Railway Board examined all railway bills – quite independently of the Parliamentary Committees – a fact that was, in the end, the Board's undoing. On 31st December, 1844, they made the announcement, as reported in the *London Gazette* of that date, that they were in favour of the Reading, Basingstoke and Hungerford lines, but against the Basingstoke and Didcot Junction. The Report of the Board appeared in the issue of the *Gazette* for 28th February, 1845.

Certain events had meanwhile occurred between the formal announcement of December and the appearance of the Report in February which changed the situation, and their relation is necessary because of a remark made in the opening part of the Railway Board's Report.

Early in 1845 the representatives of the two railway companies met. What happened may best be judged from the observations made by the chairman of the Great Western, at the half-yearly meeting of that company on 11th February, 1845. Those remarks were:

> On the decision being given the directors of the Great Western Company entered into immediate negotiations, and it is but justice that I should state that we were met in the most cordial spirit by the directors of that – the London & South Western – company and their professional colleagues. The result of this arrangement was the agreement, the heads of which are stated to you in the report which will be submitted today. Important as this agreement is in itself I think it is more important in creating a good feeling and understanding between the South Western company and ourselves.

The terms of the agreement, as recited in the Report, briefly were that the South Western would offer no opposition, directly or indirectly, to the lines promoted by the Great Western, of which the Railway Board had expressed its approval in its decision of 31st December, 1844. The Great Western, on the other hand, had relinquished, with the entire concurrence of the Southampton & Dorchester company, the lease of that line to the London & South Western in order that the latter company might work it with its own line.

The concurrent report of the South Western company said as to the decision of the Railway Board:

> It is scarcely necessary, at this date, to inform the proprietors that the Board of Trade have reported against the lines proposed by this company. Neither does it appear useful to offer speculations as to the principles which have guided that honourable board to this result. Such a course of criticism might involve some expression of dissatisfaction and imply feelings of disrespect which your directors have, by a general acquiescence in the earliest, and one of the most important, of the decisions promulgated by that tribunal, given substantial proof that they do not entertain.
>
> After giving the whole subject, as it affects the several lines projected for the use of the great district under consideration, and to the report of the Board of Trade thereon, a most patient and careful re-examination, your directors determined to avail themselves of the opportunities to establish friendly relations with the Great Western company and to become lessees of the Southampton & Dorchester line, thus settling, for the present, as far as these companies are concerned, the railway communications of the district. An arrangement between this company and the Great Western has accordingly been come to, with the sanction of the Board of Trade; and whilst the interposition of that authority will give sufficient guarantee that the public interests have not been overlooked, the directors have much

reliance that, worked out in a spirit of fair dealing, this arrangement will result in the mutual benefit of the two companies. To this agreement the Southampton & Dorchester company is a party and, by the terms of it, this company will lease in perpetuity, at a rental of £20,000 a year and half the surplus profits, the intended line – of 60 miles – from Southampton to Dorchester which would otherwise have been in the hands of the Great Western company.

The intended future relations of the South Western company with its neighbour can be gathered from the following extract from the speech of Mr Chaplin at the former company's half-yearly meeting on 13th February, 1845, two days after the Great Western meeting:

We might have driven a harder bargain with the Great Western company, but you may generally observe that any hard bargain is a bad bargain. I do not know what the Great Western feel, but I am sorry that we had not more to give them. They have entered into friendly relations towards us with a good grace and it is our duty to observe good faith towards them. We have arranged that if the requirements of the country generally should, at any future period, show that it ought to be accommodated with railway communication, then we go hand-in-hand with the Great Western to hear what these requirements are and mutually make the extensions under the sanction of the Board of Trade.

A fortnight later the Report of the Railway Board was published. It observed that the promoters of the South Western scheme had publicly announced their intention of abandoning the whole of their proposed lines and withdrawing all opposition to those of the Great Western. As, however, the schemes of the two companies had been fully investigated the opinion of the Board would be delivered without reference to the circumstances which had subsequently occurred.

The Report proceeded to remark that the traffic tables submitted, as well as the evidence before Parliament in 1844, showed that the principal traffic of Newbury, Hungerford, and the district to be-accommodated, was with London. The Great Western route by Reading was 8½ miles shorter than by the London & South Western through Basingstoke. The former afforded direct communication with Reading, Maidenhead, and the other towns along the line of the old Great Western Road, with which intercourse was considerable. The South Western, on the other hand, afforded no communication in that direction, but only towards Basingstoke and Southampton, in which direction the traffic was inconsiderable and even that could be given by the Great Western via Reading.

Dealing, then, with communication between the north and the south, the Board considered that the route via Oxford was preferable to that via Swindon, as it afforded a more direct route, not only to the north and north-east, but also to the Midlands and north-west. It was evident also that there was then not sufficient traffic to support two lines of communication to the north, and the advantages of that by Swindon were, to a great extent, obtained by the Great Western's proposed extension of the Wilts & Somerset line to Salisbury. The sole advantage of the Didcot line was that it would shorten the distance from Didcot to Basingstoke – in other words, from the north to South-ampton – by $5\frac{1}{2}$ miles as compared with the Great Western route by Reading. On the other hand, its gradients were very inferior and it involved the construction of $26\frac{3}{4}$ miles of railway, in great part of an expensive character through a thinly populated country, while the length of the Great Western from Reading to Basingstoke was only 15 miles.

Finally, it was observed that, had the through traffic from the north been sufficient in itself to support a line, much might have been said in favour of one from Basingstoke to Didcot on the narrow gauge, which would not only have given the most direct route, but also have afforded a prospect of attaining an unbroken connection throughout, since in that case the portion between Oxford and Didcot would alone have intervened on the wide gauge. But it appeared perfectly well established that there existed, at that time, no through traffic in that direction that could, in itself, warrant or support a line of 26 miles from Basingstoke to Didcot and a second narrow gauge line for 10 miles between Didcot and Oxford. Such a line would present itself under very different circumstances if the traffic towards Southampton should so far increase as to be capable of supporting it, but in the meantime it was evident that it could only hope to be supported by the London traffic from the Newbury district being diverted over it in the circuitous and inconvenient direction of Basingstoke.

The agreement between the two companies had been signed on 16th January, 1845. Under it the South Western undertook not to promote any competing lines westward of Salisbury or Dorchester.

Another extension sanctioned in 1844 was from Bishopstoke to Salisbury, a distance of about 22 miles. It was opened to Milford Station, Salisbury – now the goods depot – on 1st March, 1847 (27th January for goods only).

In 1844 Parliament took in hand the interests of third-class passengers, and the South Western rose to the occasion with a type of three-compartment 'Parliamentary Carriage' seating 30. Before the passage of the Act the third-class carriages consisted of open flat trucks with movable garden seats on them; and it had been the practice to attach them only to the goods trains, with the humane idea that their occupants would not be exposed to such violent winds. It is quite possible that in the earliest days, even the second-class carriages lacked roofs. That either this was the case, or that it was seriously proposed to build some thus, is shown by the following minute of the London & Southampton board:

22nd September, – 1837 Minute 784
Read a report of the Sub-Committee for carriages No. 3 dated this day. Resolved that the report be received and that it be recommended to the court of Directors to confirm and adopt the same except as to the second-class carriages without roofs – the committee of management recommended that the whole of the second-class carriages should be made with roofs and that the sub-committee for carriages have power to make arrangements for the supply of 20 more second-class carriages.

The people of Portsmouth had for some time been complaining about their railway facilities, which only consisted of a station at Gosport, on the wrong side of the harbour. To meet this, an extension of the Brighton system was proposed, along the coast taking Chichester en route. Another proposal was that of the 'Guildford Extension & Portsmouth & Fareham Railway Company', incorporated by 9 & 10 Vic., c. 252, for a railway from Guildford via Midhurst and Chichester, to join the South Western Gosport line at Fareham, with a branch entering Portsmouth. This proposal was supported by the South Western company, but powers were only granted for the sections between Guildford and the present Godalming goods station, and from Fareham to Portsmouth. In addition there was a line called the 'Direct London & Portsmouth Atmospheric Railway'.

Of these, only the Brighton company's plan was passed at first. When the mania arose all these schemes bubbled up again, and protracted inquiries were held. A good deal of light was thrown, not only on the actual line itself, which of course was never made, but on railway working generally at the time. The inquiry was held in June, 1845. Joseph, son of William Cubitt, was the engineer of the line, which was to begin at Epsom, and go by Leatherhead and Dorking to Godalming, thence by pretty well the same route as the present South Western. The estimate was nearly a million and a half; for a single line only. Where roads were crossed on a level, lifting bridges were proposed, to be turned down across the line for the road traffic; these being necessary to clear the tube. Samuda's royalty was to be £500 a mile. The Act for the Direct London & Portsmouth Atmospheric was passed, but in the slump after the mania the proposal was dropped.

William Cubitt said there was no third class on the Croydon Railway until the Bricklayers' Arms branch was made, as the Greenwich company refused to have them on their line. He also said the London and Birmingham stations had nothing but porters to push the trains about; they did not use engines in the stations. At Derby it was done by a horse.

Robert Stephenson said that on all the important lines the average trains weighed 40 to 50 tons – of course without the engine – the average speed was 30 to 40 miles an hour; more on some lines. On the question of taking third-class passengers by express trains, he said: 'They do not like to go at forty miles an hour'. He said goods trains usually weighed from 200 to 250 tons, and he had seen them with 400 tons on the South Western; their system being to concentrate all their goods trains into one or two, and run them at night.

Locke estimated the cost of running trains on the South Western Railway at 1s. per mile; five years previously it had been 16 or 17 pence. The average speed on the South Western Railway was 24 miles an hour; expresses, 40. The engines burnt 15 to 20 lb of coke per mile.

What Russell had described to the proprietors of the Great Western in February, 1845, as 'the good feeling and understanding between the South Western company and ourselves' was soon imperilled. Instead of going hand-in-hand, as Chaplin had said they intended doing, the Great Western, in the autumn of 1846, put forward a bill for extending the Berks & Hants branch from Hungerford so that it joined the Wilts & Somerset at Westbury. They also supported the bill of an ostensibly independent company, known as the Exeter Great Western, which was to build a line from Yeovil to Exeter. The London & South Western company thereupon wrote to the Board of Trade and claimed that such an action was a breach of the agreement, intimating that they regarded it as no longer binding. The Board of Trade, in those circumstances, declined to act, but admitted that the proposals altered the conditions under which the agreement was made. No harm, however, was done, as the bill, opposed by the Bristol & Exeter as well as the South Western, was rejected in the Commons.

This agreement led to the Southampton & Dorchester Railway being sanctioned in the Parliament of 1845, by 8 Vic., c. 93, as a narrow gauge railway, with powers to the London & South Western to lease it and to run over the Weymouth line as between Dorchester and Weymouth. The line, which included a branch to Poole – now Hamworthy – was 63 miles long. The section from Blechynden – renamed Southampton West* in July 1858 – to Dorchester was opened on 1st June, 1847, and from the former to Southampton Junction for passenger traffic on 29th July following. The opening

* Now called Southampton Central.

of the latter section was delayed by collapses of the railway tunnel where it intersected an old one, made for the Andover and Southampton canal, which had been acquired by the London & South Western company.

It was the practice of Parliament in those days, under the advice of the then Railway Board, to specify, in the empowering Act that authorised any single line of railway, that the railway was to be converted to double line if, and when, the gross receipts exceeded a certain amount. This was done with the Southampton & Dorchester, the amount specified being £65,000. As that figure was, in due time, exceeded, the line had to be doubled and the first widened portion was opened in October, 1857.

In 1845, by the Metropolitan Extension Act 8 & 9 Vic., c. 185, the South Western obtained powers to have its London terminus on a more convenient site near Westminster Bridge Road. This involved the construction of a new railway from Battersea, which ran thence to the south of the existing line to Nine Elms, through Vauxhall, for a distance of $1\frac{3}{4}$ miles, to what is now Waterloo station.

In the following year, by 9 & 10 Vic., c. 391, it was to be further extended, in order to serve the city, to a proposed station near London Bridge. The site selected was at Humphrey's Wharf, and the new station was also to be used by the North Kent Railway. That proposal may be disposed of here by the remark that a statement issued to the proprietors on 8th November, 1848, said that 'no contracts had been entered into for proceeding with works upon any part of the line between Waterloo and London Bridge and the directors had no intention of proceeding without giving the proprietors the fullest opportunity of reconsidering the propriety of the measure'. That opportunity was given twelve months later when, on 28th November, 1849, it was decided that, owing to a continuance of the financial depression, no application should be made to Parliament for the necessary extension of time.

In 1845 there was also sanctioned a Richmond & West End Railway which was to build a line between Richmond and Battersea – now Clapham Junction. In 1846, by 9 & 10 Vic., c. 131, the South Western company obtained powers to acquire the Richmond Railway, which had been opened on 27th July. The purchase was completed in January, 1847, in which year the Windsor, Staines & South Western (Richmond to Windsor) company was formed, for the construction of the section Richmond to Datchet. The use of the Southampton lines between the junction at Falcon Road and Nine Elms was soon found to be an inconvenient arrangement and not without danger. Powers were accordingly obtained in 1847 to widen that section of the line, so as to provide separate tracks for the Richmond trains. The additional lines were continued on the Metropolitan Extension, and therein is found the derivation of the term 'Windsor lines', as they are still called, between Clapham Junction and Waterloo.

The whole of the extension from Nine Elms to Waterloo (which was called York Road Station in the Act), a distance of 1¾ miles, was carried on arches. There were 290 arches and six under-bridges, which included a skew arch bridge of 90ft span over the Westminster Bridge Road. An intermediate station was provided at Vauxhall. It was expected that the arches would be a source of revenue, so they were carefully constructed and their dryness secured by the application of asphalt.

An undertaking had been given, or implied, to the proprietors that the extension should be completed by the end of the first half-year of 1848 and it was offered to the Board of Trade for inspection in time to redeem that promise. The line was inspected by Captain Laffan on 28th and 29th June, but, as he found the roads very roughly laid and without ballast, he refused to pass the work. The bridge over Westminster Bridge Road was, further, not to his satisfaction. As to the latter the Board of Trade inspector said:

This bridge is slighter in construction than any I have yet seen in railway structures for such a wide span – 90ft – with so small a rise – 9ft – and I do not think it right, on the slight consideration it is in my power at this moment to give to the subject, to pronounce that it is sufficiently strong.

When the railway officials heard that the Board of Trade inspection had not been satisfactory, the secretary wrote on 29th June and said that public notice had been given that the line would be opened the following day and proceeded to observe:

The anxiety of the directors to open the line tomorrow is greatly increased by the fact that if not so opened a most important alteration in the rights of proprietors, holding shares to the extent of 2½millions of capital, will be affected. I am instructed to call your attention to the clause in the Act of Parliament for making this work which declares the rights of the proprietors in this particular and which is so framed as to put it quite out of the power of the directors or of the company to remedy the injury and injustice which will arise if the extension shall be opened tomorrow, viz., before the 1st of July.

The matter appears to have been referred to Captain Simmons, the senior to Captain Laffan, who reported on 7th July that he recommended that the extension be opened. He said that he had tested the bridge over the Westminster Bridge Road with two engines, chimney to chimney, and found that the depression in the centre did not exceed $\frac{1}{4}$in and at the haunches of the arches, near the joints of the metal, $\frac{1}{8}$in. The new terminus was therefore opened on 11th July, 1848, and was at first named Waterloo Bridge. The cost of the extension was £900,000. The section from Nine Elms Junction to Nine Elms ($1\frac{1}{4}$ miles) was closed to passenger traffic the same day.

The station occupied three-quarters of an acre, the width being 280ft. The four running lines served four platform lines and two middle roads. Each of the former was about 600ft long. One of the middle roads was later continued to join the South Eastern Railway. In the centre of the station was the 'Crow's Nest' signal-box. Only temporary offices were provided at first, the permanent buildings being erected in 1853, at which time additional roofing was put at the eastern end of the station, originally left open. This roofing was of timber construction, the trusses being some of the largest in the country, with spans of 60 to 100ft. They remained until the station was remodelled in 1900.

The permanent station buildings were on the southernmost platform, and outside them was a cab yard and an approach road thence to the main entrance in Waterloo Road. West of the station buildings was the carriage loading dock, fed by a turntable in No. 1 platform road. Further west was the engine shed, three sidings and an engine turntable which remained in use for many years.

The extension to Waterloo had not been completed when the Richmond line was opened, so the trains at first ran to and from Nine Elms. One of the stations on the Richmond line was Putney. The Putney Pier Company had opposed the railway bill because the users of the steamers between there and London would be attracted on to the railway.

Taking events in their chronological order, attention must now be paid to the Exeter & Crediton Railway. That line, like the Bodmin & Wadebridge, was older in its inception than the London & Southampton, as it was sanctioned in 1832 – the same year as the Bodmin & Wadebridge – to make a line from the basin of the Exeter Canal at St Thomas, Exeter, to the flour mills at Crediton. In the same year, 1837, as the London & Southampton was sanctioned, powers were given to extend the proposed line to Barnstaple, but neither scheme materialised. Meanwhile, the city of Exeter had been given railway communication, as the Bristol & Exeter reached there on 1st May, 1844.

The opening of the Bristol & Exeter evidently revived the desire for a railway to Crediton, and that was sanctioned in 1845, but, there being no need to begin at St Thomas, the line was to be from Cowley

Bridge, by a junction with the Bristol & Exeter. As at that time the question of a standard gauge for British railways was under consideration by the Royal Commission, appointed 9th July, 1845, to inquire and report on the subject, the gauge of the line was not specified, but was ordered to be such as the Board of Trade might approve. In view of subsequent events it should here be noted that the Act also authorised the Bristol & Exeter company to purchase or lease the Exeter & Crediton, also that both companies had the same chairman – J. W. Buller, of Crediton. When, however, on 11th January, 1847, the provisional agreement was offered to the Exeter & Crediton shareholders for definite approval it was rejected by a majority, most of whom had been on the list of shareholders for less than a week. No doubt the newcomers were those who held shares, as related below, on behalf of the London & South Western Railway company.

It should now be observed that, as long ago as 1838, a railway was authorised to be built by the Taw Vale Railway & Dock company from Penhill, in the parish of Fremington, to Barnstaple, with docks in Fremington. In 1845 the powers to construct were extended and in the following year powers were obtained to continue the line to Crediton, and in 1847 to make a branch to Bideford and one to South Molton. There, again, the gauge was to be such as was approved by the Board of Trade.

The Bristol & Exeter opposed the extension of the Taw Vale to Crediton, but the opposition was withdrawn on the conclusion of a provisional agreement that, subject to the shareholders' approval, the Bristol & Exeter would take the line over. Earl Fortescue also opposed the bill, but became reconciled, he told the Railway Board, in consequence of a joint assurance from the two companies that the Taw Vale would be a continuation of the Bristol & Exeter.

The Railway Board of that period was not only all-powerful, but very interfering, and when the Exeter & Crediton meeting refused to approve of a lease to the Bristol & Exeter, wanted to know the reasons. It then came out that the London & South Western had advanced £30,000 to the Taw Vale, with which money 1,700 shares in the Exeter & Crediton had been brought, and that the South Western itself had also taken shares in the Taw Vale. As a result the Railway Board reported to the House of Commons, on 14th April, 1847, that:

Both these transactions appear to the Commissioners to involve an illegitimate application of the capital of the South Western company, but the proceeding appears to be more particularly objectionable in the case in which the funds have been more particularly misapplied for the purpose of controlling the directors and shareholders of an independent company.

It may be remarked that the South Western was far from being the only railway company which used the method to which the commissioners objected for the furtherance of their ends. As a matter of fact, in this very case the Bristol & Exeter had followed suit, but were too late in the field.

In spite of the shareholders' action in January, 1847, the Exeter & Crediton was built to the broad gauge and completed, except that the actual junction with the Bristol & Exeter, at Exeter, was not made. The line had not, however, been opened or offered to the Board of Trade for inspection. The delay was, no doubt, due to legal proceedings instituted by the supporters of the standard gauge.

The next phase was a petition, dated 27th August, 1847, from the Taw Vale Railway company, which recited that various interests were building narrow gauge railways from London to Falmouth and Penzance, and that the Taw Vale was intended to form a connection for Barnstaple and for docks at Fremington; that part of the route was over the Exeter & Crediton for which no definite gauge was laid down in its Act, and that the scheme was being imperilled by the latter railway having been made on the broad gauge. The petition alleged that the broad gauge interests had endeavoured to buy out the Taw Vale; then, failing in that, had sought to get a clause inserted in the Act that the Taw Vale was to be of the broad gauge and that, finally, a provisional agreement was made to the effect that, subject to the approval of the shareholders, the Taw Vale should be amalgamated with the Bristol & Exeter. That, it was said, was done on the assurance of a Bristol & Exeter director that he preferred the standard gauge and hoped that the Bristol & Exeter would change to it. The petition proceeded to say, without any apology for throwing over the Bristol & Exeter, that believing that the London & South Western would reach that part of the country, an agreement had been made with that company to provide one-fourth of the capital and to nominate one-fourth of the directors. The request was then made that it be agreed that the Taw Vale be a standard gauge line and that the Exeter & Crediton be altered to suit.

The petition having been sent to the Bristol & Exeter for its observations, that company replied that the Taw Vale was authorised on the strength of the provisional agreement referred to: that the line was to be leased to the Bristol & Exeter; that there was no narrow gauge railway within 100 miles of the Taw Vale; that, understanding orders, half the capital must be subscribed before any lease of the Taw Vale could be made, and that, under the Act, the Taw Vale must be completed before the Exeter & Crediton could be purchased or leased.

On 11th November, 1847, the Taw Vale informed the Railway Board that the Exeter & Crediton was changing its gauge to the standard. It also pointed out that the standard gauge was about to reach Exeter. Mention was made of the 'hearty co-operation of the London & South Western' in contrast to the unfriendliness of the broad gauge companies.

The upshot of the whole matter was that the Railway Board, on 12th December, 1847, sent Captain Simmons to inspect the line. He reported that only the original Taw Vale Railway, i.e. that at Barnstaple, was built. He took advantage of being in the neighbourhood to inspect the Exeter & Crediton, and found that the gauge was being altered, and that the line was to stop short at Cowley Bridge, where a temporary station was being built. Captain Simmons pointed out that the alleged advantages of a standard gauge line to London would be negatived by the proposed broad gauge route, with easier gradients, through Devizes, Hungerford and Reading. Moreover, communication between Exeter and Bristol – an important centre – would be cut off.

The result was that by a Minute dated 8th February, 1848, the Railway Board determined that the Taw Vale should be of the broad gauge. It also recorded that, as the Exeter & Crediton had not been offered for inspection, it had no voice in determining its gauge.

It may be added that when the Exeter & Credition was opened on 12th May, 1851, it was a broad gauge line, leased to the Bristol & Exeter, and that the Taw Vale was not opened until 1st August, 1854, and then also as a broad gauge line.

As part of the plan for invading the broad gauge territory, the London & South Western, in 1847, subscribed largely to the Sutton Harbour at Plymouth, in opposition to the Great Western (Millbay) Docks, projected the previous year.

On the 22nd July, 1848, bills for the Salisbury & Yeovil and the Yeovil & Exeter Railways received the Royal Assent. The powers, however, were allowed to lapse, and the inhabitants of these parts had to wait for some years before they were accommodated.

Reverting now to the London & South Western nearer home it is to be recorded that a branch from Weybridge to Chertsey was opened on 14th February, 1848. The powers, actually, were for a line to Egham, but the remaining portion was not built.

The Windsor, Staines & South Western Railway (Richmond to

The first of a very successful class, Joseph Beattie's 7-ft express engine *Clyde* (No. 157 of 1859), with new boiler, about 1880.   [*Locomotive Publishing Company*

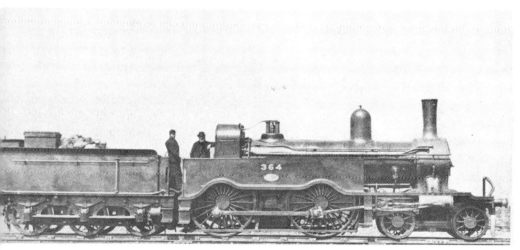

W. G. Beattie's first express class, No. 364 of 1877, built by Sharp Stewart.   [*British Railways*

The tender version of W. Adams's 4-4-0, sometimes called the 'steam-rollers'; No. 384, Beyer Peacock, 1879.

A Beyer Peacock saddle tank of 1876, No. 330. Note early type of goods brake with "birdcage" lookout on the roof.

[*Locomotive Publishing Company*

Windsor), which has already been mentioned in connection with the 'Windsor lines', was authorised by 10 & 11 Vic., c. 58, to construct a line from Richmond to Datchet, with a loop from Barnes to join the main line at what is now known as Feltham Junction. A 'Windsor, Staines & South Western (Staines and Wokingham) Railway' was incorporated by 10 & 11 Vic., c. 57, for a line from Staines, by means of a double junction with the Windsor line, to a point on the Southampton line at the 28th mile-post from London. The directors of these two companies were the same, but the second one was never constructed.

The Windsor line was to terminate on the Datchet side of the river, near Blackpots Island; and the company was required, by the terms of an agreement with H.M. Commissioners of Woods and Forests, to pay the sum of £60,000, which money, together with £25,000 to be paid by the Great Western Railway, under their Slough to Windosr Act, 1848, was expended in improving the approaches to the Castle and town of Windsor, as provided in 11 & 12 Vic., c. 53, which authorised the construction of the Victoria and Albert bridges over the river and of the roads in connection therewith, together with improvements to various streets within the town, and the removal of the old Datchet bridge. Thus the railways were made to pay well for the privilege of conferring benefits on Windsor.

The extension was opened as far as Datchet on 22nd August, 1848, and to Windsor on 1st December, 1849. The loop from Barnes to Smallberry Green – for a few months Hounslow and finally in 1850 Isleworth – was put into service on 22nd August, 1849, and the loop completed to Hounslow on 1st February, 1850.

An interesting incident associated with Queen Victoria was mentioned in the report for the first half of the year 1848. It was there said:

> The Windsor company was compelled by the Commissioners of Woods in the session of 1847 to adopt a station, certainly not so convenient for the use of Windsor as would otherwise have been selected but it was then understood that the Commissioners would allow no other to them or to their competitors. The Windsor company therefore took measures for opposition to the Great Western proposals to make a Windsor branch ending nearer the town than the one prescribed last year, but Her Majesty having graciously consented to an extension of the Windsor, Staines & South Western line from Datchet across the Home Park into the town of Windsor, every object of the Windsor company has thus been attained. The extension was authorised by 12 & 13 Vic., c. 34.

Returning to Portsmouth, the Brighton & Chichester Railway company's extension from Chichester to Portsmouth had been sanctioned in 1845, with connecting lines from Farlington Junction

and Portcreek Junction to Cosham. The Guildford Extension company, as already mentioned, had obtained powers in the same year to
construct their line from Fareham to Portsmouth, but was absorbed
by the South Western, who obtained powers in 1847 to rearrange the
junctions at Cosham, in order to obtain a connection with the
Brighton & Chichester. Subsequently the South Western and South
Coast companies agreed that there should be only one line into
Portsmouth, to be worked on a joint basis. This arrangement was
confirmed by 10 & 11 Vic., c. 244. Accordingly the section from
Cosham to Portsmouth became joint property. The South Western
powers for their separate line were abandoned by the 'L.S.W.R.
Portsmouth Extension and Godalming Deviations Act, 1847'. The
connecting link at Cosham was authorised by the L.S.W.R. Amendment Act, 1848.

The date of the openings were – Chichester to Havant, 15th
March, 1847; Havant to Portsmouth, 14th June, 1847; Fareham to
Cosham,* 1st September, 1848.

In 1846 the line from Guildford to Farnham was authorised and
was opened between Guildford and Ash Junction on 20th August,
1849; simultaneously with the Guildford–Shalford portion of the
Guildford Extension, order in to permit the Reading, Guildford &
Reigate company to commence between Dorking Town and Farnborough North on that day.

The Guildford–Shalford section included two tunnels; that nearer
Guildford was 968 yards long, bored in chalk; the northern end has
been excavated and the length reduced to 833 yards. The farther
one, under St Catherine's Hill, is 133 yards long and is in sand. The
Board of Trade Officer was very sceptical about it when he inspected
the line in August, 1849, and a couple of months later a portion of it
failed. A further failure occurred on 23rd March, 1895; necessitating the closing of the line until 1st April, during which interval
passengers were conveyed by road from the south end of the tunnel to
Guildford station. Single line working had to be used until 24th
November, 1895.

The remainder of the Guildford–Farnham branch – i.e. west of
Ash Junction – was opened on 8th October, 1849; the Godalming
Extension from Shalford Junction was also brought into use on 15th
October; the terminus of the latter at Godalming being now solely
used for goods traffic.

---

* Portcreek Junction and Farlington Junction to Cosham opened by L.B.S.C. 26th
July, 1848, but not for passengers. L.S.W.R. trains to Portsmouth via Cosham and Portcreek Junction, 1st October, 1848.

On 1st February, 1849, the Hampton Court branch was brought into use. Horse traction was used at first from the junction.

An application which had been made in 1846 for a line from Romsey to Redbridge had been unsuccessful in the Commons, who sanctioned the 'Manchester & Southampton Railway', which was to run through the same district. The latter, however, failed to pass the Lords. In the following year an Act was obtained for a line from Andover to Southampton, and for the purchase of the Andover and Redbridge Canal, which was to be turned into a railway. Arrangements were made with the Manchester & Southampton for joint ownership of the line between Andover and Romsey, the cost to be divided; and the Manchester & Southampton was to have running powers on to Southampton, via Redbridge. The ultimate outcome of the Manchester & Southampton was the Midland & South Western Junction Railway.

However, the South Western failed to make the line between Andover and Redbridge as authorised in 1847, and it was not done until 1865.

Before closing this chapter, attention may be directed to the speeds attained during the period with which it has dealt. In 1847 the fastest trains in the world were to be found on the Great Western, but

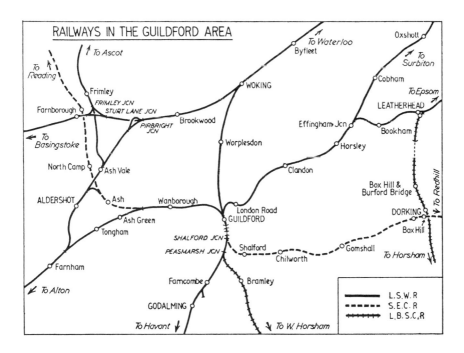

RAILWAYS IN THE GUILDFORD AREA

the South Western came easily next, and it must be remembered that its gradients were very much more severe. There were many pieces of 1 in 330, and, running down to Southampton, a stretch of 16 miles of 1 in 250. On the Great Western line as far as Swindon the worst was 1 in 660, and there was only a little of that.

From 1st January to 31st May, 1847, the Southampton expresses took two hours each way, calling at Basingstoke and Bishopstoke (now Eastleigh). On 1st June the time was made an hour and three-quarters, which was retained for the rest of the year, except during October, when the up trains were timed at 1 hour 40 minutes. The distance from Nine Elms to Southampton was 77 miles 34 chains, and the speed, therefore, on the best timing, 46.45 miles an hour. The contemporary timing between Paddington and Swindon on the Great Western (with one stop – at Didcot), 77 miles 4 chains (to the old Paddington Station), was 1 hour 37 minutes up, and 1 hour 38 minutes down, which is 47.66 miles an hour. After 1st June the stop at Bishopstoke was taken out, so far as passengers were concerned, but they must have stopped near there for the Gosport carriages.

That excessive speed was discouraged is shown by the following extract from *Rules to be observed by Enginemen and Firemen*, approved December, 1847:

No. 72. There will be delivered to every Engine man, a Time bill, shewing the time he has to keep on his trip, and every Engine man who shall arrive at any station more than three minutes before the proper time will be fined, in addition to the loss of his Trip money for the journey. In all cases where special trains are required the Engine man must take case that the distance between Nine Elms and Southampton is not performed in less time than two hours unless by special orders.

At this time the best trains on other lines averaged 31 to 35 miles an hour only, except on the Northern & Eastern, which did considerably more – on paper, at all events.

There were no accidents to speak of during the period covered by this chapter.

Fixed signals were in use in which a disc having half its centre open revolved at the top of a post. The disc applied to both directions, and some had one lamp below, whilst others had a separate lamp for each direction. The discs revolved by means of a cord, and when the closed portion of the disc was uppermost both roads were blocked; when the closed portion was on the left side, the left-hand road was blocked and the right-hand road free. When the closed portion was on the right the right-hand road was blocked and the left road free. When both roads were clear the disc was turned edgeways on. Other signals were of the 'crossbar and disc' type much favoured for many years by the Great Western; when the crossbar was turned edgeways on, and when the upper disc was presented, a clear road was intimated. Semaphores were not adopted on the South Western until 1860.

The first distant signal was put up at Kingston (Surbiton) in 1848. At that station the Guildford train had to shunt on to the wrong line to allow the Southampton express to pass, and the passengers were so afraid it would hit them that they used to get out of the carriages and wait at the side of the line until it had gone by.

Two well-known prints are in existence showing Queen Victoria, the Prince Consort and Louis Philippe, on the occasion of the return of the latter monarch from a visit to this country in October, 1844. The Queen and the Prince were on their way to the Isle of Wight, and the King was to have returned as he had come, by way of Portsmouth, crossing in the frigate Gomer; but he took fright at the stormy weather and insisted upon going to London and thence via Dover and Calais.

The following extracts from an account of the affair in *The Times* are interesting:

The royal train left Farnborough at 1.55 p.m. in heavy rain, the engine – upon which was the tricolour flag and on the tender the Royal Standard – being driven by Mr. Locke, the engineer of the line.

The royal carriage is described as a beautiful structure externally plain but light and elegant; the interior fitted up with much taste, lined with a light drab silk damask, richly trimmed with crimson and white silk lace, the ceiling formed of white watered silk, exquisitely embroidered with crimson velvet and silver in relief, forming the natural emblem of the rose, shamrock and thistle, with the Royal Crown at each corner. The carriage was entirely surrounded by light and tasteful draperies of crimson and white satin damask and lined with crimson satin richly trimmed with fringes, etc. The blinds are of a delicate peach colour, with silver tassels. The carpet is of Axminster manufacture, in colours to harmonize with the rest of the interior decorations, which reflect credit on Mr. Herring, the upholsterer of Fleet Street by whom they were executed.

Gosport was reached at 3.35 p.m., the station presenting a most animated appearance as the train came up.

The weather was so extremely bad, a gale blowing with a very heavy sea running, that it was considered undesirable for the King to make the crossing to Treport. His Majesty therefore decided to return to London, travel thence to Dover and cross the channel from that port.

Col. Bouverie was dispatched in a special train (which also took the Duke of Wellington) to London to order the special train to Dover.

At 7.45 p.m. after leave taking of the Queen and Prince Albert, the King and the Duc de Montpensier started on their return journey and reached Nine Elms at 10.35 p.m., driving at once to the Dover Railway at New Cross.

When at 11 o'clock His Majesty escorted by a troop of Life Guards drove into the Station the whole of that noble building was in flames.

A special messenger of the South Eastern Company met His Majesty and informed him that the directors of the Company regretted their inability to meet His Majesty owing to the late hour at which the notice of the altered plans had been received and offered their profound apologies for the fire.

The King in reply expressed himself perfectly satisfied with the arrangements which had been made. He expressed in strong terms his regret at the unfortunate fire then raging on the premises and concluded by hoping the Company were well insured.

At 11.15 p.m. the special train, driven by Mr. Cubitt, left the station, Dover being reached at 2.30 a.m.

His Majesty spent the rest of the night at the Ship Hotel and crossed to France next day.

The royal carriage in question is believed to be still in existence, in Kent.*

* The author presumably refers to the 'royal saloon' in use on the Kent & East Sussex Railway until its closing. This was however somewhat different from the carriage shown in engravings of the King's visit, and the one he used was almost certainly the 'royal saloon' existing on the Shropshire & Montgomeryshire Railway and which was finally broken up on the Longmoor Military Railway about 1954

VIII

The South Western in the 'Fifties

THE beginning of 1850 found the company by no means a happy family. The dividend, which had been over 8 per cent in 1846, had fallen to 3¼ in 1849, a circumstance which did not put the shareholders in a particularly good temper, and at a special meeting on 22nd December, 1849, a committee was appointed to investigate the management. The committee reported that they found much to blame and regret; the defence of the directors was that they had all along acted in the interests of the company. However, those who retired were re-elected, and harmony once more prevailed. Many of the powers which had been obtained with so much trouble, and at such heavy cost, such as for the extension to London Bridge, and the Western additions, had to be allowed to lapse for want of money with which to carry them out.

The first event during the period now under notice was the opening of the Exeter & Crediton line on 12th May, 1851, the history of which has been related in the previous chapter. At the time it was opened, the South Western, although it possessed three-fifths of the shares, had no direct interest in it. The Exeter & Crediton was an independent company, and the line, when opened, was broad gauge and worked by the Bristol & Exeter, to which company it was leased from the date of opening. It did not pass into the possession of the South Western until it was leased as from 1st January, 1862, when the Bristol & Exeter still held £47,775 of the total capital of £130,000. Not until 1876 did the London & South Western obtain powers to purchase the line, which transaction was completed in 1879.

One of the half-dozen men who had a great influence for good on the fortunes of the South Western Railway during the first fifty years of its career was Archibald Scott, and it may be put upon record at this point that he entered the company's service as traffic manager, in succession to Stovin, on 17th August, 1852. Scott started his railway career on the Dundee & Arbroath in 1838, and was with various Scottish lines until he came to the London & South Western.

On 28th July, 1852, the Guildford–Farnham line was extended to Alton, and on 15th February of the following year the North &

South Western Junction Railway company joined its line on to the London & South Western at Kew. The connection then made was for goods traffic only; passenger trains commenced to run on 1st August, 1853, provided by the North London Railway.

As its name implies, this railway was intended to join the North Western with the South Western. It was incorporated in 1851 under 14 & 15 Vic., c. 100, by an independent concern and was to be worked jointly by those two companies. It ran from West London Junction, a point just east of the present Willesden Junction, with a branch from South Acton to Hammersmith & Chiswick.

The new railway was very valuable to the London & South Western because of the mineral traffic facilities it afforded with the northern railways; it had been working goods trains over the line from 15th February, 1853. At the half-yearly meeting in February, 1854, the N.S.W.J.R. was said to have brought 4,096 tons of coal to the South Western in the previous month and was using 70 trucks a day.

In 1858 an independent line called the Brentford & Richmond Railway introduced a bill, but the House of Lords rejected it after the South Western had proposed to make improvements in the facilities for traffic between these places. As a consequence the latter company were given powers in 1859 to construct the Kew and Barnes curves, both being opened on 1st February, 1862. By sec. 32 of the South Western Act of 1859 the company were required to work a service of trains to and from the N.S.W.J.R. to Hampton Wick by way of these curves. In practice the service was to and from Twickenham (from 20th May, 1858) and later Kingston (from 1st July, 1863). It ceased on the opening of the Kensington, Richmond and Acton Junction lines in January, 1869; in accordance with sec. 60 of the L.S.W.R. (Kensington and Richmond) Act, 1864. The Barnes curve was abandoned under powers of the L.S.W.R. Act, 1864. In 1871 the South Western interest in the N.S.W.J.R. ceased, as the line was transferred to the North Western, Midland, and North London jointly.

Here it is necessary to point out that an extension of the line from Southampton to Dorchester on to Exeter would have given an alternative route from London and the south to that city, and would have constituted a determined invasion of the broad gauge territory. There must be remembered, too, in this connection, the Exeter & Crediton. There was also the Taw Vale Railway & Dock company which, as mentioned in the last chapter, had powers to build a line from the then authorised Exeter & Crediton via Barnstaple to

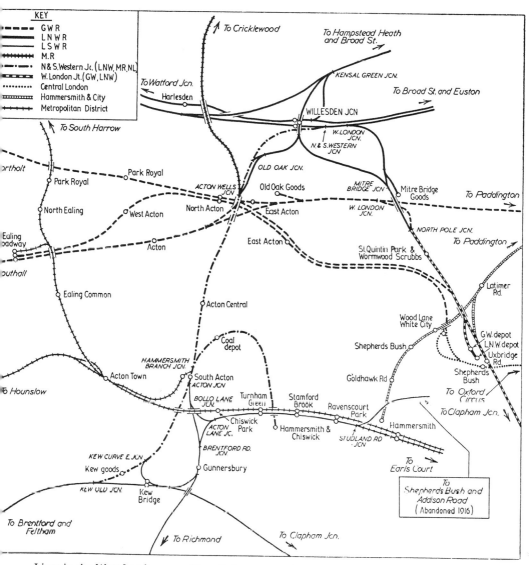

Lines in the West London area. Not all these connections were open at the same time.

the docks at Fremington Pill. By those two railways and the Bristol & Exeter there was to be railway communication between the Bristol and English Channels. With reference to the branches from Barnstaple to Bideford, and from South Molton Road to South Molton, sanctioned in 1847; the latter was not built, while the powers for the former were transferred, in 1853, by 16 & 17 Vic., c. 140, to the Bideford Extension Railway Company. In 1851, under 14 & 15 Vic., c. 83 the name of the Taw Vale company was changed to the North Devon Railway & Dock company. All the lines named were to be of the broad gauge, as they were to be worked by the Bristol & Exeter.

Reference must be made to the Wilts, Somerset & Weymouth Railway, now part of the Great Western, sanctioned in 1845. It ran from Thingley Junction, Chippenham, to Salisbury, and from Westbury – an intermediate point – to Weymouth, and thus thrust itself right into the path of the London & South Western advance to the west. Towards that advance powers had, in 1846, been given to make a line from Basingstoke to Andover and Salisbury. At that time nothing farther than Salisbury, in the Exeter direction, had been authorised, but in 1845, and again in 1847, application was made by an independent company to build the Exeter, Yeovil & Dorchester which, at the last-named place, would have joined the South Western's Southampton and Dorchester line. The Great Western successfully opposed the proposition, but in 1848, by 11 & 12 Vic., c. 85, it was carried, in the same session as the Salisbury & Yeovil, already mentioned, the powers for which were allowed to lapse.

The financial crisis of that period led to a truce between the South Western and the Great Western, and the former company held up the Basingstoke–Andover, Andover–Salisbury, Salisbury–Yeovil and Exeter, Yeovil and Dorchester. The peace was, however, in 1851, broken by, it was alleged, the Great Western proceeding with the Wilts, Somerset & Weymouth, which by that time had completed its line to Salisbury and arrived at Frome on the way to Yeovil–Dorchester–Weymouth. The South Western does not appear to have been in a hurry to retaliate. It was urged to proceed with the extensions to the west, but was obdurate. When, however, outside parties offered to build a line from Salisbury to Exeter, provided they had some financial assistance, the company undertook that, if the line were built, the South Western would work it for 50 per cent of the receipts. The company also, on its own initiative, proposed to put in hand the Basingstoke–Salisbury line. The whole length between

Basingstoke and Exeter was to be a single line, but the works were to be constructed to carry a double line. It was estimated, in 1846, that the Salisbury–Exeter double line would cost £2,275,000, but in 1851 that, as a single line, it could be done for £1,100,000, of which half was to be subscribed by landowners and other local interested parties. When, on 26th October, 1852, the directors went to the shareholders for their approval the necessary permission was refused. Chaplin thereupon resigned from the position of chairman – but retained his directorship – and was succeeded by the Hon. F. Scott.

In the following session (1853) a Bill was introduced for a Devon & Dorset Railway, which had the support of the Great Western and the Bristol & Exeter and was to run from Exeter to Dorchester and also serve Sidmouth, Honiton, and Bridport.

When, in accordance with standing orders, the South Western shareholders were asked, on 19th May, 1853, to sanction the opposition to the Devon & Dorset Bill, a resolution was carried approving such a course, and further authorising the directors to take the necessary steps towards extending the existing line from Dorchester to Bridport and Exeter. As a consequence Mr Scott, the chairman, gave the House of Commons Committee who considered the Bill a pledge accordingly. The Committee thereupon reported that in rejecting the Devon & Dorset bill:

they had not lost sight of the urgent necessity for filling up the gap in railway communication between Dorchester and Exeter nor do they doubt that the Devon & Dorset line would supply that deficiency for all purposes of local traffic. But taking a wider view of the subject and listening to evidence adduced from authorities of high consideration, your committee feel the importance of a railway communication upon one uniform gauge between Exeter and London via Axminster and Salisbury and of another from Exeter to Portsmouth and the east coast via Dorchester and believe that a communication so desirable could not be attained by that Bill and that they were best promoting the public welfare by giving an opportunity for the establishment of one uniform gauge throughout the above district. Your committee would, however, have hesitated to reject the Bill before them had it not been proved in evidence that the proprietors in the London & South Western Railway company authorised and requested their directors to pledge that company to apply to Parliament for powers to construct an extension of their railway from Dorchester to Exeter and had they not have received from the company's chairman a clear and distinct assurance, in his evidence and in a letter, that in the next session that company will introduce and use their best endeavours to obtain an Act for authorising such extension of their railway on a narrow gauge – such extension to be of an efficient character, also to comprise a double line of way. Also, immediately thereafter, to double their existing railway between Southampton and Dorchester.

It may be remarked that the 'authorities of high consideration' above referred to include Lord Hardinge, the then Commander-in-Chief; Lord Palmerston, the Secretary of State for the Home Department; Sir James Graham, the First Lord of the Admiralty; and Mr Sidney Herbert, the Secretary of State for War. They gave evidence in favour of carrying out a narrow gauge communication between the Metropolis and all the ports and arsenals of the country and testified that when the troops were removed to Chobham Camp a break in the gauge was found to be a great impediment, and the transfer from one gauge to another consumed two or three hours. Of course, the difficulties in the case of cavalry and artillery would, they said, be much greater.

At the half-yearly meeting on 18th August following – 1853 – it was unanimously resolved:

> That this meeting fully sanctions and adopts the pledge given by the Board to bring before Parliament, in the next session, an extension from Dorchester to Exeter and for making the Southampton & Dorchester Railway a double line throughout. The directors are hereby authorised and requested to take from time to time such measures as may appear to them most expedient for enabling the company to carry these pledges into practical effect.

The necessary bill was thereupon prepared and submitted to a special meeting of the proprietors on 15th November, 1853, when, by a majority of votes – as represented by the capital held – the resolutions were rejected.

One sequel to that action was that Scott and four other directors resigned. There was a large number of candidates for the vacant places on the Board, and their respective supporters agreed that Sir William Heathcote, the member for Oxford University, should select those whom he considered should fill the vacant positions. This was done, and the reconstructed Board, with Mr Chaplin once more the chairman, took office at the half-yearly meeting on 16th February, 1854. It was significant and a hopeful sign that the vote of thanks to the retiring directors was moved and seconded by their two principal antagonists.

The company was, however, not yet out of the wood – far from it. But before proceeding further it must be noted that the pledge mentioned in the above resolution as having been given to Parliament was for an extension to Exeter from Dorchester. That, perhaps, accounts for an important event that happened in 1854 – nothing less than the granting of powers to an independent company to make a railway from Salisbury to a junction with the Great Western and the Bristol and Exeter at Yeovil. Locke – who, because he did not agree with the South Western directorate over its delay to carry the line forward towards Exeter, had resigned his position of consulting engineer – was the engineer for the Salisbury & Yeovil. The line was to be single, but the Act ordered that as soon as the gross receipts for three consecutive years averaged £40,000 a year it was to be doubled.

Locke's successor on the South Western was J. E. Errington, another engineer of note, who had met the former when he was preparing the plans for the Birmingham end of the Grand Junction Railway, and became his resident engineer.

Alterations at the old terminal station at Nine Elms in the early 'fifties created a difficulty with regard to the berthing of the saloons used by Queen Victoria, which was accentuated by the construction of an additional one for the Royal children. Sidings for the accommodation of the stock when not in use were provided in 1853 in the goods yard adjacent to Wandsworth Road, and later in the year plans were prepared and approved for the erection of a private Royal station adjoining the sidings. It was removed in connection with the widening of the main line at the end of the last century.

In 1854 a Consolidation Bill was prepared, which came before the same committee who had rejected the Devon & Dorset. On 24th April the committee passed a resolution that the pledge of 1853 must be redeemed in the Consolidation Bill 'on pain of the company's dividends being stopped'. That was reported to a meeting of the proprietors four days later, when it was determined to leave the matter in the hands of the directors to act as they might consider necessary and expedient. On the 8th of the following month the company petitioned for a relaxation of Standing Order No. 131, which restricted borrowing powers to one-third of the capital. The House of Commons Committee, on the following day, consented and later inserted clauses in the Consolidation Bill to the effect that the company was to seek powers in 1856 in fulfilment of its pledge, and then, if the Bill was defeated after a bona fide effort to carry it, the President of the Board of Trade would give his certificate and relieve the company of all liability. If no bill was deposited in 1856, then that must be done in 1857, and the same condition would apply in the event of it being rejected. If, however, from want of effort, no action was taken in 1857, the ordinary dividends of the company were to be stopped until an Act was obtained, or a dispensing certificate given by the President of the Board of Trade.

There was, even yet, a strong opposition to the route via Dorchester, and the reason for that is self-evident today, as a reference to a map shows that the direct road to Exeter was through Salisbury. Many unkind things were said of Scott for having given his pledge, and when the above clauses came before the proprietors on 6th June the opposition mustered votes to the value of £1,139,734 against them, as compared with £1,546,322 in their favour. The bill passed the committee stage the following day and then its opponents pointed out that in two other important respects the standing orders of the House of Lords had not been complied with. That objection at first held, but at a special Wharncliffe meeting on 13th July the matter was adjusted, and the bill, with the penalising clauses, passed.

Leaving for a moment the consideration of the other, most important, clauses in the Consolidation Act, and continuing the history of the obtaining of powers to make an Exeter extension, we arrive at a special meeting of the proprietors on 16th January, 1856. The report of the directors on that occasion said that the question to be entertained was not in the shape of a comparison between a voluntary extension westward from Salisbury and one from Dorchester, but which would be the least onerous to the company – a compulsory extension from Yeovil or one from Dorchester. The situation had been changed in that (1) the line was open to Andover and shortly would be to Salisbury; (2) an Act had been passed enabling a separate company, known as the Salisbury & Yeovil, to continue the narrow gauge system to Yeovil; (3) Bridport, the only important place between Dorchester & Axminster, was found to be once more occupied by a broad gauge railway sanctioned in 1855; and (4) no doubt remained as to the early completion of the Wilts & Somerset Railway to Dorchester and Weymouth. It was further reported that tenders for both schemes had been received. For a line from Yeovil to Exeter the cost would be £600,000, and thus under the £700,000, required for the Dorchester & Exeter. Again, the latter would have eight miles of 1 in 80 between Dorchester & Axminster, but there would be only three miles of that gradient on the Yeovil route. A special committee of the board recommended that any extension should be from Salisbury, via Yeovil because (1) of the relative distances from important places of the system; (2) the traffic was without competition and would be less open to invasion; (3) it was less expensive and the better from an engineering point of view, and (4) on account of the great increase of traffic which would be secured permanently to the Salisbury & Basingstoke and Salisbury & Bishopstoke lines. A resolution was carried at the meeting supporting the directors in the choice of the Salisbury–Yeovil–Exeter route.

Application was, therefore, made to the Parliament of 1856 for powers to build a railway from Yeovil to Exeter, which were granted by 19 & 20 Vic., c. 120. No mention is made in the Act as to the Dorchester–Exeter scheme being abandoned; nor is it related how

the clauses in the Consolidation Act as to the dividends being suspended were to be disposed of. As, however, section 30 of the Act
of 1856 required the Yeovil–Exeter to be completed within five
years from the 31st December following, or the payment of ordinary
dividends would be suspended, it may be assumed that the Board of
Trade gave a certificate for the necessary relief.

One must now revert to the meeting of 19th November, 1853, when
the shareholders refused the necessary authority to redeem Scott's
pledge that the line should be made from Dorchester to Exeter and
that the existing single line between Southampton and Dorchester be
changed to a double line. That decision led to an article in *The Times*
of 22nd November, which began by congratulating the shareholders
on taking the management of their affairs into their own hands.
It was said that the majority of the shareholders asserted that the
Southampton & Dorchester was a losing concern, but that 'the
directors, with their packed minority of bankers, lawyers, engineers
and what not, maintain that it has returned good interest on the
capital invested'. Farther on it was observed that the chairman and
directors assert:

that they were empowered by a full meeting of the shareholders to conclude
this improvident bargain (of an extension from Dorchester to Exeter) for the
formation of the extended line within a given time. The shareholders say that
this assent was unfairly and improperly obtained from a packed meeting and
was directly contrary to the wishes of the majority of the shareholders. What
grounds for belief have the public on either side? We can but see that, when
the attention of the shareholders is called to the point, they upset the resolution
of the board, although the resolution is backed by an enormous influence which
a railway board can at any time command. We have surely heard of such a thing
as tampering with some votes and creating others of a fictitious character, for
the purpose of carrying out any scheme upon which a body of railway directors
may have set their hearts. In the absence of direct evidence, all we know is that
the directors of the South Western assert that their shareholders gave their authority
to make a bargain for them, and the shareholders came forward and said they
did nothing of the sort.

On this, criminal proceedings for libel were taken against Mr
William Harrison, the printer and publisher of *The Times*, on the
charge that the comments reflected upon the character of Mr Scott
and other directors of the London & South Western Railway company. The case was heard in December, 1854; and the jury, after a
few minutes' consideration, found the defendant guilty. Owing to
the courts rising for the Christmas vacation, sentence was not passed
until 30th January following, when Mr Harrison was fined £100.

Before dealing with the Consolidation Act of 1855 it is necessary
to mention certain openings of railways. There was the Basingstoke
and Salisbury, which had been authorised by 9 & 10 Vic., c. 370, in

1846, but its construction suspended. The work, as related above, was commenced in 1851, and it was opened as far as Andover on 3rd July, 1854. Work on the further portion to Salisbury was, however, held up until the Consolidation Act of 1855 was passed. That allowed the Andover–Salisbury to be laid as a single line, but it was to be completed within two years, or the ordinary dividends of the company would be suspended. It was opened on 1st May, 1857; the station in Salisbury being the present goods station at Milford, which was the terminus of the Bishopstoke & Salisbury.

Then came the line between Crediton and Fremington which had been completed on 12th July, 1854, but owing to the requirements of the Board of Trade Inspector with respect to signalling, the opening was delayed until 1st August. This was the property of the North Devon and a continuation of the Exeter & Crediton. Both lines it will be remembered, were of the broad gauge. For the first twelve months it was operated by the Bristol & Exeter, and then Mr Brassey worked it. On 2nd November, 1855, it was extended to Bideford. The North Devon was leased to, and worked by, the London & South Western from 1863 and acquired in 1865.

The year 1854 also saw the initial opening of a railway that was later to become part of the Somerset & Dorset Railway. The section in question was the Highbridge & Glastonbury. It was the property of the Somerset Central, which, by 15 & 16 Vic., c. 63 of 1852, was authorised to make a railway between the points named, and to purchase the Glastonbury Canal. The latter belonged to the Bristol & Exeter company, who would probably not have parted with it had it foreseen that the Somerset Central was, later, to be part of its great narrow gauge rival. The line was opened on 28th August, 1854, and was operated by the Bristol & Exeter.

Reverting to the Consolidation Act, it may be said that it embodied all the legal powers of the London & South Western in one Act. After correcting certain irregularities in the creation of portions of the ordinary share capital, it fixed the amount at £7,354,650 and, further, defined the borrowing powers at £2,772,082. It sanctioned certain new works, extended the time for the completion of others, penalised the company in the event of its not completing the Basingstoke & Salisbury within two years and, finally, had the clauses as to the extension to Exeter already mentioned.

Under the Staines, Wokingham & Woking Junction Railway Act, 16 & 17 Vic., c. 185, an independent company was authorised to build a line to run from Staines on the London & South Western Windsor line to Wokingham on the Reading, Guildford and Reigate.

The larger-wheeled (7ft 1in) version of Adams's 1880 express type, No. 449, Robert Stephenson, 1883

The last of Adams's finest express class, the T6 class 4-4-0, No. 686, built 1896.

T1 class 0-4-4T, No. 68, built at Nine Elms in 1889; the standard branch-line engine for fifty years.
[*British Railways*]

A 'Jubilee' class 0-4-2, No. 644, Neilson, 1892.

There was to be a branch through Chobham to Woking, but that was abandoned. The line was opened to Ascot on 4th June, 1856, and to Wokingham on the 9th of the following month. Running powers were exercised thence to Reading over the Guildford and Reigate line. The opening of the new line led to absurdly low fares between London and Reading by the new route and via Reigate, also by the Great Western, but they were stopped by an agreement made in 1858. The railway was worked by the London & South Western, to which company it was leased for 42 years as from 25th March, 1858, and, later, became part of the South Western system.

On 20th January, 1857, the Wilts, Somerset & Weymouth – a broad gauge subsidiary of the Great Western – was completed and, having been laid with the mixed gauge, the South Western, under powers given when the line was authorised in 1845, ran over it from Dorchester to Weymouth. To reciprocate, the London & South Western company laid mixed gauge for eight miles from Dorchester in the Wareham direction; but there is no record that they were used by broad gauge trains.

As already related, the Basingstoke & Salisbury was carried forward from Andover to Milford Station, Salisbury, on 1st May, 1857. It did not reach its present station in that city until later, as the plans had to be rearranged so as to accommodate also the Salisbury & Yeovil, which was to enter at the west end, together with the branch from Westbury of the Wilts, Somerset & Weymouth, which latter entered Salisbury on 30th June, 1856. Powers for these improvements were given in 1857 by 20 & 21 Vic., c. 135.

These lines promised considerable improvement in the facilities for transporting the produce of the surrounding country to the ancient market at Salisbury, but, owing to the lack of suitable accommodation, this state of affairs was viewed with mixed feelings by the citizens who held the market rights and rather anticipated that dealers would be tempted, after experience of the deficiences, to desert Salisbury for other more convenient markets. Accordingly, by 19 & 20 Vic., c. 93 (1856), a company was incorporated to construct a Market House, with rail connection and improved approaches within the city. The variation in the levels of the line from Basingstoke, necessitated by the decision to eliminate a level crossing proposed at Fisherton Street, also involved a modification of the Market House railway and the junction with the Salisbury & Yeovil. Powers to this end were obtained by the L.S.W.R. Co. in the following year. That the anticipated increase in trading due to the improved accommodation actually came about is shown by an Act of 1864, authorising an increase of the Market House Railway capital for the provision of still further facilities. This little railway remained an independent concern, worked by the Southern.

On 3rd May, 1858, the Somerset Central line, mentioned above, from Highbridge to Glastonbury was extended, in a northerly direction, to reach Burnham-on-Sea. At the latter place a pier was built in the hope of a steamship service to and from Cardiff.

The Lymington Railway was sanctioned in 1856, by 19 & 20 Vic., c. 71, and was opened on 12th July, 1858. The line was, and still is, a single line running off the main line a little beyond Brockenhurst, and terminated at the present Lymington Town station. The following year, under 22 & 23 Vic., c. 15, that independent company was authorised to acquire the ferry between this place and the Isle of Wight. It may be added that the property was vested in the London & South Western in 1879.

Until 1858 all trains that passed through Southampton had to do so by means of the London & Southampton terminus – Southampton Town Station. That state of affairs was then remedied by the opening of the curve between Northam Junction and Tunnel Junction, on which there is a speed limit of fifteen miles an hour.

The same year saw the earliest first-fruits of the attempt of the broad gauge interests to reach Southampton. To appreciate the situation, it must be known that by the Berks and Hants Extension of the Great Western, the broad gauge had arrived at Basingstoke on 1st November, 1848. In 1858 an apparently independent concern – the Andover & Redbridge – obtained powers to convert the Andover canal into a railway and to make a line of broad gauge railway between Andover and Redbridge – the latter place is just outside Southampton on the Dorchester line. The South Western had obtained similar powers, as has been related in the previous chapter, in 1847, but had allowed them to lapse. This time they opposed the proposal, but unsuccessfully. It should be noted that in the previous session – 1857 – a bill had been rejected which sought for authority to make a broad gauge railway between Salisbury and Southampton. The Committee who rejected that bill was unanimously of the opinion that 'it was not expedient to make that line, by reason that the traffic was not such as to justify so large an outlay and that there was no necessity for two lines of railway between Salisbury and Southampton'. There was no doubt but that, if possession had been obtained of the Andover & Redbridge, a broad gauge line would have been made from Basingstoke, or from Newbury on the Hungerford line.

In 1861 both the Great Western and the South Western sought, but unsuccessfully, to acquire the Andover & Redbridge. However, in 1862, as a consequence of happier relation between the two companies, it was agreed that the South Western should have it and that it should be of the standard gauge. Powers were given the following year, 1863, by 26 & 27 Vic., c. 109, under which Act the South Western company was also empowered to extend from Andover Town to the Junction station, there joining the Basingstoke–Salisbury line. Connecting junction lines were also authorised at Kimbridge and Romsey to enable the traffic to use the Romsey station on the Bishopstoke and Salisbury branch, a portion of the old route through Romsey being abandoned. It was opened throughout as a single line on 6th March, 1865, and for some facetious reason was known as the 'sprat and winkle' line. It may be mentioned that powers for the canal had been obtained in 1789, after an unsuccessful attempt in 1777.

One of the most noteworthy events of the year 1858 was the retirement, owing to ill-health, of Mr Chaplin who, more than any other man, assisted in establishing the firm foundation on which the London & South Western was built and in erecting the solid structure that rested upon it. Except for the two years when the Hon F. Scott was in the chair, and his party in power, Chaplin had been chairman from 1843 to 1858. He died on 24th April, 1859.

The first railway communication with Portsmouth had been given to Gosport by the London & South Western off the Southampton line, at Bishopstoke, and the next was by the Chichester and Portsmouth extension of the London, Brighton & South Coast. Neither of those was what could be called a direct line from London, and in the middle forties there were three schemes for a line to Portsmouth, one being, as related in Chapter VII, for an extension of the intended atmospheric system from Epsom. Nothing came of any of those schemes. In 1853, however, by 16 & 17 Vic., c. 99, a 'Direct Portsmouth Railway Company' obtained authority to build a line from Godalming to Havant, where it was to join the London, Brighton & South Coast and run over the latter's metals into Portsmouth.

This undertaking was a 'contractor's line' pure and simple – the contractor being Thomas Brassey. About this time many lines were built as a speculation, without any intention of working them, but in the certain belief that one of the existing companies would feel compelled to take them over. This line went over practically the same route as the atmospheric had adopted, from Godalming. It was built on the 'undulating principle', which was then being advocated by certain engineers; namely to follow the level of the ground as much as possible, not troubling about keeping the gradients down. One of the most prominent advocates of this system was Dr Lardner, who was considered one of the chief scientific authorities of the day, in spite of his having proved that it was impossible for a steamer to cross the Atlantic, only a short time before the feat was accomplished. In *The Steam Engine*, 7th edition (1840), after saying that moderate gradients are not essential, he gave the following reasons:

> The resistance produced by steeper gradients can be compensated by slackening the speed, so that the power shall be relieved from as much atmospheric resistance as is equal to the increased resistance produced by the gravity of the plane which is ascended. And, on the other hand, in descending the plane the speed may be increased until the resistance of the atmosphere is increased to the same amount as that by which the train is relieved of resistance by the declivity down which it moves.

It was not, however, considered judicious to press the theory to its limits, and some very heavy earthworks had to be constructed, particularly at Haslemere and Witley. There was also the Buriton tunnel, between Petersfield and Rowlands Castle, half a mile long, from which was removed 40,000 cubic yards of material. Indeed, in spite of its so-called surface character, some 1,600,000 cubic yards of soil had to be taken away before it was possible to lay down a single line – which was all it was – over the $32\frac{3}{4}$ miles between Godalming and Havant. There is a bank of 1 in 80 from the tunnel to Rowlands Castle nearly 6 miles long, with many reverse curves, put in to increase the length, and so keep the incline within bounds.

When the line was approaching completion the promoters began to have doubts as to the success of their venture. It was obviously a better proposition than most contractors' lines, providing as it did a direct route from London to Portsmouth and the Isle of Wight. But the shortening of the distance – some twenty miles less than the existing South Western route by Bishopstoke, which was $95\frac{1}{4}$ miles, while the distance via Brighton was also $95\frac{1}{4}$ – had a disadvantage. The fares would have to be reduced. There was also the fact that the South Western and Brighton companies had an arrangement in connection with the division of the receipts of the Portsmouth traffic. It occurred to the newcomers that they might, instead of working with the South Western, connect up with the South Eastern at Shalford, the latter company having (in 1852) taken over the Reading, Guildford & Reigate Railway.

Accordingly, in 1854 they applied to Parliament for powers to construct an extension from Godalming to Shalford. This line was to run on the western side of the South Western Godalming branch, and parallel with it, as far as Peasmarsh, where it was to curve eastwards towards Shalford. At the same time they asked for running powers between Havant and Portsmouth. All these powers were granted, subject to their building a new station at the latter place, if required to do so by the companies in possession. The Peasmarsh–Shalford spur was made on an embankment which still remains, much overgrown by trees, but it is not likely that any lines were ever laid upon it, although a bridge, which would have carried the line across the river, existed until about forty years ago. However, the South Eastern declined to have anything to do with the matter, alleging primly that it would be a breach of their agreement with the London, Brighton and South Coast Railway.*

The South Western, perhaps fearing that this virtuous attitude might not be maintained, eventually decided to lease the Portsmouth Railway at a rent of £18,000 a year, and to open it on 1st January, 1859. The line had been practically ready for a year, but the owners possessed no rolling stock with which to work it.

On 28th December, 1858, in anticipation of the opening, the South Western ran a train down, manned by a crowd of navvies, hoping to get through and establish a precedent. The Brighton company, however, was ready for them, and they found the rails taken up at the junction, and an engine firmly chained to the metals. After a smart skirmish these obstructions were removed, and the train proceeded, only to find more rails missing farther along. Here there was a regular fight, and the South Western train eventually had to go back, amid the cheers of the victorious Brighton railwaymen. The war was then transferred to the Law Courts, the result being that the first train via the new line arrived at Portsmouth on 24th January, 1859. After their defeat in the Courts, the Brighton company began a battle of fares, which were made at first 5s. return, then 3s. 6d. The Brighton company even attacked the Southampton traffic, by putting on a steamer from Portsmouth, and charging very low inclusive fares from London. After some months of this game, in which both the players lost heavily, the two companies made peace, and reverted to the old arrangement, under which the Portsmouth traffic was pooled, the South Western taking two-thirds, and the Brighton one-third.

Viewing the incident at this distance of time, one wonders why the companies acted as they did, seeing that both of them had been running into Portsmouth for ten years, the last portion of line being

* The powers to construct the portion between Peasmarsh and Godalming were abandoned by the Portsmouth Railway Amending Act, 1858.

jointly owned. This piece did not begin, however, until Portcreek Junction, nearly four miles beyond the point where the Portsmouth Direct joined the Brighton.

The South Western was obviously in the wrong, and as, according to the chairman at a special meeting of the proprietors on 17th March, 1859, it would cost £40,000 to build an independent line, it was agreed that the section between Havant and Portcreek Junction should also be jointly owned, which was sanctioned that year by 22 & 23 Vic., c. 44.

On 4th April, 1859, the London & South Western opened its line from Raynes Park to Epsom. It may be noted that the chairman of the Brighton railway, speaking at the half-yearly meeting in July, said that the decrease in that company's traffic for that six months was partly due to the South Western obtaining some of the Epsom Race traffic.

At last the approach to Exeter was completed. On the 2nd May, 1859 Gillingham was reached; on 7th May, 1860, the line was opened to Sherborne, and to Yeovil on 1st June. The final section was finished on 19th July, 1860, and the whole length between Yeovil and Exeter (Queen Street) was brought into use. Goods trains did not, however, commence running until 1st September.

The Somerset Central opened its extension from Highbridge to Burnham on 3rd May, 1858; and the branch from Glastonbury to Wells on 15th March, 1859. The Dorset Central, which with the Somerset Central, was later to be part of the Somerset & Dorset, must now be mentioned. The Somerset Central was empowered in 1856 to extend its line from Glastonbury to Bruton – actually to Cole – and the Dorset Central was to fill the gap between Wimborne on the South Western and Bruton (Cole). All these lines having associations with the Bristol & Exeter were of the broad gauge, so, in order to accommodate the London & South Western, the gauge on the Dorset Central was mixed.

The Dorset Central line was opened from Wimborne to Blandford on 1st November, 1860, and from Cole to Templecombe a year later; the Somerset Central completed the connection from Templecombe to Blandford on 31st August, 1863; but it was not opened for traffic until the 14th September following. Under powers given by 25 & 26 Vic., c. 225, in 1862, the two railways were amalgamated, as the Somerset & Dorset, as from 1st September, 1862, and, as will be related in due course, 'hat company was leased by the London & South Western and Midland companies in 1875. At the time of the above-mentioned amalgamation in 1862 the Somerset & Dorset was

65 miles in length, and was intended to connect the Bristol Channel at Burnham with the English Channel at Poole.

It is now necessary again to mention the Exeter extension, in order to observe that there was a gap between the Yeovil & Exeter terminus at Queen Street, Exeter, and the Cowley Bridge junction of the Exeter & Crediton and Bristol & Exeter lines, to be joined up before the Exeter & Crediton and the North Devon could be reached. In 1859 and 1860 plans towards that end were agreed to between the parties concerned, and under 23 & 24 Vic., c. 103, of 1860, the South Western extended its line to a junction with the South Devon at St David's, which was reached on 1st February, 1862; mixed gauge was laid through that station and up to Cowley Bridge and over the North Devon. On the Exeter & Crediton the narrow gauge rails, which had been allowed to fall into disrepair, were relaid, and standard gauge communication was established right through to Bideford in March, 1863. The South Western, under the last-mentioned Act, was authorised to lease both the North Devon and the Exeter & Crediton. The Bideford extension was amalgamated with the S.W.R. as from 1st January, 1865. The gradient between the South Western station at Exeter and St David's is 1 in 37, falling towards the latter.

The Exeter & Exmouth was an independent concern which, under 18 & 19 Vic., c. 122, was empowered to make a railway between the South Devon at Exeter, and Exmouth; but in 1858, by 20 & 21 Vic. c. 56, it was enacted that the line should instead join the South Western at Topsham and be a standard and not a broad gauge line. It was opened on 1st May, 1861. On 1st June the Great Western and London & South Western joint station at Yeovil was brought into use.

The most important event of the period with which we have been dealing in this chapter was the opening to Exeter. The express on 1st August, 1860, left Waterloo at 9 a.m. and arrived at Exeter 2.10 p.m.; five hours and ten minutes. So far as time was concerned, they could not compete with the Great Western; which as early as from May, 1845 to October, 1848, left Paddington at 9.45 a.m. and arrived at Exeter at 2.15 p.m.; afterwards made slower. Later on, however, the South Western competition led to the Flying Dutchman, from March, 1862 to the end of 1865, leaving Paddington at 11.45 a.m. and arriving at Exeter 4.15 p.m.; four hours and a half. This timing was not kept up after 1865.

The period covered by this chapter saw the beginning of a programme of widening the main lines; the first to be dealt with being that from Southampton to Dorchester. On 1st August, 1857, the second line of rails was opened westward to Beaulieu Road and from Brockenhurst to Holmsley; on 1st October following, from Ringwood to Wimborne. By 1st September, 1858, the sections Beaulieu Road–Brockenhurst and Holmsley–Ringwood were completed.

The South Western prided themselves on their immunity from accidents, and down to the time at which we have arrived, were well entitled to do so. On 20th June, 1858, a third-class carriage was derailed at Bishopstoke, one passenger being killed and several injured. At the inquest, the coroner observed that he had held his office longer than the railway had been in existence, but that this was the first occasion on which he had been called upon to hold an inquest on the body of a passenger, although an extensive part of the line ran through his district.

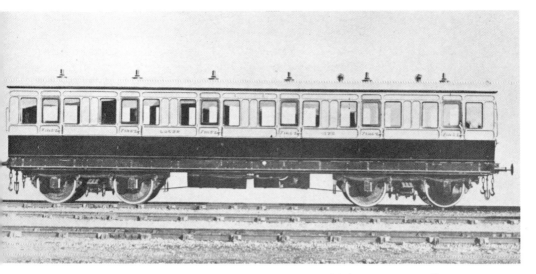

One of the first L.S.W.R. bogie coaches; note chain couplings in addition to screw couplings.
[*Locomotive Publishing Company*

The south side of Waterloo shortly after rebuilding. Note the restaurant car with clerestory roof.
[*Locomotive Publishing Company*

No. 720, Drummond's first express engine; it had four cylinders with independent drive to each axle; as fitted with enlarged boiler in 1905. [*British Railways*

Drummond's T9 class 4-4-0 of 1901, No. 773. [*British Railways*

Farthest West: the station at Padstow about 1920. Line to fish-dock and quay at right.

A 'Paddlebox' T14 class 4-6-0, of 1912, No. 458.   [*Locomotive Publishing Company*

Drummond's express tank, M7 class 0-4-4T, No. 109 of 1904.

The S11 class with smaller (6ft) wheels for hilly country, No. 395 of 1903.

IX

The South Western from 1860 to 1875

THERE appears nothing fresh to mention for 1860 and 1861, but much was done in the years immediately succeeding. It is worth recording that at the half-yearly meeting of the company on 14th August, 1862, a high compliment was paid to Archibald Scott. The chairman, Captain Mangles, said that he had been particularly requested by his colleagues on the board of directors to introduce to the favourable notice of the meeting the unceasing exertions of their traffic manager, Mr Archibald Scott. They must all appreciate what a responsibility must rest upon an officer in Mr Scott's position and he, Captain Mangles, could bear witness to the untiring zeal with which that gentleman had attended to his onerous and difficult duties.

Mention must now be made of the first important enlargement of Waterloo station. A fact that should not be lost sight of when considering the comparatively frequent expansions of that station is that it was originally intended to be a through, and not a terminal, station – the terminus was to be near London Bridge.

About this time what was known as the Windsor line station was opened, which brought into use No. 4 platform and a platform line between the latter and No. 3 platform and a new carriage siding to the north of No. 4 platform. Farther north were four other platform lines. The Windsor line station had its own station buildings, cab yard and approach road.

At that period the number of passenger trains arriving daily was about 228. All trains were stopped outside the station for the collection of tickets and, after the engine had been detached, the coaches were tow-roped into the platform road. A lever fixed near Westminster Bridge Road caused a gong near the end of the platform to sound a corresponding number of beats to the number of the platform into which the train was to run.

In 1859 the London Bridge & Charing Cross Railway was authorised, which, in 1861, was permitted also to build an extension into Cannon Street. In 1863 the proposal was taken over by the South Eastern and it will be of interest to hear that the line was mainly built in redemption of a promise made to a House of Commons committee in 1857 by Mr Byng, the chairman, that he would call the South Eastern proprietors together and recommend them to promote, or to concur in the prosecution of, such a scheme as should effectively supply access to the West End of London and to complete the system of railway communication in Kent and to the Continent. The reason that promise is mentioned here is that Mr Byng showed that such a railway could not reach the west end, but that a 'London Bridge & Charing Cross' would meet the conditions, and that it would give a direct connection with the South Western at Waterloo, and, further, thence, by means of the West London Extension, with the Great Western, North Western, and all the railways in the North.

The new railway was opened from London Bridge to near Waterloo Junction on 11th January, 1864, and the connection with the South Western was given by a line that passed between Nos. 4 and 6 platform roads in Waterloo terminus. It ran across what is now called the circulating area, and the bridge over the Waterloo Road which formerly carried the connecting line is still used for providing passenger access between the stations. When the line was out of use an opening bridge was in position to allow passengers to cross the connecting line on the level.

Except for some North Western trains, which began to run in July, 1865 (and were discontinued soon afterwards), between Euston and London Bridge, there has been no regular service of trains over the connection; it was used for 'specials' and the exchange of vehicles only.

In view of the popularity of Bournemouth it may come as a surprise to hear that there was no railway station in Bournemouth itself until 1870; there had, however, been communication through Poole (now Hamworthy) since the opening of the Southampton & Dorchester on 1st May, 1847. In 1859, however, a company known as the Ringwood, Christchurch & Bournemouth, obtained powers to construct a line between the two points first named. Although Bournemouth was included in the name of the company, authority to extend the line to that town was not given until 1863. It commenced by a junction with the Southampton & Dorchester at Ringwood, and was opened to Christchurch on 13th November, 1862, and reached Bournemouth – in the present Central goods station – on 14th March, 1870. The London & South Western worked the line from the beginning and acquired it as from 16th December 1874.

The Stokes Bay Railway company was another independent undertaking, which, in 1855, was empowered to make a line from Gosport, i.e. the terminus of the original Portsmouth extension from Bishopstoke of the London & Southampton, to Stokes Bay, 1 mile 45 chains long, and to build a pier at the latter place which could be used by the Isle of Wight steamers at all states of the tide. Thence was a ferry, belonging to another company, to and from Ryde. The line and pier were opened on 6th April, 1863, and worked by the L.S.W.R. A clause in the agreement with the Stokes Bay company provided that the terms were not to apply should either that company or the Ferry company fail to do its share. The line, pier and ferry were leased to the L.S.W.R. for 999 years from 1st June, 1872 and acquired on 17th June, 1875. The railway south of Gosport Road station and the pier were sold to the Admiralty on 3rd March, 1922.*

On 1st February, 1862, the South Western took over the Exeter & Crediton Railway from the Bristol & Exeter. There were also two other smaller independent railways. One was the Chard, 3 miles long, to give a connection with that town from Chard Junction and to build a tramway to the canal. It was authorised in 1860, opened on 8th May, 1863, and acquired in 1864. The other was the Bishop' Waltham, 3½ miles long, from Botley on the Bishopstoke–Gosport line, to Bishop's Waltham, with branches to some clay-pits at that place. It was sanctioned in 1862, brought into use on 6th June. 1863, and acquired in the latter year.

As yet there was no railway communication with the ancient county town of Kingston-on-Thames, so, in 1859, the London & South Western secured powers to build a branch thence from Twickenham on the Richmond–Windsor line. The terminus of this branch as originally authorised was to have been adjacent to the roadway bridge over the river, on the Middlesex bank, but in the following year powers to deviate were obtained and the railway was continued over the river into the present low level station. It was opened on 1st July, 1863. In 1865 further powers were obtained to construct a continuation from Kingston to Wimbledon, crossing under the Southampton main line at Malden. It was at first intended to cross the Richmond Road on the level, but a year later sanction was obtained to raise the line between Norbiton and Kingston so as to pass over the road, and join the existing railway on the Surrey side of the river bridge; hence the existence of the high level station. This line was opened on 1st January, 1869. Later on, when the widening from Clapham Junction to Surbiton was being carried out, the Kingston lines between Wimbledon and Malden were remodelled so

* Closed for passengers November, 1915. The railway link with the pier was broken, and the pier served by a narrow-gauge line running from a Royal Naval depot at the east end of Gosport.

as to form a part thereof; the up line being transferred to the up side of the main line, by means of a connection at Malden.

Mention must now be made of what may be called a strategical railway, in that it afforded through communication between the main lines on the north side of the Thames, in particular the London & North Western and the Great Western, and those on the south side. It was known as the West London Extension Railway, being, in fact, an extension of the West London, a line originally sanctioned in 1836, under the name of the Birmingham, Bristol & Thames Junction Railway, which began by a junction between the North Western and Great Western at North Pole Junction, Wormwood Scrubbs, and ended at Chelsea. It was opened in 1844 and leased to the L.N.W.R. and G.W.R. jointly in 1845.

The 'Extension' was authorised in 1859, being a joint affair, held in the following proportions: L.N.W.R., one-third; G.W.R., one-third; L.S.W.R. and L.B S.C.R., one-sixth each. In consisted of a line 4 miles 6 chains long, from a junction with the West London at Kensington (Chelsea Dock Junction), crossing the Thames to Battersea, terminating by a junction with the West End and Crystal Palace line at Longhedge. Two branches connected with the South Western lines (one in each direction); a third spur joined the West End line at Clapham Junction South; there was also a branch to the docks at Chelsea. It was opened on 2nd March, 1863. The connection to the South Western, at West London Junction, fell out of use on the withdrawal of the train service between Waterloo and Richmond via Kensington in June, 1916, and was later removed entirely, after being used for a few special trains. One of these occasions was to allow the passage of the train conveying the body of the late Field Marshal Earl Haig, on it way to Scotland, after the funeral in London, on 3rd February, 1928.

In order to accommodate the Great Western trains the West London was laid with mixed gauge. For the same reason, in order that the Great Western could run into the Chatham & Dover side of Victoria station – of which it was, until 1932, part owner – the lines of the Extension, except those joining the South Western, were also of mixed gauge.

One consequence of the West London Extension was the service of trains by the London & North Western between Euston and the South Eastern station at London Bridge, mentioned earlier in the chapter. The trains ran via Willesden, Addison Road, West London Junction, Waterloo, Waterloo Junction and over the Charing Cross Extension to London Bridge.

The Petersfield Railway was from that town to Midhurst, and it was originally proposed that powers should be obtained by the Mid-Sussex & Midhurst company to construct this line. But attention was drawn to the fact that the L.B.S.C.R. were financially interested in the Mid-Sussex, and any assistance rendered by them might be construed by the South Western as an encroachment on their territory. Accordingly, the Petersfield Railway went forward as an independent company. During the progress of the bill through Parliament some friction arose between the Mid-Sussex company and the promoters of the Petersfield Railway, in consequence of which a deviation was ordered at the Midhurst end, and a clause was inserted in the Act – 23 & 24 Vic., c. 173 – expressly forbidding any physical connection between the two lines. Nevertheless, the connection was made a few years later. The Petersfield Railway was authorised in 1860, acquired by the South Western in 1863 and opened on 1st September, 1864. The Thames Valley Railway was promoted by an independent company in order to join the Twickenham–Kingston line at Strawberry Hill to Shepperton. It was sanctioned in 1862, brought into use on 1st November, 1864, and taken over by the South Western in 1865. Alton had been reached from Farnham on 28th July, 1852, and in 1861 the Mid-Hants company, originally known as the Alton, Alresford & Winchester, was authorised to make an extension thence to the London & Southampton main line at Winchester Junction, two miles north of Winchester. It was opened on 2nd October, 1865, and acquired in 1876.

In 1864 powers were obtained to extend the Epsom & Leatherhead Railway, which had been authorised in 1856, opened on 1st February, 1859, and acquired the following year by the South Western, in order to connect it with the Brighton company's Dorking–Epsom line. The extension was opened 23rd December, 1866. The former joint station on the Epsom side of the Kingston Road bridge at Leatherhead was closed, and each company opened a new station; similarly there were two separate stations at Epsom. These parallel lines were combined some years after Grouping and the L.S.W.R. station at Leatherhead and the L.B.S.C.R. station at Epsom were closed (see Appendix, Vol. 2).

The Weymouth & Portland Railway was sanctioned in 1862, to extend the Wilts, Somerset & Weymouth Railway to the harbour in the last-named town and to construct a line from Weymouth to the Isle of Portland. The latter was put into service on 16th October, 1865, and was jointly leased to the South Western and Great Western companies. For the accommodation of the latter, the line was laid with mixed gauge, but when the Great Western lines in that neighbourhood were converted to standard gauge in 1874, the broad gauge rail was removed. The Weymouth Harbour Tramway was opened at the same time, for goods, but not for passengers until 1st July, 1889. The Portland Breakwater Railway which opened on 29th May, 1874, was leased by the Admiralty, in respect of the part between Portland and Church Hope Cove; in 1868 work had begun on a railway from Easton, as the south end of the peninsular, to Church Hope; work ceased in 1874, restarted in 1888, and on 1st October, 1900, a through goods service over these two lines from Portland to Easton was started. Passenger service began on 1st September, 1902, by which time the E.C.H.R. was in the hands of a Receiver. The two lines continued to be worked as an extension of the Portland branch, service being frequent as far as Portland, with somewhat less than half the trains continuing to Easton. There was a further railway from near Easton to Portland Harbour, but this was operated by the stone merchants.

Mention was made in Chapter VIII of the attempt, backed by the Great Western, to get the broad gauge into Southampton by the purchase of the Redbridge canal. The happier relations with the Great Western which subsequently came about, permitted the South Western to obtain powers in 1863 to build the line from Andover Junction to the terminus of the Andover & Redbridge in the town, and the necessary lines at Romsey to connect with the Bishopstoke & Salisbury.

Among the changes that were made in 1866 was the exercise, by the London & South Western, of running powers over the London, Chatham & Dover into the City by virtue of money advanced for the latter company's Metropolitan Extension. The advance was made under 28 & 29 Vic., c. 278 of 1865, and the amount authorised was £400,000 in shares and £133,300 on loan. In order to exercise these powers from the main line a connection was laid in between Lavender Hill Junction, Clapham, and Factory Junction, Wandsworth Road. This allowed L.S.W.R. trains to run to and from Ludgate Hill, and services commenced on 3rd April, 1866, from Richmond via Addison Road, and three years later from Wimbledon via Tulse Hill. In addition to being used at the present day by through goods trains, it has served as a direct line for passenger trains from the North of England to the Kent Coast resorts.

Three other lines or extensions were brought into use during that year – 1866. So far there was no direct route between Southampton and Portsmouth, passengers having to change at Bishopstoke. The first step for a direct line between those points was the construction under powers given in 1861, 3 and 4, of a line from Portswood (St Denys) to Netley. The scheme was taken over by the South Western in 1865 and the line opened on 5th March, 1866. It was to be twenty years before the gap between Netley and the Gosport line at Fareham was closed. The second new line, authorised in 1864 and brought into use in 1866 – on 1st October – was an extension of the Weybridge–Chertsey branch to Virginia Water, there joining the Staines, Wokingham & Woking Railway. The last of the three new lines was the Salisbury to West Moors, where it joined the Southampton and Dorchester. It was opened on 20th December, 1866, but fell into financial difficulties and was not acquired until 1883. It had been authorised in 1861, under the name of the Salisbury & Dorset Junction Railway. This saved 3.5 miles in the journey from Salisbury to Poole Junction (Hamworthy Junction).

We have now reached the stage in the history of the London & South Western Railway when it made its great advance into farther Devon and North Cornwall. In 1862 the Okehampton Railway company was authorised to make a railway from Coleford Junction, just west of Yeoford on the North Devon Railway, to Okehampton. The following year the same company was given powers to continue the proposal so as to join the Launceston & South Devon – a broad gauge line, worked by the South Devon company between Tavistock and Launceston – at Lidford – now spelt Lydford. In 1865 the Okehampton was authorised to build a further 41 miles by a line from Meldon Junction to Bude, also a branch to Torrington. The powers, however, were allowed to lapse until 1873, when the Meldon Junction–Holsworthy powers were re-enacted. It was opened on 20th January, 1879, and acquired by the South Western in 1880. At the same time the name of the company was changed to the Devon & Cornwall.

It may here be noted that the highest point on the South Western system occurs just beyond Meldon Junction, where an altitude of no less than 950ft is reached. The adjacent viaduct spanning the valley of the West Okement River has a maximum height of 150ft from rail to ground level.

In 1864 the Launceston, Bodmin & Wadebridge Junction was incorporated to make a railway from Launceston to join the Bodmin & Wadebridge at Wadebridge. The following year there was an Act for a railway from the end of the Bodmin & Wadebridge company's Ruthern Bridge branch to Truro. Under the latter Act the name of the L.B.W.J. company was altered to the Central Cornwall.

The half-yearly report of the South Western for January–June, 1865, said that an Act had been obtained for making new railways from the westernmost extremity of the line to Truro. The report observed that the undertaking was one which could not be without interest to the proprietors, as, by means of it, and by railways already authorised, a through narrow gauge system of railways would be established between Okehampton and the extreme west of Cornwall.

As the Central Cornwall was to terminate at Truro, some explanation appears to be necessary for the remark that the narrow gauge would reach the extreme west of Cornwall. When the West Cornwall, i.e. the line between Truro and Penzance, was built there already was in service a narrow gauge line – the Hayle Railway, opened in 1839 – and the West Cornwall was, therefore, of mixed gauge, so as to suit the narrow gauge rolling-stock of the Hayle Railway and the broad gauge of the Cornwall Railway from Plymouth.

A year later, the half-yearly report for January–June, 1866, said:

By several decisions of Parliament parties now constituting the Devon & Cornwall and Central Cornwall have obtained powers to construct narrow gauge railways from Okehampton to the Launceston & South Devon at Lidford and from the last-mentioned line to the Bodmin & Wadebridge – owned by this company since 1845 – at its eastern extremity and from the western end of the Bodmin & Wadebridge to the Cornwall at Truro. . . . In the session now closing those companies sought for powers, including the compulsory use of this company's lines between Okehampton and Exeter and of the principal station in Exeter. This application, notwithstanding a strong opposition by the several companies concerned, was, in the House of Commons, successful and thereafter negotiations ensued with a view to the working of the railways of the Devon & Cornwall and the Central Cornwall . . . and to the establishment of satisfactory arrangements as to the traffic of those districts between this company and the Great Western, Bristol & Exeter, South Devon and the Cornwall.

The report concluded the subject by saying that there was not time to complete the matter during the session and that the question would come before Parliament the following year.

In the session for 1867 there was, therefore, a bill deposited by the Great Western, Bristol & Exeter, South Devon and South Western companies which provided for traffic and other arrangements amongst themselves, and with other companies and persons and for the appointment of joint committees; certain specified Acts were to be amended or repealed. Provisions were made in the bill for the broad gauge lines, south and west of Exeter, to be open to the London & South Western, and for that company's lines, together with the Devon & Cornwall and the Central Cornwall, to be free to the broad gauge. The parties, however, did not agree and the bill was, therefore, withdrawn.

The purpose of the 'Quadruple Treaty' proposed by the bill of 1867 may best be judged by the following extract from the report for July–December, 1871, of the South Devon – which company was one of the four concerned – when it was desired to revive the proposal:

In August, 1867, the proprietors were informed that the bill which had been, in that session, introduced into Parliament, at the joint instance of the three associated broad gauge companies (Great Western, Bristol & Exeter, and South Devon) for effecting traffic and other arrangements, had been withdrawn, in consequence of the Bristol & Exeter board having decided to proceed no farther therein. Matters remained thus in abeyance until November last, when the board of this company was invited to a conference by the Great Western directors; this last has resulted in the re-deposit of the Quadruple bill, with the assent of all four companies; it being clearly expressed that the conditions which had been discussed in 1866 should now be modified so as to meet the present views of the respective parties. The proprietors having, in 1867, approved of what was then submitted to them and given to the directors large discretionary powers with reference to those very important arrangements, the board had no difficulty in assenting to the resumption of the negotiations, feeling convinced that by the arrangements which are now under discussion, the best results in the interests of the public and all concerned may be ensured and the traffic of the important districts served by the respective lines more efficiently developed.

The next stage, as regards the area in question, was that the Central Cornwall, in 1867, secured a further three years for the completion of the works. Nothing was, however, done during the extended period and, therefore, the powers lapsed in 1870. The Devon & Cornwall then alone held the field as regards new railways, and its powers, it may be repeated, were for a line from Coleford Junction, through Okehampton, to Lydford, and one from Meldon Junction to Bude, together with a branch to Torrington.

In 1863 the London & South Western concluded an agreement with the Devon & Cornwall which was confirmed in 1866, and the line was acquired by the former company as from the end of 1871.

The four companies concerned deposited, in 1872, a further bill to confirm the Quadruple Treaty. As showing some of the aims the Treaty had in view and that it had a wide field than Devon & Cornwall, the following extracts therefrom may be noted:

16. The South Western to convey by their engines and in charge of their servants and under their regulations on their line between Basingstoke and Southampton such passenger and goods trains – not exceeding three each way daily unless the traffic require four – of the Great Western as that company appoints; the trains to be narrow gauge and to convey traffic between Southampton and stations on the Great Western narrow gauge lines north of Basingstoke and Reading.

34. It is also the intention that without the necessity of application being made to the Board of Trade to sanction the laying down of any narrow gauge rails or any parliamentary proceedings or any litigation for that object, there shall be full and efficient through narrow gauge communication and running powers, with all requisite and all usual facilities for that purpose, between Lidford and Plymouth. . . . It is also the intention that the South Western are to have full and efficient narrow gauge communication and running powers, with all requisite facilities for the purpose, over and through that portion of the Bristol & Exeter which lies between the Exeter Junction of the South Western and Cowley Bridge Junction, including the use of St David's station and the necessary junctions.

The Treaty also provided against opposition to the London & South Western acquiring fourteen railways, such as the Sidmouth, the Salisbury & Yeovil and the Poole & Bournemouth, named therein, and that the 'Associated Companies' – the Great Western, the Bristol & Exeter and the South Devon – not be opposed if it was proposed that they of any or them acquire twenty-seven companies, also named therein.

To understand the fate of the bill for confirming the Quadruple Treaty it must be known that in the same year the London & North Western were proposing to amalgamate with the Lancashire & Yorkshire, while the Midland wished to absorb the Glasgow & South Western. Other amalgamations were in the air, so the Government appointed a select committee to inquire into and report upon the whole question. The possible results therefrom hindered the progress of the bill for confirming the Quadruple Treaty and after many delays it was eventually withdrawn on 8th August, 1872.

The London & South Western report for the first half of 1872, in recording the fact, said:

The House of Commons saw fit, early in this session of Parliament, to suspend the progress of this, and of all other bills for effecting similar objects, pending their consideration by a select committee, and that committee has not as yet presented its report. The directors remain of opinion that the arrangements contemplated by the bill would, if completed, operate beneficially alike to the public and to the companies.

The chairman of the South Devon, speaking on 22nd August, 1872, said on the same subject:

that he was happy to say that since the withdrawal of the bill conferences had taken place between gentlemen representing the four boards and there was every reason to hope that terms might be agreed upon substantially the same as those for which parliamentary sanction was sought and which might result in benefit to the Bristol and Exeter and, he trusted, to the other companies.

Similarly, the chairman of the Bristol & Exeter said, on 4th September:

The South Devon had been in communication with the London & South Western and he believed the directors of that company and the directors of the associated companies were entirely in accordance as to the course of operation that ought to be pursued in their district and there would be no difficulty whatever in carrying out the arrangements based upon the principle of the Quadruple bill, either at an early period or a later one. The objects of the Quadruple bill had been greatly misunderstood and, as far as it went, he was quite satisfied that if the bill had passed they would have been enabled to make arrangements for the whole of the locality which would have been of great importance to the trade and commerce of the district served and would not have been either oppressive or unjust to any one.

The lines in question were opened thus: Coleford Junction–North Tawton, 1st November, 1865; North Tawton–Okehampton Road (later Belstone Corner, and finally Sampford Courtenay), about a mile from Okehampton, 8th January, 1867; Belstone–Okehampton, 3rd October, 1871; Okehampton–Lydford, 12th October, 1874; Meldon–Holsworthy, 20th January, 1879.

Another reference has to be made to the Bodmin & Wadebridge. In 1865 powers were obtained to modernise that line, but in view of the proposed new railways in Cornwall the work was not put in hand. The South Western chairman, in making an intimation at the half-yearly meeting on 14th August, 1873, that the work was then to be commenced, spoke of the Bodmin & Wadebridge as the company's foothold in that part of the country. The improvements were not, however, made until 1887.

With regard to the Quadruple Treaty it seems that there was a certain amount of aggressiveness on the part of the South Western; on the other hand there was considerable lethargy among the broad gauge companies. The 'stirring up of the dry bones' led to extensions and expenditure of capital, but there was no wasteful competition and all was to the public good. Moreover, it was not only the South Western that gained by the happier relations. The South Devon made several extensions without opposition, and the views of that company's chairman have already been quoted.

Reverting now to the events immediately subsequent to 1866 it is necessary to remember that the portion of the South Eastern company's Charing Cross line which lay to the south of the river Thames had been opened in January, 1864, and was connected with the South Western at the point where the South Eastern passed the east end of Waterloo station. The former company, during 1867, urged the South Eastern, in anticipation of the opening of the line into Charing Cross station, to provide a proper passenger station at the junction at Waterloo and asked that all its trains should stop there, so as to serve passengers from and to the South Western Railway.

The South Eastern at first declined, but eventually agreed, and the station was opened on 1st January, 1869.

The Seaton & Beer Railway was independently constituted in 1863 to build a line from Colyton Junction – now Seaton Junction – to Beer – now known as Seaton. It was opened on 16th March, 1868, but its transfer to the L.S.W.R. was not authorised until 1880, and was effected in 1885.

On 1st October, 1868, the Midland company's line between Brent sidings and Acton Wells Junction on the North and South Western Junction was opened. Reciprocal running powers were given, so that the Midland reached the L.S.W.R. over the North and South Western Junction lines, and the South Western ran to Brent. On 1st January, 1869, two other important lines were opened in the Metropolitan area. The first, authorised in 1864, was from Kensington – now Addison Road – through Turnham Green, Gunnersbury and Kew Gardens to Richmond. The station at Kensington (Addison Road) was on the West London Extension Railway from Clapham Junction, and which was jointly owned with the L.B.S.C.R., L.N.W.R. and Great Western. The South Western granted running powers over the Richmond line from Hammersmith, when the District arrived at that point in 1877, the trains operating from City (Mansion House). The District also employed these running powers when in 1879 it opened its line from Turnham Green to Ealing. The actual point of junction between the District and the South Western was at Studland Road Junction, and after the South Western line from Kensington was abandoned, the portion from Studland Road to Richmond, although L.S.W.R. property, was operated by trains of the District company; stations from Gunnersbury to Richmond were also called at by trains of the N.S.W.J.R., an extension of the North London line from Broad Street, which made contact with South Western metals at Acton Junction, just north of Gunnersbury (Brentford Road until 1872), the link having been opened with the branch. The line from Wimbledon to the Twickenham-Kingston branch at Kingston, authorised in 1865, also opened on 1st January, 1869.

In 1865 the Waterloo & Whitehall Railway company was authorised to build what would now be called a tube railway from near Waterloo station, under the Thames, to Charing Cross. It was to be worked on what was described as the 'pneumatic principle'. Arrangements with the London & South Western were sanctioned, but except that two of that company's directors were on the board of the Whitehall, there was no official connection. After spending about

£70,000 in laying two tubes under the river – which remain there to this day – the powers lapsed in 1871.

The year 1868 saw the opening, on 1st October, of the Tooting–Wimbledon railway, connecting the Brighton company's Peckham and Sutton line with the South Western, for which powers had been granted in 1864 and 1865, the line from Wimbledon to Lower Merton (Merton Park) being L.S.W./L.B.S.C. joint. Trains ran from Ludgate Hill and London Bridge to Wimbledon, both via Merton Abbey and Haydens Lane (Haydons Road).

Mr John Strapp, who had been the chief resident engineer since 1856, retired in November, 1870. He was an assistant to Thomas Brassey in the construction of the Nine Elms–Surbiton section in 1837 and joined the South Western in 1844. In the same year the company lost the services of two important officers who were taken over by the Post Office when they acquired the telegraphs, namely the telegraph superintendent, Mr – later Sir William Preece, and his assistant, W. E. Langdon, who eventually became the telegraph superintendent of the Midland Railway. Both were very able electrical engineers, and had produced a system of interlocking the signal levers and the block instruments, which they were unable to develop after their transfer to the Post Office.

The company lost another valuable servant by the death, on 18th October, 1871, of Joseph Beattie, the locomotive superintendent. He came to the line in 1837 as an assistant to Locke and, later was given charge of the carriages and wagons and, in 1850, was appointed locomotive superintendent. In 1851 his attention was drawn to the great waste of fuel that occurred during the process of manufacturing coke. As a consequence he designed a fire-box, also a feed-water heater, which will be described later, whereby the fuel bill was reduced by £30,000 a year. The shops at Nine Elms were designed by him in 1863–4. He was succeeded by his second son, W. G. Beattie, whose name became noteworthy because of his method of fastening tires and wheels. Instead of the tire being weakened by holes for rivets or bolts, the wheel and tire were held together by a wedge-shaped key. In his annual report for the year 1858 Captain Douglas Galton drew attention to the success which attended Beattie's efforts and further good results were noted in the report by Captain Tyler on a fatal derailment at Sittingbourne on 4th December, 1861, owing to a broken tire.

As already related, the Ringwood, Christchurch & Bournemouth was extended from Christchurch to Bournemouth on 14th March, 1870. On 2nd May of the same year the line between Pirbright

Junction, Brookwood, and Farnham was opened. It had been authorised in 1865 and gave direct access between London and Aldershot and Farnham.

The East Cornwall Mineral Railway was empowered in 1869 to build a line between Callington and Calstock which, later, was to be joined to the Plymouth, Devonport & South Western at Bere Alston. It was opened between Callington and Calstock Quay on 7th May, 1872. The gauge was 3ft 6in. How the line was converted to standard gauge and connected to the main line at Bere Alston in 1908 will be related in due course.

In 1865 the London & South Western was authorised to carry its Bideford extension on to Torrington, where it was to meet the already sanctioned branch of the Devon & Cornwall. When the Quadruple Treaty was withdrawn from the consideration of Parliament in 1867, the London & South Western sought powers the following year to abandon its intended extension to Torrington. Parliament refused to sanction the withdrawal, so the work was proceeded with and the line brought into use on 18th July, 1872. In 1866 a branch from Poole New Junction – now Broadstone Junction – to Poole was sanctioned. It was opened on 2nd December, 1872. This enabled both L.S.W.R. and S. & D. trains to run direct through the present Poole station to Bournemouth, although of course S. & D. trains still at this time needed to reverse at Wimborne; and it was to be another two years before in fact the line beyond Poole to Bournemouth was opened. The former station at Poole, west of the harbour, became Hamworthy Goods Station.

In his speech on 13th February, 1873, Mr Castleman made some interesting remarks on the subject of the price of coal, which had gone from 16s. in 1872 to 24s. 6d. in 1873, as follows:

He believed the time was coming when coal would be regarded as a perfect luxury. If ever there was a time when Government ought to interfere in this matter it was the present, because the present prices were causing great privation to the middle classes and almost starvation to the poorer classes, thousands of whom would be thrown out of employment in the manufacturing towns if the increased prices continued. The increase fell with special hardship upon the proprietors of stock in railways, because, in addition to the large outlay which it caused them in their own households, it caused them also a loss in dividends, for this company could have declared 1 per cent more upon the year than they had done if it had not been for the extra £24,000 which they had expended for coal. He would repeat that the Government ought to interfere in some way or other to regulate this sort of attempt to trammel the whole business of the country and destroy its commercial prosperity.

In 1873 the L.S.W.R. and L.B.S.C.R. companies obtained powers to construct an extension of their joint Portsmouth line from a point north of the then Portsmouth station to Portsmouth Harbour. The new joint station here was adjacent to the steamer quay, and the steamers themselves were purchased by the railway companies in 1880. Previously the Isle of Wight traffic was worked from the terminal station over a tramway leading to Clarence Pier; a slow and inconvenient route, since it involved travelling through the streets of the town. The new line, which was opened on 2nd October, 1876, required the erection of a new high level station at Portsmouth Town and the construction of siding connections with the South Dockyard and Gun Wharf at the Harbour station and a deviation of the North Dockyard line at the Town station.

At the period now under review there was no direct railway communication between Poole and Bournemouth; the latter town could only be entered on the east side. Its growth was fostered by railway communication, and a connection to the West was bound to accelerate the process. In 1865 a line between the points named was authorised and on 15th June, 1874, was opened. It was transferred to the South Western company, 31st October, 1882.

On 20th July, 1874, the Somerset & Dorset – an amalgamation, as from 1st September, 1862, of the Somerset Central & Dorset Central – completed its northern extension by opening the line between Evercreech and Bath. As it had running powers between Poole and Bournemouth, through communication between the Midland Railway and the latter town was established. Moreover, by means of a junction at Templecombe, it provided narrow gauge connection between Plymouth, Exeter, and the South Western and the Midland Railway.

Also on 6th July, 1874, the branch from Sidmouth Junction to Sidmouth, built as a light railway by the Sidmouth company under powers given in 1871, was brought into use. Previous powers had been obtained in 1862 to construct this line, and had been partly carried out. For some reason the works became derelict, and the line of 1871 followed the earlier route. In 1870 the Barnstaple & Ilfracombe company was empowered to build a line between those two points and it was brought into use on 20th July, 1874. The seal on the left is that of an earlier company which failed.

The company sustained a severe loss by the death, in September, 1874, of W. M. Williams, the superintendent of the line. He had been mainly responsible for the inauguration of the block system. He was one of the first to issue diagrams of the signalling to the drivers, guards and signalmen, and that issued when the Kensington–Richmond and Wimbledon–Kingston lines were opened on 1st January, 1869, attracted considerable attention in the railway world generally. Thus the *Railway News* on 2nd January, 1869, spoke of the carefully digested and admirably explicit directions prepared for the observation and guidance of superintendents, station agents, inspectors, enginemen, guards, signalmen, pointsmen, porters and all concerned. The directions filled twenty-seven foolscap sheets and included a diagram of all the signals, a day and night code of head-signals for engines, the whistles to be given at the junctions, and various other particulars. He was succeeded by E. W. Verrinder.

The first signal box at Waterloo was built over Nos 2 and 3 platform roads, and was known as the 'Crow's Nest'. It formed part of the original station, and was taken down in 1911.

The Waterloo 'A' box had always been considered one of the wonders of the (signalling) world. It was first built in 1867, and renewed in 1874, when there were 109 levers. There was another box on the Windsor line side with 47 levers which is also no longer in existence.

Some interesting history relating to Plymouth calls for inclusion here. In 1819 the Plymouth & Dartmoor company had been incorporated for the construction of a tram road from Crabtree, at the northern end of the Laira at Plymouth to the prison at Princetown, now know as 'Dartmoor', and in the two succeeding years had obtained authority to extend its line to the Cattewater and Sutton Harbour respectively. It carried stone from the quarries on Dartmoor to Plymouth; the return traffic being lime, coal and timber; and served the district until the advent of the Tavistock & South Devon Railway in 1859. Subsequently the portion between Princetown and Yelverton was taken over by the Princetown Railway, and its route was utilised for that line. The section Yelverton–Marsh Mills fell into disuse and was ultimately dismantled, the land being sold. Southwards from Marsh Mills to a point close to the present Laira Bridge road it passed into the hands of the South Devon company, as did also the Sutton Harbour branch.

The opening of the Lee Moor China Clay Works provided a new sphere of usefulness for this old line and a tramway was laid down to connect with it at Plym Bridge, about a mile north of Marsh Mills; by which means china clay was brought direct to the Cattewater for shipment. A short length of the tramway adjacent to Laira Bridge was acquired by the South Western under the Railways Act, 1921. This line remained horse-worked as to its lower half until closed in 1947.

The Plymouth & Dartmoor company constructed various branches connecting with the South Devon; among them may be mentioned the Friary–Cattewater line authorised in 1875 and an extension thereof (1882); the Laira Bridge–Plymstock–Turnchapel line of 1883, power for part of which had to be revived in 1891, and an extension eastwards from Plymstock, authorised in 1888. This latter was acquired by the G.W.R. company. Mention may be made here of a connection from the Friary branch to the Sutton Harbour, authorised by the Sutton Harbour Acts of 1872 and 1874; opened 22nd October, 1879.

Down to the period now under review, the record of the London & South Western in respect of accidents had been so good, that it has been said that many people were induced to live in the country served by the line, on account of its exceptional safety. This state of affairs, however, did not continue.

On 29th January, 1861, there was an accident near the present Raynes Park station in which Dr Baily, Physician Extraordinary to Queen Victoria, was killed, and several other passengers injured. The tender ran off the line, and fell over the bridge into the road, while several of the carriages ran down the embankment. It is interesting to note that the track at this time was laid on longitudinal timbers.

On 5th June in the same year, a curious accident happened to a goods train which was travelling from Salisbury to London. On arriving at Andover the driver found he had left part of the train behind. He thereupon proceeded to back in search of it. Unfortunately the stationmaster at Grateley, where the wagons had been left behind, had decided to take them on to Andover by gravity, it being downhill for four miles, with a rise of half a mile which they expected to get up with the impetus gained by the descent. The resulting collision caused the death of the stationmaster, and severe injuries to the brakesman.

A fortnight later a collision occurred at Hampton Court Junction between the up Southampton express and an empty train from Hampton Court, which had overrun the junction and got on to the main line. No-one was killed, but a guard and some passengers were injured, and much rolling stock was damaged.

A climax was reached on 7th June, 1864, when there was a very serious collision at Egham during Ascot races, in which seven passengers lost their lives. The first of the two trains involved in the accident left Ascot at 7.10 p.m. and the first stop was to be at Egham; the second left at 7.15 and its first stop was to be at Staines. Nothing was said to the driver of the latter as to the first train calling at Egham, which is on the Ascot side of Staines. The driver, when 200 yards from the signal, saw the distant at danger, but it was only 513 yards from the station, on a falling gradient, and the load was 16 coaches, including two vans in which guards were riding. The block system was not in use and, of course, there was no continuous brake. As a consequence the second train ran into the first, with the result already stated.

As typical of the remarks often, at that time, made in the Board of Trade reports on accidents, the following comments by Colonel Yolland on the Egham collision may be of interest:

In my opinion it is time that such a system of working should be done away with. If railway companies cannot be induced voluntarily to alter their system and to introduce those improvements which Science has placed within their reach, then the legislature should interfere and compel them to do so. Apparently these matters are looked at entirely in a commercial point of view, and generally, it is deemed more expedient to run the risk of sacrificing human lives and inflicting dreadful injuries to individuals and to accept the liabilities which such occurrences involve in the shape of heavy compensations, than to incur the certain cost of making a change in an established system to one that may be somewhat more expensive though it will certainly be more safe.

Asked at the half-yearly meeting on 18th August, 1864, about the collision, Mr Archibald Scott said as to the block system:

It was true that in some cases block telegraph was used, but that system, as well as every other, had its disadvantages as well as advantages, and the greatest misfortune that ever occurred took place at Lewisham* on the South Eastern, which was worked entirely on the block telegraph system. On some lines, such as the Metropolitan, the working by that system was indispensable. The block system was very well when used on short lines, but when they came to long lines, few companies saw their way to the adoption of the system because of the delay it involved, of which the public were impatient. Moreover, this system meant an increase in the number of signals, of signalmen and other servants; consequently an increased risk from human fallibility. He therefore said that though he was disposed to recommend its adoption by the directors on this line he was not there to say that it would be a security against accidents.

It was in consequence of this and other accidents, that on 27th December, 1864, Queen Victoria wrote her famous letter, in which she asked railway directors to take as much care for the safety of her subjects as they did when she travelled by train.

There was a bad accident near Guildford on 9th September, 1873. An express from Portsmouth, when between Peasmarsh and Guildford, ran against a bullock which had strayed on to the line. All the carriages (ten) were thrown off the line. In the words of the *Illustrated London News*, 'the engine and tender, breaking the chains by which they

---

* See Volume 2. Twelve passengers lost their lives. It was, of course, quite inaccurate to call it 'the greatest misfortune that ever occurred'.

were coupled to the train, sprang over the body of the animal; and the engine, remaining on the rails, was enabled to run on to Guild-ford, and to convey news of the disaster'. Three persons were killed instantly, and many injured. At the inquest the jury gave a verdict of accidental death, with a recommendation that there should be a communication between the first and rear vans, and continuous brakes.

During the years to which this chapter refers, the work of laying a second line of rails on the Southampton and Dorchester line was completed on 1st August, 1863. Similar work was completed on the Basingstoke and Exeter by 1st July, 1870. From Epsom to Leatherhead was doubled by 4th March, 1867. On March 31st, 1870, a third road was finished between Kew Bridge and Brentford, enabling trains from the N. and S.W. Junction Railway to reach Brentford without interfering with traffic on the loop line from Barnes to Hounslow.

X

The South Western from 1876 to 1900

AT last, the 17th May, 1876, saw the realisation of one of the dreams of the supporters of the London & South Western Railway – it entered Plymouth. What was originally the Okehampton Railway, and was afterwards known as the Devon & Cornwall, carried communication from Yeoford, on the North Devon, to Okehampton and Lydford. A junction was made, in October, 1874, at the latter place with the Launceston & South Devon branch of the South Devon company, but, as that was a broad gauge line, the running of L.S.W.R. trains into Plymouth was not possible.

In 1866, however, powers had been given to the South Devon to convert the Launceston & South Devon into mixed gauge whenever the Devon & Cornwall asked for it to be done. The application was in due course made and, at the same time, the South Western, which company had meanwhile absorbed the Devon & Cornwall, constructed a line from the west end of the triangle outside Millbay station, Plymouth, to its own station at Devonport, with a branch line towards Stonehouse Pool; later extended by the Stonehouse Pool Improvements Act, 1876, to the waterside. On completion of the alterations to the gauge and of the new branch, South Western trains ran forward from Lydford – on, as has been said, 17th May, 1876. A joint station at North Road was being built by the South Devon at the cost of the South Western, but was not ready at the time, and was not opened until 28th March, 1877. Not for another thirteen years – until 2nd June, 1890 – did the South Western enter Plymouth over separate rails and then, strange to say, it did so in a west–east direction in contrast to the Great Western east–west.

In spite of the invasion of the London & South Western into the broad gauge territory the relations at that time between the various companies were more cordial than had long been the case, and it was evident that the spirit of the Quadruple Treaty continued to prevail. Proof of that may be seen in the following extract, relating to the absorption, as from 1st August, 1876, of the Bristol & Exeter by the Great Western, from the South Western report for the half-year January–June, 1876:

The directors hope that this union of interests – not always hitherto in concert when arrangements connected with this company were under negotiation – will be productive of satisfactory results. It will be the earnest desire of this board to continue to cultivate good relations with a neighbouring company with which it is necessarily in contact so frequently and under such important conditions.

These good relations had, however, been somewhat strained, at least on the broad gauge side, during the previous twelve months, in connection with the lease, by the South Western and Midland, jointly, of the Somerset & Dorset Railway. The amalgamation of the Bristol & Exeter with the Great Western possibly suggested to the Somerset & Dorset people that they too might be absorbed. They, therefore, saw Grierson, of the Great Western, and Wall, of the Bristol & Exeter, and those gentlemen, having, perhaps, the spirit of the Quadruple Treaty in mind, told Scott, of the South Western, of the proposals. The last-named said he would immediately discuss the matter with his directors, but it was alleged, he went at once to Derby and saw the Midland people, with the result that an offer was jointly made by the L.S.W.R. and Midland for the lease of the line, which the Somerset & Dorset accepted. This affair is characterised by MacDermot in his *History of the Great Western Railway* as 'an unpleasant episode', and it does appear that the two leasing companies inspected the line and its books, and made a better offer than that of the Great Western, with indecent haste, and possibly in contravention of the spirit in which the Paddington and Bristol managements originally revealed the situation to the South Western officers.

This line was an amalgamation of the Somerset Central and the Dorset Central. The former furnished the section between Burnham and Cole, and the latter that between Cole and Wimborne. They were joined in 1862, and the combined company carried the line northwards to Bath, on 20th July, 1874, where it met the Midland. As from 1st November, 1875, the lease to the South Western and Midland companies took effect, and was sanctioned by Parliament in 1876.

It may be observed that the Great Western company took the proposed sharing of the Midland, in the lease to the Railway and Canal Commission, as a breach of an agreement, of 17th March, 1863, between the Midland and themselves, that the former company would not go beyond Bath or Bristol. The Commission found that the agreement applied only to the Midland's proposed line between Mangotsfield and Bath – opened 4th August, 1869.

The lay-out of the Windsor lines at Clapham Junction involved a level crossing at Plough Lane; and as the traffic was increasing, powers were obtained in 1874 to divert these lines to the northward and pass the lane under the railway, the work being completed in March, 1876.

The South Western suffered a further loss in its higher administration by the death, on 17th July, 1876, of Charles Castleman, who had been a director since 1855, was deputy chairman from 1857 to 1872, and chairman until he retired from the office, shortly before his death, owing to ill-health. In 1877 W. G. Beattie retired from the position of locomotive and carriage superintendent and was succeeded by W. Adams from the Great Eastern. The latter year saw the withdrawal of the broad gauge train service on the North Devon Railway (after 1st May).

The Metropolitan District Railway joined the Addison Road–Richmond branch at Studland Road Junction, near Hammersmith, on 1st June, 1877, and ran a service of trains from Mansion House to Richmond. One of the conditions under which those running powers were given was that the District, while using the line, was not to have a line of its own to Richmond, Kew, Barnes and Putney.

On 18th March, 1878, that section of the line between Ascot and North Camp, Aldershot, sanctioned in 1873, that lies between Ascot and Sturt Lane Junction, was brought into use, and the remainder on 2nd June, 1879.

In 1874 and 1877 powers were obtained to widen the approaches to Waterloo and for the station to be enlarged. The works were in hand during 1877, 1878 and 1879, and were brought into service in the first half of the last-named year. The new portion of Waterloo thus opened was known as the South station and consisted of those two platform-lines which, later, were numbered 1 and 2. At the same time some of the lines in the main station were rearranged and the platforms raised and widened. The alterations in the approaches to Waterloo included a diversion of the main line to allow for a widening and extension of the goods yard at Nine Elms. In 1878 the 'A' signal box was enlarged by having a new one built round it, after which the previous one was taken out, 35 levers being added, making a total of 144.

In 1878 the South Western bought the Salisbury & Yeovil Railway, for which they had to pay at the rate of £260 stock for every £100 of the latter. They probably regretted that they had not made it themselves, which they had been empowered to do, thirty years earlier.

On 20th January, 1879, the line from Meldon Junction (Okehampton) to Holsworthy was brought into service.

In 1879 the London & South Western sought powers definitely to absorb the Bodmin & Wadebridge but, the Great Western opposing, they were refused. Sanction was, however, obtained in 1886, in view of the extension from Launceston to Wadebridge. The work of modernising the line was completed on 3rd September, 1888, when an improved service of trains was introduced. But not until 1st June, 1895, was it connected to the South Western system. The Bodmin & Wadebridge was, however, joined to the Great Western on 26th May, 1887, when that company's branch from Bodmin Road to its own station in Bodmin was opened and a connection, built by the Great Western, laid in between that branch and the Bodmin & Wadebridge at Boscarne Junction.

On 1st January, 1883, the curve connecting the Twickenham and Hounslow lines was opened and allowed a circular service via Richmond or via Kew Bridge.

Speaking at the half-yearly meeting on 9th August, 1883, Mr R. H. Dutton, who had succeeded to the chair, referred to widenings of the line between Clapham Junction and Surbiton and between the former place and Barnes, and said that they were making progress. The former was brought into service on 1st April, 1884, and involved the rearrangement of the main and Kingston lines between Wimbledon and Malden, with a diversion of the up Kingston line at Malden.

Archibald Scott, after thirty-two years' service, resigned the office of general manager on 10th November, 1884, and was made a director. He was succeeded on 1st March, 1885, by Charles Scotter, who had been the goods manager of the Manchester, Sheffield & Lincolnshire.

The Surbiton–Cobham–Guildford line and its branch from Leatherhead to Effingham Junction were brought into use on 2nd February, 1885. This line was made in consequence of proposals which were backed by the Metropolitan District Railway company to come to Guildford. In 1880 and 1881 a bill for a railway in this district was before Parliament under the name of the Guildford, Kingston & London Railway. At the same time the South Western sought powers for a similar line. The one authorised, which was built by the S.W.R. company, comprised parts of both schemes.

A line from Fratton to Southsea, authorised in 1880, was opened on 1st July, 1885, and worked jointly by the South Western and Brighton companies. It was reduced from double to single in 1903 and in 1904 the original East Southsea station was abandoned and a

5-chain deviation built to a new terminus. The line was closed on 8th August, 1914, and not re-opened after the war, the track being removed in 1924.

On 20th May, 1885, the line between Wareham and Swanage was opened, and on 1st June the connecting line from the main line at Hurstbourne to the Andover–Romsey line at Fullerton Junction. The latter was constructed as a double line, to accord with the doubling of the Andover & Redbridge, which at this date was nearly completed. It was, however, reduced to a single track in 1913, and in 1934 the portion between Hurstbourne Junction and Longparish was put out of use. The Somerset & Dorset curve between Corfe Mullen Junction and Broadstone Junction, which gave direct access from that line to Bournemouth, instead of going through Wimborne, was put into service on 14th December, 1885; and the North Cornwall line from Halwill, on the Holsworthy extension, to Launceston was opened on 21st July, 1886.

The most important change of this period at Waterloo was the opening, on 12th March, 1885, of the North station. It was to the north – actually almost due west – of the Windsor line station and contained six platform lines.

Meanwhile the station was served by the four running lines originally laid when the London terminus was transferred, in 1848, from Nine Elms to Waterloo, the inadequacy of which can be appreciated when it is realised that there were four lines between Surbiton and Clapham Junction and four between Barnes and Clapham Junction. It was, therefore, necessary, in 1884, to obtain powers to increase the number of running roads between Nine Elms and Waterloo from four to six and have them allocated thus: one up Windsor line, two down Windsor lines, two up main lines and one down main line. Through Vauxhall station there were, for ticket-collecting purposes, two up Windsor lines. These alterations, of course, affected the 'A' signal box. In 1885 additional levers were put in, and the levers were then arranged in two parallel frames – back to back – connected by intermediate locking. The total number was thereby increased to 200.

With such a complicated machine, the element of human error was of course an important one. Ordinary interlocking went a long way towards eliminating its possibility, but a great step in advance was taken in 1889, when the first Sykes interlocking bar, of which there were later as many as 350, was introduced. This appliance consists of a hinged bar lying parallel, and close, to the inner side of one of the running rails, which is depressed by the flanges of the wheels of a

D15 4-4-0 built at Eastleigh in 1912.

A four-cylinder 4-6-0, No. 335 of 1907, rebuilt seven years later as a two-cylinder locomotive and classed H15.   [*Locomotive Publishing Company*

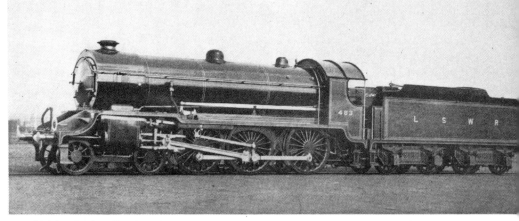

Urie's mixed traffic class of 1914 (H15), No. 483.

Urie's passenger 4-6-0, the N15 of 1918, later embodied in the 'King Arthur' class.

[*Locomotive Publishing Company*

G16 4-8-0T of 1921, designed by Urie for hump duties at Feltham marshalling yards.

vehicle standing on it, and prevents any movements of levers while the line is occupied. It has now been to a great extent superseded by 'track circuiting', in which a low tension current, which is sent through one rail of a 'block', and returned by the other, is short-circuited by a pair of wheels and axle standing or running over the rails.

The last 'A' box dated from 1892. When installed it had 220 levers.

The end of the nineteenth century found Waterloo station with eleven platforms and sixteen platform lines; all the latter were available for either arrival or departure. There was an engine shed, with its turntable and necessary sidings. Outside, on the north side, were seven engine and carriage sidings, another engine turntable and four coaling stages. The area covered by the station was nearly 16 acres.

The traffic handled had greatly increased. The average number of trains, including engines and empties, entering and leaving the station at that time was about 700 daily. On Whit Monday, 1890, the total reached 819, and on the occasion of the Wimbledon Review of 13th July, 1892, it was 849. A year later the number of trains on several occasions exceeded 800 per day and on Saturday, 16th July, 1892, there were 879 movements, made up of 505 loaded ordinary trains, 68 loaded specials, 156 empty trains and 150 engines, of which total 261 arrived on the up main and 183 on the up Windsor.

The necessity for the modernisation of the station was gradually impressed upon the company, and, in 1899, powers were obtained, and in 1900 further powers, to enlarge the station and its approaches. Briefly, the work required an area of a further 6½ acres, the closing of seven streets, the displacement of 1,750 people and the erection of six blocks of new buildings to receive them, and the removal of All Saints' Church in the Lower Marsh. As the consequent work was an event of the present century it will be dealt with in the next chapter.

On 4th July, 1887, the curve line at Staines, which had been authorised in 1883, and permitted direct running from Windsor to the Reading line, was brought into use.

On 26th May, 1887, William Jacomb died. A pupil of I. K. Brunel, he succeeded Strapp as resident engineer in 1869. He was an uncle of J. W. Jacomb-Hood, the chief engineer from 1901 to 1914.

In 1881 powers were given to a Kingston & London Company to build a railway from Surbiton through Wimbledon Common, across the Thames at Putney, to join the Metropolitan District at

Fulham, i.e. at the present Putney Bridge station. On 17th June, 1881, the South Western chairman announced that the line was to be between Putney and Wimbledon instead – an announcement that greatly relieved the users of Wimbledon Common, as its beauties were threatened – and that the South Western and Metropolitan District were to build it jointly. In 1882 a separate company was incorporated, called the Wimbledon & West Metropolitan Junction company, to make the line. Powers for the abandonment between Putney and Kingston were not obtained until 1886 and the undertaking was then vested in the London & South Western solely, subject to running powers for the District Company. The line was opened on 3rd June, 1889, and the curves between East Putney and the Clapham Junction – Barnes line at Point Pleasant Junction brought into use on 1st July, following. The section from Putney Bridge to East Putney, which included a trellis-girder bridge over the Thames, was never used by L.S.W.R. trains, but only by those of the District.

A direct line between Portsmouth and Southampton was provided at last when the extension of the Southampton–Netley to Fareham (under powers obtained in 1883) was opened on 2nd September, 1889. This involved a long plate-girder viaduct across the river Hamble at Bursledon; among new traffic tapped was considerable market-gardening and strawberry-growing around Swanwick.

In the previous year access to Bournemouth had been greatly improved by the opening, on 5th March, of a direct line from Brockenhurst to Christchurch and a junction line from the old terminus at Bournemouth East to the West station. Considerable difficulties were experienced on the former in constructing the embankment at Sway, the base of which is about 500ft wide, owing to the earth slipping during its formation, although the height is only 60ft. Before this line was made the Bournemouth trains were combined with those for Weymouth, and were detached at Ringwood Junction; the distance from Waterloo being about 116 miles. The new line reduced the distance to $107\frac{1}{2}$ miles. The popularity of Bournemouth has been greatly developed by the excellent train service. With a view to adding to the comfort of travellers, a Pullman car was placed in the service on 21st April, 1890. This was not the first introduction of Pullmans on the South Western, as one had been tried as early as 1880, on the Exeter route, but did not at that time attract travellers. Patronage diminished with the introduction of corridor stock and dining cars on the Bournemouth trains, and the Pullmans were gradually withdrawn, 1905 to 1911.

The years 1890–92 saw great developments in the Plymouth area. The main feature was the opening, on 2nd June, 1890, of the Plymouth, Devonport & South Western line from Lydford, through Tavistock and Bere Alston to Devonport thus avoiding the necessity to enter the City over the mixed-gauge Launceston & South Devon. Then on 1st April, 1891, the Great Western opened the Lipson Junction–Mount Gould Junction curve, which gave direct access to Sutton Harbour, and the South Western brought into use, on 1st July, 1891, the Friary station, as a passenger station – it had been used for goods since 1878. Then came, on 21st July, 1892, a further invasion of Cornwall by the inauguration of the Launceston–Wadebridge extension as far as Tresmeer.

Before concluding these references to Plymouth, it should be put upon record that, coincident with the opening of Friary station, the Midland, with the co-operation of the South Western, introduced through carriages between Leeds and Plymouth via Bath, the Somerset & Dorset, and Templecombe. The experiment was not a success and the coaches were soon withdrawn. Mention of the Somerset & Dorset gives an opportunity to say that the important town of Bridgwater was reached from Edington Junction on 21st July, 1890, by the railway authorised in 1882. This line was the property of the Southern Railway, and leased to the Somerset & Dorset Joint Committee.

The half-yearly report for July–December, 1890, announced that the widening between Waterloo and Nine Elms was completed. It had involved the enlargement and rearrangement of Vauxhall station and had been in hand for six years. The whole work cost £600,000.

In 1890 the National Rifle Ranges were transferred from Wimbledon Common to Bisley. The N.R. Association obtained an order in that year for the construction of a tramway from Brookwood station to the new site, which was opened on 14th July.

For many years the Great Western had desired to have access to Southampton, and had constructed a line as far as Winchester (Cheesehill). On 1st October, 1891, a connection onwards to Shawford gave them the facility they had been seeking.

The year 1892 was one of the outstanding ones in the history of the London & South Western Railway, as, in that year, power was given for the acquisition, as from 1st November, of Southampton Docks.

In 1895 the important case of the Mansion House Association *v.* the London & South Western Railway came before the Railway and

Canal Commission. It has always since been known as the Southampton Case. Briefly, the charge was undue preference for imported traffic in contrast to home produce. The clause in the Railway and Canal Traffic Act, 1854, relied upon by the complainants, comes in the middle of section 2 and reads:

no such company shall make or give any undue or unreasonable preference or advantage to or in favour of any particular person or company, or any particular description of traffic, in any respect whatsoever, nor shall any such company subject any particular person or company or any particular description of traffic to any undue or unreasonable prejudice or disadvantage in any respect whatsoever.

The answer of the railway company was to be found in the concluding words 'in respect of the same or similar services' in the following proviso attached to section 27 (2) of the Railway and Canal Traffic Act, 1888:

Provided that no railway company shall make, nor shall the court of the commissioners sanction, any difference in the tolls, rates or charges made for, or any difference in the treatment of, home and foreign merchandise, in respect of the same or similar services.

The company was able to show that the imported traffic in question – mostly meat, bacon, cheese and butter – was taken direct from ship to wagon and conveyed in full train loads. Much was consigned to one firm, so the clerical labour was considerably less. The home produce, on the other hand, was in small consignments, for numerous firms; occupied much more space in the wagons; and hundreds of items would have been necessary to secure a full train load. There were not, therefore, the 'same or similar services', and the Court gave judgment accordingly.

Many important changes were made in the administration in the last seven or eight years of the nineteenth century On 8th October, 1892, Mr Dutton died and was succeeded in the chairmanship by Mr – afterwards Sir – Wyndham S. Portal. On 23rd July, 1893, E. W. Verrinder, the superintendent of the line, died after 42 years' service and was succeeded by G. T. White. After holding the office of general manager for 13 years Scotter retired and was made a director on 5th August, 1897, being succeeded as general manager by Charles J. Owens.

W. Adams, the locomotive superintendent, was suffering from ill-health in 1895 and wished to retire. The directors therefore appointed, as his successor, Dugald Drummond, whose railway career had included some years with Stroudley at Inverness and at Brighton. Adams left at the end of the year.

On 13th October, 1898, F. J. Macaulay, the secretary, after forty-eight years' service, also retired and was elected to the board. His successor was Godfrey Knight, the assistant secretary, who, prior to July, 1894, when he took up the last-named appointment, was a solicitor in the firm of Bircham and Company, the L.S.W.R. solicitors. G. T. White, the superintendent of the line, died on 17th March, 1899, and was succeeded by Sam Fay, an old servant of the company, but then the secretary and general manager of the Midland and South Western Junction Railway. In 1899 Mr Portal gave up the chairmanship of the company and Lieut-Colonel H. W. Campbell was elected in his stead, being succeeded, as deputy chairman, by Mr Scotter.

The branch from Hamworthy Junction to Poole, known as the Holes Bay curve, was authorised in 1890, and brought into service on 20th May, 1893. The Hamworthy station was the original Poole station; the present one having been brought into use in 1872. The Holes Bay curve, across shallow tidal water, allowed the Weymouth trains to pass through Bournemouth. On 1st June, 1893, a short curve was made at Branksome which obviated reversing the Weymouth trains at Bournemouth West. Then, in various stages, the Cornish coast at Padstow was reached thus: Launceston-Tresmeer, 28th July, 1892; Tresmeer-Camelford, 14th August, 1893; Camelford–Delabole, 18th October, 1893; Delabole–Wadebridge, 1st June, 1895; Wadebridge–Padstow, 27th March, 1899. Bude, farther north, was reached from Holsworthy on 10th August, 1898.

The Lee-on-the-Solent – a light railway from Fort Brockhurst, promoted by a private company and sanctioned in 1890 – was opened on 12th May, 1894. It was worked by vehicles of a tramway type hauled by light locomotives (for many years the L.S.W.R. locomotives *Scott* or *Lady Portsmouth*); as some of the halts had no platforms the cars were provided with steps. Another private effort was that of the Budleigh Salterton Railway, for a line to that seaside resort, from Tipton St John's on the Sidmouth branch. It was authorised in 1894 and opened on 15th May, 1897.

A new departure in keeping with the times was the Waterloo & City Electric Railway. It was the creation of a separate company, backed by the London & South Western. Power for its construction was given in 1893 and the line was put into service on 8th August, 1898. It was the second electrically-operated line to be opened in London; the first having been the City and South London, on 18th December, 1890. The Waterloo & City was mechanically signalled by the Railway Signal company, but the electrical equipment was supplied by W. R. Sykes, of whom mention is made in Volume 2. The latter work included five electrically-operated signals in the under-river section, electrical detection for points, fouling bars, etc. The signals in the tunnel consisted of a frame, carrying a red and a green glass, which, when raised electrically, showed a green light. On the train passing over an electrical contact the current to the signal was cut out and the frame was released so that it fell to normal and the red light was again exhibited.

Considering that the period covered by this chapter is a quarter of a century, there are not very many serious accidents to record. The commencement of the joint control of the Somerset & Dorset was marred by a bad collision between two trains on a single line, head-on, which occurred on 7th August, 1876, at Foxcote signal-box, between Radstock and Wellow. Twelve passengers and a guard were killed.

As an outcome of this accident, and an earlier one of a similar character at Norwich in 1874, Edward Tyer invented his method for controlling train movements on single lines, under which each train carries a token which can only be obtained by the co-operation of the signalmen at each end of the section, and as long as a token is out another cannot be obtained. A token that has been withdrawn can be returned to the instrument in either box. Tyer's system was, at first, used only by the Scottish companies but, when the English railways took it up the Somerset & Dorset adopted it extensively, and of the 72 miles of single line there were 50 miles so protected by the end of 1886 and 70½ miles by the end of 1888. It is generally known as the 'tablet' system.

Another form of protection for single lines, known as the electrical train staff, was introduced in 1889 on the London & North Western by Webb and Thompson. It appealed to railway men in that it made use of the train staff to which they were accustomed. It was introduced on the London, Brighton & South Coast in 1892, and on the London, Chatham & Dover in 1897.

Returning to the subject of accidents on the South Western; on 11th June, 1877, one passenger was killed in a collision at Woking. A bad one occurred on 11th September, 1880, at the Nine Elms Locomotive Yard box. A light engine arrived, and stood on the main line waiting to enter the shed. The signalmen were exchanging duty at the time, and the light engine was forgotton, and a passenger train was allowed to run into it. Five passengers, a driver and fireman were killed, and 42 passengers injured. The only brake power was on the engine, and one van in the centre of the train. In 1882 it was decided to adopt the automatic vacuum brake, and the stock was gradually fitted, at a cost of £100,000.

Weak permanent way led to a derailment at Downton on 3rd June, 1884, when five passengers were killed.

A collision occurred at Hampton Wick on 6th August, 1888, by which two passengers lost their lives. A light engine, instead of passing through a crossover-road, set back on the facing, or wrong, line and met a passenger train head-on.

There was a collision at Bournemouth on 25th January, 1890, one passenger being killed. A train ran into a vehicle standing at the buffer-stops.

That the 'Southern' companies had been doing all they could to increase the safety of their lines is shown by the fact that the interlocking return made, under the Act of 1873, on 31st December, 1888, showed that the London, Brighton & South Coast and the London, Chatham & Dover were interlocked to the 100 per cent level, the London & South Western to 99.5 per cent, and the South Eastern to 71 per cent. The return as to the extent to which the block system had been installed showed that the South Western had the block system on all its 582½ miles of double line and on 214 out of 232 miles of signle; the Brighton & South Coast reported all its 339 miles of double and all the 121 of signle as equipped; the South Eastern did the same with its 347¾ miles of double and 41¾ miles of single and the Chatham & Dover had the same report as to its 175 miles of double and 10 of single.

The policy of widening important routes was pursued during the years covered by this chapter, many being so dealt with. The lines in question were Portsmouth Direct, completed 1st March, 1878; Thames Valley, 9th December, 1878; Crediton–Lydford (including the Meldon Viaduct), 22nd December, 1879. Andover and Redbridge, 20th November, 1885; Ilfracombe–Barnstaple, 1st July, 1891, and Ascot to Frimley Junction, 11th June, 1893. The opening of a second line on 25th October, 1886, between Poole and Bournemouth West completed the double track to Weymouth via Bournemouth. On 19th November, 1882, a third track was opened from Andover Junction to Red Post Junction, thus continuing the single line from Swindon to Andover without fouling the South Western line. The installation of four tracks between Clapham Junction and Hampton Court Junction was completed on 5th November, 1885.

The intersection of the main line by diverging branch lines which crossed on the level was an undesirable feature, causing frequent delays, and steps were taken for their elimination by means of 'fly-over' and 'dive-under' lines. The first flying junction on the South Western Railway was made in 1882, when the up Kingston line at Twickenham was carried over the Windsor lines. Two years later, the up Leatherhead road was taken down under the main line at Raynes Park.

XI

The South Western from 1901 to 1922

THE opening of the twentieth century found the London & South Western Railway in a very consolidated position, both financially and physically, and what is related in the present chapter concerns the development of the existing system rather than any new extensions.

After forty-four years' service with the company E. Andrews, the chief engineer, retired on 1st March, 1901. He was succeeded by J. W. Jacomb-Hood, the Exeter divisional engineer, who was a son of R. Jacomb-Hood, at one time the engineer and later a director of the London, Brighton & South Coast Railway.

Allusion must next be made to some pioneer work done by the South Western in relation to light railways and immediately after the Light Railways Act, 1896, was passed. In January, 1897, the Light Railway Commission inquired into a proposed line between Basingstoke and Alton, the Order for which was issued on 9th December following. The first sod was cut by Mr Ritchie, the President of the Board of Trade, on 22nd July, 1898, and the line opened on 1st June, 1901.

Among many other minor railways the Basingstoke & Alton was closed on 1st January, 1917, and when railway material was required for use overseas, the track was lifted and sent out. When hostilities ceased the company decided not to restore the line, and in 1923 powers were sought to abandon it. The reasons given for that step were that the line did not pay for its upkeep, and that the House of Commons Committee appreciated that fact was shown by its refusal to allow the clause to be withdrawn. The opinion was, however, expressed that the line should be restored and, when the bill was before the House of Lords, the company, on 5th June, agreed to restore the railway and test the results for ten years. That was accepted, the line was restored and reopened on 18th August, 1924. In 1933 the company again sought sanction to abandon the portion between Bentworth and Alton, this time being successful.

On 1st August, 1901, vestibuled trains of corridor coaches with dining or luncheon cars were provided for the West of England service, three trains being put in service. Although not part of the South Western system, it may not be inappropriate to mention that the Bideford & Westward Ho! Railway was opened on 28th August, 1901. Like the Basingstoke & Alton, it was closed during the First World War, and never re-opened.

In March, 1902, Sam Fay, the Superintendent of the Line, was given the appointment of General Manager of the Great Central Railway, being succeeded by H. Holmes.

Mr Fay, who was knighted when, on 22nd July, 1912, the King opened the Immingham Docks of the Great Central, had been with the South Western from 1872 to 1892, when he left to become the General Manager of the Midland & South Western Junction Railway. He returned to the South Western as Superintendent in 1899, and went almost at once to the United States to study the railway operating methods over there. He also went again in 1901 with Mr Jacomb-Hood, to examine large railway stations with a view to the rebuilding of Waterloo. An immediate result of his earlier visit was the first installation of automatic signalling on a steam-worked railway in this country. An order to equip the line between Andover Junction and Grateley with automatic signals and the operation of the points and signals at Grateley by pneumatic power was given in October, 1900. The power operation was opened on 31st July, 1901, and the automatic signals were brought into use on 20th April, 1902. The operation was perfectly satisfactory, though rather costly. During the First World War a temporary junction for military purposes had to be put in, which interfered with the automatic signalling, and the power operation was given up at the same time for the sake of economy.

A sequel to the appointment of Fay to the Great Central was a through service, inaugurated on 1st July, 1902, between Bournemouth and Newcastle upon Tyne, via Basingstoke, Oxford, the Great Central Railway and York.

On 29th April, 1902, the branch line from Grateley to Amesbury on Salisbury Plain was brought into use. It had been authorised as a light railway in 1898. Powers for an extension to Bulford were obtained in 1903 and it was opened on 1st June, 1906; the connecting line permitting direct access to the Plain from Salisbury was authorised in the same year and opened 7th August, 1904.

At the half-yearly meeting on February 5th, 1903, the chairman mentioned that Sir Wyndham Portal, who gave up the chairmanship in 1889, and Mr Archibald Scott had retired from the directorate. The former died on 14th September, 1905, and the latter on 6th December, 1910. One of the new directors appointed when the gentlemen named retired was Mr Evelyn Cecil – later Lord Rockley.

In 1903, to meet the competition of electric tramways, a number of railways began experimenting with light self-propelled units of various kinds. One of the first of such services, was tried on the Southsea branch, jointly owned by the South Western and Brighton companies.*

Another interesting enterprise set on foot at this time was the running of a motor omnibus between Exeter and Chagford. After trials had been made of the route, the South Western Railway company purchased a Milnes-Daimler omnibus second hand, and began a service on 1st June, 1904, which ran through the summer months and was taken off in the winter. Two of Clarkson's steam omnibuses were put on the next year, running till 1908, when they were replaced by Thornycroft machines.

As already recorded, **Budleigh** Salterton was given railway communication in 1897, by a connection from Tipton St John's, on the Sidmouth branch. That connection was extended to Exmouth on 1st June, 1903, under powers obtained in 1898, and allowed for a circular service from Exeter to Exmouth and home via Sidmouth Junction, or vice versa. On the same date the Meon Valley line, authorised in 1897, from Alton to the Bishopstoke and Gosport at Fareham, was brought into use. The diverging line at Knowle Junction authorised by the same act, to avoid Fareham tunnel, was opened on 2nd October, 1904. On 23rd August, 1903, the Lyme Regis branch from Axminster was opened. The last-named was a private undertaking authorised as a light railway in 1898, and was acquired by the South Western as from 1st January, 1907.

Another change in the chairmanship was made on 24th March, 1904. Colonel Campbell, who had held the office since 1892, resigned and Sir Charles Scotter now became the head.

In April, 1904, Sir Charles Owens (the South Western General Manager) was a member of a committee appointed by the Board of Agriculture and Fisheries to inquire into the alleged preference shown to imported produce. The conclusion arrived at was that:

> The evidence tendered has failed to show that the railway companies are giving undue preferential treatment to foreign and colonial produce as compared with Home produce, contrary to the intention and effect of existing legislation.

Improvements in speed and coaching stock came about this year, initiated by the competition with the Great Western that arose when

* First public service 1st June, 1903, but had previously been given a trial on the G.W.R. Designed by Dugald Drummond, with vertical boiler, the car was the forerunner of seventeen steam railcars built 1903–1906. A second improved car was put in service on the Southsea branch in 1904; two rail-level halts were built to be served by these cars.

the latter made a bid for the American Line traffic from Plymouth – so far the Great Western carried the mails, but the South Western, the bulk of the passengers. In order to retain them as far as possible new corridor coaches were constructed, six inches wider than their predecessors. Since the 'Ocean Specials' – as they were called – ran at uncertain times, dependent on the arrival of the steamers, sleeping cars were provided – an innovation which did not survive the Ocean Specials, whose existence was of short duration. The first of these took only 78 minutes 9 seconds to cover the 83 miles 50 chains from Salisbury to the stop at Waterloo: the total time for the whole journey of 230 miles 5 chains was 4 hours 24 minutes 29 seconds, including four stops, which consumed 10 minutes 27 seconds in standstills. The competition continued for over two years, till on 1st July, 1906, the Salisbury accident occurred, and the boat specials were made to conform with the running of other expresses, and stopped at Exeter and Salisbury, instead of once only (Templecombe). The time was increased to 4 hours 28 minutes.

The restaurant car service was extended to Plymouth on June 1st, 1905. The light railway between Bentley and Bordon (for Longmoor Camp) was put into service on 11th December of the same year.

W. Panter, the carriage and wagon superintendent, who came to the line from the L.N.W.R. works at Wolverton in 1885, retired at the end of the year and was succeeded, as from January 1st, 1906, by Surrey Warner, the assistant carriage and wagon superintendent of the Great Western. Panter died on 11th June, 1928.

The adverse influence of the motor car on railway passenger traffic was making itself felt about the period now under review. As an example of the traffic lost to the railways it may be noted that 1,166 motor cars were seen at Ascot on the Royal Hunt Cup day of 1907.

The Waterloo and City was acquired by the company as from 1st January, 1907. The East Cornwall Minerals Railway was converted to standard gauge, extended from Calstock to Bere Alston and so joined the main line on 2nd March, 1908. Powers for that purpose had been obtained in 1900 by the Plymouth, Devonport & South Western Junction Light Railway, who were also authorised to equip the whole line for passenger traffic. About the same time there was completed a widening between Queen's Road and Clapham Junction, which gave four lines of way for the whole of the fifty miles between Waterloo and Worting Junction, Basingstoke. On 24th January, 1909, the first section of importance, of the rebuilt and enlarged station at Waterloo, was opened. It consisted of the five most southern roads in the station.

The London and South Western Orphanage at Woking was inaugurated by the Duchess of Albany on 5th July, 1909. It replaced the original orphanage in Jeffreys Road, Clapham, which was opened in March, 1886.

The year just mentioned – 1909 – saw the completion of the removal of the locomotive shops from Nine Elms to Eastleigh.* At the half-yearly meeting in February, 1910, Sir Charles Scotter, the chairman, said that Mr Drummond, the chief mechanical engineer, had reported:

> The locomotive works at Nine Elms are now closed and the men and machinery are removed to Eastleigh. The works are designed to reduce to the minimum the handling of material, and the process of manufacture and the machinery are the finest that can be procured for our requirements. This transfer has been accomplished without an employee of the department being one hour out of work or the output of the work interfered with. I have no hesitation in saying that the company posesses the most complete and up-to-date works owned by any railway company.

The period is now approached which saw a most interesting event – a traffic agreement between the South Western and the Great Western companies. What had been accomplished in that direction by other rivals no doubt initiated the steps which led to this agreement between the two competitors for the West of England traffic. The first companies to come together, and to agree to cease the costly competition between them, were those old rivals in Scotland, the Caledonian and North British. Peace between these antagonists was brought about in 1907. That was a great achievement, but a greater – when the size of the concerns and the area which they covered are considered, perhaps the greatest possible – was accomplished in 1908 when the London & North Western and the Midland made an agreement as to competitive traffic. The following year the Lancashire & Yorkshire – with which company the North Western had such an agreement since 1862 – was joined and the arrangements became tripartite.

At this stage it is necessary to mention Mr Lloyd George. When the Campbell-Bannerman Government was formed in December, 1905, he was made President of the Board of Trade. In view of his frequent praises for German railways and criticism of the British lines the appointment was an interesting one. Threatened trouble with the railway servants, in 1906 and 1907, to which reference will be made,

* The works is described in Volume 2.

led Mr. Lloyd George to make a closer acquaintance with railway administrators and to learn, for the first time, and to appreciate, some of their difficulties. A result of that was the appointment, in February, 1908, of what was known as the Board of Trade Conference which, to quote its report, was constituted:

Without any rigid terms of reference but with the object of reviewing some of the more important questions that, from time to time, have been raised between the railway companies on the one hand and the traders and general public on the other.

It may be remarked that Sir Charles J. Owens, the then general manager, was a member of the Conference and was one of the eight railway representatives on a committee of the Conference appointed to consider certain questions, who contributed memoranda thereto. The subject of Sir Charles's memorandum was 'The Disadvantages of Competition'.

In 1909 a bill was deposited for the sanction of a working union between the Great Central, Great Eastern and Great Northern companies. Such conditions were, however, threatened, that the companies withdrew the bill, but it had the interesting sequel of the appointment, in June, 1909, of a departmental committee on the general question of agreements amalgamations and working unions. Sir Charles Owens was nominated by the Railway Companies' Association as its main witness, and the report of the committee said that he 'rendered us great assistance on all the principal matters connected with our inquiry'.

When such competitors as have been named could come to terms, there seemed no reason why something similar should not be put into operation between the London & South Western and the Great Western, and negotiations to that end were begun in 1909. At the latter company's half-yearly meeting in August, Viscount Churchill stated that a move had been made, which was confirmed by Sir Charles Scotter in February, 1910. On 13th May following, the agreement was signed. It provided for the pooling of all competitive traffic, based on the figures for 1908, and was for ninety years. One immediate result was the cessation of the L.S.W.R. Ocean Mails specials from Plymouth to London.

In 1906 the South Western had obtained power to widen their North Devon line between Copplestone and Umberleigh, in order to complete the two lines of way westward to Barnstaple. The work was begun, and earthworks and bridges were completed, but in consequence of the working agreement just mentioned, the additional rails were never laid.

Another sequel to the agreement was a through service from Birkenhead, Manchester, Birmingham and other points on the Great Western to Bournemouth via Basingstoke. This service, opened on 1st July, 1910, was important, inasmuch as the towns in question had hitherto only been directly connected with Bournemouth via the Midland and the Somerset & Dorset. The Midland in the latter service did not, however, provide through carriages from Liverpool & Manchester – only from Leeds and Bradford – so the North Western later met the new competition by through carriages, as from 1st October, 1910, which were handed to the Midland company at Birmingham, and joined that company's train from Bradford and Leeds to Bournemouth.

After the army manœuvres of September, 1910, the South Western carried 25,080 officers and men, 6,722 horses, and 1,174 guns from stations in the manœuvres area to their depots within 48 hours and at a time when holiday traffic was particularly heavy.

A great misfortune befell the company in the death, on 13th December, 1910, of Sir Charles Scotter. Of the many events of note during his connection with the company the most outstanding was the purchase of the Southampton Docks; worthy of special mention also, but in a minor way, were his efforts to retain second-class traffic. Two of his activities outside the London and South Western may be noted. Sir Charles, together with Sir Ernest Paget, the chairman of the Midland, represented the railway interests on the Royal Commission of 1899 on Accidents to Railway Servants, over which Lord James of Hereford presided. He was also the chairman of the Viceregal Commission of 1906–1910 which inquired into the future of the railways of Ireland. In the latter connection Sir Charles surprised his friends by being included in the majority report in favour of State Purchase. He was made a baronet in 1907.

In February, 1911, it was announced by the South Eastern & Chatham Railway that in connection with the rebuilding of the South Western company's Waterloo terminus, the physical junction at Waterloo Junction, on the line of the former company, was to be removed.* From 1st May, 1911, through carriages between Manchester and Southampton by the L.N.W.R., Midland and the Midland & South Western Junction were introduced, and on 3rd July the service of two-hour expresses between Waterloo and Bournemouth was commenced.

---

* In fact, only the portion of the spur which lay within the boundaries of the new L.S.W.R. Station was removed, the remainder lying unused for twenty more years.

The general strike of railwaymen occurred on 18th and 19th August, 1911, which was an event that calls for special mention. The relations between the administration of the London & South Western Railway and its staff had nevertheless been very happy; in fact, it is safe to say that on no railway in this country or abroad did better feelings, in that respect, prevail.

The duplication of the lines between Studland Road Junction and Turnham Green, which gave the Metropolitan District two lines for its exclusive use, was completed on 3rd December, 1911. The then existing stations at Ravenscourt Park and Turnham Green were replaced by new ones with two island platforms, and an additional station on the Metropolitan District lines was provided at Stamford Brook.

Some remarkable results of the fish traffic from Padstow were published in 1912. That port was reached on 27th March, 1899, and, in 1900, the fish traffic sent thence weighed 24 tons and brought in £65 receipts. In 1911 the weight was 3,074 tons and the receipts £6,879.

In view of the retirement, after fifty years' service with the company, of Sir Charles Owens, Mr Herbert Ashcombe Walker was appointed general manager as from 1st January, 1912. Brigadier-General Drummond, in announcing the fact to the shareholders in February, 1912, spoke of Mr Walker as one of the rising and most capable of the younger railwaymen of the country. It may be noted that when his name was included in the New Year Honours of 1915 he received the exceptional one of being created a K.C.B. In November, 1912, Sir Charles Owens was made a director of the company.

The locomotive engineering world, and the London & South Western company in particular, were the worse by the death, on 7th November, 1912, of Mr Dugald Drummond, the company's chief mechanical engineer since August, 1895. Drummond, an Ayrshire man, was born on the New Year's Day of 1840; the son of a permanent way inspector on the North British Railway. By the time he was 30 years of age he had seen service on three railways in Scotland and, when only 27, was Stroudley's works manager at Inverness. When that engineer left the Highland to go to the London, Brighton & South Coast, he took Drummond with him to be his assistant. In 1875 the latter went to the North British as locomotive carriage and wagon superintendent and, seven years later, accepted a similar position on the Caledonian, leaving there, in 1890, in the expectation of taking up a post which did not, however,

L.S.W.R. three-coach electric sets as delivered at Strawberry Hill; the nearest set is No. E1.

[*H. C. Casserley*

I.O.W.R. 2-4-0T *Sandown* (Beyer Peacock, 1864) at Ventnor.   [*Locomotive Publishing Company*

Ex-North London Railway 4-4-0T as I.W.C.R. No. 7.   [*Locomotive Publishing Company*

One of the two Slaughter Gruning 'singles' of the I.W.C.R.; No. 2, built 1861, shown after withdrawal in 1904.   [*Locomotive Publishing Company*

A Beyer Peacock 2-4-0T, No. 8 of the I.W.C.R., built 1898.   [*Locomotive Publishing Company*

materialise. Drummond was succeeded by R. W. Urie, the Works Manager.

In October, 1913, it was announced that the Government had appointed a Royal Commission to inquire into the relations between the railways and the State. Lord Loreburn was the chairman and, again, Sir Charles Owens was one of the principal witnesses for the railways. The inquiry stood adjourned for the summer vacation when war broke out, and on 21st January, 1915, it was abandoned.

In February, 1914, as a result of an amendment to the Reply to the King's Speech, it was decided to appoint a departmental committee to inquire into the working of a Railway Employment (Prevention of Accidents) Act, 1900. After evidence had been given by the Board of Trade and by representatives of the men's unions, the inquiry was adjourned until 6th October for the companies to prepare their reply, but the war prevented the inquiry being resumed.

On 6th March, 1914, the Chief Engineer, Mr J. W. Jacomb-Hood, was found dead by the side of his horse when out hunting at Dulverton. He was succeeded by Mr A. W. Szlumper, the London Divisional Engineer, who, on the formation of the Southern Railway, became, and was until 30th June, 1927, its Chief Engineer, afterwards being Consulting Engineer.

The next event to be noted is the outbreak of war on 4th August, 1914. Not only did that affect the London & South Western seriously, on account of the use made of Southampton Docks, but Sir Herbert Walker was the chairman, and Major Gilbert Szlumper the secretary, of the Railway Executive Committee, who, on behalf of the Government, administered the whole of the British Railways from the time the Government control commenced on 5th August, 1914, to the resignation of that Committee on the inauguration of the Ministry of Transport in 1919. The achievements of the South Western Railway during the war will be dealt with presently.

Following the lead of the London, Brighton & South Coast Railway, the South Western began to electrify its suburban services. The first* installation was between Waterloo and East Putney, which was brought into service on 25th October, 1915. Before it was begun, Mr Herbert Jones, the electrical engineer, visited the United States. As a result of his visit, and with the concurrence of Sir Alexander Kennedy and Partners – later Messrs Kennedy and Donkin – it was decided to adopt the direct current third rail system.

* Apart, of course, from the District Railway's electrification of the L.S.W.R. line from East Putney to Wimbledon.

The power house was built on the up side of the line to the east of Durnsford Road bridge, Wimbledon. The boiler house was 237ft long and 130ft wide and contained, originally, sixteen Babcock and Wilcox boilers, and later twenty, arranged in two rows, with the firing floor between them. The coal bunkers, with a capacity of 1,400 tons, are on a floor above the boiler house and are fed by trucks which come from the railway sidings near Durnsford Road bridge by a viaduct.

For the original installation there were nine sub-stations, at Waterloo, Clapham Junction, Raynes Park, Kingston, Twickenham, Barnes, Isleworth, Sunbury, and Hampton Court Junction. Seven more were provided for the later extension to Guildford and Dorking.

The sections opened during the time the South Western preserved its individuality were, after East Putney in 1915; Point Pleasant Junction–Shepperton and Clapham Junction–Wimbledon–Strawberry Hill on 30th January, 1916; Hounslow loop on 12th March, 1916; Malden–Hampton Court 18th June, 1916, and Surbiton–Claygate, 20th November, 1916.

The rolling stock was of the usual compartment type; in fact steam coaches were converted for electrical traction being made up into three-coach sets, each end coach having one motor bogie. They were fitted with the Westinghouse brake, the air for which was compressed by motor-driven pumps, switching in automatically when the pressure falls to a pre-arranged figure.

On 14th July, 1915, the Hampton Court flying junction was opened. By it the Hampton Court down line was carried over the four main lines. The girders of the principal bridge were each 160ft long, 18ft deep in the centre and 12ft at the ends, and weighed 85 tons.

Mr Holmes retired from the position of Superintendent of the Line on 1st November, 1916, and was followed by Mr G. F. West.

A long delayed step was taken on 22nd July, 1918. Six years after it had been done on the London, Brighton & South Coast, the South Western abolished the second class.

Turning now to the War service of the South Western company, it may not be out of place to give here a short account of the relations between the railways and the Army.

In 1864 it was suggested by Charles Manby, the Secretary of the Institution of Civil Engineers, and an enthusiastic volunteer, that there should be an Engineer and Railway Volunteer Staff Corps; for the purpose of directing the application of railway transport and skilled labour to the work of National Defence, and for preparing, in time of peace, a system on which such duties should be conducted.

The Corps was constituted in January, 1865, and Manby was made the Adjutant, with the rank of Lieut.-Colonel. Its first Colonel was Colonel McMurdo who, on the initiation, in 1860, of the Volunteer movement, had been made Inspector-General of Volunteers. The corps was composed of a certain number of engineers, several of the great contractors and the general managers of most of the principal railways. The contractors formed what was called the Labour Branch of the Corps.

The late Sir George Findlay, in a paper, *The Transport of Troops by Rail within the United Kingdom*, read before the Royal United Service Institution on 20th June, 1890, said of the duties of the Engineer and Railway Volunteer Staff Corps:

> The intention is that, in case of invasion, the officers this corps would superintend the working of the railways, as they do in peace, but acting under the directions of the military commanders. The railways of the country, as far as may be necessary, and wholly if need be, would have to be, for the time being, given up to the service of the State, and by thus using the means and appliances which are at all times available, and making a free use of the perfect organisation and large resources of the great railway companies, it is believed that no difficulty need be anticipated in concentrating a considerable body of troops within a brief period upon any part of our shores that might be threatened by a foe.

The Engineer and Railway Volunteer Staff Corps was, however, too large properly to solve the problems associated with the possibilities of invasion. A better course was taken in 1896, when the Army Railway Council was formed. It consisted of two representatives of the Navy and four of the Army, a Board of Trade Inspector of railways, six railway general managers and two members of the Engineer and Railway Volunteer Staff Corps who were not railwaymen. The Army Railway Council was able to discuss the questions with greater freedom and to come to conclusions more quickly than the body it replaced, and generally, to prepare the necessary programmes with promptitude and secrecy.

The Agadir incident of July, 1911, led to the question of railway communications in the time of war being considered. At that time Sir John Seely was the Under Secretary of War, and on 1st August, 1911, he held a meeting with the general managers of six of the principal companies – of which the South Western was one – to consider the provision of means for the feeding of London in the event of war. Those gentlemen undertook to develop schemes towards that end, but it became manifest that there was a possibility of various interests clashing: for example, the conveyance of food from Liverpool might interfere with the transport of naval coal from South Wales to the north-east coast.

As a consequence of representations made thereupon, a Board of Communications was established, which was composed of the six general managers just mentioned and representatives of the Admiralty, War Office, Board of Trade, Home Office and Treasury.

In October, 1912, there was a further development. The Commitee on National Defence recommended that a committee be formed whose duty it should be to put into effect that part of the Regulation of the Forces Act, 1871, which, in effect, gave the Government control over all or any of the railways should an emergency arise. On 5th November a meeting was held at the Board of Trade, under the presidency of Mr Sydney – afterwards Lord – Buxton, which led to the formation of the Railway Executive Committee, of which the President of the Board of Trade was the nominal chairman. The acting chairman was Mr – later Sir – Frank Ree, the General Manager of the London & North Western, and the secretaries were Mr Stanley G. Spencer, of the Railway Accidents Branch of the Board of Trade, and Mr L. W. Horne, the Superintendent of the Line, London & North Western Railway. On the death, in February, 1914, of Sir Frank Ree, Mr H. A. Walker was made the acting chairman. Simultaneously, Mr Spencer and Mr Horne retired from the secretaryship and were succeeded by Major Gilbert Szlumper. The Railway Council ceased to exist when the Railway Executive was formed.

The London & South Western was the only one of the three southern companies to be represented on the Committee, but Mr Francis H. Dent, from the South Eastern & Chatham, was added in May, 1913, and on 7th August, 1914, Mr William Forbes from the London, Brighton & South Coast. In June, 1919, Major Szlumper, on his removal to Southampton, resigned his position as secretary and was succeeded by Mr Geo. H. Wheeler. The Ministry of Transport was formed under the Act of 1919 and came formally into being in September of that year. At the request of Sir Eric Geddes, the first Minister of Transport, the Railway Executive Committee continued in office until December.

One of the first sequels to the outbreak of hostilities, and one that particularly affected the 'Southern' companies was that the ports of Dover, Folkestone and Southampton were at once closed against public traffic and most of the cross-channel steamers withdrawn.

The greatest event in the early days of the war was the dispatch of the British Expeditionary Force – an event intimately connected with the port of Southampton. War was declared as from midnight of Tuesday–Wednesday, 4th–5th August, and the War Office gave the Railway Executive Committee sixty hours in which to get together the necessary locomotive power and rolling-stock wherewith to convey the 'striking force' to Southampton. Within forty-eight hours, however, the intimation was sent that all was ready, and at 7 p.m. on the following Sunday, 9th August, embarkation was begun. The dispatch of the British Expeditionary Force was completed by 31st August, and during that period of three weeks there were shipped from Southampton: 5,006 officers, 125,171 men, 38,805 horses, 344 guns, 1,574 other limbered vehicles, 277 motor cars and other motor vehicles, 1,802 motor cycles and 6,406 tons of stores. The total weight shipped was 18,064 tons and 711 trains were used.

The busiest day was Saturday, 22nd August, when 73 trains had to be dealt with, the first due to arrive at 10.12 the previous evening and the last at 6.12 p.m. on the 22nd. Eight trains were timed to arrive between 6.12 and 7.36 a.m., another eight between 12.12 and 1.36 p.m., and twenty-one in the four hours between 2.12 and 6.12 p.m. They carried 537 officers, 16,268 men, 4,586 horses, 72 guns, 309 other limbered vehicles, 187 four-wheeled vehicles, 202 two-wheeled vehicles, 275 motor cycles and 1,503 tons of stores. The total weight shipped was 4,067 tons. Sixteen transports were used on that occasion for the conveyance of the troops overseas, and each train was taken direct to the berth where the designated transport lay by the engine that had brought it to Southampton.

On 18th August the Press Bureau announced:

The Expeditionary Force, as detailed for foreign service, has been safely landed on French soil. The embarkation, transportation and disembarkation of men and stores were alike carried through with the greatest possible precision and without a single casualty.

On 25th August Lord Kitchener, in his first speech as Secretary of State for War, said:

The railway companies, in the all-important matter of the transport facilities, have more than justified the complete confidence resposed in them by the War Office, all grades of railway services having laboured with untiring energy and patience.

In his first dispatch – of 7th September, 1914 – Sir John French said:

The transport of the troops from England, both by sea and rail, was effected in the best order and without a check. Each unit arrived at its destination in this country (France) well within schedule time. The concentration was practically complete on the evening of Friday, the 21st ultimo.

Finally, it must be put upon record that Mr Asquith, the then Prime Minister, speaking on 16th November, 1914, in the debate on the second vote of credit, said that he quite agreed that no praise could be too high for the manner in which the railway companies of the country discharged the duty of transport of the Expeditionary Force and the various matters in which they were engaged.

Southampton was one of the principal ports for hospital ships, and 1,234,248 wounded, requiring 7,822 trains, were dealt with there. After the battle of the Somme on 1st July, 1916, there were 29 trains, with 6,174 wounded, dispatched on one day – 7th July – and during the week ended 9th July there were 151 trains with 30,006 wounded. On the first-named day 13 ambulance trains were used and they were supplemented by nine corridor trains. The other seven trips were executed by some trains making a second journey.

The first contingent of troops from Canada, in 33 transports, arrived in this country on 15th October. They had to be conveyed to Salisbury Plain, and the troopships were intended to come to Southampton, but at the last moment were diverted to Plymouth. As 92 trains were required for their conveyance it will be appreciated that some fine organisation had to be forthcoming. The men were entrained at either Friary Station, Plymouth, or Devonport, and all were on their way to camp by the 23rd.

The mention of camps prompts the remark that there were no fewer than 176 camps on the London & South Western system. Incidentally, the men going on leave for the week end greatly taxed the resources of the company. It was found that an average of about 16,600 men travelled on either Friday evening or during Saturday, and they required about 21 special trains.

Besides the well-known ferry from Richborough there was also one at Southampton, for which a jetty 100 yards long was built in stone about 100 yards to the west of the Royal Pier. The jetty has now been removed, as it was in the way of the extension works at Southampton Docks. At the end of the jetty was a bridge, hinged at the land end so as to be adjustable through a vertical range of 12ft.

The authority given to the Government, under the Act of 1871, to acquire a railway company's plant included its steamers, and one of the earliest actions of the State was to acquire most of the railway-owned steamships, mainly, at first, to be used as hospital ships. Others, later, were used as transports, boarding vessels, mine layers, sea-plane carriers, etc. Not all returned to their original owners, as out of 126 vessels requisitioned by the Government from all the railways, 31 were lost by enemy action or otherwise, while four were lost on their ordinary railway services.

Two of these four were the *Normandy* and *South Western* of the L.S.W.R. fleet. The former was torpedoed on her regular run to Cherbourg on 25th January, 1918, and the latter when going to St Malo on 16th March following. The *Sarnia* of the same fleet became an armed boarding vessel, and, while employed as such in the Mediterranean, was sunk by an enemy torpedo on 12th September, 1918. The cargo steamer *Guernsey* was lost on her way from Guernsey on 9th April, 1915, being wrecked on the French coast owing to the light on Cape La Hogue being extinguished as a war measure. The *Duchess of Richmond*, of the Portsmouth–Ryde joint service, was a post-war loss, as she was mined in the Mediterranean on 28th June, 1919. The *Cæsarea* – the sister ship to the *Sarnia* – *Princess Ena*, *Victoria*, *Lydia* and *Lorina*, were also engaged in war service.

Out of 24,270 men employed by the South Western Railway 6,552 joined the colours, of whom 585 were killed.

The Locomotive workshops of Eastleigh contributed the following items, among others: about 2,600 fittings of a varied character for 6-in howitzer carriages; 650 fittings for 2-in trench howitzers; 47,430 adapters for 18-pounder shell, and 36,200 nose caps and 40,130 base plates for 6-in shell. Over 61,000 copper bands were made for shells; 735 forged nickel steel cranked axle-trees for 4.5-in howitzers. For the 600 mm. narrow-gauge railways in France, 200 turnouts were machined and fitted together. Various ship fittings, to the number of about 20,000, were supplied to Harland and Wolff and Thornycroft and Co. for boats they had in hand at Southampton.

The Carriage and Wagon Department supplied ambulance stretchers, general service wagons, open vehicles for carrying aeroplanes, bodies for lorries and many kinds of miscellaneous small parts, also two complete ambulance trains, and six specially fitted ambulance coaches for home use, and two complete ambulance trains for service overseas. Two more were in hand when the war came to an end, and were countermanded.

The company also provided fifty six-coupled goods engines, of which thirty-six went to Egypt, nine to Mesopotamia and five to Salonika, also eleven tank engines for home use, with much other rolling-stock, among which were sixteen corridor vehicles which were converted into an ambulance train. Four of the goods engines mentioned above did not reach their destination, as they were sunk in the *Arabic* when she was torpedoed in the Mediterranean. None of the engines came back.

Resuming now the consideration of general events on the London & South Western, during the year 1922 the concentration yard at Feltham was completed. Direct access is given from Feltham to any part of the South Western system and vice versa, also to what was the London & North Western and the North London at Willesden, the Great Central and Metropolitan at Neasden, the Midland at Brent, and the South Eastern and Chatham at Clapham Junction.

The yard is on the down, or south, side of the line. Up trains enter by facing points worked from Feltham Station East box and run into one of the eight reception sidings, six of which accommodate 65 wagons each while two hold 68 wagons. The engine is then placed in the rear of the train and it is pushed up the hump of 1 in 140 and the wagons are distributed by gravity down the 1 in 50 of the hump into one of 19 up marshalling sidings. The operation of the points is done electrically by push-button machines. As many as 3,390 wagons have been dealt with in 24 hours, and it has been found possible to sort completely a train of 70 wagons, involving 56 'cuts' in 12 minutes.

At the end of 1922 the total length of route running line on the London & South Western was 1,019 miles. Of that, 324 miles were single track, 695 miles had a double line, 79 miles had a third track, 65 had a fourth track and there was a total length of 37 miles on those sections that had over four lines. The sidings were of a total length of 486 miles.

The great station at Waterloo remains to be described. It has been already recorded that Mr Jacomb-Hood went to America for the purpose of seeing what there was to be learnt over there about large terminal stations. The plan laid down on his return was carried out practically as at first conceived. The result was a commodious station, well adapted for long-distance, suburban and excursion traffic, at the same time extremely simple in its layout and operation.

There were 13 platforms and 21 platform lines – eight of the platforms having two platform faces. Four of the platform faces were of a length of from 843 to 860ft, whilst ten – Nos. 1 to 10 inclusive – varied in length from 683 to 765ft, and were of an average length of practically 720ft. Between Nos. 11 and 12 platform lines were three loading docks, the only sidings in the station. On the north side, and outside the station walls, were the carriage sidings, engine sidings, coaling stages and engine turntable, as before reconstruction. There were yet more extensive carriage sidings and a turntable and other accommodation for engines on the down side immediately on the other side of Westminster Bridge Road.

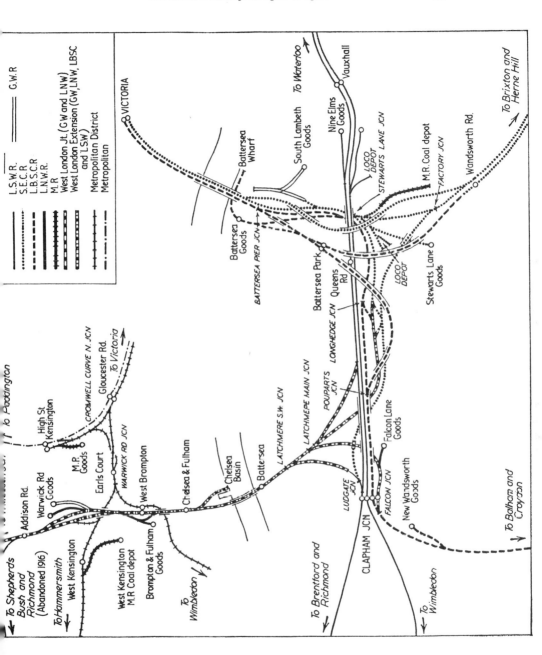

Key (legend):

L.S.W.R.
S.E.C.R.
L.B.S.C.R
L.N.W.R.
M.R
West London Jt. (G W and L N W)
West London Extension (G W, L N W, L B S C and L S W)
Metropolitan District
Metropolitan
G.W.R

VICTORIA

To Paddington
To Victoria
CROMWELL CURVE N. JCN
Gloucester Rd.
High St Kensington
Addison Rd.
Warwick Rd Goods
M.P. Goods
WARWICK RD JCN
Earls Court
West Brompton
West Kensington
West Kensington M.R Coal depot
Brompton & Fulham Goods
To Hammersmith
To Shepherds Bush and Richmond (Abandoned 1916)
Chelsea & Fulham
Chelsea Basin
Battersea
To Wimbledon
LATCHMERE S.W. JCN
LATCHMERE MAIN JCN
POUPARTS JCN
LONGHEDGE JCN
Queens Rd
Battersea Park
BATTERSEA PIER JCN
Battersea Goods
Battersea Wharf
South Lambeth Goods
To Waterloo
Nine Elms Goods
Vauxhall
LOCO DEPOT
STEWARTS LANE JCN
LOCO DEPOT
Stewarts Lane Goods
M.R. Coal depot
FACTORY JCN
Wandsworth Rd.
To Brixton and Herne Hill
LUDGATE JCN
FALCON JCN
CLAPHAM JCN
Falcon Lane Goods
New Wandsworth Goods
To Brentford and Richmond
To Wimbledon
To Balham and Croydon

The running lines outside the station at this time numbered eight: two down main, three up main, two down Windsor and one up Windsor.

Of the 21 platform lines, Nos. 1 to 6 and Nos 16 to 21 inclusive were at this time equipped for electric traction. No. 11 being the longest, was usually used for outgoing boat trains and Nos. 12, 13, 14 and 15 for main line arrivals. Every road was provided with hydraulic buffer stops which had a total stroke of 7ft and were capable of withstanding the impact of a 400 ton train at 10 miles an hour. One of the main exits is by the 'Victory Arch', leading from the north-east corner of the station to the approach to York Road. The group of sculpture above the centre of the archway represents Britannia holding the torch of Liberty; that on the left is Bellona, the Goddess of War, and is marked '1914', whilst that on the right is marked '1918' and represents Peace. Inside the archway are four bronze tablets recording the names of the 585 servants of the company who died *Pro Patria* in the Great War.

The King had intended to honour the London & South Western Railway and its fallen heroes by opening this new entrance and formally inaugurating the new station on 21st March, 1922, but as he had a chill, and it was a very cold day, his place was graciously taken by the Queen. Her Majesty entered from the York Road, and, ascending the steps, cut a silken cord and so opened the station.

There were, of course, further developments in the 'A' signal box. When the rebuilding of the station was undertaken, a new box was built alongside the existing one, on the main line side, in which it was proposed to provide a new lever frame. This was not carried out, the existing frame being altered and extended, then having 266 levers.

It only remains to mention the accidents which occurred during the period covered by this chapter. There was a curious one at Waterloo on 5th May, 1904. A signal linesman was executing some repairs, when he accidentally stepped on a wire. As a result, a signal was irregularly put to 'clear' which the driver of a train of milk empties accepted as a signal to move. He did so and his train came into collision with an arriving passenger train and a passenger was killed.

The most serious accident experienced on the London & South Western occurred at Salisbury on 1st July, 1906, when a special train from Plymouth, with passengers from the *St Louis* was de-railed. Of the 42 passengers on the train 24 were killed and seven seriously injured. Four employees also were killed. The train had called at Templecombe, where the engine was changed, and it was timed to make a non-stop run to Waterloo. There was a speed restriction of 30 miles an hour through Salisbury and there were also two circulars that had been issued to drivers instructing them that they must run those special trains to schedule time and that any man running in advance of the timing would be taken off his engine.

It was the first time the driver concerned in the accident had driven one of these specials, and, possibly, he had not previously run through Salisbury without stopping. If that was the case he would always have entered upon the severe curve at the London end of the station from 'dead' and perhaps not have appreciated its severity. Anyhow, instead of passing through the station at 30 miles an hour he travelled at 50 or 60, and was derailed at the curve, which was a reverse one of $7\frac{1}{2}$ chains radius (165 yards).

The accident, naturally, caused considerable concern to the company, and the chairman at the half-yearly meeting soon afterwards pointed out that since the Hampton Wick collision of August, 1888, they had carried 1,220 million passengers in safety. The damages paid by the company to passengers amounted to nearly £60,000.

A collision at Vauxhall on 29th August, 1912, when two passengers were killed, illustrated the increased dangers that arise out of a multiplicity of lines. There are eight running lines through Vauxhall station, and the fifth line from the north was the up main local and the sixth the up main through. A light engine left the shed at Locomotive Junction, Nine Elms, and was turned there on to the up main through line, and the starting signal lowered for it. The next box was Vauxhall West, where the signals for the up main through were at danger, as a train from Aldershot was in the station. The signals for the up main local were, however, at clear for a train from Earlsfield. Apparently the driver of the light engine was under the impression that he was on the latter line and he took the Earlsfield train's signal as his, overlooked his own and ran into the standing passenger train. There was no question of confusion of signals. The driver read them correctly, but was not on the road on which he thought he was.

The widenings during this period were, Farnham to Butts Junction (Alton), 2nd June, 1901; Wadebridge to Wadebridge Junction, 3rd February, 1907, and Exmouth Junction to Topsham, 31st May, 1908; these being from single to double line. A third line was laid from Newton Tony Junction, continuing the line from Amesbury into Grateley station, completed 24th April, 1902. On the 4th May following, the main Southampton line was quadrupled between St Denys and Northam Junction, and on 4th June of the same year similar lines were opened between Weston and Wallers Ash (north of Winchester). In July, 1905, the provision of four lines of way between Clapham Junction and Basingstoke was completed, and shortly afterwards there were seven running roads between Vauxhall and Waterloo.

A great improvement was made on 30th June, 1901, when the up line from Aldershot was connected with the up main line at Pirbright Junction, Brookwood, by a flying junction. The work necessitated a bridge over the four roads of the main line. In 1903 the down Chertsey line was passed under the main line at Byfleet Junction. At Hampton Court Junction the up Guildford line (from Claygate) was similarly dealt with in 1908, and the down Hampton Court line taken over the other lines in 1915. The up Southampton line had also been raised and passed over the others in connection with the Basingstoke–Worting widening.

NOTE: Dendy Marshall did not deal in the pre-grouping part of his book with two minor lines acquired at amalgamation, although they were mentioned briefly. Further details are as follows:

PLYMOUTH DEVONPORT & SOUTH WESTERN JUNCTION. This line was the subject of various Acts from 1884 onwards; in 1887 the transfer to it of the East Cornwall Mineral Railway was provided for, and later part of this line, which was of narrow gauge, was reconstructed as a standard gauge passenger light railway from a junction with the L.S.W.R. at Bere Alston to Calstock, opened 2nd, March 1908. Locomotives: 0-4-2ST rebuilt from E.C.M.R. Neilson 1872, 0-4-0ST; *A. S. Harris*, 0-6-0T Hawthorn Leslie, 1907; *Earl of Mount Edgcumbe* and *Lord St Leven*, 0-6-2T Hawthorn Leslie, 1907.

LYNTON & BARNSTAPLE. This was a narrow-gauge (1ft 11½in) line from a junction with the L.S.W.R. at Barnstaple Town to Lynton. It was authorised on 27th June, 1895, and opened 11th May, 1898. Locomotives: *Yeo*, *Exe* and *Taw*, 2-6-2T Manning Wardle, 1897; *Lyn* 2-4-2T Baldwin, 1899. All had 2ft 9in driving wheels, but while the English engines had 10½ × 16in cylinders, the diameter in the case of the American engine was 10in. This was a pretty and well-run line, whose green engines and brown-and-cream carriages (of a normal compartment type except for some observation saloons) seemed dwarfed at Barnstaple Town by the towering standard gauge machines across the platform. There were considerable works including a long brick viaduct at Chelfham. Traffic suffered somewhat from the fact that by geographical necessity the line stopped well above and back from the chief tourist attraction, the village of Lynmouth.

XII

South Western Locomotives

THE first Locomotive Superintendent was Joseph Woods. The first engine was a four-wheeled single built by E. Bury and Co. in 1835, of their well-known standard pattern, named *Lark*, which was taken over from contractors in 1838. Next followed three very similar engines built by Nasmyth and Co. in the latter year: *Hawk*, *Raven*, and *Falcon*. These had disappeared by August, 1845; except the *Raven*, which lasted till 1851.

It was wisely decided that six-wheeled engines were more suitable. In the *Public Works of Great Britain*, by F. W. Simms, 1838, a copy – probably condensed – is given of the specification which was drawn up. It begins by saying 'General Form. The engines to be constructed with two horizontal cylinders working to a double cranked axle in the driving wheels, very similar in form to the "Shark" now in use on the Grand Junction Railway.'

The cylinders were to be 13 by 18in and driving wheels 5ft 6in. The number of engines ordered is not stated, but later it says there were to be ten tenders similar to those on the Grand Junction.

The *Shark*, chosen as a pattern, was built by R. Stephenson and Co. in 1837. An illustration is given of one of the above engines, on page 215, in Brees' *Railway Practice* (1849).

There is some evidence that Jacob Perkins, the apostle of high-pressure steam, was building an engine for the Southampton Railway about this time, on his closed water-tube principle, but it does not appear to have materialised; at all events it was not taken into the stock of the company. The *Railway Magazine*, Vol. I, November, 1836, p. 375, says:

Mr Perkins is constructing some locomotive engines with the new – we think we may call them everlasting – boilers to bring to a decisive test on the Southampton Railway. If the invention succeeds, we shall have no trouble hereafter about incrustations nor consequential danger of bursting.

In accordance with the usual practice at the time, the engines were not numbered, but merely bore names. The numbers given in brackets are those which were subsequently allotted.

Four six-wheeled singles by G. and J. Rennie came in 1838:

Garnett, London, Victoria, and *Reed,* which were never numbered. In the same year Tayleur and Co. delivered six more:

Sussex (1)	Tartar (2)	Transit (3)
Thetis	Tiger	Locke (4)

It may be mentioned that in giving evidence in connection with the Direct Portsmouth Atmospheric Railway, Locke said that the first three or four South Western engines were no good, and were laid aside until they were rebuilt a few years later. He was probably referring to the four-wheelers mentioned at the beginning of the chapter.

Nine came in 1838 from Sharp, Roberts; of their standard design:

Venus (7)	Aurora (10)	Orion (13)
Vesta (8)	Minerva (11)	Mercury (14)
Chaplin (9)	Jupiter (12)	Mars (15)

Five very similar ones were supplied by Rothwell and Co:

Vivid (35)	Arab (37)	Wizard (39)
Comet (36)	Vizier (38)	

In 1839 there were five more from Tayleur and Co.:

Pegasus	Renown	Ganymede (5)
Sam Slick	Cossack (6)	

Of this batch, those without numbers were sold, together with the *Thetis* of the previous year, to Fairbairn and Sons in 1842.

Two odd single engines acquired about this time were *Fly* (40) and *Southampton* (16, afterwards 176), which is set down in an official list as from Millbrook Foundry, 1840. In that year Fenton, Murray and Jackson, sent four singles:

Leeds (31)	Eclipse (32)	Phoenix (33)	Crescent (34)

All the foregoing engines had single driving wheels 5ft 6in in diameter and most of them cylinders 13 by 18.

In 1840 two front-coupled engines were supplied by Jones and Potts, *Ajax* (41) and *Atlas* (42). They were sent to Wadebridge about 1854 by sea, to work the Bodmin & Wadebridge Railway. Two similar 'luggage' engines came from Sharp, Roberts and Co.: *Milo* (43) and *Pluto* (44).

In a return issued by the Board of Trade in November, 1841, the London & Southampton Railway is said to have had 48 locomotives, four of which were four-wheeled. Those which had been given above, which are all that appear in the company's records, and in a long series of articles in *The Locomotive Magazine* beginning in 1903, come to four with four wheels and 39 with six. There are consequently five missing. The writer had a MS. 'Report and Repairs Book', dated June, 1849, which shows, incidentally, that the engines were numbered by then, and mentions five engines in existence by that time, which are almost certainly those required; especially as their numbers are not to be found among those already given, namely:

17 Queen	19 Briton	(21) Prince
18 Albert	20 Princess	

The first one, *Queen*, was clearly in existence by 1841, because the *Railway Times* of 4th December, 1841, says she opened the Gosport branch. As for the others, they were in need of repairs in 1849, and the book mentions that *Princess* was 'ballasting', therefore probably old. Who the makers could have been one cannot say, but they were certainly six-wheelers, and no doubt singles. Their existence in 1844 in confirmed by the Gauge Commissioners' Report, to which reference will be made in due course.

John Viret Gooch succeeded Woods on 1st January, 1841. He was a brother of Daniel Gooch, of the Great Western, and had been the engineer of the Manchester & Leeds Railway.

In 1842 two more 'luggage' engines, similar to the *Milo* and *Pluto*, came from Sharp, Roberts; *Titan* (45) and *Minos* (46). Nos 45 and 41 (*Ajax*) were sold to the Swedish Government in October, 1855, for £900 each.

In 1843 five single engines were delivered by Fairbairn, with 5ft 6in wheels as usual:

Giraffe (22)	Elk (24)	Gazelle (26)
Antelope (23)	Reindeer (25)	

The history of these engines is rather difficult to make out satisfactorily. The first four were rebuilt at the Millbrook Foundry, Southampton, in 1852, and then had outside cylinders – the *Giraffe* is thus illustrated in *The Locomotive Magazine*, Vol. VIII, p. 181 – but it is clear from the Gauge Commission Report that they must have originally had inside cylinders. The *Gazelle* is not given in the company's records, but is wanted to agree with the Report, and there is a tradition that she was made into a tank in 1852.

The *Elk* ran from Southampton to Nine Elms – 78 miles – in 93 minutes in 1846.

Gooch then built four engines at Nine Elms, with 6ft 6in driving wheels, and outside inclined cylinders 14½ by 21:

Eagle (27) 1843	Falcon (29) 1844
Hawk (28) 1844	Vulture (30) 1844

London Bridge Station in 1844.

The opening of the Shoreham branch of the Brighton Railway in 1840.

Brighton Station in 1841. *[British Railways*

No. 65 of the Brighton Railway, a 'Jenny Lind' engine by E. B. Wilson, 1847. The print is enlarged from a daguerreotype. *[British Railways*

The above had the largest wheels which had so far been put on the narrow gauge.

The next were four goods engines with six-coupled wheels and outside frames:

Bison (49)	Elephant (51)
Buffalo (50)	Rhinoceros (52)

Two small rear-coupled engines were also turned out this year (1844, but perhaps the second not till 1845): *Taurus* (47) and *Hercules* (48). They had 5ft driving wheels.

We are now in a position to compare results with the Gauge Report, which gives the stock as at 31st December, 1844.

There are only four engines with outside cylinders (obviously Nos. 27–30, as the exact dimensions are given). With inside cylinders, there is one with four wheels (*Raven*); 36 singles with 5ft 6in wheels, which must be 1 26 and 31–40; six coupled with 4ft 6in wheels (Nos. 41–46), and one with 5ft wheels, which must be the *Taurus*.

While on the subject of this report, the following reference to carriages is given, as it is of considerable interest:

> The most commodious carriages on the narrow gauge lines, such as those on the South Western, weigh less than 5 tons; seven such carriages would therefore weigh about 34 tons, and being capable of containing 126 first-class passengers, weighing, with their luggage, 12½ tons, the total load would be only 46 tons.

In 1845 and 1846 the company built eight singles with outside cylinders, the wheels being 6ft 6in, and cylinders 15 by 22 (afterwards 53–60):

Mazeppa	Mentor	Sirocco
Medea	Meteor	Sappho
Medusa	Sultan	

Two others, dated December, 1847, with cylinders only 14¼, were *Snake* (61) and *Serpent* (62). The safety valve, which was invented by Gooch, also acted as a pressure gauge; rising gradually for some distance before allowing the steam to escape.

In 1846 and 1847 ten singles with outside cylinders, similar to the *Mazeppa* class, were supplied by Fairbairn & Sons (afterwards 63–72):

Alecto	Aeolus	Ariel
Acheron	Apollo	Alaric
Achilles	Argus	Arrow
Actaeon		

Meanwhile, between December, 1846, and the end of 1848 Rothwell and Co. were delivering a batch of twenty-eight singles of their standard design with inside cylinders; 6ft; 15 by 22 (afterwards 73–100):

Fireball	Siren	Charon
Firebrand	Styx	Cyclops
Fire King	Saracen	Camilla
Firefly	Shark	Centaur
Hecla	Stentor	Castor
Hecate	Sirius	Pegasus
Harpy	Saturn	Plutus
Hornet	Sybil	Phlegon*
Herod	Spitfire	Python
Sultana		

These engines do not appear to have been rebuilt, except the *Firefly*, which was converted into a tank in 1862. The *Hecla* was renamed *Wildfire* in 1852, when No. 120 came out.

In 1848 six more goods engines of the *Bison* type, with 4ft 9in wheels, were built at Nine Elms (101–106):

Lion	Tiger	Leopard
Lioness	Tigress	Panther

The three last were rebuilt in the 'sixties, and not broken up till the 'eighties.

In 1847 Stothert and Slaughter were allowed to try some engines of the well-known 'Crewe' pattern (singles), which they had built for an Italian railway, on the South Western line, and they were so successful that the latter company arranged to take two of them over, *Gem* (107) and *Ruby* (108). The pressure was 80 pounds. Both engines met with disasters to the boiler about twelve years later, that of the *Gem* bursting at Andover in 1857.

During 1848 and 1849 six single engines were built by Christie, Adams and Hill, of the Thames Bank Iron Works. The writer does not know of any other instance of this firm having built locomotives; possibly they were only intermediaries. The engines were (109–114):

Rocklia	Test	Stour
Avon	Trent	Frome

The driving wheels were 6ft 6in, and cylinders $14\frac{1}{4}$ by 21.

In December, 1849 Nine Elms turned out a single express engine, which was Gooch's *chef-d'œuvre* so far as the South Western was concerned. The driving wheels were 7ft, and cylinders 15 by 20;

---

* An error for *Phlegethon*, which was a river in hell, the waters of which were always burning (repeated on the new engine of 1868).

namely, 118 *Etna* (numbered at first for a short time 40). Altogether there were eight of the class, the rest being mostly finished after Gooch had retired, and being as follows:

116 Stromboli	1850	115 Vulcan	1851	121 St George	1853
117 Volcano	1851	120 Hecla	1852	122 Britannia	1853
119 Vesuvius	1851				

About the middle of 1850 Gooch resigned, and went to the Eastern Counties Railway. He was succeeded by Joseph Beattie, who had been previously the carriage and wagon superintendent. The latter at once began by renewing the stock, much of which was old and obsolete. When he replaced an engine, the new one took the same name and number, so that, as was the case on the North Western Railway, sometimes there were as many as three generations of engines bearing names associated with the original numbers.

His first engines, built at Nine Elms, were rear coupled, with 5ft 6in wheels, and inside cylinders, namely:

43 Milo	1851	47 Taurus	1851	31 Leeds	1852
46 Minos	1851	48 Hercules	1851	40 Windsor	1852

They mostly lasted till the 'eighties.

In 1852 six tanks with single driving wheels 6ft 0$\frac{1}{2}$in diameter, outside cylinders 14$\frac{1}{2}$ by 20, were built by Sharp, Roberts and Co.:

2 Tartar	13 Orion	18 Albert
12 Jupiter	17 Queen	33 Phoenix

They were broken up in the early 'seventies. Eight similar engines were constructed the same year at Nine Elms, except for the wheels, which were 5ft in the first three, and 5ft 6in in the rest:

1 Sussex	4 Locke	20 Princess
14 Mercury	6 Cossack	36 Comet
15 Mars	19 Briton	

These also disappeared in the 'seventies. For the present, if no maker is mentioned, Nine Elms may be assumed. Four more of the *Milo* type followed in 1853: 21 *Prince*, 32 *Eclipse*, 37 *Arab*, and 42 *Atlas*. They were followed by an express with single driving wheels 6ft 6in; outside cylinders 15 by 21; 123 *The Duke*.

In 1854 and 1855 the last of the *Milo* type were built:

5 Ganymede	35 Vivid	41 Ajax (1855)
26 Gazelle	44 Pluto	

Outside cylinders were then made universal, except for six-coupled engines (and remained so till 1887). In 1855 a new type for mixed traffic was designed, with cylinders 15 by 24, and 5ft coupled wheels, known as the *Dane* class:

124 Saxon	126 Dane	128 Samson
125 Norman	127 Goliath	129 Albion

This year Beattie altered an engine, 134 *Ironsides*, which had just been built as a single, to coupled. It was very successful, running until June, 1885, when it was sold. Five more singles came out in 1856, with 6ft 6in wheels and 15 by 21 cylinders:

130 Harold	132 Conqueror	135 Canute
131 Rufus	133 Crescent	

The *Canute* is illustrated in a rare book, *The Permanent Way and Coal-burning Locomotive Boilers of European Railways*, by Colburn and Holley (New York, 1858). The boiler savours of Beattie's predecessor, not having the large bell-mouthed dome over the firebox which he almost always used. It shows two specialities of his, namely the feedwater heater in front of the chimney, and the method – peculiar to him – of hanging outside bearings to the leading wheels from the slide-bars, without any framing to carry them.

The following interesting episode in her history is related in Colburn's *Locomotive Engineering*, page 253. (The 'writer' is D. K. Clark.)

With Mr Beattie's permission the writer, in 1856, balanced the 'Canute' engine on the London & South Western Railway. This engine had previously a balance-weight of 85 lbs applied within the rims of the driving wheels. New weights were put in, weighing 186 lbs for each wheel, and balancing the whole mass acting at the crank pin. The engine ran so much more steadily and freely with the new balance-weights, as to take the engineman by surprise. On the first day after the alteration, it considerably overshot the stopping stations, although the steam was shut off and the brakes applied at the usual distances from the stations.

Two more single tanks came out in 1856: 9 *Chaplin* and 10 *Aurora*, together with four coupled ones (afterwards made into tender engines): 11 *Minerva*, 34 *Osprey*, 16 *Salisbury*, and 39 *Wizard*.

In December, 1857, six 'Danes' appeared:

136 Goth	138 Vandal	140 Gaul
137 Hun	139 Lombard	141 Celt

In 1857 and 1858 there were five singles resembling *Canute*:

142 Eugenie	150 Havelock	152 Marmion
149 Napoleon	151 Montrose	

Three single tank engines (the last) appeared in December, 1858: 143 *Nelson*, 144 *Howe*, and 145 *Hood*; also three express engines with

6ft coupled wheels: 146 *Tweed*, 147 *Isis*, and 148 *Colne*. In June, 1859, the last single express engine on the line was turned out, 153 *Victoria*, which was also the last of this type to survive, being sold in June, 1885. After three coupled tanks, 154 *Nile*, 155 *Cressy*, and 156 *Hogue*, there came the first three of a very fine class of engine, which ran the expresses for nearly a quarter of a century; namely 157 *Clyde*, 158 *Lacy*, and 159 *Castleman*.

Until the 'fifties, coke had been practically the universal fuel for locomotives, owing to the strict prohibition of smoke. Many attempts were made to produce a firebox which would burn coal successfully, of which two of the most prominent were Beattie's on the South Western and Cudworth's on the South Eastern (which will be described later). Beatties' experiments began in 1853, and comprised a double firebox; earlier designs contained a mass of perforated firebricks in the combustion chamber. The heaviest firing was done in the back part of the firebox; in the front a bright incandescent fire was kept, which consumed the smoke from the rear portion. Of this firebox (as fitted in 1859 to the *Clyde* for example) Ahrons says:*

> This was probably the most fearful and wonderful boiler and firebox ever placed in service on a large scale, and must have caused the running shed boiler repairing staff furiously to think. But it was undoubtedly most efficient as a means of extracting heat units from the fuel, and there were no locomotives in the kingdom which could touch Beattie's for fuel economy.

In January, 1854, Beattie read a paper *On an Improved Locomotive Engine* at a meeting of the Institution of Mechanical Engineers held in Birmingham. He said the *Britannia* burnt on the average 17 lb per mile between Southampton and London; the gradients averaging 1 in 250 for 17 miles; 'the Southampton, Portsmouth, Gosport and Salisbury trains being all joined at Basingstoke, and taken in one train to London, which generally contains from 20 to 26 carriages'. A uniform pressure of 120 lb per square inch was maintained up all the gradients.

The regulations as to emitting smoke seem to have been strictly enforced about that time. In the course of the discussion on the paper, William Fairbairn said that in Manchester regular inspectors were appointed to carry them out; any chimney was reported that emitted black smoke for longer than three minutes after firing, and they were limited at other times to what was called 'Parliamentary smoke', or such that allowed an object to be seen through it.

* *The British Steam Locomotive 1825-1925*, p. 134.

The combustion chamber was discarded about 1863, and only the double firebox remained, until 1877, when that too went.

A series of articles on Beattie's inventions was published in *The Locomotive* for 1934, beginning in April, and continued in 1935.

The final solution of the problem, which turned out to be very simple, was reached on the Midland Railway in 1860; being the standard design of brick arch and firehole deflector, but Beattie and Cudworth refused to be convinced.

Probably much of the economy of Beattie's engines was due to the hot feed. The first type of heater he used was a jet condenser in front of the chimney, sometimes double. In a later form, which was used for something like twenty years, the chamber in front of the chimney was discarded, and exhaust steam pipes ran along outside the boiler, through which the feed water circulated, without being allowed to mix with the steam.

The *Castleman* lasted until June, 1887, and ran a total of 869,000 miles. The dimensions of these engines were outstanding for the period; namely, driving wheels 7ft; cylinders 17 by 22; heating surface 1,004 plus 98, total 1,102 square feet; weight, engine 35 tons 11 cwt, tender 20 tons 15 cwt, total 56 tons 6 cwt. The cylinders were afterwards enlarged to 18 inches.

In June, 1859, three more 6ft coupled engines were put to work: 160 *Thames*, 161 *Shannon*, and 162 *Severn*. In September, another of the seven-footers appeared: 169 *R. H. Dutton*.

A smaller edition of the last-mentioned type, with 6ft 6in wheels, were constructed between December, 1859, and June, 1860, twelve in all:

163 Undine	167 Atalanta	172 Zephyr
164 Psyche	168 Electra	173 Nymph
165 Circe	170 Cupid	174 Naiad
166 Ariadne	171 Sylph	175 Hebe

About this time eleven engines were taken over from the North Devon Railway, which had been opened in 1854 on the broad gauge. When the South Western took it over, they proceeded to 'mix' the gauge, eventually converting it to narrow. These engines were as follows:

176 Creedy	four coupled	5ft	outside cylinders
177 Yeo	single	6ft	,,
178 Dart	,,	6ft	,,
179 Venus	four coupled	5ft	inside (?) cylinders
180 Star	single	6ft 6in	inside cylinders
181 Barum	,,	6ft	,,
182 Exe	,,	6ft	,,

183 Tite	single	6ft	inside cylinders
184 Mole	,,	6ft	,,
185 Dreadnought	six coupled	4ft	,,
186 Defiance	,,	?	,,

Most of the above engines were built at the Canada Works, Birkenhead, by Messrs Brassey and Co. Brassey had been working the line for seven years. The names were not used again.

No more new engines were turned out from Nine Elms until December, 1862, when three 6ft 6in coupled appeared: 27 *Eagle*, 28 *Hawk*, and 30 *Vulture*. There followed six four-coupled goods engines with 5ft wheels (1862–3):

107 Gem	56 Mentor	78 Hecate
55 Medusa	57 Meteor	67 Aeolus

Also a 6ft coupled express, 29 *Falcon*; and two 6ft 6in, 69 *Argus* and 71 *Alaric*.

During the next year Beyer, Peacock and Co., delivered the first eighteen of the celebrated little engines known as 'Beattie's well-tanks', of which altogether eighty-three were built. The numbers of this batch, which had no names, were 177 to 194. After some twenty years of service they were converted into tender engines, some with new boilers, and ran for another ten years or so.

The next engines built at Nine Elms were three six-coupled goods engines, which came out in 1864: 101 *Lion*, 102 *Lioness*, and 103 *Tiger*. Three 7-ft expresses followed: 73 *Fireball*, 74 *Firebrand*, and 75 *Fire King*, and three 6ft 6in: 68 *Apollo*, 70 *Ariel*, and 72 *Arrow*. There were six more well-tanks from Beyer, Peacock, Nos. 195–200.

In 1865 there were four 6ft 6in passenger engines: 77 *Wildfire*, 79 *Harpy*, 80 *Hornet*, and 81 *Herod*; and three goods: 52 *Rhinoceros*, 53 *Mazeppa*, and 54 *Medea*. Beyers supplied six more tanks, 203–208.

Two engines were bought this year from G. England and Co. and numbered 201 and 202. They were outside cylinder four-coupled 'long boiler' engines, and were afterwards transferred to a separate list known as the Engineers' Department engines, when they became 9 *Harrison* and 10 *Bidder*.

In 1866 there were four 6ft 6in passenger engines: 82 *Sultana*, 83 *Siren*, 84 *Styx*, and 85 *Saracen*. Three 6ft engines; 63 *Alecto*, 64 *Acheron*, and 66 *Actaeon*. Three goods: 58 *Sultan*, 59 *Sirocco*, and 60 *Sappho*; and another dozen tanks from Beyer, Peacock: Nos. 209–220, most of which afterwards had tenders given them; and from the same makers, twelve goods engines, all of which lasted into the 'nineties:

221 Scotia	223 Colossus	225 Hibernia
222 Cambria	224 Gallia	226 Anglia
	237–242 without names.	

The *Cambria*, when scrapped in 1898, had 870,000 miles to her credit. Beyers also supplied six passenger engines with 6-ft wheels, numbered 231–236, of which No. 234 was sold in 1897, after a mileage of 960,950 miles, together with 235.

Four engines were bought this year from Robert Stephenson and Co., numbered 227–230. The first two were 2-4-0 engines with outside cylinders, the wheels being 6ft; the other two were six-coupled goods engines with 5-ft wheels and 18-in cylinders. They were transferred later on to the Engineers' Department (see the end of the chapter).

In 1867, from Nine Elms came three 6ft 6in engines: 86 *Shark*, 87 *Stentor*, and 88 *Sirius*; and three goods: 92 *Charon*, 93 *Cyclops*, and 94 *Camilla*; also twelve well-tanks from Beyer, Peacock: Nos 243–254.

In January, 1868, three 6-ft engines came out: 89 *Saturn*, 90 *Sybil*, and 91 *Spitfire*; followed by six seven-footers:

| 95 Centaur | 97 Pegasus | 99 Phlegon |
| 96 Castor | 98 Plutus | 100 Python |

Most of the above ran about a million miles before being broken up, 1895–9.

In July, 1868, eight more well-tanks came from Beyers: Nos 255–262.

Early in 1869 there were six goods from Nine Elms:

| 108 Ruby | 110 Avon | 112 Trent |
| 109 Rocklia | 111 Test | 113 Stour |

Next came four 6-ft coupled: 114 *Frome*, 115 *Vulcan*, 116 *Stromboli*, and 117 *Volcano*. In December three with 6ft 6in wheels: 119 *Vesuvius*, 121 *St George*, and 122 *Britannia*.

In 1869, two 6ft coupled: 61 *Snake* and 62 *Serpent*.

In 1870 there were the following from Nine Elms:

Passenger, with 6ft 6in wheels:

| 1 Sussex | 15 Mars | 6 Cossack |
| 14 Mercury | 2 Tartar | |

Goods, with 5-ft wheels:

65 Achilles	3 Transit	9 Chaplin
120 Hecla	7 Venus	10 Aurora
176 Dragon	8 Vesta	

In 1871, Passenger, 6ft 6in:

| 4 Locke | 19 Briton | 17 Queen |
| 18 Albert | 20 Princess | 21 Prince |

Goods, 5ft:

| 12 Jupiter | 22 Giraffe | 23 Antelope |
| 13 Orion | 38 Vizier | 24 Elk |

Also eight tanks from Beyer, Peacock: Nos. 263–270.

In 1871 Joseph Beattie died, and was succeeded by his son, W. G. Beattie, who continued for several years on the same lines as his father, but usually discarding the large dome on the firebox in favour of a plain one in the middle of the boiler, with Ramsbottom safety-valves on the firebox. In February, 1872, there were three standard tanks: 33 *Phoenix*, 36 *Comet*, and 76 *Firefly*. In, 1872, Beyer, Peacock delivered six powerful goods engines, Nos. 273–278. There were also three goods engines from Nine Elms: 16 *Salisbury*, afterwards *Stonehenge*, and Nos 271 and 272. These were followed by three 6-ft passenger engines of the Snake class: 25 *Reindeer*, 26 *Gazelle*, and 118 *Etna*.

In March, 1873, there were three more of the last mentioned type: 5 *Ganymede*, 11 *Minerva*, and 31 *Leeds*. At the same time, three light six-coupled engines were bought from Beyer, Peacock and Co., known as the 'Ilfracombe goods', numbered 282–284 (No. 282 was renumbered 349 in 1899).* This year (1873) there were six passenger engines with 6ft 6in wheels: 279, 280 *Persia*, 281, 32 *Eclipse*, 35 *Vivid*, and 294. Also three goods: 291–293. Six more goods engines came from Beyers: 285–290.

In 1874 there were twelve passenger 6ft 6in engines:

37 Arab	295–297	42 Atlas
39 Wizard	315–317	43 Milo
40 Windsor	41 Ajax	

For a number of years, no more new engines were built at Nine Elms. Six more well-tanks were delivered by Beyer, Peacock: 201, 202, 34 *Osprey*, 298, 299, and 314. Of these, Nos. 298 and 314 survived long enough to be renumbered 3298 and 3314, and later taken into B.R. stock, along with No. 329 of 1875; all withdrawn 1962, being still in use on the Wenfordbridge branch, where very light engines are essential. In 1874 Beyer, Peacock also supplied two Ilfracombe goods, 300 and 301; and twelve large goods engines, Nos. 302–313, in which the outside frames, which had always been used before, were discarded.

* Two of these engines were sold as late as 1910 and 1914, to the Kent & East Sussex Railway, being then numbered 0349 and 0284; under the new owners they became 7 *Rother* and 8 *Juno*. They survived for another 20 years or more. One similar engine was also sold to the East Kent Railway and two to the Shropshire & Montgomeryshire Railway; L.S.W.R. 0324, S.M.R. *Hesperus*, was not scrapped until 1942.

About this time the successful working of the Metropolitan engines, the credit for the design of which is usually given to Sir John Fowler, but really belongs to Beyer, Peacock and Co., attracted so much attention that several railways, of which the South Western was one, ordered similar engines, and in January, 1875, six were supplied, Nos. 318–323. No. 318 was improved later on by being fitted with an Adams bogie; the very short bogies on the Bissell plan with which they were originally fitted being the only serious fault in the design. No. 320 lasted until the end of 1913. During 1875 Beyers supplied also another Ilfracombe goods, No. 324; and the last six of the little well-tanks, 44 *Pluto* and 325–329.

In May, 1876, they sent six saddle tanks,* 330–335, known as the 'Saddlebacks', and twelve goods engines, 336–347.

By this time the standard express engines were beginning to feel the increasing loads, and W. G. Beattie tried his hand at designing a new class, with a leading bogie and 6ft 7in wheels. There were twenty of them, Nos. 348–367, built by Sharp, Stewart and Co. in 1876 and 1877. They were the last engines to be fitted with Beattie's patent firebox, and at first had piston valves. They were not very successful, the boilers being too small for the $18\frac{1}{2}$in cylinders, which were afterwards reduced to 17in.

In 1877 there were two more saddle tanks from Beyer, Peacock, 227 and 228, afterwards 316 and 328. This year, W. G. Beattie retired, owing to ill-health. Of his engines, the only remaining ones were twelve goods from Beyers.

151 Montrose	160 Thames	229, 230
152 Marmion	162 Severn	368–373

Two more Ilfracombe goods, Nos. 393 and 394, which came in 1880, may be mentioned here. There are a few 'oddments' which may also be conveniently dealt with now. In December, 1877, two little four-wheeled saddle tanks were purchased from Shanks and Co. for use at Southampton Docks. They were named *Cowes* and *Southampton*, and were numbered many years later 108 and 109. Two years later a similar one was taken over from the Dock company, named *Ritzebuttel*. Another little engine which has not been mentioned was the *Bodmin*, an 0-4-0 saddle tank built by Fletcher and Jennings of Whitehaven, and sent to the Bodmin & Wadebridge about 1864.

It will also be convenient to give particulars here of the engines in the Engineers' Department list, to which reference has already been

---

* Several of these engines enjoyed a very long life: No. 335 was sold to the Kent & East Sussex Railway in 1932.

made. They were used for ballasting work, etc. Sketches of most of them were given in *The Locomotive*, Vol. XXXVI (1930), pp. 349 and 385.

The first seven were four-coupled 'long boiler' engines with outside cylinders, built by G. England and Co., 1857–64, as follow:

1 Hawkshaw	4 Locke	6 Telford
2 Brunel	5 Smeaton	7 Fowler
3 Stephenson		

The last was bought from the Somerset & Dorset Railway (on which line it was No. 14). It will be noticed there were two engines on the system '4 *Locke*'.

No. 8 *Mina* was a small four-wheeled tank built by J. Walker of Wigan in 1872. Nos. 9 and 10, *Harrison* and *Bidder*, were similar engines to the first batch, built by England and Co. in 1862; they have already been mentioned, as when bought in 1865 they were put into the ordinary stock as 201 and 202. The next four were the engines bought from R. Stephenson and Co. in 1866, also previously mentioned; named after the four Government Inspectors:

11 Yolland and 12 Tyler; six-coupled (229 and 230)
13 Rich and 14 Hutchinson; four-coupled (227 and 228)

Three others were taken over from the Somerset & Dorset Railway, on which line they were Nos. 11–13, namely 15 *Scott* (afterwards 21), which was a small 2-4-0 tank, with the distinction of having figured in the 1862 Exhibition, and two long boiler engines taken over about 1880 and at first called 147 *Isis* and 148 *Colne* in the main list, but transferred in 1884 to the Engineers' Department, where they took the numbers and names of the original Brunel and Stephenson.

Another old 2-4-0 engine by England and Co. is mentioned in the books as having worked for the Engineers' Department, named *Hesketh*. It may have been only hired.

The above engines were painted green. The earliest piece of evidence on the subject of the colours of the ordinary stock is a painting of the first *Stromboli*, built in 1850, which was in the Directors' room at Waterloo, and showed a deep crimson colour. During the greater part of the Beattie regime, however, the engines were dark brown, with polished brass domes.

The new Locomotive Superintendent was William Adams. The son of a fine engineer of the same name, he had for twenty years held the same post on the North London Railway, where he designed most admirable engines; so much so, that they remained the standard pattern until the end of the Great War. He then went to the Great Eastern Railway for five years, where he was by no means a success, none of his engines being particularly efficient; his legacy to that company being fifteen 'Mogul' goods engines which were delivered after he had left, in 1878 and 1879, and were so unsatisfactory that they were all broken up 1885 to 1887. Nevertheless, he did magnificent work for the South Western.

He began with twelve large bogie tanks, built by Beyer, Peacock. They were numbered 46, 123, 124, 130, 132, 133, and 374–379. All were lengthened a few years later, with a pair of radial wheels at the trailing end. They were called the 'Ironclads'.

Another dozen engines followed by the same makers, Nos. 380–391, which were similar, except that they had tenders instead of tanks. These were known as the 'steam rollers' on account of their small solid bogie wheels.

In 1880 the type was enlarged into a class of fine express engines, Nos. 135–146, also from Beyers. They had 6ft 7in wheels, and 18 by 24 cylinders, weighing 73 tons complete.

In July, 1880, a shunting tank was bought, which had been built by Manning, Wardle and Co. in 1862: No. 392 *Lady Portsmouth*, the name being afterwards removed.

In 1881–2 a dozen large goods engines were built by Neilson and Co.: Nos. 395–406. Two more shunting tanks were bought in September, 1881, (Manning, Wardle, 1876): 407 *Pioneer* and 408 *Jessie*.

In 1882 Beyer, Peacock and Co. supplied twelve saddle tanks similar to those of 1876, which were of their own design, numbered 127, 128, 131, 149, 150, 161, and 409–414. Three of them lasted till 1932.*

In 1882 the same firm delivered twelve large ten-wheeled tanks, Nos. 415–426, of a type which remained standard for a number of years, and took the place of the small well-tanks, which were beginning to find the work too heavy for them.

In 1883 Neilson and Co. built 24 more goods engines like the previous ones: Nos. 153–159, 163–167, and 433–444. At the same time Robert Stephenson and Co. supplied eighteen of the 4-4-2 tanks: Nos. 427–432, 45, and 47–57. From the same makers also came twelve express engines, Nos. 445–456, which were a development of those of 1880, having 7ft 1in wheels. Two more little saddle tanks were bought this year, No. 457 *St Michael* (Manning, Wardle, 1871) and 458 *Jumbo*, built by the same firm in 1862.

* No. 127 was sold to the East Kent Railway and was scrapped in 1941.

In 1884 Adams turned his attention to compounding, and a trial took place on the South Western line of some of the 445 class and Webb's No. 300 'Compound' of the L.N.W.R. The latter burnt more coal and had a difficulty in starting from stations. The matter was allowed to rest until 1888, when No. 446 was altered into a compound of the Worsdell type, by putting a 26-in low-pressure cylinder on one side. The possibility of having so large a cylinder outside was due to the fact that the connecting rod worked inside the coupling rod. The results were not satisfactory, and the engine was made 'simple' again three years later.

In January, 1884, another little engine was bought, similar to *Jumbo*, and named *Sambo*, No. 459.

Ten more express engines with 6ft 7in wheels were delivered in 1884 by Stephenson and Co., Nos. 147 and 470–478; and ten by Neilson, Nos. 460–469, together with ten radial bogie tanks by Dubs and Co., 169–171, 173, and 490–495. Side by side with the acquisition of all these fine engines many of the earlier ones were rebuilt, keeping Nine Elms busy, so that the locomotive stock was enormously strengthened, as compared with ten years earlier. And the stream of new engines went on. In February and March, 1885, Neilson and Co. delivered eleven of the standard ten-wheel tanks, Nos. 479–489.* In 1885–6 the same firm sent thirty-four goods: 496–515, 27–30, 69 (afterwards 83), 71 (afterwards 84), 101, 105, 134, 148, 168, 172, 174, and 175. Ten more tanks were supplied by Stephensons – the numbers in brackets being alterations: 67 (58), 77 (59), 78 (60), 82, 104, 106, 107, 125,† 126, and 129. Another ten were built by Dubs, Nos. 516–525.†

In 1886 Messrs Stephenson wished to exhibit an engine at the Newcastle Exhibition of the following year, and obtained permission to build one similar to the expresses supplied in 1884 – which obtained a gold medal. It was taken over by the railway company afterwards, and numbered 526.

So far, no engines had been built at Nine Elms under Adams's regime, but in 1887 construction began again. At the same time, he made a remarkable change in his designs, no doubt influenced by the success of the 'Gladstone' class on the Brighton Railway. From this time onwards, all tanks and mixed traffic engines were made more compact by being coupled in front. The mixed traffic engines,

* No. 488 had a varied history; after being used on War work and then on the East Kent Railway, it was taken back into S.R. stock in 1938, and finally sold in 1961 to the Bluebell Railway in Sussex where it is still running in 1963.
† Nos. 3125, 3520 survived to become B.R. stock, working on the Lyme Regis branch.

known as the 'Jubilee' class ('A12'), had 6ft 1in wheels and 18 by 26 cylinders. Thirty were built at Nine Elms in 1887–9, Nos. 527–556; forty by Neilsons in 1892–3, 607–646; and twenty more at Nine Elms in 1892–5, 597–606 and 647–656.

In June, 1888, the first four-coupled trailing bogie tank was turned out at Nine Elms, with wheels 5ft 7in, and cylinders 18 by 26. Of this class ('T1') there were in all fifty, built 1888–96. The numbers were 61–80, 1–20, and 358–367.

Side by side with the above were sixty of a smaller pattern ('O2') with wheels only 4ft 10in diameter, and 17 by 24 cylinders, built 1889–95, and numbered 177–236. No. 185 for a few years bore the name *Alexandra*, having been used for the opening – by the then Princess of Wales – of the Brookwood and Bisley Camp Railway in July, 1890.

In that year some magnificent express engines appeared, the design being a great advance on the previous ones, good though they were. The wheels were 7ft 1in and cylinders 19 by 26. Of these (class 'X2') there were thirty, built 1890–3: Nos. 577–596. These engines had forty rather smaller sisters (class 'T3'), with 6ft 7in wheels, built 1892–6: Nos. 557–576. After Mr Adams retired in 1895 two slightly larger types (again a large and small-wheeled version) appeared, the 'T6' (Nos. 677–686) and the 'X6' (657–666).

In 1894 ten six-coupled tanks were built there, Nos. 257–266, and four more in 1896, Nos. 267–270. Similar engines turned out later were 271–278, 1897–8; 162 and 348, 1900. They are known as the 'G6' class.

No mention has yet been made of a group of twenty little four-wheeled tank engines built 1891–3 at Nine Elms for shunting purposes at the docks, etc. ('B4' class). They had side tanks and outside cylinders. Most of them afterwards received names, as follows:

81 Jersey	91 — 92 —	98 Cherbourg
85 Alderney	93 St Malo	99 — 100 —
86 Havre	94 —	102 Granville
87 — 88 —	95 Honfleur	103 —
89 Trouville	96 Normandy	176 Guernsey
90 Caen	97 Brittany	

These conclude the engines designed by Adams, who as stated retired in 1895. During his seventeen years of office over 520 engines were built for the company. Until 1887 they were painted dark green, which was then changed to a light shade for the passenger engines.

It may be mentioned that the purchase of Southampton Docks in 1892 brought in eight small tank engines; two built by Hawthorn and Co., 457 (afterwards 734) *Clausentum* and 458 *Ironside*; two by the Vulcan Foundry, 118 (afterwards 111) *Vulcan* and 408 *Bretwalda*; three by Shanks and Co., *Sir Bevis*, *Ascupart*, and *Arbroath*; and *Canute*, built by Dick and Stevenson of Airdrie.

Adams was succeeded by Dugald Drummond, who had been on several of the Scottish railways, as related in Chapter XI, where he had done excellent work. The first engine of his design was a four-coupled tank with trailing bogie, which appeared early in 1897. The design became practically a standard one, subsequent engines only differing in detail. Some were fitted with exhaust pipes for heating the water. All were built by the company, 1897–1911. There were 105 of them, known as the 'M7' class: 21–60, 104–112, 123–133, 241–256, 318–324, 328, 356, 357, 374–379, 479–481, and 667–676. No. 126 was rebuilt by Urie in 1921 with superheater and 19 by 26 cylinders.

The same year thirty goods engines were built by Dübs and Co. They were originally numbered 687–716, but about a year later the following alterations were made:

702–306	707–325	712–350
703–308	708–326	713–352
704–309	709–327	714–355
705–315	710–339	715–368
706–317	711–346	716–459

The above were known as the '700 class'. They were the last 0-6-0 tender engines built for the South Western Railway.

Drummond then produced his first express engine for the line, which was of a startling originality. It had four cylinders, with independent driving wheels, the latter being 6ft 7in in diameter, which became the maximum for the railway. The cylinders were 16½in, but were found too large, and reduced. The first example was No. 720. In 1905 she was fitted with a much larger boiler, as shown on another page. Five similar engines came out in 1901, Nos. 369–373, but the divided drive proved unsatisfactory, and they had to be put to light work, and all disappeared in the nineteen-twenties.

In 1898 the first of a series of 4-4-0 expresses appeared, which were of orthodox design, very much like engines which Drummond had put on the Caledonian: Nos 290–299 ('C8' class; 18 by 26in cylinders).

Continuing the history of the 4-4-0 expresses, in 1899 and 1900 Nos. 280–289 and 113–122 ('T9' class) were built at Nine Elms. The fireboxes were very long, necessitating 10-ft coupling rods; 18½ by 26 cylinders.

There also came a batch from Dübs and Co., Nos. 702–719 and 721–732, and 773 (later 733). These had the Drummond cross tubes in the fire box. From Nine Elms followed 303–305, 307, 310–314, and 336–338. All the above engines were classed 'T9'.*

During 1903 and 1904 ten 4-4-0 engines appeared with 6ft wheels (all the preceding having been 6ft 7in), Nos. 395–404 (class 'S11'; 19 by 26 cylinders), intended for the hilly west country. Twenty more of the larger-wheeled class followed, 415–434 (class 'L12').† These two classes put the L.S.W.R. in a better position to compete with the accelerated G.W.R. services to the far West. Some of the 'L12' class however, were also used on the Bournemouth lines. No more express engines were built until 1912, when the 'D15' class 4-4-0, with 20in cylinders came out (463–472), built at Eastleigh. These were put on the Bournemouth trains. Although fitted with Drummond's smoke-box superheater at first, Urie superheaters were later fitted, and finally standard Maunsell superheaters.

In 1900 some mixed traffic engines were brought out, similar to the bogie expresses, but with 5ft 7in wheels only. There were two sizes, the 'Small Hoppers', 1900–3 (class 'K10'), and the 'Big Hoppers', 1903–7 (class 'L11'); forty of each:

Small: 135–146, 149–153, 329, 340–345, 347, and 380–394.
Large: 134, 148, 154–159, 161, 163–175, 405–414, and 435–442.

The 'K10s' carried a C8 type boiler, and 'L11s' a T9 boiler; the former carried 9-ft coupling rods against the 10-ft rods of the later class.

We now come to his 4-6-0 engines with four cylinders. The first were 330–334, which were turned out of Nine Elms towards the end of 1905. The coupled wheels were 6ft in diameter, with four cylinders 16 by 24; the total heating surface 2,727 square feet. When new, they were the largest passenger locomotives in the British Isles. No. 335 followed in 1907, with slight modifications, including $16\frac{1}{2}$-in cylinders, a superheater, and, it is said, water pick-up apparatus in the tender, although the line had no troughs! All were drastically 'rebuilt' as two-cylinder engines, and later formed part of the 'H15' class.

In 1908 five more were built at Nine Elms, numbered 453–457, followed by a further five from Eastleigh (after the locomotive works had been removed) in 1910 and 1911: Nos. 448–452. They were generally similar to the '330' class, but slightly smaller, and lighter, with 15-in cylinders. They were broken up in 1925, being replaced

* Later superheated and cylinder diameter increased from $18\frac{1}{4}$ to 19.
† Later superheated and fitted with shorter chimneys: from 1925 many worked on former S.E.C.R. and L.B.S.C. lines, as also did the 'T9's.'

L.B.S.C. No. 164 *Spithead*, formerly No. 153, a 'single' built in 1862 and here shown rebuilt by Stroudley.

An early type of L.B.S.C. signal box (Lovers' Walk) and a Stroudley rebuild of a Craven 2-4-0T No. 378 (formerly No. 12 of 1858), taken about 1882.

A Stroudley G class single passing Wandsworth Common about 1898.

One of the famous 'Gladstone' class Stroudley 0-4-2 in original form.

by the first of the 'King Arthur' class, which took over their tenders.

The last batch had 6ft 7in wheels: Nos. 443–447, in 1911, and 458–462 the next year. Their broad splashers led to the nickname 'Paddle-box engines'. A few years later they were rebuilt with extended smoke-boxes and Eastleigh superheaters, and in 1931 had the 'Paddle-boxes' removed and the footplate raised clear of the motion; classed 'T14'.

The only other engines by Drummond to be recorded are some very small ones, namely four-wheeled tanks: 746 (101) *Dinan*, 747 (147) *Dinard*, and Nos. 82–84 (classed 'B4' with the earlier batch).

He was the pioneer of the modern revival of the steam rail car, as was mentioned in Chapter XI. He also designed ten little 2-2-0 tanks for auto-train work in 1906, numbered 736–745, class 'C14'. During the war, seven of them were taken over by the War Office, and three by the Admiralty, the latter, Nos. 741, 744, and 745 being returned and rebuilt as 0-4-0 engines. A curious little inspection engine, No. 733, which he used as a kind of private motor car, was of interest as being of the Bristol & Exeter wheel arrangement, 4-2-4 (later No. 58S).

As recorded in Chapter XI, Drummond died in November, 1912, and was succeeded by Robert W. Urie, the works manager. He had been previously Chief Draughtsman to the Caledonian under Drummond.

The latter had introduced a complete revolution in South Western engines, using inside cylinders practically for all classes, and bringing up the weight and power to a high pitch. Among his special innovations were, firstly, cross water-tubes in the firebox, which in theory are excellent, but have been gradually removed, for reasons connected with maintenance. About 1901 he built an engine with an all-water-tube boiler, but it was not successful. He also had a scheme for heating the water in the tender, and a peculiar form of spark arrester; and at one time used a steam drying arrangement in the smoke-box.

With Urie came another revolution in design. No more four-coupled engines appeared, and the cylinders went outside again. During the ten years he had charge only five types of engines were built, all largely interchangeable as to parts. Walschaert's valve gear became the standard, and all the engines had high footplates, exposing the running gear.

The first engines were 4-6-0, with 6-ft wheels, Nos. 482–491, which appeared in 1914 ('H15' class). Of these the first four had Schmidt superheaters: the next four, Robinson, and the last two at first ran on saturated steam. The cylinders were 21 by 28.

The next design was similar, but with 6ft 7in wheels, Nos. 736–755, which appeared gradually from Eastleigh during 1918–1923 (class 'N15'). These engines, after some modifications which greatly improved their performance, formed the basis of the famous 'King Arthur' class of the Southern Railway.

During 1920 and 1921 there were twenty more 4-6-0 engines, but with 5ft 7in drivers, for work on heavy goods trains, numbered 496–515 (class 'S15').

Two large tank engine classes came out in 1921: the first, consisting of four engines, Nos. 492–495, were 4-8-0 with wheels 5ft 1in ('G16'). The other class had 5ft 7in wheels; 4-6-2; Nos. 516–520 ('H16').

All the Urie engines, except as mentioned above, were fitted with his 'Eastleigh' superheater.

On the formation of the Southern Railway, he retired, and the office of Chief Mechanical Engineer devolved upon Mr R. E. L. Maunsell, C.B.E., who had held that post with distinction for nine years on the South Eastern & Chatham.

XIII

South Western Steamer Services

FINALLY, mention must be made of the L.S.W.R. steamer services; an interesting article on the early services was contributed to the *Railway Magazine* in June, 1911, by Mr Thomas C. R. Orme, late assistant marine manager at Southampton to the Southern Railway. Speaking of the Channel Islands' service, he says that the Government stationed a swift sailing cutter at Southampton in 1781, which left every fortnight. This, however, was only a temporary expedient during a period of war, when private boats were afraid to run. The first regular mail service to the Channel Isands was established by an Act of 28th March, 1794. It granted 'rates of postage' – which previously did not exist to the Islands, and established Weymouth as a port. According to the sixth Report of the Commissioners of Post Office Enquiry (1836), at that time there were three Post Office steam packets stationed at Weymouth: *Flanner*, *Watersprite* and *Ivanhoe*.

About this time there were two companies running steamers between Southampton and Havre, and the Channel Islands; the South of England Steam Navigation Company, and the British and Foreign Steam Navigation Co. In 1845 the South Western Railway being, like the rest, unable to run steamers themselves, formed the South Western Steam Navigation Company, to run from Southampton to the Channel Islands, Havre and St Malo. As soon as operations commenced, the mails were withdrawn from the Weymouth route, and transferred to the new company. The latter acquired two wooden paddle boats, the *South Western* and *Transit*, which had been running on the Weymouth service, and had been built in 1843 by Ditchburn and Mare, the predecessors of the Thames Iron Works. They also built a steamer for the new company called the *Wonder*, of iron, with a gross tonnage of 250, which was put on the Havre service. She was fitted with powerful condensing engines on Seaward's atmospheric principle, with three cylinders 53-in diameter and 42-in stroke, with open tops. She was one of the fastest boats on the Channel at the time, running at the exceptionally high speed of 14 knots.

In 1847 the Western Railway of France completed its line to

Havre. That year saw a great improvement in the Islands' service, by the introduction of three new iron boats: the *Courier*, *Dispatch* and *Express*, built by Ditchburn and Mare, engined by Maudslay. On the 30th September, 1859, the *Express* struck a rock in Jailer Passage, near the Corbière Lighthouse, and became a total wreck.

The South Western Railway Company obtained powers in 1848 to own, maintain and work steam-vessels, but at first decided only to lease them. Two further steamers were the *Grand Turk* and the *Alliance*. The latter was built in 1855 on the Thames, with Seaward's engines of 857 I.H.P. She was fitted with compound oscillating engines in 1878, and not broken up until 1900. The following year, 1856, the *Havre* was acquired, on similar lines, but was wrecked near Guernsey in 1875.

In 1857 a Channel Islands' concern – the Weymouth and Channel Islands' Steam Packet Company – established a rival service, centred on Weymouth, which prompted the South Western Navigation Company to send its steamer the *Wonder*, referred to above, to work from and to Weymouth. In 1860 she reverted to the Southampton service.

By the London & South Western Railway Act, 1860, that company had its steamboat powers, given in 1848 for fourteen years, made perpetual and in August, 1862, it absorbed the Navigation Company entirely. In 1888 the Weymouth and Channel Islands' Steam Packet Company was bought by the Great Western Railway Company and the two railway companies thus became competitors for the Channel Islands' traffic. The conveyance of the mails remained, though, with the South Western. It may be mentioned that the Channel Islands' traffic was pooled between the two companies as from December, 1899.

Returning to the steamers: in 1860 the *Southampton* was obtained from Palmer's, of Jarrow-on-Tyne. She was 475 tons gross. Twenty years later she was lengthened and given new engines and boilers, and lasted until 1898.

Then followed two much larger boats: the *Normandy* in 1863, and *Brittany* in 1864, built by J. Ash and Company, on the Thames. The former was lost by collision in a fog on 17th, March 1870, thirty-three persons being drowned. A memorial to the gallantry of the crew on that occasion stands facing the entrance to the harbour at St Helier. Thirty-one survivors were saved by the steamer that ran into her. The *Brittany* continued work until 1900.

In 1865 a steamer named *Dumfries* was purchased to inaugurate a new service from Southampton to Honfleur. In 1867 the railway bought a French steamer named *Comet*, which they re-christened *Granville*, and began a service between Jersey, Granville, and St Malo. In 1870 two steamers called *Alice* and *Fanny*, which had been engaged in blockade-running during the American Civil War, were bought, and proved very useful, lasting until 1898 and 1890 respectively.

In 1871 the last paddle steamer for this service was purchased: the *Wolf*, which had been built eight years earlier by Napier. The *South Western*, built in 1874, was torpedoed in 1918.

In 1903 (June, 24th) Professor (afterwards Sir John H.) Biles read a paper on Cross-Channel steamers before the Institution of Naval Architects, in which there is the following interesting account of South Western boats:

The speeds are high in relation to the length and the vessels are, therefore, among the most interesting problems in modern naval architecture. The development may be seen by tracing the changes in any of the fleets. Take that of the London & South Western Railway with which the author (Professor Biles) has been most familiar. In 1889 the fastest vessel in this fleet was the *Dora*, of 1,114 tons displacement, on 10.1 feet moulded draught and 16½ knots speed, having engines which developed 2,250 i.h.p. on 109 revolutions. In 1890, three new vessels, the *Frederica*, *Lydia* and *Stella*, were built, for which the owners issued tenders for vessels having 17 knots speed, with natural draught, and 18 knots with forced draught. The vessels built obtained 19½ knots, on a six hours' trial, for 5,500 i.h.p. on 1,630 tons displacement, the engines running at 172 revolutions. The cost of each was about double that of the *Dora*.

Those vessels were succeeded in 1894 by two others – the *Columbia* and *Alma* – which obtained 19.3 knots for 3,750 i.h.p. on 1,350 tons displacement, the engines running at 190 r.p.m. With this change were introduced separate cabins, instead of open berths in the saloon, and also a much more minute system of subdivision. These vessels were built of much lighter scantlings, the total hull weight being 16 per cent lighter than in the earlier ships. Prolonged experience has shown that, arduous as the service is, the scantlings are quiet satisfactory. The later vessels have been of 19½ and 20 knots speed, with 4,500 i.h.p. and with increased accommodation and weight-carrying capacity. All these vessels have forced draught with closed stokeholds, the ratio of weight of machinery to i.h.p. being approximately 1 to 10; all except the *Frederica* type having four-cylinder triple expansion engines. It is interesting to note that none of these engines have water tube boilers, nor have any serious difficulties been experienced with the forced draught. These vessels have, in common with all channel steamers, to run for comparatively short distances and then to cease steaming. To that extent there is variation in the service of the boiler, though the rapid changes in speed of ships and the consequent comparatively sudden changes in the air pressure in the boilers, so common in Navy boilers, does not exist in these cases.

Readers who are familiar with the terribly dangerous nature of the approaches to the Channel Islands, will perhaps not be surprised at the number of ships which have been lost near there, generally in foggy weather. The *Stella* was wrecked on 30th March, 1899; running on the 'Black Rock', near the Casquets, in thick weather, the captain and 104 persons being drowned. On 18th, November 1905, the *Hilda*, on her way from Southampton to St Malo, struck a rock at the entrance to the latter harbour during a snowstorm, and rolled off into deep water. There was great loss of life; 128 persons were drowned, including the captain and every member but one of the crew.

Excluding four small cargo boats, there were in 1911 thirteen vessels: *Ella* (1881), *Laura* (1885), *Frederica* (1890), *Lydia* (1890), *Alma* (1894), *Columbia* (1894), *Vera* (1898), *Alberta* (1900), *Ada* (1905), *Bertha* (1905), *Princess Ena* (1906), *Caesarea* (1910), and *Sarnia* (1910). The *Alberta* was taken out of commission on 13th December, 1929, after having run 750,000 miles and having carried 700,000 passengers. One of the four small ones was a second *Normandy*, torpedoed in 1918.

Of the above the last three call for special mention. The *Princess Ena* was built by Messrs Gourlay Brothers. She was a twin-screw vessel of 1,198 tons with triple-expansion engines. Her builders launched her in less than four months from laying her down, and while the contract called for a speed of 16 knots, she often made 19 knots. She was destroyed by fire in August, 1935. The *Caesarea* and *Sarnia* – the Roman names for Jersey and Guernsey – were built by Cammell Laird, and fitted with turbine machinery of the usual type of that period. It consisted of three Parsons' reaction blading turbines, driving, as in the *Queen*, three shafts direct. The designed power for each vessel was 6,350 equivalent i.h.p. at 500 r.p.m., and that was exceeded on trials, when a speed of 20½ knots was obtained. Both vessels were 284ft long, with a beam of 39ft, and each carried 980 passengers.

The *Hantonia* and the *Normannia* followed in 1911. They were built by the Fairfield Shipbuilding and Engineering Company, and each was of 1,560 tons and fitted with geared steam turbines of the Parsons' type, of which use in passenger vessels the London & South Western company was the pioneer.

Four vessels in the L.S.W.R. fleet were, as was related in chapter XI, lost in the war. One of these was replaced in 1920 by the *Ardena*, built, in 1915, as a war vessel and known as the *Peony*. She was converted for her later use by the Caledon Steamship and Engineering Company; was a single screw, 263ft 4in long, with a beam of 33ft, and of a tonnage of 1,092.

In 1918 Messrs Denny sent out the *Lorina*, a geared turbine boat, 300ft long, a beam of 36ft, and tonnage of 1,504. For twelve months she was engaged in conveying troops across the Channel. She was reconditioned by the Caledon Company, and came to her intended owners in 1919.

XIV

The Isle of Wight Railways

THE first railway in the Island was the Cowes and Newport, which was incorporated in 1859, and opened on 16th June, 1862. It was only four and a half miles long, but was nevertheless very useful, as it connected the capital of the Island with the sea. In 1877 the company built Medina Wharf, near Cowes, where all the coal and heavy goods for the Island were landed. In 1887 it formed part of an amalgamated line, called the Isle of Wight Central Railway, which preserved its independence until 1923.

The Cowes & Newport Railway possessed three engines, afterwards 1, 2 and 3 on the I. of W.C.R. Two were named *Pioneer* and *Precursor*; built by Slaughter, Gruning and Co., of Bristol, in 1861, and scrapped in 1904. The third engine was a small front-coupled saddle tank, built in 1870 by Black, Hawthorne and Co. It worked for many years at shunting at the wharf, and later on with a twelve-wheel bogie coach bought from the Midland Railway, as a relief to a rail-motor, being sold in 1918.

The next line was the Isle of Wight Railway, running from Ryde (St John's Road) to Ventnor; incorporated 1860, opened to Shanklin, with a short branch from Brading to a quay, 23rd August, 1864; opened throughout, 10th September, 1866. This company was financially successful, and also lasted till the end.

It started with a stock of three engines built by Beyer, Peacock and Co. in 1864, named *Ryde*, *Sandown* and *Shanklin*; 2-4-0 inside cylinder tanks. A similar one, the *Ventnor*, was purchased in 1868, and another, named *Wroxall*, in 1872. In 1879 a rather more powerful one (*Brading*) was acquired from the same makers, and of the same type, and a still bigger one, called *Bonchurch*, in 1883. This last one, by the way, they managed to drop into the sea coming over. There was also a little saddle tank, with six coupled wheels of 3-ft diameter, built by Manning, Wardle and Co. in 1875, which they bought in 1882, named *Bembridge*, which went to Mesopotamia in 1917. Six of the engines were used for a time by the Southern Railway and numbered as follows:

Ryde W13	Ventnor W15	Brading W17
Shanklin W14	Wroxall W16	Bonchurch W18

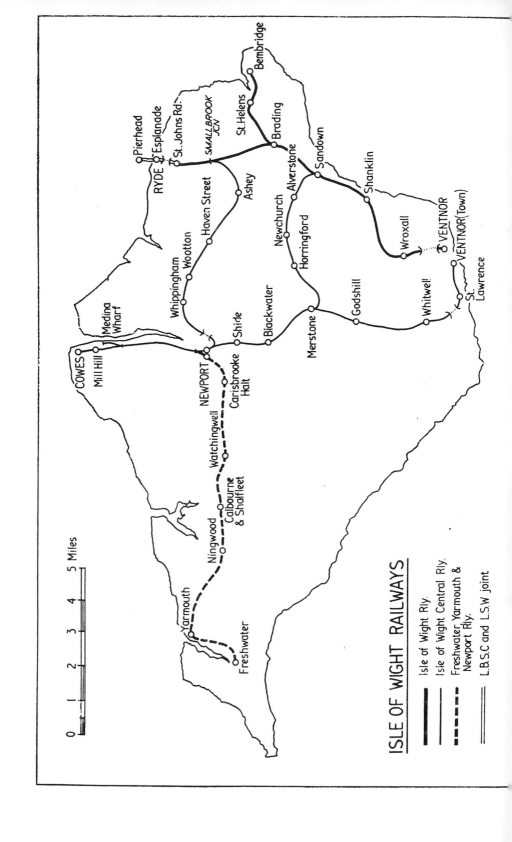

ISLE OF WIGHT RAILWAYS

Isle of Wight Rly.

Isle of Wight Central Rly.

Freshwater, Yarmouth & Newport Rly.

L.B.S.C and L.S.W joint

5 Miles

0 1 2 3 4 5

Pierhead
Esplanade
RYDE
St. Johns Rd.
SMALLBROOK JCN
St. Helens
Bembridge
Brading
Alverstone
Sandown
Shanklin
Wroxall
VENTNOR
VENTNOR (Town)
St. Lawrence
Whitwell
Godshill
Merstone
Horringford
Newchurch
Blackwater
Shide
Carisbrooke Halt
NEWPORT
Watchingwell
Calbourne & Shalfleet
Ningwood
Yarmouth
Freshwater
Mill Hill
COWES
Medina Wharf
Whippingham
Wootton
Haven Street
Ashey

The *Ventnor* was scrapped in 1925, after a life of 57 years, during which she ran 1,348,548 miles. The *Ryde* lasted till July, 1932, with a total mileage of 1,556,846.

In 1868 the Isle of Wight (Newport Junction) Railway was authorised to make a line from Sandown to Newport, a distance of nine miles. The first section, from Sandown to Horringford, was offered for the Board of Trade inspection in June, 1872; but Colonel Yolland raised very serious objection to the use of second-hand double-headed rails which had been turned and re-used by the South Western company, and then bought by the Newport Junction company, who shortened them and laid them on this section. The Colonel's report stated that quite a number were cracked at the ends, and the fish bolts were too short. A further inspection was made by Colonel Rich in August, 1874, the faulty rails having been replaced by flat-bottomed ones; but permission to open was still withheld on account of unfinished works. It was not until February of the following year that Colonel Rich reported that the line could be opened with safety. His inspection this time included the section from Horringford to Shide, which was pronounced satisfactory. The third section, Shide to Pan Lane, was offered to Colonel Hutchinson in August, 1875, and condemned, but was passed in the following October. The same Inspector declined to pass the last section, Pan Lane to Newport, in March, 1879, until certain faulty arrangements had been altered, and the line was not opened into Newport until 1st June, 1879. It fell into the hands of a Receiver that year; being taken into the Isle of Wight Central in 1887.

It only possessed one decrepit tank engine of its own, which had been originally built by R. and W. Hawthorn for the Whitehaven Junction Railway in 1861. It was a 2-2-2 inside cylinder well tank with outside frames, named *Newport*. It had been called *Queen Mab* earlier in its existence. Eventually it became No. 6 on the I. of W. Central Railway, and was broken up in 1895. Its efforts were supplemented by engines of the I. of W.R., and a tank with single driving wheels hired from the South Western (36 *Comet*).

The next undertaking was the Ryde & Newport Railway, which was sanctioned in 1872, and opened on 20th December, 1875. On completion, it was administered as a joint concern with the Cowes and Newport line, under an agreement dated 4th December, 1872.

Two engines were built for it in 1876 by Beyer, Peacock and Co.: 2-4-0 tanks with inside cylinders, named *Cowes* and *Osborne*, which became 4 and 5 on the 'Central', and W4 and W5 on the Southern.

The joint committee bought a 4-4-0 tank from the North London Railway in 1880, built by Slaughter, Gruning and Co. in 1861, which became No. 7 of the I. of W.C.R., and was scrapped in 1906.

We now come to an invasion of the Island by the Mainland railways. Passengers from the boats at Ryde Pier were taken to the station by a horse tramway. The London & South Western and London, Brighton & South Coast Railway, both much interested in the Isle of Wight traffic, and seeing that no improvement in this state of affairs was likely to be made unless they took a hand, obtained powers jointly to construct a new pier carrying a railway half a mile out to sea, and inland to connect the pier railway to the Island lines at St John's Road; which involved tunnelling under the Esplanade, and then rising at 1 in 50. It was opened on 12th July, 1880.

The original pier at Ryde was constructed under an Act of 1812, which incorporated the 'Ryde Pier Company'. In an Act of 1865 it is recited that by then a double line of tramway had been laid along the eastern side of the pier. It was worked at first by horses, and later by locomotives,* when a connection had been made via adjacent streets under the Act of 1865, with the Isle of Wight Railway at St John's Road. This connection was replaced by the joint line of 1880, mentioned above.

In 1874 a company called the Brading Harbour Improvement & Railway Company was incorporated for the construction of a line from Bembridge to Brading, where it joined the Isle of Wight company's Quay branch. This piece of line was opened on 27th May, 1882. Powers were also granted to make an embankment about a mile long from Bembridge to St Helens; the effect of which was to reclaim a considerable area of the harbour;† sluices being provided to control the outlet of the river Yar. The effect of these works was unsatisfactory, difficulty being experienced in keeping the harbour open, on account of the accumulation of silt. Further powers were obtained in 1896, which defined the harbour limits and permitted the company to improve the access thereto by dredging.

In early times the south-east corner of the Isle of Wight formed a separate island. In the year 1338 the construction of an embanked

---

* Experimentally in 1864 with a Manning Wardle, and in 1876 with a Merryweather, and regularly 1881–1886; then again by horses until electrified in March 1888; in 1927 motive power altered to petrol, with two Drewry cars, which are still at work.

† A train-ferry operated 1882–1888 from St. Helens on this branch, to Langston Harbour, Hayling Island.

causeway at Yar Bridge created the harbour of Brading, and had the effect of reclaiming a large area of land north-east of Sandown. Further reclamation work was carried out in the sixteenth century, which left the map of the Island practically the same as it is today.

So far, the western half of the Island was without any railways, but a line was authorised in 1881, called the Freshwater, Yarmouth & Newport Railway. Its route was altered in 1887 to allow Freshwater to be reached from Yarmouth in the opposite direction to that originally intended, which would have been from the westward. The line was inspected by Major-General Hutchinson (as he had become), who reported that, owing to incompleteness of works it must not be opened, and accordingly the Board of Trade ordered a postponement of one month. On 19th July, 1890, the opening was provisionally agreed to, but the line was not passed as finally satisfactory until the following December. Nearly all the concrete used was made of burnt clay, which made the Inspecting Officer rather anxious, and, in consequence, the company was asked to arrange for a careful watch to be kept on the structures. The railway was worked by the I. of W. Central until 1913, when it terminated the arrangement.* It then bought a saddle tank which had been built by Manning, Wardle and Co. in 1902, and one of the celebrated 'Terriers' from the L.B.S.C.R., which had been originally built at Brighton in 1876, and was No. 46 *Newington*; having been sold to the L.S.W.R. in 1903, who used it on the Lyme Regis branch, numbering it 734. These two engines, apart from a petrol rail motor, were the only ones the Freshwater line ever possessed. They finally became W1 and W2.

The last section of line constructed in the Island was the Newport, Godshill & St Lawrence Railway, which ran from Merstone on the Newport–Sandown line, through the places named, to Ventnor, where it arrived in 1900. It was worked by the Central Railway, and absorbed by the same in 1913.

The gradients in the Isle of Wight are severe, and impose very hard work on the locomotives. The following account of them has been taken from *The Railways of the Isle of Wight*, by P. C. Allen (Locomotive Publishing Co., 1928).

On the Isle of Wight Railway the line is only 9ft above sea level between Brading and Sandown, yet, 6½ miles farther on, at the mouth of the Ventnor tunnel, the line has risen 300ft; in this section of the line is the famous Apse

---

* This forced the F.Y.N.R. to build their own station at Newport (just on the Yarmouth side of the junction); from 1914 however some F.Y.N.R. trains again worked into Newport station proper, a reversal being necessary as the junction faced Cowes.

bank between Shanklin and Wroxall, where the line rises steadily for nearly 3 miles of 1 in 70. On the other lines gradients are even more severe. Between Ryde and Newport, on the Central line, there are stretches of 1 in 61 each side of Wootton, while between Whitwell and St Lawrence there are 1¾ miles of 1 in 55 falling towards St Lawrence, and sections of 1 in 55 and 1 in 56 between St Lawrence and Ventnor Town.

The steepest grade on the I.W.C.R. is, however, between Alverstone and Sandown, where the line rises for half a mile of 1 in 54 into Sandown Junction.

On the Freshwater, Yarmouth & Newport Railway, 1 in 66 is common, and there are stretches of 1 in 63 between Ningwood and Calbourne, near Watchingwell private station, and between Carisbrooke and Newport, while 1 in 64 is found at Wellow siding, near Yarmouth, and between Calbourne and Watchingwell. The most severe gradient in the whole island is, however, on the S.W.R. and L.B.S.C.R. joint metals, as this line had to make a very sudden drop in order to negotiate Ryde Esplanade, so that a descent of 1 in 50 is made from Ryde Esplanade station to the mouth of the tunnel.

We have still to deal with the locomotive history of the Isle of Wight Central Railway.

The first seven engines, taken over from the old companies, have already been described. In 1890 a new 4-4-0 tank was ordered from Black, Hawthorne and Co., and became No. 6; the old 6 being made a duplicate. No. 8 was a 2-4-0 from Beyer, Peacock and Co. in 1898.

The next additions were four 'Terriers':

9 (75 Blackwall,* 1872) 1899 11 (40 Brighton, 1878) 1902
10 (69 Peckham, 1874) 1900 12 (84 Crowborough, 1880) 1903

In 1906 a steam rail-motor was introduced, and numbered 1 in the place of the old Cowes and Newport engine. The locomotive part was sold in 1918.

In 1908 a 2-4-0 inside cylinder engine was bought from the Midland & South Western Junction Railway (built by Beyer, Peacock in 1882) and numbered 7 to replace the old North London engine.

In the following year an 0-4-4 tank was bought from the North Eastern Railway, and numbered 2. It was found too heavy, and was sold in 1917.

The engines of the Central line numbered from 4 to 12 at the time of the amalgamation kept the same numbers with the prefix W added.

The native engines of the Isle of Wight were mostly all soon replaced by locomotives from the Brighton & South Western railways, as set forth in the list on the following page.

They were named, in accordance with the Island custom. Nos. 1

---

* Previous writers have said that this engine was 74 *Shadwell*, but the records show that it was 75. No. 74 was renumbered 674 and sold, with 673, to the Edgehill Light Railway in June, 1920.

to 4 were Stroudley's Ei goods tank engines, the other six-coupled engines being Terriers.

ISLE OF WIGHT ENGINES, 1934

No.	Name	Wheels	Originally	
W 1	Medina	0-6-0	L.B.S.C.R.	136
2	Yarmouth	,,	,,	152
3	Ryde	,,	,,	154
4	Wroxall	,,	,,	131
8	Freshwater	,,	,,	46
9	Fishbourne	,,	,,	50, (650)
10	Cowes	,,	,,	69
11	Newport	,,	,,	40
12	Ventnor	,,	,,	84
13	Carisbrooke	,,	,,	77, (677)
14	Bembridge	,,	,,	78, (678)
17	Seaview	0-4-4	L.S.W.R.	208
18	Ningwood	,,	,,	220
19	Osborne	,,	,,	206
20	Shanklin	,,	,,	211
21	Sandown	,,	,,	205
22	Brading	,,	,,	215
23	Totland	,,	,,	188
24	Calbourne	,,	,,	209
25	Godshill	,,	,,	190
26	Whitwell	,,	,,	210
27	Merstone	,,	,,	184
28	Ashey	,,	,,	186
29	Alverstone	,,	,,	202
30	Shorwell	,,	,,	219
31	Chale	,,	,,	180
32	Bonchurch	,,	,,	226

NOTE: Since this text was written the Ei goods tanks and the 'Terriers' – which had worked on the island with Drummond chimneys in most cases and with enlarged bunkers – have been withdrawn. Services are now worked entirely by the 'O2' class 0-4-4T engines (also with enlarged bunkers), some of which are those mentioned above, but with many detail changes of names and numbers.

Mention must be made of the only two other possible alternative methods of arriving at the Isle of Wight, namely, burrowing under the sea, and flying through the air. On several occasions, the question of making a tunnel has been mooted. Test borings were made in the 'seventies. A few years before the 1914 war the subject was taken up again; Sir Blundell Maple being a prominent supporter of the scheme. Under the name of the 'South Western & Isle of Wight Junction Railway', a tunnel was to be made under the Solent from the Lymington branch of the L.S.W.R. to the F.Y.N.R. The last attempt to arouse interest in the scheme was after the amalgamation;

but the Southern Railway, having spent a great deal of money on new boats and pier reconstruction, did not encourage it; and the County Council and Chamber of Commerce vetoed it, chiefly owing to the cost.

In 1933 there was a certain amount of passenger traffic by air, and on 1st May, 1934, a service was inaugurated by Railway Air Services, in conjunction with Spartan Air Lines Limited. Passengers were conveyed from Imperial Airways, adjoining Victoria station, to Croydon Air Port by motor car, and thence by air to Cowes; the whole journey taking an hour and a half.

PART III

THE LONDON, BRIGHTON AND SOUTH COAST RAILWAY

Laval, No. 310, D2 class for mixed traffic work, 1876.   [*Locomotive Publishing Company*

Poplar, a member of the famous 'Terrier' class 0-6-0T, taken in 1880,   [*Locomotive Publishing Company*

One of the Stroudley D1 class tanks 0-4-2T, No. 269.   [*Locomotive Publishing Company*

A Stroudley C class 0-6-0 goods of 1874, shown here rebuilt and renumbered 416.

[*Locomotive Publishing Company*

B2 class 4-4-0, No. 206, *Smeaton* of 1897.

[*Locomotive Publishing Company*

R. Billinton's B4 class 4-4-0, No. 54, *Empress*, later *Princess Royal*, and here temporarily renamed *La France*.

[*Locomotive Publishing Company*

XV

The London and Brighton Railway

LIKE that of so many lines, the history of the Brighton Railway has to begin with William James. The first published proposals for a communication between London and Brighton by railway are contained in an essay of 1823, published by him. On the cover there is a drawing of the kind of locomotive which he proposed to employ, being, in fact, George Stephenson's colliery type of about 1816.

His line consisted of two portions running north and south, and another extending in a north-easterly direction all the way from Portsmouth to Rochester. The first section was to begin at the south end of Waterloo bridge, joining the Surrey Iron Railroad near Tooting, 'which being improved and altered to an Engine Rail-road, will be continued by Croydon to Mesterham' (i.e. Merstham), where the new line would begin again, and run down to a place called New Chapel, three miles north of East Grinstead, where it joined the Portsmouth line. The other section left the latter at a place called Holmbush, a little west of Crawley, and went nearly due south through Bramber to Shoreham, where it turned east along the coast about as far as Southwick, according to his map; but in the text he speaks of going to 'Brighthelmstone'. The Portsmouth line went through, or close to, Havant, Petworth, Horsham, Crawley, Edenbridge, passing about two miles south of Sevenoaks, straight to Strood.

These ideas were before their time, and seem to have attracted little attention.

Sir John Rennie now comes on the scene. He was the second son of the great engineer of the same name, who executed a vast number of canals, harbours, bridges, etc.; the most spectacular of his works being the Plymouth breakwater.

The son first learnt surveying under Francis Giles, and then began work on the Waterloo, Vauxhall and Southwark bridges under his father. On the death of the latter in 1821 he stepped into his shoes, and became the engineer for London Bridge, at the opening of which, in 1831, he was knighted. His autobiography, which is very interesting, was published in 1875.

When giving evidence before the House of Commons Committee in 1836, he said that he was first connected with a route to Brighton in the year 1825, when he was employed by a company called the Surrey, Sussex, Hants, Wilts & Somerset Railway Company. He selected two possible routes, one nearly the same as that which became known as the 'direct line', and was eventually adopted, and the other by Dorking, Horsham and Shoreham, which he afterwards gave up. He employed Vignoles to survey the latter route, which was to approach London by Wandsworth, to Nine Elms. He also employed a surveyor named Jago.*

This all-embracing company, the capital of which was only £650,000 for the immense tract of country which they proposed to cover, came to nothing. Rennie was employed by another company in 1829, but 'the public at that time were not at all prepared for a railroad', and the scheme lay dormant for a while, until 1833, when the subject was revived, and it was considered advisable to take the direct line, which was re-surveyed under Rennie's direction by Giles and others, and the plans were deposited in Parliament; but it was again abandoned. At the beginning of 1835 it was taken up once more.

In the meantime two other lines had been brought forward. One was by Vignoles, which was quite different to the one he had surveyed for Rennie. The other was promoted by Nicholas Wilcocks Cundy, who had surveyed one of the routes for a ship canal from London to Portsmouth, and was distinguished as a civil engineer. He designed the Pantheon in Oxford Street. His scheme was to leave London by the Southampton Railway, branching off at Wandsworth, and proceeding by Leatherhead, Dorking, Horsham and Shoreham. In December, 1834, the London & Brighton committee asked Robert Stephenson to decide which of the lines was in his opinion the best. He reported in favour of the general route taken by Cundy, but said that the actual line as laid down was useless, as it was full of errors. In the *Life of Robert Stephenson*, by Jeaffreson (vol. I, p. 223), it is said that Cundy had merely relied on the Ordnance maps. Whether this is correct or not, one cannot say, probably not. It is not quoted as a definite statement of Stephenson's.

The latter then drew out a line of his own, and entered the field as a competitor.

The fight that ensued was tremendous, and was of a different

---

* This, no doubt, is the explanation of the name 'Jago' sometimes found on the engine on Staffordshire pottery mugs. But the writer has never found evidence that Jago rose to any particular eminence, nor that there was ever an engine named after him.

character to the Parliamentary contests on previous occasions. With the earlier lines, by the time they had come to applying for an Act, the route had been settled, and the opposition they had to meet came from landowners who wished to stop the railway altogether, and the die-hards who said that the crops would not grow, nor the cows give milk, and so forth. In this case it was a regular scrimmage between five or six different sets of persons, all desirous of making the line.

A map shown on a little card issued by the South Eastern Railway – who were also in the field – shows five of the proposed lines clearly. It is dated February, 1837. On the back the advantages of the S.E.R. route are set forth. The writer also has a 'Report by Mr Gibbs' – the engineer of the Croydon Railway – which had a large folding map showing in addition an alternative line of his own going from Croydon to Betchworth and joining the one above at Capel. It also includes Vignoles' line, which went by Croydon and Merstham, then took a slightly westward slant, and went through the Shoreham gap. The South Eastern scheme to reach Brighton also appears, called Mr Palmer's line – he being the engineer – but it differs from the line of 1837 shown on the card, in that it runs from Lindfield to Clayton, thence closely parallel with Rennies'; the latter, by the way, not going by the line finally chosen, but passing through Hurstpierpoint and the Newtimber gap.

Herapath's *Railway Magazine* for April, 1836, gives the following account of the proceedings:

Probably no subject has so much occupied the attention of the rail-road public of late as the rival lines to Brighton. Not less than six were some time since in the field at once – one by Sir John Rennie, a second by Mr Vignoles, a third by Mr Cundy, a fourth by Mr Gibbs, a fifth by Mr Stephenson, and a sixth by Mr Palmer, to which might be added the wild whims of some others that hardly arrived to a name before they died.* At length the first two ceased to exist; Mr Cundy's, through sheer mismanagement, got hid under a cloud, and there only remained before the public the three last. Among these the fight was expected to be, when all at once Mr Palmer turned off from going to Brighton, to Dover, and left Messrs Stephenson and Gibbs to contend for the victory. Scarcely was this known to the public, before Mr Gibbs, owing to some irregularity or neglect, it is said, on the part of his subalterns, found himself so involved in dilemmas from non-compliance with the standing orders of Parliament, that his committee thought it needful to withdraw their intention of going for a Bill this session, and Sir John Rennie sprang up again to contest the point with Mr Stephenson. In this Bobbin-Joan sort of style it is that things have been going on with the Brighton lines, and such is the state in which they at present stand.

* Among the 'wild whims' there was Vallance's scheme, whose system was mentioned in Chapter V. He proposed to blow, or suck, the trains through a tunnel extending the whole way.

Cundy also bobbed up again, in conjunction with a man named Mills, and mingled in the fray when they went to Parliament in the session of 1837. The *Railway Magazine* for June, 1837, said:

Brighton Railways. These lines are still in Committee. A union has been formed between the direct Brighton, Rennie's, and the South Eastern Brighton. We sincerely wish they would all do so. Petition against petition has been presented by parties connected with one against the other, and now they are all got into 'Warburton's dissecting-room' or 'Railway cess-pool', as it is sometimes called, to have their subscription lists sifted. Near £300,000 has already been spent in the two sessions on these lines. Is Parliament doing right to permit such immense sums of private individuals' money to be squandered for merely obtaining their sanction, which is, after all, only a yes or no; and is as likely to be given to the worst as to the best line?

There was some tremendously hard hitting. On the two facts that Stephenson had seen Cundy's plans, and that his line went through the same part of the country, the latter's supporters based an accusation that he had stolen the plans, and only made deviations for the sake of appearances, such alterations, moreover, being all for the worse. Cundy's counsel said Stephenson was like a gipsy, 'who having purloined the child of another person, covers it with rags and dirt in order that he may pass it as his own, when he starts forward on his mendicant expedition'!

The absurdity of the suggestion that a man of Robert Stephenson's fine character would steal anyone's plans is manifest on the fact of it. With regard to the deviations, it is sufficient to say that his quantities, both of excavation and embankment, were less than half those of Cundy's line, although passing through the same country.

It may be remarked that the line afterwards made (in 1861) from near Horsham to Shoreham did not follow Stephenson's line exactly, but resembled it fairly closely.

On 13th May, 1837, it was reported to the House that Sir John Rennie's scheme was the most favoured. Lord George Lennox, the chairman of the committee, however, said that the committee stage had lasted 27 days and the average daily attendance of members was 20, but on the day on which the reports were to be considered they were honoured by the presence of 45 members, six of whom voted for Rennie's line, although that was the first day on which they had been present and they had not heard a particle of the evidence. He, therefore, moved an amendment to the effect that an Ordnance engineer be appointed to survey all four lines and report thereon. The amendment was carried by 164 votes to 157. The Home Office thereupon, on 2nd June, appointed Captain Robert Alderson, R.E. Meanwhile, on 13th June, Lord George Lennox informed the House that the promoters of the four schemes had united to put forward an agreed plan, and on the following day it was resolved to send that plan, with the four others, to Captain Alderson.

His report, which is very interesting, but too long to reproduce in full, was dated 27th June. It deals with Rennie's, Stephenson's, Gibbs' and the South Eastern – Cundy having retired from the field. Captain Alderson began by saying that he had no hesitation in stating that the line proposed by Stephenson, considered from an engineering point of view alone, was preferable to any of the others.

Availing himself of the valleys of the rivers Mole and Adur he avoids the heavy cuttings necessarily consequent on forcing a passage through the chalk ridges known as the North and South Downs; and, with the exception of two short tunnels, one at Epsom and the other at Dorking, arrives at Brighton, via Shoreham, having only such ordinary difficulties to contend against as are necessarily consequent on undertakings of a similar nature and extent.

As the towns passed through are of minor consequence, compared with Brighton, the termini become of paramount importance. At the London end,

each of the proposed lines avails itself of a terminus already constructed, or for which an Act of Parliament has been obtained. Mr Stephenson adopts the terminus of the London & Southampton Railway at Nine Elms, a little above Vauxhall Bridge, with a depot on the banks of the Thames, branching from this line at Wimbledon Common, five miles and a half from the terminus. The 'direct' line and Gibbs' adopt the Greenwich Railway terminus at London Bridge and avail themselves of railway communication already sanctioned and now constructing as far as Croydon. The South Eastern also has its terminus at London Bridge and, in addition to the Croydon, avails itself of 12 miles of the Dover railroad branching off at Oxted.

He decides that London Bridge is to be preferred, and mentions that the Greenwich Railway has sufficient ground to enable the line to be widened.

He then makes a curious remark. It is quite isolated, without any further reference to the subject:

There is still, however, an objection of some importance to any new line adopting either this or the Southampton terminus – the necessity of limiting the distance between its rails to that of the lines already laid down.

Did he consider the standard gauge too narrow? The subject is not mentioned once in the engineering evidence, but Sir John Rennie has stated elsewhere (Autobiography) that if the Liverpool & Manchester Railway had been given him to make, he would have adopted 5ft 6in. Evidently Captain Alderson had no inkling of the troubles with which a break of gauge was beset.

The result of a consideration of the various termini proposed at

Brighton – into the sites for which it is unnecessary to go – was that he preferred Rennie's, as being the most central.

The latter line was also the best as regards branches to Lewes, Shoreham and Newhaven. On the comparative merits as regards branches, he says:

> The Shoreham branch of the 'direct' line appears to be incomplete in not communicating with the wharfs like that to Newhaven. Stephenson's and Gibbs' lines give a communication with Shoreham, liable to the same objections as that of the 'direct' line, and in a greater degree, and altogether exclude Lewes and the port of Newhaven. The South Eastern gives a communication with Lewes and Newhaven but excludes Shoreham and has therefore a corresponding disadvantage in this respect to Stephenson's. Had this line, however, adopted the terminus of the 'direct' line in Brighton, with the addition of its branch to Shoreham, and been able to select a better route from Oxted it would, from having the smaller quantity of railroad to construct, have been the most desirable. On the other hand, had Stephenson's line more central termini and, instead of making the coast at Shoreham, proceeded direct to Brighton, it would have had strong claims to consideration and, if there were no other lines already constructed south from London, deserve a preference over all the others. Gibbs' line appears to unite the principal objection to the 'direct' line, viz. the extensive cutting at Merstham, with that of Stephenson's line in going round by Shoreham; and though it preserves a better gradient than the 'direct' line yet, from its circuitous route, works to less advantage than any of the others.

He proceeds to examine in detail the works necessary for the construction of the various lines, to the disadvantage of Rennie's, but ends this part of the report by saying:

> In comparing these objections, in an engineering point of view, with the advantages the 'direct' line possesses I am of opinion the latter are not too dearly purchased and that it is the best line between London and Brighton.

Now we see what the 'agreed plan' put forward by the four candidates was; the following extract being the conclusion of the report:

> It is proposed in this joint line that there should be two termini in London; one at London Bridge and the other at Nine Elms near Vauxhall; also two lines going south, one through the Valley of the Mole and the other through the Merstham Pass, meeting at or near Capel and from thence there should be one line for Brighton, via Shoreham, adopting at Brighton the terminus and branches of the 'direct' line.
>
> It is thus intended to construct between London and Brighton nearly seventy miles of railroad, independent also of using upwards of fourteen miles of railway constructed, and this, too, through a country possessing neither manufactories nor minerals and with no town on the line, excepting Croydon, of more than 5,000 inhabitants and which, therefore, must principally look for support from the towns of its termini, nearly fifty miles apart.
>
> In the present uncertain state of the return which railways will make for the capital expended and the absence of any great national advantages proposed to be obtained, I cannot think it advisable to venture on so great an outlay of capital or that the traffic is such between London and Brighton as to demand it.
>
> The Company proposing, therefore, as a part of their plan, to come to Croydon through the Merstham Pass to Earl's Wood Common, the distance from

thence to Brighton – twenty-nine miles – by the 'direct' line is all that is required to be constructed to render the communication complete between the two great termini; whereas, in the proposed joint line, nearly seventy instead of about forty-two miles of railroad will have to be constructed and maintained as well as a second terminus and depot, without any additional traffic except what may be afforded by the towns on the line.

Under these circumstances it appears to me that continuing the route proposed by the 'direct' line from Earl's Wood Common to Brighton is better for the interests of the Company and affords to the public all the accommodation required. I, therefore, adhere to the opinion already given in favour of the 'direct' line.

In the Patent Office Library there is a copy of a *Reply to Captain Alderson's Report*, by Robert Stephenson, 1837. He, of course, expresses disapproval of the 'direct line', and mentions that he had never advised the addition of a line to Lewes and Newhaven, although well aware that Parliamentary interest would have been gained by doing so, because he was satisfied that it would never pay the cost of its maintenance.

On 15th July, 1837, the Royal Assent was given to the proposals for the direct line by 7 Will. IV, c. 131. It was not only for a line from a junction with the London & Croydon Railway, near Croydon, to Brighton, but for branches to Shoreham, Lewes and Newhaven. Power was, in addition, given to purchase the Croydon, Merstham & Godstone Railway – see Chapter I – as its route was followed between Croydon and Merstham.

The following arrangement was entered into.*

Company	Directors	Shares	New for Old	
Stephenson's	7	11,000	11 ,,	10
Rennie's	5	11,000	11 ,,	16
South Eastern	5	6,600	1 ,,	2
Gibbs'	3	5,400	1 ,,	5
Mills' or Cundy's	—	2,000	1 ,,	5
	20	36,000		

The shares were £50 each. Why Stephenson's company, whose line had been rejected, should have done so well in the share-out, does not appear. It will be observed that Cundy was in at the death.

In the year 1836 the South Eastern Railway company was incorporated, with authority to build a line from the terminus of the London & Croydon Railway to Dover. By 1 Vic., c. 93 of the following year, it was altered to commence at the Jolly Sailor (Norwood Junction), pass to the east of the Croydon Railway, and through what is now East Croydon, through Godstone Road (Purley) and Oxted to

* Scrivenor's *Railways of the United Kingdom* (1849), p. 262.

Edenbridge. The Brighton line was also to commence at the Jolly Sailor.

Parliament appreciated that, for some distance south of the junctions with the London & Croydon, there would be two separate railways paralleling each other. It, therefore, related, by section 135 of the Brighton Act of 1837, that as 'by the abandonment of the parallel part of the line of the said South Eastern Railway much expenditure of money and much intersection of the country might be very advantageously avoided', the South Eastern might, within two years, divert its line so as to form a junction with the London & Brighton on, or to the north of, Earlswood Common and, further, to purchase that part of the Brighton line which lay between that junction and the junction with the London & Croydon, at cost price. The South Eastern accepted this advice, but in 1839, by 2 & 3 Vic., c. 91, the proposal was amended and the line between the two junctions was built jointly, the South Eastern contributing £327,334 towards the cost. The latter company, under the Brighton Act, could have bought the whole section but, to the advantage of both companies, the railway was divided; the South Eastern taking the southern end up to Coulsdon, and the Brighton the other part.

In this connection it may be observed that the report for the half-year ended 31st July, 1838, read at the meeting of the London and Croydon company on 6th September, 1838, said, in relation to the Brighton Railway:

> After a lapse of three years, during the greater part of which the proprietors of this company have encountered obstacles to a rapid progress of their works, arising out of the Brighton contest, the directors have now to congratulate the proprietors that the line to Brighton – more particularly that portion of it extending from Croydon Common to Merstham – which, by carrying the combined traffic of Surrey, Kent and Sussex, will give the whole traffic of the south and south-east to the Croydon Railway, is, at this time, in a state of active progress; the capital being ample and the company liable to no obstruction or discouragement, all opposition being thoroughly extinguished, there is no doubt that the works will be carried on with all the energy which has been directed within the last six months to the Croydon line.

The resident engineer for the London & Brighton Railway was John Urpeth Rastrick, of Stourbridge, whose previous connection with railway work had been of an extremely interesting, and quite unique character.

In 1808 he was a partner of John Hazeldine, of Bridgnorth, in an engine-making business. In that year they built the celebrated 'Catch me who can' for Trevithick, which was run in London on a circular railroad, carrying passengers at five shillings a ride. It was the third engine constructed to run on rails, and about the seventh or eighth self-moving machine in the world.

In 1816 he built a beautiful cast-iron bridge over the Wye at Chepstow, which is still in existence; and left Hazeldine and joined William Foster at Stourbridge. In 1822 he became engineer to the Stratford and Moreton Rail Road Company, a horse line of about 16 miles in length, between Stratford-on-Avon and Moreton-in-the-Marsh, which had been made by James.

In 1828 Foster and Rastrick constructed three locomotives which were sent to America; one, the *Stourbridge Lion*, was the first railway engine to turn a wheel in the Western Hemisphere; and in the following year built the *Agenoria* for the Shutt End Railway, which is now preserved at South Kensington. Another important employment at this time was to report – in conjunction with James Walker – on the question of fixed engines versus locomotives to the directors of the Liverpool & Manchester Railway. He was also one of the three judges at the Rainhill trials of 1829, and later became engineer to a great number of railways. He left the Brighton company in 1846, except for continuing to act as Consulting Engineer for one year; at the end of which he retired altogether from active work, dying in 1856. He lies in the cemetery at Brighton under a massive granite monument which overlooks the railway. No portrait of him is known to exist.

Returning to the railway, it left the Croydon line at a point about ½ mile south of the present Norwood Junction, and was 41 miles 59 chains long. There were five tunnels – Merstham, 1,831 yards; Balcombe, 1,141 yards; Haywards Heath, 249 yards; Clayton, 2,259 yards; and Patcham, 492 yards. The viaduct over the Ouse Valley was 1,475 ft long, with 37 semicircular arches, each of 30-ft span, and of an extreme height of 96ft.

Every effort was made to push forward the work. The strength employed was as follows:

	Men	Horses	Locomotives
July, 1839	4,769	570	—
Jan., 1840	4,370	695	5
July, 1840	6,206	960	5

In Erredge's *History of Brighthelmston* it is related that the first permanent rail of the line was laid on 4th February, 1839, at 'Hassocks' Gate', by Mr Alfred Morris.

The Brighton–Shoreham section was completed and opened first – on 12th May, 1840 – for which the engines were conveyed by sea; the line from the junction at Norwood to Haywards Heath was brought into use on 12th July, 1841, and thence to Brighton on 21st September, 1841.

The ruling gradient was 1 in 264, which is equivalent to a pull of 8½ lb per ton, and was considered to double the resistance exactly going uphill. There was, of course, the New Cross bank of 1 in 100 on the Croydon line which had to be negotiated. The gauge was laid ½in wide, namely 4ft 9in.

The exact cost is impossible to make out from the published accounts, because by the time the line had been fully completed other expenses were running, which were unconnected with the actual construction, but it was over two millions, or something like £40,000 per mile.

When the line was opened throughout, the fastest booked time was 1 hour 45 minutes. Return fares were: first class, 14s. 6d.; second, 9s. 6d.; children in second class, 6s. 6d. No mention of thirds.

For a number of years, how many it is impossible to ascertain, the tunnels were lit by gas. The gasworks adjacent to Hassocks Station were originally built for the purpose of lighting Clayton Tunnel. The *London & Brighton Railway Guide* (1841) thus describes Merstham Tunnel:

It is, as the other tunnels on this line are, whitewashed well throughout, and plentifully lighted with gas, which, though not of much value to the passenger (though, in him, it induces a feeling of confidence and cheerfulness), is, to the engine driver, of utmost moment, enabling him to see the road throughout as well almost as in broad day – so well, indeed, that any obstruction existing, which otherwise could not be observed, will by him be perceived and guarded against.

The first chairman of the London & Brighton Railway was John Harman. His reign lasted till June, 1843, when dissatisfaction on the part of the shareholders, which had been seething for some time, boiled over, and a completely new board was elected, the chairman at first being J. M. Parsons, and after a short time Rowland Hill, the Post Office reformer. He had been dismissed from the P.O. on a change of government, but returned there in 1846. During the three years' interval he devoted his energies to improving the position of the Brighton Railway. There is an interesting account of his experiences as a director in Chapter XIII of his 'Life', which is really an autobiography. He says:

The rigorous examination immediately set on foot showed the existence of practices now too well known in railway management, whereby the appearance of prosperity is maintained amidst progress towards real insolvency. Dividends had been paid when there were in fact no profits to divide, and meantime the resources of the Company were being drained and narrowed by waste, mismanagement, and inattention to public convenience. Distrust and dissatisfaction had gone so far that the value of the shares, originally £50, had fallen to £35.

By July, 1845, they had risen to £76.

One of the features of his policy was a strict enforcement of penalties on every discovered breach of a rule – whether any accident happened or not – on the principle that the amount of blame was nowise affected by the result. Another useful practice was to diffuse throughout the company's force full information as to the cause of accidents, wherever they might occur. For that purpose he had slips printed by one of the railway papers of all accounts of accidents, for distribution.

But the principal innovation due to Hill was the introduction of excursion trains. In his Autobiography he claims express trains also, but one 'express', i.e. a train stopping only once – at Croydon – was instituted right at the beginning, and was so called in the advertisements.

The first excursion train to Brighton was run on Easter Monday, 1844. It consisted of 45 carriages, drawn by four engines; at New Cross six more carriages and another engine were attached, and another six carriages and a sixth engine at Croydon. The train with its 57 coaches and six engines arrived at its destination at 1.30 p.m., after a journey of four and a half hours.

At the half-yearly meeting of the proprietors in February, 1845, it was announced that the company had increased the speed of its trains, and that the distance between London & Brighton was being covered in 90 minutes.

When the summer train service came into operation there were from London: a first-class only train at 10.30 a.m., and another at 5 p.m. which performed the journey in 1½ hours; first- and second-class at 9.30 a.m., 12 noon, 2.0 p.m., and 3.0 p.m., that ran in two hours, and an all classes at 7.40 a.m. and 6.30 p.m. which required 2½ hours. On Saturdays an additional first-class left at 4.0 p.m.

In 1844 the Brighton & Chichester Railway company was constituted to build a line from Shoreham to Chichester, and, under the same Act, to sell the undertaking to the London & Brighton company. The line was opened to Worthing on 24th November, 1845, to 'Arundel', now Ford Junction, on 16th March, 1846, and to Chichester on 8th June of the same year.

One of the works on this line which is worthy of mention is the drawbridge over the river Arun immediately on the London side of Ford Junction station and between there and the actual junction, from the Portsmouth direction, for Littlehampton. (The bridge recently reconstructed as a 'fixed' bridge was not the structure provided when the line from Shoreham was opened.) It was described in *Our Iron Roads*, by F. S. Williams (1852), in the following words:

> There is a kind of bridge on the South Coast Railway which is worthy of notice. It is over the Arun, below Arundel, and is the first of its kind. At this point the Company was bound to leave a clear waterway of sixty feet for the passage of shipping, and this had to be accomplished by a contrivance called a telescope bridge. The rails, for a length of 144ft, are laid upon a massive timber platform, strengthened with iron, and trussed by means of rods, extending from its extremities to the top of a strong framework of timber, rising 34ft above the level of the roadway in the middle of the platform, the frame-work being ornamented so as to appear like an arch. Beneath this central framework and one-half of the platform are mounted 18 wheels, upon which the whole structure may be moved backwards and forwards, so as to be either clear of the river, or to project its unsupported half across it, to form a bridge for the passage of trains. To provide for moving this platform, when it is necessary to open the waterway, a second portion of the railway, 63ft long, is laid upon a moveable platform, which may be pushed aside laterally, while the end of the larger platform is pushed longitudinally into its place. Two men and a boy are able to open this bridge in about five minutes, the operation being performed by toothed wheels and racks, wrought by winches.

Under the same Act, a road from the town of Arundel to the station at Ford Junction was constructed by the company; a distance of 1¾ miles. The following year (1845), an extension of the line to Portsmouth was sanctioned.

Although the London & Brighton company had powers to build branches to Lewes and Newhaven as well as to Shoreham, only the last was constructed at the time. It was left to the Brighton, Lewes & Hastings company in 1844, by 7 & 8 Vic., c. 91, to secure the authority that actually enabled the line between Brighton and Lewes to be made, and under the same Act the property was sold to the London & Brighton. It was opened to Lewes on 8th June, 1846, and on to St Leonards (West Marina) on the 27th of the same month. Access to Hastings itself did not come until 13th February, 1851, over a line made by the South Eastern.

On 27th July, 1846, the Royal Assent was given to an Act which amalgamated the London & Croydon and the London & Brighton, under the name London, Brighton & South Coast Railway.

Within a fortnight of the opening to Brighton there was, on 2nd October, 1841, a derailment in Copyhold Cutting just north of Hayward's Heath, in which four passengers and two of the company's servants were killed, which is of some historical importance, since it occasioned a great controversy as to the comparative safety of four-

and six-wheeled engines, and a Board of Trade enquiry was held to investigate the subject – without, however, coming to any definite conclusion, one way or the other.

The train engine had six wheels, and there was a four-wheeled engine as pilot, which ran off the line. The road was, of course, newly laid, and there had been a large quantity of rain, and there is little doubt that it gave way under the weight of the two engines, which appear to have been travelling at over thirty miles an hour, although a watchman had been posted to warn them to reduce speed.

William Lucas, the writer of *A Quaker Journal*, from which some remarks were quoted at the end of Chapter VI, was in the accident, of which he gives a graphic account. His party felt very little of the concussion, although they were in the first carriage that was not thrown off the line. He says they were going at a terrific rate.

The jury returned a verdict of accidental death, but added that in their opinion the four-wheeled engines used on this line were not of a safe construction, and recommended their discontinuance.

The Board of Trade, however, were not so sure. They issued a circular letter to the principal railway companies asking how many four-wheeled and how many six-wheeled engines were in use. The replies showed that, with a total of 1,330½ miles open on 1st January, 1841, there were 224 of the former and 605 of the latter. The conclusion of the Board of Trade was:

> From the returns made by the different railway companies it will appear that a very general opinion is entertained that four-wheeled engines are rather more unsteady and subject to oscillatory movements and especially to vertical movements, which, in extreme cases, may lead to jumping off the rails, while, on the other hand, six-wheeled engines are thought to be less adapted for going round sharp curves; and if constructed with outside bearings which are generally used with this description of engine, to be more liable to fracture their axles than four-wheeled engines with inside bearings.

> The fact that the two railways which, in proportion to their amount of passenger traffic, have been perhaps more free from serious accidents, viz. the London and Birmingham and the Grand Junction, use, in the one case, four-wheeled and, in the other, six-wheeled engines exclusively, appears quite sufficient to show that any attempt at legislative interference to enforce the adoption of any peculiar construction would be, in the present state of experience on the subject, altogether misplaced.

On the 9th October, 1841, an advertisement appeared in the *Railway Times*, announcing that the express train would take a quarter of an hour longer on the road, and that, 'in deference to the recommendation of the jury at Haywards Heath on the 4th inst. the Directors have issued orders that no four-wheeled engines be used on the line, and they have also ordered that a LUGGAGE VAN be placed between the tender and the first passenger carriage in each train'.

It may be remarked that in the appalling accident at Versailles in 1842 – almost the worst that has ever occurred – there was the same combination of a four-wheeled engine in front of a six, and a similar controversy raged on the other side of the Channel.

The writer has a copy of *Regulations for observance by officers and servants of the London & Brighton Railway Company, 1845*. It gives three colours for signal lamps (green for caution) and three semaphore positions. Detonating fog signals were in use (Cowper's). There was a code of lamps differentiating between Brighton, Croydon & Dover trains. Every train passing through the long tunnels was to carry two red tail lights. A red tailboard by day, or a third red lamp at night, indicated that a special or extra train would follow.

The stop signal was to be maintained for five minutes after a train had passed; here there is a footnote to the effect that the interval was three minutes only on the Croydon line. In the event of an accident the guard was to proceed half a mile from the train to warn a following one. Regulation 20 is curious:

> When necessary to stop a Train from any obstruction on the Line, or other cause, the Engineman shall give a tremulous sound of the Whistle as a Signal for the Guard to apply the Brakes; and should the Guard wish to attract the attention of the Engineman, he must do so by suddenly and repeatedly checking the Train by means of his Brake.

The foreman of platelayers was to inspect, tighten up keys, etc., all over his district not less than twice each day. In slippery weather the platelayers were to sand the rails, heaps being provided at short distances all along the line for that purpose.

XVI

The London, Brighton and South Coast down to 1860

THE line from Croydon to Epsom via Sutton, which as mentioned in Chapter V, was to have been on the atmospheric principle, was completed as a steam line, and opened on 10th May, 1847. The extension of the coast line from Havant to Portsmouth, the last $4\frac{1}{2}$ miles of which were jointly owned with the South Western, was opened on 14th July, 1847.

In 1845, by 8 & 9 Vic., c. 52, the Brighton, Lewes & Hastings company was granted authority to build the Keymer branch, which joined the London–Brighton main line at Wivelsfield to the Brighton–Lewes–Hastings at Lewes, and gave Lewes and St Leonards direct access to London. The branch was opened on 2nd October, 1847. In 1845, by 8 & 9 Vic., c. 200, an extension from Hastings to Rye and Ashford was sanctioned, but this line was transferred to the South Eastern. The London & Brighton, in 1845, was also authorised to build a branch from its main line at Three Bridges to Horsham, which was brought into use of 14th February, 1848. Three branches off the Lewes–Hastings line were authorised in 1846. They were: (1) To Newhaven, opened on 8th December, 1847; (2) to Hailsham and (3) to Eastbourne, both the latter being brought into use on 14th May, 1849.

Under 9 & 10 Vic., c. 234, of 1846, the London & Croydon obtained powers to make the Deptford branch, which was opened on 2nd July, 1849. It was from New Cross, crossed the Surrey Canal by a lift bridge and went to Deptford Wharf on the Thames, where the riverside dock had a frontage of 400ft and the inner dock a length of 500ft. It adjoined the Government Arsenal at Deptford.

In the same session as that just mentioned, 9 & 10 Vic., c. 281, the London & Brighton obtained powers to make the Wandsworth branch, as it was called, from Croydon. It was intended to join the South Western at Wandsworth, near the present Earlsfield station, in order, it would appear, to run into Waterloo; a *quid pro quo* for the joint ownership at Portsmouth. A remark made by Mr Chaplin, the

L.S.W.R. chairman, at the opening of the Waterloo terminus on 11th July, 1848, probably refers to this intention, as follows:

We have placed on the railway four distinct lines of way in order that we may have no trouble or inconvenience in the future with the traffic, be it what it may, but ability to let others come and hire, that we may benefit by our enterprise and industry on our property.

This forecast is interesting, in view of the fact that on this section today there are eight lines, solely carrying the traffic of the former South Western system, and there is considerable difficulty in working it conveniently.

The Wandsworth branch was never constructed, and it was not until March, 1858, that the London, Brighton & South Coast reached the South Western line, and even today there is no direct access from the Brighton lines towards Waterloo.

Mr C. P. Grenfell was the first chairman of the London, Brighton & South Coast Railway, and was succeeded in 1848 by Samuel Laing, then the Law Clerk in the Railway Department of the Board of Trade. The first secretary was T. J. Buckton, who was followed, in October, 1849, by F. Slight. Peter Clarke, who was originally a 'creature' of George Hudson, and came from the Leeds & Selby after the Railway King's collapse, was the first manager, and R. Jacomb-Hood the first resident engineer. The last-named, whose father had added the name of Hood to the original Jacomb, was destined to be connected with the company for fifty-four years and then to die in its service. His diary, which runs from 1822 to 1894, has been very kindly lent to the writer by Mr S. Jacomb-Hood, one of his sons, and has furnished much valuable information. The following entries are of interest:

8th February, 1847. Returning to Brighton from Board at London Bridge by 5 p.m. express, was snowed up below Three Bridges. Passed the night in train. With four engines and all men available, got through to Brighton by 1.20 p.m. on the 9th.

May, 1847. Atmospheric line from New Cross to Croydon condemned. Taken up and converted to a locomotive line by 19th August.

2nd October, 1847. Company in financial difficulties; orders given to stop all new works in progress and to reduce wages.

28th December, 1847. Received notice to leave and ordered to give notice to whole staff, with a view to general reduction.

3rd January, 1848. Sent in resignation, which was accepted.

18th March, 1848. Reappointed engineer.

Works gradually resumed in the summer after the financial disturbance.

In the meantime, on 14th February, great dissatisfaction was expressed at the general meeting, when the results of the previous half-year were submitted, and a committee of seven shareholders was

R. Billinton E4 class 0-6-2T, No. 514 of 1901, *Barcombe*, with a block train of suburban stock when new, about 1906.   [*Locomotive Publishing Company*

Reboilered 'Gladstone' 0-4-2, No. 197, on the "Sunny South Express", comprising L.N.W.R. stock, near Balham.

L.B.S.C. 'balloon' type railmotor car, working with two standard coaches and a D1 class 0-4-2T.

[*H. Gordon Tidey*

H1 class 4-4-2, No. 40, on the four-car "Southern Belle" passing Balham Intermediate box.

An I3 Class 4-4-2T No. 22 on the "Southern Belle" near Streatham Common.　　　[*E. R. Wethersett*

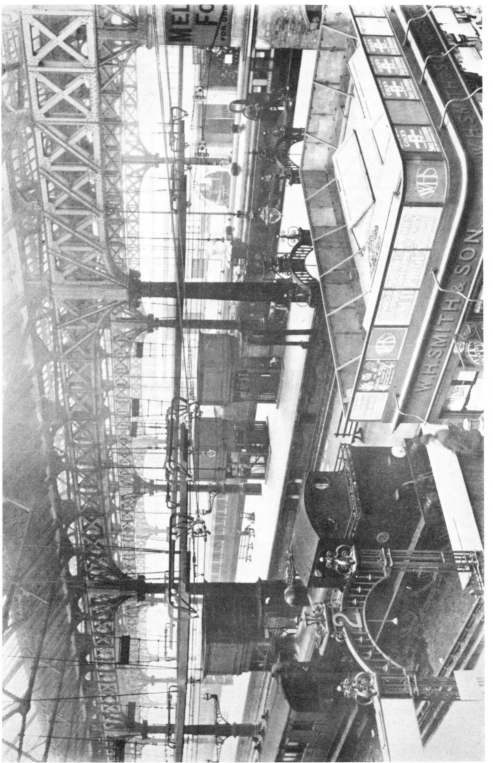

Victoria Station in its rebuilt form with an E5 class radial tank in the foreground, and a Marsh 'Atlantic' on the right. Notice the catenary

appointed to investigate; strong complaints being made of Peter Clarke's administration.

The committee reported to a special meeting on 17th April, 1848. The document in question is of interest today, as it showed the rates of expenditure to receipts of three of the companies in which the present readers are interested; also that of the Eastern Counties – later the Great Eastern. The figures were:

	1845	1846	1847	*Average*
London & South Western	38.49	39.11	42.75	38.78
London & Brighton	28.11	31.55	39.39	33.01
South Eastern	32.46	29.39	28.62	30.15
Eastern Counties	38.88	34.98	36.26	36.70

As to Peter Clarke, the report observed:

While fully admitting his abilities and knowledge of railway business, we are nevertheless of the opinion that there should be an efficient head of each department, who should be immediately responsible to the directors, and that it is undesirable that any one servant should interfere with the management of every other department, thereby destroying the responsibility of the officers so interfered with and impairing the efficiency of the Board itself.

The chairman entered into a spirited defence of Clarke, who, however, solved the difficulty by resigning soon afterwards, being succeeded by George Hawkins.

In July, 1849, the Willow Walk goods depot was opened, adjoining the Bricklayers' Arms station on the north side. The origin of the latter was dealt with in Chapter IV.

The encouragement given to London business men to reside in Brighton was always one of the main features in the policy of the London, Brighton & South Coast company. In that relation the chairman mentioned at the half-yearly meeting on 24th January, 1851, that a train was running from Brighton to London Bridge which performed the journey in 1 hour 15 minutes and arrived at 10.0 a.m. It returned to Brighton at 5.0 p.m., and was said to run with such punctuality that a man could set his watch by it.

The year 1851 was a happy one for the Brighton & South Coast company. The new terminus at London Bridge was completed; there was a huge traffic to and from London for the Great Exhibition, and it was intended to remove Paxton's remarkable masterpiece to Sydenham, to become the well-known Crystal Palace. The 1851 Exhibition led to a better service of boats on the Newhaven–Dieppe route, which brought in the greater part of the £42,000 increase, as compared with those of 1850, in passenger receipts. It may be remarked that there was no apparent extra traffic until low fares were instituted.

For the opening of the Crystal Palace in 1852 a new station was required at Sydenham, and on 10th June, 1854, a branch authorised in 1853, was opened from Sydenham to the Crystal Palace. At the half-yearly meeting on 27th July, 1854, Mr Laing gave a great account of the traffic that was being carried. He said they were having a 'Derby Day' traffic every day and taking 10,000 people, and often more, to the Crystal Palace and back.

About the year 1851 there were several independent schemes for railways in that part of the London area which lay between the South Western and the Brighton lines. One was a proposal for a railway from Wandsworth, near the present Clapham Junction, to Croydon. It reached the committee stage in the House of Commons in 1852, where it was opposed by the two companies named and withdrawn on their undertaking that if a Wimbledon–Mitcham–Croydon line were built the two companies would work it. An agreement to that effect was approved by the boards of the companies, and was confirmed by the Brighton shareholders but rejected by the South Western. The line was, however, authorised in 1853, and the route followed the line of the old Surrey Iron Railway for some distance. It was opened on 22nd October, 1855, and was at first worked by Mr G. P. Bidder, but in 1856 was leased to the London, Brighton & South Coast and acquired by that company in 1858, subsequently being vested in a joint committee of the South Western and Brighton companies by 29 & 30 Vic., c. 281 (1866).

As early as 1851 proposals were made which might have resulted in the formation of the Southern Railway. The idea of amalgamation, which had been under discussion, was postponed in consequence of a committee being appointed in December, 1852, over which Mr Cardwell presided, to consider the principle of the amalgamation of railways, and of canals with railways.

The L.B.S.C.R. half-yearly report for January–June, 1853, said:

The directors continue strongly of the opinion that a complete union of the three companies (L.B.S.C.R., L.S.W.R., and S.E.R.) on equitable terms would be a measure most conducive to the safety and convenience of the public as well as most beneficial to the proprietors. They will, therefore, be prepared to renew the negotiations, both with the London & South Western and South Eastern, at the first favourable opportunity.

Jacomb-Hood's diary records that he was much occupied during 1853 in promoting the Weald of Sussex Railway (Horsham to Midhurst). The name was afterwards changed to Mid-Sussex.

The year 1853 saw the commencement of one of the most important developments in the history of the London, Brighton & South Coast

Railway, namely, its entrance into the West End of London, eventually to Victoria Station. A 'West End of London and Crystal Palace' company received powers in 1853 to build a railway from the South Western line at Wandsworth to the Crystal Palace, with a branch to the London, Brighton & South Coast at Norwood and another branch to near Chelsea suspension bridge, together with a wharf and pier on the south side of the river Thames. An agreement was made with the London, Brighton & South Coast, which company's report for July–December, 1853, said that there was a necessity for a terminus in the West End. That report further remarked that a junction could be made with the London & South Western, the trains using Waterloo terminus. Negotiations towards that end were begun and the L.S.W.R. agreed to join in the promotion of a bill for that purpose. The idea, however, was not popular, so the London & South Western, on the ground that it could not accommodate the traffic, withdrew from the scheme in 1855.

The line from the Crystal Palace to Wandsworth Common was opened on 1st December, 1856, and thence to Battersea Wharf on 29th March, 1858. The former section included a considerable tunnel in clay. The junction line between the Croydon main line at Norwood Junction and the Crystal Palace station was brought into use on 1st October, 1857. The West End and Crystal Palace line was leased in 1858 and purchased in 1859, except for an extension to Farnborough, Kent, which went to the London, Chatham & Dover in 1860.

A still more important phase was entered upon in 1858, when the Victoria Station and Pimlico Railway was sanctioned, which was to join the West End and Crystal Palace Railway near the Battersea terminus and carry it across the river Thames into a general station 'near Victoria Street, Pimlico'. Sir John Fowler was the engineer. The first stone of the bridge over the Thames was laid on 9th June, 1859, and the first locomotive crossed on the same day of 1860. There was some delay owing to a dispute with the Board of Trade, and the line was not opened until 1st October, 1860.

The London, Brighton & South Coast subscribed half the capital and was entitled to one half of the station. Under an agreement, confirmed by Parliament in 1861, the other half was leased to the London, Chatham & Dover, and the Great Western jointly. For the benefit of the last-named company mixed gauge lines were laid.

The booking of passengers to the seaside at cheap rates was always a prominent part of the Brighton company's policy. Speaking on that subject, Laing observed at the half-yearly meeting on 26th January, 1854:

> He would refer shortly to the excursion system, upon which the line depended so much for its prosperity. It was a bold experiment to take people from London to Brighton and back at 3s. 6d. a head. This experiment had, however, been completely successful, and the best evidence which could be afforded of its success was given by Sir Richard Mayne, the chief constable of the Metropolitan Police, who, on being examined before the committee of the House of Commons which sat to investigate crime in the Metropolis said it was a positive fact that since the system of excursion trains had been carried out to such an extent crime had, to his own personal knowledge, very greatly diminished.

A possible explanation of this curious phenomenon is that the thieves took advantage of the cheap tickets, and pursued their avocation farther afield.

The East Grinstead Railway was built by an independent company under powers given in 1853, and ran from Three Bridges. It was opened on 9th July, 1855, and in 1878 was acquired by the London, Brighton & South Coast.

The report for the half-year July–December, 1857, said that the whole line between London and Brighton had been relaid and provided with fish-plates* and that the timbers, where necessary, had been replaced by creosoted sleepers. At the next half-yearly meeting it was observed that since 1854, when London Bridge station was last enlarged, the number of passengers, including season-ticket holders, had risen from 5,187,348 to 6,062,716 in 1857.

Mr Laing, having received an appointment in India, resigned the chairmanship in April, 1855, and was succeeded therein by Mr Leo Schuster.

The Lewes and Uckfield was, like the East Grinstead, built by an independent company. The powers were given in 1857 and the line was brought into use on 11th October, 1858; the opening being celebrated by a public dinner at Uckfield. It was purchased by the Brighton & South Coast in 1864, who obtained powers in the same year to construct the Lewes and Uckfield Junction line, 3 miles 44 chains long, to the eastward of, and nearly parallel with the Keymer branch, which enabled trains from Uckfield to enter Lewes from the opposite direction, thus avoiding Lewes tunnel. It was opened on 3rd August, 1868; 2 miles 31 chains of the old line being put out of use.

---

* Fish-plates were patented by W. B. Adams and R. Richardson in 1847. Before their introduction the ends of adjacent rails were supported in a special joint-chair. At first they were only used as wedges. The earliest bolted ones were applied on the Eastern Counties Railway by J. Samuel, at the beginning of 1849.

The Epsom and Leatherhead line was sanctioned in 1856 and opened on 1st February, 1859. There was a question whether it should be acquired by the South Western or the Brighton & South Coast, but under an Act passed in 1860 the former company took it. It was, however, jointly worked and, until the establishment of the Southern Railway, was administered by an Epsom and Leatherhead Joint Committee, as was also an extension authorised by the South Western Act of 1864, from the terminus at Leatherhead to the river Mole, where a junction was formed with the Brighton company's Leatherhead–Dorking line, authorised in 1863. It is mentioned here because it was part of the Brighton company's route to Portsmouth.

The Mid-Sussex company was authorised in 1857 to build a line from Horsham to Pulborough and Petworth. The line was brought into use on 10th October, 1859, and was acquired in 1862.

The Working Time-table dated February, 1858, shows that the practice of slipping carriages was adopted on 1st February of that year, with a coach slipped at Haywards Heath off the 4 p.m. express from London to Brighton. This appears to have been the introduction of the practice; the Great Western following at the end of the year.

F. D. Banister was made resident engineer in place of R. Jacomb-Hood – who had resigned, and later on became a director – on 3rd December, 1860. Banister was to hold that office for thirty-five years.

Coming to the subject of accidents, on 24th August, 1846, there was a collision at Pevensey. A passenger train from Brighton to Hastings ran into a train of ballast wagons which was standing in a siding; the points not having been changed. There were no deaths, but a number of passengers were injured.

On 6th June, 1851, a passenger train, with the engine running tender first, was going down a steep incline between Falmer and Lewes, where it was usual to descend with steam shut off and the hand-brake applied. About half-way down there is a bridge, known as the Newmarket Arch, over an occupation road. When the train was within about 80 yards of the arch, the tender and engine suddenly left the rails, and bearing to the right, passed over the up line to the south side of the railway, and, forcing down the parapet wall, fell with a tremendous crash into the road beneath, a depth of 25ft, dragging a second and third-class carriage with it. Three passengers and the fireman were killed on the spot, the driver dying three days later. The accident was attributed to a local boy having wilfully placed a sleeper across the outer rail on the north side of the down line. The case not being proved, the boy was acquitted, but, re-markable to relate, one year later, exactly to a day, he was killed within a short distance of the spot.

On 27th November, 1851, a passenger train collided with a cattle train at the drawbridge over the river Arun, near Ford station, and went over the embankment. Two passengers and the fireman of their train were injured, the latter so severely that he died a few days afterwards. The driver of the cattle train jumped into the river to save himself, and the other driver, to whose negligence in disregarding the signals the accident was due, attempted to commit suicide by cutting his throat; but failing to accomplish this, he leapt into the river, out of which he was dragged by the guard.

A derailment at some facing points at London Bridge on 1st May, 1857, caused the death of one passenger and injuries to four others.

On 3rd October, 1859, a remarkable explosion occurred. A heavy goods train drawn by a 'long boiler' engine, consisting of 45 loaded wagons, was proceeding up the heavy bank of 1 in 80 from Lewes to Falmer, assisted at the rear by another engine, when the firebox suddenly blew up. The driver and fireman were both thrown a con-siderable distance ahead, sustaining severe injuries, from which the former did not recover. The explosion bent the rails down where it occurred. Next to the engine was a wagon loaded with hops, and behind that a cattle truck truck containing two cows. This truck was forced over the hop wagon and on to the leading engine, by the propulsion of the engine in the rear. When the truck was lowered down and the cows taken out, they quietly began to graze on the embankment, not a bit the worse for their adventure.

It is due to the London, Brighton & South Coast company that at this early stage in its history it should be said that it always was pre-eminent in the adoption of safety appliances. The originator of the semaphores in railway signalling, Charles Hutton Gregory, speaking at the Institution of Civil Engineers on a paper *The Fixed Signals on Railways*, read by R. C. Rapier on 31st March, 1874, said:

He was engaged as resident engineer on the Croydon Railway and was actively employed in the mechanical details of railway working. During that time mechanical inventions were introduced by very slow degrees, and while the period of the first introduction of the semaphore was correctly fixed (by Mr Rapier) at the end of 1841 or the beginning of 1842, and its use was soon extended from the Croydon railway to the Brighton and the South Eastern railways, it was some time before it was adopted into general use. The Brighton railway was opened from Croydon to Haywards Heath in 1841, but it was not till the summer of 1844 that a double semaphore with signal-locking apparatus was put up at the Brighton junction, a few months after the erection of the Bricklayers' Arms Junction signals (by Mr Gregory in 1843). The arrangements at the

Brighton junction, as well as at the Greenwich and Croydon junctions, were, at first, of the simplest character. A signalman, with two flags by day and hand-lamps by night, worked the whole of the traffic, which, as far as the Greenwich junction was concerned, was a very large one. In order to show that such simplicity of working was not only adopted by railway companies but met with the approval of the Government authorities of the day, he quoted a short extract from the report of Sir Frederick Smith, relating to the opening of the Brighton railway dated 10th July, 1841: 'The points of junctions with the Croydon and Greenwich lines are also matters of some anxiety; for, unlike the ordinary junction of other railways, these occur where there are no stations and consequently the safety of the traveller depends mainly on the switchman at each place. . . . The selection of good men and good administration were considered the best safeguard, rather than the introduction of new mechanical appliances.' To show the correctness of Sir Frederick Smith's judgment it might be stated that for a long period, from 150 to 200 trains per day passed the Greenwich junction without the slightest accident.

As early as the half-yearly report for July–December, 1851, it was observed:

> The experience of the past year has impressed upon the directors the importance of directing a thorough and minute investigation at every point of the line, with a view to ascertain whether any additional securities could be introduced for the prevention of accidents. The result has been the commendation, in a joint report from the resident engineer and the superintendents of the traffic and locomotive departments, of several works, consisting mainly of fresh sidings, crossings and signals; extension of the electric telegraph; check rails at curves; extensions of platforms and improved arrangements at stations and the erection of cottages for such servants as switchmen and signalmen whose duties required them to live in the immediate vicinity of the lines.

Eighteen months later – on 25th July, 1853 – the chairman at the then half-yearly meeting said:

> The goods trains were much longer than when they (the railways) were originally constructed and were too long for the sidings originally intended for them. A strong recommendation was made to the directors that the sidings should be so enlarged as to admit the goods trains in their increased proportions. The directors therefore gave orders to the locomotive superintendent to go all over the line with a view to ascertain what steps might be taken to remedy the evil pointed out. The directors had thus a duty to the public to discharge as well as to the shareholders, but it would not do for them to allow themselves to be shot at with verdicts of manslaughter, on the ground that they had not taken the necessary precautions. Additional sidings were costly, but the directors were bound to study the safety of the public and therefore they had felt it right to incur an expense in extending the sidings.

The Brighton & South Coast Railway was closely identified with John Saxby and John Stinson Farmer, who, about 1860, founded the world-renowned firm of signal engineers called by their names, now the Westinghouse Brake and Saxby Signal Co. The former was in the engineer's department and the latter in the traffic department.

Jacomb-Hood's appointment ceased at the end of 1860. He records that in November, 1863, 'Bidder and self took Brighton Company's engineering on new lines'. Twenty years later he became a director.

XVII

The London, Brighton and South Coast from 1861 to 1880

In 1858 the Brighton company had obtained powers to build a line from Shoreham to Henfield. It was opened as far as Partridge Green on 1st July, 1861. Under powers acquired in 1859 it was extended so as to join the Horsham–Pulborough line at Itchingfield junction (near West Horsham), and brought into use on 16th September, 1861.

In May, 1862, the Brighton company built what was practically an extension of East Croydon station, which was for many years known as 'New Croydon'. Treating it as a separate station, they established a lower rate of fares than those charged at the old station, to which the South Eastern, under an agreement of 1848, which will be mentioned again later on, were bound to conform. The extremely weak reply to the not unnatural complaint of the South Eastern was that 'one of the chief objects for that arrangement was to avoid the inconvenience which had resulted from the admission of Croydon ticket holders to our Main Line trains, causing a number of carriages to be attached which were used for ten miles only'. The South Eastern rejoinder was that it was the reduction of the fares to which they objected, not the existence of the station. From their point of view it was neither more nor less than a piece of sharp practice. In fairness to the Brighton company, it may be pointed out that being the owners of the original London & Croydon Railway, they had a certain amount of claim to do as they liked about the Croydon traffic.

What has proved to be a very useful line, in that it is part of the main route between Victoria and the south, was opened on 1st December, 1862. It was a connection between Balham and Windmill Bridge Junction, Croydon, authorised in 1860, which had the advantage of giving almost the same time in running to and from Victoria, as to and from London Bridge. The line ran across Streatham Common and through open country which was to be rapidly developed for building, thus providing excellent season ticket revenue in the years to come.

A further reference has to be made to the West London Extension Railway, which was mentioned in Chapter IX, and, as related there, was opened on 2nd March 1863. It joined the West End and Crystal Palace at Longhedge Junction, and the London & North Western company, by having running powers over the Victoria Station and Pimlico, was able to use the Brighton side of the terminus, just as the Great Western used the London, Chatham & Dover side. There was, however, the considerable difference that the G.W.R. was there by ownership and not by virtue of running powers.

It was soon found that the accommodation was not sufficient, and in 1863 the Brighton company was authorised, in conjunction with the Dover company, to widen the line on the east side. As the report for January–June, 1866, said:

> This company will possess, for its exclusive use, three lines of rails from Victoria to the point south of the Thames where its lines will diverge – i.e. at Battersea Park – to the South London system on the one hand and towards Clapham Junction for its main line system on the other and the new main lines will be carried by a viaduct over the South Western, entirely obviating the present junction with the lines used by the London, Chatham & Dover and the Great Western at Stewarts Lane Junction and avoiding the passage of all main line and suburban trains round the severe curve at that spot.

It will be noticed from the latter part of the above quotation that there was to be a new approach from Clapham junction. This began at Pouparts Junction and after crossing the lines to and from Stewarts Lane in a south-westerly to north-easterly direction it re-crossed them, also the South Western, in a south to north direction. The new widening was opened on 1st December, 1867. The work was done under powers of 1864, as was also the construction of a high level viaduct; a brick structure 45 chains long, which carries the South London line from Factory Lane Junction to Battersea Pier Junction, and was opened 1st May, 1867.

A stiff Parliamentary contest was waged during the session of 1863 over the proposals of a private company – with the encouragement of the London, Chatham & Dover – to build a railway between Beckenham, Lewes and Brighton. The proposals were under the consideration of a committee in the House of Commons for twenty-five days and then rejected. Nevertheless, the bill was again deposited in 1864, but was at once negatived without a division. The line has already been mentioned; it was to start near Beckenham, running down due south through East Grinstead to Lewes, whence it was to curve gradually round into Kemptown.* It led to the Brighton company obtaining powers to construct lines to fill up that district.

---

* A short branch from Brighton to Kemptown was opened on 2nd August, 1869.

One such line, the Ouse Valley, was partly constructed, but was abandoned in 1866, as will be related presently.

It was, and probably still is, generally assumed that the traffic to and from Brighton was the corner-stone of the business of the London, Brighton & South Coast company. Judging, though, by a statement made by the chairman at the half-yearly meeting on 29th January 1863, such was not – at that time, at all events – the case. He said that during 1862 they carried 12,258,302 passengers, including Volunteers – of whom they had a large number – and excursionists, but only 693,000 were to or from Brighton itself. Although theirs was called the Brighton Railway the great bulk of their traffic did not arise from Brighton itself, which only furnished £220,000 out of the £1,025,400 gross receipts.

During the year 1862 the station at Brighton was enlarged at a cost of £92,450.

In connection with Volunteers, it may be recorded that on the occasion of the Volunteer Review at Brighton on the Easter Monday of 1863, nine trains were dispatched from London Bridge within 2 hours 41 minutes, carrying 6,922 volunteers; and within 2 hours 50 minutes, seven trains, carrying 5,170, left Victoria. Two thousand were also conveyed to Brighton from other places.

At this time the route between London and Portsmouth by the L.B.S.C.R. was via Brighton and Worthing. Afterwards, of course it was by Sutton and Horsham, but at the period with which we are dealing, the latter town was only reached via Three Bridges, and the line westward of Horsham led through Pulborough to Petworth. From Pulborough to the Brighton–Worthing–Chichester–Portsmouth line was a distance of 11 miles, so, in order to fill that gap, the company, in 1860, went to Parliament for what was called 'A Deviation of the Coast Lines, with new bridges over the Arun and Ouse, abandonment of portions of existing lines and of existing bridges; new lines to the Mid-Sussex, to Arundel, Littlehampton and Bognor; new channel for the Arun'. The Act was 23 & 24 Vic., c. 171. In passing it should be said that the reference to the river Ouse related to the line from Lewes to Hastings, and the 'new lines' included the Mid-Sussex Junction, and the Littlehampton branch.

The line from Hardham Junction to Ford, otherwise the Mid-Sussex Junction, was opened on 3rd August, 1863, and the branch to the terminus in Littlehampton on the 17th of the same month. Ford station was no longer said to be 'for Arundel', and the Littlehampton station on the Worthing line was re-named Lyminster.

The deviation at Ford, as the parliamentary notice recited,

necessitated a new bridge over the Arun, and that was the unique structure to be found there until the electrification. The bridge was 190ft long and of three spans. The eastern span was 30ft, the western of 70ft, and the centre span of 90ft. The last was the movable span and its western end overlapped the eastern end of the western span. The structure was a drawbridge in the strictest sense of the term as, when it had to be opened for river traffic, the central span was drawn by manual gear on to the western span. When fully open a clear space of 40ft was provided. From eight to ten men were required to draw the span out, but it returned more or less by gravity. The time taken to open the bridge, for the vessel to pass, and for the span to return, was about thirty minutes. The bridge was costly to maintain, and yet it had not been used for waterway traffic between 22nd September, 1919, and 4th May, 1928.

The report for the second half of 1862 said about the Pulborough–Ford line:

it would complete a new direct route to Portsmouth, shortening the distance by nearly ten miles, a result which, while materially improving the communication between that port and dockyard and the great arsenals on the Thames, will give greater facilities to the general traffic of Bognor, Arundel, Chichester, Havant and Portsmouth.

The report for July–December, 1863, in mentioning the opening of the Littlehampton branch, observed that steamers were already running thence to the Channel Islands and that the company had applied to Parliament for steamboat powers for Littlehampton. Those powers were given in 1864.

The extension from Newhaven to Seaford, authorised by 25 & 26 Vic., c. 78, was opened on 1st June, 1864; on which day the line to Bognor was also brought into use. It had been authorised in 1861 as an independent company, and was acquired by the L.B.S.C.R. in 1870.

The Banstead & Epsom Downs of 1862 was an independent company for a railway from Sutton. It was acquired by the London, Brighton & South Coast in 1864 and brought into use on 22nd May, 1865. At the time, the London, Chatham & Dover had a scheme for a line between Herne Hill and Epsom, but it was withdrawn on the Brighton company offering through bookings, without change of carriage, for the traffic for Epsom and the intermediate stations; the taking over of the Banstead line being part of the bargain.

The Horsham & Guildford Direct – an independent company – built, under powers given in 1860, the branch between West Horsham and Peasmarsh Junction, Guildford. It was acquired in 1864, and opened on 2nd October, 1865. The Board of Trade withheld permission at first, owing to incompleteness of works, and to the fact that Rudgwick station was situated on a gradient of 1 in 80. In order to meet the latter objection, the station was not brought into use until the embankments on either side of it had been altered sufficiently to introduce a piece of line through the station on a grade of 1 in 130.

Under the date 11th October, 1864, Jacomb-Hood records 'Brighton Co. in financial difficulties and all work stopped'. There is a similar entry for 29th May, 1866.

The next item to be noticed is the opening of the South London line, which had been sanctioned in 1862 and 1863, from London Bridge, through Old Kent Road, Peckham Rye and Loughborough Park, to a junction with the Herne Hill and Victoria line of the London, Chatham & Dover at Brixton. Thence, by their Act of 1864, the latter company were required to duplicate the line up to Wandsworth Road, from which point the South London would be carried on, by independent rails, to Battersea Park Junction on the L.B.S.C.R. main line, as mentioned above. Between Peckham Rye and Brixton there were also to be four lines of way, provided by the Brighton company. The northern two between Peckham Rye and Wandsworth Road were also for the use of the L.C.D.R. company's trains off the Crystal Palace and Greenwich Park lines, which joined the northern lines by an end-on connection at Cow Lane Junction. The railway was opened from the London Bridge end as far as Barrington Road Junction at East Brixton on 13th August, 1866, and thence to Battersea Park, including the L.C.D.R. additional lines, on 1st May, 1867. To carry the additional traffic the L.B.S.C.R. station at London Bridge was again enlarged (on the south side) and the viaduct approach further widened. The latter work was completed in 1867. As the report for January–June, 1866, observed:

> The company have obtained, for the first time, an independent access to London Bridge by three additional lines of rails controlled by their own signals.

In the session of 1864 a bill was deposited by a semi-independent company, which, by an arrangement with the London, Brighton & South Coast, was withdrawn, as was also a bill of the South Eastern for a line between Croydon and Eastbourne. An agreement between the two companies as to their respective spheres of activity had been signed on 2nd March, 1864.

A new bill was, nevertheless, lodged by the Surrey and Sussex Junction company in the 1865 session, which was passed. It was for a line from Croydon to Tunbridge Wells, and the London, Brighton

& South Coast was to work it. The South Eastern claimed that the scheme was a breach of the agreement of March, 1864, but the Brighton company replied that that document provided against any inroad into the system of each other. What was proposed, the latter company said, only connected two parts of the Brighton line – at Croydon and at Groombridge – and thereby shortened the distance to St Leonards and Hastings in exactly the same way as the South Eastern was doing in its new line through Sevenoaks. Further, the allegation that the agreement was being broken has been considered by the Committees of both Houses before they passed the bill. An Act obtained in the following session by the South Eastern and London, Chatham & Dover jointly for a London, Lewes & Brighton Railway was the sequel to that reply. It was never of course built.

Neither did the Surrey and Sussex Junction ever materialise. There were many irregularities over the purchase of land, and disputes arose between the two companies interested, with the result that the Duke of Richmond was called in to act as arbitrator. His award was made on 22nd March, 1869, and it was reported to the half-yearly meeting of June, 1869, that the loss to the Brighton company was £500,000. An act was obtained in the same session to confirm the award and to transfer the railway to the London, Brighton & South Coast Company, which was to proceed to complete the railway under a penalty of £50 a day. The Brighton company thereupon, in the 1870 session, sought for powers to abandon the line, but they were refused. The company was therefore in the position of having to build a line, at a cost of between one and two millions, that would never pay its working expenses. The directors did not feel justified in taking that step and preferred to pay the penalty of £50 a day, which was limited to a total of £32,250. The result was that the powers automatically lapsed, but not until after a good deal of work had been done. Jacomb-Hood records under the date 6th August, 1866, 'Serious riot at Edenbridge against the Belgians brought over by Messrs Waring to assist in the Surrey & Sussex Railway works'.*

In 1864 the Brighton company obtained powers to construct the 'Ouse Valley' line from the Ouse Viaduct, north of Haywards Heath, to the Lewes and Uckfield at Uckfield and the Hailsham branch at Hailsham. In 1865 an extension of the Ouse Valley line to St Leonards was authorised, with deviations in the 1864 route and junctions with the Tunbridge Wells and Eastbourne; further powers

* Some of the works were used twenty years later by the Croydon—Oxted—Groombridge lines.

to vary these lines being granted in 1866. Construction was begun, but the financial position of the company and the necessity for economy led to the abandonment of these lines, powers to that end being obtained in 1868. Traces of the works are still to be seen.

Mr Schuster was succeeded in the chair in January, 1866, by Mr P. N. Laurie who, in turn, was followed in April, 1867, by Colonel Barttelot. Mr Laing had, meanwhile, returned from India and was again made chairman in July, 1867. He found the finances in a very bad state and, with the July–December, 1867, report, issued a statement in which he said:

> As regards the past I have only to say that when I was the chairman twelve years ago I left the Brighton in a sound and prosperous condition; when I came back to it in July last I found it practically insolvent, having spent 8 millions of additional capital without any net return; working at 75 per cent of the receipts which did not leave enough to pay half the preference interest and with further pressing liabilities of upwards of 2 millions on deposit account, to meet which there was not a sixpence left in cash or credit. In six months the board over which I have presided has reduced the liabilities from over 2 millions to ¾ million and the working expenditure from 69 to 57 per cent for the corresponding half year.

The causes of the decline were said to have been: (1) During the period in question the original capital of £7,700,000 was increased to upwards of £18,000,000 without anything like a corresponding increase in the net profits; (2) The average receipt per train-mile fell from 7s. to 5s., so that, with an average expense of about 3s. 6d. per train-mile, the net receipts fell from 3s. 6d. to 1s. 6d. or less than a half. The goods traffic, it may be noted, did well. It had increased from 5s. to 9s. per train-mile, but the passenger traffic fell from 7s. 6d. in 1853 to 4s. 10½d. in 1866 – the last complete year of the old management. Passenger traffic had increased 60 per cent in money, but the train mileage increased 170 per cent, so the average train-mile receipts dropped 40 per cent. The new Board, which was appointed in 1867, reduced the passenger train mileage from 3,605,302 in 1866 to 3,312,372 in 1868 or 8 per cent, and raised the average receipts per train-mile from 4s. 10½d. to 5s. 8¾d. The expenditure per train-mile was reduced from 3s. 10d. or 64¼ per cent, to 3s. 3¼d. or 51½ per cent of the receipts. It may be added that in 1869 those figures were 2s. 11d. and 49 per cent respectively.

The new lines and extensions opened about that time were all promoted by independent companies. They were: the East Grinstead, Groombridge and Tunbridge Wells, sanctioned in 1862 and acquired by the London, Brighton & South Coast in 1864; opened 1st October, 1866: the Brighton, Uckfield & Tunbridge Wells, authorised in 1861, acquired in 1864 and opened from Groombridge to Tunbridge

Wells on 1st October, 1866; and from Groombridge to Uckfield on 3rd August, 1868; the latter section including Crowborough tunnel, 1,020 yards long, built in clay: the Mid-Sussex and Midhurst Junction, i.e. Petworth and Midhurst, authorised in 1859, acquired in 1862 and opened 15th October, 1866: the Horsham, Dorking and Leatherhead, sanctioned in 1862, acquired in 1864, opened from Dorking to Horsham on 1st May, 1867: Hayling – authorised in 1860 and modified by Acts of 1864 and 1867, for a line from Havant to Hayling – opened 16th July, 1867, and leased as from 25th December, 1871; which included an opening bridge at Langstone. A Chichester & Midhurst Railway was authorised in 1864, with an extension to Haslemere in 1865, but this scheme came to nothing, until 1876, when it was revived by the Brighton company.

The Leatherhead–Dorking line of the independent Horsham, D. and L. was never made, and a line between the two places was constructed by the Brighton company under powers of 26 & 27 Vic., c. 137, and was opened on 11th March, 1867.

In 1864 the L.B.S.C.R. company, with a view to tapping the shopping centre of Croydon, obtained powers to construct a short spur from the New or East Croydon station to a point adjacent to Park Lane, which was carried over the spur line. A terminal station, known as Croydon Central, was provided; but the venture was not a success, owing to the close proximity of East Croydon. It was opened in 1868, but was closed in 1871. At the request of the Croydon Council it was reopened in 1886, but was finally abolished on 8th September, 1890. Later, the site was sold to the Council for the erection of a new Town Hall.*

On 27th November, 1867, an agreement between the London & South Western, London, Brighton & South Coast and South Eastern was signed, which, again, nearly brought the Southern Railway into existence. In the following session the bill for its confirmation passed the House of Commons, but it was withdrawn when in the House of Lords, because the committee there insisted, as a condition of union, on limiting the tolls over the whole system to the maximum tariff sanctioned for the Brighton company. The South Eastern would not agree, as it stood to lose £60,000 a year, so all three companies consented to withdraw the bill.

The London, Brighton & South Coast and the South Eastern thereupon made, on 1st September, 1867, a new agreement, one section of which provided for the abandonment of the S.E.R. and

---

* The shallow cutting however, used for some years as a car park, was only built over in 1962.

L.C.D. railway to Lewes and Brighton which, as previously related, those companies had secured in retaliation for the Surrey and Sussex Junction. As the Brighton company's report for July–December, 1868, observed:

It will avert what must otherwise have been a serious competition between the two companies on the opening of the South Eastern short line to Tunbridge.

The agreement was for ten years, and was approved by Parliament in 1870.

The Tooting, Merton & Wimbledon was promoted by an independent company which was authorised, in 1864, to build the line from the London, Brighton & South Coast at Streatham. In 1865 it was transferred to the L.S.W.R. and L.B.S.C.R. jointly and on 1st October, 1868, it was opened, including the loop from Tooting to Merton Park via Merton Abbey. In 1863 the Brighton company had obtained powers to make a line from New Cross to the Croydon & Epsom at Sutton which intersected the Wimbledon & Croydon at what became Mitcham Junction, but in 1864 powers were obtained to divert it to Peckham in lieu of New Cross. It was opened on 1st October, 1868.

The report for January–June, 1869, complained that the public was not spending as much money as it did in former years on pleasure excursions. Great decreases in the number of excursionists to Brighton, and of visitors to Epsom races, were given as illustrations.

J. P. Knight, the traffic manager, was made the general manager as from 1st January, 1870. The same day saw the introduction of workmen's cheap tickets on the Brighton railway. On 5th December, St Leonards station – Warrior Square – was first used by Brighton trains. The end of the year 1871 saw an important reduction in the price of annual tickets between London and Brighton and other watering places on the south coast, and an acceleration in the train services.

During the next year or two there was no event of great importance. A number of short 'spur' lines were opened; most important being the at Stone Cross, 1 mile 8 chains in length, which provides direct access between Eastbourne and Hastings.

In 1875 there was an important rearrangement of capital, which took the form of creating a consolidated guaranteed 5 per cent stock of £1,955,860; and a consolidated preference stock of £6,190,315.

The report for the second half of 1875 submitted to the meeting on 26th January, 1876, showed that during the six years 1870–1875 the gross revenue had increased from £1,283,765 to £1,736,868, an in-

C2 class 0-6-0, No. 435, in post-grouping livery as 2435 at Gomshall. [*H. M. Madgwick*

Worthing Pullman express near Worthing about 1920. E5 class radial tank No. 568.
[*E. A. Gurney-Smith*

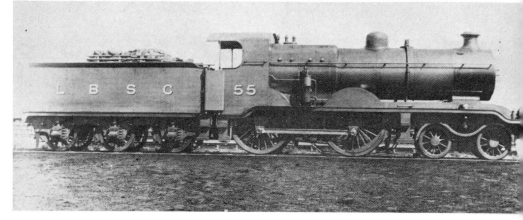

B4x class 4-4-0, No. 55; a rebuild of one of the Sharp Stewart engines of 1901.

[*Locomotive Publishing Company*

Above
The ultimate in Brigh
tank engines, L. Billint
L class 4-6-4T, No. 327
[*Locomotive Publis
Com*

Left
Three-car L.B.S.C. ov
head electric set in its o
inal form, before fitt
wire guards round the c
rent-collecting gear.

crease of 36 per cent, which had been earned by an increase of only 29 per cent in the train mileage.

The year 1876 opened with a new scheme before the public for a rival line between London and Brighton. It was to begin by a double junction with the South Eastern and the London, Chatham & Dover at Beckenham, and was to proceed to a central station opposite the Pavilion in Brighton, a distance of $46\frac{1}{2}$ miles. It was anticipated that through traffic from the northern lines would be possible over the widened lines of the Metropolitan and over the London, Chatham & Dover. It was said that neither the latter company nor the South Eastern was associated with the scheme. It, however, failed to appeal to the public and was therefore dropped.

The East London Railway may be mentioned here. It was incorporated in 1865 with a view to linking up the railways north and south of the Thames. It utilised the tunnel which had been constructed under great difficulties by the Brunels during the years 1824 to 1843 for horse and pedestrian traffic, and was opened on 6th December, 1869, between New Cross* and Wapping on the north bank of the river. It was extended to the Great Eastern line at Bishopgate on 10th April, 1876, thereby allowing Brighton trains to have direct access to Liverpool street, a privilege only used for a short time by main line trains. It was leased to six railways, and worked by the L.B.S.C.R. On 1st October, 1884,† Metropolitan & District trains began running over it, and it was afterwards electrified.

In 1873 the London, Brighton & South Coast and the London & South Western companies jointly received powers to extend the Portsmouth line to the harbour. The new line of fortifications at Hilsea had allowed the old ones at Portsmouth to be removed and the railway to be extended across the site, beignning at the new high level platform in the Town station. A branch to the dockyard for the use of troops was provided. The extension was opened on 2nd October, 1876, and greatly improved the journey to the Isle of Wight.

Among the traffic items of interest about that time there may be mentioned that, on 29th March, 1877, an agreement was concluded with the South Eastern as to a division of the London–Eastbourne traffic. It was scheduled to the South Eastern Act of that year. The working cost for the year 1877 was 2s. $7\frac{1}{2}$d. per train-mile; a figure that was the lowest for the previous ten years. The Croydon, Oxted and East Grinstead proposed railway was before Parliament in 1878.

* Originally from a separate New Cross station lying to the east of New Cross (L.B.S.C.R.). The public opening was on 7th December.

† Until 6th October only for local service from St. Mary's to New Cross.

It was agreed with the South Eastern that the two companies jointly should own the line between Croydon and Crowhurst Junction East, and the L.B.S.C.R. that south from Crowhurst Junction North. The Act was obtained accordingly. An agreement of 1st February, 1869, between the Brighton company and the South Eastern as to the Coulsdon–Redhill traffic expired in 1879 and was renewed for a further ten years. It had covered a gross traffic of £2,500,000. The agreement with the London & South Western as to the Portsmouth traffic was also renewed. It had given that company 63 per cent of the receipts, but under the new agreement they were divided equally. In 1878 the rights which the South Western acquired, in 1865, in the Tooting, Merton & Wimbledon were bought by the London, Brighton & South Coast for £28,000, and the line became wholly the property of the Brighton company.

The Cliftonville curve between Preston Park and Hove, authorised in 1875, which gave direct access between London and Worthing, was brought into use on 1st July, 1889. It included a tunnel 535 yards long, through chalk, which, by the way, failed during the First World War, putting the curve out of use for some time.

In 1873 powers had been given to a Tunbridge Wells & Eastbourne company to build a line between Groombridge and Hailsham, and in 1876 the undertaking was vested in the L.B.S.C.R., who were authorised to divert the line between Waldron and Hailsham. It was opened from Hailsham to Heathfield on 5th April, 1880, and thence to Eridge, where it joined the Uckfield & Tunbridge Wells, on 1st September following.

The period covered by this chapter includes the worst accident which had up to then taken place on a British railway. The best description with which the writer has met is that in *Historic Locomotives and Moving Accidents*, by A. R. Bennett, which is the chief basis of the following account.

The disaster was the product of a series of mishaps and misapprehensions, due to the primitive signalling arrangements then in use, and the factor of human fallibility. On Sunday, 25th August, 1861, three trains were dispatched from Brighton for London: an excursion train from Portsmouth due to leave Brighton at 8.5 a.m., an excursion from Brighton of seventeen coaches, due away at 8.15, and an ordinary stopping train, supposed to start at 8.30. Actually they were dispatched at 8.28, 8.31 and 8.35. The first one got through Clayton tunnel, but before the fact had been wired to the signalman at the southern end, the second train was seen approaching. There was a signal commanding the entrance to the tunnel, 305 yards away, which was a very early example of an automatic signal, being so arranged that a passing train put it to danger by a treadle worked by the wheel flanges, in which position it remained until pulled off by the signalman. Unfortunately it failed to act, and the signalman was unable to change it. He therefore showed a red flag. The driver immediately did all he could to stop, whistling for the brakes, reversing his engine, and sanding the rails, and succeeded in pulling up in about 400 yards. By the rules he should have stayed where he was, and sent the rear guard back to enquire what was wrong, but it appeared by the balance of testimony that he began to back out of the tunnel. In the meantime the southern signalman, thinking the driver had failed to see the flag, telegraphed to the north signalman enquiring whether the train had passed. The latter, taking the question as referring to the first train, replied 'Yes', with the unhappy result that the third train ran into the tunnel without being checked, and crashed into the Brighton excursion train 220 yards within it; the last two coaches being completely demolished, and the tunnel rendered impassable by wreckage. Twenty-three persons were killed and a hundred and seventy-five more injured, many desperately. A Brighton grocer named John Lynn, who was a passenger in the smashed train, made his way out of the south end of the tunnel and ran over Clayton Hill to the north end, arriving in time to prevent a train from London, already at Hassocks, from proceeding.

The jury at the inquest returned a verdict of manslaughter against the stationmaster at Brighton, for dispatching trains so quickly one after the other; but the grand jury at the Lewes Assizes the following March threw out the Bill of Indictment. This accident cost the Brighton company an enormous sum of money. Ministers of all denominations made it a text for the denunciation of Sunday travelling.

The Board of Trade was represented at the inquiry by Captain (afterwards Sir Henry) Tyler, R.E., and it is remarkable as an instance of intelligent foresight that he recommended that an interval of space should be observed between trains (the block system), instead of the interval of time (five minutes, which was not adhered to in this case) then in general use. He also advocated the use of continuous brakes, no doubt referring to the chain brake, which was the only one available at the time.

The following passage from the company's reply to his report is of interest.

The directors feel bound to state frankly that they have not seen reason to alter the views which they have so long entertained on this subject and they still fear that the telegraphic system of working recommended by the Board of Trade will, by transferring much responsibility from the engine-drivers, augment rather than diminish the risk of accident. Indeed, they think it is open to grave doubt whether the circumstances of the serious collision in question did not, when fairly considered, tend to prove that the increasing practice of multiplying signals and thus lessening the responsibility of the engine-driver who is in charge of the motive power and whose own life is at stake, has not resulted in reducing rather than increasing the safety of railway locomotion.

On 29th May, 1863, an accident occurred near Streatham, which was notable in several ways. The Victoria portion of the 5 p.m. express from Brighton consisted of sixteen vehicles, containing two companies of the Grenadier Guards, under the command of Colonel Burnaby, afterwards the hero of the ride to Khiva. Near the bottom of a gradient of 1 in 126, on entering a curve of 80 chains radius, the engine, a tank, began to oscillate violently, and on the driver shutting off steam in alarm, went off the road with all the carriages. After continuing for 224 yards on the ballast, it rolled right over. The dome hit a rail, and the boiler exploded. The driver, a lady and two soldiers were killed, and 59 people injured. The cause was considered to be excessive speed, and a controversy arose, which has cropped up again and again, as to the safety of running tank engines fast.

A collision occurred at New Cross on 23rd June, 1869, which, although no-one was killed and no bones were broken, cost the company £74,010. A goods train over-ran its signals and collided with an excursion train. There were 600 passengers in the train and 360 of them sent in claims for personal injury. Out of the latter the company was led into 126 actions at law. Some of the awards made by the juries in the cases that went to trial were significant. One passenger claimed £5,000 and received £10; another also asked for £5,000 and was awarded £125. A claimant for £1,500 got £100, and one for £3,000 received £250.

On 22nd August, 1873, an accident occurred at Eastbourne station. A train from Hastings to Brighton, due at Eastbourne 1.59, was seven minutes late, while the 2 o'clock express from Eastbourne to London was six minutes late in starting. At the approach to the station, trains from Hastings had to cross the up line. The London train was started, and met the one from Hastings at the point of intersection. A little girl was killed and one or two passengers injured. It appeared that the driver of the London train started on receiving 'all right' from the platform, without looking at the signal, which must have been against him, as they were interlocked, and could not be 'off' for both trains at once.

On 27th September, 1879, there was a boiler explosion at Lewes, resulting in the death of the driver and serious injuries to the fireman and guard.

During this period (1860–1880), great strides were made in the direction of adopting safety appliances. John Saxby, who had fixed a locking frame – i.e. one in which the point levers and signal levers controlled one another – at Bricklayer's Arms in 1856, patented an improved system in July, 1860. The first frame of this pattern was fixed at the 'Hole-in-the-Wall' signal box, where the Brighton and L.C.D.R. lines divided just before entering Victoria station. One of the 1860 pattern frames, with 37 levers, was fixed at Brighton North Box in 1861–2. Another box was at Stewarts Lane Junction (Battersea).

Interlocking made great progress on the Brighton line, and the first Interlocking Return – under the Regulation of Railways Act 1873 – showed that on 31st December, 1873, concentration of points and signals had been effected at 261 places out of 332 – which included those on branch lines – and interlocked at 290 places out of 303. The block-system was not, judging from some remarks made in 1863, welcomed at first. Speaking on the paper *Railway Telegraphs*, read by W. H. Preece, at the Institution of Civil Engineers on 13th January, 1863, George Hawkins, the traffic manager, said:

the Brighton company was not opposed to train signalling by telegraph. He had endeavoured to carry it out on that line but as an auxiliary only, for, in his opinion, anything which had a tendency to lessen the caution incumbent upon an engine driver would increase the danger, rather than diminish it. That was the reason why he had not adopted the electric telegraph so fully as he might otherwise have done. Although on the crowded portions of that line other precautions than the ordinary signals were required and adopted, yet he considered that the block system of working would be impracticable, except with such a large number of signals and signalmen, as to increase the liability to mistake and so render the alleged additional safety very questionable.

In the subsequent discussion, Bartholomew, the company's telegraph superintendent, said that his instruments had been in operation for eight years on the most crowded part of the Brighton line, including all the Crystal Palace traffic. It may be noted that by 1873 the whole of the line was equipped. The block system was applied throughout by the last day of 1874.

To the London, Brighton & South Coast belongs the credit for distinguishing the arm of a distant signal so that by day it would not be confused with a stop signal. That was done by 'fish-tailing', i.e. cutting a notch out of the end of the arm, and was first adopted on the suggestion of W. J. Williams, the outdoor superintendent, at Norwood Junction in August, 1872.

Intercommunication between passengers and servants in charge of the train was, for long, a very vexed question. It was recommended by a select committee in 1857 and by the Royal Commission of 1865. A private bill to enforce it was introduced in 1866, but consideration thereon was postponed and in 1868, by the Regulation of Railways Act, 'such efficient means as the Board of Trade might approve' was ordered. Most companies adopted the very unsatisfactory cord system put forward by T. E. Harrison of the North Eastern Railway which, though approved of in 1869, was condemned in 1873. The London, Brighton & South Coast company did so at first, but afterwards changed to an electrical system of which Stroudley, the locomotive superintendent, was one of the patentees. It was submitted to the Board of Trade; was approved in April, 1877, and remained the standard passenger communication on the Brighton system until the line became part of the Southern Railway.

In continuous brakes the London, Brighton & South Coast was one of the prime movers. It sent an engine and a train, of fifteen four-wheeled coaches, fitted with the Westinghouse vacuum brake, to the Newark brake trials, which were carried out, in June, 1875, under the supervision of the 1874 Royal Commission on Railway Accidents. Tests were made of nine different types of brake, on trains supplied by five companies. A full report is given in Michael Reynolds' *Continuous Railway Brakes* (1882). The Westinghouse company were also offering their air brake, which was demonstrated on a Midland train, and soon abandoned the vacuum principle. In reply to a circular of 19th December, 1877, the Brighton company informed the Board of Trade that it had determined to adopt the Westinghouse automatic (i.e. air) brake, and that 50 engines and 500 carriages were being so fitted. This brake remained its standard until it was absorbed into the Southern Railway. Though the Westinghouse is almost universal outside Great Britain, it is now for practical purposes confined in this country to electrically-operated trains. owing to the preference shown by the larger systems for the vacuum brake, and the necessity for uniformity when amalgamation came about.

It may be observed that the report for the second half of 1877 said that the block system and the interlocking of points and signals was complete throughout the whole of the Brighton railway system, and that arrangements were in progress for equipping all passenger trains with the Westinghouse brake.

While discussing the question of safety it may be remarked that in 1878 it was considered that the Brighton side of London Bridge station must again be enlarged. Such an enlargement would, however, have been very costly and Messrs Saxby and Farmer were therefore approached as to whether they could make any suggestion whereby the existing station could remain. As a consequence of the platforms being carried further outwards, each of the platform lines was made to accommodate two trains at the same time, whilst connections in the yard were altered and added to so as to allow for each platform to be used for both arriving and departing trains.

The admission of a second train into an already occupied platform was controlled by the arrival signal having a lower distant arm. When the platform line was free up to the buffer stops both arms were lowered; when the line was occupied but there remained room for another train the distant arm remained 'on'.

There were also provided, on the ordinary signals, what are today called route indicators. They were letters or numbers, and indicated, when the outgoing signal was lowered, for what route the points were set.

The account of this period may be concluded by mentioning that there was a two days' strike of enginemen on 26th and 27th March, 1867 – the time of the Epsom Spring races! – which caused considerable discussion in the Press, and called forth a proposal that the Royal Engineers and Royal Artillery should all be trained as engine-drivers.

The majority of the lines forming the L.B.S.C.R. system were constructed as double tracks. The provision of the third and fourth lines between London Bridge and Norwood was mentioned in Chapter V. By the opening of the 'New Croydon' section in 1862 these additional lines were continued southwards, and extended to South Croydon in 1864.

XVIII

The London, Brighton and South Coast from 1881 to 1900

THE line between Chichester and Midhurst, which, as related in the last chapter, had been commenced by an independent company, was abandoned in 1868. In 1876 the powers were revived by the Brighton company; altered junctions being provided for under their Act of 1877. It was opened on 11th July, 1881.

The Uckfield & Tunbridge Wells was completed on 18th May, 1881. The junction at the latter place with the South Eastern Hastings line was opened 1st February 1876 (for goods 1870 or earlier).

To the London, Brighton & South Coast belongs the honour of being the pioneer of the electric lighting of trains, as on 14th October, 1881, a Pullman car so equipped was put upon the Victoria–Brighton trains. It was fed by accumulators, which were changed at Victoria.

It will be remembered that the London & Brighton Railway entered London Bridge over the rails of the London & Greenwich, which became – for practical purposes – the property of the South Eastern, which ran from Croydon to Redhill on its way to Dover, over the line jointly owned with the London, Brighton & South Coast. Now, the latter company was carrying a greater suburban traffic into and out of London Bridge than was the South Eastern and, possibly through jealousy, the South Eastern sought powers in 1882 to exercise their alleged right to use the up Croydon line north of Corbett's Lane. The Brighton company protested to the Board of Trade that they had had the sole user for over thirty years, and the introduction of joint working would jeopardise the safety of the public. The Board replied that their remedy was to petition against the bill, but this course proved to be unnecessary, as the proposal was dropped for the moment.

A further controversy arose in October, 1883, when the South Eastern called on the Brighton to remove some connections at London Bridge laid by the latter in 1878 to enable their trains to enter the terminus from the up main line. As the Brighton demurred, the South

Eastern removed them arbitrarily, at the same time introducing a connection near Corbett's Lane which enabled them to use the up Croydon line. This last straw sent the Brighton company to the Court of Chancery, for an injunction to restrain such user. Judgment, however, was given in favour of the South Eastern company.*

Attention was then turned to the Croydon–Redhill section, as in the South Eastern report for July–December, 1884, the following remark was made:

> For many years past your train service over the joint lines between London Bridge and Redhill has been greatly restricted by the excessively large service of the Brighton Company. Your directors contend for your right to an equal participation in the usable capacity of the joint lines and discussions of a friendly character have been undertaken with a view to an equitable settlement of this long-pending question which so seriously affects your interests.

The 'equitable settlement' was a long time coming. What was known as the 'Southern Lines Controversy' dragged along until it was mutually agreed to refer the dispute to the arbitration of Sir Henry Oakley, the then general manager of the Great Northern Railway. He made his award in July, 1889, which was in favour of the South Eastern to the extent that, instead of the Brighton Company paying about £14,000 a year, it had to pay about £20,000. Speaking on 24th July, 1889, within a fortnight of the receipt of the award, Laing said that their dividends would be affected by about £5,000 or £6,000 a year. He need not tell the proprietors that he thought the advantages of peace were very cheaply purchased at that price. He could not say what a relief it was to feel that time would not be taken up in Parliamentary contests, or in preparing for them, and that they were at peace with all their neighbours and able to attend to their own affairs. In the session of 1890 the London, Brighton & South Coast company secured Parliamentary sanction to the agreement.

Reverting to the middle 'eighties it may be recorded that on 1st June, 1885, a day service was given on the Newhaven–Dieppe route. The working expenses for that year were at the rate of 2s. 5d. per train-mile or $47\frac{1}{3}$ per cent of the receipts – the lowest ratio on record.

In 1885 there was the important trial of Hall v. The London, Brighton & South Coast Railway Company, which established the right of railway companies to charge what are known as terminal

---

* This passage is not very clear. At this time it would appear that the utilisation of lines east of London Bridge was (north to south): Greenwich Up, Greenwich and S.E. Main Down, S.E. Main Up, S.E. and Brighton Down, S.E. and Brighton Up, Croydon Local Up, South London Up, South London Down, South London Up. The disputed line was presumably No. 6, which has been laid in 1842, being at that time provided for the Up trains of the S.E., Croydon, and Brighton companies.

charges, i.e. it laid down that station accommodation, the use of sidings, weighing, checking, clerkage, watching and labelling were 'other services of a like nature' mentioned in section 15 of the Regulation of Railways Act, 1873. The question was subsequently adjusted by the Railway and Canal Traffic Act, 1888.

Under powers given, in 1877, to a private concern, and vested in the Brighton Company in 1878, a Lewes & East Grinstead Railway, with a branch from Horsted Keynes to the main line at Haywards Heath, was built. It was between Culver Junction, near Barcombe, and East Grinstead, and was opened throughout on 1st August, 1882.* The branch was brought into use on 3rd September, 1883.

In 1883 Brighton station was again enlarged and the same principle of signalling adoped as at London Bridge. The Brighton South box had 240 levers in one continuous frame.

The Croydon, Oxted & East Grinstead Railway was mentioned in the last chapter as being partly constructed jointly with the South Eastern. It was opened from South Croydon to East Grinstead on 10th March, 1884, and the curve from that line at Crowhurst Junction North to Crowhurst Junction East on the South Eastern on the same day.† The Oxted Tunnel, on the first section, is 2,261 yards long. It should be noted that this line was partly constructed on the abandoned works of the unfortunate Surrey & Sussex Junction Railway, also mentioned in Chapter XVII. Joseph Firbank was the contractor. At different times he executed a number of lines for the Brighton Railway. In Chapter XI of his 'Life' (by F. McDermott, 1887), there is a most interesting account of the making of the Lewes–East Grinstead, Croydon–East Grinstead, and Oxted–Groombridge lines. The latter also made use of some of the workings of the Surrey & Sussex Junction of twenty years before.

In 1884 powers were obtained to remodel the lines in the vicinity of Lewes station. The latter was reconstructed, and new connections were provided between the Brighton and Hastings and the Brighton and Uckfield lines. The exit from the tunnel on the Keymer branch was improved and all the curves were considered flattened.

The Fratton and Southsea Railway, brought into use on 1st July, 1885, and worked jointly with the L.S.W.R., has been mentioned in Chapter X. The Woodside & South Croydon was from Woodside

---

* The present two-level station being opened on the same date. This was the third station at East Grinstead, the first being near the London Road (closed 1st October, 1866), and the second actually on the London Road (closed October 1883).

† Also a curve from St. Margaret's Junction to the High Level station at East Grinstead, permitting through running to Tunbridge Wells.

on the South Eastern's Addiscombe Road branch to South Croydon.† It was promoted by a separate company and sanctioned in 1880. In 1882 it was acquired by the London, Brighton & South Coast and the South Eastern companies jointly, and was brought into service on 10th August, 1885.

The curve between Arundel and Ford that gave direct access from the east to Littlehampton was put into traffic on 1st January, 1887. One mile of route between Angmering and Ford Junction was abandoned to allow resiting of the Junctions. On the 27th of the following month the Betchworth tunnel near Dorking fell in. It was constructed in sand and had to be relined for its whole length of 384 yards.

The Dyke branch, authorised in 1877 and 1885, was brought into use on 1st September, 1887. The Oxted & Groombridge Railway was promoted by a private company and sanctioned in 1881. It was taken over by the London, Brighton & South Coast in 1884 and opened from Hurst Green Junction – on the Croydon – East Grinstead line – to Edenbridge on 2nd January, 1888, and was completed to Groombridge on 1st October following. On the latter date the Withyham spur was also brought into use. It is a short link, 72 chains in length, connecting the Oxted and Groombridge and the Tunbridge Wells and Uckfield lines; having been authorised in 1878.

A train, composed wholly of Pullman cars, commenced to run from Victoria to Brighton and back on 10th December, 1888. Pullman cars had been attached to the Brighton company's trains since November, 1875, but this was a complete Pullman train.‡ It will be convenient to add here that the 'Sunday Pullman Limited' commenced on 2nd October, 1898, to make the journey from Victoria to Brighton, also the return, in an hour.

J. P. Knight, the general manager, died on 20th October, 1886, and was succeeded by Allen Sarle, who had been the secretary for twenty years.

Two other well-known Brighton men passed away within the next five years. Stroudley, the locomotive superintendent, was taken ill and died on 20th December, 1889, and W. J. Williams, who had held the office of traffic superintendent, on 22nd, July, 1891. Stroudley was succeeded by R. J. Billinton, then chief locomotive draughtsman on

† Strictly, to Selsdon Road Junction (Selsdon since 1935) which lies ½ mile S.E. of South Croydon station, on the Oxted Line.

‡ As a matter of fact, it was not the first, as one was run in 1881, but discontinued the next year.

the Midland Railway, but who, up to 1872, when he went to Derby, had held a similar position on the Brighton Railway.

An accident occurred at Norwood Junction on 1st May, 1891, that caused considerable concern, not only on the Brighton railway, but on all other systems. A bridge, in which cast-iron girders were used, failed and one result was a circular from the Board of Trade to all the companies on the subject. So far as the Brighton was concerned it may be noted that Sir John Fowler and Mr F. D. Banister examined all the bridges on the system and the renewals and repairs necessary to remove all probable future similar trouble were expected to cost £60,000. In the end the work cost nearly £100,000 and was finished by the end of 1895. Although there were no fatalities arising out of the above accident, a considerable amount was paid for injuries. It was the only one in which an engine of the '*Gladstone*' class was ever involved.

In the summer of 1893 an outbreak of typhoid fever occurred at Worthing, due, it was supposed, to a defective water supply. The effect on the Brighton Railway may be judged from the fact that at the end of August, when the season should have been at its height, it was said in *The Times* – of 29th August – that it was believed that there was not a single visitor then in Worthing. The loss in railway receipts was £15,000. The agreement with the Western of France as to the Newhaven–Dieppe service was renewed and scheduled in the Brighton Company's Act of 1893.

Considerable progress had been made by this time in the use of electric light. By 1893 some 300 coaches in 'block' trains were so lit. An interesting experiment made at Brighton Works in 1894 was the preparation of an armour-plated truck for certain artillery tests carried out by the 1st Sussex Artillery Volunteers on behalf of the Committee on National Defence, by which the feasibility of firing heavy ordnance from railway permanent way on a suitable vehicle was established.

Despite the arbitration award of Sir Henry Oakley, mentioned earlier in the chapter, disagreement with the South Eastern continually occurred over the Croydon–Redhill line, and Laing said, on 26th July, 1893, that the only way out of the trouble appeared to be to widen the line. Powers were obtained for that purpose in 1894, and the report for January–June, 1894, said that the bill had met with very little opposition, owing in a great measure to all questions with the South Eastern Railway Company having been amicably settled in a spirit of mutual conciliation.

An entirely separate line was made, leaving the main track about

400 yards north of Coulsdon station, on the up side, crossing over the old line, and running close-by (but invisible) on the down side to rejoin the L.B.S.C.R. main line at Earlswood, after passing in tunnel underneath the S.E.C.R. Redhill–Tonbridge line. The work entailed some very heavy cutting through the chalk, and boring three tunnels, namely 'Covered Way' (417 yards), Merstham (2,113 yards), and Redhill (649 yards). It was opened in April, 1900. The covered way went through ground belonging to the Cane Hill Asylum, and was insisted upon by the London County Council, out of their tender care for the lunatics under their charge.*

The new line was constructed to plans prepared by Charles L. Morgan, who, on 1st February, 1896, came from the Great Eastern Railway to be chief engineer to the Brighton company on the resignation of F. D. Banister. The latter started his connection with the Brighton Railway as an assistant to Robert Jacomb-Hood in 1846. He left railway service in 1849, but returned to the Brighton Company as successor to his former chief in 1860, and was chief engineer to that company for nearly 36 years. He died on 22nd December, 1897.

It may be added that Jacomb-Hood died suddenly on 10th May, 1900, in his 79th year, thus severing a connection of well over half a century. Although, as has been recorded, he resigned in 1860, he continued to work for the company, becoming a director in March, 1883, and remained on the board until his death. It may truly be said that he died in harness, as on the day of his death he conducted some business for the railway company. He had been a member of the Institution of Civil Engineers since March, 1847.

At all the half-yearly meetings of the company for some few years Laing had found it impossible to make his voice sufficiently heard and his speech was read for him by the secretary. At the meeting on 29th January, 1896, he was not present and in the address read to the meeting intimated that he had desired to retire but had been persuaded to remain. That statement prompted Sir George Russell, at the South Eastern meeting the following day, to remark that he hoped it would be considered no detraction from other gentlemen to say that he regarded Mr Laing as possessed of the finest intellect and most cultivated mind of any man then left who was actively engaged in railway work. The very fact of the concerns of a neighbouring company being in the hands of such a man must be an advantage to the South Eastern company, and he hoped that when Mr Laing eventually retired from the Brighton company it would

* The roof has now been removed.

be fortunate enough to find a successor who would pursue the same course in the interests of both his own company and its neighbours.

Laing did, however, retire during the following half year. He had been chairman of the Brighton company from 1848 to 1855, when he went to India and, on his return to England, was again made chairman in 1867. He had then to take the drastic measure of issuing £1,250,000 of ordinary stock at a discount of 55 per cent. In 1867 the capital was £17,013,405 and no dividend was paid on the ordinary stock; in 1895 it was £25,478,324 and paid 6 per cent dividend. A bright feature in Laing's career was the interest he took in the welfare of the staff.

The shareholders voted Laing an annuity of £1,000, but he did not enjoy it for long, as he died on 6th August, 1897. He was succeeded in the chairmanship by Lord Cottesloe.

In December, 1897, Sarle retired from the position of secretary and general manager and was made a director. He had joined the company in 1849 and became the secretary in 1867. J. F. S. Gooday, the Continental traffic manager of the Great Eastern, was the new general manager and J. J. Brewer, the chief assistant solicitor, was made the secretary. The former post was soon again vacant, as when Sir William Birt resigned his position of general manager to the Great Eastern, Gooday returned there on 30th September, 1899, to succeed him. The new general manager was Mr – afterwards Sir – William Forbes, formerly the traffic manager of the London, Chatham & Dover. He had been bred and brought up in the railway world. His father was general manager of the Midland Great Western Railway of Ireland, and his uncle was James Staats Forbes, the chairman of the London, Chatham & Dover from 1873 to 1904. The company was indeed fortunate to have a man of this wide experience and brilliant abilities to steer it through the beginnings of its career as an electric railway, and, what is more, through the vicissitudes of the War period. He retired, with many honours, when his line was absorbed by the Southern.

During 1897 two Royal saloons and associated brake vans were built at Brighton, and in 1898 the decision was made that all future main line stock should be bogie vehicles.

In 1899 the London, Brighton & South Coast sought powers to acquire some property at Victoria for the enlargement of the station there. Strong opposition was offered, there being seventeen petitions against the bill. Included in the scheme was the purchase of two houses, belonging to the Grosvenor Hotel, which had to be acquired in order to make a cab exit. The attitude of the lessees of the hotel was so obstinate that the only solution was to buy them out, which was done for £230,000. The Brighton company had been the ground landlords since 1872. The hotel was subsequently leased to the Gordon Hotels for fifty years. At the half-yearly meeting on 26th July, 1899, the chairman paid a high compliment to Mr – later Sir – Charles Morgan, the engineer, for the way in which he had presented the case to the Parliamentary Committee.

On 1st September, 1897, there was a derailment at Mayfield, resulting in the death of the driver, and injuries to a number of people. The engine turned completely over, and the wheels continued to revolve until steam was shut off, but when lifted and put on the rails again, it was found to be little the worse for its mishap.

On 19th December, 1899, the company had its second fatal accident to a passenger for twenty-five years, during which period it had carried 65 million people. In a dense fog a passenger train standing in Bermondsey station was run into by another one and two passengers were killed. A more serious accident occurred four days later, in the same fog, at Wivelsfield. The up Continental boat train had been pulled up, and whilst standing there was run into by an express from Brighton, the driver of which overran the signals. Five passengers were killed.

The London, Brighton and South Coast from 1901 to 1922

At the half-yearly meeting on 29th January, 1902, it was announced that land had been purchased at Lancing whereon to erect shops for building and repairing wagons; a step which was necessary, owing to the accommodation at Brighton being insufficient.

In consequence of the schemes of various promoters for electric railways to Brighton the company decided to develop one for converting its line to electrical traction. Towards that end Major Philip Cardew, R.E., who, a few years previously, had retired from the position of Electrical Adviser to the Board of Trade, was appointed a director.

On 4th June, 1903, Sir Allen Sarle died. After having been the secretary for twenty years he became general manager in 1886 and retired therefrom and became a director in 1897.

On Sunday, 26th July, 1903, two remarkable runs were made by the engine *Holyrood*, by way of showing what the steam trains could do. The distance between Victoria and Brighton is 50 miles 73 chains, and there was much talk of the possibilities of doing it in 50 minutes with electric trains. On the day mentioned, the 'Pullman Limited' was made up of three cars and a brake van, totalling about 130 tons behind the tender. The down trip was run in 48 minutes 41 seconds, start to stop, at an average of 63.4 miles an hour, the maximum attained being 90, near Horley. The return journey occupied 50 minutes 21 seconds; average 60.8, maximum 85.

R. J. Billinton, the locomotive superintendent, died on 7th November, 1904. His successor was D. Earle Marsh, who came from the Great Northern Railway, and entered upon his new duties on 1st January, 1905.

In July, 1904, Great Western trains began running between Birkenhead and other northern towns and Brighton, etc.

On 1st March, 1905, the 'Sunny South Special' train was inaugurated. It provided through accommodation between Liverpool, Birmingham and other places in the north of England with the South Coast resorts, and at the time of its introduction was somewhat of a novelty in the way of cross-country connections. It was worked by London & North Western as far as Willesden, where it was handed over to the Brighton.

The Brighton & South Coast, like most of the railways, was suffering from the competition of tramways, and it was that which was the main cause of studies on possible electrification which Major Cardew, Mr E. J. Houghton and Sir Philip Dawson undertook. The result of their investigations was that it was decided to adopt an overhead wire, instead of a third rail, as the means whereby current was conveyed to the train. For suburban working the third rail was considered better, but for long distances, overhead line was at that time considered preferable and, as it is quite possible that the Brighton authorities had in mind not only electric trains to Brighton but perhaps by the coast line to Portsmouth, the adoption of the overhead line in preference to the third rail may be understood. That the system was, after amalgamation, removed and replaced does not imply that it was in any way a failure, but merely that it was economically necessary to have the same method of operation on all the sections of the Southern Railway.

The South London Railway between Peckham and Battersea Park was the part chosen for the initial venture, powers therefore being obtained in 1903, and tenders having been called for, the contract was let in 1905 to Messrs Robert Blackwell and Co., the material coming from the Allgemeine Elektricitats Gesellschaft – usually known as the A.E.G. – of Berlin. Later, it was decided to carry the work into London Bridge and Victoria. Six platform lines and three approach roads were equipped at the former station and five platform lines and two running roads at the latter. Then, in August, 1910, it was decided to convert to electric traction the line from Battersea Park, through Crystal Palace, to Selhurst and that from Peckham Rye to West Norwood. The total length of line equipped, including sidings, was 62 miles. Repair shops were provided at Peckham Rye, at which place, and at Norwood Junction, there were carriage sheds.

The overhead construction was of the double catenary type, carried on side pole, centre pole or girder structures. In some places cantilever structures had to be provided. The coaches were of the compartment type, at first 6oft long and 9ft wide but, owing mainly to the Crystal Palace tunnel, were afterwards made 54ft by 8ft.

All trailer coaches had a driving compartment at one end, and therefore a train could be of one motor and one trailer, or one motor and a trailer in front and in rear. A two-coach train carried 144 passengers; a three-coach 218 passengers and a four-coach – two motors and two trailers – 288. The motor coaches had four 150-h.p. motors, which were ied by current collected from the contact wire by means of a bow collector. Power was taken from the London Electric Supply Corporation's power-station at Deptford, and supplied to the railway at Queen's Road station switch-cabin.

The section between Victoria and London Bridge, via the South London line, was put into service on 1st December, 1909. The line from Battersea Park, through Clapham Junction and Streatham Hill, to Crystal Palace was brought into use on 12th May, 1911, and that from Peckham Rye to join the Crystal Palace line at West Norwood on 3rd March, 1912. On the last-named date electrical working was extended through Norwood Junction to Selhurst. The war prevented the completion of the further extensions which were in hand.

The Brighton was one of the companies which made extensive use of rail motor trains. Speaking on 1st August, 1906, the chairman said:

> The experience gained by those of the services which had been working long enough to enable a judgment to be formed was very encouraging and it was intended to extend them as might be found desirable. The company possessed a considerable number of small engines,* built over thirty years ago, which were found to be well adapted for these services. By an alteration which the locomotive engineer had been able to make, these engines could be driven from the further end of the trailer car so that reversing was unnecessary.

It may be observed that there was nothing novel in the arrangement referred to in the concluding sentences of Lord Cottesloe's remarks; what was new was that the controls from the motor compartment, when the engine was in the rear, were pneumatically operated, instead of being actuated by wires or chains.

What may be described as the monumental work of the Brighton company during the present century was the widening of the line between Grosvenor bridge and Victoria station and the reconstruction of that terminus, powers for which were, as related in the last chapter, obtained in 1899, after a severe fight.

The original station at Victoria, i.e. the terminus of the Brighton company and distinct from the adjoining 'Chatham' station, extended from the existing front of the station to Eccleston Bridge and was bounded on the east by the above-mentioned 'Chatham' station and on the west by the Grosvenor Hotel and some private property facing Buckingham Palace Road. It was 800ft long, 230ft wide, and

---

* The reference is probably to the 'Terrier' class, used for this work sometimes with leading coupling rods removed. Later D1 class 0-4-2T engines were fitted for auto-train work, also D3 0-4-4T; the first two E2 0-6-0T engines were also used for a time between two trailer sets.

covered an area of 8½ acres and had eight platform roads and two sidings. These were served by one arrival road, one departure road and a siding. The new station extended to Elizabeth Bridge, as far again, and was 1,500ft long, 320ft wide and, with the yard outside, covered 16 acres. There were nine platform roads with a total length of platform face of 2¼ miles. A novel and interesting feature was that four middle roads were provided for the southern half of the station. These came between the platform lines and allowed trains, entering or leaving, to pass others standing at the platforms in the southern end of the station.

The whole of the property along the Buckingham Palace Road between the Grosvenor Hotel and Ebury Bridge had to be demolished to provide room for the extension to the west of the station, and a portion of the Grosvenor canal filled in. The annexe to the Grosvenor Hotel had to be rebuilt, most of which is on a foundation of 1,200 timber piles in London clay. The whole scheme – station approaches and hotel enlargement – was a very ingenious one and reflects the greatest credit on its designer, Sir Charles Morgan.

On 10th June, 1906, a portion of the new station was brought into use, in order to turn over the former station to the contractor. On 10th February, 1907, nine platforms were put into service, the entrance being by what is now the cab-exit in Buckingham Palace Road. Two additional lines over Grosvenor Bridge were also brought into use on that date and the ticket-collecting platform there dispensed with. On 1st July, 1908, the new station was formally opened.

One of the changes introduced when Victoria was being opened was the transference of the suburban traffic from the west to the east side of the station. The change was one in accord with the volume of traffic, as the greater portion of the suburban traffic came from places to the east of the main lines – that is, regarding the lines to Brighton and Portsmouth as main lines. As a consequence the platforms at Balham, Wandsworth Common and Clapham Junction had to be altered.

David Greenwood, the superintendent of the line, retired on 30th June, 1907, and was succeeded by F. Finlay Scott. Lord Cottesloe retired from the chairmanship at the half-yearly meeting on 5th February, 1908, and was succeeded by the Earl of Bessborough. On 2nd November, 1908, a new train of first-class Pullman cars only was introduced, and christened the 'Southern Belle' – now renamed the 'Brighton Belle' – which made two journeys daily between Victoria and Brighton in exactly one hour.

The agreement with the South Eastern, originally made in 1867, and extended from time to time as required, expired on 31st December, 1908. It was again renewed, with small amendments, for five years on 5th January, 1909. That proved to be the final agreement as, when due for renewal in 1914, negotiations were still in hand when war broke out and all the railways passed under the control of the Government. When that control ceased the formation of the Southern Railway had been sanctioned by the Railways Act, 1921.

It was recorded in the last chapter that Gooday resigned his office as general manager of the London, Brighton & South Coast in order to return to the Great Eastern to succeed Sir William Birt. For reasons of health Gooday had to give up his position there and, in 1910, became again connected with the Brighton – as a director. Second-class bookings in suburban services were abandoned as from 1st June, 1911, and in all services on 1st June, 1912.

A remarkable feature in railway operation was accomplished on 30th June, 1911. The King and Queen gave a fête at the Crystal Palace, in commemoration of their coronation, to 100,000 London school-children. Ninety-six trains were employed to convey the party to their destination and twenty-one stations had to be closed for part of the day owing to the running lines being used as standing room for empty carriage trains. The traffic was handled at the High Level and Low Level stations at the Crystal Palace, also at Penge and Sydenham Hill.

Marsh retired from the position of locomotive superintendent towards the end of 1911 and L. B. Billinton, the son of the former's predecessor, was promoted to succeed him.

As already recorded, the Peckham Rye–Tulse Hill–West Norwood electrification was opened on 1st June, 1912, and at the next half-yearly meeting the chairman said that since the opening of the South London section in December, 1909, there had been nearly 14 million additional passengers. At the half-yearly meeting in February, 1913, it was observed that before electrical operation was introduced there were 496 trains into and out of Victoria, but that then there were 739. The corresponding figures for London Bridge were 663 and 901. Allowing for an 18 hours' day, those stations were accommodating an average of 50 trains per hour.

As indicative of the suburban traffic of the company at that time it may be noted that figures, ascertained in connection with the proposed further electrification, showed that in June, 1913, there were 259 trains per day timed to run over the main lines between Clapham Junction and Balham, and 347 over the suburban lines. Between

Sydenham and Norwood Junction there were 236 over the main lines and 191 over the suburban.

On 25th June, 1913, the day service between Victoria and Paris, in both directions, was reduced to practically eight hours, a saving of nearly an hour. That was made possible mainly by the opening, by the French State Railways, of the direct route between Dieppe and Paris, through Pontoise, which reduced the rail journey by 20 miles. Of nearly equal assistance was the placing into service, on the New-haven–Dieppe route, of the new 24-knot turbine steamers *Rouen* and *Paris*, which crossed in 2¾ hours. On 12th September, 1915, third-class Pullman cars were provided on many trains.

The benefits of Gooday's great railway experience were not long at the service of the London, Brighton & South Coast, as he died, after a brief illness, on 16th January, 1915. His seat on the board was filled by Sir Robert Turnbull, who had recently retired from the position of general manager to the London & North Western Railway.

Sir Charles Morgan, to whom the present Victoria station is a lasting memorial, was the chief engineer from 1st February, 1896, to February, 1917, a period of 21 years. A vacancy in the directorate having occurred in the previous November, he was appointed a director and retired from the position of chief engineer in the latter month. His successor was J. B. Ball, of the Great Central Railway, but the company only had the advantage of his services for a period of 3½ years, as he died with great suddenness on 16th September, 1920. O. G. C. Drury was appointed to follow him as chief engineer. An equally sudden death deprived the company, on 1st December following, of its chairman, Lord Bessborough. The new chairman was Mr C. C. Macrae, a son-in-law of Samuel Laing, but he only occupied the chair for two years, as he died, in his eightieth year, on 28th November, 1922. Mr G. W. E. Loder – Lord Wakehurst – succeeded Mr Macrae in the chair.

A bad accident occurred at Stoat's Nest (now Coulsdon) on 29th January, 1910. A wheel shifted on its axle, causing its coach and others to be derailed. Five passengers, also two other persons who were on the platform of the station, were killed, and forty-two were injured.

When, on the outbreak of war, special duties were assigned by the Government to the railways they had taken over, the function allotted to the London, Brighton & South Coast, apart from the ordinary movements of troops, etc., was that of the dispatch from Newhaven – to which port Littlehampton was added some months later – of the bulk of munitions and war stores for France and overseas generally. Newhaven passed under naval and military control at once, the Harbour station being closed to the public altogether.

New sidings had to be provided on an extensive scale, also a new signal box and power station, warehouses, etc. The total number of special goods trains to Newhaven was 19,750: consisting of 866,021 loaded trucks 336,153 of which carried munitions, and 529,868 stores. The total tonnage shipped at Newhaven was 6,018,465, namely 2,682,756 tons of ammunition and 3,335,709 of other stores.

The tonnage through Littlehampton was 787,345. There were 9,061 transports loaded at Newhaven and 2,098 at Littlehampton.

A large number of wounded men were taken in at the Royal Pavilion, Brighton, and at other centres in the town. As a consequence there were 233 ambulance trains run there, carrying 37,070 patients. To other stations on the L.B.S.C.R. system there were 445, conveying 42,337.

At Brighton works some very interesting work was done in the way of making turning swivels and links for paravanes. Many hundreds of these were made. Another job was a series of 18-ft saddle plates for fixing to the bows of transports for the paravane attachment. Billinton and his staff brought great credit upon themselves over the manufacture of some 9,000 four-pronged grapnels. These had been made elsewhere in large quantities, but proved unsatisfactory as they could not stand the 5 cwt test of each arm. They were, however, made at the Brighton works without a weld and not one gave the slightest sign of distress under the test. Another item was 2,000 sets of finely executed drop forgings for the various lugs, bracing eyes, swivel eyes, forks, etc., in connection with the chassis of the Handley-Page aeroplane. Finally, ten thousand Mills' hand grenades were made.

A good deal of emergency work for the Admiralty ships and transports was done, consequent upon the nearness of the Brighton works to the harbour of Newhaven. One typical job was a new rudder and rudder post for the transport *Koolga*. It was intended to have sent the vessel to her builders in the North of England, but that would have meant an absence of some weeks and, possibly, loss by enemy action. The work was, however, done in the shops at Brighton and completed in six days. The rudder and its post were 26ft high, the blade was of $\frac{7}{8}$in steel, the total weight being 7 tons.

The ambulance train given by Lord Michelham and known as Queen Mary's Ambulance Train was constructed at Lancing, and another was built for the Government.

A serious accident, which might have had terrible results, occurred to a Brighton company's train conveying ammunition on 18th April, 1918, in Redhill tunnel. A goods train from Eastbourne became divided and the van and last three wagons came to a stand in the tunnel. The breakaway was not noticed by the signalman at the box at the farther end of the tunnel and a second goods train was allowed to follow, which ran into the standing vehicles and derailed them. Its engine and first three trucks were also derailed. The fireman of the latter train attempted to pass, in order to protect the down line, but hearing a train approaching, he had to get out of the way. The train he heard was a special down train carrying munitions which ran into the wreckage. Both engines were badly damaged and 26 wagons were destroyed or more or less broken up and about 40ft of the tunnel was filled to the crown with trucks and debris. Colonel Pringle enquired into the accident and said that the tunnel was cleared of the wreckage and opened to traffic within forty hours of the collision, which spoke well 'for the manner in which the emergency was met and for the excellent work done by the breakdown gangs in so confined a space and in trying and dangerous conditions'.

Of the London, Brighton & South Coast fleet six were engaged, either as hospital ships or in the transport of troops across the Channel. Six cargo boats were also in the Government service, and two of them – the *Maine* and the *Anjou* – were lost. The passenger vessels *Rouen* and *Sussex* were torpedoed but were not lost; the cargo boat *Cherbourg* struck a mine and was damaged beyond repair.

The total number of the Brighton Railway staff who enlisted was 5,635, being 34.6 of those in the company's service at the outbreak of war. Of these 532 were killed.

In addition to a war memorial at London Bridge, the Brighton Company gave the name *Remembrance* to the large tank engine No. 333, which also received bronze memorial tablets engraved 'In grateful remembrance of the 532 men of the L.B.S.C.R. who gave their lives for their country 1914–1919.'

Twelve E4 class 0-6-2 tank engines were sent to France in 1917, all of which came back in 1919.

This chapter may be completed by saying that on 24th July, 1904, the widening to double track of the line between Newhaven and Seaford was completed; four lines of way between Victoria and Windmill Bridge (near Croydon) were placed in service during 1907; the stations on this section, such as Norbury and Thornton Heath, may be taken as examples of the spacious and solidly-built structures that the Company considered worth while erecting at this time. The completion of the quadruple from London to the north end of

Balcombe Tunnel was accomplished by the opening of the widened section between Three Bridges and Balcombe on 22nd May, 1910. A fifth track, on the down side, between Norwood Junction and South Croydon was completed on 3rd January, 1908. At the end of 1922 the total length of route running line on the London, Brighton & South Coast was 457 miles. Of that, 100 miles were single tracked, 357 had a double line, 47 miles had three tracks, 35 miles had four tracks, and there was a total length of 14 miles of track on those sections that had over four lines. The sidings had a total length of 355 miles.

XX

Brighton Locomotives down to 1869

THE thirty-one engines originally belonging to the London & Brighton Railway which were handed over to the Joint Committee, and became Nos. 45–75, have been given in Chapter V.

Three others were used in the very early days, which were either borrowed from contractors, or were sold almost at once, namely two singles, *Brighton* and *Shoreham*, by Rennie, and one named *Kingston*, which, according to the *Railway Times* (vol. iv, p. 390), opened the Shoreham branch on 10th May, 1840.

When the Joint Committee was dissolved, and the engines were divided up, the Brighton company took 51, renumbering them as shown in the list below. Numbers in brackets are subsequent alterations. Particulars of the engines will be found in Chapter V.

Brighton	J.C.	Brighton	J.C.	Brighton	J.C.
1	61	18 (13)	74	37 (16)	96
2	63	19 (14)	75	38 (17)	97
3	65	20 (15, 7, 292, 367)	124	39 (34, 115, 260)	113
4–6	21–23	21 (20)	4	40 (35, 96)	114
7	66	22	1	41 (36, 97)	115
8	0ı	23	3	42 (37, 98)	116
9 (96)	38	24	30	43	60
10 (97)	83	25	8	44 (39)	6
11 (98, 100)	110	26	85	45	47
12 (99)	112	27	89	46 (40)	54
13 (8)	53	28–32	91–95	47 (41)	68
14 (9)	50	33	42	48 (42)	69
15 (10)	52	34 (38)	48	49 (44)	72
16 (11)	28	35 (18)	98	50 (45)	88
17 (12)	49	36 (19)	99	51 (46)	90

The new numbers were not allotted in quite so haphazard a manner as appears; the underlying idea being to keep engines by the same makers together. Renumberings complicate the locomotive history of this line enormously, as the sensible plan of adding O or A to the number of an obsolescent engine was not adopted, and every time the number of an engine was wanted in order to keep members of a new class together it was changed.

In compiling the following account, use has been freely made of Mr F. Burtt's excellent book on the subject, which was published anonymously in 1903, and where much additional information as to details, rebuildings, etc., will be found. The writer has also had the advantage of being able to collate Mr Burtt's account with two old books belonging to the Company, where additional items have been found. In cases of disagreement – which are extremely few – the latter have been followed.

The first locomotive superintendent was named Statham, followed by John Gray in 1845, who was succeeded from February to December, 1847, by S. Kirtley. In the latter month John C. Craven was appointed, and remained until the end of 1869.

The only engine that calls for remark among the first 51 is No. 20, which was originally built by Bodmer, with two opposed pistons in each cylinder. It was rebuilt with normal cylinders, and named *Seaford*, lasting until 1876. Some further information about it will be found in an article on Bodmer's engines, *The Locomotive*, XVI, p. 60.

The first new engines to come were twelve singles with 6-ft wheels and 15 by 25 cylinders designed by Gray, also two 2-4-0s. The writer has a copy of the elaborate printed specification issued in connection with these engines, which is a most remarkable document, reading in many places just like one of the present day. The valves were on the tops of the cylinders (inside), at an angle of 45 degrees, and were fitted with his peculiar 'horse-leg' gear. The engines were built by Hackworth and Co., and numbered 47–60, the coupled ones being 48 and 55. Renumberings were: 47 (55), 48 (110), 55 (114). Although they are said to have run well and fast, they were all transformed into coupled engines, six being made into tanks. Nos. 56 and 58 were converted experimentally into 'Cramptons', with dummy crank shafts, but not for long.

At the same time as these engines were arriving (1846–8), ten of the celebrated 'Jenny Lind' class were supplied by E. B. Wilson and Co., numbered as follows:

60 (70, 101, 273)	63 (301, 351)	68
61	64–66	69 (295)
62 (302, 402, 501)	67 (296)	later named Lewes

No. 60 is said to have been the first of this admirable type of engine, which was designed by David Joy, and adopted by a number of railways.

The driving wheels were 6ft; cylinders 15 by 20in.

In 1847 and 1848 Sharp, Roberts supplied fifteen engines, numbered as follows; 71, 84 and 85 being coupled (the last two 'long boiler' type), and the rest singles:

71 (274)	80 (281)	85 (109)
72 (275)	81 (282, 407)	86 (77, 278)
73 (276)	82 (283)	87 (78, 279, 408)
75 (277)	83 (284, 406, 502)	88 (79, 280)
76	84 (108, 111)	89 (74)

The numbers of 84–89 were altered almost at once.

Twelve engines came in the above years from Stothert and Slaughter, 90 and 91 coupled, the rest singles:

84	87	90 (64)
85	88 (57)	91 (65, 300)
86	89	92–95

Two long-boiler, six-coupled goods by the same makers were 73 (107, 113)* and 74 (106, 112). Eight engines of the same type by Longridge and Co. were:

70 (101)	75 (104)	100 (108)
71 (102)	96 (106)	105
72 (103)	97 (107)	

Nine Sharp singles were supplied in 1849, which were given odd low numbers, replacing previous engines:

19	35	39 (361)
21	36 (299)	43
34	37 (360)	47

Burtt adds 20, on p. 29; but this engine is dated 1838 in the official list, and was originally 21 (No. 4, J.C.). He omits it on p. 39, but puts in 45, which he dates (correctly) 1844 on p. 29. It was formerly 50 (88 J.C.). He also mentions a Sharp No. 110, of which he could obtain no particulars. The present writer is in the same position, and thinks it is either a myth, or an unknown renumbering.

We now come to the beginning of locomotive building at Brighton, which was carried on for seventy years. In future, if a maker is not mentioned, Brighton may be assumed. Cylinders are practically all inside. When names are given, they were added in later years by Stroudley. The first engines to be turned out were a pair of single-wheel well-tanks; Nos. 14 (60, 278) and 26, in May and June, 1852. In December a single express with 6-ft wheels was built: No. 48.†️ Three more singles were built in 1853, with 5ft 6in wheels: 24, 41, and 10 (290). In 1854 came two six-coupled goods engines, wheels

---

* Burtt says afterwards 400, but this is extremely unlikely.

†️ Burtt is wrong in saying 274 and 412. These numbers were given to No. 84 of 1861, afterwards 48.

4ft 9in, cylinders 16 by 24; 44 (271, 303, 401) and 46 (272, 304, 403). There were also two small singles, 23 (266) and 38. Two four-coupled engines were built by the company in September, 1854, with 5ft 9in wheels and cylinders 16 by 24, Nos. 16 and 20 (264). These two engines, which were sold in 1874, are said by Burtt to have been built by Sharp, Stewart and Co., but this appears to be a mistake.*

Six engines of the same type were obtained from that firm during 1854–6, which may as well be dealt with together, as follows:

Nov., 1854	July, 1855	April, 1856
13	6 (289, 390)	42 (355)
40 (260, 464)	116 (356)	100 (257, 505)

No. 40 was fitted with a Stroudley boiler in 1871 and named *Epsom*, being sold in December, 1891.

In November, 1854, there were also two more coupled engines built at Brighton with 5ft 6in wheels; but only 15 by 22 cylinders, 1 (285, 391) and 2 (286, 389), which were called the 'Croydon engines'.

In the same month two extremely powerful goods engines were bought from the Manchester, Sheffield & Lincolnshire Railway which had been built by Sharp, Stewart and Co. They bore the numbers and names 117 *Orestes* and 121 *Europa*, and were the most powerful engines in the country, having no less than 1,572.5ft of heating surface; wheels 5ft and cylinders 18 by 24. No. 117 was renumbered 362 and 398; and 121, 370; being scrapped in 1885 and 1886 respectively.

Eight engines were built at Brighton in 1855; two 'long boiler', 5ft coupled, 3 (287) and 5 (288); two similar, but 5ft 6in, 8 (291) and 9 (18,† 293); two front-coupled tanks, 11 (294) and 22; and two 5-ft goods, 118 and 119.

In 1856 there were six: four single expresses

125 (372) (Ventnor) July	122 (—) Sept.
126 (373) (Shanklin) July	123 (Drayton) Sept.

and two four-coupled, long-boiler engines, 120 (297) and 124, in December. Of the above singles, the first pair, with 6ft 6in wheels and 16 by 22 cylinders, closely resembled Sharp's in appearance, while the other two (6ft, 15 by 20) were copies of the 'Jenny Lind' type.

---

* They are put down to Brighton Works in an official list of 1869, See also *The Locomotive*, XVI, 79.

† See *The Locomotive*, XV, 48.

In 1858 seven tanks were built, the numbers of which are difficult to unravel. They appear to have been:

> 12 (131, 378)   15 (277)
> 105 (291 according to Burtt; but see No. 8 of 1855 above)
> 127 (106, 292, 367). The alteration of this engine to 106 is certain, as it appears in two or three places in the books; hence Burtt's suggestion of 106 for No. 15 must be wrong. 107 does not appear in the books as a tank.
> 128   129 (376)   130 (377)

The date of all these engines in the books is June, 1858, except 130, which was much smaller, and came out in October. For June, 1858, the books also give an engine omitted by Burtt, namely 105, four-coupled 5ft 6in, 16 by 20; built by the company, rebuilt August, 1862.

In September there was a similar one, 101 (258, 506) (*Rouen*), which lasted till 1885.

The year 1859 began with two singles: 132, 6ft, 16 by 22; and 133 (405), 5ft 6in, 15 by 22 (*Penge*). They were followed by four goods, the first 5ft, 16 by 24; the others 4ft 9in; 134 (384), 102 (259, 311, 500), 107 (281, 393) and 135. In June of this year an extraordinary little engine made its appearance, being an outside cylinder bogie saddle tank, No. 136. The following month there were two small singles, 137 (382) and 138 (383), followed by another in December, 108 (285, 391). The year 1859 finished up with a single-wheeler tank, 98 (298, 214) (*Seaford*).

In January, 1860, there were first two singles, 6ft and 6ft 6in: 139 (385) and 140 (386). Two small goods engines were bought of Slaughter and Co., 103 and 114. In May a small outside cylinder single tank engine was built, 25 (268, 399); also a four-coupled tender engine with 5ft 6in wheels, 59 (276, 410) (*Leatherhead*). Two goods came out in October, 141 and 142, with 4ft 9in wheels.

The year 1861 began with a 5ft goods, No. 143, followed in February by a four-coupled engine, No. 89 (61) with 5ft 6in wheels, which was a 'hash-up' of two old engines. Burtt does not quite agree with the official books here. He also omits a similar engine, No. 97 (285), which was built by the company in June.* In the same month a neat little tank with outside cylinders and leading bogie, No. 144, appeared; also a long-boiler coupled, No. 145 (503). In September two fine single engines were turned out, with 6ft 6in wheels and 17 by 22 cylinders, 146 (*Lancing*) (451), and 147 (*Worthing*) (452);

---

* See *The Locomotive*, XIII 183, for a discussion on, and sketch of, this engine.

followed by two more with 6ft wheels and 15-in cylinders, Nos. 84 (48, 274, 412) and 86 (49).

In January, 1862, a single tank was built, No. 4 (104, 295, 365), which, according to Bennett,† originally had outside cylinders, but was afterwards drastically rebuilt. In one of the company's old books it is named Lewes. There has been some confusion here with the '*Jenny Lind*' (69) of 1848, which was also named *Lewes* and renumbered 295 (and 365 according to Burtt); 365 *Lewes* is entered in the book as a tank, built 1862. But in another place there is '69 *Lewes* single Wilson 1848 altered to 295'. It is unlikely that No. 69 ever became 365.

Some coupled engines followed: two with 5ft 6in wheels, Nos. 32 (275, 411) and 148 (*Ryde*) (453); and four with 6-ft wheels, Nos. 149 (454), 150 (455), 151 (120, 363) and 152 (456). All these six engines are dated April in the company's book. In May a couple more long-boiler engines were built, which were the last of this detestable design: 45 (277, 409) and 99 (298?). In July there were two fine singles with 6ft 6in wheels, which may be described as enlarged '*Jenny Linds*', 153 (*Spithead*) (164) and 154 (*Southsea*) (165), lasting till 1890 and 1891 respectively. In August two engines came out which foreshadowed the future, being of the o-4-2 type: Nos. 155 (504) and 156. The wheels were 5ft 6in, cylinders 16 by 20. The second one was made into a stationary engine in 1878, for hauling wagons up the incline from the wharf to the railway at Kingston-on-Sea, near Shoreham. The year 1862 finished with three goods engines, 110 (353), 157 and 158; and a single express, 31 (*Little-hampton*) (259).

In March, 1863, two 6-ft 2-4-0 engines were turned out, 159 and 160. In September there was a 6-ft single, 161 (*Havant*). In the following month Craven produced his *chef d'œuvre*, in the shape of a pair of singles with 7-ft wheels, 162 and 163 – the largest that ever ran on the L.B.S.C.R. – cylinders 17 by 22. They were never re-numbered, but were named by Stroudley at first *London* and *Brighton*, later *Penge* and *Sandown*. The last two months of 1863 saw the following: two o-4-2, 164 (299, 368) and 165 (297, 364); two o-4-2 saddle tanks, 166 and 167; two goods, 168 (477) and 169; and two 2-4-0 side tanks, 170 and 171.

The year 1864 opened with two single expresses (6ft 6in), Nos. 172 (*Chichester*) and 173. In March, April and May twelve 2-4-0 expresses were received from Beyer, Peacock and Co., with 6-ft wheels and

† *The Locomotive*, XV, 191.

16 by 22 cylinders, which were numbered 178–189; the only ones to be renumbered being 185 and 189, which became 465 and 466, these two lasting till 1890, when the boilers were taken for the electric light plant at Brighton. In June four similar engines were turned out at Brighton, Nos. 174–177. Of these No. 174 was afterwards 488 and 454; No. 175, 455. No. 177 was named *Hayling* later on.

Two small singles with only 5ft 6in wheels followed in June, Nos. 190 (24, 267, 485) and 191 (33, 280, 392). In July there were two goods engines: 192 (382, 475) and 193 (383, 476).

Twelve large single engines were also delivered July–November, by R. Stephenson and Co. They had 6ft 6in wheels and 16½ by 22 cylinders. Their history is somewhat complicated, but interesting. They were originally numbered 194–205. A few months after they had started running, Nos. 194, 196, 197 and 202 were bought back by the makers to fill a 'rush order' by the Egyptian Government. The other eight remained unaltered until the advent of Stroudley, who named 195, *Portsmouth* (later 486); 200, *Dieppe* (later 490); 201 was renumbered 111, then 197, named *Cavendish*, finishing up as 487 *Chichester*. 205 was renumbered 198 and named *Drayton* (later 488). Nos. 198, 203 and 204 were rebuilt with Stroudley boilers in 1871 and 1872 – the old boilers being used for other engines – 203 as a single and the other two as coupled engines; 198 becoming 205 *Kensington* (later 505); 203 being named *Sussex* (503); and 204 *Westminster* (504). The year 1864 concluded with three goods engines from Brighton: 54 (136, 381); 206 (271, 396, 476); and 207 (272, 397).

Four more goods followed in February and March, 1865: 208 (380, 474); 209 (387, 463); 210 (388, 464); and 211 (394). In July there were two front-coupled tanks, 212 (413) and 213 (414). Two little 5ft 6in single engines were added to the stock in September: 29 (293, 366) and 30 (19, 263, 486). Two 6ft 6in singles came out in November: 194 (*Glynde*) (484) and 196 (*Pevensey*) (485); also two little 0-4-2 well-tanks: 214 (369) and 215 (371, 497).

The year 1866 opened with four 0-4-2 side-tanks: 216 (376, 498) and 217 (377, 499) in February; and 17 (261, 465) and 218 in March. In the latter month two 6-ft singles were built, Nos. 197 and 202. No. 197 was named *Solent* by Stroudley and renumbered 266 and 484. There is possibly some confusion here with a single built in 1854, originally 23, which Burtt tells us also bore the numbers 266 and 484. No. 202 was renumbered 112 and 354. In March also two goods engines were purchased from Manning, Wardle and Co., Nos. 219 (386) and 220. The following month a large goods engine came out at Brighton, No. 221 (389). In May there were two side-tanks with single driving wheels, 222 and 223, the former afterwards named *Egmont*. In June there were two goods, followed by two more in July, 224 (390, 465); 225 (391, 466, 514, 614); 226 (392, 467) and 227 (393). In August two six-wheel coupled saddle-tanks were built, 228 (351) and 229 (352); followed in October by an o-4-2 side-tank, No. 230; and an o-4-4 tank of the S.E.R. type, No. 231 (466). At the end of the year four 6-ft singles appeared: 232 (485); 233 (*Horsham*) (487); 234 (474) and 235 (*Dorking*) (475).

In April–June, 1867, six single expresses with 6ft 6in wheels were received from Nasmyth, Wilson and Co. as follows:

236 (Arundel) (476)	239 (Polegate) (479)
237 (Reigate) (477)	240 (St Leonards) (480)
238 (Shoreham) (478)	241 (Eastbourne) (481)

Six 2-4-0 expresses came from Dübs and Co.: 242–247 (457–462). In October two large goods engines with Cudworth fire-boxes were built at Brighton, 190 and 191.

In February, 1868, a small 2-4-0 engine was purchased of Kitson and Co. It had been shown at the Paris Exhibition of 1867, and was furnished with a peculiar cab with an enormous roof, which looked as if the makers were hankering after an Egyptian order. It was numbered 248, named *Hove* by Stroudley, and renumbered 463, lasting till 1893. In March a six-coupled wing-tank came out, 52 (269, 395). In July a curious little four-wheeled tank, with outside cylinders, was built for the Hailsham branch: No. 27 (400); a pair of trailing wheels was added with a view to steadying it, and afterwards, when it was taken for shunting in Brighton works, removed. In October six goods engines were obtained from Slaughter and Co., Nos. 249–254 (468–473). In the same month the last of the Craven singles came out at Brighton; the wheels being 6ft 6in – he never repeated the 7-ft experiment – Nos. 255 (*Hastings*) (482) and 256 (*Victoria*) (483). In November there were two 2-4-0's, one 6ft, one 5ft 6in; Nos. 12 (124, 371) and 28 (283, 377). In December a heavy six-coupled wing-tank was provided for piloting trains up the New Cross bank, No. 58 (273, 398).

In May, 1869, a small o-4-2 saddle-tank was supplied by Kitson and Co., No. 76 (*Bognor*) (358, 496). In October, Sharp, Stewart and Co. supplied a small 2-4-0 side-tank, No. 96. It was later named *Kemp Town*, and afterwards *Hayling Island*, subsequent numbers being 115, 359 and 499. Finally it had a small saloon added at the back, with an additional pair of wheels, for inspection purposes, being then

481 *Inspector*. The Craven series of engines built at Brighton were concluded in November by two tanks (2-4-0): Nos. 51 (132, 379) and
109 (352).

Two more single expresses remain to be chronicled, which were
built by Dodds and Son, being part of an order for six, placed in
1866. Owing to the firm going into liquidation in consequence of the
Spanish Government failing to pay them for engines supplied, only
two were built, and were not received until 1871. They were fine
6ft 6in engines with 17 by 22 cylinders: Nos. 127 (*Norwood*) (374)
and 128 (*Croydon*) (375).

At the end of 1869 Craven retired. During his rule the engines
were painted green.

XXI

Brighton Locomotives, 1870 to 1922

WILLIAM STROUDLEY, when the directors decided to appoint him locomotive superintendent, was rather a 'dark horse'. He had only held comparatively unimportant posts – gaining a wide experience nevertheless – until 1861, when he was made works manager of the Cowlairs shops of the Edinburgh & Glasgow Railway. In 1865 he became locomotive and carriage superintendent of the Highland Railway, but even there had but little scope for his abilities. However, the choice proved a wise one.

He did very little rebuilding, but let the old engines run themselves out, and produced new ones of great originality of design, comprised in only about half a dozen classes, in which the principle of inter-changeability was carried as far as it was possible to go. For neatness they were quite unsurpassed.

In March, 1885, he read a paper before the Institution of Civil Engineers, which has become a classic amongst the literature of the locomotive. The commencement of the paper is as follows:

The Author, on his appointment to the London, Brighton & South Coast Railway in 1870, had to consider what kinds of locomotive engine and rolling-stock would best meet the requirements of the service; as, owing to the great increase and complication of the lines and traffic, the original primitive engines and rolling-stock were not able to do so.

This railway system offers some peculiarities, when compared with its neigh-bours, in having no less than 90 miles within the Metropolitan area, 15 of these having three or four lines of rails. Some of the lines have very heavy gradients, and curves as small as 6½ and 7 chains radius; there are ninety-four junctions, and twenty terminal, stations and from some of these latter, the line rises with gradients of from 1 in 64 to 1 in 80. These features, together with a crowded passenger-traffic moving at irregular intervals, over about twenty hours out of the twenty-four, cause the working to be very difficult. Some of the engines are attached to as many as sixteen trains in one day; the loss of time in running on and off, and in standing waiting, tending to increase the cost of working, as compared with those railways having more continuous lines. The great distance from the collieries also renders the fuel costly.

Before beginning the subject of his engines, mention must be made of one which Burt omits: No. 66, 'six-wheel coupled tank, Manning Wardle, June, 1871 (purchased of Mr Chappel)'. In another place the engine is given again, with a pencil note 'sold to Mr Chappel'. Either this is a mistake, or they did not like the engine, and sold it back again. Nothing more is known about it. Chappel seems to have been a locomotive dealer, as in 1882 the South Western bought an engine named *Jumbo* from him.

In the following account, if no maker is mentioned, Brighton may be assumed; also cylinders 17 by 24 except if otherwise specified. A '6—' in brackets signifies that the number was increased subsequently by 600. When the amalgamation first came about, the Brighton engines were distinguished by a B placed above the number, but from June, 1931, 2000 was added to them as they came in for heavy repairs. The standard pressure of the Stroudley engines was at first 140, afterwards 150 lb per square inch.

The first engines he produced were a pair of small 0-4-2 tanks, 18 (262,* 373) and 21 (265, 467), which came out in December, 1871; together with two very fine goods engines with 5-ft wheels and $17\frac{1}{2}$ by 26 cylinders, afterwards enlarged to $18\frac{1}{4}$in diameter. They were designated class 'C', the first two being numbered 84 and 85, the latter of which was soon altered to 83. Further engines of this type are given in the following list; Nos. 77–84 being built at Brighton, and 85–96 by Kitson and Co.

77	March 1873		86	July	1873		92	April	1874
78, 79	April	,,	87	Sept.	,,		93	June	,,
80–82	June	,,	88, 89	Oct.	,,		94	Sept.	,,
83, 84	Dec.	1871	90	Dec.	,,		95, 96	Nov.	,,
85	June	1873	91	March	1874				

They were renumbered 401–420 in the early 'eighties, and scrapped 1901–4.

In October, 1872, the first of the famous 'Terriers'† appeared. They were designed for working the East London Railway, which had bad gradients and very light rails; also for the South London line between Victoria and London Bridge; and were beautiful little engines, doing remarkable work, considering their diminutive size. The wheels were 4ft, and cylinders 13 (some 14) by 20; the weight being only 24 tons 7cwt, nearly equally divided. Altogether there were 50, known as the 'A' class, as follows:

35 (6—)	*Morden*	June 1878		40 (WII)	*Brighton*	Mar.	1878
36	. *Bramley*	,, ,,		41	. *Piccadilly*	June	1877
37 (6—)	*Southdown*	May ,,		42 (6—)	*Tulse Hill*	,,	,,
38 (6—)	*Millwall*	,, ,,		43 (6—)	*Gipsy Hill*	June	1877
39	. *Denmark*	Mar. 1878		44 (6—)	*Fulham*	,,	,,

* 261 (Burtt) is a mistake. The engine of this number was formerly 17, built in 1866.

† One of the few nicknames to receive official recognition; in 1953 a board was erected half-way down the Newhaven East Harbour branch stating that beyond that point it was restricted except for 'Terrier class engines'.

45	.	Merton	June 1877	66	.	Hatcham	June 1874
46	(W8)	Newington	Dec. 1876	67	(6—)	Brixton	,, ,,
47	(6—)	Cheapside	,, ,,	68		Clapham	Aug. ,,
48	.	Leadenhall	,, ,,	69	(WIO)	Peckham	,, ,,
49	(6—)	Bishopsgate	,, ,,	70	.	Popular	Nov. 1872
50	(6—) (W9)	Whitechapel	,, ,,	71	(6—)	Wapping	Oct. ,,
				72	(636)	Fenchurch	Nov. ,,
51	.	Rotherhithe	,, ,,	73	(6—)	Deptford	,, ,,
52	(6—)	Surrey	,, 1875	74	(6—)	Shadwell	,, ,,
53	(6—)	Ashtead	,, ,,	75	(W9)	Blackwall	,, ,,
54	(6—)	Waddon	,, ,,	76	.	Hailsham	June 1877
55	(6—)	Stepney	,, ,,	77	(6—) (W13)	Wonersh	,, 1880
56	.	Shoreditch	,, ,,				
57	(6—)	Thames	,, ,,	78	(6—) (W14)	Knowle	,, ,,
58	.	Wandle	Nov. ,,				
59	(6—)	Cheam	Oct. ,,	79	(6—)	Minories	,, ,,
60	.	Ewell	,, ,,	80	(6—)	Bookham	,, ,,
61	(6—)	Sutton	,, ,,	81	(6—)	Beulah	July ,,
62	6—()	Martello	,, ,,	82	(6—) (380S)	Boxhill	,, ,,
63	(6—)	Preston	,, ,,				
64	(6—)	Kemp Town	June 1874	83	(6—)	Earlswood	Aug. ,,
65	.	Tooting	,, ,,	84	(W12)	Crowborough	Sept. ,,

Of the above about half were later sold, amongst which the following may be mentioned: 46 and 68 to the South Western (734 and 735); 54 to the South Eastern & Chatham (751), and 72 to the Newhaven Harbour Co., besides those mentioned as going to the Isle of Wight in Chapter XIV. Amongst the light railways which acquired this class of engine (some through the War Stores Disposal Board) were the Shropshire & Montgomeryshire (two), the Edge Hill (two), the Kent & East Sussex (two), and the Weston Clevedon & Portishead (two). The last-named had the curious distinction of being taken into stock by the Great Western Railway (becoming Nos. 5 and 6) when the W.C.P.R. closed.

It is interesting to note that eight engines were built of the same design in Australia in 1875, for the New South Wales Government Railway.

In November, 1872, two 2-4-0 express engines with outside frames were built, which were practically identical with the two coupled rebuilds of the Stephenson singles of 1864 (*Kensington* and *Westminster*), namely, 201 *Belgravia* (501) and 202 *Goodwood* (502, 602). There were only two more of the class, which came out in November and December, 1875; 206 *Carisbrooke* (506, 606) and 207 *Freshwater* (507, 607).

A small 2-4-0 tank engine, built by Sharp, Stewart in 1872, was bought in 1873. The cylinders were only 12 by 17in. It was named and numbered at different times, *Bishopstone* and *Fratton*, 53, 270, 357 and 497.

* Withdrawn 1927. No. 50 (W9) sent to IoW. in 1930.

On 25th November, 1873, the first of the well-known 'D' class tanks began work, No. 1 *Sydenham*. They were an exceedingly success-ful design; 0-4-2 with 5ft 6in driving wheels. The total wheel-base was only 15ft, unusual features being the large 4ft 6in trailing wheels, and the long overhang – 7ft 10¼in – at the rear end. About fifty of them were later adapted as 'motors'; i.e. permanently attached to one or two carriages, and running in either direction; out of a total number of 125, which were all practically identical, and were named and numbered as follows – Nos. 233–267 being built by Neilson and Co., and the rest at Brighton:

No.		Name	Date		No.		Name	Date
1 (684)		Sydenham .	Nov. 1873		223	.	Balcombe .	June 1885
2 (75, 298)		Wandsworth	Dec. ,,		224	.	Crowhurst .	May ,,
3	.	Battersea .	,, ,,		225	.	Ashburne .	,, ,,
4	.	Mickleham .	,, ,,		226	.	Westham .	,, ,,
5 (6—)		Streatham .	,, ,,		227	.	Heathfield .	Dec. 1884
6 (76, 299)		Wimbledon	,, ,,		228	.	Seaford .	,, ,,
7 (6—)		Bermondsey	Mar. 1874		229	.	Dorking .	Nov. ,,
8	.	Brockley .	,, ,,		230	.	Brookhouse .	Oct. ,,
9	.	Anerley .	,, ,,		231	.	Horsham .	June ,,
10	.	Banstead .	,, ,,		232	.	Lewes .	,, ,,
11	.	Selhurst .	,, ,,		233	.	Handcross .	Mar. 1883
12 (6—)		Wallington	June ,,		234	.	Rottingdean	Oct. 1881
13 (77, 77A,		Pimlico .	Dec. ,,		235	.	Broadwater	Nov. ,,
347, 214)					236	.	Ardingly .	,, ,,
14 (6—)		Chelsea .	,, ,,		237	.	Cuckfield .	,, ,,
15 (6—)		Brompton .	,, ,,		238	.	Lindfield .	,, ,,
16 (6—)		Silverdale .	Mar. 1875		239	.	Patcham .	,, ,,
17 (6—)		Dulwich .	,, ,,		240	.	Ditchling .	,, ,,
18 (78, 78A,		Stockwell .	May ,,		241	.	Stanmer .	,, ,,
348, 215)					242	.	Ringmer .	,, ,,
19 (6—)		Belmont .	June ,,		243	.	Ovingdean .	,, ,,
20 (79, 79A,		Carshalton .	,, ,,		244	.	Hassocks .	,, ,,
349, 216)					245	.	Withdean .	,, ,,
21 (6—)		Beddington	,, ,,		246	.	Bramber .	,, ,,
22	.	Addington .	,, ,,		247	.	Arlington .	,, ,,
23 (6—)		Mayfield .	Aug. 1875		248	.	Ashurst .	,, ,,
24 (6—)		Brambletye	Oct. ,,		249	.	Hilsea .	,, ,,
25 (6—)		Rotherfield	Mar. 1876		250	.	Hoathly .	,, ,,
26 (6—)		Hartfield .	,, ,,		251	.	Singleton .	,, ,,
27 (6—)		Uckfield .	April ,,		252	.	Buckhurst .	,, ,,
28 (6—)		Isfield .	,, ,,		253	.	Pelham .	,, ,,
29 (6—)		Lambeth .	,, ,,		254	.	Hambleton	,, 1882
30 (6—)		Camberwell	,, ,,		255	.	Willingdon	,, ,,
31 (6—)		Borough .	May ,,		256	.	Stanford .	,, ,,
32 (80, 80A,		Walworth .	,, ,,		257	.	Brading .	,, ,,
350, 217)					258	.	Cosham .	,, ,,
33 (6—)		Mitcham .	,, ,,		259	.	Telford .	,, ,,
34 (6—)		Balham .	June ,,		260	.	Lavington .	,, ,,
35 (298, 698)		Southwark	,, ,,		261	.	Wigmore .	,, ,,
36 (299, 699)		New Cross	,, ,,		262	.	Oxted .	,, ,,
221	.	Warbleton .	,, 1885		263	.	Purley .	,, ,,
222	.	Cuckmere .	,, ,,		264	.	Langston .	,, ,,

265	.	*Chipstead* .	Nov.	1882	288	.	*Effingham* .	June	1879
266	.	*Charlwood*.	,,	,,	289	.	*Holmbury* .	,,	,,
267	.	*Maresfield*.	,,	,,	290	.	*Denbies* .	,,	,,
268	.	*Baynards* .	June	1880	291	.	*Deepdene* .	,,	,,
269	.	*Crawley* .	May	,,	292	.	*Leigham* .	Nov.	1877
270	.	*Warnham*.	,,	,,	293	.	*Norbury* .	,,	,,
271	.	*Eridge* .	,,	,,	294	.	*Rosebery* .	,,	,,
272	.	*Nevill* .	,,	,,	295	.	*Whippingham*	Oct.	,,
273	.	*Dornden* .	,,	,,	296	.	*Osborne* .	,,	,,
274	.	*Guildford* .	Dec.	1879	297	.	*Bonchurch* .	,,	,,
275	.	*Cranleigh* .	,,	,,	298	.	*Southwark*.	,,	,,
276	.	*Rudgwick* .	,,	,,	299 (6—)		*New Cross* .	,,	,,
277	.	*Slinfold* .	,,	,,	351 (218)		*Chailey* .	Dec.	1885
278	.	*Groombridge*	,,	,,	352 (219)		*Lavant* .	,,	,,
279	.	*Tunbridge Wells*	,,	,,	353 (220)		*Keymer* .	,,	,,
280	.	*Grinstead* .	Oct.	,,	354	.	*Lancing* .	April	1886
281	.	*Withyham*.	,,	,,	355	.	*Worthing* .	May	,,
282	.	*Rowfant* .	,,	,,	356	.	*Coulsdon* .	June	,,
283	.	*Aldgate* .	,,	,,	357	.	*Riddlesdown* .	,,	,,
284	.	*Ashburnham*	,,	,,	358	.	*Henfield* .	Oct.	,,
285	.	*Holmwood*.	,,	,,	359	.	*Egmont* .	Dec.	,,
286	.	*Ranmore* .	June	,,	360	.	*Leconfield* .	,,	,,
287	.	*Buryhill* .	,,	,,	361	.	*Upperton* .	,,	,,
					362	.	*Kidbrooke* .	Mar.	1887

Notes: 259 renamed Barnham   1898
       272   ,,   Goring   1897
       294   ,,   Falmer   ,,
       296   ,,   Peckham   1901
As the derivation of the name 'Brookhouse' (230) is probably known
to very few people, it may be mentioned that it was the residence
of Mr Stephenson Clarke, at Ardingly; the writer's father-in-law.

In November, 1874, the first of a very similar type, class 'E',
appeared: No. 97 *Honfleur*. They were six-coupled, with 4ft 6in
wheels, for goods traffic. Altogether there were 72, as follows:

85 (6—)	*Cannes* .	Feb.	1883	103 (695)	*Normandy* .	Oct.	1876
86 (6—)	*Geneva* .	Mar.	,,	104 (696)	*Brittany* .	,,	,,
87 (6—)	*Bologna* .	,,	,,	105 (697)*	*Morlaix* .	,,	,,
88 (6—)	*Rhine* .	,,	,,	106 (606)	*Guernsey* .	,,	,,
89 (89A, 689)	*Brest* .	April	,,	107 (607)	*Alderney* .	Nov.	,,
90 (6—)	*Berne* .	,,	,,	108 (608)*	*Jersey* .	,,	,,
91 (6—)	*Fishbourne*.	Oct.	,,	109 (609)	*Strasbourg*.	Mar.	1877
92 .	*Polesden* .	,,	,,	110 (610)*	*Burgundy* .	,,	,,
93 .	*Calbourne* .	,,	,,	111 (611)	*Montpellier*	,,	,,
94* .	*Shorwell* .	,,	,,	112 .	*Versailles* .	April	,,
95* .	*Luccombe* .	Nov.	,,	113 .	*Granville* .	,,	,,
96* .	*Salzberg* .	,,	,,	114 .	*Trouville* .	May	,,
97 .	*Honfleur* .	,,	1874	115 .	*Lorraine* .	June	,,
98 .	*Marseilles*.	,,	,,	116 .	*Touraine* .	,,	,,
99 (610)*	*Bordeaux* .	Dec.	,,	117 .	*Florence* .	Aug.	,,
100 (692)	*Calvados* .	April	1875	118 .	*Trocadero* .	Sept.	,,
101 (693)	*Orleans* .	,,	,,	119 .	*Rochelle* .	,,	,,
102 (694)	*Cherbourg* .	,,	,,	120 .	*Provence* .	,,	,,

121	.	*Verona* .	July 1878	139	.	*Lombardy* .	Mar. 1879
122	.	*Leghorn* .	Aug. ,,	140	.	*Toulouse* .	,, ,,
123	.	*Seine* .	,, ,,	141	.	*Mentone* .	,, ,,
124*	.	*Bayonne* .	,, ,,	142	.	*Toulon* .	,, ,,
125	.	*Navarre* .	,, ,,	143	.	*Nuremberg*	,, ,,
126	.	*Gascony* .	,, ,,	144	.	*Chambery* .	April ,,
127	.	*Poitiers* .	Oct. ,,	145	.	*France* .	Oct. 1880
128	.	*Avignon* .	,, ,,	146	.	*Havre* .	,, ,,
129	.	*Alencon* .	,, ,,	147	.	*Danube* .	,, ,,
130	.	*Rennes* .	,, ,,	148	.	*Vienna* .	,, ,,
131 (W4)		*Gournay* .	,, ,,	149	.	*Lucerne* .	,, ,,
132	.	*Epernay* .	,, ,,	150	.	*Adriatic* .	Nov. ,,
133	.	*Picardy* .	,, ,,	151	.	*Helvetia* .	Dec. ,,
134	.	*Ancona* .	Dec. ,,	152 (W2)		*Hungary* .	,, ,,
135*	.	*Foligno* .	,, ,,	153	.	*Austria* .	Mar. 1881
136 (W1)		*Brindisi* .	,, ,,	154 (W3)		*Madrid*	,, ,,
137	.	*Dijon* .	,, ,,	155	.	*Brenner* .	,, ,,
138	.	*Macon* .	,, ,,	156	.	*Munich* .	,, ,,

Notes: No. 113 was renamed Durdans in 1883.
The eleven engines marked * were rebuilt after the amalgamation as 0-6-2 (class E1/R) to work the North Devon & Cornwall Light Railway.

In December, 1874, Stroudley built his first single-wheel express engine, *Grosvenor*. The driving wheels were 6ft 9in, which he reduced in the succeeding engines to 6ft 6in. The carrying wheels were the standard size of 4ft 6in. The total heating surface was 1,210 square feet, in later engines, 1,184. In January, 1877, he produced a smaller one, *Abergavenny*, with cylinders only 16 by 22, and heating surface 1,074 square feet. At the end of 1880 he settled upon standard dimensions, which were between those of the two already mentioned, and the whole class, known as 'G', were as follows:

151 (326)		*Grosvenor* .	Dec. 1874	338	.	*Bembridge* .	Oct. 1881
325	.	*Abergavenny*	Jan. 1877	339	.	*London* .	Dec. ,,
327	.	*Imberhorne* .	Dec. 1880	340	.	*Medina* .	,, ,,
328	.	*Sutherland* .	,, ,,	341	.	*Parkhurst* .	,, ,,
329	.	*Stephenson* .	June 1881	342	.	*St Lawrence* .	,, ,,
330	.	*Newhaven* .	,, ,,	343	.	*Wilmington* .	,, ,,
331	.	*Fairlight* .	,, ,,	344	.	*Hurstmonceux*	,, ,,
332	.	*Shanklin* .	,, ,,	345	.	*Plumpton* .	Mar. 1882
333	.	*Ventnor* .	,, ,,	346	.	*Alfriston* .	,, ,,
334	.	*Petworth* .	,, ,,	347	.	*Dallington* .	,, ,,
335	.	*Connaught* .	Sept. 1881	348	.	*Lullington* .	April 1882
336	.	*Edinburgh* .	,, ,,	349	.	*Albany* .	,, ,,
337	.	*Yarmouth* .	,, ,,	350	.	*Southbourne* .	,, ,,

Notes: Nos. 326, 335 and 336 were sold to the Italian State Railways in 1907.

In September, 1876, a class of 0-4-2 tender engines was introduced for mixed traffic, with 5ft 6in wheels, fourteen in all; called 'D2';

300 *Lyons* . . .	Sept. 1876	307 *Venice* . . .	Mar. 1878
301 *Caen* . . .	Mar. 1877	308 *Como* . . .	June 1883
302 *Turin* . . .	Dec. ,,	309 *Splugen* . . .	,, ,,
303 *Milan* . . .	,, ,,	310 *Laval* . . .	,, ,,
304 *Nice* . . .	,, ,,	311 *Rhone* . . .	,, ,,
305 *Genoa* . . .	,, ,,	312 *Albion* . . .	,, ,,
306 *Naples* . . .	Mar. 1878	313 *Paris* . . .	,, ,,

As these engines gave very satisfactory results,* Stroudley then ventured upon some similar engines for express work, with 6ft 6in wheels, which was a very bold experiment, fully justified by results; in spite of many predictions that they would never stay on the road. These engines, which were the forerunners of the '*Gladstone*' class, had cylinders 17½ by 26, and were known as 'D3'. They were the following:

208 (508, 608) *Richmond*	Oct. 1878	211 (511, 611) *Beaconsfield*	Mar. 1880
209 (509, 609) *Devonshire*	July 1879	212 (512, 612) *Hartington*	,, ,,
210 (510, 610) *Cornwall*	Oct. ,,	213 (513, 613) *Norfolk*	,, ,,

No. 210 was renamed *Belgravia* in 1902; 211, *Cavendish* in 1885. They were all scrapped 1901–4.

In June, 1882, some large goods engines, class 'C', known as 'Jumbos', began to come out, of which there were twelve altogether; the cylinders being 18¼ by 26; one of these (428) was sold in 1920 to the Stratford & Midland Junction Railway (No. 7).

421 (691) . . .	June 1882	425	Oct. 1882
422 (692) . . .	,, ,,	426	Nov. ,,
423	Sept. ,,	427–429 . . .	May 1884
424	,, ,,	430–432 . . .	June 1887

The first of the magnificent 'B' or '*Gladstone*' class appeared at the end of 1882. As an example of neat and compact designing they were quite unrivalled, and were the most powerful engines ever built for their weight, which was only 38 tons 14 cwt, of which 28 tons 6 cwt was available for adhesion. The cylinders were 18¼ by 26in, cast in pairs, with the valves underneath. The total heating surface was 1,485 square feet, grate area 20.65. There were 36 in the class, the last ten coming out after Stroudley's death in December, 1889, as follows:

172 .	*Littlehampton*	April 1891	179 .	*Sandown* .	May 1890
173 .	*Cottesloe* .	,, ,,	180 .	*Arundel* .	Mar. ,,
174 .	*Fratton* .	Dec. 1890	181 .	*Croydon* .	Feb. ,,
175 .	*Hayling* .	,, ,,	182 .	*Hastings* .	Dec. 1889
176 .	*Pevensey* .	Nov. ,,	183 .	*Eastbourne*	Nov. ,,
177 .	*Southsea* .	,, ,,	184 .	*Carew D. Gilbert*	Sept. ,,
178 .	*Leatherhead*	June ,,	185 .	*George A. Wallis*	,, ,,

* Though this class only lasted thirty years.

186	.	*De la Warr*	June	1889		197	.	*Jonas Levy*	May	1888
187	.	*Philip Rose*	,,	,,		198	.	*Sheffield* .	Dec.	1887
188	.	*Allen Sarle*	April	,,		199	.	*Samuel Laing*	,,	,,
189	.	*EdwardBlount*	Mar.	,,		200	.	*Beresford* .	,,	,,
190	.	*Arthur Otway*	Dec.	1888		214	(618)	*Gladstone* .	,,	1882
191	.	*Gordon-Lennox*	Nov.	,,		215	.	*Salisbury* .	,,	1883
192	.	*Jacomb-Hood*	Oct.	,,		216	.	*Granville* .	,,	,,
193	.	*Fremantle* .	,,	,,		217	(620)	*Northcote* .	,,	,,
194	.	*Bickersteth*	June	,,		218	.	*Beaconsfield*	Oct.	1885
195	.	*Cardew* .	,,	,,		219	(619)	*Cleveland* .	,,	,,
196	.	*Ralph L. Lopes*	May	,,		220	.	*Hampden* .	Dec	1887

Notes: 184 was afterwards named Stroudley.
189 was shown at the Paris Exhibition of 1889.
214 is now in the Railway Museum, York.

The last survivor of this class was No. 172, which was only withdrawn from service in 1933.

In October, 1884, a 0-6-2 goods tank engine was brught out which was a development of the 'E1' 0-6-0T, No. 157 *Barcelona*. She lasted till 1922. Stroudley's intention of laying down a class of these engines was carried out by his successor in office.

During the Stroudley period the passenger engines were yellow,* and goods very dark green. This practice was continued by his successor. Each engine had its own driver, whose name was painted inside the cab. As the now universal practice of 'pooling' locomotives has been receiving some criticism lately, the following remarks which Stroudley made in the course of the discussion on his paper mentioned at the beginning of this chapter are interesting: he

considered it of great advantage to keep separate engines for the drivers. He had always believed that if an engine was made as carefully as possible, it would respond to the attention it got afterwards; that the driver would be proud of its appearance and of the duty he could get out of it; and doubly proud to be able to perform a great duty with a small amount of expense.

It was to be found that the same man would not take the care of another engine, should he have to work one for a time, as he did of his own; and those engines which had unfortunately to be entrusted to several drivers deteriorated in quality, consumed more coal, and got dirty and out of repair much more rapidly than those which were appropriated to particular men.

He was of the opinion that it was better for a railway company to spend more capital and have more engines, so that one locomotive could be retained for each driver, as the total cost for stores and maintenance would in that case be less.

In February, 1890, Robert J. Billinton was appointed locomotive, carriage and wagon superintendent. At first he had to complete a number of engines which had been put in hand by his predecessor.

---

* The yellow colouring has a base of yellow ochre, tinted with orange chrome, burnt sienna, and bronze green. For some reason the mixture was known as 'Scotch green'.

Besides some of the 'B' class, which have been already dealt with, there were several 0-6-2 goods tanks. One came out in December, 1891: No. 158 *West Brighton*. There were six more of the 'E' class, which were slightly modified by the new chief:

159	.	*Edenbridge*	June 1891		162	.	*Southwater*	Nov. 1891
160	.	*Portslade* .	,, ,,		163	.	*Southwick*	Dec. ,,
161	.	*Aldrington*.	Nov. ,,		164	.	*Spithead* .	,, ,,

Experience on the Midland Railway had taught Billinton the value of a bogie, and the first engines of his own design were a series of 0-4-4 tanks, of which there were 36 in all. The wheels were 5ft 6in and 3ft; cylinders 18 by 26 (some later $17\frac{1}{2}$):

363 *Goldsmid*	.	.	May 1892		381 *Fittleworth*	.	.	Oct. 1893
364 *Truscott*.	.	.	,, ,,		382 *Farlington*	.	.	,, ,,
365 *Victoria*	.	.	June ,,		383 *Three Bridges* .	.	Dec. ,,
366 *Crystal Palace* .	.	.	,, ,,		384 *Cooksbridge*	.	.	,, ,,
367 *Norwood*	.	.	,, ,,		385 *Portsmouth*	.	Jan. 1894
368 *Newport*	.	.	,, ,,		386 *Chichester*	.	.	,, ,,
369 *Burgess Hill* .	.	Oct. ,,		387 *Steyning*	.	.	May ,.
370 *Haywards Heath*	.	,, ,,		388 *Emsworth*	.	.	,, ,,
371 *Angmering*	.	.	Dec. ,,		389 *Shoreham*	.	.	,, ,,
372 *Amberley*	.	.	,, ,,		390 *St Leonards*	.	.	,, ,,
373 *Billingshurst* .	.	Jan. 1893		391 *Drayton*	.	.	June ,,
374 *Pulborough*	.	.	,, ,,		392 *Polegate*	.	.	,, ,,
375 *Glynde* .	.	.	April ,,		393 *Woodside*	.	.	Mar. 1896
376 *Folkington*	.	.	,, ,,		394 *Cowfold*	.	.	,, ,,
377 *Hurstpierpoint* .	.	June ,,		395 *Gatwick*	.	...	April ,,
378 *Horsted Keynes*	.	,, ,,		396 *Clayton*	.	.	,, ,,
379 *Sanderstead*	.	.	,, ,,		397 *Bexhill*	.	.	Nov. ,,
380 *Thornton Heath*	.	,, ,,		398 *Haslemere*	.	.	,, ,,

The next class, designed at Brighton, was a series of goods engines at first called class 'C' later 'C2' and 'C2X', the latter being rebuilt with much larger boilers. They were all built by the Vulcan Foundry:

443, 444	.	.	.	June 1893		535-540	.	.	.	Nov. 1900
445-452	.	.	.	Dec. 1894		541 .	.	.	Nov. 1901
521-523	.	.	.	Aug. 1900		542-546	.	.	.	Dec. ,,
524-527	.	.	.	Sept. ,,		547-550	.	.	.	Jan. 1902
528-534	.	.	.	Oct. ,,		551-555	.	.	.	May ,,

In 1894 some 0-6-2 radial tanks came out, which were a development of the 'E3' type. These proved very useful engines, and a large number were built. The first batch had 4ft 6in wheels, and 18 by 26 cylinders:

165 *Blatchington*	.	.	Nov. 1894		170 *Bishopstone*	.	.	Dec. 1894
166 *Cliftonville*	.	.	,, ,,		453 *Broadbridge*	.	.	May 1895
167 *Saddlescombe*	.	.	,, ,,		454 *Storrington*	.	.	,, ,,
168 *Southborough*	.	.	,, ,,		455 *Brockhurst*	.	.	,, ,,
169 *Bedhampton*	.	.	Dec. ,,		456 *Aldingbourne* .	.	,, ,,

457	*Watersfield*	.	. Oct. 1895	460	*Warminghurst* .	. Nov. 1895
458	*Chalvington*	. .	,, ,,	461	*Staplefield*	. . ,, ,,
459	*Warlingham*	. .	,, ,,	462	*Washington*	. . ,, ,,

In 1895 the first of a quite new type for the Brighton company appeared, being an express engine with leading bogie and 6ft 9in coupled wheels, the cylinders being, as usual, 18 by 26 (class 'B2'). They were handsome engines, but would have been better if the boilers had been larger, a fault which was amply corrected in succeeding ones. The heating surface was only 1,342 square feet in all. They were afterwards rebuilt with much larger boilers (class 'B2X'):

314	*Charles C. Macrae*	. June 1895	203	*Henry Fletcher* .	. Mar. 1887
315	*Duncannon*	. . ,, ,,	204	*Telford* .	. ,, ,,
316	*Goldsmid*	. ,, ,,	205	*Hackworth*	. April ,,
317	*Gerald Loder* .	. June 1896	206	*Smeaton*	. April 1897
318	*Rothschild*	. . ,, ,,	207	*Brunel* .	. June ,,
319	*John Fowler* .	. Sept. ,,	171	*Nevill* .	. ,, ,,
320	*Rastrick*	. ,, ,,	208	*Abercorn*	. Aug. ,,
321	*John Rennie*	. . ,, ,,	209	*Wolfe Barry* .	. Sept. ,,
322	*G. P. Bidder* .	. Oct. 1896	210	*Fairbairn*	. Oct. ,,
323	*William Cubitt*	. Dec. ,,	211	*Whitworth*	. Nov. ,,
324	*John Hawkshaw*	. ,, ,,	212	*Armstrong*	. Jan. 1898
201	*Rosebery*	. Jan. 1897	213	*Bessemer*	. . ,, ,,
202	*Trevithick*	. Feb. ,,			

Note: No. 315 was renamed J. Gay and No. 319, Leconfield.

In 1897 another set of six-coupled radial tanks were commenced, with 5 ft wheels, being intended for use on passenger work. There were 75 in all, class 'E4'; several were later fitted with class 'I2' boilers, and classified 'E4X'.

463	*Wivelsfield*	. Dec. 1897	482	*Newtimber*	. Dec. 1998
464	*Woodmancote* .	. ,, ,,	483	*Hellingly*	. Feb. 1899
465	*Hurst Green*	. Mar. 1898	484	*Hackbridge*	. Mar. ,,
466	*Honor Oak*	. ,, ,,	485	*Ashington*	. ,, ,,
467	*Berwick*	. April ,,	386	*Godalming*	. April ,,
468	*Midhurst*	. ,, ,,	487	*Fishergate*	. May ,,
469	*Beachy Head* .	. May ,,	488	*Oakwood*	. ,, ,,
470	*East Hoathly* .	. ,, ,,	489	*Boxgrove*	. June ,,
471	*Forest Hill*	. June ,,	490	*Bohemia*	. ,, ,,
472	*Fay Gate*	. ,, ,,	491	*Hangleton*	. Sept. ,,
473	*Birch Grove*	. July ,,	492	*Jevington*	. ,, ,,
474	*Bletchingly*	. ,, ,,	493	*Telscombe*	. Oct. ,,
475	*Partridge Green*	. Sept. ,,	494	*Woodgate*	. ,, ,,
476	*Beeding*	. ,, ,,	495	*Chessington*	. Nov. ,,
477	*Poynings*	. Oct. ,,	496	*Chiddingfold* .	. ,, ,,
478	*Newick* .	. ,, ,,	497	*Donnington*	. April 1900
479	*Bevendean*	. Nov. ,,	498	*Strettington*	. ,, ,,
480	*Fletching*	. ,, ,,	499	*Woodendean*	. May ,,
481	*Itchingfield*	. Dec. ,,	500	*Puttenham*	. ,, ,,

501 *Stoat's Nest*	.	.	June 1900	520 *Westbourne*	.	.	June 1901
502 *Ridgewood*	.	.	,, ,,	556 *Tadworth*	.	.	Aug. ,,
503 *Buckland*	.	.	Aug. ,,	557 *Northlands*	.	.	,, ,,
504 *Chilworth*	.	.	,, ,,	558 *Chiltington*	.	.	Sept. ,,
505 *Annington*	.	.	Sept. ,,	559 *Framfield*	.	.	Oct. ,,
506 *Catherington*	.	.	Oct. ,,	560 *Pembury*	.	.	,, ,,
507 *Horley*	.	.	Nov. ,,	561 *Walberton*	.	.	Nov. ,,
508 *Bognor*	.	.	,, ,,	562 *Laughton*	.	.	Dec. ,,
509 *Southover*	.	.	Dec. ,,	563 *Wineham*	.	.	,, ,,
510 *Twineham*	.	.	,, ,,	564 *Nettlestone*	.	.	,, ,,
511 *Lingfield*	.	.	Jan. 1901	565 *Littleton*	.	.	Jan. 1902
512 *Kingswood*	.	.	Feb. ,,	566 *Durrington*	.	.	Feb. ,,
513 *Densworth*	.	.	,, ,,	577 *Blackstone*	.	.	June 1903
514 *Barcombe*	.	.	Mar. ,,	578 *Horsebridge*	.	.	,, ,,
515 *Swanmore*	.	.	,, ,,	579 *Roehampton*	.	.	,, ,,
516 *Rustington*	.	.	April ,,	580 *Shermanbury*	.	.	,, ,,
517 *Limpsfield*	.	.	May 1901	581 *Warningcamp*	.	.	Sept. ,,
518 *Porchester*	.	.	,, ,,	582 *Horndean*	.	.	,, ,,
519 *Portfield*	.	.	June ,,				

The year 1899 saw the first of a still larger type of 4-4-0, which were very fine engines. The wheels remained 6ft 9in, but the cylinders were made 19in in diameter, and cast together, with the valves below. They were classed 'B4' and B4X', the latter rebuilt and superheated. Nos. 47–51 and 55–74 were built by Sharp, Stewart and Co., the rest at Brighton:

42 *His Majesty*	.	.	May 1902	59 *Baden Powell*	.	.	Aug. 1901
43 *Duchess of Fife*	.	.	,, ,,	60 *Kimberley*	.	.	,, ,,
44 *Cecil Rhodes*	.	.	June ,,	61 *Ladysmith*	.	.	,, ,,
45 *Bessborough*	.	.	,, ,,	62 *Mafeking*	.	.	,, ,,
46 *Prince of Wales*	.	.	July ,,	63 *Pretoria*	.	.	,, ,,
47 *Canada*	.	.	June 1901	64 *Windsor*	.	.	,, ,,
48 *Australia*	.	.	July ,,	65 *Sandringham*	.	.	,, ,,
49 *Queensland*	.	.	,, ,,	66 *Balmoral*	.	.	,, ,,
50 *Tasmania*	.	.	,, ,,	67 *Osborne*	.	.	Sept. ,,
51 *Wolferton*	.	.	,, ,,	68 *Marlborough*	.	.	,, ,,
52 *Siemens*	.	.	Dec. 1899	69 *Bagshot*	.	.	,, ,,
53 *Sirdar*	.	.	Jan. 1900	70 *Holyrood*	.	.	,, ,,
54 *Empress*	.	.	Feb. ,,	71 *Goodwood*	.	.	,, ,,
55 *Emperor*	.	.	July 1901	72 *Sussex*	.	.	,, ,,
56 *Roberts*	.	.	Aug. ,,	73 *Westminster*	.	.	Oct. ,,
57 *Buller*	.	.	,, ,,	74 *Cornwall*	.	.	,, ,,
58 *Kitchener*	.	.	,, ,,				

Notes: No. 49 was renamed Duchess of Norfolk.
     No. 52   ,,   Sussex.
     No. 53   ,,   Richmond.
     No. 54   ,,   Princess Royal.
     No. 64   ,,   Norfolk.
     No. 66   ,,   Billinton.
     No. 70   ,,   Devonshire.

The other names were removed in 1906 and following years.

In 1902 experiments were carried out with oil fuel for locomotives, Milburn's system being employed. Twelve engines in all were so equipped. The experiment was not satisfactory so far as four tank engines were concerned, and they were converted back to coal in 1903, but the tests were continued with the other engines until 1904, when they were dropped owing to the cheapening of coal supplies having made oil fuelling no longer economical.

Some large six-coupled radial tanks appeared next, with 5ft 6in wheels; the boiler centre pitched at 8 feet from the rail; thirty in all, ('E5'), several received 'C3' class boilers later (class 'E5X'). These were sometimes used on important passenger duties, including the Newhaven boat trains.

399	*Middleton*	.	.	June 1904	574	*Copthorne*	. .	Feb. 1903
400	*Winchelsea*	.	.	,, ,,	575	*Westergate*	. .	Mar. ,,
401	*Woldingham*	.	.	,, ,,	576	*Brenchley*	. .	,, ,,
402	*Wanborough*	.	.	Sept. ,,	583	*Handcombe*	. .	Nov. ,,
403	*Fordcombe*	.	.	Oct. ,,	584	*Lordington*	. .	,, ,,
404	*Hardham*	.	.	,, ,,	585	*Crowborough*	. .	Dec. ,,
405	*Fernhurst*	.	.	Nov. ,,	586	*Maplehurst*	. .	,, ,,
406	*Colworth*	.	.	,, ,,	587	*Brighton*	. .	,, ,,
567	*Freshwater*	.	.	Oct. 1902	588	*Hawkenbury*	. .	,, ,,
568	*Carisbrooke*	.	.	,, ,,	589	*Ambersham*	. .	Mar. 1904
569	*Kensington*	.	.	Nov. ,,	590	*Lodsworth*	. .	April ,,
570	*Armington*	.	.	,, ,,	591	*Tillington*	. .	,, ,,
571	*Hickstead*	.	.	Jan. 1903	592	*Eastergate*	. .	,, ,,
572	*Farncombe*	.	.	,, ,,	593	*Hollington*	. .	May ,,
573	*Nutbourne*	.	.	Feb. ,,	594	*Shortbridge*	. .	June ,,

The last of R. J. Billinton's engines were a dozen 0-6-2 tanks, classed 'E6'; similar to the 'E5' class, except that the coupled wheels were only 4ft 6in (two received 'C3' boilers, reclassified 'E6X'):

407	*Worplesdon*	.	.	Dec. 1904	413	*Fenchurch*	. .	July 1905
408	*Binderton*	.	.	,, ,,	414	*Piccadilly*	. .	Aug. ,,
409	*Graffham*	.	.	,, ,,	415	.	. .	Sept. 1905
410	*Chilgrove*	.	.	Feb. 1905	416	.	. .	Oct. ,,
411	*Blackheath*	.	.	April ,,	417	.	. .	,, ,,
412	*Tandridge*	.	.	May ,,	418	.	. .	Nov. ,,

In November, 1904, Billinton died, and was succeeded in January, 1905, by Douglas Earle Marsh, who had been assistant to Ivatt at Doncaster, and had become steeped in Great Northern ideas. He took the very radical steps of substituting dark umber for the yellow colour of the passenger engines, adopting black for the goods, and abolishing names, except in a few special cases.

In 1905 two bogie-steam motor coaches were obtained from Beyer, Peacock and Co., numbered 1 and 2, and two four-wheeled petrol units from Dick, Kerr Ltd. Further experience led, however, to the adoption for rail-motor work of a distinctive type of unit consisting of an 'A' class tank engine working with a specially designed trailer coach; this style of motor train proved successful, and many were made in the years 1906 to 1908, the 'halts' on the routes they served being constructed at this time. 'D1' and 'D3' class engines were later fitted for rail-motor work.

At the end of the year a huge 4-4-2 express engine appeared, which was a copy of those in use on the Great Northern Railway. The coupled wheels were 6ft 7½in; cylinders 18½ by 26. Five were supplied by Kitson and Co., known as 'H1' class. Two (later all) had 19-in cylinders and all were later superheated. They came out as follows: 37, Dec., 1905, 38, Jan., 1906, and 39–41 in February. From 1909 to 1923 No. 39 bore the name *La France,** being so christened on the occasion of a visit of the French President to this country. After being taken into the Southern Railway they were named as follows:

37 Selsey Bill	40 St Catherine's Point
38 Portland Bill	41 Peveril Point
39 Hartland Point	

Ten large six-coupled goods followed, with 17½ (Nos. 305–9; 18in) by 26 cylinders ('C3' class):

300	.	.	.	.	Mar. 1906	305, 306	.	.	. July 1906
301, 302	.	.	.	May ,,	307, 308	.	.	. Aug. ,,
303, 304	.	.	.	June ,,	309	.	.	. . Sept. ,,

In September, 1906, the first of a new class of engine came out, namely a 4-4-2 tank, classed 'I1' (all later rebuilt as 'I1X'); followed by three more classes, 'I2', 'I3' and 'I4'. There were 62 in all.

Class 'I1'. Wheels, 5ft 6in; cylinders, 17½ by 26; pressure, 180 lb.

595	.	.	.	. Sept. 1906	1	.	.	.	. June 1907
596	.	.	.	. Nov. ,,	2, 3	.	.	.	. July ,,
597	.	.	.	. Dec. ,,	4	.	.	.	. Aug. ,,
598	.	.	.	. Jan. 1907	5	.	.	.	. Sept. ,,
599	.	.	.	. Feb. ,,	6, 7	.	.	.	. Oct. ,,
600	.	.	.	. Mar. ,,	8	.	.	.	. Nov. ,,
601, 602	.	.	.	April ,,	9, 10	.	.	.	. Dec. ,,
603, 604	.	.	.	June ,,					

Notes: Nos. 1–10 had a shorter wheelbase than the earlier ones; it is said wheels and motion off scrapped 'D1' class were used.

* The same name had been borne by B4 4-4-0 No. 54 in August, 1905 in connection with the visit of the French fleet to Portsmouth.

Class 'I2'. As above, but pressure 170 lb.

11	Dec. 1907	16,17 . .	. May 1908
12, 13 . .	. Feb. 1908	18, 19 . .	. June ,,
14 . .	. Mar. ,,	20 . . .	. July ,,
15 . . .	. April ,,		

Class 'I3'. Wheels, 6ft 7½in (No. 21, 6ft 9in); cylinders, 19 to 21 by 26; pressure, 180 lb.

21 . . .	. Sept. 1907	80, 81 . .	. Nov. 1910
22 . . .	. Mar. 1098	82 . .	. June 1912
23, 24, 25 .	. Dec. ,,	83, 84 .	. July ,,
26 . .	. Jan. 1909	85 .	. Aug. ,,
27 . .	. Feb. ,,	86 .	. Sept. ,,
28 . .	. Oct. ,,	87 .	. Oct. ,,
29 . .	. Nov. ,,	88 .	. Nov. ,,
30, 75 . .	. Jan. 1910	89 .	. Dec. ,,
76 . . .	. Feb. ,,	90 .	. Jan. 1913
77 . . .	. Sept. ,,	91 .	. Feb. ,,
78, 79 . .	. Oct. ,,		

Most of the above were superheated from the first.

Class 'I4'. Wheels, 5ft 6in; cylinders, 20 by 26; pressure 160 lb; superheated

31 . . .	. July 1908	34 . . .	. Oct. 1908
32 . . .	. Sept. ,,	35 . . .	. Nov. ,,
33 . . .	. Oct. ,,		

The engines of the 'I3' class were the first tanks to be regularly used for main line express traffic in this country, and led to the practice being extended to other lines, also to the adoption of superheaters elsewhere, as well as to the introduction of gigantic tank engines on a number of railways, which was so noticeable just before the grouping. In particular, the running of Nos. 23 and 26 on the Sunny South Special between Rugby and Brighton, which they did on alternate days with an express engine of the L.N.W.R., showing a considerable economy over the latter, both of fuel and water, had, there is very little doubt, a strong influence in favour of superheaters, which were afterwards adopted by the North Western.

Encouraged by the performances of these engines, Marsh produced an enormous tank engine of the 4-6-2 type with outside cylinders 21 by 26in, coupled wheels 6ft 7½in: No. 325 *Abergavenny*, which appeared in December, 1910. She was followed by another in February, 1912, No. 326 *Bessborough*, which was similar, except for having Walschaert's gear instead of the ordinary link motion.

In 1911 six more 'Atlantics' were produced at Brighton, with 21-in cylinders. The names given on the following page were bestowed on them after the amalgamation.

421 *South Foreland*	. July 1911	424 *Beachy Head*	. Sept. 1911
422 *North Foreland*	. ,, ,,	425 *Trevose Head*	. Dec. ,,
423 *The Needles* .	. Aug. ,,	426 *St Alban's Head*	. Jan. 1912

On 1st January, 1912 the duties of Locomotive Superintendent were taken up by L. B. Billinton, the son of the chief of 1890–1904 who had been in the service of the company ever since he left school. After completing engines ordered by his predecessor he built five six-coupled tanks followed later by five more, classed 'E2':*

100	.	.	.	. May 1913	105	.	.	.	. May 1915
101	.	.	.	. June ,,	106	.	.	.	. June ,,
102	.	.	.	. July ,,	107	.	.	.	. Jan. 1916
103	.	.	.	. Aug. ,,	108	.	.	.	. June ,,
104	.	.	.	. Dec. ,,	109	.	.	.	. Sept. ,,

In 1913 he introduced a powerful type of 'Mogul' goods engine known as class 'K', with 5ft 6in wheels and 21 by 26 cylinders (outside); superheated. There were seventeen in all:

337	.	.	.	. Sept. 1913	345, 346	.	.	. Dec. 1916
338	.	.	.	. Dec. ,,	347	.	.	. Oct. 1920
339	.	.	.	. Mar. 1914	348	.	.	. Nov. ,,
340	.	.	.	. July ,,	349, 350	.	.	. Dec. ,,
341	.	.	.	. Dec. ,,	351	.	.	. Jan. 1921
342	.	.	.	. Oct. 1916	352	.	.	. Feb. ,,
343, 344	.	.	. Nov. ,,	353	.	.	. Mar. ,,

In April, 1914, the first of class 'L' appeared, which was a colossal tank engine of the 'Baltic' or 4-6-4 type, of which in all there were seven. The driving wheels were 6ft 9in, cylinders 22 by 28.

327 *Charles C. Macrae*	. April 1914	330, 331 —	. . Dec. 1921
328 —	. . . Sept. ,,	332 —	. . Feb. 1922
329 *Stephenson*	. . Oct. 1921	333 *Remembrance* .	. April ,,

Nos. 329 and 333 were the only Brighton engines which retained their names after the grouping, although, as has already been mentioned, the Atlantics were given names later on. Owing to the increase of electrification, there was eventually no scope for the above tanks, and it was decided in 1934 to rebuild them as tender engines, with the following names (329 and 333 as before):

2327 Trevithick	2331 Beattie
2328 Hackworth	2332 Stroudley
2330 Cudworth	

A number L.B.S.C.R. engines were fitted with top-feed in the 'twenties: examples of the 'C2X', 'C3', 'E6X', 'B2X', 'B4', 'B4X' and 'K' class were seen at various times so fitted.

---

* These rather curious little engines used boilers intended by Marsh to be fitted on 'D1' and 'E1' engines to give them more power, but only one 'D1X' and one 'E1X' were ever so fitted. having a very 'overboilered' appearance.

XXII

London Brighton & South Coast Railway Steamer Services

THE Brighton company's steamer services must now be considered. Regular communication was established between Brighton and Dieppe towards the end of the eighteenth century. A placard printed in 1790 shows that the *Princess Royal* packet crossed from 'Brighthelmston' to Dieppe every Tuesday and returned on Saturday. She contained two elegant cabins, eight beds in each. It is pointed out that the route to London (presumably from Paris) is 90 miles nearer than by way of Dover and Calais.

In the early years of the nineteenth century, according to *Brighton in the Olden Time*, by J. G. Bishop (1880), the number of packets was out of all proportion to the passengers, and the Revenue officers had a strong suspicion that business of another character was carried on by them.

In conjunction with the London & Brighton company's trains, the General Steam Navigation company put on the *Menai* on 6th April, 1844, to run every Wednesday and Saturday from Shoreham to Dieppe, calling at Brighton. In the same year they also put on the *Fame*. They had been running steamers from Newhaven to Dieppe, calling at Brighton pier,* since June, 1825. It may be remarked, however, that the G.S.N. Co. was more a competitor than a coadjutor of the railways, as they ran steamers from London to Margate, Boulogne and Ostend.

Although, as related in the last chapter, the Select Committee of 1847–48 had signified their approval of giving the L.B.S.C.R. powers to own steamers, under certain limitations, the recommendation was not carried into effect for some years.

Much of the following information has been taken from a paper read before the Institute of Marine Engineers by Mr G. W. Buckwell, entitled *History of the Newhaven and Dieppe Service*, on 10th November, 1891.

* This was, of course, the old Chain Pier, which was opened on 25th November, 1823, and considered one of the great engineering works of the day. Erredge's *History of Brighthelmston* says the first steamer employed in the service was the *Swift*, of 80 horse-power.

Like the other companies in the same position, the L.B.S.C.R. proceeded to form an independent one, in 1847 – the Brighton and Continental Steam Packet Co. As the Brighton pier was very unprotected for the departure and arrival of the boats, and as, to quote Mr Buckwell, the Shoreham harbour authorities 'took too high a hand', Newhaven was chosen for the port on the English side. The vessels engaged in the service were the *Brighton, Newhaven* and *Dieppe*.

There was this difference between the two nominally independent steamship companies that worked with the South Eastern and Brighton companies respectively: the former had no railway money directly invested in it, but the Brighton had. As a consequence of action taken by the South Eastern Railway company the Brighton and Continental Steamship company had to be dissolved and the service between Newhaven and Dieppe was undertaken by the private firm of Maples and Morris. The three vessels just named were not, however, taken over, but Maples, instead, obtained a fleet from the Clyde. It so happened that at that time William Denny and Brothers had on their hands some old river paddle-steamers, known as the Castle fleet of Messrs Burns. The new service of Maples and Morris was opened in 1851 by the *Ayrshire Lassie*, and other boats were started the following month.

During the discussion on Mr Buckwell's paper, Captain E. Blackmore remarked:

> There was no Board of Trade supervision then. The harbour of Newhaven was a mere creek, with only two or three feet of water upon the bar at low water, and it was impossible to use larger vessels. The fares being much cheaper than by the South Eastern route, the boats were crowded, and the miseries endured by deck passengers were very great; they were often landed more like drowned rats than human beings.

Among the boats in Maples' fleet were the *Paris* and *Rouen*, which were put into service in 1852, and of which it may further be related that they were engaged in blockade running during the Crimean War. The *London* and the *Dundroon Castle* followed in 1853, the *Brighton, Lyons* and the *Orleans* in 1856. The last two were sister ships, built of iron by Scott Russell, on the same model, as regards the hull, as his *Great Eastern*. They had paddle wheels, and, in their palmiest days, made the crossing in 4 hours and 20 minutes.

In 1858 Maples' contract expired, but as the railway company had not, as yet, any steam-vessel powers, the agreement was renewed, and in 1863 the *Alexandra* was added, built by Caird and Co., of Greenock. Her tonnage was 369 gross; two oscillating engines, 52in diameter by 57 stroke; n.h.p., 170; i.h.p., 872. She ran ashore on the French coast in 1865, and was very badly damaged, fortunately without any loss of life. She was sold in 1883, and actually received a new set of engines in 1893. She was followed by the *Rouen II* and the *Sussex*, both twin screw.

In 1862 the Brighton railway obtained powers to build, own and operate steamer services between Newhaven and Dieppe, which were enlarged in 1864, to operate from Littlehampton to certain parts in France and to the Channel Islands. The powers for the Newhaven–Dieppe service were operative as from 13th July, 1863, and were shared by the Western railway of France. The working of the boats remained, however, with Maples until 1867, when he withdrew, taking with him the *Paris*, *Rouen I*, and the *Dieppe*. The vessels that the joint companies took over were the *Brighton*, *Lyons*, *Orleans*, *Rouen II*, *Sussex* and the *Alexandra*. The Littlehampton service belonged solely to the Brighton Railway, and that company opened it, in 1867, to St Malo, and in 1870 to Jersey. A service to Honfleur was taken over by the company in March, 1870.

The *Marseilles* was added to the Newhaven fleet in 1864 and the *Bordeaux* in 1865; both were paddle steamers built by Charles Lungley of Deptford, and were capable of a speed of 13 knots. In 1875 the *Paris II* was constructed by John Elder and Company. The last-named vessel, though generally admitted to be one of the handsomest vessels that ever crossed the Channel, did not come up to expectations in speed. Mr Buckwell related that, in a cupboard on the top engine-room platform of the *Paris*, a sovereign was put at the commencement of every trip which the firemen were to have if the passage were made in under five hours, but the men never won it. Strange to relate, in March, 1888, when nearly thirteen years old, she crossed in 4 hours 50 minutes – the first time under five hours. In the same year as the *Paris* was delivered – 1875 – the *Dieppe* and the *Newhaven* were put into service. They were screw cargo boats built by the Société des Forges et Chantiers, Havre. In 1878 – the year of the Paris Exhibition – the *Honfleur* (built 1875) and *Rennes* ran between Littlehampton and Dieppe; the following year they were in the Newhaven service, but were again at Littlehampton in 1880, where they remained until 1882, when they left that port for good and went to Newhaven, to which port the service to Honfleur was that year transferred.

In 1878 John Elder and Company delivered the *Brighton* and the *Victoria*. They were the first steel vessels in the fleet, and had the first steam steering gear – fitted on the bridge – to be seen at Newhaven. The former vessel, in June, 1878 – three months after delivery – crossed in 3 hours 54 minutes, and eleven years later – in January,

1889 – made the trip in 4 hours 2 minutes. In 1882 the same firm – by then the Fairfield Shipbuilding and Engineering Company – provided the *Normandy* and the *Brittany*, which were capable of 1½ knots greater speed than the *Brighton* and *Victoria*. In June, 1885, the *Brittany* crossed in 3 hours 37 minutes, and in July, 1885, the *Normandy* took 17 minutes less time. In 1888 the Fairfield yard supplied the *Rouen III* and the *Paris III*. They were 250ft long, had a beam of 29ft; forced draught was an innovation, and they were the last paddle steamers to be built for that service. On 11th September, 1888, *Paris III* made the trip in 3 hours 25 minutes, but the following day her sister ship beat that record by five minutes, i.e. in 3 hours 30 minutes.

It may be mentioned that the speed of the steamers about this time was partly due to the introduction of a very efficient type of feathering paddle wheel, invented by Stroudley, the Locomotive Superintendent.

There were also two other screw cargo boats, *Italy* and *Lyons*, the latter built by Elder in 1885.

During the Easter holidays of 1887 the *Victoria* went ashore on the French coast during a dense fog and subsequently became a total loss. Nineteen passengers lost their lives by the upsetting of a lifeboat, caused by a lady's wrap getting entangled in the ropes. In 1881 a change was made in the flag under which the Newhaven–Dieppe boats ran. They were, as already said, jointly owned by the Brighton and the Western of France – the latter now the greater part of the French State Railways. All the boats, though, sailed under the British flag, but in the year just named the cargo boats – the *Dieppe*, *Newhaven*, *Italy*,* and *Lyons** – were placed under the French flag, whilst the passenger vessels – the *Bordeaux*, *Paris*, *Victoria*, *Brighton*, *Brittany* and the *Normandy* – remained under the British flag. Up to 1891 only the cargo boats were regarded as French boats, but in that year, as a consequence of a decision that the Western of France should share in the passenger and mail traffic, the *Seine*, a passenger boat which had been built at Havre, was put on the route and sailed under the French flag. On 8th August, 1891, the *Seine* crossed in 3 hours 11 minutes. The *Tamise* of 1893, the *Manche* of 1897, and the *France* of 1898 were also built at Havre and flew the French flag.

The *Seaford* was supplied in 1894 by William Denny and Brothers, but was unfortunately lost in a collision during a fog on 20th August, 1895.† She was succeeded by the *Sussex* – also built by Denny's –

---

* Altered to *Italie* and *Lyon*.

† No lives were lost. The passengers (250) were transferred to the *Lyon*, and taken back to Newhaven.

which made the passage in 3 hours 3 minutes on her trial trip. In 1894 the same firm supplied the *Calvados* and the *Trouville* for cargo service between Newhaven and Caen, followed in 1896 by the *Prince Arthur*. These three were sold to the S.E.R. Co., the *Calvados* being at once resold to the General Steam Navigation Co., and the other two being renamed *Walmer* and *Deal*. All these steamers since the *Paris III* were twin-screw. In 1900 Messrs Denny supplied the passenger steamer *Arundel*.

The London, Brighton & South Coast company lost no time in following the lead of its neighbour in the matter of the turbine. The S.E. & C. *Queen* ran her trials over the Skelmorlie mile on 12th June, 1903, and on the following day Denny's launched, for the Newhaven–Dieppe service, the turbine-driven *Brighton*, which further assisted in establishing the economy and popularity of the new method of propulsion, especially in rough weather. The *Brighton* was rather smaller than the *Queen*, having a length of 280ft and a beam of 34ft. Her turbines, driving three shafts, were of 6,000 i.h.p. and the speed realised was 21.37 knots. It was said in the discussion on a paper by Messrs Parsons and Stoney at the Institution of Civil Engineers, that the trials of the *Brighton*, with turbine engines, as compared with her sister vessel, the *Arundel*, having triple expansion engines, showed a saving of 10 per cent by the turbines at the same usual speed and when carrying equal loads; also that the turbine vessel had a considerable advantage in point of speed on the same coal consumption.

In 1905, as a consequence of the success of the *Brighton*, the L.B.S.C.R. company ordered the *Dieppe*, built and engined by the Fairfield Shipbuilding and Engineering Company. As with the *Brighton*, severe limitations were imposed, in connection with the design of the vessel, by the dimensions and draught of water in the harbours. She had, therefore a length of only 284ft, a beam of 34ft 8in, and a depth of 22ft 1in. Despite these limitations, on her final trial to and from Dieppe, she attained a mean speed of 21.64 knots, which was about half a mile in excess of that required by the contract. Her astern turbines were of somewhat greater efficiency than in previous vessels, and it was found that, when steaming at 12 knots, she could be stopped in a distance equal to one and a half times her length, and in 31 seconds time. It was proved that, in their runs, the *Brighton* and *Dieppe* gained from three to four minutes over the boats with reciprocating engines in fine weather, and about five minutes when the weather was rough. In 1911 the French partners furnished the *Newhaven*, and in 1912 the *Rouen*. In 1913 Messrs W.

Denny and Brothers delivered the *Paris*, which was 300ft long, with a beam of 35ft 6in, a tonnage of 1,774, and capable of a speed of 25 knots, and of crossing in 2¾ hours. Her arrival was coincident with the opening, by the French State Railways, which the Western had now become, of the new route through Pontoise, whereby the rail journey between Dieppe and Paris was reduced by 20 miles.

The war services of the Brighton company's fleet were briefly described in Chapter XIX, but further mention may be made of the torpedoing of the *Sussex*, which was an outstanding event of the war. She was on the way from Folkestone to Dieppe, on 24th March, 1916, when she was torpedoed by a submarine, and though she remained afloat, her forepart was blown up and some 80 passengers were killed and injured. This event helped materially to bring the United States into the war.

In August, 1921, the French partners made another addition to the fleet – the *Versailles*; 305ft long, with a beam of 36ft, a tonnage of 1,903, and, like the *Paris*, a speed of 25 knots.

Three cargo steamers remain to be mentioned, which were twin-screw, and owned by the French State Railways, namely *Brest* (1900), *Portsmouth* (1902), and *Bordeaux* (1912). The *Maine* (1910) was torpedoed in 1917.

There were two fine modern tugs at Newhaven, which could be used for fire-fighting and salvage work: the *Richmere* (1921), and *Foremost* (1922); the latter built in Holland.

PART IV

THE SOUTH EASTERN AND CHATHAM RAILWAY

XXIII

The South Eastern Railway
down to 1850

WHAT appears to have been the earliest proposal for a passenger railway to enter London was the Kentish Railway. The prospectus was published in full in *The Times* of 21st December, 1824, the engineer being Thomas Telford. The line was planned to run from London to Dover and Sandwich, by way of Woolwich, Chatham, and Canterbury; there were to be branches to Maidstone and to Margate. The capital was £1,000,000, and the London board consisted of eighteen directors. The line was to be worked 'by locomotive machines', but the company would 'in addition thereto make use of the assistance of horses'.

According to a 'General Statement of the position and projects of the Company', issued by the South Eastern directors in December, 1845, the construction of a railway through the county of Kent was first projected in 1825 – doubtless referring to the above – and again in 1832 and 1835. The Phillimore collection contains a prospectus of the 1832 scheme, which is of the greatest rarity, and contains some remarkably interesting features. The line was to run nearly due east, much of the same route as that of 1824 – in fact, following closely the London and Dover road. It is entitled 'Prospectus of a proposed Rail Road between London and Dover, with a steam Boat Ferry across the River Thames, forming a communication between the counties of Kent and Essex, and a Steam Boat Dock, connected by the Rail Road with the Metropolis. London, 1832.'

After expatiating on the advantages of the scheme, pointing out the importance of bringing into contact with the metropolis, and each other, the military depots of Woolwich, Chatham, Sheerness and Dover, it proceeds:

The proposed Rail-road will commence near Limehouse, and pass through the Essex marshes to a point on the bank of the Thames, a little below Woolwich; here the train of carriages will run on to the deck of a Steam Ferry-boat, which will convey them to the opposite bank, where without having subjected the passengers to the inconvenience of quitting their seats, or to the delay of removing a single article of luggage, they will resume their course on the Railroad, proceeding in nearly a straight line over the marshes by Erith to Greenhithe putting out a branch to Dartford. Near Greenhithe, the line will leave the marshes, and be continued to the southward of Gravesend till it reaches the Medway, near Upnor Castle; here a branch Steam Boat will afford a ready means of communication with Sheerness. Crossing the Medway, by a Ferry-boat, to the north side of Chatham Dock Yard, the line running between Milton and Sittingbourne, will be nearly direct to Faversham; from hence a small divergence is necessary to pass Boughton Hill on the south side and approach Canterbury, where it will form a central point, for radial roads to Herne Bay, Margate, Broadstairs, Ramsgate, Sandwich and Deal to the north, and Folkstone, Sandgate, Hythe, Wye and Ashford to the south. Between Canterbury and Dover there is scarcely anything to cause a diversion from the direct line, except the consideration that may be due to the parks and pleasure grounds of the proprietors of the land.

* * * * *

In addition to the improvement in the line of road, it is proposed so to adapt the carriages that run upon it, as to render them equally fit for passage over ordinary roads, with those constructed for that object solely; so that at whatever point it may be convenient to diverge from the Rail-road, it will only be necessary to disengage the particular carriage, and attach horses, without disturbing either passengers or luggage.

The interesting points in the above account are, firstly, the proposal for a train ferry, and secondly, the suggestion of running passenger carriages on rail and road indifferently. How the latter feat was to be accomplished does not appear; probably a 'plate-railway', with the flanges on the rails, was intended. The survey was made by or under Henry R. Palmer, then vice-president of the Institution of Civil Engineers, who had published a book in 1823 describing a scheme for a monorail line.

The project, however, was before its time. It met with no local encouragement from the towns, and with violent opposition from most of the landowners. The passage of the Medway at Rochester was considered an almost insurmountable barrier, and the matter dropped for a time. The crossing of the Thames could have easily been avoided, of course, by starting south of the river.

In Herapath's *Railway Magazine* for April, 1836, the following reference to the South Eastern Railway occurs:

In May, 1834, a prospectus was issued by the solicitors to the present South Eastern line, containing proposals to form a line of railway of which Mr Green was the secretary, and Colonel Landmann* the engineer. Six months later the same solicitors sent out a new prospectus, retaining, I believe, Colonel Landmann, but replacing Mr Green by a Mr Yeats.

* * * * *

They then turned their kind attention towards the fashionable Brightonians, hooking on another engineer, Mr Palmer, instead of Colonel Landmann. At length, a strong gale having sprung up from the west, by Stephenson and Rennie, they once more veered round towards Dover.

* Of London & Greenwich fame.

The aspirations of this company in the direction of Brighton have already been mentioned in Chapter XV.

In 1836, by 6 & 7 Will. IV, c. 75, a railway from the terminus of the London & Croydon, through Oxted, Tonbridge and Ashford to Folkstone and Dover was sanctioned. By 1 Vic., c. 93, of the following year, the junction with the London & Croydon Railway was to be in the parish of Penge.

The London & Brighton Act received the Royal Assent on 15th July, 1837, and the arrangement for sharing the line from Norwood to Redhill has been described in Chapter XV. At that time Parliament considered that there should only be one entrance into London from the south; hence the concentration of these lines at Croydon, or, as provided by section 135, the junction could be made at Redhill, which was done, under 2 & 3 Vic., c. 79. The deviation joined the line of 1836 at Chiddingstone, near Edenbridge. There is a tunnel – at Bletchingley, 1,326 yards long – and there were three viaducts over the river Medway and one over the river Stour. The most remarkable feature of the line was that the 46 miles to Ashford were practically straight throughout and on almost a dead level. Those features, moreover, were not obtained by expensive cuttings or embankments, such as Brunel found necessary for the Great Western between Paddington and Swindon. Considerable deviations from the original line between Smeeth and Dover were authorised before construction.

William Cubitt was the engineer, and as he was one of the first to use the modern transverse sleeper road, the following remarks thereon by the Board of Trade Inspector will be noted with interest:

The peculiarity of Mr Cubitt's construction consists in using transverse triangular sleepers, between 8 and 9 feet in length, with the vertex of the triangle undermost, which renders them much easier to arrange by the process technically termed packing, than the more usual forms either of a rectangular section or of half spars round at top but flat at bottom. The upper part of these triangular sleepers is planed true, over which the chairs and rails are fitted into their places by iron gauges, the chairs being fixed to the sleepers by trenails of compressed oak whilst the rails are confined in their places by side wedges (keys) of compressed ash. The trenails usually attract some moisture, which causes them to swell a little, and thus they keep the parts so firmly together that on lifting a rail the chairs and sleepers are raised along with it, without their mutual hold of each other being loosened. The chairs are heavier than those in common use, and therefore nearly twice as expensive, but being stronger in proportion very few of them break in comparison with the latter, and those used over the joints of adjoining rails are so formed as to prevent the ends from rising. The rails weigh about 71 lbs to the yard, and are made with equal flanges at top and bottom, but not with a view to taking them up and turning them when half worn. The chairs and the mode of fixing them were on a plan patented by Messrs Ransome and May of Ipswich, and triangular sleepers were used before but never transversely, so that the combination of all these particulars, but not the invention of any of them, is due to Mr Cubitt. The sleepers being formed by sawing Baltic fir timber diagonally, less wood is expended than in any other arrangement, and I am inclined to believe that this plan will prove more economical than any other, and superior to all in smoothness of motion, except perhaps the rails laid on longitudinal sleepers. I cannot help remarking on this subject that it appears to me to be a great advantage that railway companies are independent in their arrangements, so that as no two of their engineers think alike as to these details, new plans are being continually tried which cannot fail to lead to a knowledge of the most advantageous construction in the end. Thus, for example, fish-bellied rails, which were at first conceived the most perfect, have been entirely given up, and the stone blocks of the first railways seem also to be becoming obsolete. The travelling on Mr Cubitt's rail is certainly very easy, though he assures me that the contractors' waggons without springs have carried ballast for months along a portion of the line upon his permanent rails, which have not been at all deranged by this severe trial.

The line was opened from Reigate (Redhill) to Tonbridge on 26th May, 1842, to Headcorn in August, to Ashford on 1st December, 1842, and to Folkestone on 28th June, 1843.

At Folkestone a temporary station had to be provided. The valley, through which a mill stream passed on its way to the harbour, was crossed by the Foord Viaduct – of nineteen arches of a maximum height of over 100ft – which had to be completed before the town could be reached (on 18th December, 1843).

Between Folkestone and Dover there were the Martello, the Abbot's Cliff, the Shakespeare and Archcliff tunnels. The first-named, 530 yards long, crossed under the ridge separating the Weald of Kent from the undercliff next the sea. At that point the gault and greensand, which underlie the chalk, crop out, thus rendering either cutting or tunnelling at that place a most difficult and expensive operation. From the Martello tunnel to Abbot's Cliff is the Warren cutting, 2 miles long, where was another extraordinary formation of undercliff. Abbot's Cliff tunnel is 1,933 yards long and thence to Shakespeare tunnel, 2 miles, was a sea-wall 30-ft thick at the base and from 50 to 70-ft high. The Shakespeare tunnel is 1,392 yards long.

Between the Abbot's Cliff and Shakespeare tunnels was the Round Down cliff, the summit of which was 375ft above high water; of this a thickness of about 70ft had to be removed for a length of about 300ft. It was estimated that to do that by ordinary means would have cost £8,000, so Cubitt decided to blow up the cliff. He had three shafts sunk, off each of which was a gallery 300ft long, and at the foot of each shaft was a chamber, 14ft by 4ft 6in and 5ft high. In the chamber of each of the outer shafts was a charge of 5,500 lb of gunpowder, and in that of the middle shaft one of 7,500 lb. Each charge had a battery fixed in a shed on the cliff and connected thereto by 1,000ft of wire. Cubitt saw General Pasley, of the Board of Trade, and explained what he proposed to do; on the General's advice the services of Lieut. Hutchinson, R.E., were obtained to superintend the firing, as that officer had been employed under Pasley as executive engineer in the removal of the wreck of the Royal George, and so knew how to fire the three great charges simultaneously.

The explosion was made on 26th January, 1843, and the correspondent of *The Times* described it as follows:

At exactly 26 minutes past 2 o'clock a low, faint, indistinct indescribable moaning rumble was heard and immediately afterwards the bottom of the cliff began to belly out and then almost simultaneously about 500 feet in breadth of the summit began gradually, but rapidly, to sink. There was no roaring explosion, no bursting out of fire, no violent and crushing splitting of rocks and, comparatively speaking, very little smoke, for a proceeding of mighty and irresponsible force it had little or nothing of the appearance of force.

The Folkestone–Dover section was inspected, on behalf of the Board of Trade, by General Pasley, whose report, dated 1st February, 1844, said

The extraordinary and novel character of this portion of railway, which has been partly conducted along the bottom of a lofty range of chalk cliffs, with the sea either near to, or bordering upon parts of, the line, whilst the rest of it has been led through tunnels cut in the same high ground, induced many persons to believe that it would either be impossible to complete this portion of the railway according to Mr Cubitt's original plan or that, if finished, it would be liable to be overwhelmed by the fall of the cliffs above it or be destroyed by the eruptions of the sea.

Having examined the whole of the ground above the railway with the greatest attention, in order to discover the unsound parts of the chalk cliffs, if any, which may be known by cracks at the surface, I am of opinion that there is not the smallest ground for apprehension in respect of the first alleged source of danger because the two tunnels cut through chalk have been formed, in the soundest part of it, with a considerable height or thickness of solid chalk, not only above, but between them and the sea. . . .

In respect to the second alleged cause of danger, the two short portions of the railway formed along the beach, each bounded by projecting headlands of chalk, have been protected – one by a massive concrete sea-wall, similar to that at Brighton, with foundations of brick and cement and substantial counterforts, and the other by a strong timber viaduct, on piles driven into the solid chalk below, both of which are of sufficient height above high water to prevent them from being injured by the sea; at the same time the tides have no tendency to wash away the beach in those small portions of the coast.

The timber bridge survived until 1927, when it was removed in connection with the demolition of the Archcliff Fort and other alterations at Dover. The line is now carried on an embankment behind a concrete wall.

The terminus at Dover was at what was afterwards known as Dover Town station, and the line was opened on 7th February, 1844.

Folkestone Harbour was built by Telford in 1809, but never was a success. It was bought for £18,000 by the South Eastern in 1843. The Folkestone Harbour branch, after being in use for five years as a goods line, was offered to the Board of Trade for inspection and passed as a passenger line on 31st December, 1848, after the provision of suitable accommodation.

Although the real name of the railway was South Eastern from the first, it was usually called the Dover Railway, even in official publications. The writer has a time-sheet, dated 1st February, 1843, when it was only open as far as Ashford, headed 'London & Dover Railway', which gives the following particulars.

The distance – round by Reigate – was 66 miles (now 56 direct); the fastest train, which ran through six of the stations, took 2 hours 50 minutes. An interesting note on the sheet is as follows:

The packets from Boulogne, Calais and Ostend arrive at Dover in time for the Coaches to the last Up Train, which will enable passengers to reach London the same day, and under ordinary circumstances the journey from Boulogne to London will be made in 9 hours. The Proprietors of the Boulogne Packets have decided to run at reduced Fares, on and after 1st December. Six shillings for deck passengers, forward, and eight shillings for cabin passengers.

Third-class passengers were only to use New Cross as a terminus. Gratuities and smoking were forbidden.

An excellent feature of the principal stations on the S.E.R. was the arrangement of through fast lines, with loops for the platforms on each side. This design was used at Redhill, Tonbridge, Paddock Wood, Ashford and later, at Canterbury.

The Bricklayers' Arms branch, to which reference was made in Chapter IV, was, as there stated, opened in May, 1844. In September, 1849, a connection, 55 chains long, was constructed from this branch to a line which will be dealt with almost immediately called the North Kent.

The Bricklayers' Arms station, in spite of its plebeian name, was sometimes spoken of as the Grand West-End Terminus of the South Eastern Railway. Its glory paled into complete insignificance, so far as passengers were concerned, when Charing Cross station came into being. A great day in its history was the arrival of Princess Alexandra of Denmark on 7th March, 1863, for her marriage with the Prince of Wales. Her Royal Highness arrived at Gravesend by steamer, and travelled by special train to Bricklayers' Arms, whence she drove to Paddington and proceeded by train to Windsor.

Returning to the course of events, a branch from Maidstone Road, which was 4½ miles east of Tonbridge, to Maidstone, was sanctioned in 1843 and brought into use on 25th September, 1844. The line was ten miles long, and followed the course of the Medway. It was at first only single, and was equipped with the electric telegraph, the South Eastern being thereby among the pioneers of the employment of the telegraph to ensure safety in working; the utility of which was so marked, that its extension all over the system was decided upon two years later. The branch was soon afterwards doubled. On the day prior to the normal opening the Directors, Officers and invited guests were conveyed by special train from Bricklayers Arms, and on the same day trains ran backwards and forwards all day between Maidstone and Paddock Wood, as Maidstone Road was then re-named, carrying people gratis. Though the route from London was very indirect, namely 21 miles south, 25 east and 10 north, making in all 56, as against 34½ by road, the coaches soon had to succumb, and the railway took all the traffic.

A branch line from Tonbridge to Tunbridge Wells was opened on 20th September, 1845.* It runs uphill all the way, the gradients being never less than 1 in 108, except for one short stretch of 1 in 188, and has frequent curves. A short cut into Tonbridge station, made in 1857, approaching it in the opposite direction, and thereby obviating reversing, which was previously necessary, is at 1 in 53. There was a fine viaduct, called the Colesbrook, or the Southborough Viaduct (254yds).

The Ashford, Canterbury & Margate line, authorised in 1844, was opened from Ashford to Canterbury on 6th February, 1846, to Ramsgate Town on 13th April and to Margate Sands on 1st December, 1846. A branch thereof from Minster to Deal was brought into service on 1st July, 1847.

In 1824 a canal had been finished, which had been authorised in 1800, joining the Thames at Gravesend to the Medway opposite Rochester. On it were two tunnels, 1,530 and 2,329 yards long, with an open space of 50 yards between them. In 1845 a single line of railway was opened, laid along the towpath. In the following year it was purchased by the South Eastern company for £310,000, who filled it up through the tunnels and opened a double line from Denton, about half a mile east of Gravesend, to Strood, forming part of what was called the North Kent line, on 23rd August, 1847. It may here be remarked that the portion of the canal between the north end of the tunnel and the south end of Gravesend basin was only abandoned, under powers obtained by the Southern Railway, in 1934. The North Kent line, also known as the Greenwich and Gravesend,

* Temporary station: present station opened 25th November, 1846.

had been authorised in 1845. As objections were raised against the line going near Greenwich Observatory, it had to take a southern course, and commenced at what is now North Kent East Junction, about 1¼ miles west of Greenwich on the London & Greenwich Railway.

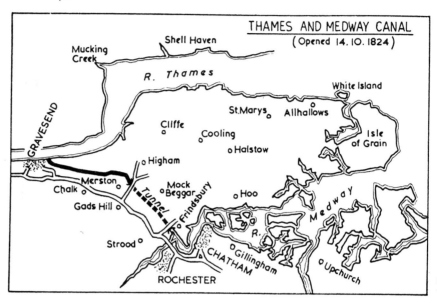

The South Eastern did not obtain their powers to make the North Kent line without a fight. In the session of 1845, in addition to their scheme – which was evidently brought forward to keep strangers away – two others were in the field, which were mentioned in Chapter V: one promoted by a company called the 'London, Chatham & North Kent Railway', also known as 'Vignoles' Line' – he being the engineer; and the 'Chatham & Gravesend', which was put forward by the London & Croydon Railway. The evidence given before the committee is very interesting. George Parker Bidder, in conjunction with Robert Stephenson, had laid out the South Eastern line. Vignoles was to start from a new station to be built at Bricklayers' Arms. He was in difficulties at Woolwich, as he had to cross the ground where guns were tested, involving a very shallow tunnel. In consequence – although he would not admit it was a reason – he proposed to make his locomotives with chimneys only 12ft from the rail, and informed the committee that 12ft 6in was the usual height; also that the lower they were, the better. Bidder exaggerated slightly in the opposite direction, giving 13ft 6in as the ordinary height, and saying that reducing it would be injurious to the engine in its operation. The Croydon line was to branch off to the east at Sydenham, and was to be on the atmospheric system, with a ruling gradient of 1 in 50. Cubitt was the engineer. Owing to this piece of activity, the South Eastern directors dispensed with his services in 1844, and appointed P. W. Barlow as their engineer.

The Reading, Guildford & Reigate was made by an independent company. It ran from Ash Junction, near Aldershot, through Guildford to Shalford Junction over the London & South Western metals. Two sections – the Reading–Farnborough and the Dorking–Redhill were opened on 4th July, 1849, and the rest on 20th August (except the Guildford-Shalford section which was opened 15th October). It was carried over the Wey at Shalford by a wooden bridge, which lasted until 1912.

The Folkestone Harbour branch, which as already mentioned, was opened for passengers at the end of 1848, is 1,328 yards in length, and as the station is 111ft below the level of the main line the branch has an average gradient of 1 in 36, with a maximum of 1 in 30. Four engines – two pulling and two pushing – have been sometimes required to work the trains up the branch. Heavier engines could not be employed because of the small carrying capacity of the swing bridge over the entrance to the inner harbour. The original bridge of the late 'forties was replaced in 1893, and once again, this time by a steel one, in May, 1930, but up to the end of 'Southern' days the heavier classes of engine were prohibited, the 'R' class 0-6-0T being normally used.

The station at Canterbury was that now known as Canterbury West. The Canterbury & Whitstable Railway was in the path of the Ramsgate line to the east of Canterbury West station, and the latter line crossed the Canterbury & Whitstable on the level. A junction was, however, put in on the Whitstable line, to join it to the Ramsgate line, so that the Whitstable trains could use the West station. The level crossing remained in use until the end of the nineteenth century.

It has already been related in Chapter XVI, that the London & Brighton company was authorised, in 1845, to extend the Brighton, Lewes and Hastings line, then being constructed, to Rye and Ashford, but under the same Act permission was given to hand over the extension to the South Eastern. Those powers were exercised and the line opened on 13th February, 1851. The Act provided that there should be a swing- or drawbridge over the river Rother, near Rye. The former was adopted, and remained in use until 1903, when the River Authorities agreed that it should be replaced by a fixed bridge. There was a stipulation that the railway company was to hand over £10,000 to the Paymaster-General, to be expended on improving Rye harbour. Another condition was that the company should assume financial responsibility for the drainage of the Royal Military Canal in the Romney Marsh Level.

A branch from Rye* to Rye Harbour was later authorised by 9 & 10 Vic., c. 55, of 1846, and opened in March, 1854.

By c. 56, of the last-named session, authority was given to build the locomotive, carriage and wagon works at Ashford at a capital expenditure of £500,000. The half-yearly report of January, 1849, said, as to this scheme:

> The completion of the Ashford locomotive station and works is deemed to be of great consequence to the welfare of the Company, as a large portion of the future expenditure on revenue account will be incurred there.

In the same session, again, by c. 64, the branch from the Dover main line at Tonbridge to Tunbridge Wells which, as already noted, was opened on 20th September, 1845, was authorised to be extended to Hastings. The extension was opened to Robertsbridge on 1st September, 1851; carried on to Battle on 1st January, 1852, and to Hastings on 1st February, 1852. The opening of this last link completed a continuous direct line of railway all the way from Ashford to Salisbury, via Brighton.

In the 1847 session a widening of the line between London Bridge and Corbett's Lane was authorised. London Bridge station was enlarged to deal with the increased traffic expected from the North Kent line.

In 1849 an agreement was concluded between the South Eastern and the London, Brighton & South Coast companies which put an end to a matter that was a constant source of friction between them. The former company obtained access to London over the London & Croydon line from the junction at Croydon to the point where the London & Croydon joined the London & Greenwich at Corbett's Lane. In 1846, as already recorded, the London & Croydon became part of the London, Brighton & South Coast. Later, as just mentioned, the Greenwich line between London Bridge and Corbett's Lane was widened. For that work the South Eastern had a claim on the Brighton company for £25,000. The agreement of 1848 provided that, in return for free running powers over the London, Brighton & South Coast from Croydon to Corbett's Lane, the payment of the £25,000 should be remitted and the L.B.S.C.R. should have the use of nearly

---

* Actually from a west-facing junction west of Rye.

five acres of land adjoining Bricklayers' Arms for a goods depot, afterwards known as Willow Walk. The South Eastern undertook not to make or work new competing lines to Brighton, Horsham, Chichester or Portsmouth, but to complete its line from St Leonards to Hastings and to give the Brighton company an entrance into the latter town. The South Eastern was to be allowed to call with its trains at the stations between London and Croydon for the purpose of picking up or setting down passengers. It should be put upon record that the agreement was unanimously accepted by the South Eastern shareholders at their half-yearly meeting on 2nd March, 1848. On the other hand, at the half-yearly meeting of the Brighton company on 25th July, 1849, we find the chairman criticising an agreement come to between Robert Stephenson and Cubitt for the division of London Bridge station. The Brighton company was entitled to two-thirds of the value of the station, but it had only one road and one platform. The opening of the North Kent Railway had, it was said, brought a big increase in the South Eastern traffic and the accommodation was not sufficient for the needs of the two companies. The independent station for the London, Brighton & South Coast company was brought into use in 1850.

From 1841 to 1845 J. Baxendale was the chairman. Previously he had been for nine months general superintendent of the London & Birmingham Railway. For twenty years he had been the head of the firm of Pickford and Co., the carriers; but he turned that business over to his sons and devoted himself to railway work, just as Chaplin had done on the South Western. There is an interesting reference to him, and to the line generally, in a severely critical article on railways in the *Westminster Review*, vol. xlii (1844), as follows:

We do not mean to assert that all railway directors are rapacious in fares, and regardless of the public welfare. We must take the conduct of the Dover line as an example to the contrary. The axiom put forth by the benevolent and liberal-minded chairman, Mr Baxendale, at one of their meetings – *a hard bargain is ever a bad bargain for the apparent gainer* – cannot be too strongly impressed on the attention of railway directors. It is the disregard of this maxim in the disposition to give the public as hard a bargain as possible that has caused the public outcry. The Dover Chairman and Directors, and the gentlemanly Secretary, seem to have impressed the whole management and officers with their own spirit. The public, rich and poor, is treated like a gentleman; and we have no doubt that the highway between London and the rest of Europe will ever be among the most prosperous lines, while the principle is recognised that efficient public service at a cheap rate is the true bond of union between a railway company and the public.

Later on in the same article there are some quotations from evidence given before the Commission on Railways, which afterwards led to the 'Parliamentary' trains, and roofs for third-class carriages. Baxendale was asked what sort of accommodation he gave to third-class passengers; his reply being as follows:

> We give them seats; we give sides above four feet high; in fact, we give such accommodation that the number of what we term the broad-cloth is far greater than the lower class; they find the accommodation so good that you cannot travel along the line without discovering that class of person there to a great extent; I must say that I, going as chairman, often by choice take my seat in a third-class carriage, if the weather is at all tolerable.

Hudson, the 'Railway King', seems to have considered that third-class passengers came into the same category as sardines. In the course of the same enquiry, he said: 'I do not know what number of passengers are put into the third-class trucks, because there is a great difference in the way of packing them!'

On 29th July, 1845, a very unusual accident occurred. When the evening train from Dover had arrived at Tonbridge, the last carriage was taken off, and the tail lights were not transferred. By an excess of zeal, an engine was sent after the train with the lamps, which ran into it when stopping at Penshurst, and telescoped three carriages, injuring about thirty persons. The driver of the light engine said that he did not see the train until too late to stop.

On 10th January, 1846, a train between Tonbridge and Penshurst was passing over a wooden bridge resting on brick abutments, across a side stream of the Medway, when the bridge gave way, precipitating the engine and part of the train into the water, killing the driver and causing much damage to the stock. The accident was attributed to heavy rains, the stream being greatly swollen and the foundations undermined.

Peter W. Barlow, who was the engineer from 1844 to 1851, had his own peculiar ideas on the subject of permanent way. He was not the inventor of the well-known 'Barlow rail', which was of a saddle-shaped section resting directly on the ballast, and was introduced by W. H. Barlow. Peter's principle was to support the rails on short, independent longitudinal sleepers made of cast iron, the chairs being integral, and the gauge being preserved by transverse iron bars. The arrangement is illustrated in D. K. Clarks' *Railway Machinery*, vol. i, p. 283. He began with two miles, which were laid by May, 1850, and extended until 61 miles were in existence by 1851. Dissatisfaction then became apparent with his methods, and a Committee of Investigation was appointed by the Directors, who reported that the work in connection with his cast-iron road 'has unduly engrossed his attention to the exclusion of the company's affairs', and further, that he had refused to give details to the committee to enable them to judge of its value, but that failing such, they were of opinion that 'the company has been misled as to the importance of the Iron Road for purpose of repairs, and that it can be used advantageously only for the purpose of relaying. . . .' As a result of this controversy Barlow resigned on 10th July, 1851, and from that date no more cast-iron sleepers were laid, renewals being carried out by his successor, Thomas Drane, with 'creosoted Memel timbers'.

XXIV

The South Eastern from 1851 to 1875

At the beginning of the period upon which we are now entering, a dispute arose with the Brighton company. It has been related in the last chapter how the South Eastern reached Folkestone and Dover through Ashford, and obtained powers to build a line from the latter place to Hastings; also that the London, Brighton & South Coast was to use the South Eastern station at Hastings. The trouble in question originated in the Brighton company applying, in August, 1850, for an injunction to restrain the South Eastern from departing from the levels laid down in the Act. The injunction was not granted, but the South Eastern was given, instead, an opportunity of making an application to the Railway Board for a variation, which was done on 4th October, 1850. The line was completed by the end of that year, and it was proposed to open it on 1st January, 1851. The London, Brighton & South Coast opposed the opening on the ground that the station was incomplete, inasmuch as there was not room for its traffic. The South Eastern replied that it was not surprised at the further desire of the Brighton company to oppose the opening of the line. The difficulty was apparently smoothed over, only to be followed by an allegation from the Brighton that the proposed working was unsafe.* The South Eastern then retaliated by asking the Brighton company by what right it was going to be there; if as an assignee of the Brighton, Lewes & Hastings – to which company, previous to its absorption by the London, Brighton & South Coast, running powers were given – the deed of transfer must be produced. The line was opened on 1st February, and when the Brighton company attempted to use it the South Eastern wilfully obstructed it. Matters were, however, immediately afterwards adjusted, and an agreement was entered into for pooling the fares and allowing return tickets by either route.

---

* They had to go through the 'Bo-Peep' tunnel, which, though laid with a double track, was so narrow that it had to be worked as a single line. It has since been opened out to full gauge.

About the middle 'fifties there was a spirit of unrest and a feeling of discontent among the shareholders of the South Eastern. Mr James Macgregor, M.P., was then chairman, but the 'Liverpool party', who were the financial mainstay of the concern, had no confidence in him. One particular grievance was the purchase, in 1852, on most extravagant terms, of the Reading, Guildford & Reigate. A proposed railway from Bromley to Lewisham brought matters to a head and Macgregor resigned, many of the former directors were not re-elected, and in March, 1855, a new board was formed, Samuel Smiles, of 'Self Help' fame, being secretary. It was announced that the policy of the new board was to be 'to improve the existing property, to increase traffic, lower expenses and improve dividends'.

Smiles said, in his Autobiography: 'Our company was generally at war with the adjoining companies. On one side there was the Brighton, and on the other, the East Kent. They had always to be watched, as they watched us'. The East Kent, afterwards the London, Chatham & Dover, had obtained an Act in 1853 for giving railway accommodation to the district between Chatham and Canterbury; and in 1855, powers to extend to Dover.

As related in the last chapter, the South Eastern had established communication with Reading. A junction between their station and that of the Great Western was completed in August, 1855, but for some time no effort was made by the latter company to provide a mixed gauge, and so the hopes of the South Eastern that it would be part of a main route between the North and South remained unrealised. A year or two later, the Great Western made suitable arrangements, and the new connection between the Midlands and North and the south-eastern ports, and through them to the Continent, was completed.

On the 19th May, 1855, the news reached London from Paris that three large boxes containing bullion to the value of £14,000 had been robbed on their journey between the two places; the weight of the bullion bars having been replaced by shot. The mystery was solved rather more than a year later, and the guilty parties, two of whom were employees of the company, brought to justice; the ringleader being a well-known criminal called 'Jim the Penman'. The story is related in detail in Smiles' Autobiography.

At this time the South Eastern had no officer occupying the rank of general manager. Captain R. H. Barlow was the 'Superintendent', but left in 1855, and on 1st November of that year C. W. Eborall, until then general manager of the East Lancashire Railway, was invested by the board 'with the united functions of manager and superintendent', as the chairman put it.

In 1853 the company was authorised to make a line from Strood to Maidstone, which was opened on 18th June, 1856. The following session – 1854 – the Caterham Railway company was given powers to build a line from the L.B.S.C.R. and S.E.R. Croydon–Reigate line at Godstone Road, (renamed Caterham Junction, now Purley), to Caterham. It was brought into use on 5th August, 1856, and in 1859 was sold to the South Eastern* for £15,200 – it had cost £40,000 to build. The Mid Kent & North Kent Junction Railway was also an independent concern, sanctioned in 1855, to build a line from Lewisham on the North Kent Railway to Beckenham, on the Farnborough extension of the West End & Crystal Palace Railway. It was opened on 1st January, 1857. In 1862 an extension from New Beckenham to Addiscombe Road was sanctioned. That was opened on 1st April, 1864, and under powers given in the same session the line was leased to the South Eastern

At the half-yearly meeting on 1st September, 1859, mention was made of proposed changes at Dover whereby, with the consent of the Admiralty, trains could run direct on to the Admiralty Pier and so provide special facilities for the conveyance of passengers, luggage and mails to and from the Continent.

The great work of the South Eastern in bridging the Thames and entering the City at Cannon Street, and the West End at Charing Cross, has now to be described.

In addressing the proprietors on 24th February, 1859, the chairman, Mr Byng, said that in 1857 he was asked by a Committee of the House of Commons to give a pledge to call the proprietors together and to recommend them to promote or to concur in the prosecution of such a scheme as should effectively supply access to the West End of London and to complete the system of railway communication in Kent and to the Continent. Byng showed the Committee that the company could not get to the West End; it could go to Waterloo, but that would be very inconvenient and expensive in working. A London Bridge & Charing Cross Railway would meet the conditions, and it could give a direct connection with the London & South Western at Waterloo and with the Great Western and the London & North Western and all the railways in the North via the West London Extension. He proceeded to recommend to the proprietors that the company should vote £300,000 towards the new railway, which was agreed to.

The railway in question – known as the Charing Cross – was promoted by an independent company and sanctioned in 1859. Two

* Previously worked with rolling stock hired from L.B.S.C.R.

The swing bridge on the South Eastern Railway at Rye.   [*British Railways*

Canterbury Station, S.E.R., in 1846, showing the Canterbury & Whitstable Railway crossing.
[*BTC Collection*

Above: Two S.E.R. outside-cylinder Cramptons; No. 85 (*left*) as built in 1849, No. 92 (*right*) rebuilt by Cudworth from a Nasmyth 2-2-2. [*British Railway*

Below: Charing Cross station when first built, showing cab road. [*BTC Collection*

A carriage formerly used on the Canterbury & Whitstable, and later put at the disposal of the Duke of Wellington by the S.E.R. *[BTC Collection*

The carriage built by the S.E.R. for Queen Victoria. *[BTC Collection*

Cudworth 'I' class 0-6-0 No. 129, 1864.

[*Locomotive Publishing Company*

S.E.R. Watkin 2-4-0 class 'L', Avonside 1876.

years later an extension into Cannon Street was authorised. Amalgamation with the South Eastern was permitted in 1863.

The passage of the bill through Parliament was strenuously opposed by the Brighton Railway and, even more violently, by the Trustees of St Thomas's Hospital (then situated in High Street, Southwark). The line crossed a corner of the grounds, without touching the buildings, and a provision was inserted in the Act that the railway company should, if called upon, purchase the whole of the hospital buildings and grounds.

The Hospital Authorities have kindly allowed the writer to see the report of the arbitration case. Only one-sixth of an acre was actually required. The governors made it a *sine qua non* that the whole site and buildings should be bought, and asked at first £750,000 (the capital of the Charing Cross Railway company at that time being £800,000). Most of the evidence was given by surveyors, etc., and turned on the question of values. Only one engineer was called, John Hawkshaw One piece of his evidence is a little gem in the way of 'expert evidence'. In order to keep down the noise, the railway company were intending to use longitudinal sleepers, so that no metal would intervene between the rail and the ground. He was asked: 'Does not the noise principally arise from the blows of the driving wheels on the rail?' to which he replied: 'No, it arises from the action of the driving wheel causing the rail to hammer on the iron support.' Counsel tried again; 'Is there not the hammer of the wheel on the iron?' Answer: 'No, never, the rail lies too close.'

The arbitrator fixed the total sum to be paid at £296,000. The report ends thus:

> Having paid that sum into the Bank of England, the company on the morning of the 21st January (1862) applied by their solicitor to the hospital authorities to give up possession, and upon this being refused, the Company's workmen forced open a small gate leading into the hospital grounds and took possession. The governors then filed a bill in Chancery, and obtained an injunction from Vice Chancellor Wood. Upon appeal to the Lord Chancellor, a compromise was suggested by the Court, and ultimately agreed to by both parties, by which the Company obtained possession of the portion of the hospital grounds required for the contruction of their railway, and the governors of the hospital retained possession of the hospital itself till the month of July, 1862, when the last of the patients was removed and the whole buildings given up to the company.

The work cost a great deal more than was expected, and at the half-yearly meeting on 26th February, 1863, the South Eastern chairman explained that in order to provide sufficient accommodation for the traffic there were to be three lines of way in all cases where two only had been intended, and land was to be purchased for four lines and, where practicable, five. Hungerford Bridge was to have four lines instead of two; Charing Cross station was to be much larger than was intended, the width being increased from 130 to 170ft and the length to 900ft. Hawkshaw was the engineer.

Anticipating events somewhat, it may be noted that the lines from London Bridge to Blackfriars (S.E.R.) were opened on 11th January, 1864. The chairman, at the half-yearly meeting held immediately after that date, said that the opening was of a merely partial character; the general manager had urged upon the board the necessity for acting with great caution in making the requisite preliminary arrangements, and that they should proceed step by step in opening out the line for traffic and only the Greenwich & Mid Kent trains would be handled at first. The chairman added that they were carrying 40,000 a week. The line into Charing Cross was opened for local traffic by the Greenwich and Mid Kent trains on 11th January, 1864, and North Kent trains on 1st April and for Main Line trains on 1st May following. The station at Waterloo Junction, adjacent to the L.S.W.R. station, was opened in 1869.

Cannon Street was opened on 1st September, 1866. The bridge over the Thames, in the approach to Cannon Street, was designed by Hawkshaw. There are two side spans of 131ft each, and three middle ones of 148ft; the width is 66ft 8in. The piers are of cast-iron columns of 18-ft outside diameter below the bottom of the river and 12ft above. The cost of the bridge was £193,000.

From the northern end of the bridge to the public highway in Cannon Street was a distance of 855ft, of which a length of 680ft was occupied by the platforms in the station; the booking office took 85ft, and outside that was the forecourt, 90ft wide. The width of the station was 201ft 8in outside the walls, and 187ft wide inside at platform level. The area of the station, exclusive of the forecourt, was 152,632 square feet. The cost of the station buildings and platforms was £157,262.

The chairman of the South Eastern, at the half-yearly meeting on 26th February, 1863, reported that the previous year had produced the largest gross revenue since the establishment of the company, in spite of the competition of the London, Chatham & Dover. No doubt, to some extent, the International Exhibition of 1862 contributed towards that end. He added that an agreement had been made with the Chatham & Dover that there should be no competition in fares; observing that the directors of that company had met those of the South Eastern in a fair and honourable spirit.

In 1863 the London, Chatham & Dover was seeking powers to

make an extension to Woolwich. The proposal in its original form was withdrawn on the conditions that the South Eastern extended its Greenwich branch to a junction with its North Kent line at a point eastward of Blackheath tunnel and gave the Chatham company running powers over it to Woolwich Arsenal. In exchange, the South Eastern was to have running powers over the Chatham to Forest Hill, Sydenham and Crystal Palace, High Level.

From 20th June, 1863, the S.E.R. and L.C.D.R. companies jointly commenced to convey the English mails between Dover and Calais A yet more thorny point was disposed of on 10th August, 1865, when all traffic via Dover and via Folkestone was put into a joint account and divided. In 1866 the South Eastern proportion was 64 per cent, but the Chatham, year by year, carried more traffic, so that, in 1872, it was agreed that thenceforward it should be divided evenly.

An event which had a great effect on South Eastern history was the arrival of that stormy petrel in railway politics, Sir Edward Watkin. Watkin entered railway service in 1845 and was connected with the Trent Valley. Thence he went to Euston and received no little insight in railway administration under Captain Mark Huish, going afterwards to the Manchester, Sheffield & Lincolnshire Railway. Certain influential interests on the South Eastern wanted to have his services on their line, but there was no vacancy. A director named Whatman thereupon resigned his seat on the board, and Watkin was made a director in 1864, deputy chairman in February, 1865, and chairman in 1866.

In 1862 the South Eastern was authorised to make a line from New Cross to Tonbridge and from what was later Hither Green on the new main line to Dartford on the North Kent, called the Dartford Loop Line (opened 1st September, 1866). The former was opened to Chislehurst on 1st July, 1865, thence to Sevenoaks on 2nd March, 1868, and the remainder on 1st May, 1868. It included the Polhill tunnel, 2,610 yards, and the Sevenoaks, 3,454 yards. The line was also characterised by long stretches of high embankment, and several very considerable brick bridges; everything was to the standard expected for a new 'Main Line', designed to strike fear into the neighbouring L.C.D.R. by reason of the much faster schedules now possible between the new London termini and the Channel ports.

An early new departure under the Watkin administration was the issue of workmen's tickets. They were introduced at the end of the year 1868 and were from Plumstead, Woolwich and intermediate stations to London at 4d. per day. There were weekly, also fortnightly, tickets, and 53,094 were issued during the first half-year – January–June, 1869 – after their adoption. In 1873–74 there was an agitation for a nine hours' day, and on 30th July, 1874, Sir Edward Watkin announced:

> Workmen's trains did not pay, and considering the advance in wages and that workmen were not inclined to work more hours than pleased themselves, he did not see that they were entitled to special privileges at the expense of their small 5 per cent dividend, and therefore it was intended to discontinue these trains after 1st October.

Except as regards the block system, the South Eastern did not make the same good progress in the provision of safety appliances that their neighbours did. In the matter of the block system it may be said that the South Eastern was one of the first to use it, and certainly made more progress in its adoption than any company. In fact, the report for the half-year January–June, 1869, said that the Board of Trade had recently recommended the adoption on all railways of the block telegraph, 'which has been in operation on this company's line for many years'. Further, Watkin, in commenting on that report at the subsequent half-yearly meeting on 26th August, said that the South Eastern was the first to use the block system and the first to use passenger communication. It is doubtful whether the former claim can be sustained. There is a record of block bells, without visual signals, being introduced on the South Eastern in January, 1852, by C. V. Walker, the then telegraph superintendent, who also brought out a miniature semaphore in 1854 wherein, when 'line clear' was sent, the arm was lowered, and when 'train on line' was acknowledged, the arm was placed to the horizontal. It was in that year, though, that Edwin Clark used, on the London & North Western, the needle and the indications 'line blocked', 'line clear' and 'train on line' on the dial of the instrument.

In a paper on 'Safety in Railway Working', read before the Society of Arts in 1874, Captain – afterwards Sir Henry – Tyler observed that at the request of the railway company he made a preliminary inspection of the signalling at Charing Cross before the station was opened, and said:

> It was proposed by the company to work the Charing Cross by bells only, as other parts of the South Eastern were worked, without block instruments. But the author ventured to dissent from that proposal and to express the opinion that, considering the importance of the line and the nature of the traffic which it was likely to accommodate, it was absolutely necessary to provide visual as well as audible instruments; to give the signalmen, in fact, the advantage of a record before their eyes as to the condition of each block length – whether it was obstructed or whether it was clear – in place of trusting to their memories as to the last signal which they had received or transmitted on their bells or

gongs. . . . The talented electrical superintendent of that company – Mr C. V. Walker – accordingly contrived and provided, before the opening of the line, the miniature semaphore signals which are working in the cabins. . . . The use of Mr Walker's semaphores has since been extended to all other portions of the South Eastern.

An amusing incident occurred when Cannon Street station was opened. Saxby and Farmer did the signalling and provided an interlocking frame. The men who had to work it were, apparently, not given any opportunity to 'learn the frame', and at the time of opening such confusion ensued that Eborall gave instructions for the interlocking to be taken out, as the traffic could not be worked with it in. Fortunately, action in that direction was delayed and in twenty-four hours the men had become accustomed to it.

It will be convenient, as the subject of safety is being dealt with, to mention here that the South Eastern carriage and wagon superintendent for over thirty years was R. C. Mansell, the inventor of the Mansell wheel. The principle he employed was a wooden disc which was forced on to a bevelled inner face of the tire by hydraulic pressure. Two grooves were formed in the tire and two securing rings were fixed in the grooves – one on each side – and all were bolted together by screw bolts and nuts at frequent intervals. Mansell's first patent was taken out in 1848 and was renewed in 1862. Further improvements were patented in 1866. In the Board of Trade report on a serious disaster at Shipton-on-Cherwell, Great Western Railway, on 24th December, 1874 – due to a broken tire – it was stated that 3,944 sets of wheels had been made under the 1848 patent and, up to the end of 1874, 16,816 under the 1866 patent, and that no case of the failure of a Mansell wheel had been reported to the Board of Trade. Mansell retired on 31st January, 1882.

Addressing the half-yearly meeting on 23rd February, 1871, Sir Edward Watkin said that the company had run 666 trains a day, independently of light engines. They made 4,083 stoppages daily, passed 1,096 signals, travelled over 1,635 sets of points, and 5,700 men were concerned in their movements. To him it was not a wonder that there were so many accidents, but that there were so few.

In one respect the South Eastern and its neighbour, the London, Brighton & South Coast, were in advance of all other railway companies, and that lay in their having begun to comply fully with that section of the Regulation of Railways Act, 1868, which required an efficient means of communication between passengers and the servants in charge of the train. Reference was made in Chapter XVII to Stroudley's system on the Brighton line. That on the South Eastern was also an electrical device, and had been designed by the before-mentioned C. V. Walker, the telegraph superintendent. It was introduced first on 24th January, 1866, was tested on 23rd March, 1866, by Captain Tyler, and official approval was sent by the Board of Trade on 2nd January, 1869. Captain Tyler's annual report on the accidents of 1871, in dealing generally with the subject of passenger communication, gave drawings and a description of Walker's apparatus and said that at the end of 1871 it had been fitted to 56 engines and 550 coaches at a total cost of £2,212.

After the Act of 1871 was passed, which enlarged the powers of the Board of Trade as to accidents, annual reports were prepared. The first was on those of the year 1870 and therein Captain Tyler said, in his general remarks:

> The South Eastern, having regard to its mileage and gross receipts, takes the lead among the 'no accident' companies and the London, Chatham & Dover, as a Metropolitan line, deserves also to be specially referred to.

After mentioning other companies, whose names were included among the 'many accident' lines, Captain Tyler proceeded:

> But it is worthy of observation at the outset – though I do not wish to lay too much stress on the experience of a single year – that the South Eastern and the London, Chatham & Dover Railways, on which no accidents have needed investigation, are worked by the telegraph block system.

This subject of safety may be closed by observing that on 31st December, 1873, there were 232 connections interlocked and 436 not interlocked, and that all the 335 miles of double line had the block system. The Board of Trade was told in reply to the circular letter of 19th December, 1877, as to the use of continuous brakes, that both the Westinghouse and Smith's vacuum had been tried and that 16 engines and 85 carriages were equipped with the vacuum brake, and 15 engines and 85 further carriages were to be added. When the Act of 1889 was passed, making interlocking, the block system, and continuous brakes for passenger trains compulsory, there were 661 connections interlocked and 272 not interlocked, the block system was on the whole of the 366 double lines, and 237 engines and 23 per cent of the carriages had the vacuum brake.

In 1869 a pamphlet was published, entitled *London and Europe, or the South Eastern Railway*. It states that at that time the S.E.R. possessed 243 engines, of which 45 were in reserve. The carriages were replaced on an average every 12 years, and wagons every 15. It speaks disparagingly of the service on the Northern of France; 5 trains daily between Boulogne and Paris as against 23 between London and Dover.

In January, 1870, the South Eastern company received £200,000 from the Post Office for the purchase of its telegraphs. This line was unique amongst the railways, in that it issued stamps for payment of telegrams sent by the public, which were of a very handsome design, and are now of great rarity.

On 19th December, 1873, C. W. Eborall died. On the 31st December the board decided to abolish his office, namely that of General Manager, and it was arranged that the chairman (Sir E. Watkin) should undertake, in addition to his other duties, to conduct all the Parliamentary business and negotiations of agreements with other companies, including supervision of the general Committees, and that he should exercise general authority of approval and veto usually delegated to the General Manager. The offices of Manager and Secretary were combined.

It was in the early 'seventies that various proposals were made for meeting the disadvantages of crossing the English Channel. In that connection it may be noted that a bill for a Channel Ferry was rejected in the Parliament of 1872. Also that on 11th March, 1875, the South Eastern agreed to make a grant of £20,000 towards trials to test the possibilities of a Channel Tunnel. There was a proviso that the vote was conditional on the London, Chatham & Dover doing the same, and that the company would not be bound to any further expenditure.

As has been recorded earlier in this chapter, the South Eastern had arranged to continue the Greenwich Railway to join the North Kent (at Charlton), and deposited a bill to that effect in 1865. The proposed railway was to pass under Greenwich Park and, on account of possible vibration resulting therefrom, it was opposed by the Astronomer Royal. The House of Commons therefore deleted that part of the bill and sanctioned only the two ends. In 1871 the necessary powers for the intervening portion were obtained and the western portion of the line of 1865 was altered. A condition was that the company was to pay the cost of any practical experiments as to the effect upon Greenwich Observatory of a tunnel through the Park, but the point was never pursued. Thus, on 1st January, 1873, the eastern end, from Maze Hill to Charlton, was opened and that from Greenwich to Maze Hill on 1st February, 1878. On 9th October, 1874, the Hythe & Sandgate, which actually commenced at Sandling Junction, and was sanctioned in 1864, was brought into use.*

One more line may be mentioned, which was also sanctioned in 1864, but, unlike the Hythe & Sandgate, came to nothing, namely the

---

* The South Eastern also operated a horse-tram from Hythe to Sandgate.

Weald of Kent Railway. It was to run from Paddock Wood to Hythe, via Cranbrook, Tenterden and Shorncliffe, a distance of 20 miles. Various deviations were authorised by a second Act of 1865, but no attempt appears to have been made to construct the line, and the powers were allowed to lapse. The present Paddock Wood–Hawkhurst branch follows the line of the Weald Railway for part of its length.

The end of the 1851–1875 period was noteworthy in that the fusion of the South Eastern and London, Chatham & Dover was agreed to. That, at least, was what an official announcement of the South Eastern said in April, 1875. Differences, however, arose in May and the scheme was dropped. The proposal was to be a fusion of the net receipts, but the Chatham wanted it to be of the gross receipts. The South Eastern would have agreed to the latter if its net revenue, as in 1874, had been guaranteed, but that was considered too much to ask.

The accidents to be chronicled which occurred during the period covered by this chapter seem rather numerous, but it must be remembered that it covers a quarter of a century.

On 21st August, 1854, a collision occurred at Croydon, in which three passengers were killed. An excursion train, consisting of fifty carriages, left Dover at 8.30 a.m. for the Crystal Palace. At Ashford it was separated into two parts, being considered too long. The second part was overlooked, and ran into the engine of a Brighton company's ballast train which had moved from the down to the up line at Croydon to obtain water.

On the night of 28th June, 1857 a passenger train ran into a stationary one at Lewisham. The brake van of the latter was forced on the top of the next carriage, which was an open third, and eleven of the passengers in it were killed, together with one more elsewhere. The cause was the ignoring of a distant signal warning, due, according to the inspecting officer's report, to the 'relaxation of the discipline on the line by which "red signals" are allowed to be passed in defiance of the company's printed rules'. It was also observed that the great loss of life was due to the weakness of the third class un-covered carriages in which the passengers were placed, and to the unequal height of the buffers. The further remark was made that there could be no doubt that the absence of fatal consequences in the case of many of the collisions which occurred was mainly due to the strength with which the carriages were constructed, and that the use of open carriages and of cattle trucks for the conveyance of passengers was objectionable and unsafe.

On 30th June, 1858, a special excursion, consisting of nine coaches, left London Bridge at 3 p.m. for Ramsgate, and when the train was travelling at full speed, near Chilham, it left the rails, and as a result three passengers lost their lives. The driving axle of the engine broke, but it could not be decided whether that was a cause or an effect. On 11th August of the same year a train was being drawn from the ticket platform to the terminus at Ramsgate, by means of a rope, and was allowed to run violently into the dead end, resulting in injuries to twenty passengers.

A collision occurred at Margate on 1st August, 1864, between a down train out of control and a stationary one, in which there was one death, and a number of people injured. On 16th December of the same year there was a collision in the Blackheath tunnel, between a ballast train and a passenger one. The rails were very slippery, and the former could not proceed. An express ran into the rear of it, killing five platelayers who were in the ballast brake-van.

The most disastrous accident in the company's history occurred near Staplehurst, on 9th June, 1865. A bridge was under repair, in the course of which two lengths of rail were removed, when the up boat express was seen approaching. There was a flagman 150 yards from the obstruction, but the brake power was insufficient to stop the train, and nearly all the carriages fell over into the stream, resulting in the death of ten passengers and injury to fifty more. The ganger, who was arrested, said that he had mistaken the day of the week, and did not expect the express so soon – the running varied from day to day, according to the tide. Charles Dickens was a passenger, but fortunately escaped unhurt. In the 'Postscript' to 'Our Mutual Friend', he refers to the accident thus:

On Friday the Ninth of June in the present year, Mr and Mrs Boffin (in their manuscript dress of receiving Mr and Mrs Lammle at breakfast) were on the South Eastern Railway with me, in a terribly destructive accident. When I had done what I could do to help others, I climbed back into my carriage – nearly turned over a viaduct, and caught aslant upon the turn – to extricate the worthy couple. They were much soiled, but otherwise unhurt. The same happy result attended Miss Bella Wilfer on her wedding day, and Mr Riderhood inspecting Bradley Headstone's red neckerchief as he lay asleep. I remember with devout thankfulness that I can never be much nearer parting with my readers for ever, than I was then, until there shall be written against my life, the two words with which I have this day closed this book:–THE END.

The railway company presented Dickens with a piece of plate, as an acknowledgement of the valuable help which he rendered on the occasion.

There is an interesting reference to the speed of the trains in Sir Cusack Roney's *Rambles on Railways*, published in 1868. Speaking of mail trains, he says:

For a short run, involving only one stoppage for the engine to take water, the most rapid on the narrow gauge in England is between London and Dover, by the South Eastern Railway, 88 miles in 2 hours and 5 minutes, 42 miles an hour. But on Australian mail nights (the 26th of each month), the Post Office employs, in addition to the ordinary down mail, a special one for the conveyance of such bags and boxes as can be got ready by 7 p.m. This train travels between London and Dover in 1 hour and 45 minutes. There is one stop for water. The rate of speed, including the stop is a little over 50 miles an hour, excluding it, the rate is 54.

As will be seen later, special engines were built for these trains, called the 'Mails'.

An elaborate 'rule-book' was issued in 1857. A copy seen by the writer has a supplement of 1860 bound up with it, making over 400 pages altogether. There is a good deal of interesting information therein, together with some amusing passages.

It appears that disc signals were still in use on the S.W.R., and crossbar ones on the G.W.R. in 1857. Luggage was still put on the tops of the carriages in 1860. There is an instruction that 'as far as possible luggage for the terminal stations is to be *roofed*, so as to make the vans available for intermediate stations'.

The method of working a single line in 1857 was as follows: before a train was allowed to leave, it had to be ascertained by telegraph that the line was clear; then the telegraph clerk wrote out a pass, which the stationmaster signed, and the driver took with him, giving it up at the other end.

The regulations for working the incline at Folkestone Harbour were that all trains going up were to have a 'harbour brake-van' attached behind; when descending it was put next the engine. It mentions 'the new large carriages', which were 8-wheeled composite, 6-wheeled first- and 8-wheeled second-class. The 8-wheelers were almost certainly two 4-wheelers jointed together.

One rule, to which the Trades Unions would object nowadays, was 'If an Engine-driver or Stoker be not required for his full time on the line, he is to employ the remainder of his time in the shop, under shop rules, and at *any work* the foreman may give him.'

Racing between trains on the main line and those on the Croydon, North Kent and Greenwich lines is strictly prohibited.

Smoking, either by employees or passengers, was a deadly sin. The proprietors of refreshment rooms were not allowed to sell cigars or tobacco – cigarettes, of course, were unknown except to the Crimean veterans.

One of the stationmaster's daily duties was to inspect a certain apartment, in order to remove any unseemly writings or sketchings.

The supplement contains very elaborate instructions for telegraph operators. At this time – ten years before they were taken over by the Post Office – private telegrams were mixed up with those sent on the railway service. Everyone liable to see the contents of a telegram had to sign a 'Secrecy Form', declaring that he would not divulge the same 'unless compelled to do so by some court of law or equity or other competent tribunal'.

With regard to service messages, the telegraph was not to be used on every trivial occasion (for fear of wearing out the wires?).

If a reply was required to any 'chap' telegram, the sender had to deposit 5s. or more. In the absence of an explanation of the term 'chap', one is led to wonder whether telegrams addressed to ladies were allowed to be replied to free; but later on, from a list of abbreviations, it appears that 'chap' meant 'charges all paid here'. Another was 'cup', which meant 'Charges unpaid. Reply to chap paid for by sender'.

XXV

The South Eastern from 1876 to 1898

THE first event on the South Eastern during this period, worthy of being recorded, was a great improvement inaugurated on 1st March, 1876, at Folkestone Harbour, whereby the trains ran alongside the steamers, and passengers, luggage and mails passed directly between the one and the other.

An event that bid fair to be of yet greater importance, but which has altogether failed to realise its promoters' hopes, was the opening, on 10th April, 1876, of the East London Railway, to which allusion has been made in Chapter XVII. The chairman was Sir Edward Watkin, and the line formed part of his dream of a direct through route between the North of England and the Channel Ports.

The company was dissatisfied with the train service provided by the Brighton company, who worked it under arrangement, and lodged a complaint with the Railway and Canal Commission. It made a grievance of the fact that passengers had to change at New Cross, and that the fares to Liverpool Street were higher than to London Bridge. The Railway Commission, in August, 1876, ordered a train service that would not detain passengers at New Cross more than a reasonable time and that there should be one through, reasonably quick, train to Brighton and back, and two to Croydon. On 2nd July, 1877, in response to a further complaint, judgment was given to the effect: (a) that the London & Brighton company had power only to use Liverpool Street for East London local traffic, i.e. not for beyond New Cross; (b) the Railway Commission had no power to order the Brighton company to run through trains to Croydon, Brighton, etc; the duty of that company was limited to giving good connections at New Cross and at Old Kent Road, and it was running two through trains from Croydon and back; also one from Brighton, which left at 9 a.m. and arrived 10.58 and returned at 5.40 p.m., due to arrive in Brighton 7.15. It was recommended that the up train be quickened so as to approximate with the down journey and that, as Old Kent Road was hardly suitable for an exchange station, Peckham Rye should be adopted instead. As a result, from 1st August, the train service was improved; better communication with the South London was made and improvements effected at Croydon, and there were 25 trains instead of 19.

In 1879 the South Eastern company gave six months' notice of its desire to participate in the working, and on 1st April, 1880, they commenced running sixteen trains a day between Addiscombe Road* and Liverpool Street. In 1882 the line was leased in perpetuity to the Great Eastern; the London, Brighton & South Coast; the South Eastern; the London, Chatham & Dover; the Metropolitan and the Metropolitan District, and, on 1st October, 1884, a junction was made with the latter two companies at Whitechapel and through passenger trains commenced on 6th October.

On 1st June, 1878, the junction with the London, Chatham & Dover at Blackfriars was made, which gave the South Eastern access to the Metropolitan Railway, and thence on to the Great Northern for Finsbury Park and the Alexandra Palace. The Great Northern, in exchange, ran to Woolwich, until the end of July, 1880. On 1st August South Eastern trains began running to Enfield and Muswell Hill (later Alexandra Palace).

The line between Folkestone and Dover was completely blocked by a serious slip at the southern end of the Martello Tower tunnel on 12th January, 1877. A storm washed away the foot of the cliff, 400ft high, and brought down 60,000 cubic yards of earth into a cutting 116ft deep, burying and killing three men. The summits of some of the other cliffs were subsequently blown up and reduced, so as to prevent further falls. A single line was put into operation on 12th March, and ordinary working resumed on 30th May.

In the autumn of 1877 there were some unfortunate incidents in the higher circles of the company. The services of Cudworth, the locomotive superintendent, had been dispensed with in 1876, without the knowledge of the directors, in order, it was alleged, to find room for A. M. Watkin, who was the son of Sir Edward, and a director of the Manchester, Sheffield & Lincolnshire and of the Metropolitan Railways. Moreover, again without the board being consulted, he was allowed to be a Parliamentary candidate for Grimsby—and was elected. The ground of offence lay in the fact that, some time previously, Eborall, the general manager, without mentioning the matter to anyone, had consented to act as arbitrator between the

* By way of a spur line from each side of New Cross (S.E.) joining the original East London beside the Surrey Canal, using locomotives with shortened chimneys and condensing gear ('Q' class 0-4-4T).

Caledonian and the North British Railways. The latter act was apparently a great sin in the eyes of Watkin, who thereupon persuaded the board to pass a resolution that all servants should devote themselves fully to the services of the company. Cudworth was an old servant, but Sir Edward claimed that the efficient discharge of the duties and the public safety required a greater amount of zeal and energy. Probably those qualities were to be found in his son, but the directors declined to avail themselves of them and he was relieved of his appointment. Sir Edward, further, was censured by the board for having induced his son to act in contravention to the spirit and letter of the agreement he had himself inspired.

In December, 1878, Mr Mewburn, who was the mover of a vote of confidence at the half-yearly meeting in February, 1878, issued a circular to the proprietors asking them not to vote for the re-election of Messrs John Bibby, Nathaniel Buckly and Henry Rawson, obviously on the grounds that they were opposed to Sir Edward Watkin. That was followed by a special report as to the differences at the board, naming eight directors, with a total holding of £284,150, who concurred in the report, and four, including Watkin, with a total holding of £10,940, who did not concur.

The report for the half-year July–December, 1878, which appeared soon after, complained of a letter from Watkin that had recently appeared in *The Times*, in which he said:

I have been entirely superseded in the executive management. All my recommendations for improvements have been ignored. During nearly the whole of the year a locomotive committee – upon which Mr Nathaniel Buckley has been appointed chairman and Mr Mellor principal member – have managed or, I must say, mismanaged, without interference of any kind from me, the whole locomotive department. Some time ago, too, a traffic committee with Mr Rawson as chairman, was appointed, with whose labours I have in no manner whatever interfered. I say, therefore, that it is to the inexperienced operations of these gentlemen who have now had their own way for about a year, that all the mismanagement which the company is suffering from is due.

A remarkable sequel to the foregoing was seen at the meeting on 1st February, 1879, when the chairman, instead of, as usual, recommending the adoption of the report, left that duty to the deputy-chairman and he himself then moved an amendment that the report be not received. The amendment was carried. A poll was demanded on the question of the election of directors, which showed Watkin's opponents at the bottom of the poll. With Sir Edward again in the ascendant peace once more reigned.

The Bromley Direct Railway was ostensibly an independent company, but had South Eastern directors and officers. It was empowered, in 1874, to build a line from Grove Park to Bromley – now Bromley

North. The railway was brought into use on 1st January, 1878, and vested in the South Eastern in 1879.

As related in Chapter XXIV, the line between Greenwich and Maze Hill was opened on 1st February, 1878. It had necessitated the diversion of the main southern outfall sewer of the Metropolitan Board of Works for 1,700ft. Besides the difficulty as to Greenwich Observatory, also previously mentioned, there was another item of interest about the opening of this line, in that it closed the then existing Greenwich station, which was the original terminus of the first railway out of London.

In 1878 the Hastings Corporation brought the South Eastern before the Railway and Canal Commission on a complaint as to facilities. Judgment was given in favour of the applicants, and the railway was ordered to carry out many works at Hastings and St Leonards, involving a capital expenditure of a considerable amount.

The question of improving the harbour at Boulogne had been under the consideration of the French Government for several years, and at last it was announced, in 1878, that a deep-water harbour and port was to be made. On 20th January, 1881, Sir Edward Watkin said that he anticipated that when the improvements were completed a fixed service would be possible which would place that company in the same position as the London, Chatham & Dover, who had commenced a fixed service between Dover and Calais in 1880, when the Brussels Exhibition was opened. Improvements were also made by the South Eastern at Folkestone in anticipation; a new pier was commenced in October, 1881, and completed in May, 1883. It was not, however, until 1886 that a fixed service was introduced. Meanwhile, Sir Edward Watkin having expressed a desire to be relieved of some of the duties of a Great Panjandrum, a reshuffle of offices took place as from the 1st January, 1880. A General Manager was once more installed, Myles Fenton being appointed to the post. He had begun his career on the Kendal & Windermere Railway, and was at the time on the Metropolitan. His later history may be summarised here by saying that he was knighted in 1889 and retired from the general managership in 1896, when he was made a 'consulting director'.

In dealing later with the London, Chatham & Dover Railway, mention will be made of the animosity created by that company erecting a pier at Queenborough at the mouth of the Medway. In 1879 a private company was given the powers to build the Hundred of Hoo Railway from a junction with the South Eastern Gravesend–Strood line near Higham to a place called Stoke, a distance of 9 miles. The following year an extension of $3\frac{1}{2}$ miles was granted which would carry the line to the banks of the Medway. The South Eastern then appeared on the scene and acquired the railway in 1881 and, under further powers in 1883, built a deep water pier, 400ft long, which, seeing that the rival port on the other side of the Medway was called Queenborough, was named Port Victoria. The section of line from the junction with the main line to Sharnal Street was brought into use on 31st March, 1882, and the remainder on 11th September, 1882.

The Westerham Valley, a private venture, was for a line from Dunton Green to Westerham. It was sanctioned in 1876, acquired by the South Eastern in 1881, and opened on 7th July of that year. The Lydd Railway was another nominally separate concern which, under powers given in 1881, was to build a line from Appledore, on the Ashford–Hastings line, to Dungeness, and, by further powers in 1882, to build a branch to New Romney. The Appledore–Lydd section was brought into use on 7th December, 1881, the Lydd–Dungeness, for goods only, on the same day, and for passenger traffic on 1st April, 1883, and the New Romney branch on 19th June, 1884. The railway was vested in the South Eastern in 1895. The West Wickham & Hayes Company was incorporated in 1880; it was acquired by the South Eastern in 1881 and the line opened on 29th May, 1882. The Elham Valley company was for a line from Shorncliffe to Canterbury. It was sanctioned in 1881, vested in the South Eastern in 1884, opened to Barham on 4th July, 1887, and completed on 1st July, 1889.

A tunnel under the Channel has long been the dream of many Englishmen and Frenchmen, and the height of the agitation for it was in the early 'eighties. The railway companies who stood most to gain by it were enthusiastic over it; namely the South Eastern and Northern of France. In that relation mention may be made of the vote of £20,000 made, as recorded in Chapter XXIV, in 1875. It should also be stated that in 1882 the South Eastern & Channel Company was incorporated.

One of the conditions under which the grant just mentioned was made was that the London, Chatham & Dover should contribute a similar amount. At the half-yearly meeting of the latter company on 10th August, 1881, a shareholder asked what was the then financial position of the company in that respect. The chairman replied:

It is quite true that the board were authorised some years ago to contribute a sum not exceeding £20,000 towards the initiation of that enterprise. A good many disturbing causes have arisen since then. At that time the Emperor

L.C.D.R. No. 55, *Africa*, built by Sharp Stewart in 1873.   [*Locomotive Publishing Company*

L.C.D.R. No. 62, rebuilt by Martley from a Hawthorn 4-4-0ST, and here seen rebuilt **again** by Kirtley in 1876.

S.E.R. Stirling 'O' class 0-6-0 No. 108, Ashford 1897.   [*Locomotive Publishing Company*

Above: S.E.R. Stirling 'F' class 4-4-0 No. 206, Ashford 1885.

Below: L.C.D.R. 'R' class 0-4-4T No. 199, Sharp Stewart 1891.

Above: L.C.D.R. 'M' class 4-4-0 engines; No. 24, 'M3' class, Longhedge 1893, in foreground.
[*Locomotive Publishing Company*

Below: Stirling 'Q' class 0-4-4T, S.E.R., No. 405, Sharp Stewart 1894. [*Locomotive Publishing Company*

Wainwright 'H' class 0-4-4T, S.E.C.R., No. 550; Ashford 1904.

Above: 'C' class 0-6-0, Wainwright's standard goods class for the S.E.C.R.; No. 712, Sharp Stewart 1900.

Below: S.E.C.R. 'D' class 4-4-0 No. 736, Ashford 1901, with rolling stock from the 'Folkestone Car Train'. [*Locomotive Publishing Company*

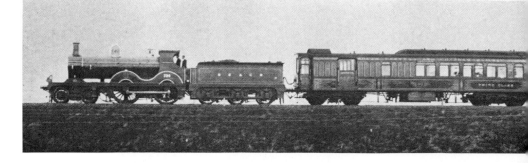

Napoleon was supreme in France, and I have only just to mention that fact to show you the character of the causes which have put a stop to all that sort of thing since. We have never been in a position to aid in the thing from that time, for the simple reason that it was all suspended, both in France and England. It has been revived lately and in a very tangible form. The French people have made a number of experiments and, I believe, have satisfied themselves as to the entire practicability of the matter. Some of the funds of the South Eastern have been devoted to a Channel Tunnel scheme, but it was not the scheme of Sir John Hawkshaw or of the associated French and English companies.

A series of collisions in Cannon Street yard on 22nd February, 1883, led to Colonel Yolland saying of Cannon Street that it was:

evidently intended in the first instance as a terminal station for the city, but it has been converted into a mere road station, and I believe it to be the very worst in the Kingdom. There are eight or nine lines of railway, independent of crossover-roads, on the bridge over the Thames at the south end of the station, and any passenger train, either in the act of entering or of leaving that station, must cross those lines of railway on the level and, except for the security which is obtained from the interlocking of the points and signals, by preventing the signal-man from making mistakes, the station would be unworkable.*

In 1881 the Rochester & Chatham Extension, about a mile long, was sanctioned. Part of it was brought into use on 20th July, 1891, and the remainder on 1st March, 1892. It was an expensive line to build, as a considerable portion was on viaduct, including a long four-span bridge over the Medway parallel to the similar viaduct of the L.C.D.R. The Cranbrook & Paddock Wood company was authorised in 1877, to build a line from the main line at Paddock Wood to Cranbrook, and, in 1882, an extension to Hawkhurst was sanctioned. Neither of these powers were exercised. The lines were constructed under the S.E.R. Acts of 1887 and 1892 respectively, and opened to Goudhurst on 1st October, 1892, and to the terminus at Hawkhurst on 4th September, 1893.

At the beginning of the present chapter mention was made of Sir Edward Watkin's dream for a through railway from the North to the Channel ports. That was to be realised by the Manchester, Sheffield & Lincolnshire, the Metropolitan, the East London and the South Eastern, of all of which Sir Edward was chairman.

In that connection the following extract from the South Eastern report for January–June, 1890, is instructive:

The importance to this company of forming a closer connection with the northern railway systems has continued to occupy the attention of the board. They hope, in the next session of Parliament, in concert with their allies in the north of London, to submit a mature and practical scheme, either by means of a separate undertaking or otherwise.

* To understand this, it must be appreciated that most trains were being worked into Cannon Street and then round the west side of Borough Market triangle to Charing Cross, and, of course, back the same way.

A great event happened on 31st May, 1894, which marked the beginning of the end of the constant friction with the Chatham company. Sir Edward Watkin, owing to ill-health, resigned and was succeeded by the Hon. James Byng. The latter had been chairman from 1855 to 1866, when he was displaced by Watkin. Sir Edward remained a director and was voted £1,000 a year. An agitation followed for a change in management. A circular was issued by Mr John Abbott, Mr Nathaniel Spens and others, who, among other things, wanted the appointment of E. M. G. Eddy, formerly of the London & North Western and Caledonian railways, and at that time the Commissioner for the New South Wales Railways. A special meeting of the proprietors was held on 10th January, 1895, in order to discuss the circular in anticipation of the half-yearly meeting. The latter meeting was held a fortnight later and the directors then accepted a proposal that a committee of six be appointed to assist the board. No more was heard of the agitation to appoint Eddy and, as events proved, it was as well. Happier relations, all round, followed Watkin's retirement, and eventually the Chatham & Dover and the South Eastern came together in 1898.

At the above-mentioned meeting on 24th January, 1895, Byng, who had been connected with the railway for forty-seven years, resigned the chairmanship and was succeeded therein by Sir George Russell. Byng died in May, 1897, and Sir George also passed away on 7th March, 1898. It was said of the latter by the *Railway Times* that:

upon his succession to the chair he initiated a policy wholly new to that company, the salient features of which were peace with its neighbours and an energetic development of its own resources.

Mr H. Cosmo O. Bonsor was elected chairman on Sir George Russell's death.

William Wainwright, the carriage and wagon superintendent, died on 21st May, 1895, and was succeeded by his son, Harry S. Wainwright. On Sir Myles Fenton's retirement – already referred to – W. R. Stevens was appointed the 'secretary and chief officer'. Two years later those duties were divided and Stevens became the chief officer, and the deputy secretary, Charles Sheath, was appointed the secretary.

The Bexleyheath line was authorised under powers obtained in 1883 by an independent company. It was to run from a junction with the Dartford loop line near Hither Green to one on the North Kent line near Slades Green; but in 1887 amended powers provided that it should commence a quarter of a mile east of Blackheath on the North Kent. It was brought into use on 1st May, 1895, and absorbed in 1900.

No mention has so far been made of widenings on the South Eastern Railway. The policy of this company was to construct a double track from the first, unlike that of the South Western, which provided a single line originally in most cases. The only recorded instance in which single lines were doubled later are two;* in both cases the lines had been promoted independently. One was the Caterham Railway, which had been opened in 1856, and was not doubled until the end of 1899. The other was the Chipstead Valley (opened 1897, from a point on the Caterham branch just South of Purley, to Kingswood), where the second track from Purley to Tadworth was not introduced until 2nd July, 1900, the single line having been extended from Kingswood to Tadworth on the preceding day, and to Tattenham Corner a year later.

The only serious accidents during this period occurred in dense fogs, one on 21st March, 1890, when a passenger train ran into one standing in St John's station. Three passengers were killed and about twenty injured. The other was on 9th October, 1894, when a goods train ran into a wagon full of hop-pickers on a private level crossing between Canterbury and Chatham. Seven of them were killed and eight injured. The verdict of the jury was 'accidental death'; it was clearly due to lack of care on the part of the horse driver.

* The Maidstone branch was opened single, but was doubled as early as 1846.

XXVI

South Eastern Locomotives down to 1898

AT the time of pooling the engines with the Croydon Railway, the South Eastern company possessed twenty-six engines built 1841–1843, which, as recorded in Chapter V, became Nos. 9–34 of the Joint Committee. For the list, see Vol. I. Benjamin Cubitt was the first Locomotive Superintendent, and controlled the Joint Committee. On the dissolution of the latter, the South Eastern took over 71 engines, retaining the same numbers, with two exceptions. All the names were removed, unless that had already been done. The numbers were as follows: 2, 5, 7, 9–20, 24–27, 29, 31–37, 39–41, 43–46, 51, 55–59, 62, 64, 67, 70, 71, 73, 76, 77, 79, 80, 82, 84, 86, 87, 101–109, 111 and 117–123; details of which have been given in Chapter V.

Nos. 2, 7, and 46 were evidently worn out, as they were replaced almost at once.

An interesting episode in the history of No. 27 was that in 1849 it was fitted with long cylinders with a central exhaust port uncovered by the piston, this being an anticipation of the Stumpf 'uniflow' system tried on the North Eastern in 1913 and 1919.

On being taken over, Nos. 45 and 51 were numbered 4 and 10, on a system that was adopted for a year or two of having a separate series of numbers for engines allotted to the Greenwich service. This arrangement was dropped in 1848, and they became 130 and 133. Five other engines taken over from the Greenwich line itself – Nos. 1, 2, 3, 8 and 9 thereon – were then numbered 127–129, 131 and 132.

The Bodmer double-piston engine, No. 123, met with misfortune on 23rd May, 1846, when it ran off the line with an up Dover express near Pluckley, probably owing to a stone on the line. The driver was killed. Attempts were made to throw the blame on its peculiar construction, but strong evidence was given to the effect that it was the steadiest-running engine on the line. It was not broken up until 1880, but had probably been reconstructed before then.

James I'Anson Cudworth was appointed Locomotive Superintendent in 1845, at the age of only twenty-eight. At first he followed the usual custom of purchasing engines designed by the makers. No satisfactory account of the early South Eastern engines has ever been published, nor is there very much in the way of official records. For details down to 1855, the writer has relied on a copy of an Ashford list of that date, for which he is indebted to Mr A. C. W. Lowe.

The 'long boiler' type was in great favour in the early years, Cudworth having become attached to it during his previous service on the North Eastern Railway. Crampton's designs were also given a trial.

They began by filling up the blank numbers. In 1846 Hick and Co. supplied Nos. 1–4, long boiler singles with 6ft or 5ft 6in wheels; cylinders 15 by 22; afterwards altered to coupled engines. In the same and following year they sent Nos. 6–8, long boiler coupled, with driving wheels on 4ft 6in.

At this time Forrester was also supplying 21–23, 28, 30, 38, 42, 45–54, 60, 61, and 63; 2-4-0 long boilers, the driving wheels being 5ft 6in. All the above had outside cylinders.

Six more long boiler singles came from Bury and Co. in 1847, Nos. 68, 69, 72, 74, 75 and 78. They had 6-ft wheels (next the firebox); four (believed to be Nos. 72 onward) were later on converted to rear-drive Cramptons.

Nine long boiler singles were supplied by Nasmyth, with 5-ft driving wheels (in the middle); Nos. 88–94, 110 and 112; and by the same makers, six coupled ones with 4ft 6in wheels, Nos. 95–100. These engines were much altered in the course of rebuilding; 88 and 89 were converted to coupled; 92 to a Crampton, while 90 and 93–95 were made into tanks, known as 'swallow-tails'. No. 117, by Jones and Potts, met with the same fate.

Four engines were taken over from the Gravesend & Rochester Railway in 1847; 113–115, by Stephenson, the first two coupled and the last a single; and 116, built by Fossick and Hackworth, type doubtful, originally named *Van Tromp*.

Nos. 124 and 125 were 0-6-0 engines built by Kitson, Thompson and Hewitson in 1846. No. 126 was a little four-wheeled engine with vertical boiler, nicknamed the 'coffee-pot', built at Bricklayers' Arms in 1850.

In 1849 three Crampton expresses with 7-ft wheels behind the firebox were supplied by Tulk and Ley, of Whitehaven: Nos. 81, 83 and 85.

In 1851 large additions were made to the stock: Nos. 65 and 66 were Kitson, 0-6-0. Ten express engines were supplied by Robert Stephenson and Co., Nos. 134–143. They were Crampton's type with

6-ft driving wheels behind the firebox, coupled to an intermediate dummy crankshaft (i.e. without any wheels on it). No. 136 was named Folkestone,* and shown at the Great Exhibition. They were all converted afterwards to ordinary coupled engines. Then came eight singles of normal pattern, designed by Cudworth and built by Sharp: 144–151. Nos. 152–156 were tanks intended for the Folkestone harbour incline, built by Stephenson. They had 4ft 6in wheels, driven by a dummy crankshaft, with the then large dimension of 16 by 24 cylinders, and were called the 'Bulldogs'. The first three were altered to 0-6-0 tanks, and the other two made into tender engines.

We now come to the first engines built at Ashford. They were a series of ten (157–166) known as the 'Hastings' engines; 2-4-0, long boiler, 5ft 6in wheels and inside cylinders 15 by 20, with outside frames and a compensating beam above the bearings. No. 157 appeared in 1853, the rest in 1854. In the latter year four similar engines came from Stephenson's, Nos. 167–170, and in 1855 the first Cudworth goods engines, with 4ft 9in wheels and 16 by 24 cylinders, were built at Ashford, Nos. 171 and 172, together with another 157 type, No. 59.

Like Beattie on the South Western, Cudworth had his own scheme for burning coal, which he brought out about 1856. He used a double firebox; no less than 7ft 6in long, with a sloping grate, divided by a longitudinal water partition. There were two firing doors and each side was fired alternately. The shaking of the engine, when running, caused the incandescent fuel gradually to descend along the sloping grate to the front and the gases, passing over the fuel, to be properly consumed. The partition was cut away near the tube-plate so that the gases from the two compartments could combine before entering the tubes.

From the year 1855 the designs became more or less standard, and the rest of the Cudworth engines can be dealt with in large groups. All the cylinders were inside, and practically all engines had double frames. The goods were as follows, all built at Ashford (53):

171–174 .	.	.	.	1855–7	1, 168 .	.	.	.	1868
108, 111	.	.	.	1859	106, 124, 169, 170	.	.	1869
76, 77, 80, 107	.	.	1860	51, 98, 100, 155–157	.	1870
39, 82	.	.	.	1861	6, 8, 48, 50	.	...	.	1872
127, 128	.	.	.	1863	47, 65, 66, 95–97	.	.	1874
109, 129	.	.	.	1864	254, 255	.	.	.	1875
99, 126	.	.	.	1866	49, 125, 256–258	.	.	1876
3, 7, 44, 46, 69, 123	.	1867			

* But the plate was cast as 'Folkstone'.

In 1856 and 1857 five 6-ft singles were built at Ashford, Nos. 175–178 and 36. In the latter year, six 2-4-0 engines with 6-ft wheels, numbered 179–184, were supplied by Wilson and Co.; the type, slightly improved, became the '118 class', of which there were 110, as follows:

Built at Ashford:

118	.	.	.	.	1859	11, 101	.	.	.	1865
4, 20, 22, 30	.	.	.	1860	13, 29	.	.	.	1866
52, 53, 63	.	.	.	1860	31, 32, 78, 94, 103, 105	.	1871
21, 23, 60, 88	.	.	.	1861	37, 54, 71, 89, 104, 114	.	1872
17, 26, 28, 34, 35	.	.	1862	38, 45, 56, 61, 110	.	.	1873
42, 62, 64, 79, 102	.	.	1862	113	.	.	.	1874
25, 86, 91, 112, 130, 133	.	1863	57, 68, 74, 75, 90, 92	.	1875
9, 18, 24, 33, 87, 132	.	1864	93, 117, 142, 145, 252, 253	1875

By outside firms:

185–196 Vulcan Foundry	1859–60	225–234 Dübs & Co.	1866
219–224 „ „	1866–7	242–251 „	1874–5
215–218 England & Co.	1865		

No. 232 was named *Joan of Arc*.

There were also six smaller engines with 5ft 6in wheels ('19' class), all built at Ashford: 19, 55 (1858); 5, 67, 70, 131 (1859).

In 1861 the first of some very fine single express engines appeared, with 7-ft wheels, which were known as the 'Mails'. There were sixteen of them, those of 1861 and 1862 having cylinders 17 by 22; while the later ones were only 16in:

27, 116 Ashford	.	.	1861	2, 43, 72 Ashford	.	.	1865
197–200 Vulcan Foundry	.	1862	81, 83, 85 „	.	.	1866
201–204 Kitson & Hewitson	1862		

No. 81 was named *Flying Dutchman*.

There were four classes of tank engine designed by Cudworth: the first being 0-4-2 with 5-ft wheels, cylinders 15 by 20; Nos. 12 and 16 at Ashford (1863 and 1864), and 205–214 by Slaughter, Gruning and Co. in 1864. Another batch was built at Ashford with 5ft 6in wheels in the 'sixties: 10, 14, 15, 40, 41, 73. He then produced some 0-4-4 tank engines: the first to have this wheel arrangement, which afterwards became so popular. They were Nos. 235–241, built at the Canada Works, Birkenhead, in 1866, and had 5ft 6in wheels and 15 by 20 cylinders. The last tank engines he designed came out in 1877, being three, numbered 152–154, for the Folkestone Harbour incline. They had six coupled wheels 4ft 6in diameter, with 17 by 24 cylinders, which, though inside, were horizontal; there being twin piston rods, one above and one below the leading axle.

Owing to disputes arising in 1876, to which reference was made in Chapter XXV, Cudworth resigned; his duties being for a short time assigned to A. M. Watkin. At this juncture twenty engines were built, known as the '259' class, and familiarly as the 'Ironclads'. In all essential details they were North Western 'Precedents', except that the splashers were open. Nos. 259–268 were by Sharp, Stewart and Co., and 269–278 by the Avonside Engine Co., of Bristol. The dimensions were 6ft 6in and 17 by 24.

As has already been related, Watkin was not permitted to retain the appointment, and the locomotives were for a time placed in the charge of R. C. Mansell, the carriage and wagon superintendent. He designed three goods engines, similar to Cudworth's, but with cabs: Nos. 59, 70 and 150, which appeared in 1879; and nine 0-4-4 tanks ('144' class): Nos. 58, 84, 115, 144, and 146–149.

In 1878 James Stirling was appointed Locomotive Superintendent He came from the Glasgow & South Western Railway, and was a brother of Patrick Stirling, of the Great Northern. The brothers were alike in dispensing with domes, but whereas Patrick never used a bogie unless it was very difficult to avoid doing so, James employed one whenever it was possible. During the twenty years of his appointment he only introduced six classes of engines, in four of which the boilers were interchangeable, and many parts were common to all. He invented a particularly neat and successful form of steam reversing gear, and a very original type of bogie, with the side motion controlled by rubber pads, which worked satisfactorily, though it would possibly have been better if the wheel base, which was only 5ft 9in, had been longer. His standard pressure was 150 lb per square inch.

His first class of engine was a 4-4-0, with 6-ft wheels and 18 by 26 cylinders. Of these there were twelve 'A' class, all built at Ashford: 165, 157, (1879); 163, 166, 160, 176, 159, 179, 19, 67, 36 (1880), and 175 (1881).

Then came the standard goods engine, with 5ft 2in wheels and the same sized cylinders, of which there were 122, as follows: ('O' class*)

* No. 372 was sold to the East Kent Light Railway in 1923, also No. 376 in 1928, and No. 383 in 1935. No. 372 ran on the E.K.R. until 1933 with domeless boiler and chimney as cut down for Whitstable branch. No. 376 became an oddity in having a Wainwright boiler fitted but retaining Stirling cab. Nos. 279-298 had 5ft. 1in. wheels.

279–298 Sharp, Stewart & Co.	1878–9		14, 41, 48	.	Ashford	1893
314–318 .	. Ashford	1882		167, 170, 238	.	,,	,,
119–122 .	. ,,	1883		46, 106, 258	.	,,	1894
55, 131, 171, 207	,,	1884		3, 52, 64, 65	.	,,	1896
299–301 .	. ,,	,,		96, 109, 111, 123		,,	,,
331, 332	. ,,	1886		142, 248, 251	.	,,	,,
333, 334	. ,,	1887		425–439 .	. Sharp	1897
1, 15, 144	. ,,	1890		39, 66, 80, 93, 108 Ashford	,,
369–378 .	. Sharp	1891		44, 49, 51, 254	,,	1898
379–398 .	. ,,	1893		7, 8, 98–100	.	,,	1899

This was a remarkably successful class, being used on passenger as well as goods duties, and many examples were still at work at the end of the Southern era. Almost all the 'O' class were rebuilt by Wainwright with domed boilers, some retaining the wings of the front end over the sandboxes, others having rounded smoke-box plates and new sand-boxes under the running plate.

In 1880 three 4-4-0 tanks of the Metropolitan type were acquired from Beyer, Peacock and Co., and numbered 299–301, but did not run very long on the S.E.R., being taken over by the Metropolitan Railway in 1884.

In 1881 a little crane engine was supplied by Neilson and Co., numbered 302, and a saddle tank by Manning, Wardle, No. 313. They were later 234S and 225S.

In the same year Stirling introduced his Q class 0-4-4 tanks, of which there were 118; numbers as below:

303–312	. Neilson	1881		23, 82, 85, 220	Ashford	1889
5, 158, 161, 162	Ashford	,,		343–352 .	. Neilson	,,
164, 177, 178, 181	,,	,,		354–368 .	. ,,	1891
27, 180, 182, 184	,,	1882		58, 73, 115	. Ashford	,,
319–328 .	. Neilson	1882–3		134, 146, 224	. ,,	,,
329, 330	. Ashford	1885		135, 136, 138	. ,,	1892
12, 26, 40, 72	. ,,	1887		6, 50, 95 .	. ,,	1894
129, 193, 200	. ,,	,,		399–408 .	. Sharp	1893–4
235, 237, 239	. ,,	,,		76, 160, 169	. Ashford	1895
16, 81, 83	. ,,	1888		410–424 .	. Neilson	1897
141, 173	. ,,	,,				

None of the above engines survived after 1930. The first twelve, built at Ashford, were fitted with a condensing pipe for underground working. The steam only went into the left-hand tank, which was connected to a pump, thus leaving the other tank cool for an injector. Many were rebuilt with domed boiler, classed 'Qi'.

In 1883 the first of the well-known 'F' class bogie expresses with 7-ft wheels appeared. A few at first had 18-in cylinders, afterwards enlarged to 19in, but the rest had the latter diameter from the first. They were later reduced to 18in. There were 88, all built at Ashford, of which 78 were running in 1928, after which year they began to drop away rather quickly.

205	1883	60, 130, 137, 139, 140, 215	1891
116, 183, 198, 208, 212, 214	1884	79, 133, 232 . . .	1892
43, 104, 199, 201 . .	1885	9, 97, 156, 172, 187, 231 .	1893
203, 204, 206, 209 . .	,,	24, 25, 31, 94, 196, 226 .	1894
2, 32, 78, 114 . . .	1886	11, 29, 89, 110 . .	1895
202, 210, 211, 213 . .	,,	117, 118, 216 . . .	,,
20, 35, 56, 190 . .	1888	42, 45, 103, 105 . .	1896
28, 91, 148, 151 . .	1889	53, 62, 87, 88, 188, 192 .	1897
194, 236, 240 . . .	,,	195, 222, 228, 230, 249, 250	,,
74, 84, 143, 149, 197, 241	1890	22, 30, 185, 233 . .	1898

No. 240 was shown at the Paris Exhibition of 1889. Almost all eventually received new boilers with domes, classed 'F1'. Both this class and the 'O' class had tenders with springs above the footplate, later necessitating smaller numerals on the side than normal.

In 1888 a class known as 'R', namely six coupled tanks, was produced, of which there were twenty-five, all from Ashford:

335–338	1888	153, 154, 174 . . .	1892
339–342	1889	47, 125, 126, 127 . .	1895
10, 77, 147 . . .	1890	69, 70, 107, 155 . .	1898
124, 128, 152 . . .	1892		

Most were reboilered by Wainwright, some retaining the wings to the smoke-box over the sand-boxes. Several were fitted with short chimneys for the Whitstable branch (one by Bulleid with a short stove pipe).

In 1898 an enlargement of the 'F' class of bogie expresses appeared, having the same size wheels and cylinders, but larger boilers and tenders, and greatly improved cabs. There were twenty, built by Neilson and Co., Nos. 440–459; and nine at Ashford, Nos. 13, 21, 101 and 217 in 1898, and 17, 34, 132, 186 and 189 in the following year. They were known as 'B' class and 'B1' class after rebuilding with Wainwright boiler.

Mention should be made of a second saddle tank, No. 353, obtained from Manning, Wardle and Co. in 1890, and another crane engine, No. 409, Neilson, 1896.

On the establishment of the South Eastern and Chatham Joint Committee, Stirling resigned.

Generally speaking, the South Eastern engines have always been green, but in Stirling's time many, including the goods and tanks, were painted black.

The company exhibited a very remarkable carriage at the Great Exhibition of 1851, which is described in the extra volume for that year of the 'Year-book of Facts in Science and Art'. It was 44ft long, on eight wheels; built on Adams' patent and separable into two four wheeled carriages, but so coupled that the combined bodies formed a perfectly rigid frame. Provision was made for going round curves by giving lateral play to the wheels. There was accommodation for 80 passengers, in four first and four second-class compartments, also one for the guard and luggage.

Another bold experiment was made in the early 'eighties, when they built an all (or mostly) metal carriage, and covered the panels with nickel plate. It did not suit the London atmosphere, and had to be painted in the usual way.

The development of S.E.R. suburban stock, partly due to the need for light four-wheelers on the Metropolitan services, lagged behind other lines, but some six-compartment six-wheelers and seven-compartment bogies were built in the 'eighties, and before the fusion the well-known Wainwright high-roofed bogies, with the guard's look-out in a raised "birdcage" at the brake-ends, began to appear.

XXVII

The London, Chatham & Dover Railway to 1870

AT the beginning of the South Eastern history, in Chapter XXIII, accounts were given of schemes of 1824 and 1832 for lines through North Kent, which failed. In the *Autobiography of Sir John Rennie*, particulars are given of another line, projected in 1838, of which he was the engineer, called the Central Kent, which had much in common with the line afterwards known as the London, Chatham & Dover. Rennie says:

> It had long been considered a desirable object to connect Dover and London by a railway for the Continent, and the South Eastern had already obtained an Act to make a line by Redhill, thence to Tunbridge, Ashford and Folkestone to Dover, the distance being 86 miles, whereas the old coach road was only 72. Moreover the South Eastern avoids all the principal towns and population in Kent; so much so, that it was considered to be very objectionable, and that it would not pay. I was accordingly requested by a most influential committee to examine the country of Kent carefully, and endeavour to find out a better line. I was not long in discovering one, namely to commence at London Bridge, thence by Lewisham, Eltham, the Crays, the Darent, 4 miles above Dartford, thence by Gravesend, through Gad's Hill, crossing the Medway a mile above Rochester, thence, within a mile of Maidstone, to Eastwell, where it has to separate into two branches, one to Ashford, and thence on to Folkestone and Dover; another to Canterbury, thence to Sandwich, where it was to terminate; while from the Darent another branch was intended to run up the valley of that river, with a tunnel at its head, and thence to Sevenoaks and Tunbridge.

This line – according to Rennie – was so obviously the best for Kent and the sea coast, that when submitted to the South Eastern company, who had not commenced theirs, they received it with open arms, and said they would make terms with the promoters for carrying it into effect. The negotiations, however, fell through, Sir John Rennie hints, through the opposition of Maidstone and the landowners; and the South Eastern made their line by Reigate and Tonbridge, as originally intended.

Before anything further was done in this direction, the North Kent line of the South Eastern was made via Gravesend to Strood, as recorded in Chapter XXIII. Then it occurred to Crampton and Morris, who had been assistants to Rennie, that it would be a good speculation to promote a shorter line to Dover once more, and they persuaded Lord Harris, who had considerable property between Sittingbourne and Canterbury, and some other landowners on the line, to form a company to make a line from Rochester to Canterbury, and were joined by George Burge, the contractor of the St Katherine's Docks and the Herne Bay pier. Burge had invested a considerable sum of money at the latter place, and looked forward to the railway improving its value. Morris, who afterwards became one of the contractors of the South Eastern, and made a good deal of money there, had had the sagacity to buy Folkestone Harbour, it was said for £10,000; reaping a handsome profit when he sold it to the S.E.R. for £18,000. Crampton was the well-known locomotive engineer.

They obtained their powers in 1853, the line being known as the East Kent Railway, and commenced with comparatively little support for so large an undertaking. They experienced very great uphill work; so much so, that Burge became alarmed, and Morris and Crampton bought him out. They struggled on, and then Morris retired, and Crampton was left alone. At last he induced Peto and Betts to join him, and then they went ahead. Lord Sondes, a large landowner in Kent, joined them, and they then completed the original line, which started from Strood, crossing the Medway to Rochester. A branch to Faversham Quay, and another to Chilham were also authorised.

The Act gave the East Kent Railway the right to use the South Eastern stations at Strood and Canterbury. They did not obtain running powers over the North Kent section of the S.E.R., as they would have liked to have done, but merely a 'facilitation clause', which laid down that the S.E.R. were to transmit the East Kent traffic with the same facilities as their own. Indications occur later on that this clause was not obeyed to the satisfaction of the East Kent people. The latter obtained a most valuable advantage in the House of Lords in connection with their intention to push on to Dover at the earliest possible moment. The South Eastern were at the time seeking powers to extend their line from Strood down to Maidstone, which would have necessitated a parallel length of line for some distance through Strood. The East Kent company agreed that their line should begin in Strood station, so that only one was necessary. For this small concession, if it can be called one, they obtained, by direction of the House of Lords Committee, an undertaking that the South Eastern would not in any future session oppose any bill introduced for powers to construct a railway from Canterbury to Dover. It must be realised that at that time the

S.E.R. looked upon the East Kent as merely an extension to its North Kent section, through a part of the country well away from its own line; moreover, they expected to obtain a considerable traffic from it at Strood. If the directors of the South Eastern had had any idea that the East Kent was going later on to seek an independent line to London, doubtless they would have done anything rather than allow their hands to be tied in this way. Parliament, on a number of occasions, showed itself extremely favourable to the company whose history we are now narrating; so much so, that it was called 'the spoilt child of the legislature'.

The South Eastern directors little realised what was going to happen, when, in January, 1849, in their 'statement to the proprietors', they said that their company 'holds, from its natural position, the key to the land traffic passing from Europe into Great Britain and cannot be dispossessed of it'.

In 1855, the coveted powers to extend to Dover were obtained by the East Kent company. The various sections were opened thus: Strood–Chatham, 29th March, 1858; Chatham–Faversham, 25th January, 1858; Faversham Creek branch, 12th April, 1860; Faversham–Canterbury, 9th July, 1860; Canterbury–Dover Town – now Dover Priory – 22nd July, 1861; Dover Town–Dover Harbour, 1st November, 1861. This was the genesis of the London, Chatham & Dover, but the East Kent did not get that name until 1859 and after an extension into London had been sanctioned. The Chilham branch was not made, nor was there any connection with the S.E.R. at Canterbury. One was put in temporarily during both Wars.

The engineering features of the Strood–Canterbury line included a bridge over the Medway between Strood and Rochester, and four tunnels. The bridge, which was designed by Joseph Cubitt, had four spans, one of which had to be made to open, but was later on made fixed, as opening it was found to be unnecessary. The line through Rochester and Chatham was very costly, as it passed through valuable property, and three tunnels had to be made in a short distance: the Fort Pitt tunnel, 1,200ft in length, approaching Chatham station from Strood; the Chatham tunnel (795ft); and the New Brompton tunnel (2,685ft) to the east of the station. There was hardly any level line. The worst part was between Faversham and Canterbury, which involved a rise of about a mile and a half at 1 in 110, then, after a short level piece, two miles at 1 in 100, up to the Selling tunnel, which was 1,188ft long, falling at 1 in 183. After the tunnel there is a stretch of over four miles down hill of 1 in 132; the remaining three-quarters of a mile into Canterbury being level.

The extension from Canterbury to Dover also necessitated much heavy work. The gradients from Canterbury include a rise of a mile at 1 in 105, succeeded by shorter lengths of 1 in 168 and 188; a fall of nearly a mile at 1 in 132, with a rise at the same rate of about the same length. Half a mile west of Adisham a bank commences of $3\frac{1}{2}$ miles long, at 110, 132 and 273. This attains the Shepherd's Well tunnel, 2,376 yards long, from which the line falls for $6\frac{1}{2}$ miles to Dover, five miles at 1 in 132, and the last mile at 106.

In 1856 the East Kent opened their attack on London, by a bill seeking powers to run over the South Eastern from Strood to Dartford, thence by a new line through Lewisham, to join up with the West End of London & Crystal Palace Railway, which, as related in Chapter XVI, was to carry the London, Brighton & South Coast up to Battersea on its way to Victoria. In 1854 the West End company had been authorised to build an extension, in an easterly direction, from Norwood through Beckenham and Bromley, to Farnborough, Kent; but this particular line did not get farther east than Shortlands.

The South Eastern, thoroughly alarmed, offered vigorous opposition, and this first attempt fell to the ground. The East Kent, however, was determined to reach London by a route of its own; arguing that the South Eastern said that the North Kent had all the traffic it could carry – which they had stated when opposing the running powers sought – also that the London Bridge station was inconveniently crowded, and that a West End terminus was highly desirable, which the South Eastern did not at that time possess. All this had its effect on Parliament, and eventually the first definite stage of the Chatham & Dover march on London was authority, given in 1858, to build a line in a westward direction from Strood to Bickley opened on 3rd December, 1860. The West End Railway was, as said above, authorised to make a line from Norwood Junction to Shortlands and the gap between St Mary Cray and Shortlands was to be filled by the Mid Kent company under powers given in 1856. The latter piece was made partly by the Mid Kent and partly by the East Kent, and opened for traffic on 5th July, 1858. Thence, London was reached by the London, Chatham & Dover under running powers to Battersea given by the West End of London & Crystal Palace Company and, into Victoria, by the Victoria Station and Pimlico Railway. The Mid Kent line was leased by the L.C.D.R. in 1863.

In 1860 the L.C.D.R. obtained powers to build a line of its own from Penge Junction to Battersea, and at the latter place to join the Victoria Station and Pimlico.

The line all the way from Strood to London was just as disadvantageous from the point of view of gradients as that from Strood to Dover. Roughly speaking, there is a five mile climb of 1 in 100 up to Sole Street, thence the line all the way to Penge is like the teeth of a saw, the slopes being mostly 1 in 100. The extremely uneven character of the line severely handicapped it in competing for the Dover traffic with the South Eastern.

The Penge tunnel, which is 2,200 yards long, went through the London clay, which had the disadvantage of being very treacherous to work in, but provided excellent material for bricks, supplying 33,000,000 of them, all of which were used in lining it. It was unfortunately made to rather small dimensions, and for some seventy years, imposed limitations on the stock which could be permitted to use it.

As said above, Battersea was reached, at first, by running powers over the West End Railway (via Bromley Junction and through Crystal Palace and Balham), and the Chatham & Dover entered Victoria on 1st December, 1860. As its own half was not then ready temporary arrangements were made until 25th August, 1862, on which date the Chatham company's line from Herne Hill was also opened. Beckenham and Herne Hill were connected on 1st July, 1863.

By the same Act as sanctioned the extension to Victoria, a line from Herne Hill to Blackfriars and thence to the Metropolitan Railway at Farringdon Street was authorised. The south side of the Thames was reached at the present Blackfriars goods station on 1st June, 1864. The bridge over the Thames had been approved by the Admiralty, but the consent of the City Corporation was not as readily forthcoming.

Moreover, the latter body was very concerned as to the viaduct over Ludgate Hill, as it was said that it would obstruct the view of St Paul's Cathedral. The company, therefore, had to be satisfied with a temporary station at Ludgate Hill, opened on 21st December, 1864. The permanent station was brought into use on 1st June, 1865. The Metropolitan Railway then hindered further progress, but eventually that line was joined at West Street Junction, Farringdon Street, on 1st January, 1866.

Near Ludgate Hill, the line absorbed the site of the notorious Fleet Prison, which dated back to Norman times, but had been pulled down in 1844. The contribution of the South Western to these City lines by virtue of which they obtained running powers to Ludgate Hill, was mentioned in Chapter IX. The Great Northern also supplied £300,000.

S.E.R. 'B' class 4-4-0, Stirling's final express class; No. 217, built at Ashford 1898 and seen here after rebuilding by Wainwright as class B1.

S.E.C.R. motor-train with 'P' class 0-6-0T and ex-L.C.D.R. bogie stock.

[*Locomotive Publishing Company*

Charing Cross station about 1908 after re-opening with new roof; 'D' class 4-4-o No. 591 right on Continental train, re-

Down main line S.E.C.R. train near Chislehurst, after widenings about 1905, headed by a 'D' class 4-4-0 No. 57. The train is formed of early bogie stock, the first coach is a 1st and 2nd class brake compo with coupe.   [*Locomotive Publishing Company*

Down main line S.E.C.R. train near Grove Park with 'L' class 4-4-0 No. 767; the train comprises 11 6-compartment thirds, one four-compartment first, two brakes and an ex-L.C.D.R. parcels van, all six-wheeled, and is probably an excursion.

'N1' class 2-6-0 No. 822, Ashford 1922; the only three-cylinder example built before amalgamation.

A rebuilt 'F' class No. 62 leaving Cannon Street station about 1910.

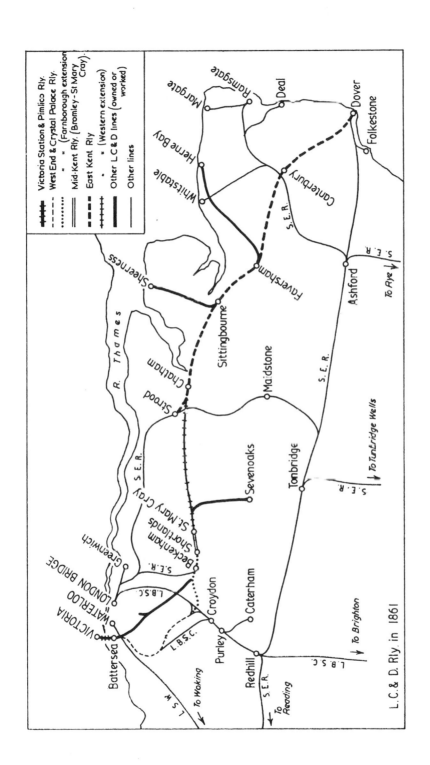

L.C. & D. Rly. in 1861

Victoria Station & Pimlico Rly.
West End & Crystal Palace Rly.
"   " (Farnborough extension)
Mid-Kent Rly. (Bromley-St Mary Cray).
East Kent Rly
"   " (Western extension)
Other LC & D lines (owned or worked)
Other lines

In the meantime promoters were busy in other directions. An Act was passed, without any serious opposition, in 1856, repealing a somewhat similar one of the previous year, for a branch railway from the East Kent at Sittingbourne, to Sheerness, in the Isle of Sheppey, which was destined to be of great importance, quite unrealised at the time. An interesting feature of it was the bridge across the Swale at King's Ferry, which carried both road and rail, thus superseding the ferry; the Sittingbourne and Sheerness Railway, in consideration of providing the road bridge, acquiring the ancient rights of the 'wardens and jury of the King's Ferry'. The line was opened on 19th July, 1860 (extended to Queenborough pier in 1876). It was worked by the L.C.D.R., and leased to them in 1866. The loop giving through running from London without reversing in the station at Sittingbourne was opened in 1863.

Another subsidiary line which became a very prominent part of the L.C.D.R. was the Herne Bay & Faversham Railway, which obtained powers in 1857·to construct a line between the points named, through Whitstable, a distance of 10 miles 48 chains. This time the South Eastern offered strenuous opposition, as it was carrying the Herne Bay passengers as far as Sturry, six miles away, whence they proceeded by omnibuses.

It was opened from Faversham to Whitstable on 1st August, 1860; the company, having the previous year obtained powers to extend to Margate and changing its name to the Margate Railway. It was also arranged for the L.C.D.R. to do the working. It arrived at Herne Bay on 13th July, 1861, having by then acquired authority to push on to Ramsgate, and calling itself the Kent Coast Railway. The extension to Ramsgate included a tunnel at the latter place, 1,630 yards long, on a falling gradient of 1 in 75, the total length of this severe gradient being one and a half miles, which necessitated very careful handling of the trains. It was opened on 5th October, 1863, and acquired by the L.C.D.R. in 1871, having been leased as from 1861. The original terminus provided at Margate was never used, and some years later was converted into a 'Hall-by-the-Sea'.

What was known as the Sevenoaks Company was empowered in 1859 to build a line from Sutton-at-Hone – now Swanley Junction – to Sevenoaks. It was opened on 2nd June, 1862. In the latter year an extension to Maidstone was authorised which was opened on 1st June, 1874, from a north-facing junction near the present Otford station. A connection between Sevenoaks L.C.D.R. (Bat & Ball) and the S.E.R. station (Tubs Hill) had been opened on 1st August, 1869, and a shuttle service worked from Tubs Hill to a platform at the Maidstone line junction until 1880, after which all Maidstone trains ran via an east curve which completed the triangle at the junction in and out of Bat & Ball. In 1882 the present Otford station was opened and Maidstone trains ceased to call at Sevenoaks. From 1885 to 1898 there was no passenger service on the connecting line between the two Sevenoaks stations.

The name of the company had been changed in 1862 to Sevenoaks, Maidstone & Tonbridge, with the idea of going on to the last named place, but the connection between the L.C.D.R. and the S.E.R. at Sevenoaks had rendered unnecessary the proposed line to Tonbridge, and it was abandoned. The line was absorbed in the Chatham system in 1879.

In 1861, James Staats Forbes, who had been on the Great Western Railway before he became the resident manager and a director of the Dutch Rhenish Railway – practically a British company – came to the Chatham as general manager. There were to be, during the following nearly forty years, many disputes between Mr Forbes and his neighbour Sir Edward Watkin of the South Eastern. They were both extremely autocratic, and past masters in railway strategy.

In 1862 the Chatham company executed a master stroke by obtaining the contract for the conveyance of the mails between Dover and Calais. For eight years previously it had been held by a Mr Churchward, of Dover, who had steamers of his own; being conveyed between London and Dover, of course, by the South Eastern.

At that time the L.C.D.R., like the S.E.R., had no power to own and work steamboats, so they arranged with Churchward to make use of his steamers. In 1864 they obtained the necessary powers, and acquired the boats. As was mentioned in Chapter XXIV, they carried the mails jointly with the South Eastern after June, 1863, and entered into a pooling arrangement covering all Continental traffic via Dover and Folkestone two years later. At the same time, competition, so far as passengers were concerned, still went on; in consequence of a clause in the agreement making an allowance to each company in respect of every passenger carried. The 'Continental Agreement', as it was called, went on until 1899.

In the session of 1862 the London, Chatham & Dover obtained sanction for a line from Dover to Deal; a continuation of their line at Dover to the Admiralty Pier; and a junction with the West London Extension (which gave the G.W.R. access to Victoria).

In connection with the Admiralty Pier extension, an amusing quotation from a daily paper of the period is as follows:

It is generally a moot point whether the express from Charing Cross or Victoria shall be the first alongside the steamer at Dover. The fact has been noted by the idlers on the pier, who have devised a new form of gambling, and bets are freely laid as to which train shall be first past the post. The difference in actual mileage from London is comparatively nothing, and the betting is accordingly even. When the signals have fallen on both tracks the excitement becomes intense. The S.E.R. has a clear run in by the shore and when the train shoots out of the tunnel the backers of Charing Cross are jubilant: but, as often as not, Victoria suddenly shoots round the corner and wins, like a well-ridden thoroughbred, by a short head.

About this time the idea of having a goods station at Blackfriars began to be considered, as the company's London goods had to be dealt with by the Brighton company at Willow Walk, for which rather heavy charges were made. Parliamentary sanction for the construction of Blackfriars goods depot was obtained in 1864. The area obtained was quite inadequate for sorting and marshalling the trains there, so fourteen acres of land were acquired between Herne Hill and Loughborough for the purpose of making up the goods trains, the trucks of which were dealt with at Blackfriars. The Herne Hill sidings were probably the first 'sorting sidings', as previously all marshalling had been done in yards close to the goods stations. Forbes said that the G.N.R. supported the L.C.D.R. plan of a riverside goods station at Blackfriars, as they wished to use it for the purpose of shipping coals. With regard to the Blackfriars passenger station, he said both the Metropolitan and the Great Northern companies thought so highly of it that they proposed to start many of their trains from there; and as a *quid pro quo*, the Chatham company's trains were to have the use of Farringdon Street and King's Cross stations free of charge. The use of Blackfriars Station by passengers was given up in 1885.

The first train passed over Blackfriars Bridge on 6th October, 1864. The bridge is 933ft between the north and south abutments; of the lattice girder type, with five spans.

G. F. Holroyd, who had been Secretary since the incorporation of the company, resigned the position, and was elected a director in August, 1863. W. E. Johnson, the accountant, was appointed secretary.

The Chatham & Dover's suggestion of going to Epsom Downs was mentioned in Chapter XVII.

The Crystal Palace High Level branch from Peckham* was opened

* Owing to the later opening of the Greenwich branch and the Catford Loop, this branch appeared to start at Nunhead, and it was later closed from Nunhead to Crystal Palace, remaining open from Peckham Rye to Nunhead for the Catford Loop trains and trains by that time running via the Lewisham Loops to the Dartford Loop and Bexleyheath line.

on 1st August, 1865. It involved the Crescent Wood tunnel, 362 yards, and the Crystal Palace tunnel, 430 yards.

In 1865 the London, Chatham & Dover introduced workmen's trains. The *Illustrated London News* described the innovation thus:

The Metropolitan Extension of the London, Chatham & Dover Railway Company, which connects Blackfriars and Ludgate Hill with the Victoria station at Pimlico by a line through Walworth, Camberwell, Brixton, Stockwell and Battersea-fields, has been made the scene of an interesting experiment in social economics during the last two months. On Monday the 27th February, commenced the running of two trains daily throughout the week, from each terminus of this line to the other, for the exclusive accommodation of artisans, mechanics and daily labourers, both male and female, going to their work, or returning from work to their houses.

.   .   .   .

The morning trains from each end of the line start at five minutes before five o'clock, and arrive at the other end shortly before six. The evening trains, on five days of the week, start at a quarter past six, but on Saturdays at half past two.

The running of these trains aroused comment at the next half-yearly meeting. One shareholder denounced them, saying the receipts would not pay for the coke. Another thought it 'highly creditable to be the first to run these trains', and even suggested putting on later ones for the benefit of clerks, etc. Forbes said that they were run under an obligation imposed on the company by Act of Parliament. He proceeded:

The company was described as a great destroyer of house property in London, and was charged with turning the working man out of his habitation. To meet this state of feeling it was thought advisable to make a graceful concession on the part of the company; they therefore volunteered to run cheap trains for the benefit of workmen, and a clause was inserted in the Act of Parliament for that purpose. That Act fixed both the hour at which the trains should be run, and the fares to be charged, and the company had strictly adhered to the Act in these particulars. He believed those trains would be successful and prove both beneficial to the working classes and advantageous to the company.

There can be no two opinions about the benefit to the working classes, but whether they were advantageous to the railways is another matter. After this concession volunteered by the Chatham & Dover, it became usual for Parliament to insist on the provision of workmen's trains whenever a railway was seeking powers to do anything which involved the removal of urban dwelling houses.

In 1864 the finances of the company were in a very serious state, and in December of that year a circular was issued which began by observing:

The position of the company having recently been the subject of much mis-representation, the board think it incumbent on them to afford some information to the proprietors without waiting until the general meeting in February.

It observed, *inter alia*, that

The authorised capital of the company is, in the opinion of the board, sufficient to complete all the company's works, including the junction with the Metropolitan, discharge all their liabilities and leave a surplus to meet demands for additional rolling stock and siding accommodation for increased traffic.

.   .   .   .   .

An arrangement has been made with the South Western, subject to confirmation by Parliament, by which the traffic of their whole system will, on payment of adequate tolls, obtain access over the Metropolitan Extension lines to Ludgate Hill station and thence over the City Junction to the Metropolitan at Farringdon Street and the Great Northern and Midland and King's Cross. The arrangement also embraces the provision of additional accommodation at Farringdon Street for the South Eastern, at their cost, upon land already acquired by this company.

.   .   .   .   .

The recent traffic receipts of the Metropolitan Extension have been represented as discouraging and tending to preclude any hope of adequate return upon the capital expended. Such a representation is, in the judgment of the board, without any foundation; and it must be obvious to the proprietors that any opinion formed on the basis of existing traffic must be fallacious. The Metropolitan Extensions were designed to convey passengers, goods and minerals between the Great Northern, Midland, Great Western and Metropolitan, the south of London, the Kent Coast, the South of England and the Continent. Therefore, until the last important link in this chain of communication is completed none of this vast traffic can be brought upon the lines of the company.

The circular wound up by saying that in the course of the following summer the junction with the Great Northern and Metropolitan would be opened.

Matters were made worse in 1865 by some allegations as to the sale, in April, 1863, of the steamer *Eugenie*. A committee of investigation looked into the matter who, whilst clearing the board of all suspicions of irregularity, showed that the money received had not been clearly indicated in the accounts. It was also said that the legitimate questions of a shareholder had not been treated with proper respect; had a contrary course been taken the matter would have been cleared up.

In 1866 the company could not meet its obligations. In order to avert a disaster a circular was issued in August appealing for abstention from individual action by any shareholder or section of shareholders. An application had, however, been made in Chancery for the appointment of a receiver and manager, and J. S. Forbes and W. E. Johnson – the secretary – were appointed jointly. The board, further, assigned to certain creditors the rolling stock, plant and movable chattels, so as to prevent their seizure by special creditors. An application to Parliament for special powers for the debenture holders and shareholders was unsuccessful, on the ground that it was too late in the session.

The half-yearly report for January–June for 1866, issued about the same time, said that the causes of the trouble were: (*a*) The delay in the completion of the Metropolitan Extensions and the City and Victoria station works beyond the period originally fixed, which had postponed the receipt of income and aggravated the amount of interest; (*b*) the increased cost of the Metropolitan and City lines; (*c*) the state of the money market, and (*d*) the very heavy working expenditure required for the efficient conduct of the traffic, coupled with the incompleteness of the line, which necessarily limited its amount.

The writer has an allotment letter dated 21st April, 1866, and brokers' receipts, showing that 'consolidated stock' was being issued at the rate of 27½ (for £100 stock).

At the subsequent half-yearly meeting on 31st August the chairman said that the board would welcome the appointment of a committee of shareholders. The offer was accepted and a report was presented and agreed to at a special meeting held on 12th October. A scheme of rearrangement was prepared by the board and issued to the shareholders in November and accepted by them at meetings held on 26th and 27th November.

The sequel to the scheme was the Arrangements Act of 1867, which granted exceptional powers for raising capital, provided for the claims of creditors and of debenture holders, gave a moratorium of ten years, created a board of eight directors, of whom four represented the shareholders and four the debenture holders, and allowed for the creation and issue of debenture stocks of three classes, all of which were chargeable on the entire undertaking and not, as previously, on separate sections.

A further Act – the Arrangements Act, 1869 – was necessary to adjust the financial situation, and under it the Marquis of Salisbury and Lord Cairns were appointed arbitrators. They sat for ten days at the beginning of November, 1869, and made their first award soon afterwards and their final one in 1871.

That the company had turned the corner was shown by the gradual growth of the receipts and the reduction in the ratio of working expenses. In 1866 the receipts were £168,175 at 70.66 per cent expenditure; in 1867 they were £219,842 at 65.33 per cent; and in 1868 they were £231,062 at 64.46 per cent.

It should be mentioned that in the bill of 1868, which, as mentioned in Chapter XVII, nearly brought the Southern Railway into existence, the L.C.D.R. had power to join, which it was willing to do; but for reasons already given, the scheme fell through.

The reward to the London & South Western for having advanced money for the Metropolitan Extensions came on 3rd April, 1866 when LSW trains from Kingston via Clapham reached Ludgate Hill. From 1st January, 1869, services were from Wimbledon, via Tulse Hill and Richmond via Addison Road. This necessitated a curve from Tulse Hill on the Brighton to Herne Hill on the Chatham. It was sanctioned in 1864 and opened on the inauguration of the new service. A line was also made from Wandsworth Road to the South Western at Clapham Junction.

It was mentioned above that the Great Northern also came to the help of the L.C.D.R. The return for its £300,000 was a service of Great Northern trains to and from Victoria via Brixton, which was inaugurated on 1st March, 1868.

Under the Metropolitan Extension Act a connection was, it will be remembered, made with the Metropolitan. It was in both an easterly and westerly direction – the easterly to join the 'widened lines' of the Metropolitan and so run into Moorgate, and westerly lines for the King's Cross direction. The negotiations for reaching Moorgate were very protracted, and although the Chatham and Metropolitan were joined at West Street Junction on 1st January, 1866, and access thus obtained to King's Cross, it was not until 1870 that an agreement was arrived at as to Moorgate. The service was commenced on 1st September, 1871.

A peculiar arrangement was made in 1870, which was that Forbes, the general manager, was allowed to be also the managing director of the Metropolitan District. A condition laid down was that he was to give a rebate, of not less than £2,500 a year, of the salary he received from the District, and that the Chatham had the first call on his services, The anomaly, it may be added, became less marked when, in March 1871, he ceased to be the general manager and became a director of the Chatham. On 1st October, 1873, the agreement expired and was thereupon renewed, accompanied by his elevation to the office of managing director at £2,500 a year. His connection with the District remained undisturbed, and he was at liberty to devote as much of his time to that company as necessary.

If the Chatham company had many anxieties in various directions, it could pride itself upon its record as to freedom from accident. In that connection it received commendation from Captain Tyler in his report on the accidents of the year 1870. On 4th December, 1861, a broken tire led to the derailment of a passenger train at Sittingbourne, one passenger being killed. Another accident occurred at Faversham on 9th May, 1862, when, owing to weak track, a train left the rails and three passengers lost their lives.

XXVIII

The London, Chatham & Dover from 1871 to 1898

THE line from Nunhead on the Crystal Palace Branch to Greenwich, which had been sanctioned in 1863, was opened from the junction at Nunhead as far as Blackheath Hill on 18th September, 1871. It did not reach Greenwich Park until 1st October, 1888.

In 1871 the company obtained powers to build a station on Holborn Viaduct, in view of the completion of the latter. It was also agreed that there should be a hotel, and at a subsequent meeting the chairman announced that a contract had been made with Messrs Spiers and Pond to work the hotel on payment yearly of 6 per cent of the cost of the building, and 10 per cent of the profits from the business. The new station was put into service on 2nd March, 1874. It had four platforms, each 400ft in length. The station called Snow Hill, on the through line passing beside and under Holborn Viaduct, was opened on 1st August following. The hotel was inaugurated on 17th November, 1877.

In 1870 the company had received what the chairman described as a 'nest egg' in the shape of £100,000 from the Post Office for its telegraphs, which came in useful at this juncture. The Franco-German War seriously affected the Continental traffic, the loss to the L.C.D.R. during the second half of 1870 amounting to £28,000. Immediately the war was over, the traffic to and from the Continent grew considerably. In consequence of a shortage of rolling stock on the French railways, the Chatham and South Eastern companies each lent the Northern of France twenty passenger carriages, to accommodate the Anglo-French traffic.

During 1871 progress was made in relaying the line with steel rails weighing 84 lb to the yard, in substitution for iron rails weighing 70; the cost being charged to revenue.

In the latter half of 1872 the contract with the French Government for carrying the mails from Calais to Dover expired, and was let to two Frenchmen. They began operations from 1st October, but their boats were not suitable for passengers, and the South Eastern's

Folkestone–Boulogne route benefited. The L.C.D.R., after about six months, succeeded in making arrangements to carry the mails once more, though at a lower price.

As was mentioned in the last chapter, J. S. Forbes became supreme in 1873, being made Chairman and Managing Director, a position which enabled him to meet Watkin on equal terms in their many disputes. One severe one came to a head about this time, in connection with the 'Continental Agreement', under which, it will be remembered, a percentage was allowed for each passenger to the line that carried him. As the Folkestone traffic was included, the South Eastern carried the larger number, and sought to have the percentage increased. It was decided to resort to arbitration, and T. E. Harrison, of the North Eastern Railway, was appointed arbitrator. He increased the percentage of the carrying company from 25 to 41½, the new allowance to be for two years, dating back from 1st January, 1872. Neither company was satisfied, Sir E. Watkin saying that he would apply for a fresh arbitration immediately the two years had expired. In later years, when Forbes' nephew – now Sir William of that ilk – was Continental Manager, the tide set the other way, Victoria becoming the chief gateway for passengers going abroad, instead of Charing Cross.

In 1873 powers were sought for the construction of a branch line into the Government Dockyard at Chatham, the estimated cost being £57,000. As there was considerable traffic between Woolwich Arsenal and Chatham the South Eastern sought powers at the same time for a line to Chatham and the Dockyard. The L.C.D.R. scheme was sanctioned, and the line was finished in February, 1877. The South Eastern plan failed.

The year 1874 was a bad one financially for the Chatham & Dover company, owing principally to the high price of coal, which cut both ways, increasing the locomotive expenses, and causing people to economise by decreasing their consumption. The Great Northern and Midland railways conveyed coal over the L.C.D.R. to their depots in South London, paying toll for every ton carried. The reduction in these tolls alone was £11,733 for the first half of 1874.

At the General Election in January, 1874, J. S. Forbes was a candidate for Dover, but failed to obtain the seat, in spite of having tried to obtain the support of the employees at Dover. No doubt his Parliamentary ambition was partly due to the fact that his great rival, Watkin, was M.P. for the adjoining borough of Hythe.

The Dover to Deal line, powers for which, as mentioned in the last chapter, had been obtained in 1862, having failed to materialise, in 1874 was brought forward once more, this time as a joint line with the S.E.R. The bill received the Royal Assent, but the line was not begun until 1878, and then, though only 8½ miles in length, it took three years to complete.

On 6th February, 1874, William Martley died. He had been Locomotive Superintendent and Marine Engineer almost from the time the first part of the line was opened. He was succeeded by William Kirtley, a nephew of the then Locomotive Superintendent of the Midland Railway.

The Midland company began to run trains, similarly to the Great Northern, to Victoria on 1st July, 1875, and on the same date the Chatham company's existing services, which ended at Finchley Road, were extended to Hendon.

By this time Pullman cars had been introduced on the Midland, and Pullman's competitor, Mann, arranged to run a 'Palace Car' between Victoria and Dover. It was divided into four sections – a drawing-room saloon, a smoking saloon, a small family saloon, and a 'honeymoon compartment' for two. It was a considerable advance on the usual first-class carriages of the period. Most of the Chatham & Dover firsts at this time were four-wheeled vehicles, with four compartments, 25ft long over the frames. The second-class were the same length, but with five compartments.

On 15th May, 1876, an important addition was made to the train services by commencing the running of boat expresses to and from Sheerness in connection with the Flushing steamers. A branch nearly a mile long, with a station on the Queenborough pier, was constructed for this traffic.

During the years 1875 to 1878 negotiations proceeded in connection with the amalgamation of the South Eastern and Chatham railways. On 15th February, 1877, the terms were actually approved by separate meetings of the proprietors, but the Standing Orders Committee of the House of Commons refused to allow a late bill to be deposited. The proposals at that time were that the Chatham should have 31 per cent of the net receipts for the first year, and that the proportion be increased yearly up to 33 per cent for the fifth and each subsequent year. There was to be a joint committee of three members from the South Eastern and two from the London, Chatham & Dover.

When, however, the matter came up again a year later, a meeting of the Chatham proprietors on 14th February, 1878, rejected the proposals almost unanimously, and the idea was abandoned for a time.

Towards the end of 1876 the Mayor of Chatham, a Mr Toomer commenced proceedings before the Railway Commissioners to compel the L.C.D.R. and the S.E.R. to provide facilities for passengers by running trains between Strood (S.E.R) and Chatham (L.C.D.R.), by means of an existing loop connecting the two systems just west of the Medway at Strood. This loop, which was the commencement of the original East Kent Railway, had been disused (save for one goods train each way daily) for eighteen years. Orders for through trains were made, in spite of many objections raised by the L.C.D.R., finally imposing a penalty of £60 a day on that line, and £15 on the S.E.R. if the service was not put into operation by 1st April, 1877. The loop was afterwards called the 'Toomer loop'.

The failure of the 'fusion' scheme led to fresh competitive lines being projected. One such was the Maidstone & Ashford Railway, which, in spite of strenuous opposition on the part of the South Eastern, passed in 1880. There was a separate terminus at Ashford, but permission was given for a junction with the S.E.R., and running powers into the latter's Ashford station. Another scheme was for a line 9½ miles long, from Lenham on the Maidstone–Ashford line up to Faversham, which was authorised in 1880. The five years allowed for construction by the Act expired, and a further one was obtained, extending the time to 1891; nevertheless, the line was never made; probably the sole reason for its projection was to keep the South Eastern out of the district.

The first sod of the joint Dover–Deal railway was cut by Earl Granville (the Lord Warden of the Cinque Ports), on 29th May, 1878. Leaving the L.C.D.R. main line at Buckland Junction, 73 chains east of Dover Priory station, the line rises for 2¾ miles at 1 in 70. Near the top it passes through the Guston tunnel, 1,425 yards long, and then falls with varying gradients to Deal. The junction at Buckland was the wrong way for the Chatham & Dover trains from London to Deal, so in 1881 they obtained powers to make the 'Kearsney loop'. The Dover-Deal line was opened 15th June, 1881, and the loop in 1882.

When the Brussels Exhibition was held in 1880, a fixed, instead of a tidal, boat service was run between Dover and Calais. The work of improving the harbour at the latter place had been in hand for some time then and two-thirds of the work had been completed. Evidently that was sufficient for a fixed timing for the small boats of the period, and so it was practicable to give it in the Brussels service. It also became possible in the Paris service in 1882, when trains left London and Paris at 10 a.m. regularly. The journey by Calais was still handicapped by the want of the curve near Tintelleries outside Boulogne. At the half-yearly meeting on 1st August, 1883, Forbes said that the French Government had insisted on the Northern of France making the curve, and in 1888 it was completed.

An extension into the town of Sheerness was brought into use on 1st June, 1883. On 1st July, 1884, the Maidstone–Ashford line, mentioned above, was completed. In the latter year, still prosecuting its war against the South Eastern, the Chatham Railway promoted a bill to continue its Ashford extension to Folkestone, but as such a line would have been parallel with the existing S.E.R., Parliament refused to sanction it. Another form of attack was a bid for the hop traffic carried from the Kentish gardens to the Borough, which at the existing rates was very lucrative. The Chatham, by a considerable reduction of rates, attracted a large amount of the traffic away from the S.E.R.

A flank attack, sanctioned in 1881 and completed in 1886, was a line from Fawkham to Gravesend. In those days there was a considerable river passenger traffic during the summer, but this mostly used Tilbury pier on the other side of the river, as the South Eastern station was away from the river at Gravesend. The L.C.D.R. determined to try for the river traffic, and crossing the S.E.R. line, reached the riverside, where they erected a pier. It was not a profitable venture, as the fares on the London, Tilbury & Southend Railway were so cheap – a halfpenny a mile – that they carried most of the Gravesend traffic, although that route involved crossing the river; and only very few steamers were attracted to the new pier.

On 10th May, 1886, the station at St Paul's, approached by a new bridge over the Thames, was completed. The new bridge had five spans, which, reading from the Surrey side, were 183, 175, 185, 175, and 185ft. It had a clear width of 81ft between the parapets and accommodated seven roads. The parapets widen out on the Middlesex side so as to provided for the platforms, and the width there was 123ft.

In the 1886 Parliament the London, Chatham & Dover deposited a bill for a fusion with the London, Brighton & South Coast. The attitude of the latter may be best seen by the following extract from its report for the half-year July–December, 1885:

A bill has been introduced by the Chatham company for powers to make working agreements with this company and for the working of the two railways as one system under a joint committee. The policy of your directors remains the same as has been frequently expressed, viz., to cultivate friendly arrangements with all neighbouring companies, but to retain the independent position of the Brighton company. They cannot, therefore, recommend, the proprietors

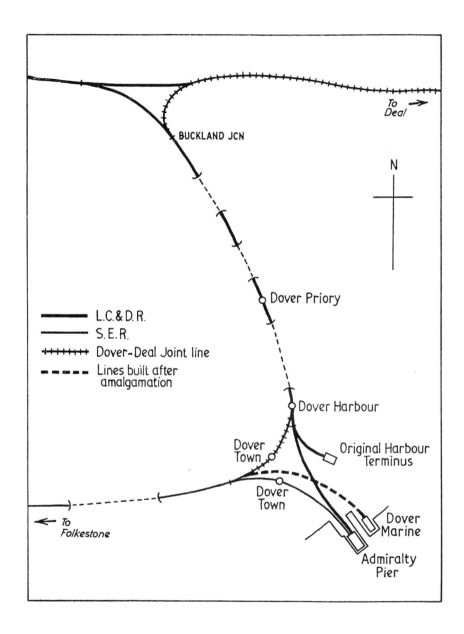

To
Deal

N

BUCKLAND JCN

Dover Priory

L.C.&D.R.
S.E.R.
Dover-Deal Joint line
Lines built after
amalgamation

Dover Harbour

Dover
Town

Original Harbour
Terminus

Dover
Town

Dover
Marine

To
Folkestone

Admiralty
Pier

to assent to these provisions of the bill which contemplate the working of the lines of the two companies as one system, but they approve any reasonable clause for authorising working agreements similar to those which they have with the South Eastern and South Western companies for the division of traffic at competitive points and joint use of certain lines and stations.

The report of the South Eastern intimated, on this subject, that it had received from the Brighton company a declaration that it dissented and would oppose any proposal for working the two companies together as one concern. The matter, however, came to an end by the action of the Chatham company itself. Its report, after saying that the principle of a working union had been in existence since 1868, observed that the Brighton company would appear to have altered the views it so strongly advocated in 1868. As its consent was indispensable, it would be useless to proceed with the bill.

A really big fight in the law courts between the London, Chatham & Dover and the South Eastern began on 19th January, 1886. It was mainly based on the 'Continental Agreement'. Two points stood out pre-eminently and were constantly made the ground for a special grievance by each company. That of the South Eastern was that Queenborough was outside the agreement, as it did not lie between Margate and Hastings, whilst the complaint of the Chatham company was that Shorncliffe was in Folkestone and not outside the agreement as to cross-channel competitive traffic to and from Folkestone and Dover, as claimed by the South Eastern on the ground that it was not 'Folkestone'.

On 19th January, 1886, arguments on points of law as to Queenborough were begun in the Chancery Division, and on 2nd February Mr Justice Chitty gave judgment on all points in favour of the applicants – the Chatham. The other side took the case to the Court of Appeal, where it was dismissed on 31st July, 1886, and the same fate awaited it in the House of Lords, where judgment was given on 14th May, 1888. The South Eastern report for January–June, 1888, said that the company accepted the judgment. The board, it added, was of opinion that the time was opportune for renewed efforts to settle the dispute, so they had made a suggestion to the Chatham company. If that was not acceptable the Chatham company had been requested to make a counter offer.

Meanwhile the dispute as to Shorncliffe had been dragging its way slowly through the courts. It began in the Chancery Division on 14th November, 1887, and was decided in favour of the applicants – again the Chatham company. The other side took it to the Court of Appeal, where it was dismissed on 11th November, 1888, but in the

House of Lords, on 28th July, 1890, the original judgment was restored, but modified as to the amount of interest payable.

The half-yearly report of the South Eastern that appeared soon after, said that as the litigation had terminated, the company was at liberty to reopen negotiations with the London, Chatham & Dover for the consolidation of the two undertakings.

It may be added that at no time subsequently were there any serious differences between the companies, which agreed to a fusion a few years later.

A development in the Dover–Calais service occurred on 3rd June, 1889, when the harbour works at Calais were opened by the French President. A sequel was the running of the 'Club Train', which left London at 4.15 p.m., the French connection being due in Paris at 11.15. It was first-class only, coupled with an extra fare of 16s., all of which latter was taken by the Wagons-Lits Company. Forbes admitted, on 3rd August, 1892, that the train was a very serious loss, except to the Wagons-Lits. On 1st October, 1893, it was withdrawn. The rolling stock was of the Pullman type, provided by the International Sleeping-Car Company. In connection with the improvements at Calais, the French Government decreed that the French mails must be carried not only in boats flying the French flag, but in steamers built and owned in France, and manned by French crews; an outburst of patriotism that proved expensive, as the payment to the L.C.D.R. for the conveyance of the Calais—Dover mails was £4,000 a year, but the Nord Railway received £12,500 when its steamers provided the service, having to borrow some of the Chatham boats in the first instance.

As a result of the completion of the improvements at Calais Harbour, and the employment of compound locomotives by the Nord Railway to haul the Paris–Calais trains, the day mail was, from July, 1895, accelerated nearly an hour. The departure from London was made at 9 a.m. instead of 8 a.m., while the arrival at Paris was only nine minutes later, the London arrival being only six minutes later. On 12th June, 1896, passengers by a special train did the journey from London to Paris in 6 hours 25 minutes.

On 12th August, 1889, after efforts lasting five years, powers had been obtained for a line from Nunhead to Shortlands, which was opened for traffic 1st July, 1892. It was worked by the L.C.D.R., and became their property in 1896. It was a welcome improvement, as it gave an alternative route avoiding Penge tunnel.

In July, 1894, a bill promoted by the L.C.D.R., with the approval of the South Eastern, was passed. It gave authority to the two companies to enter into arrangements for sharing the competitive traffic not covered by the Continental Agreement. The measure came into force on 1st January, 1895, and produced increases of fares between various places.

The next few years were both peaceful and successful. Undivided attention could be given to developing and improving the traffic; while new passenger coaches to the value of £110,000, which were put into service 1897-8, and more punctual and faster services, helped to console travellers for the increased fares that had come into operation.

The position of the London, Chatham & Dover gradually became more prosperous financially, and negotiations for a closer approach with the South Eastern took definite shape in 1898. H. Cosmo Bonsor was now chairman of the South Eastern, and although J. Staats Forbes still occupied the Chatham & Dover chair, the discussions were much more amicable than they had been in the past, so much so, that not only was the necessary bill for sanction deposited for the 1899 session, but from 1st January of that year the two systems were worked as one in anticipation of Parliament granting the requisite powers.

The comparative freedom of the Chatham & Dover from serious accidents continued through the period covered by this chapter. The worst accident, however, that ever occurred on the line took place at Sittingbourne on 31st August, 1878. A heavily laden 'cheap fast' from the Kent Coast to London was approaching Sittingbourne at full speed, when it dashed into some goods trucks standing on the line, resulting in the death of five passengers, and injuries to many. A mistake of a shunter was the cause. He pulled the wrong points, an accident which could not have occurred with modern interlocking. Previously to this time the company had not been lavish in its expenditure on safeguards. Speaking on 10th February, 1876, Forbes showed that, although from 1871 to 1875 the number of passengers had increased from 16,000,000 to 21,000,000; the tonnage of goods from 335,000 to 466,000; the tonnage of minerals from 630,000 to 1,006,000 and the receipts from £483,000 to £631,000, he had spent only £25,000 on safety appliances. He said:

> He had had these things urged upon him for some time, but he had been as reluctant as any man could be to involve the shareholders in a single shilling of outlay which could be avoided and he had required, not mere theory, but the strongest evidence that these things were required before he would allow them to be done.

In spite of that remark it is to the credit of the London, Chatham

& Dover that, like the South Eastern, all its 134 miles of double line were equipped with the block system when the first Signal Arrangements Return was compiled at the end of 1873. In interlocking, 113 places had been equipped and 152 not. The reply of the company to the Board of Trade circular of 19th December, 1877, said that it had only tried the Westinghouse continuous brake and that to a limited extent; 6 engines and 20 carriages were so fitted. When the compulsory Act of 1889 was passed, all the 175 miles of double line had the block, all the 462 places were interlocked, 81 engines and 44 per cent of the coaches had the Westinghouse brake, and 2 engines and 1 per cent of the coaches had the automatic vacuum. The Westinghouse became the standard brake on the Chatham & Dover, and it has been suggested that the obvious reason was that the South Eastern had adopted the vacuum!

While speaking of brakes, it may be mentioned that the earliest atmospheric brake to be put in regular work was one that was running for many years on the London, Chatham & Dover. It was patented in 1864 by Charles Kendall, and in an article in *The Engineer* of 9th October, 1868, it was stated that it had been in use, with little interruptions, on the Metropolitan Extension of the London, Chatham & Dover Railway and that Mr Martley, the locomotive superintendent, reported that it had never once been out of order or failed to do its duty.

Returning to the subject of signalling, it should be recorded that among the distinguished signal engineers who were at various times employed by the component companies of the Southern Railway was W. R. Sykes, who introduced many valuable improvements, and founded one of the most important signal manufacturing companies. He originally went to the London, Chatham & Dover in 1863, and one of the first new ideas he introduced was an electrical signal repeater in the shape of a miniature arm, which was provided in 1864 at Herne Hill for the distant signal from Tulse Hill.

At that time block working was, comparatively speaking, in its infancy and, naturally, there were many mistakes. Irregular block signalling frequently happened, also disputes arose as to the signals sent and received. To remedy that Sykes proposed a recording paper, actuated by clockwork, to show what signals were exchanged and at what time. The idea was, however, considered to be too expensive and was abandoned.

Sykes worked on the principle that all signalling should be done in sequence, and that was the basis of his 'lock-and-block'. He considered that the train should control the block instrument, and that the block instrument should be interlocked with the outdoor signals. In 1874 he suggested to Forbes, the managing director of the L.C.D.R., that the system should be tried at three consecutive boxes – Shepherd's Lane, Brixton and Canterbury Road Junction. Forbes would not hear of it; if it were tried it should be some where in the country; but he considered the idea foolish. The four Board of Trade inspectors – Captain Tyler, Colonel Yolland, Colonel Rich and General Hutchinson – however, thought differently. Their opinion carried weight and a trial in the three boxes named was agreed to. Sykes took out his patent for the idea in 1875 and, incidentally, coined therein the phrase 'lock-and-block'. By 1880 the following lines had been equipped: Victoria–Ludgate Hill; Cambria Junction–Crystal Palace; Herne Hill–Sydenham Hill. It may be noted that in Colonel Yolland's report on a collision on 19th November, 1875, at Ludgate Hill, that officer said he had often recommended some means to guard against signalmen making mistakes in block signalling and that he had 'great pleasure now in stating that this (the L.C.D.R.) company has now had in operation for several months at three signal-boxes an invention of the kind'. By September, 1881, the London, Chatham & Dover was equipped as far as Faversham, and by June, 1882, to Dover.

Penge tunnel is 2,170 yards in length, and there were two distant signals fixed in it which, because of the smoke and steam, were very difficult to see. Sykes, therefore, in 1875, repeated them outside the tunnels.

By 1882 the Sykes lock-and-block system was in use on some of the London lines of the London, Brighton and South Coast, and in 1884 work was done on the South Eastern as a result of adjacent L.C.D.R. boxes being joined up.

In November, 1883, Sykes provided 50 electrically-operated shunting signals at Victoria, L.C.D.R., which were actuated by the movement of a small switch. In March, 1887, similar signals were placed in service at the 'Hole-in-the-Wall' box. Those signals remained in use for many years.

In the matter of providing double track at the time of construction this company appears to have adopted a policy similar to that of the South Eastern. The record of subsequent doublings applies only to lines which had been promoted independently and were afterwards absorbed by the L.C.D.R. The line from Sevenoaks to Maidstone, opened as a single track in June, 1874, became a double line throughout on 3rd July, 1882, when the section from Otford to Wrotham was completed. Quadruple lines as far as Kent House station were opened by 2nd May, 1886, and from Shortlands to Bickley in May, 1894.

A derailment occurred at Crystal Palace on 21st May, 1881, when one passenger was killed. On the 31st August, 1891, there was an accident at Ramsgate which would have had terrible consequences had the train involved been full, instead of empty. A train of empty G.N.R. carriages left Margate for Ramsgate to form an up return special, hauled by a Chatham & Dover engine running tender first. The carriages, of course, had the vacuum brake. The engine was 'dual fitted', but had no vacuum pipe at the leading end, so no connection could be made, a fact which was not realised by the driver. The approach to Ramsgate was through a tunnel on a gradient of 1 in 75 down. It was impossible to hold the train, and it crashed through the end wall. The driver and fireman jumped clear, but a man in the street was unfortunately killed.

On 1st August, 1895, an accident occured at Herne Bay. An excursion train, being too long for the platform from which it was intended to start, was divided; the engine and the first two carriages being uncoupled and moved to the main line, in order to allow people to get in. They were run into by an up goods train from Ramsgate, one death being the result. It may also be mentioned here that on 29th November, 1897, Sheerness Pier was wrecked in a severe gale.

XXIX

London, Chatham & Dover Locomotives

APART from contractors' engines used during construction, which were also employed at the opening the earliest locomotives to work on the East Kent Railway were six singles, known as 'small Hawthorns', hired from the Great Northern Railway. Later in the year (1858) six new engines arrived from Hawthorns. They were designed by Crampton, who seems to have managed the locomotive department for the first two years. He had very original ideas, more appreciated on the Continent than here.

Until Kirtley became Locomotive Superintendent, in 1874, the engines merely bore names, to which he added the numbers given in brackets, removing the names when the engines were rebuilt. Rebuilding was very much the order of the day on the L.C.D.R.; Martley had to do so on account of so many being of bad design, and his successor went over most of the same ground again, doubtless for economy's sake. At the time of the fusion with the S.E.R., the highest number in use on that line was 459, and on the L.C.D.R., 216. They were combined into one system by adding 459 to the numbers of the latter.

The first batch of engines, just referred to, were four-coupled tanks, with 5ft 6in wheels, 15 by 20 cylinders, and a leading bogie. The cylinders were outside, behind the bogie, and drove the trailing wheels. The names were:

Sondes	Crampton	Faversham
Sittingbourne	Lake	Chatham

They were very unsatisfactory, and were replaced six or seven years later by 2-4-0 side tanks with inside cylinders built at Longhedge Works, which utilised the boilers and wheels, and bore the same names (afterwards numbers 59–64). They were known as class 'F', and survived the fusion.

Three single-wheeled tender engines were purchased from the L.N.W.R. about this time: *Gadfly*, *Hornet* and *Wasp*, which were nearly worn out, and of very little use.

A small tank, built by Neilson and Co., was used for the Sitting-bourne & Sheerness Railway, named *Cubitt*, which was lent by the contractors. Another little tank, with four wheels, was bought from Hawthorn and Co. at the beginning of 1860, named *Magnus*, after-wards altered to *Magnet* (54, 142). At the same time, a six-coupled goods engine was obtained from Brotherhood of Chippenham, named *Swale*, afterwards converted into a saddle tank (53?, 141). In the same year two single engines, with 5ft 9in wheels and 14 by 18 cylinders, were purchased from Hawthorn and Co., which had been built in 1855, namely *Meteor* (57) and *Eclipse* (58). They were made into tanks a few years later, and broken up 1875.

In April, 1860, William Martley was appointed Locomotive Superintendent. For some years he had been the district L.S. for the South Wales division of the G.W.R. under Sir Daniel Gooch. The purchase of odds and ends of engines still went on, of course owing to shortage of money.

The first engines to be delivered after Martley came on the scene were two six-coupled goods engines which had been built in 1856 by Hawthorn and Co., with 4ft 6in wheels and 16 by 24 cylinders: *Hercules* (55, 143) and *Ajax* (56, 144). They were afterwards made into saddle tanks, and broken up in 1893.

About the end of 1860, four four-coupled bogie engines, driving wheels 5ft, cylinders (outside) 16 by 20, were bought of R. Stephenson and Co.: *Æolus* (71), *Bacchus* (72), *Vulcan* (73), and *Comus* (74). They had been built for a South American Railway and were painted yellow, afterwards altered to green, the then standard L.C.D.R. colour. They were converted into saddle tanks, and were replaced by four 2-4-0 tanks in 1873, in which some of the original parts were used, and which took the same names and numbers, being rebuilt 1885-8, and eventually renumbered 530-533. The *Æolus* had the honour of running the first Chatham & Dover train into London.

In 1861 six 2-4-0 engines were bought from the Dutch Rhenish Railway, which had been built by Sharp, Stewart in 1856. They had inside cylinders 16 by 20, wheels 5ft 6in, with double frames. The domes were of plain polished brass close to the chimney, a fashion adopted later by Martley for some of his own engines. They ran the Dover boat trains for some years. Names:

| Onyx | Emerald | Diamond |
| Ruby | Amethyst | Pearl |

They were rebuilt as tanks, and numbered 65–70, afterwards 145–150, and rebuilt again, this time without names, being finally broken up 1890-1.

Twenty-four engines then came along which had been ordered before Martley's appointment, designed by Crampton. They are notable as being the first bogie engines built in this country for express work, but unfortunately turned out to be very unsatisfactory, running badly and damaging the permanent way. In arrangement they resembled the Sondes class of tank, having outside cylinders about midway along the engine, driving the trailing pair of coupled wheels. As early as 1864 Martley began altering them into 2-4-0 engines, with inside cylinders. They were rebuilt again in the 'eighties, when the names were removed. The latter were as follows:

Brassey and Co., 1861.

Falcon (3)	Swift (7)	Ostrich (10, 469. 469A)
Vulture (4)	Dottrel (8)	Petrel (11)
Heron (5)	Swallow (9, 468, 468A)	Pelican (12)
Stork (6)		

Slaughter, Gruning and Co., 1861-2.

Lynx (13)	Tiger (16)	Jackall (19)
Gorilla (14)	Leopard (18, 477)	Panther (21, 480)

Hawthorn and Co., 1861-2.

Cerberus (15)	Pegasus (22, 481)	Syren (25)
Gorgon (17)	Satyr (23)	Xanthus (26)
Harpy (20)	Sphinx (24)	

The fireboxes were of the Cudworth type; wheels 5ft 6in, cylinders 16 by 22. It will be noticed that the names of Nos. 8 and 19 were misspelt.

Two front-coupled engines, with 5-ft wheels and the same size cylinders, were supplied in 1861 by Sharp, Stewart and Co.: *Brigand* (1, 460) and *Corsair* (2, 461). The same makers also supplied six powerful goods engines with double frames, wheels 5ft, cylinders 17 by 24. They were followed by eight similar ones from R. Stephenson and Co. in 1862. All had Cudworth fireboxes. Names:

Sharp, Stewart, 1861-2 (113-118; 572-577).

Acis	Diomede	Gordius
Calypso	Fortuna	Pyramus

Stephenson, 1862 (119-126; 578-585).

Amphitrite	Iris	Tacita
Chloris	Phyllis	Thisbe
Ianthe	Nestor	

Even yet, the Crampton influence still lingered on. In 1862 five engines were delivered by R. Stephenson and Co., with dummy crankshafts, like the S.E.R. *Folkstone*, except that they had leading bogies, and large domes, The driving wheels, situated behind the firebox, were 6ft 6½in; cylinders 16 by 22. Like the rest of the Cramptons, they were very unsatisfactory, and were expensive to maintain. Martley therefore converted them into coupled engines ('K' class), retaining the bogies. The names were:

Echo (27)	Flirt (29, 488)	Sylph (31, 490)
Coquette (28, 487)	Flora (30)	

In future, unless otherwise mentioned, all engines may be assumed to have survived the 'fusion', and to have had their numbers then increased by 459.

At the end of 1862 the first engines of Martley's design appeared. They were 2-4-0; driving wheels 6ft 6in, and cylinders 16½ by 22, built by Sharp, Stewart and Co., and intended for the Continental expresses:

Dawn (32)	Herald (34)	Frolic (36)
Alert (33)	Pioneer (35)	Vigilant (37)

Six more followed from the same makers in 1863, with slight modification:

Violet (38)	Snowdrop (40)	Hyacinth (42)
Crocus (39)	Verbena (41)	Bluebell (43)

From R. and W. Hawthorn there came six 2-4-0 tanks in the above year, with 5ft 6in wheels and 16 by 22 cylinders:

Rose (75)	Thistle (77)	Narcissus (79)
Shamrock (76)	Myrtle (78)	Daphne (80)

They were broken up before the fusion.

No new engines were supplied in 1864, but in the following year there were six more expresses, rather larger than their predecessors, the cylinders being 16 by 24, from Brassey and Co.:

Reindeer (44)	Champion (46)	Talisman (48)
Elk (45)	Templar (47)	Zephyr (49)

All the above, except the last one, had an ugly square sandbox enclosing the lower part of the dome, with the idea of 'keeping the powder dry'.

In 1866 a new type of well-tank engines appeared, with four-coupled wheels in front, and a single pair of radial trailing wheels at a considerable distance away (11ft 9in). The driving wheels were 5ft 6in, and cylinders 16½ by 22. They were built by Neilson, and known as the 'little Scotchmen', fourteen in all (numbered 81–94) class 'E':

Iona	Islay	Kelvin	Tay
Bute	Staffa	Spey	Nith
Jura	Ulva	Annan	Esk
Arran	Clyde		

In the same year six very fine goods engines (class 'J') were supplied by John Fowler and Co., with wheels 5ft 3in and cylinders 17 by 24 (numbered afterwards 127–132):

Adrian	Vespasian	Pertinax
Trajan	Tarquin	Constantine

So far, Martley had retained the long sloping Cudworth fireboxes (except in the tanks), but they were all subsequently altered into ordinary ones, with horizontal grates.

In 1869 the first new engine was turned out from Longhedge Works – *Enigma* (50). It was a 2-4-0 tender engine of the usual design, but with 6-ft wheels. The name was bestowed on it by the directors, because Martley told them that it was an enigma to him how he ever managed to finish it, the work having been so often stopped for want of money. Two more followed from the works in 1870, with 6ft 6in wheels: *Mermaid* (51) and *Lothair* (52).

In 1873 four very handsome expresses with 6ft 6in wheels and 17 by 24 cylinders, which were Martley's *chefs-d'oeuvre*, came from Sharp, Stewart and Co. for the Continental mail trains, which they ran for many years: *Europa, Asia, Africa* and *America* (53–56). There were also six more radial tanks from Neilson and Co. (95–100), which had no domes, and closely resembled some on the Great Northern Railway. These were known as 'C' class engines:

Albion	Erin	Mona
Thanet	Cambria	Scotia

They were the last that Martley designed, as he died in 1874. Shortly before, two small goods engines were bought from Sharp, Stewart, with wheels 4ft 6½in and cylinders 16 by 24: *Huz* (133) and *Buz* (134). Although rebuilt by Kirtley in 1887–8 both were withdrawn in 1901.

The first engines built at Longhedge after Kirtley came were two 'Europas', already on order, which he numbered 57 and 58.

In 1875 the first engines he designed made their appearance, being eighteen 0-4-4 bogie tanks with wheels 5ft 3in and cylinders 17½ by 26, which were his standard cylinder dimensions. Nine were by the Vulcan Foundry, Nos. 65–70 and 110–112; and nine by Neilson and Co., 101–109 (class 'A').

In 1876 Kirtley designed some six-coupled goods engines (classes 'B' and 'B1') with 4ft 10in wheels, of which six were supplied in that year by Dübs and Co., Nos. 135–140; and six in 1877 by Neilson, Nos. 151–156. The latter makers also received an order for

six bogie expresses with 6ft 6in wheels, also in 1877, Nos, 157–162.*
Although not of outstanding dimensions, they were of an excellent
design, and a full description and specification was given in professor Jamieson's well-known *Textbook on Steam and Steam Engines*, as a
typical specimen of a locomotive. Another indication of the admira-
tion of contemporary engineers for these engines is the inclusion of
the specification in W. S. Hutton's *Works Managers' Handbook* (1885).

In 1880 there were twelve bogie tanks ('A1' class) by Kitson and
Co., 163–174, which had 5ft 7in wheels. In that and the following
year four bogie expresses were built at Longhedge, 175–178.*

In 1883 and 1884 Stephenson and Co. supplied six bogie tanks
(class 'A2') with 75–80. In 1884 six bogie expresses came from Dübs,
181–186; and in 1886 two were turned out at Longhedge, 179 and
180.

The last types of L.C.D.R. engines were as follows:

Class 'M3', bogie expresses, Vulcan Foundry, 187–192; and the
following at Longhedge:

14, 25 (1892)	13, 23 (1896)	4, 467 (1899)
16 (1893)	3, 5, 19 (1897)	485 (1900)
17, 20 (1894)	6, 7, 24 (1898)	468, 469 (1901)
12, 15 (1895)		

Six goods engines, class 'B2', with 18 by 26in cylinders and 5ft
wheels were built by Vulcan Foundry, 193–198 (1891); eighteen
5ft 6in bogie tanks,† Sharp, Stewart, 199–216 (1891). There remain
to be chronicled ten six-coupled side tanks shunting engines built
at Longhedge; wheels 4ft 6in and cylinders 17 by 24 (class 'T'):

141, 142 (1879)	146, 148 (1890)	143, 144 (1893)
149 (1889)	145, 147, 150 (1891)	

The standard colour for Chatham & Dover engines for many years
was green, but Kirtley changed it to black. On becoming part of the
Joint Committee's stock, ex-L.C.D.R. locomotives had their numbers
increased by 459. Twenty five years later 28 'M' class, 35 'A' class,
8 'B' class, and all the 'R' and 'T' class were taken into S.R. stock,
but only the last two classes had much further life; three 'T's' and
all the 'R's' except three achieved B.R. ownership, a creditable
sixty years stint in some cases.

---

* Class 'M1': Nos. 179–186 were classified 'M2', having b.p. 150 against 140 and
weighing 1 ton more.
† Class 'R': 17 by 24in cylinders. Their appearance was quite unlike the 'A' class.

XXX

The South Eastern and Chatham Joint Committee

As has already been said, the working union between the South Eastern and the Chatham & Dover Railways came into operation on 1st January, 1899, in anticipation of Parliamentary sanction, which was not obtained until 1st August, after having weathered a storm of opposition from various outside interests that feared their positions might be prejudiced by the absence of competition, and did not realise, or chose deliberately to ignore, the fact that the combination would result in a more efficient machine coming into existence. So many concessions had to be made, that the economics due to joint working were more than swallowed up, with the result that for several years the shareholders were in a worse position, the dividends being less than they were before the union.

The terms of the arrangement were as follows: the net receipts were to be divided as 59 per cent to the South Eastern and 41 per cent to the Chatham. The Joint Managing Committee consisted of four representatives from each board, with Bonsor as chairman and Akers-Douglas, a London, Chatham & Dover director, as deputy chairman. Forbes was retained for ten years as an adviser. He died on 5th April, 1904.

Alfred Willis was the general manager, John Morgan and Charles Sheath the joint secretaries, P. C. Tempest the chief engineer, H. S. Wainwright the locomotive, carriage and wagon superintendent, and W. Thomson the superintendent of the line. The South Eastern and London, Chatham & Dover companies retained their respective identity. Morgan, one of the joint secretaries, died in 22nd October, 1900, and Willis retired, owing to ill-health, at the end of that year, being succeeded by Vincent Hill of the Hull and Barnsley Railway. Sir Edward Watkin died on 13th April, 1901.

Various simplifications of traffic working followed the fusion, together with new services, the first of which was one of through express trains to Hastings via Sevenoaks, starting from Victoria, L.C.D.R., and worked by the latter company's stock. Several new close-coupled trains for suburban service were delivered in May, 1899, by Craven Bros., each consisting of eight four-wheeled coaches, with bodies 27ft long, electrically lighted, including the tail lamps; with the classes indicated by figures on the doors. After some experimenting, the teak colour of the L.C.D.R. was abandoned, and all passenger vehicles were painted claret, the standard colour of the S.E.R.

On 19th July, 1900, the pier at Queenborough was destroyed by fire – for the second time. It was reopened in February, 1901, but as the whole of the repairs were not completed, the night service continued to use Port Victoria until 3rd May, 1904. The Sheppey Light Railway from Queenborough to Leysdown – then an independent concern – was opened on 1st August, 1901, and was absorbed on 3rd October, 1905.

The widening of the S.E.R. between London Bridge and New Cross was completed in 1902, with a new station at Southwark Park just east of the site of the original Corbett's Lane Junction. This station had a short life, being closed early in the first war, and afterwards demolished. Many years previously a station known as Commercial Dock had for a time occupied the site. Advantage was taken of the widening to bring the running into conformity with the usual practice. Previously, as mentioned in Chapter IV, trains had run on the right-hand rails on the Greenwich line. The alterations included the reconstruction of the low level station at London Bridge so as again to be used for passenger trains.

On 4th June, 1901, the Purley–Kingswood branch was extended to Tattenham Corner, where a suitable station, with six platform roads and three middle sidings, was erected for the Epsom race traffic.

On 1st June, 1902, the Bexhill branch from Crowhurst was opened. A company had been empowered to make it in 1897.

On 3rd June the 10 a.m. service to Paris was accelerated to arrive at 6.10 p.m., and the 2.20 p.m. to arrive at 9.15. The return services at 8.15 a.m. and 4 p.m. were timed to arrive at 3.45 and 10.45 respectively. The last was a very creditable performance.

On 17th July, 1903, Chislehurst tunnel had to be closed. A new tunnel, under construction, had led to the workings being damaged. All was adjusted and the line reopened on 3rd November. This may seem a minor matter to be recorded, but it is mentioned because the benefits of the working union between the two companies were then clearly revealed, and a minimum of inconvenience resulted. The new tunnel was part of the widened lines between St Johns and Orpington, which were completed in June, 1905. The loop lines in the neighbourhood, constructed in 1902 and 1904, enabled trains from the S.E.R. to pass to the L.C.D.R. line, and *vice versa*, also heavy traffic between Victoria and Dover – mainly Continental – was able to use the more easily graded and less tortuous S.E.R. route east of Orpington. The chief advantage was that heavier locomotives could work into Victoria from Dover than had been able to do so before over the Chatham route, on which many of the underbridges were of light construction. There still remained the 'bottle-neck' of the Penge tunnel, which necessitated the through train from the L.N.W.R. to the Kent Coast going by the Catford loop. Through carriages between Dover and Manchester via Reading and the Great Western were introduced on 1st October, 1903.

Dover became a port of call for Atlantic liners from Hamburg in July, 1904. The railway lines were increased to provide the necessary accommodation, and the first steamship company to call was the Hamburg-American. At the half-yearly meeting on 3rd February, 1905, it was announced that coal had been found at Dover.

On 1st June, 1905, the light railway of the Kent and East Sussex Railway (hitherto called the Rother Valley Railway) was extended from Tenterden to Headcorn, and direct railway communication* thus afforded between the S.E.C.R. stations at Robertsbridge and Headcorn.

The L.C.D.R. station at Ashford was closed on 1st January, 1899, afterwards becoming a goods depot.

A serious disaster occurred on 5th December, 1905. One of the tie-rods of the main principal nearest the wind screen in the roof of Charing Cross station failed, and two complete bays and the large wind screen at the river end of the station collapsed. The station wall that carried the bays overturned and crashed bodily through the adjoining wall and roof of the Avenue Theatre, which was under reconstruction. No passengers, and none of the platform staff were hurt, but two men, engaged on repairing, glazing and painting that part of the roof, were killed, also one of Messrs W. H. Smith and Son's bookstall attendants and three of the men working in the Avenue Theatre.

The accident was inquired into, on behalf of the board of Trade, by Sir John Pringle, who reported that the tie-rod failed at a weld, by reason of a flaw in the welding at the time the roof was made about the year 1863. The additional weight of the temporary staging used

---

* The sparse service was, however, worked as two sections outwards from Tenterden, and little incentive was given to passengers to use this line as a through route. A number of projected further connections never got beyond the planning stage.

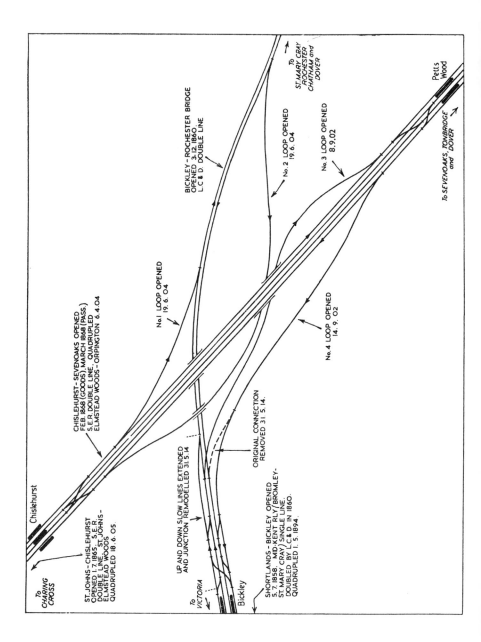

To CHARING CROSS

Chislehurst

ST. JOHNS - CHISLEHURST
OPENED 1.7. 1865. S.E.R.
DOUBLE LINE. ST. JOHNS-
ELMSTEAD WOODS
QUADRUPLED 18. 6. 05

CHISLEHURST-SEVENOAKS OPENED
FEB. 1868 (GOODS), MARCH 1868 (PASS.)
S.E.R. DOUBLE LINE. QUADRUPLED
ELMSTEAD WOODS-ORPINGTON 6.4. 04

BICKLEY - ROCHESTER BRIDGE
OPENED 3. 12. 1860.
L.C & D. DOUBLE LINE

To
ST. MARY CRAY
ROCHESTER
CHATHAM and
DOVER

No. 2 LOOP OPENED
19. 6. 04

No. 3 LOOP OPENED
8. 9. 02

No. 1 LOOP OPENED
19. 6. 04

No. 4 LOOP OPENED
14. 9. 02

Petts
Wood

To SEVENOAKS, TONBRIDGE
and DOVER

UP AND DOWN SLOW LINES EXTENDED
AND JUNCTION REMODELLED 31.5.14.

ORIGINAL CONNECTION
REMOVED 31. 5. 14.

To
VICTORIA

Bickley

SHORTLANDS - BICKLEY OPENED
5. 7. 1858. MID-KENT RLY/BROMLEY-
ST. MARY CRAY/SINGLE LINE.
DOUBLED BY L.C & D. IN 1860.
QUADRUPLED 1. 5. 1894.

for the above-mentioned repairs of the roof was the immediate cause of failure, but the stress was not in any way unreasonable and could not have been anticipated to cause danger of failure. Colonel Pringle concluded his report by drawing attention to the work carried out by the engineering staff on the railway during the days immediately following the accident. The condition of affairs was highly dangerous, and a further collapse might have occurred at any moment. The works, he said, were carried out by night and day, under very considerable risk to life and limb, and the efforts of the staff, which had the result of rendering the rest of the roof safe, called for special mention.

At the coroner's inquest a verdict of 'accidental death' was returned. Arising out of the damage done to outside property it was considered that Mr Cyril Maude, of the Avenue Theatre, had no legal claim on the company, but he was voted a grant of £20,000. The station was, of course, closed until the whole of the roof was taken down. It was reopened on 19th March, 1906. The cost of repairs was about £60,000 and there was, in addition, a loss of between £7,000 and £8,000 a week in traffic receipts.

In 1906 the Joint Managing Committee gave an undertaking to Parliament that, if the Dover Harbour Board were authorised to increase the poll tax levied on passengers using the harbour, and were thereby enabled to proceed with its enlargement, within three years of the completion of that work a marine station would be built that would be suitable for the accommodation of the traffic of the harbour. The poll tax was increased the following year, which allowed the Harbour Board to put in hand the reclamation of the land for a new station.

On 1st October, 1907, the through service between the Great Northern line and Victoria via the Metropolitan Extension was discontinued, and on 1st July, 1908, the corresponding service with the Midland line was withdrawn.

Sir Frederick Harrison, the general manager of the London & North Western Railway, retired from that position at the end of 1908 and became deputy-chairman of the Joint Managing Committee. At this time there arose an agitation for reform by what Cosmo Bonsor called a 'self-constituted shareholders' committee'. At the half-yearly meeting that summer he said that the Working Union Act had not been passed as submitted to Parliament, and the restrictions put upon the two companies rendered it absolutely impossible to close duplicate stations, rearrange their affairs, and to carry out other alterations which would have been effected had they had a free hand. Sir

Frederick Harrison also spoke and observed that the results were as satisfactory as could be expected. They had a good property which would continue to improve. He did not say that the concern was perfect, and he welcomed an active interest of shareholders in it, but strongly deprecated such interest being in a form that weakened the responsibility of the directors and officers.

On 1st October, 1910, the Great Western company began running an express service from Birmingham into Victoria. It apparently was not a success, as the trains were withdrawn soon afterwards. On 1st December following Pullman cars were put on the Folkestone route.*

Under powers obtained in 1906 considerable improvements were made at Rochester on October, 1911. The former South Eastern line and the London, Chatham & Dover line were joined near Rochester station, and the viaduct line of the former company to Chatham Central, also two stations, were closed.

Some important changes were made in the London, Chatham & Dover directorate about that time. Sir E. L. Pemberton retired from the chair and was succeeded therein by Sir William Hart Dyke, and Sir Arthur Yorke, who had just retired from the position of inspecting officer of railways for the Board of Trade, was made a director. Sir Arthur, later, also became a member of the S.E.C.R. Managing Committee. In March, 1911, Vincent Hill resigned the general managership and was made a director. He was succeeded by F. H. Dent, the goods manager. E. C. Cox followed his chief, W. Thomson, as superintendent of the line on 1st July, 1911.

In 1911 it was decided to close the former L.C.D.R. locomotive works at Longhedge and to concentrate on the works at Ashford. It was said that an expenditure of about £80,000 would be necessary.

On 1st May, 1911, the Flushing night service was transferred from Queenborough to Folkestone. On 1st June the services from the East London line to East Croydon and Peckham Rye were withdrawn in view of the East London being converted from steam operation to electric traction. They were never resumed: Metropolitan electric trains began running 31st March 1913 to both New Cross stations but not beyond. On 3rd July, 1911, through communication between places on the Great Northern main line and with the seaside resorts on the S.E.C.R. was established via Kings Cross in competition with the L.N.W.R. 'Sunny South Special'.

---

 * Pullman-type coaches had already been running from 1892 on the 'Hastings Car Train' using cars built in Troy (U.S.A.) but assembled at Ashford, and from 1897 on the 'Folkestone Car Train' using cars built by Metropolitan-Cammell. Most of these cars later ran in Pullman livery.

Above: The one, and only, 'S' class 0-6-0ST No. 685, rebuilt by Maunsell from a 'C' class, 0-6-0 for shunting at Bricklayers Arms.

[*Locomotive Publishing Company*

Below: 'K' class 2-6-4T No. 790, the only example constructed before amalgamation

[*Locomotive Publishing Company*

Above: A Continental Express in S.E.C.R. days; 'E1' class 4-4-0 as rebuilt 1919; the stock is the 1921 corridor type.

Below: S.E.C.R. City Express leaving Broadstairs with 'D1' No. 487, rebuilt by Beyer Peacock 1921.

The twin-hulled *Calais-Douvres* steamship (the first to carry that name) built 1878. [*British Railways*

Maunsell's rebuild of the ex-L.B.S.C.R. 'E1' class 0-6-0T as an 0-6-2T classified E1R for service in the West of England. [*P. Ransome-Wallis*

Maunsell's version of the inside-cylinder 4-4-0, class L1, built by the North British Locomotive Company in 1926.

Above: An L.B.S.C. a.c. electric motor coach No. 10101, built for the Coulsdon and Sutton services.
[*English Electric*

Below: Class 'N15' 4-6-0 No. E453 *King Arthur*, built 1925.

A very fine service was given to Paris as from 1st July, 1913. The route was through Dover, and the train left London at 4.30 p.m. and Paris was reached at 11.25. The 76½ miles from Charing Cross to Dover Pier was covered in 90 minutes. The trip was balanced by a sleeping car train from Paris, with a breakfast car on the train from Dover to London.

Mr H. S. Wainwright retired in November, 1913. He was the son of a former carriage superintendent of the South Eastern whom he succeeded in 1896 and, on the Working Union in 1899, was made the South Eastern & Chatham locomotive, carriage and wagon superintendent. At a meeting of the directors on 12th November, 1913, Mr R. E. L. Maunsell, who afterwards became Chief Mechanical Engineer of the Southern Railway, and was then the locomotive superintendent of the Great Southern and Western of Ireland, was appointed his successor. Mr Vincent Hill died on 24th November, 1913, and Sir Frederick Harrison on 1st January, 1915.

The outbreak of war in August, 1914, created a rather piquant situation as to ten locomotives which had been ordered from the German firm of Borsig. They were delivered in May of that year, and one of the terms of the contract was that the locomotives were to have a three months' trial before being paid for. That period expired on 5th August* – the day of the commencement of hostilities – and payment was not made until 1920, when it was handed over with interest from the date due.

Dover Marine station was opened in December, 1914, after war had broken out. The length of the land reclaimed was 2,300ft, and the maximum width thereof was 350ft. It was filled by 1,000,000 cubic yards of chalk from the East cliff, and in the foundations for the station 1,200 reinforced concrete piles were used. There were two island platforms, each 700ft long and 60ft wide.

As showing how the most generous anticipations in the way of station accommodation may be negatived by some unexpected change in procedure, it may here be remarked that when, in the spring of 1927, the question of making Customs examinations on the boat trains between Dover and London was once more raised, Sir Herbert Walker, the general manager of the Southern Railway, wrote to *The Times* of 29th March a letter from which the following extract is made:

---

* This was part of the 'L' class; it was as well that they arrived in time for the S.E.C.R. was desperately short of motive power for war work, and had to borrow 15 'Ei' 2-4-0 engines from the Great Northern, fifteen 0-6-0 engines from the Hull & Barnsley ('B' class), and six 'K8' 2-8-0 engines of Great Eastern type from the R.O.D.

When the S.E.C.R. constructed the splendid Marine Station at Dover, they spent a large amount of money in providing really adequate facilities for baggage examination, the Customs room being 360ft long, with 530ft of benches, on which is placed the baggage. The railway company thus early provided for a very large expansion in the traffic, but since the room was built, the Home Office examination of aliens has been instituted, and many more articles have become dutiable, so that the Customs regulations are now more comprehensive and rigorous as regards both luggage and merchandise. The result is that these two departments have appropriated no less than 250ft of the room and 390ft of the benches, leaving a space available for the examination of passengers' baggage of only one-third of that originally provided.

A very unfortunate accident occurred on 19th December, 1915, on the Folkestone–Dover section. Owing to the abnormal rainfall a slip on adjoining land caused the line near the Warren Halt to slide towards the sea, in places as much as 160ft. Since the railways were then under the control of the Government the repairs would have to be done at the cost of the State, and as the sum required was estimated at £250,000 it was decided to do nothing. When hostilities ceased the work was put in hand and the line was reopened, after an expenditure of £310,000, on 1st August, 1919. The repairs involved the removal of 82,000,000 yards of earth and chalk.

The north or down-stream side of Charing Cross bridge was built when the railway was constructed, at a cost of £180,000, and was opened in 1863. Consequently, the strength of some of its members was not equal to the weight to be carried later. It was, therefore, decided to strengthen it, and for that, unfortunately, Parliamentary powers were necessary, as part of the scheme was to build piers around each of the four pairs of columns in the river and that would reduce the openings. After a prolonged hearing, in 1916, the bill passed the House of Commons, but when it reached the House of Lords the London County Council succeeded in getting clauses inserted that would prevent the railway company obtaining any compensation for the additional expense incurred on the bridge should the property be acquired for public services within fifteen years of the passage of the Act. The bridge was strengthened somewhat, but without interfering with the columns.

In February, 1919, Francis Brady died. He had succeeded Peter Ashcroft as chief engineer to the South Eastern in 1870 and retired in 1897. He was a great believer in the Channel Tunnel and in the prospects of the Kentish coalfield; in both directions he was of great service to his company and to those interests.

In March, 1920, Sir Francis Dent retired and Mr Tempest, the chief engineer, was made general manager and chief engineer.

Cannon Street bridge was built at the same time as that at Charing

Cross. It, too, has been strengthened; the work took $4\frac{1}{2}$ years and cost £99,000. No Parliamentary powers were, in that case, necessary.

The 'Thanet Pullman' – a 'Sundays only' train of exclusively first-class Pullman cars – commenced running on 10th July, 1921. On 23rd February, 1922, it was announced that the company's electrification proposals were under the consideration of the Ministry of Transport.

A very unfortunate mishap occurred on 27th December, 1922. As a vessel was passing through the channel at the Swale opening bridge, Sheerness, she collided with the structure and so damaged it that the bridge could not be used. Both railway and road communication between Sittingbourne and Sheerness was thus closed and remained so until partially restored on 1st October, 1923, and fully reopened on the following 1st November. It was stated at the time of the accident that in 1902 the Joint Managing Committee had a bill in Parliament which provided for the reconstruction of the bridge, but the local authorities made such exacting conditions that the proposals were withdrawn.

From what has been said before, it will be gathered that there was practically no single track left to be doubled after 1899. In connection with the London Viaduct widenings, the New Cross Spur, opened on 13th December, 1903, was virtually a widening, though in fact upon a separate viaduct.* Quadruple tracks from Charing Cross to Orpington were brought into use in sections as completed, being opened throughout in June, 1905. On 31st May, 1914, the local lines were extended from Bickley station to Bickley Junction, in order to facilitate interchange of traffic with the South Eastern main line, via the Chislehurst loops.

Electrification on the lines we are now considering did not come about until after the amalgamation. Certain preliminary steps were taken, however, which call for mention here. The South Eastern and Chatham companies appreciated fully the benefits to be derived from electrification, and as long ago as 1903 obtained powers towards that end. There were difficulties, however, in the way of raising the necessary capital, but they were mostly overcome by the Trade Facilities Act, 1921. Under that Act the Treasury was prepared to guarantee for twenty-five years the principal and interest on £6,500,000, of which £5,000,000 was to be for the electrification and £1,500,000 for the power-house. The peculiar financial arrangements of the company, due to its being composed of three parties, led to a subsidiary company being formed to do the work. The Construction

* From North Kent East Junction to Corbett's Lane Junction.

company, so formed, consisted of five members of the Joint Managing Committee and Mr Charles Sheath and Mr Tempest. An agreement between the parties was approved, at meetings held on 2nd June, 1922, whereby the Construction company was to lease the works, rolling stock, etc., to the Joint Managing Committee.

It must now be noted that part of the scheme was the erection of a power-house at Angerstein Wharf,* which is on the river about midway between Deptford and Woolwich, and in accordance with the Act of 1919, permission had to be obtained from the Electricity Commissioners. An application was made on 23rd February, 1922, and on 30th May a public inquiry into the matter was opened. The result was a decision, on 21st August, refusing the application for an independent power-house, as an authorised undertaking would be in a position to supply power by the time the lines would be ready. No names were mentioned, but that obviously intended was the London Electric Supply Corporation.

Later; the Electricity Commissioners issued a supplementary statement in which it was observed that on 8th September the railway company informed them that the directors had unanimously resolved that no satisfactory agreement with the electric supply companies could be arrived at.

This supplementary statement concluded as follows:

The pooling of the railway company's supply and that of other classes of consumers would constitute an important contribution towards the centralisation of generation in Greater London, and the advantages due to saving in capital expenditure, increased efficiency – and hence lower cost – of generation, and enhanced reliability of supply consequent upon the eventual interconnection of the principal stations forming the centralised system, would be to the benefit not only of the railway company but also of other classes of consumer supplied from the central system. To these advantages must be added the national gain by the saving in fuel consumption.

The proposal of the railway company at this juncture to erect their own generating station, thereby involving the forgoing of all the benefits to be derived from the pooling of supplies and the centralisation of generation for all purposes, is not only contrary to the views to which railway companies and railway engineers have expressed their adherence, but in direct conflict with the fundamental basis upon which the reorganisation of electricity sypply must proceed.

On 13th December, 1922, just before the formation of the Southern Railway, the chairman of the South Eastern & Chatham, at a meeting in connection with the constitution of the grouped company, said that the decision of the Electricity Commissioners had been accepted.

* At the end of a short single-line S.E.R. branch leaving the original North Kent Line near Charlton.

The work of the South Eastern and Chatham Railways during the War was of the first importance. It possessed the two shortest cross-channel routes and had six terminal stations in London. By the Metropolitan Railway it was connected with the Great Northern & Midland; by the West London, with the North Western and Great Western; with the latter it was also connected at Reading, a route which carried a vast quantity of traffic thus enabled to avoid London; while the East London Railway gave direct access to the Great Eastern. Against all these advantages has to be set the fact that it was primarily a passenger line; in 1913 only a quarter of its traffic was goods, a circumstance which necessitated much alteration of methods, increase of wagons, and laying down new sidings, etc., as the lines had to be adapted to a heavy goods traffic, partly owing to the immense expansion of Woolwich Arsenal, and partly due to the huge development of goods traffic passing to ports, dockyards, munition works, etc., in the South Eastern district.

Ambulance traffic from Dover was taken to Charing Cross,* leave trains and mails to Victoria. In 1918 Cannon Street was closed to passengers during the middle of the day and on Saturday afternoons and Sundays; and used for the transfer of goods trains from the Midland and Great Northern lines.

After the fall of Antwerp on 9th October, 1914, large numbers of wounded and refugees were received at Dover, and when that place was full, Folkestone was made the port of reception. On one day 6,000 refugees were landed; after the seizure of Ostend on 14th October, 26,000 Belgians were landed in one week, and between 20th September and 24th October, 35,000 were received. Altogether 120,000 refugees passed through Folkestone during the war period.

The new marine station at Dover was not finished, but, in recognition of the fact that it would be a most useful port at which to receive hospital ships, orders were given in December that the station was at once to be sufficiently completed to accommodate ambulance trains. By commandeering all the available labour in and near Dover, and by working day and night, the platforms were filled in, a roof put over them and the station made fit within ten days to tranship the wounded from the ship to train. Two boats and six hospital trains could be dealt with simultaneously. From that date to February, 1919, there were 4,076 hospital ships, containing 1,260,506 wounded, received at Dover, and 7,781 ambulance trains dispatched.

In connection with the latter, it will be of interest to note that on 1st August, 1914, the South Eastern & Chatham were asked to pro-

* And some to Sidcup, where a large hospital was set up.

vide two ambulance trains, which they improvised from ordinary stock in forty-eight hours, each consisting of eleven vehicles.

For many years past, every encouragement had been given to members of the staff to obtain proficiency in ambulance work, with the result that large numbers of the company's employees had availed themselves of the facilities offered to them, and were able to render exceptionally good service in that respect – all, it should be mentioned, in addition to their regular duties.

The greatest increase in goods traffic was in connection with Woolwich. From there thousands of tons of necessaries for the army abroad went to the ports, while a ceaseless stream of materials kept pouring in. Altogether, 1,023,883 wagons went into and out of the Arsenal, and 452,352 into and out of the Royal Dockyard.

The Joint Managing Committee had its share of the strain caused by the leave traffic of the men in France. During the four years ended November, 1918, 14,871 special trains ran from Dover or Folkestone to Victoria and vice versa, which carried 6,530,482 men.

The military mail was dealt with at Victoria and conveyed via Folkestone. It required about thirty covered goods wagons each night, and, up to the end of 1918, 10,463,834 sacks of mail matter, weighing 324,596 tons, were handled. The civil mail, to and from the Continent, passed through Southampton.

In Pratt's *British Railways and the Great War*, from which much of the information in this section has been obtained, a list of the figures for goods traffic at nine stations on the system is given, which shows that the average increase of traffic at those points was 773 per cent.

Yet another cause of increase of traffic was the creation of the new port at Richborough, whence 9,644 barges loaded with war material, weighing 1,282,656 tons, were taken across the Channel. By 10th February, 1918, a train ferry was established, with Calais (35 miles) and Dunkirk (54 miles) as the termini in France. No passengers were carried, but 200,936 tons of goods were taken outwards, and 59,922 homewards; including locomotives, 'tanks', and heavy siege guns on their own mountings.

In many instances running lines were utilised for stabling wagons containing war material awaiting inspection, etc. The Greenwich Park branch line was closed to passenger traffic and largely used for this purpose. Another line, that between Welling and Bexley Heath, was for a time worked single: one road being occupied by trucks of coal. After the landslip between Folkestone and Dover, all traffic had to work via the L.C.D.R. route, and the uninjured part of the other was used for storage. Sometimes well over a hundred trucks of explosives were stabled in the Shakespeare Tunnel. Seven or eight other lines were temporarily pressed into the service, owing to the congestion which, for one reason or another, occurred at various times.

Of the South Eastern & Chatham fleet the *Empress*, *Engadine* and *Riviera* were engaged as seaplane carriers, and the *Biarritz* as a mine-layer. The *Engadine* made history: she was in the battle of Jutland and was the first ship to sight the German fleet. Subsequently she took the damaged *Warrior* in tow and, before that warship sunk, the *Engadine* took off 675 officers and men. The *Victoria*, *Invicta*, *Onward* and *Queen* carried on military passenger communication between Folkestone and Calais or Boulogne. Of those boats the *Queen* was captured and sunk on 26th August, 1916, and the *Onward* was destroyed by fire on 24th September, 1918. The *Queen* rendered noteworthy service on 26th October, 1914, when she rescued 2,300 passengers from the French ship *Amiral Ganteaume*, which was torpedoed while conveying Belgian refugees. The *Achille Adam*, a cargo boat, met the same fate as the *Queen* on 23rd March, 1917. Another cargo boat – the *Hythe* – was lost in collision in October, 1915, when serving in the Dardanelles expedition.

The expansion at the port of Boulogne which became necessary in consequence of its adoption as a military base, involving new sidings, roads, drainage, water mains, etc., was carried out by the South Eastern & Chatham Railway. Owing to the pressing needs of their own service, they made a comparatively small contribution to the rolling stock sent overseas, namely 8 locomotives, 1,042 wagons and 24 carriages. For the same reason they were unable to undertake war manufactures in their workshops to the same extent as some of the leading railways, but they nevertheless made many thousands of parts of shells, over 400 wagons, and 4,000 ambulance stretchers.

The services rendered by the South Eastern & Chatham Railway were well summed up in a letter Field Marshal Lord – then Sir Douglas – Haig wrote to Mr Bonsor, the chairman of the Joint Managing Committee, on 23rd December, 1918, from which the following is extracted.

The Army in France owes much to all concerned with the control of our railway companies in the United Kingdom, and, indeed, in the Empire. They have at all times shown the greatest willingness to help us in every possible way in their power. Track has been torn up to give us rails; engines, trucks, men, capable engineers, operations staff, etc., all have been sent abroad to us, regardless of their own special needs and the demands of the people at Home, and without a moment's hesitation.

But we have been more closely associated with the South Eastern & Chatham Railway than any other. The bulk of our armies, as well as several millions of men, as reinforcements and on leave, have passed over their system. Their sphere of duty, too, has been nearest to the shores of France and Belgium, and, consequently, more open to hostile attacks by air and fears of invasion by sea. Undisturbed by any alarms the traffic for the Armies in France has never ceased to flow. This reflects the greatest credit on all concerned with the company.

The number of S.E.C.R. men in all grades who joined the colours was 5,222, of whom 556 were killed. A beautiful war memorial was erected at Dover Marine station. It was executed by Mr W. C. H. King, and represents Victory, with wings battered in the conflict, but still holding high the torch of Truth, led by a sailor and a soldier.

The first fifteen years of the Managing Committee passed without any accidents involving the death of a passenger, but on 25th October, 1913, in a dense fog, there was a collision between two passenger trains at Waterloo Junction station, in which three passengers were killed. A train from Blackheath was in the station and standing in the rear of the signals at Waterloo Junction box and in advance of those at Waterloo station box. A light engine had preceded the Blackheath train, which for some reason was not properly block-signalled. Confusion was created thereby, and it was added to by the signalman at Waterloo station who, when he wanted to send a Mid Kent train, and not knowing, because of the fog, that the Blackheath train was still there, told the man at the Junction box that he had not freed the instrument. The latter man, without thinking, freed the instrument irregularly and the collision resulted.

A passenger train left Cannon Street on 27th June, 1914, the driver of which misread his signal and a collision resulted in which a passenger was killed. In reporting on the accident, Colonel Pringle said that the hitherto safe working of Cannon Street spoke well for the manner in which both signalmen and enginemen had performed their duties in difficult circumstances.

A serious collision occurred at Milton Range Halt on 21st August, 1922, The driver of a passenger train, on being given the guard's hand signal to start, left Gravesend without noticing that the fixed signals were not in his favour. As a consequence, his train ran into a passenger train which, owing to an accident to some of its passengers, was detained at the halt. Three passengers in the standing train were killed or died from their injuries as a result of the collision.

At the end of 1922 the total length of route running line of the South Eastern & Chatham was 638 miles. Of that, 65 miles were single tracked, 573 miles had a double line, of which 40 miles had a third track, 29 miles had a fourth track, and there was a total length of

23 miles on those sections that had over four lines. The sidings were of a total length of 384 miles.

At the last general meeting of the South Eastern & Chatham Railway, Mr Cosmo Bonsor made a most interesting speech, which summed up so well the work of the period covered by this chapter, that a rather lengthy extract will form a fitting conclusion. He said:

> I do not think I am exaggerating when I say that when the South Eastern and the Chatham companies came together they were both singularly unpopular. Their services were bad. The complaints, both public and private, as to the unpunctuality of their trains were very numerous, and I think I might almost add that they were a standing joke with the clown of the pantomime and with the comic gentlemen in the music halls.

He then proceeded to relate how one of the directors obtained the loan of a Caledonian engine, which the engineer refused to allow to be tried, saying that neither the road nor bridges would carry it, nor was there a turntable large enough to accommodate it. It was therefore sent back, but it had brought home a lesson to all concerned. Mr Tempest, who had just been appointed chief engineer, undertook the task of bringing the works and way up to a higher standard.

> It was a Herculean job. I think I am right in saying there were four tunnels that had to be reconstructed, the whole of the road, the main line road, had to be relaid with heavier rails, instead of the light rails that had been in existence since the commencement of the railway, and the ballast, which was shingle, had to be taken out and replaced with Kentish stone.
> There was another almost bigger job, that was the reconstruction, the rebuilding, and the strengthening of the whole of the bridges of the main lines. 588 bridges had to be taken in hand and reconstructed, and this, I believe cost – I hardly like to allude to the cost – it was something over one million sterling, and that work was practically completed in 1913. The War broke out and consequently the shareholders got no return from the enormous sacrifice they had made during all those years in putting their line in order. I think I might also allude to the harbours. There was Dover Admiralty Pier, and there was our own harbour at Folkstone. That harbour had not grown sufficiently to take even the moderate boats that were then crossing the Channel, and the pier was practically out of order. It was decaying. We had to undertake the rebuilding of that pier. Then we come to the question of the fleet. Well, gentlemen, a good many of us who went abroad remember the old Foam and the Petrel, and the boats that ran between Calais and Dover, and I think it was the Albert Victor, the Louis Victoria and the Duchess that made the run between Folkstone and Boulogne. Well, there again the Managing Committee were extremely fortunate. The late Captain Dixon was our new Marine Superintendent and he had energy and perseverance, and in conjunction with Denny Brothers, he practically — I was going to say – cajoled the Managing Committee into going into the enterprise of building the first turbine steamer. The Queen was the first turbine steamer of any size that crossed the Channel and became the pioneer of the turbine fleet which now exists. With the completion of the Dover Marine Station – the land was reclaimed by the Dover Harbour Board and the station built by the Managing Committee – practically our large capital expenditure came to an end. That station was finished in 1914, and if you look at the

capital expenditure of the Managing Committee since you will find that we have hardly spent any considerable sums and much less on capital than any of the other large companies. Practically that is the work we have done, and I do claim that it was a considerable public service. I do not think it would have been possible to have carried the military traffic that was thrust upon us in 1914 had we not anticipated and spent that money. It is a matter of regret naturally to me that owing to the War and so on we have not been able until today to make some sort of return on that expenditure and putting the line in order.

XXXI

South Eastern & Chatham Locomotives, 1899-1922

EARLY in 1900, owing to engines being badly wanted, arrangements were made whereby five were taken over which had been built by Neilson, Reid and Co. for the Great North of Scotland Railway. They were 4-4-0 engines with 6ft 1in wheels and 18 by 26 cylinders, with American type cabs: Nos. 676–680 (class 'G'). They were never rebuilt, disappearing about 1927.

In May, 1900, the first engine of H. S. Wainwright's design was put into service, a six-coupled goods, No. 255. By way of showing that the Joint Committee meant to smarten things up, he painted his engines a bright green, with polished brass dome covers, and bright copper caps to the chimneys. The goods engines of this type, known as 'C' class, numbered 109 in all, as follows:

At Ashford:

18	.	. 1900	54	.	. 1901	573	.	. 1903	495	.	. 1904
33	.	,,	61	.	,,	575	.	,,	498	.	,,
63	.	,,	71	.	,,	576	.	,,	499	.	,,
86	.	,,	221	.	,,	578	.	,,	508	.	,,
102	.	,,	223	.	,,	579	.	,,	510	.	,,
112	.	,,	234	.	,,	581	.	,,	513	.	,,
191	.	,,	59	.	. 1902	582	.	,,	280	.	. 1908
218	.	,,	90	.	,,	584	.	,,	287	.	,,
219	.	,,	113	.	,,	585	.	,,	291	.	,,
225	.	,,	150	.	,,	260	.	. 1904	293	.	,,
227	.	,,	242–245	.	,,	262	.	,,	294	.	,,
229	.	,,	252	.	,,	267	.	,,	297	.	,,
255–257	.	,,	253	.	,,	268	.	,,	298	.	,,
4	.	. 1901	68	.	. 1903	270–272	.	,,	317	.	,,
37	.	,,	572	.	,,	277	.	,,	588–590	.	,,
38	.	,,									

At Longhedge:

592	.	. 1901	461	.	. 1902	580	.	. 1903	480	.	. 1904
593	.	,,	486	.	. 1903	583	.	,,	481	.	,,
460	.	. 1902									

No. 685 was converted into a saddle tank in 1917, and was called class 'S' of which it was the only representative.

At the end of 1900 Sharp, Stewart and Co. delivered fifteen very smart-looking 0-4-4 tanks, 5ft 6in, $17\frac{1}{2}$ by 24; Nos. 696–710, known as 'R1' class. (A development of the L.C.D.R. 'R' class.)

Neilson, Reid and Co.: 681–695, 1900
Sharp, Stewart and Co.: 711–725, 1900

Another design of 0-4-4T, but with cylinders 18 by 26, was built at Ashford, as under (known as class 'H'):

540–542	.	1904	500 .	.	1905	320 .	.	1907	239 .	. 1909
544 .	. ,,		503 .	. ,,		324 .	. ,,		279 .	. ,,
546 .	. ,,		530–533	. ,,		327 .	. ,,		295 .	. ,,
548 .	. ,,		553 .	. ,,		518–523	. 1908		319 .	. ,,
550–552	. ,,		305–310	. 1906		158 .	. 1909		322 .	. ,,
259 .	. 1905		312 .	. ,,		161 .	. ,,		512 .	. ,,
261 .	. ,,		321 .	. ,,		162 .	. ,,		517 .	. ,,
263–266	. ,,		326 .	. ,,		164 .	. ,,		543 .	. ,,
269 .	. ,,		328 .	. ,,		177 .	. ,,		554 .	. ,,
274 .	. ,,		329 .	. ,,		182 .	. ,,		16 .	. 1915
276 .	. ,,		5 .	. 1907		193 .	. ,,		184 .	. ,,
278 .	. ,,		311 .	. ,,						

We now come to Wainwright's first 4-4-0 expresses. When they came out, they were of extremely smart appearance, shining with polished brass. They were known as 'D' class, and were 51 in all, about half of which were later rebuilt with Belpaire fireboxes and superheaters, these latter being called 'D1'. The wheels were 6ft 8in, and cylinders 19 by 26, pressure 175 lb. The first were a batch of ten from Sharp, Stewart and Co. in 1901: Nos. 726–735; the last one was shown at the Glasgow Exhibition of that year. Others from outside firms were 741–745 from R. Stephenson and Co., and 746–750 from the Vulcan Foundry; and the following from Dübs and Co., all in 1903: 75, 92, 145, 247, 489, 492–494, 501 and 502.

Twenty-one were built at Ashford:

736–740	. 1901	470 .	. 1906	577 .	. 1906	505 .	. 1907
57 .	. ,,	509 .	. ,,	477 .	. 1907	574 .	. ,,
246 .	. ,,	545 .	. ,,	487 .	. ,,	586 .	. ,,
488 .	. ,,	549 .	. ,,	496 .	. ,,	591 .	. ,,
490 .	. ,,						

From 1915, one 'D' class, all 'E' class, and 'F' and 'B' as rebuilt, were fitted with extended smokebox.

The purchase of a 'Terrier' from the L.B.S.C.R. (No. 654),

mentioned in Chapter XXI, occurred in 1904. It was numbered 751, later 680S, being for some years Brighton Works shunter.

In 1905 Wainwright produced his second type of express engine, class 'E'. The wheels were reduced to 6ft 6in, and the cylinders increased to 19in. They were fitted with Belpaire fireboxes from the first. Eleven of them were rebuilt with larger boilers, superheaters and piston valves (classified 'E1'): one at Ashford, and the rest by Beyer, Peacock and Co. All were built at Ashford:

273 .	.	1905	176 .	.	1907	19 .	.	1908	507 .	.	1908
275 .	.	1906	491 .	.	,,	36 .	.	,,	516 .	.	,,
506 .	.	,,	497 .	.	,,	67 .	.	,,	547 .	.	,,
157 .	.	1907	504 .	.	,,	159 .	.	,,	163 .	.	1909
160 .	.	,,	514 .	.	,,	175 .	.	,,	315 .	.	,,
165 .	.	,,	515 .	.	,,	179 .	.	,,	511 .	.	1910
166 .	.	,,	587 .	.	,,						

NOTE—No. 516 was shown at the Franco-British Exhibition of 1908.

Nos. 36 and 275 were fitted in 1912 with Robinson and Schmidt superheaters respectively with 20½in cylinders, but remained class 'E'.

About this time a number of rail-motors* were introduced for branch lines, but were superseded later by standard engines arranged to 'pull and push'.

Early in 1909 the first of a class of small 0-6-0 side-tank engines was turned out at Ashford, of which there were eight in all – much on the lines of the Brighton Terriers; with wheels 3ft 9in and cylinders 12 by 18 (class 'P'):

753 (556)	1909	27 .	.	1910	323 .	.	1910	555 .	.	1910
754 (557)	,,	178 .	.	,,	325 .	.	,,	558 .	.	,,

The last engines built by Wainwright at Ashford were five 0-6-4 tanks in 1913; wheels 5ft 6in, cylinders 19½ by 26; fitted with Schmidt uperheaters: Nos. 207 (595), 129 (596), 597, 611 (598) and 614 (599).

The weakness of the bridges had prevented the use of engines with more than 18 tons on an axle on the Continental trains, but by 1914 improvements had been made in this respect, which allowed Wainwright to design a large 4-4-0 express with the driving axle carrying 19¼ tons. Twenty-two were ordered, twelve from Beyer Peacock, Nos. 760–771, and ten from Borsig of Berlin, Nos. 772–781. The latter

---

* Kitson, 1904–5, eight in all, with 10 by 15in cylinders and 3ft 7in driving wheels. The coach portions were dismounted 1911–14 and made into four pull-and-push sets, two of which were articulated and used on the Sheppey Light.

were erected at Ashford by Borsig's men, the last being barely finished when the War broke out. The wheels were 6ft 8in, and cylinders $20\frac{1}{2}$ by 26. The English ones had Robinson superheaters, and the German, Schmidt. They were known as class 'L'.

During the time that Mr Maunsell was in charge, which of course, covered the war period, only two new designs were produced, one of which was extremely successful, so much so, that it was chosen by the Government when they decided to build locomotives at Woolwich, to alleviate the unemployment caused by the cessation of activity after the end of the war. They were 2-6-0 tender engines, with large taper boilers carrying 200 lb of steam; 5ft 6in wheels and 19 by 28 cylinders. Those built before the end of 1922 – all at Ashford – were (class 'N') : 810, 1917; 811–815, 1920; 816–821, 1922, to which must be added No. 822, with three cylinders 16 by 28 (class 'N1'). All had Maunsell superheaters.

The other class, known as 'K', was a 2-6-4 tank engine, very similar to the 'N's', but with 6-ft wheels, No. 790. The engine, together with twenty other similar ones built after the amalgamation, were converted into tender engines. After the war she was given the name *River Avon*, which was removed when the conversion took place. The development of these designs into the 'U', 'U1', and 'W' classes is detailed in a later chapter.

XXXII

South Eastern, & Chatham and Dover Steamer Services

Of all the sea routes from England, that narrow stretch lying between Dover and Calais – the narrowest that divides Britain from any other country – has always been the most traversed, from the days of the Romans and the Normans, through the times of alternate peace and war with France, down to today. Dover, being also the port of departure for Ostend, has well been called the 'Gateway to the Continent'.

When an organised service was first set up is not known. Joyce, in his *History of the Post Office*, says that it seems certain that Dover was a packet station long prior to 1686, going on thus: 'In that year the arrangements, whatever they were, for carrying the mails between England and France came to an end, and a new service was established between Dover and Calais and between Dover and Ostend, or Nieuport.' The contractor was to receive £1,170 a year, to provide the boats and to manage the 'letter office' at Dover. In 1689, owing to the breaking out of the war with France, the packets ceased to run, being reinstated in 1697, only to be discontinued again on the resumption of hostilities in 1702. And so it went on. After the close, in 1782, of the American War of Independence, in which France supported Washington against George III, there was a service twice a week in each direction which operated until 1793. According to the *Kentish Companion* of 1784, there were four English and four French vessels in the service which sailed every Wednesday and Saturday. The names of the English vessels were the *Union*, *Dispatch*, *Prince Frederick* and *Courier*. There were also vessels to Ostend. The outbreak of the French Revolution in 1793 – which was followed by the Napoleonic Wars – caused communication with France to cease – that with Ostend was, however, maintained, but Harwich was used as the English port.

In Dover Museum there is a fine model of the *King George* – one of the three packets which conveyed passengers and mails between Dover and Calais. By starting from Dover as soon as there was sufficient water, these vessels were able, given a tolerably fair wind, to reach Calais in three hours and to enter that port on the same tide. The mails were carried in a weighted box, so that, if attacked by a French privateer, the box could be thrown overboard and saved from falling into enemy hands.

Communication through Dover was reopened after Napoleon's defeat at Waterloo in 1815. Steam had, by that time, been adopted, to a small extent, for the propulsion of ships.

The first steamboat placed on the cross-Channel service was the *Rob Roy*, of 90 tons burthen and 30 horse-power. She had been built by William Denny, of Dumbarton – the founder of the famous firm of that name – in 1818, and engined by David Napier, who ran her between Glasgow and Belfast. Two years later he sold her 'to two gentlemen, holding a third if her myself, to run between Dover and Calais'. The quotation is from his autobiography. It goes on:

The *Rob Roy* was therefore not only the first steamer that proved the practicability of navigating the open sea by steam, but was also the first to connect France and England by steam.* Her success there was so complete as to induce the Government again to employ Boulton and Watt to make engines for two steamers for that station, which the little *Rob Roy* so thoroughly beat, particularly in stormy weather, that the French Government took such a fancy to her that they purchased her, that vessel being the first steamer they possessed, and with which they were so well pleased that, with a priest and some holy water, they formally transformed the Scotch freebooter into a French king, i.e. Henri Quatre.

The *Rob Roy*, it may be remarked, had an elliptical funnel.

About 1822 J. and W. Hayward, of Dover, began running two steamers of about 100 tons, fitted with side-lever engines of 32 nominal h.p. by Maudslay, named the *Sovereign* and *Monarch*. In 1823 a vessel named the *Spitfire* was placed on the route – by whom it is not known – with Boulton and Watt engines of 40 n.h.p.

The mails at this time were conveyed in steamers belonging to the Post Office. In the Sixth Report of the *Commissioners appointed to Enquire into the Management of the Post Office*, published in 1836, it is stated that there were five packets: three employed on the Dover–Calais route, and two running to Ostend, to which place mails were sent four times a week. The names of the boats were *Arrow*, *Crusader*, *Ferret*, *Firefly* and *Salamander*; the first being 155 tons and the others 110; the h.p. being 50–60. The packets to Calais conveyed the outward mails only, the French Post Office delivering their own at Dover. The British boats carried the Ostend mails both ways, the

* Actually the first steam passage across the Channel was made by the Majestic in 1816, but that was an isolated performance.

Belgian Government contributing £1,000 a year towards the expense. The Report mentions that the harbour at Dover was dry at low water. In 1837 the packets were all taken away from the Post Office, and handed over to the Admiralty.

The *Firefly* occasionally crossed to Calais in 2½ hours, but, more often, took over three. The *Arrow* performed what was considered a great feat on 5th February, 1834, by making Ostend in 5 hours 47 minutes.

On 11th May, 1844, the General Steam Navigation Company put the *Magician* on the route between Dover and Boulogne. She was built of iron, being the second vessel so made to be owned by the company – the first had been the *Rainbow*, built by Laird, which was the first iron sea-going steamer ever constructed. The *Magician* crossed regularly in two hours. She was joined by the *City of London*, an old wooden vessel, and the two ran in competition with the Hayward boats mentioned above, *Sovereign* and *Monarch*.

No sooner had the South Eastern Railway reached Folkestone in 1843, than the company entered into arrangements with the New Commercial Steam Packet Co. to run a regular day service to Boulogne; three vessels belonging to the latter company being the *City of Boulogne*, *William Wallace*, and *Emerald*. On arrival the following year at Dover, the railway company wished to run packets of its own, but as it had no powers to do so under its Act, a subsidiary company was formed in August, 1845, call the 'South Eastern and Continental Steam Packet Company', which ran steamers from Dover and Folkestone to Calais, Boulogne and Ostend. Its first boats were the *Princess Mary*, *Princess Maud*, *Queen of the Belgians*, *Queen of the French*, all built by Ditchburn and Mare, with Maudslay's annular engines, and the *Prince Ernest*, built by Laird and engined by Forrester, of Liverpool (side lever). According to one account, these boats had been ordered by the Haywards, which is quite likely. In 1846 and 1847 they added three more by Laird and Forrester: the *Princess Helena*, *Princess Clementine*, and *Lord Warden*. They made the passage of the Channel in about 2¼ hours in fair weather.

In 1844 a steamer named the *Ondine* was built by Miller and Ravenhill for the Dover Royal Mail Steam Packet Co. – a firm which does not seem to have been as important as would appear from its name. A condition of the contract was that she was to beat all the boats of her class. She was of about 260 tons, with a pair of oscillating engines of 106 n.h.p., the cylinders being underneath the shaft. They are illustrated in *Tredgold on the Steam Engine* (Marine Engines and Boilers), vol. ii. Her speed was about 12½ knots. When tried against the *Princess Maud*, she lost by one minute, which is very remarkable considering the great difference in design of the engines. She was bought by the Admiralty in 1847, who altered the name to *Undine*.

In 1846 the Belgian Government entered the field, and began to carry the mails from Ostend to Dover, the South Eastern and Continental Co. taking them the other way – a daily service. At an early stage they seem to have gone from Ramsgate. In Bradshaw's *Descriptive Guide to the South Eastern Railway*, by E. L. Blanchard, published in 1846, the following passage occurs:

> Being now the station for the Ostend steam-boats, which usually perform the voyage in about four hours and a half, Ramsgate has received an impetus which must eventually make it the most important packet station on the south-eastern coast.

The above prophecy was, of course, not realised, as the service was taken back to Dover after a year or so. As a matter of fact, there is no indication in the company's records that there was any definite intention of transferring the Dover–Ostend service to Ramsgate. The service thence may have been merely an occasional one, and the passage quoted above was perhaps based on a suggestion which was not put into effect.

The question as to whether railway companies should be allowed to step outside what had hitherto been regarded as their sole province, and own and run steamers, beagn to assume great importance. The attitude taken by Parliament and the Government in respect of the incorporation of companies was that the privilege, with the extinction of individual liability incidental to it, was not granted to companies for carrying on any trade or enterprise which could effectively be carried on by individual capitalists, private partnerships or unincorporated companies.

In the session of 1848 bills were deposited by four railway companies: the Chester & Holyhead – which railway was then approaching completion – Furness, London & South Western, and London, Brighton & South Coast – seeking for powers to own and work steam vessels. The bills were referred to the Select Committee which had been appointed on 26th November, 1847, to decide what procedure should be adopted with the host of railway bills then before Parliament. The Committee sent an intimation to the Board of Trade and to the Board of Railway Commissioners that their views on the subject of railway companies owning steam vessels would be welcomed.

The report issued by the Board of Trade and the Railway Commissioners recommended that powers should be given to the Chester

& Holyhead, on various grounds, of which the most important is the following:

The transit from Holyhead to Dublin may be fairly considered as a portion of the railway enterprise; but for the railway to Holyhead there would be little opening for any profitable employment of steam vessels in that passage; and but for securing the transit of passengers to and from Dublin_the railway to Holyhead would never have been constructed.

Sanction was also given to the Furness scheme, which was not an ambitious one.

After disposing of the above, the report proceeded:

With regard to the London & South Western company's bill, now under consideration, the provision respecting steamboats is of a very extensive character and no protection whatever is given to the public against any excessive fares which, as owners of steamboats, the railway company might charge to the public. The provision empowers the railway company to build, buy, hire and use, maintain and work steamboats and other vessels for navigating between the ports of Southampton, Portsmouth, Gosport, Lymington, Poole and Weymouth, or any of them, and France, or any one or more of the Channel Islands, and to contribute by loan or holding of shares towards the capital of any company engaged in steam navigation between any of such ports or places and may take tolls and fares in respect of such steam packets and other vessels.

.   .   .   .   .

The passenger traffic from Southampton, and the other ports mentioned, to France and the Channel Islands, although advantageous, is not essential to the support of the South Western Railway, nor can Havre or any other French port be regarded as a kind of terminus to the South Western Railway, in the way that Dublin is justly regarded as a terminus of the Chester & Holyhead Railway.

It must be borne in mind, however, that there already exists an incorporated company – the General Steam Navigation Company – possessing great capital, which, to a considerable extent, can prevent or put down competition of individual steamboat owners; and it may therefore be a question worthy of the attention of the committee, whether the permission to the South Western Railway company to establish steamboats may not prevent, instead of creating, a monopoly, the more especially as if the like permission be given to the Brighton and to the South Eastern steamboat companies – the latter of which already exercises indirectly but practically the same powers – several competing lines will thus be established from London to the Continent, which will keep down prices to their proper level.

If the Committee should be of opinion that this permission should be granted, it would seem advisable that the voyages to be undertaken by the South Western company be defined and limited to Havre and to the Channel Islands and parts of France immediately adjacent; that the powers should only be granted for a limited period and that arbitration of fares, similar in principle to that on the Chester & Holyhead Railway, be inserted; and that the company be not empowered to lend money or subscribe to any other steam-vessel company. This indirect arrangement which, while it seems open to many of the objections applicable to the ownership of steam-vessels by railway companies, appears to afford no compensating advantages, and the Board of Trade and Railway Commissioners decidedly disapprove of it. It should likewise be necessary that, in addition to the clauses limiting the fares, a clause should be framed and inserted for securing equality of treatment to passengers who use the steam-vessels of the company but not the railway.

With respect to the London, Brighton & South Coast Railway bill, the power relating to steamboats is of a somewhat indefinite character. It authorises the directors, with consent of a meeting of the company, to subscribe or advance or guarantee the subscription of, or expend any sum of money not exceeding £100,000 for, or towards, or in, or about the establishment of, steam communication with any port with which the said London, Brighton & South Coast Railway communicates and any port or town in the Kingdom of France, in such a manner and upon such terms as the directors may think proper. The observations which have already been made upon the London & South Western Railway company's bills are applicable also to this bill. If the Committee should acquiesce in the London & South Western Railway company establishing steamboats to France, they would probably be of opinion that such permission, in a definite form and due regulation, might be given for a limited period, to the London, Brighton & South Coast Railway, confining, however, its voyages to Dieppe and possibly to Havre.

The recommendations of the Board of Trade and the Board of Railway Commissioners were accepted by the Select Committee and, subsequently, by both Houses of Parliament.

In 1853, under 15 & 16 Vic., c. 156, the South Eastern Railway company obtained powers. The bill met with considerable opposition in Parliament, but the Commons Committee reported 'that the convenience and advantage to the public will be better secured by the concession of such powers to the extent limited between Folkestone or Dover and Calais or Boulogne'. The railway company acquired, for £99,406, eight of the South Eastern and Continental Steamship company's vessels.

It may be noted here that the Admiralty Pier at Dover was commenced in 1847 and completed in 1875. It was first used, in an unfinished state, by the *Onyx*, one of the Admiralty mail packets.

In 1854 an important change came about. The Government decided to put the mail services out to contract, and that for the mails from Dover to France and Belgium was awarded to Messrs Jenkins and Churchward. The latter seems to have been the prime mover in the firm. His son, Captain A. W. Churchward was marine superintendent at Queenborough for about thirteen years, having charge of the Queenborough and Flushing service. In 1889 he was appointed Paris agent to the London, Chatham & Dover Railway, continuing in the same post under the joint Committee until the end of April, 1914. He died on 17th October, 1929.

The contractors worked the mail service as a company, known as the English, French and Belgian Royal Mail Co. They began with the following packets which they took over from the Admiralty: the *Onyx*, *Violet*, *Undine* and *Garland*. The *Onyx* and *Undine* were afterwards sold, the latter to the proprietor of the *Morning Herald* for conveying dispatches. There was great rivalry in those days between the various newspapers for the publication of news from the Continent, and for that reason some of the fastest vessels were retained for the sole use of couriers with foreign intelligence. In this connection it may be mentioned that in 1848, before there was a telegraph to London, both *The Times* and the *Herald* paid £5 a day and £5 a night for an engine to stand in steam ready to take news from Paris up to London the moment the boat arrived.

Returning to the Churchward steamers, the *Violet* was wrecked with great loss of life in a violent storm on the Goodwins on 5th January, 1857, when on her way from Ostend to Dover.

The firm lost no time in obtaining new vessels, of which the first were the *Queen, Empress, Prince Frederick William*, and *John Penn*. The first two were of 300 tons, with engines of 100 nominal h.p., giving them a speed of 12 to 13 knots; average time for crossing about 1 hour 55 minutes. The *Prince Frederick William* was about 30 tons larger, with 120 n.h.p. engines, indicating about 600 h.p., which drove her at 15 knots. But these were easily surpassed by the *John Penn*. She was 171ft 8in long, beam 18ft 7in, with oscillating engines giving 800 i.h.p., having two cylinders 46 by 50in. On her first run she crossed from Dover to Calais in 1 hour and 23 minutes. As will be seen later, she was transferred to the L.C.D.R., but soon sold to the Belgian Government, who renamed here *Perle* and placed her on the Ostend Dover service. In 1872 the French Government bought her, and she ran between Calais and Dover once more, continuing to do so for a number of years.

The Fourth Report of the Postmaster General mentioned that during the Indian Mutiny the mails frequently travelled from Paris to London in less than nine hours, and acknowledged with thanks 'the zealous co-operation of the Directors of the English, French and Belgian Royal Mail Company, and of the South Eastern Railway Co.'

In 1862, it was decided not to renew the Churchward contract, and the mail service was offered to the South Eastern Railway, but was declined. Here, there is no doubt, they made a grave mistake. The directors considered that, holding the Folkestone route in their own hands, they had the key of the whole Continental traffic; paying, apparently, no attention to the fact that a new and formidable competitor had arrived at Dover the year before. The latter, meaning, of course, the L.C.D.R., stepped in and secured the mail contract. The consequence was that the S.E.R. decided to restrict their activities entirely to the Folkestone–Boulogne route, and the two services became distinct until the fusion of the companies in 1899. Incidentally, the small firms who had spasmodically run services from Dover found it impossible to compete with the railway company, and soon took off their boats. Another change that came about was that the Belgian Government alone worked the Ostend–Dover route.

It must be mentioned that for much of the above, and succeeding details, the writer is indebted to an excellent book published in 1934, by Mr Frank Burtt, entitled *Cross Channel and Coastal Paddle Steamers*.

In order to present a connected narrative as far as possible, the history of the Dover services will be carried on, and for the time being, therefore, the L.C.D.R. will hold the stage.

They took over most of the Churchward fleet, to which they soon made the following additions: *Maid of Kent*, *Foam* and *Scud*, from Samuda Brothers; and *Samphire* and *Petrel*, from Money, Wigram and Co. In 1863 and 1864 they added the *Breeze* and *Wave*, from the latter builders, and the *Prince Imperial* (afterwards *Prince*) and *France*, from J. Ash and Co. The *Samphire* had diagonal engines, with two cylinders 50 by 45in; boiler pressure 28 lb; 160 n.h.p. The *Petrel* and *Foam* had engines of 240 nominal h.p.; the cylinders being 62 by 54.

The *Maid of Kent* and *Samphire* had been laid down to Church-ward's order. Of the former, it is said, in *Mail and Passenger Steamers of the Nineteenth Century*, by Capt. Parker and F. C. Bowen, that she was of 346 gross tonnage, engines by J. Watts and Co., of Birmingham, with the following note:

She was one of the earliest of the new pattern packet steamers, which broke away from the old yacht lines, and was originally the property of Messrs Church-ward. Soon after the Railway company took her over, they scrapped the old side-lever engines and refitted her with diagonal oscillating engines by Messrs Ravenhill, Salkeld & Co., supplied by tubular boilers, a move which considerably improved her speed. She ran very successfully, and was in existence long after she was outclassed on her station, not being broken up till 1899, when she was sold to the Dutch.

With the exception of the *Scud*, which was hired by the Belgian Government in 1863 and withdrawn from service in 1866, these boats all continued in regular service for thirty years, and then were kept in reserve, not being turned out until the fusion with the S.E.R. The *Foam* actually remained till 1901.

Although the Chatham company had the advantage of a shorter sea-passage, it suffered from the fact that its passengers, on arrival at Calais had to take the diligence to Boulogne, as railway communication with Paris began there. The line between Calais and Boulogne was opened in 1867.

The discomforts of the passage in the comparatively small boats experienced by passengers unaccustomed to the sea was so great that in the 'seventies inventors began to bring forward schemes by which they hoped to make things more comfortable, and some experimental boats appeared.

The first was the *Castalia*, designed by Captain Dicey for the English Channel Steamship Company. She was launched on 2nd June, 1874, from the yard of the Thames Ironworks Company at Blackwall. She had two parallel hulls, or perhaps one should say, half-hulls, each 290ft long, with a beam of 17ft. They were separated by a gap of 26ft, and united by a superstructure of upper deck 183ft long by 60ft wide. Two paddle wheels worked in the space between, driven by indepent diagonal engines, one in each hull. The total engine power was 250 nominal, which only produced a speed of eleven knots. She was pronounced a failure, and was sold to the Metropolitan Asylums Board as an isolation hospital for infectious diseases.

For four or five years Mr (afterwards Sir) Henry Bessemer had been working at the problem of producing a ship with a saloon which could be moved relatively to the hull, so as to remain stationary in space, so far as rolling and pitching were concerned. The result was that he designed an arrangement whereby the saloon was hung on a horizontal axis, and could be revolved by means of vertical hydraulic cylinders on each side. They were to be controlled by a man watching a spirit-level. Had the scheme succeeded, he proposed to substitute automatic control, by the application of a gyroscope driven by a steam turbine, an idea which, considering it was conceived sixty years ago, was brilliantly original.

A company was formed, and a steamer, named the *Bessemer*, was built by Earle's Shipbuilding Company at Hull, to the designs of Mr (afterwards Sir) E. J. Reed. She was 350ft long, 40 ft wide over the deck, and 65ft across the paddle-boxes, with a draught of only 7ft 6in of water. The saloon occupied the whole of the centre, for a length of 70ft. She had very low freeboard at the ends – which were alike, to save turning – with the idea that heavy seas would pile up on them, and prevent pitching. Owing to the position of the saloon, the engines and paddle-wheels were duplicated, being located fore and aft of it.

There have been various more or less inaccurate accounts of her short and disastrous career, but the true facts are related in Chapter XX of Sir Henry Bessemer's 'Autobiography', and are these:

The vital part of the invention, namely the swinging saloon, was not the cause of the failure, as it was not tried in a completed state; in fact, the controlling machinery was never even finished. A public trial was arranged for on 8th May, 1875, and on the occasion of a private rehearsal three weeks before, she crashed into the pier at Calais, breaking one of the paddle-wheels; the consequence being that all efforts had to be devoted to repairing the damage. The saloon was therefore clamped temporarily to the ship so that it could not move, and the arranged trial took place – on a perfectly calm day – with the result of a precisely similar accident, showing she was hopelessly unmanageable. The fact was that she would not steer properly, a circumstance quite unconnected with the saloon, except possibly in so far as its size and location may have hampered the designer. The saloon was then still in existence, as a lecture hall in Kent. A large amount of money might have been saved if trials had been made before the decorations were put in, which were most lavish.

In parenthesis, it may be of interest to recall at this point another extraordinary attempt to 'rule the waves' which was made in 1897, when a French steamer named the *Ernest Bazin* was built, which had the hull supported on six huge rollers.

In comparison with the *Bessemer*, the *Castalia* might almost be described as a success, her chief fault being her slowness. Her owners ordered another double-hulled vessel from Hawthorn, Leslie and Co., which they called the *Express*. She was taken over by the London, Chatham & Dover Railway Co., and re-christened *Calais–Douvres*. The hulls, 302ft long, were each complete, unlike those of the *Castalia*, which had the inner sides straight. The paddle-wheels were in the space in between.

She was placed in service in May, 1878, and proved very popular with travellers. Her speed was 13 knots. She attracted considerable traffic from the South Eastern, and at the half-yearly meeting in February, 1883, it was said that the *Calais–Douvres* had amply justified the large expense of her original purchase, the working cost and the novelty of the experiment. Faster boats, on the same route and between Folkestone and Boulogne, revealed that she was too slow for the service and she was withdrawn in 1887, when Mr Forbes admitted that her coal consumption was extravagant, her operation, generally, expensive, and that her peculiar construction often created difficulties in handling.

The next steamer was the *Invicta*, built in 1882, of normal design, by the Thames Iron Works. She was of 1,197 gross tonnage, with oscillating engines by Maudslay, Son and Field, giving 4,000 indicated h.p. On the measured mile she did $18\frac{1}{2}$ knots; and made the passage from Dover to Calais in 1 hour 12 minutes. In accordance with an Anglo-French diplomatic arrangement that the mails should be carried jointly, she was chartered in 1896 by the Northern Railway of France, manned by Frenchmen, and passed under the French flag.

In 1886 the *Victoria* was placed in service, built by the Fairfield Shipbuilding Co., of rather less tonnage, but 1,000 more horse-power. She was also loaned to the French. She was followed in the next year by the *Empress*, from the same builders, which was larger and faster, doing on her trials 20.4 knots, with compound diagonal engines of 5,000 i.h.p. She once did the passage in a fraction of a second under the hour.

In view of the Paris Exhibition of 1889, a magnificent boat was obtained from the Fairfield Company, also named the *Calais–Douvres*. Her gross tonnage was 1,212; i.h.p. 6,450; quickest passage, 57 minutes (22.63 knots).

In 1896 it was decided to withdraw the small boats, which were over 30 years old, from the night services and replace them with modern ones. For that purpose, three sister ships were obtained from Denny Brothers, of Dumbarton, the *Calais*, *Dover* and *Lord Warden*. They were single funnel boats of 1,002 gross tonnage, with triple expansion diagonal engines, speed 19.65 knots, and were extremely economical.

The story of the Dover–Calais service has now been brought down to the time of the fusion of the two railway companies, except that there remain to be noticed two fine boats put on by the Northern of France company in 1898, *Le Nord* and *Le Pas de Calais*, which were valuable acquisitions to the service, and ran the morning mails: the L.C.D.R. taking the midday and night services. It may be mentioned that *Le Nord* rammed a German submarine during the War, and *Le Pas de Calais* had sunk a French one accidentally in 1910.

We left the South Eastern in 1862, when they retired to the Folkestone–Boulogne route, and must take up the story from then. About that time, or perhaps just before, they obtained two boats, the *Victoria*, and *Albert Edward*, from Samuda Brothers, who built all the S.E.R. steamboats for thirty years. The engines were oscillating, by John Penn and Sons. They crossed under favourable conditions in an hour and a half. They were very handsome, with a pair of belltop funnels, a feature peculiar to the South Eastern boats for many years. The tonnage was 374. In 1864 there came a smaller boat, the *Alexandra*. In 1865 another, similar to the first two, was added, the *Napoleon III*.

In 1880 the company obtained the *Albert Victor* and *Louise Dagmar*, which were much larger than their predecessors. They had steel hulls with straight stems, of 782 gross tonnage, and Penn's oscillating engines, giving 2,800 i.h.p. Two years later a very similar boat was acquired, the *Mary Beatrice*. Samuda supplied a small cargo steamer in 1887, the *Achille Adam*. The last boats built by Samuda for the South Eastern Railway were two small ones in 1891, the *Edward William* and *Myleta*, which were used for coastal excursion trips.

In 1895 the *Duchess of York* was built by R. and H. Green, of London, of 996 tons gross. She only lasted nine years. In 1898 Laird Brothers supplied the *Princess of Wales*, of 1,009 tons, and with three-cylinder compound engines of 4,000 indicated h.p. She averaged on trials 19.1 knots. She was followed by a beautiful boat named the *Mabel Grace*, from the same builders, which was made as large as just to be able to enter Boulogne harbour safely. Her gross tonnage was 1,215; indicated h.p., 5,500. Steam was supplied by six boilers, at 120 lb per square inch. She was not put into service until after the fusion, and was the last paddle boat running between Folkestone and Boulogne.

The consolidation of the fleets which came about in consequence of the fusion of the two companies on 1st January, 1899, permitted a number of old boats to be laid aside, and only the more modern ones to be retained in service. Among these a new-comer was the *Maidstone*, a single-screw goods boat, which had been ordered from Denny Brothers by the L.C.D.R., and was delivered in 1899. Five boats with twin screws may be mentioned here, which were mostly used for cargo: the *Walmer* (1894), *Deal* (1896), *Canterbury* (1900), *Folkestone* (1903), and *Hythe* (1905). The *Walmer* and *Deal* had been bought from the Brighton Company. They were originally named *Trouville* and *Prince Arthur*.

The South Eastern boats continued after the fusion on the Folkestone–Boulogne service.

By the beginning of the twentieth century the Parsons turbine had showed itself to be a practical and economical method of propulsion. The results obtained from two boats, the *King Edward* and *Queen Alexandra*, on the Clyde aroused the interest of railway companies, and the South Eastern and Chatham Joint Managing Committee placed an order in 1902 with Denny Brothers for a turbine steamer named the *Queen*. On her trial trip on the Clyde she steamed 21.76 knots ahead and 13 knots astern. Starting and stopping trials were also carried out and, when steaming 19 knots, the *Queen* was brought to a dead stop in 1 minute 7 seconds from the time that orders were given from the bridge, while the distance travelled was less than two and a half times the length of the ship – namely 770ft. It was also observed that she gathered way from rest more quickly than paddle steamers. She was 323ft long by 43ft beam.

The results were so satisfactory that the *Onward* and *Invicta* followed in 1905, and the *Victoria* and *Empress* in 1907; all turbine-driven, and from the same builders. The following report, quoted by Sir Alexander Richardson in his book, *The Evolution of the Parsons Steam Turbine*, is of interest as to the cost of the wear and tear of the *Queen, Onward,* and *Invicta*:

The tonnage of the turbine steamer is 27 tons greater and the number of passengers carried 64 per cent higher than in the case of the steamer with compound diagonal engines, while the speed is 22 knots against 17 knots. The labour cost of making repairs in a season was, for the turbine £176, and for the main engines of the paddle steamers £273, including, in both cases, the cost of opening out the machinery for the Board of Trade surveys. These sums do not include the cost of material, in respect of which the result is equally favourable to the turbines. The only renewal in three years in the turbines was one set of glands, costing about £90, whereas, in paddle steamer, renewal of piston packing rings, brasses or bushes, or some such detail, has been required every quarter. It is true that the paddle steamers are older by four or five years, but the comparison of labour cost is made for a year, during which the turbine steamer made 520 trips against a paddle steamer which made 288 trips. Thus the turbine has clearly a most distinct advantage over ordinary engines in respect to wear and tear. In the same period the coal consumption was 24 per cent in favour of the turbine vessel.

In 1911 the *Riviera* and the *Engadine* were added to the S.E.C.R. fleet. They were rather larger than their predecessors, being 315ft long, with a beam of 41ft, a tonnage of 1,676, and having a speed of 23 knots. The *Biarritz* was launched in December, 1914, i.e. during the war, and was at once made use of by the Government. She was 348ft long, with a beam of 42ft. After the war she was reconditioned by Vickers and came to her original owners in December, 1921. The *Maid of Orleans* was launched in March, 1918, as a sister ship to the *Biarritz*. She, too, was used by the Government during the war. All the four vessels named above were the work of W. Denny and Brothers Limited.

There is no record of any passengers having been lost in accidents to steamers on the Dover or Folkestone routes since they belonged to the railway companies; which is a wonderful thing to be said, when one considers the thousands of journeys that must have been made under appalling weather conditions of storm or fog, across the crowded Channel.

The war service of the South Eastern & Chatham steamers has been dealt with in Chapter XXX.

Although the Flushing service has never been run by railway owned steamers, it is so intimately connected with the history of the railways that a short account of it must be given.

In 1874 Prince Hendrik of the Netherlands, the Dutch Government and the Dutch State Railways proposed to establish a steamer service to England in competition with the Belgian State service from Ostend. Forbes, of the L.C.D.R., no doubt through his Dutch connections, was able to get in ahead of Watkin, and join up with the new company that was formed, the (in English) Zeeland Steamship Co. The nearest port from Flushing would have been Ramsgate, a distance of about 95 miles. But the 'Continental Agreement' with the S.E.R. covered receipts from all places between Margate and Hastings. Forbes therefore induced the company to adopt Queenborough, which was served by the Sittingbourne & Sheerness Railway, a line already leased to the L.C.D.R. The service was inaugurated in July, 1875, at first from Sheerness, but the results were disappointing, and it was withdrawn the following November. It was re-opened in May, 1876, the boats running from Queenborough, where the pier had by then been completed. Shortly afterwards they obtained the mail contract for Holland. When the pier was burnt for the first time, in 1882, Dover was used until it was repaired. Again, in December, 1897, they had to go to Dover owing to floods damaging the Queenborough railway. By 1900, when the unlucky pier was burnt again, the fusion had come about, and the boats used Port Victoria for a time.

In 1911, owing to the competition of the Great Eastern Hook of Holland service, which had been accelerated, the night service was removed to Folkestone; the day boats still used Queenborough.

The service was discontinued during the war. Afterwards the Zeeland company only ran a day service, from Folkestone, but the S.E.C.R. arranged a night service to Holland via Gravesend, by utilising the Batavier company's steamers. The story may be finished by saying that at the end of 1926 the Zeeland company, having made arrangements with the London & North Eastern Railway company, transferred its English port to Harwich, thus terminating its connection of over fifty years with the L.C. & D.R., S.E.C.R., and S.R. companies. Its boats have always been among the finest of that class of steamer, and were all British built.

PART V

THE SOUTHERN RAILWAY

XXXIII

The Southern up to 1934

THE 'Railways Act, 1921' received the Royal Assent on 19th August of that year. It laid down that the railways of Great Britain were to be merged into four groups, each group containing certain 'constituent companies', these being the chief components, and a number of subsidiary companies which were to be absorbed, and were the smaller ones. The responsibility for working out the details was placed upon an 'Amalgamation Tribunal', consisting of Sir Henry Babington Smith, G.B.E., Lord Plender, G.B.E., and Mr G. J. Talbot, K.C. The secretary to the Tribunal was Sir Henry Allan Steward.

The Act spoke of five 'constituent companies' in the Southern Group, namely, (1) the London & South Western; (2) the London, Brighton & South Coast; (3) the South Eastern; (4) the London. Chatham & Dover; (5) the South Eastern & Chatham Railway Companies' Managing Committee. Strictly speaking, the latter should not have been included, as it was not a company, and possessed no stockholders (whose consent was supposed to be required).

The terms on which it was proposed to amalgamate were worked out by the companies themselves.

At a special general meeting of the proprietors of the London, Brighton & South Coast on 16th November, 1922, the scheme was accepted and, on the following day, those of the London & South Western followed suit. The South Eastern and the London, Chatham & Dover respective acceptances were on 13th December. At the meeting of the last-named there was considerable opposition. The hearings before the Amalgamation Tribunal occupied the whole of 11th and 12th December, but the proposals, with some minor exceptions, which stood over for consideration, were approved.

Before dealing with the amalgamation scheme, the Tribunal sanctioned two absorption schemes of subsidiary companies put forward by the South Western and Brighton companies. The former absorbed the Bridgwater; Isle of Wight; Isle of Wight Central; North Cornwall; Plymouth and Dartmoor; Plymouth, Devonport and South Western Junction, and Sidmouth railways. In the Brighton scheme there were only two small subsidiaries, the Hayling and the Brighton and Dyke companies. The Hayling was absorbed, but no agreement was reached with the latter, which was in the hands of a receiver. Of these undertakings, the Bridgwater was being worked by the S.D.J.R., the North Cornwall, Sidmouth and such parts of the Plymouth and Dartmoor as remained by the L.S.W.R., the Hayling and Dyke by the L.B.S.C.R., and the others were working their own lines.

After the amalgamation had been passed, the Greenwich, Mid Kent, and Victoria Station and Pimlico (all, of course, worked lines) came in. The last lines to be absorbed were the Lee-on-the-Solent and the Freshwater, Yarmouth and Newport. In the case of the Lee-on-the-Solent, the Southern contended that it was of no value. It was using stock hired from the L.S.W.R., receipts never exceeded £1,400 a year, and it was built on land leased from the War Office which could be recovered without any compensation. There were outstanding liabilities exceeding £14,000 which, as the company was insolvent, could not be paid, and the Southern objected to their being transferred. The Tribunal, however, decided on 16th May, 1923, that the liabilities must be taken along with the railway, but a case was stated for the Court of Appeal. It was dismissed there in July, 1923, and the Southern Railway then proposed to take it to the House of Lords, but did not do so. The Freshwater case came before the Tribunal on 20th June. The main point for consideration there was whether allowance could be made for possible future prosperity to be derived from the proposed Solent tunnel, but the Tribunal refused to allow it to be taken into consideration.

The Brighton & Dyke Company also went to the Court of Appeal. There again, it was a question of debts. Eventually all three schemes were passed by the Tribunal.

The new group commenced business on 1st January, 1923, with the following: capital issued, including nominal additions, £149,443,229; capital issued, excluding nominal additions, £145,488,788: capital expended; on railways, £131,672,135; on horses and railway vehicles, £102,054; on steamboats and marine workshops, £1,967,908; on canals, £77,700; on docks, harbours and wharves, £6,618,669; on hotels, £1,384,739; on electric power stations, £565,600; on land, property, etc., not forming part of the railway or stations, £5,387,164; on subscriptions to companies other than railway companies, £150,000; on other items, £284,530; total capital expended, £148, 210,499. The net receipts for 1922 had been £5,815,905, which included £5,455,236 from railway business, £256,418 from steamboats, £73,831 from docks, harbours and

Maunsell's 'Z' class 0-8-0T engine, No. 953, Brighton 1929. Latterly used for banking between Exeter St. Davids and Exeter Central. *[Locomotive Publishing Company*

Class LN 4-6-0, No. 850, *Lord Nelson*, built at Eastleigh in 1926. *[British Railways*

Above: Eastern Section 3-SUB electric unit, No. 1491, rebuilt from former S.E.C.R. steam stock.

Below: 3-SUB unit rebuilt from former L.B.S.C.R. steam stock on Victoria–Orpington service near what was then known as Orpington Junction. [*W. V. Orford*

'King Arthur' class 4-6-0 No. 772 (built by North British in 1925) with experimental smoke-deflectors.
[*Locomotive Publishing Company*

Class U 2-6-0 No. 799 rebuilt from a 'River' class 2-6-4T on Eastbourne express in 1930.
[*Locomotive Publishing Company*

Continental Boat Train at Newhaven; the train engine is a 'B4' 4-4-0 and the pilot Class H2 4-4-2 No. 2424 *Beachy Head*.

Two 4-LAV units leaving Brighton; originally built for semi-fast work on the Brighton line electrification in 1930.

[*H. C. Casserley*

wharves, and £32,452 from hotels, refreshment rooms and cars. The gross receipts from railway business for 1922 had been £25,481,042 and the expenditure thereon £20,025,806.

There were 2,178 miles 9 chains of first track and 4,175 miles 49 chains of total track of running line, and 1,205 miles 60 chains of siding. The number of locomotives was 2,281, of passenger-carrying vehicles 7,500, and of wagons 36,749. The steamboats were 41 in number, with a net registered tonnage of 15,454; the length of quay on the docks, wharves, etc., was 57,587ft; there were 11 hotels owned by the company. The coaching mileage was 38,759,550 and the freight mileage 6,359,418. The number of passenger journeys was 173, 954,186, of which 122,695,833 were third-class and 45,588,044 were at workmen's fares. Of season tickets the equivalent of 163,569 annual tickets were issued, of which 102,608 were third-class.

The first chairman was Brigadier-General Sir Hugh Drummond, and the vice-chairmen were Brigadier-General the Hon. Everard Baring and Mr Gerald W. E. Loder – afterwards Lord Wakehurst. In the new management Sir Herbert Walker, Mr Tempest and Sir William Forbes retained their positions by being appointed joint general managers. The last-named retired on 30th June, 1923. Mr Tempest, who received a knighthood in the Birthday Honours of 1923, was the joint general manager for the latter part of 1923 and retired at the end of the year. As from 1st January, 1923, Sir Herbert Walker became sole general manager.

Among those who did not join the new company were Lord Henry Nevill, deputy chairman of the L.B.S.C.R., Sir William Portal and Sir Robert Williams of the South Western – the latter being known as the Father of the Board. Sir Henry Cosmo Bonsor also retired. He had been the deputy-chairman of the South Eastern from 1895 to 1898, when he became its chairman, and was the chairman also of the Joint Managing Committee from its formation in 1899.

Sir Hugh Drummond died on 1st August, 1924. He was succeeded in the chairmanship by Brigadier-General the Hon. Everard Baring. Viscount Pirrie died on 7th June of the same year, and on 1st March, 1925, Sir Robert Turnbull passed away. The three vacancies thus created on the board were not filled. On 19th April, 1925, Sir David Salomons, the senior director as regards length of service, died. Sir George L. Courthope, Bart., M.P., was elected in his place

The three sections of the line were known as the Western, Central and Eastern divisions. The Central was the former Brighton, and the other two were the South Western and the S.E.C.R.

Many old officers of the constituent companies retired on, or in anticipation of, the new organisation coming into force. From the South Western there retired Mr G. F. West, the superintendent of the line since November, 1916, Mr R. W. Urie, the chief mechanical engineer since November, 1912; the retirements from the Brighton & South Coast included Mr O. G. C. Drury, the chief engineer since October, 1920, Mr L. B. Billinton, the locomotive superintendent since January, 1912, Mr Finlay Scott, the superintendent of the line since July, 1907, the solicitor, Mr E. A. Scanes, and Mr R. H. Houghton, the company's telegraph and electrical engineer.

Mr R. E. L. Maunsell, Mr G. Ellson, Mr A. D. Jones, Mr A. Raworth, Mr E. C. Cox, and Mr F. H. Willis went from the South Eastern to the Southern to fill respectively the positions of chief mechanical engineer, deputy chief engineer, locomotive running superintendent, electrical engineer for new works, chief operating superintendent and indoor commercial manager, whilst Messrs H. A. Sire and A. H. Panter went from the Brighton as, respectively, chief commercial manager and deputy assistant mechanical engineer for carriages and wagons. Among the London & South Western officers who joined the Southern there were Mr A. W. Szlumper, who became the chief engineer, Mr S. Warner, who received the title of assistant mechanical engineer for carriages and wagons, Mr G. S. Szlumper, who, as docks and marine manager, took over all the docks, steamers, etc., Mr H. Jones, who became the electrical engineer, Mr G. T. Hedge, the outdoor commercial manager, and Mr C. J. Francis, the stores superintendent.

An interesting feature that followed upon the grouping of the southern lines was that the wide stretch of lines outside London Bridge belonged to the same company. From London Bridge to Blue Anchor signal-box, 1½ miles, there were for the greater part of the way, twelve running lines, and for the remainder, eleven. At Blue Anchor the three tracks of the South London diverged and, a few chains further on, at Corbett's Lane, the Brighton section parted company with the South Eastern. All these lines were on brick arches above the street level. Similarly, approaching Clapham Junction from Waterloo and Victoria there was a stretch of twelve running lines. It is doubtful whether any other railway system in the world could furnish a parallel to these examples.*

In 1923 Parliamentary powers were obtained to acquire the Lynton & Barnstaple Railway, and for the transfer to the Southern and London, Midland & Scottish companies jointly of the Somerset

* In practice, these lines have remained largely as pre-1923. There is still, for example no traffic from former L.B.S.C.R. lines running into Waterloo, or vice versa.

& Dorset Railway, which had hitherto been leased. Both these proposals were outside the Railways Act – the Lynton & Barnstaple because it was not a standard gauge line, and the Somerset & Dorset because the Act did not cover jointly-owned railways.

In the 1923 session, the interests of the Southern Railway were considered to have been threatened by the proposals of the City & South London Railway to extend that line from its then terminus at Clapham Common to a junction with the proposed Wimbledon & Sutton Railway. This had been privately promoted, and was sanctioned in 1910. The new railway was to commence end-on with the East Putney and Wimbledon section of the South Western company and be a continuation of the bay lines on the north side of Wimbledon station, used by the trains of the Metropolitan District, and run to a proposed station alongside that of the Brighton company at Sutton. The District Company was to work the line. The only opposition came from the London, Brighton & South Coast, but that was ineffectual, and, as related, the line was sanctioned.

The Wimbledon & Sutton Railway, however, lay dormant until the City & South London proposals in 1923. The Southern company opposed that scheme on the broad ground that it was exceeding the limits of the facilities that tube railways were expected to provide. The Southern had no objection to an extension as far as Tooting and, if the Wimbledon & Sutton was considered to afford any justification for the City & South London going further, it – the Southern – would relieve the situation by taking over the Wimbledon & Sutton. As a result of conversations between the parties the City & South London was empowered to extend its line to Morden, but not to the proposed junction with the Wimbledon & Sutton, and the latter line was to be taken over by the Southern. It only remains to be added that powers for the latter acquisition were granted in 1924, and that the extension of the City & South London was opened on 13th September, 1926. The Wimbledon–Sutton line was not opened throughout until 5th January, 1930, and was electrically-operated from the start.

The service between Ludgate Hill and Wimbledon was suspended during the war. Owing to tram and omnibus competition, and the fact that it was mainly used by workmen travelling at reduced fares, the traffic did not pay, and the trains were not restored. No doubt this was an inconvenience so, as some appreciation for the concessions made by Parliament, the trains not only were restored on 27th August, 1923, but a new service between London Bridge and Wimbledon was inaugurated.

Second-class bookings were withdrawn from the trains on the

South Eastern section, except the Continental trains, from the end of September. On 7th October, the London–Paris services were co-ordinated to suit the grouping of the three systems.

In January, 1924, a commencement was made to remove the divisions that separated the Brighton station from the Chatham at Victoria, openings being made in the walls so that the public could go to and fro. The circulating area in the Chatham station was to be enlarged and towards that end and to allow for the openings to be made, No. 1 road – the nearest to the Brighton station – was shortened. The buffer-stops on Nos. 2, 3, 4 and 5 roads were put in alignment with those in No. 1. What was No. 6 road was taken out and the platform on the east side of No. 5 road widened and brought up to No. 7, which was converted from a siding into a platform line. Later, the platforms in both stations were renumbered, the most eastern in the Chatham station becoming No. 1, and the most western in the Brighton station No. 17.

Vast improvements at Dover Priory were outlined in an interview between Sir Herbert Walker and the Dover Corporation on 24th June. It was, he said, proposed to rebuild that station. The engine depot would be removed to near the Marine station; the Harbour station would be demolished; a new goods yards provided, and it was intended to improve the railway near Archcliffe Fort so as to give a double line thence to the Marine station. The whole work would cost half a million pounds. It may be remarked that in the demolition of the works near Archcliffe Fort a gun of the Napoleonic period was disclosed.

During the latter half of 1924 and the first half of 1925, there were serious complaints from the public as to congested compartments, the late running of trains, etc. The trouble possibly began from the revised train service introduced in the summer of 1924. Therein an effort was made to co-ordinate the facilities, of the South Western and Brighton sections in particular, and that led to some places, which had perhaps been more favoured than their importance deserved, getting less attention.

In self defence, the Southern Railway company put an advertisement in a prominent position in the principal daily papers of 22nd January, 1925, which set forth briefly what they had done during the war, and the difficulties with which they had had to contend since. It made a good impression, and the complaints soon afterwards died out. It was followed by the explanation of the chairman, at the annual meeting on 27th February, that one reason for the congestion was that hundreds of carriages had had to be withdrawn from service so that they could be converted for electric traction. The charges as to late running were refuted by the statement that during that month 113,709 trains had been run each weekday, of which 93 per cent had arrived on time or less than five minutes late; five per cent were over five, but less than ten minutes late, and only two per cent were over ten minutes late. The chairman further reported that the company, in 1923, carried 59 millions more passengers than in 1913, an increase of 26 per cent, and that the Continental passengers in 1924 numbered 1,850,000 as against 1,650,000 in 1923. There were 250,000 passengers entering the London stations of the company daily, of which 163,000 arrived between 7 and 10 a.m. As typical of what the company could do, he mentioned that a Rugby match at Twickenham brought 30,000 people, who had to be carried there during the rush hours on a Saturday.

The question of the strengthening of bridges still remained a serious one. At the annual meeting on 27th February, 1925, the chairman said that, in 1912, the South Eastern & Chatham Joint Managing Committee commenced to spend large sums of money on that work, and when the Southern Railway came into existence that company had to allocate £250,000 so as to strengthen the bridges on the Eastern Section in order to carry any type of engine used on the Southern Railway. He added that he hoped that the work would be finished by the end of 1926.

A year later – on 25th February, 1926 – General Baring again mentioned the subject, and on that occasion said:

Between Victoria and Folkestone and Dover there are three boat train routes. One, via Folkstone, is already open for the *King Arthur* class* of engine, the bridges thereon having been brought up to the requisite strength and standard. The second route, via Swanley and Maidstone, will be ready for these engines by next month – March, 1926 – and the third one, via Chatham, will be ready for the summer traffic of next year – 1927. On that section the capabilities of the line are governed by the strength of the bridges over the Medway. The bridges on the boat train route between Victoria and Newhaven are also receiving attention so as to enable '*King Arthurs*' to be used thereon, and by July next – 1926 – will be brought up to the necessary strength. This will also allow these engines being worked to Brighton and Eastbourne, as well as to Newhaven.

The same engines can traverse the routes from Waterloo to Exeter, Southampton, Bournemouth and Portsmouth, so that we shall shortly reach a very desirable uniformity of strength in bridges over the whole of the principal routes between London and the coast. I told you last year that we hoped to be able to run heavy modern engines, hauling big loads, throughout the system by the end of 1926, and I think we are well up to, if not in advance of, our programme.

* A new 4-6-0 class by Maunsell developed from Urie's last passenger class for the L.S.W.R. It weighed 81 tons against the 51 tons of a 'D1' or 'E1' 4-4-0, then working the Continental trains.

In the earlier pages of the present work there have been several references to the Channel Tunnel. In the years immediately following the cessation of hostilities the subject was revived. Sir Percy Tempest was the then chief engineer for that work, and in August, 1923, he published a memorandum on the subject and estimated the cost of the work at 29 millions sterling, saying that, based on the then traffic, the results should provide over 5 per cent on that sum. The boring machine which would be used would provide a heading 12-ft diameter at the rate of 120ft a day, or a mile in ten weeks. Two such machines, starting simultaneously from each side, should meet in $2\frac{1}{2}$ years. Allowing six months for the preliminary shafts, and eighteen months, after the headings had met, to complete the work, the tunnel should be opened in $4\frac{1}{2}$ years.

The subject was shelved, but, as will be related later, it was revived – and again put aside, not to be seriously revived until after nationalisation.

A light railway between Totton, Hythe and Fawley, on the west side of Southampton Water, was opened on 20th July, 1925. The South Western had obtained powers to construct it as far back as 1903, but had never done so. In 1921 the proposal was revived and an independent company was incorporated for the purpose, whose powers were transferred to the Southern Railway in 1923.

Another light railway, opened on the 27th July, 1925, was the North Devon & Cornwall Junction, between Torrington and Halwill. It was authorised in 1914 and was leased to the Southern Railway company. It occupied most of the road-bed of the 3-ft gauge Torrington–Marland mineral railway between Torrington and Dunsbear. The somewhat shaky wooden viaduct over the River Torridge at Torrington was replaced by an iron structure.

The undertaking of the East London Railway, mentioned in an earlier chapter, was transferred to the Southern Railway Company by Section 46 of the Southern Company's Act of 1925. The London Passenger Transport Board took over the former Metropolitan and Metropolitan District interests, under the London Passenger Transport Act 1933, amounting to $17\frac{1}{2}$ per cent each.*

At the Southern annual meeting on 26th February, 1926, the chairman said that 49 stations had either been entirely reconstructed or substantially improved since the beginning of the previous year, and operations were in hand for 40 others.

---

* During the Southern Railway's ownership, the line was worked by the 'Hammersmith & City' electric stock, followed (when the service became self-contained instead of working to Hammersmith) by the red trains of the former District Railway.

Mention must be made of the general strike of May, 1926. In the mining industry wages were the subject of long-period agreements. During the summer of 1925 there were numerous discussions between the Mining Association and the Miners' Federation without any agreement being reached. The Government then set up a court of inquiry which made certain recommendations, but none sufficiently helpful to remove the *impasse*, and eventually, on 31st July, the day the agreement expired, the Government persuaded the parties to agree to 'carry on'. In return, there was to be a subsidy to to meet the increased expenses of the coalowners, and an inquiry into the coal mining industry. The subsidy expired on 30th April, 1926, and the men's agreements came to an end concurrently. With a view, undoubtedly, to the coercion of the Government, either to continue the subsidy, or to force the Mining Association to give way, a general strike broke out on 4th May.

As a matter of historical interest, it must be recorded that in the cessation of railway labour the strike was most complete and the loyalty of the railwaymen to each other, and to the cause of the miners, was remarkable. But, regarded from the point of view of a stoppage of railway communication it was the very opposite – almost a complete failure. The services offered and, where possible to accept them, rendered, by volunteers and the success that came from their efforts, were a far greater surprise than the solidity of the railwaymen, and, although other reasons were given for the general strike being called off there can be no doubt that the men's leaders recognised that not only was public opinion strongly against them, and they were inflicting unintentional injuries on their fellow workers, but that, as far as the railways were concerned, the cause was lost. The general strike was withdrawn on 12th May, but it was not until Friday, the 14th, that the railway companies agreed to the men resuming work.

Meanwhile, electrification had been proceeding fast. The programme laid down by the Brighton company for its suburban area was proceeded with. On 1st April, 1925, the line from Balham, through Streatham Common, Selhurst, and East Croydon, to Coulsdon North, and that from Selhurst, through West Croydon and Wallington, to Sutton were opened on the overhead system. The length of track, including sidings, dealt with was 82 miles and the cost was £680,000. The units there employed were a bogie motor vehicle, without passenger compartments, between two leading and two trailing coaches. At each end of the five vehicles was a driving compartment.

Power was, as before, obtained from the London Electric Supply Corporation and fed in at New Cross Gate. Thence it was conveyed to a main distributing centre at Gloucester Road Junction, Croydon.

On 12th July, 1925, an enormous piece of work was inaugurated; in fact, there were two very big installations – one on the old South Western, and one on the former South Eastern & Chatham. The former work involved the conversion of 67 miles of track, including sidings, and the work cost between £800,000 and £900,000. The lines treated were: between Claygate and Guildford; Raynes Park and Dorking; Leatherhead and Effingham Junction.

Power was obtained from Durnsford Road power-house at 11,000 volts, three phase, 25 cycles, and conveyed to sub-stations at Oxshott, Clandon, Guildford, Epsom, Effingham Junction, Leatherhead and Dorking, by approximately 60 miles of cable.

The second important undertaking referred to above was the initial stage of the Eastern section scheme. It embraced the line between Victoria and Orpington; Holborn Viaduct, together with St Paul's, and Herne Hill; Loughborough Junction and Shortlands; Nunhead and Crystal Palace.

Power was obtained from the London Electric Supply Corporation, and fed into a main distribution station at Lewisham. Sub-stations for the initial installation were provided at Lewisham, Victoria, Holborn Viaduct, Loughborough Junction, Upper Sydenham, Shortlands, Chislehurst, Nunhead and Catford. For this service, the stations at Elephant, Brixton, Loughborough Junction and St Pauls required alteration, the platforms at Loughborough on the Nunhead line being removed. Nunhead station was rebuilt as a single island platform on the London side of the triple junction.

The next stage was to give, on 28th February, 1926, electrically-operated trains to and from Charing Cross and Cannon Street. That covered the line between those stations through London Bridge, New Cross and Hither Green, and the junction with the Victoria line north of Orpington; between Lewisham and Hayes; New Beckenham and Beckenham Junction; Elmers End and Addiscombe. The additional sub-stations for the further services were at Cannon Street, Grove Park and Elmers End.

In anticipation of the above services, and to provide them with better facilities, considerable alterations were made in the track and connections at, and between, Charing Cross and Cannon Street. One change made was that between Metropolitan Junction and Charing Cross the four up and down lines alternated instead of the two outer lines being for up traffic and the two inner for down.

A further stage in the programme for the conversion from steam operation to electric traction on the Eastern section, commenced in July, 1925, was opened on 19th July, 1926, and involved the North Kent and Dartford lines. These were: from North Kent East Junction, through Greenwich, Plumstead and Erith to Dartford; Lewisham, through Blackheath to Charlton; Blackheath, through Bexley Heath to Slades Green; and from Hither Green, through Sidcup to Dartford Junction. The new sub-stations were at Eltham, Bexley, Dartford, Shooters Hill, Barnehurst, Charlton, Plumstead and Belvedere. This opening was rather bedevilled by the General Strike; because of this a few electric services to Dartford ran from 10th May to 16th May, but steam working was resumed. Then Cannon Street station was closed from 3rd to 28th June, owing to trackwork alterations, and to ease the situation some electric services were again run during this period.

During the year 1927 the total number of passenger journeys by the electrical services was 166,294,231 and the receipts therefrom £3,737,946. The former figure, compared with 1924, was an increase of 4.63 per cent, and the latter figure one of 4.87 per cent.

On 9th August, 1926, the final decision to abandon the overhead equipment on the Brighton section was announced. Not only was it to be replaced by third-rail operation, but a further programme of electrification on the Central – or Brighton – section was also intimated. The lines to be dealt with were:

Streatham Junction–Mitcham Junction–Sutton–Epsom, to join the Raynes Park–Dorking.
Sutton–Epsom Downs.
Streatham Junction–Haydons Road–Wimbledon.
Herne Hill–Tulse Hill.
London Bridge–Brockley–Forest Hill–Norwood Junction.

In view of the substitution of third rail operation for overhead working on the line to Coulsdon North, it was found convenient to equip the two lines on the Eastern section that leave the Croydon–Earlswood line at Purley, viz the Purley–Caterham, and Purley–Tattenham Corner. The rolling stock was dealt with as follows: South London trains converted to third-rail without other alteration, the bogie locomotives demotored and converted to brake vans, the trailer coaches rebuilt and incorporated into three-coach D.C. sets, except for a number retained as trailers in two coach sets for strengthening peak-hour trains.

The result of that decision was that when the work was done all the lines in the London area, except the Wimbledon–Mitcham–

Croydon and the Tooting–Haydons Road, had electrical services running over them. The cost of the further work was estimated at another $3\frac{3}{4}$ millions. The train mileage on the lines affected by the order of August, 1926, was 2,038,556 for the steam and 2,377,973 for electric. These new services involved an electric train mileage of 7,636,000, providing 100 per cent more trains on the steam-worked sections and 50 per cent more on what was the overhead electric.

On 2nd July, 1926, new lines were brought into use and certain others abandoned, in the Ramsgate, Margate and Broadstairs district; the competitive situation here had resulted in awkward terminal stations at Margate on the S.E.R. and Ramsgate on the L.C.D.R., and a reversing stations at Ramsgate on the S.E.R. The only one of the four stations retained was Margate L.C.D.R., the other three being closed and a new line built from a point south of Broadstairs L.C.D.R. to St Lawrence on the S.E.R. lines, allowing through running between Chatham & Ashford via these resorts. An entirely new station was built at the back of Ramsgate, and also one at Dumpton Park.

Powers were obtained in 1926 to acquire the property of the Newhaven Harbour Commissioners.* Their rights were purchased for £383,000. It was also decided to take up the unissued capital of the East Kent Light Railway in view of the developments of the Kent coalfield. The chairman, at the annual meeting on 26th February, 1926, spoke very highly of the prospects there. Three independent collieries were at work and a new pit was being sunk.

The Folkestone–Flushing services were discontinued this year.

On 11th October the London and Home Counties Traffic Advisory Committee began an inquiry into the travelling facilities in south-east London. It reported at the end of February, 1927, and among the conclusions affecting the Southern Railway were the following:

Complaints of overcrowding during the rush hours were general, particular reference being made to the conditions prevailing at London Bridge station especially during the evening rush hours. The company recognised that more seating capacity is necessary during the rush hours and assured the Committee that it was making every effort to cope with the situation. It admitted that it was not satisfied with the present situation, and stated that the programme of services under electrified working will continue to be improved to the fullest possible extent.

> .   .   .   .   .

Although the existing facilities are inadequate the position has been greatly ameliorated by the action of the Southern Railway in electrifying its suburban

---

* There are two harbour branches at Newhaven; one from the Town station over the Town Bridge and down the west side of the harbour and along the mole; the other from the Harbour station sidings along the Bishopstone shore to near Seaford.

lines. The Committee is of opinion that when the electrification programme is complete, and more experience has been gained of its working, still better services will be provided. The Committee has been much impressed by the evidence given on behalf of the company in regard to the electrification of its suburban lines and the proposed works of improvement and extension shortly to be undertaken, and is satisfied that the company is making a notable effort to provide all the facilities which are reasonably necessary for the travelling public whom they have undertaken to serve. In carrying out its programme of electrification the company has certainly shown initiative and a regard for the public convenience.

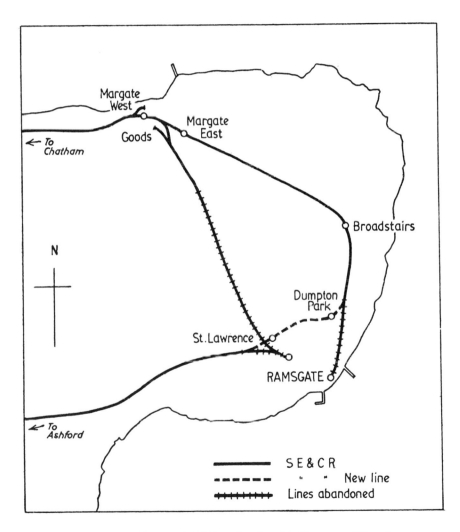

Map showing new lines, and old lines abandoned in Ramsgate, Margate and Broadstairs district 1926.

The bridge across the Thames at Charing Cross is not, all must admit, a thing of beauty but, seeing that from 90,000 to 100,000 passengers were being carried over it daily, it served a very useful purpose. Many proposals, some helpful, but most revealing a lack of knowledge, have been made as to what should be done to, or with, the bridge. The question of the strengthening, rebuilding or abolition of Waterloo bridge and the apparent need for other cross-river bridges led to the appointment of a Royal Commission to inquire into the subject, who reported on 30th November, 1926; recommending, as regards Charing Cross bridge, that a double-deck steel bridge be erected which should provide on its lower level for six railway tracks and have a roadway on the higher level. The roadway should begin outside Waterloo station, at platform level, and terminate near the south end of St Martin's Lane. A new station should be built at Charing Cross and the existing bridge and station be dispensed with. The Report added that the Southern Railway had acquiesced in these proposals, also in those as to a new Ludgate Bridge which would affect St Paul's, Ludgate Hill, and Holborn Viaduct stations.

In March, 1930, a bill was submitted to Parliament by the London County Council (and agreed to by the Southern Railway company) which was unsuccessful. It involved the abolition of Charing Cross station altogether, the trains stopping south of the Thames. Matters, however, rested as they were.

A noteworthy signalling development was that done at Blackfriars, Holborn, Charing Cross, Cannon Street and in the London Bridge area in connection with electrification, which included all-electric operation of points and signals throughout and the automatic working of signals. Many of the running signals were four-aspect day colour-light signals.

The Holborn Viaduct–Elephant and Castle section was controlled by seven manually-worked signal-boxes, which were reduced to two power-worked boxes. From Charing Cross to Cannon Street the route was also controlled by seven boxes, for which there were substituted two power-worked and one manual.

The work was carried out with great expedition, as is shown by the following extract from the *Railway Gazette* of 16th July, 1926:

It is well known that in new work the signal engineer is nearly always last. That is because he cannot complete – and, often, cannot commence – his work until the roads are in. It is true that at Cannon Street, where the station was closed on 3rd June, the new signal-box had been built, the all-electric frame of 143 levers was in position, many signals were erected and a good deal of the work on the switches had been done at New Cross while the track lay there;

but in the intervening three weeks motors had to be fixed at the points and coupled up, the remainder of the signals placed in position and their lights focussed and approved, track circuits laid, illuminated diagrams installed, and all coupled and tested. That the end was so successfully won is greatly to the credit of the Southern Railway signal department and to the Westinghouse Brake and Saxby Signal Company – the contractors for the supply of the material.

The light signals on the Charing Cross and Cannon Street lines were extended through London Bridge, Spa Road, and North Kent East Junction to Greenwich, and from North Kent East Junction through New Cross and to Blackheath, Hither Green and Ladywell. The new box at London Bridge contained a Westinghouse and Saxby frame of 311 levers, and that at North Kent East Junction one of 83 levers.

The London & South Western Railway was the first railway in this country to adopt the automatic telephone system for railway service. In 1921 a 50-line system was installed at Waterloo, and in 1923 a 300-line equipment – later extended to 500 lines – was provided at Southampton Docks, together with a 60-line system at Eastleigh.

These equipments proved so successful that in October, 1925, an automatic telephone system for the inner London area was installed by the Southern Railway. It had provision for approximately 1,000 lines, with facilities for extension.

The annual meeting for the year 1926 was held on 22nd February, 1927. The chairman, on that occasion, summarised what had been done, since the amalgamation of the four companies, towards standardisation. General Baring's remarks on that subject were as follows:

You will remember that the Southern Railway was formed only four years ago. At that time we were faced with an amalgamation of three entirely separate undertakings, each with its own organisation, its own methods of construction and operation, and its own ideals, and I may say, perhaps its own prejudices. Today, all that has been changed; the whole concern, under the control of the general manager, has been blended into one entity, and each department has been placed in the charge of the very best man we could find amongst the three constituent companies. . . .

At the time of the amalgamation we found that the various constituent companies had no less than 135 different types of locomotives; the elimination of these types must be a gradual process, but considerable progress has already been made and nine types of locomotives have been designed as most suitable to meet the requirements of the line. Most of the important parts of these types will be interchangeable, and all new engines are being built to these standard designs.

A similar state of affairs existed in regard to carriages and wagons, and a similar campaign of simplification has been embarked upon, with the result that today all our new coaching stock, for both steam and electric services, is built to standard designs and has been fully tested and proved.

Each of the separate constituent companies had its own idea as to the proper construction of the permanent way, each had its own particular type of rails and innumerable kinds of fastenings of every description; these are all in the process of being brought down to standard type.

The bridges on the different systems were constructed to carry only the weight of engines considered, at the time when they were built, suitable for the particular traffic that passed over them, and we have found that very few of the routes were able to take the heavier engines which in future will form our standard. This is all in process of being put right, and very large sums of money have already been spent in the reconstruction of bridges in order to render possible the interchangeability of our engines and so enable them to be worked to the best advantage.

The various manufacturing plants under the control of the former chief mechanical engineers of the three companies were all being used, of course, for the same purposes, so that at the time of amalgamation, and for some period thereafter, there was, and there could not help being, a great deal of overlapping. That is gradually being overcome, and it is our intention to concentrate on the manufacture of new wagons at Ashford, new locomotives at Eastleigh, and new carriages at Eastleigh and Lancing.

Reference was also made to the strengthening of bridges dealt with in his speech a year before, in which he mentioned that the capabilities of the line to Dover via Chatham were governed by the Medway bridge. West of the Medway the original London, Chatham & Dover line crossed the South Eastern Strood & Maidstone line by a three span bridge, which was renewed on 19th June, 1927. In Chapter XXV mention is made of a line between Strood and Chatham which was opened on 1st March, 1892. That necessitated a bridge over the Medway paralleling the earlier bridge provided for the L.C.D.R. Another change made at that point was to put in a connection between the two lines that allows trains on what was the L.C.D.R. to use the other (ex-S.E.R.) bridge over the Medway.

An improvement, put in hand in 1927, was the conversion of the double line between Kent House and Beckenham Junction into four lines of way, so abolishing a bottle neck that delayed the up boat trains and hindered the development of certain electrical services.

Through goods trains from the former Midland and Great Northern Railways run to Hither Green Sidings and back for exchange purposes. They used to journey from the Metropolitan Railway, through Ludgate Hill, and then via Metropolitan Junction, London Bridge, New Cross and St Johns to Hither Green. There were about forty of these trains daily, and their running had to be confined to the slack hours of the day and to night time. It was appreciated that the situation would be relieved and more electrical trains rendered possible if use could be made of the L.C.D.R. lines through Elephant and Castle and Nunhead, and that was made practicable by two curves at Lewisham, one from the Greenwich Park line to the St Johns–Blackheath line, and another from Lewisham Junction to the

Hither Green line. These new connections not only allowed the trains to be doubled in number, but also gave direct access between the West London Extension line and Hither Green and so allowed the 20 or 30 trains a day from the Great Western and L.M.S. that formerly exchanged elsewhere to do so at Hither Green. The engineering work involved was probably the largest undertaken in the company's London area for some time. These curves were opened as follows: for goods, 7th July, 1929; for passengers (steam) Lewisham Junction to Hither Green, 7th July, 1930; electric, 16th July, 1933; Nunhead–Lewisham Junction 30th September, 1935. The electric service comprised morning and evening trains down the Bexleyheath and the Dartford Loop lines; they ran virtually empty for some years, because of the longer time taken by these trains, although they called only at Peckham Rye and Elephant after leaving Lewisham. Some terminated at St Pauls. Some confusion was caused at first at St Pauls, for this was before the days of public address systems, and the cry of the porters 'Loop Line Train' meant the Catford Loop, and not the Dartford Loop as migrant passengers from the Cannon Street trains supposed.

A new station at Riddlesdown on the Croydon and Oxted line was opened on 5th June, 1927, whilst on 10th July two new stations were brought into use – West Weybridge, between Weybridge and Byfleet, and Sunnymeads between Wraysbury and Datchet.

On 30th June, 1927, Mr A. W. Szlumper retired. On the formation of the Southern Railway he had become its chief engineer, and on his retirement was succeeded by Mr G. Ellson, who had come from the South Eastern & Chatham, and was given the rank of deputy chief engineer.

On 1st July, 1927, Mr Gilbert Szlumper, the assistant general manager, relinquished the duties he also performed as docks and marine manager and Mr G. R. Newcombe, the deputy docks and marine manager, was confirmed in the higher appointment, Mr W. J. Thorrowgood, the Signal and Telegraph Superintendent, retired on 30th September. His successor was Lieut.-Colonel G. L. Hall, one of the inspecting officers of railways.

On 24th August, 1927, an express train from Cannon Street to Deal hauled by a 'River' class tank engine was derailed near Sevenoaks, and thirteen passengers lost their lives, while 48 others were more or less seriously injured. Sir John Pringle conducted a most searching inquiry into the circumstances. His report was thus commented upon by General Baring at the next annual general meeting, in the following words:

We have recently received the report of the Ministry of Transport Inspecting Officer, who inquired into the circumstances of the accident. He has come to the conclusion that the derailment was caused by the oscillation of the engine which may have been set up by certain defects of the road. I personally visited the spot within a few hours of the accident and spent a good deal of time there with the experts, including the inspecting officer, on the morning following the accident. All I can say is that if there were any defects in the road they were quite invisible to the naked eye, but measurements taken since proved that the superelevation of the rail on the curve was slightly out of adjustment in some places, that is, not exceeding an inch at any one point over a distance of 200 yards. It may have been sufficient to set up the oscillation, as the inspecting officer thinks possible.

It must be remembered that last year was the wettest season on record in the South of England for very many years. The whole area was water-logged, and it is not surprising that the task of the permanent way staff of maintaining the road in the highest possible state of efficiency has been a most anxious and trying one. You may remember that on that very morning, 24th August, there were three unusually heavy storms.

During the last few years we have spent heavy sums of money in adapting our permanent way and bridges to enable them to carry the heavier engines which are how being used on the fast expresses, and we propose to continue the practice in the future in order that, as far as possible, we may make our road bed and permanent way immune from the effects of such weather as we have lately experienced.

As a result of tests carried out after the accident and the knowledge of certain other derailments by the 'River' class, the entire series of locomotives was converted to 2-6-0 tender engines. In their rebuilt form they were put to work on Western section expresses with complete success. The further series of 'River' Class engines then being built emerged as tender engines: both series were classed 'U' (U1 for No. A890, the three cylinder 'River').

On 21st February, 1928, the fifth annual meeting was held, presided over by Brigadier-General Baring. He began by giving some interesting figures of the results of the year 1927, saying that it would be a waste of time to compare them with those of the previous year, owing to the disturbed conditions arising out of the general strike and the coal stoppage that lasted till nearly the end of the year.

Comparing 1927 with 1925, instead, the railway receipts were found to be nearly £500,000 down, due, almost entirely, to the falling-off in passenger revenue. They must remember that the Southern was a 75 per cent passenger line and therein differed from the other big lines of the country. The ancilliary businesses were up by £88,000 and so the loss, compared with 1925, was £412,000. Against that there had been a reduction of £378,000 in expenditure, notwithstanding that the coal supplied during the first three months of 1927 had, owing to the contracts having to be made during the stoppage, been at a very high price.

The chairman proceeded to say that the number of passengers carried in the electrified area was still going ahead by leaps and bounds. Further, notwithstanding the opening of the City and South London tube to Morden – which had taken four million passengers from the Southern during the year – there was an increase of $7\frac{1}{4}$ millions as compared with 1925. The expansion in the areas opened in 1925 and 1926 had brought in £257,000 more in 1927.

After referring to the Sevenoaks accident in words which were quoted at the end of the last chapter, he went on to say:

> Owing to the effect of the bad weather, the heavy storms and snow at Christmas and since, we have had to impose speed restrictions on many of our lines. Many people ask me why the trains are not running as punctually as they were, and this is the fact. The abnormally wet weather has caused more percolation of water into a number of tunnels than has been known in living memory. In Sevenoaks Tunnel drainage works have been executed and the tracks reballasted; 5,000 tons of stone has been used for this purpose. In Polhill Tunnel, work of a similar character is just finished; in Clayton Tunnel, on the main line to Brighton, it has been necessary to renew a large culvert right through the tunnel – the work has all been carried on at night, with the men up to their waists in water; while at Abbot's Cliff Tunnel, near Dover, and at Gillingham on our main line to the West of England, also at many other places, there are speed restrictions, due to repair and drainage works. Wherever a big repair work is going on we have to put on speed restrictions, and there are several speed restrictions on our main line which make it impossible for the train to be run actually on time. The effect of this is that, whereas up to Christmas our service over the whole system – that is to say, the working of our 180,000 trains a month – was running most punctually, being under two minutes late on the average – that is where we had got to – we were rather knocked out by that big storm at Christmas, and we have never really got into our stride since. Our engineers are pressing on with the work for all they are worth, and we hope to resume normal working within the next few months.

On 25th March, 1928, the electrical operation of trains was extended so as to cover the section between London Bridge–Norwood Junction–Caterham and from Purley to Tattenham Corner. Incidentally, that allowed for the specials for the 'Derby' to and from the last-named place to be electric.* The section between Sutton and Epsom Downs was opened on 17th June. On the same day a new direct current service was inaugurated between London Bridge and Coulsdon North and between Norwood Junction, Sutton and Epsom Downs, via Wallington. Circular services were also provided in two directions from and to London Bridge: (1) via Forest Hill, Norwood Junction, Thornton Heath and Tulse Hill; and (2) via Forest Hill, Crystal Palace Low Level and Tulse Hill.

The conversion of the Victoria–Crystal Palace line followed on 3rd March, 1929, and of the Victoria–Coulsdon North line on 22nd

---

* The Pullman trains remained steam-worked.

September. As part of the conversion programme of the overhead electric, South Bermondsey station had been moved 200 yards to be beyond the junction, and the middle line of the three was taken up between there and Old Kent Road. The reversible-working middle South London line was also converted between South Bermondsey and London Bridge to a down line, the third South London line becoming available for Croydon trains.

The decision was also taken to restrict trains from the Caterham and Tadworth branches to Charing Cross to the off-peak hours. The reason for this was that these trains ran in on the Croydon lines until just beyond the former Spa Road Station, then crossed to the South Eastern lines, thus fouling the down fast Croydon line: in the reverse direction they fouled the up fast South Eastern lines. Peak hour services were therefore terminated at London Bridge (Low Level).

Mr C. J. Lucas, who came to the Southern board from that of the London, Brighton & South Coast, died on the 17th April and was succeeded as a director by Sir G. Rowland Blades, afterwards Lord Ebbisham. Two other changes in the directorate were announced at the annual meeting on 6th March, 1929: Messrs E. W. Mellor and William Mewburn, both old South Eastern directors, retired and were replaced by Sir John Thornycroft and Sir Edward Hilton Young.

On the occasion just named, the chairman reported that, compared with 1927, the receipts had decreased by £584,000, but those from passengers actually increased by £11,400. He observed that the number of passenger journeys at full fares over the whole system decreased by 12,000,000, whereas the passenger journeys at cheap fares increased by 10,500,000. The number of journeys at workmen's fares showed an increase of 4,500,000, and season ticket journeys advanced by 5,000,000. There was, therefore, a total increase in passenger journeys, as compared with 1927, of nearly eight millions. Altogether 306,673,000 passengers were carried. In the electrified area passenger journeys increased by no less than six millions, as compared with 1927, and the receipts improved by £213,000.

On the subject of the decrease in the goods train receipts General Baring said that they had suffered, as all other railway companies had suffered, by the general depression in trade and the increasing diversion of traffic on to the road. They were doing everything that possibly could be done, within reason, by way of reduced rates, better services and improved methods, to recover some, at any rate, of this traffic, and he was glad to say that the efforts had been attended by a fair measure of success. They were making extended use of containers, not only for traffic within this country, but also in connection with Continental traffic. Prior to the institution of containers, a considerable proportion of the meat traffic between Southampton and London was lost, inasmuch as the road carriers were able to pick up the meat at the docks and carry it through to destination in refrigerator cars, often delivering it into cold storage in London five or six hours after it left Southampton. By the provision of insulated containers, which had been a great success, they had, however, to a large extent, recovered this traffic, and were now conveying the bulk of the meat for five of the six large importers of meat traffic using Southampton.

The subject of the reconstruction of Charing Cross bridge and of a new station on the south side of the river was mentioned, and the chairman said that on 1st August, 1928, a letter was sent to the Minister of Transport to the effect that the Board, though still opposed to the removal of Charing Cross station to the south side of the river, would be prepared to consider such a proposal and to submit to it the shareholders, provided they were assured that the Government was satisfied that the provision of an additional bridge over the Thames was a matter of national importance, and that the removal of the station to the south side of the river was vital to any such scheme.

It was stated that the bill permitting the company to own and operate road services had received the Royal Assent on 3rd August. One of the main objects was to secure co-operation with existing road-transport concerns which, it was believed, would produce a better result for all parties than could be attained by entering into active competition.*

It was also announced that the line from Wimbledon to West Croydon was to be converted to electric traction, and those from Twickenham to Windsor and from Dartford to Gravesend.

On 3rd March, 1929, electrically-operated trains began running between Holborn Viaduct and Wimbledon on weekdays. On Sundays the service was to Victoria. Of greater importance was the extension of electric trains from Victoria and London Bridge, via Mitcham Junction and Sutton, to Epsom Town. On that date there was opened a new station at what used to be Epsom Junction. It was renamed as Epsom, and the former 'Town' station on the Brighton system was closed. The new station had two island platforms which could serve trains to and from the Sutton direction in contrast

* Bus transport in Southern England was emerging from a period of some chaos. Well known companies in which the S.R. acquired an interest are listed on page 428.

to only to and from the Wimbledon direction, as was previously the case. At the west of the station facing connections into sidings on the down and up sides of the line allowed for trains that terminated at Epsom quickly to reverse and to be ready to return.

The 'Golden Arrow' all-Pullman service was inaugurated on 15th May. The journey from London to Paris was covered in 6 hours 35 minutes. There was no increase in the speed on land or sea, but the time saved was gained by improved Customs examination. In the reverse direction, forty minutes was saved over the old timing, by accelerations and elimination of Customs examination at Dover.

The work of reconstructing Wimbledon station was completed during the year. Among its outstanding features were the greater length of the platforms; better accommodation for the Metropolitan District trains; the closing entirely of the former L.B.S.C.R. station, and the modern style of architecture adopted.

The annual meeting to review the events of the year 1929 was held on 27th February, 1930. The chairman's speech opened with an expression of regret at the death, on 29th April, of Viscount Younger, who came to the Southern board from that of the London, Chatham & Dover. It was announced that Viscount Folkestone, afterwards the Earl of Radnor, had been elected a director in his stead. Sir George Murray and Sir Charles Owens intimated that they desired to retire; Major Eric Gore-Browne and the Hon. Oliver F. G. Stanley were elected directors to fill the vacancies.

To make amends for a loss of £156,000 in passenger receipts the goods traffic returns were up £145,000. There was, further, a reduction of £273,000 in railway working expenditure.

The announcement was made that the line between Purley and Brighton and thence to Worthing was to be converted to electric traction on the third-rail method. The cost was estimated at £2,700,000. The chairman added:

In order to cover the increased cost of the additional mileage, and provide for depreciation and for interest on the capital, it will be necessary to increase our traffic by 6 per cent compared with the existing traffic on the lines affected by the extension of the electrification. We are absolutely confident that this result will be achieved, and we shall be very much surprised if it is not achieved in the first year of working. When this scheme is completed, as I expect and hope it will be by the year 1932, the Southern Railway company will be the pioneers in this country of long-distance electric traction, as they were the pioneers in the matter of suburban electrification.

Actually an increase of over 19 per cent in the gross traffic receipts was achieved during the first year of operation.

The Wimbledon and Sutton Railway, which had been opened

from the former end as far as South Merton on the previous 7th July, was brought into use throughout on 5th January, 1930. It allowed for a through service of electrically-operated trains between Holborn Viaduct and West Croydon; actually an extension, from Wimbledon, of the services inaugurated on 3rd March, 1929.

During the week-end 10th–12th May the opening bridge over the inner harbour on the Folkestone Harbour branch was replaced by a new steel bridge. Electrical operation of trains to Windsor and to Gravesend and from Wimbledon to West Croydon commenced on 6th July, adding fifty miles to the length of railway on the Southern where electric traction was in force and costing £600,000. New stations were opened at Whitton between Twickenham and Feltham, and at North Sheen between Mortlake and Richmond. It may be added that Birkbeck station, between Crystal Palace and Beckenham Junction, had been brought into use on 2nd March, and Hinchley Wood, between Surbiton and Claygate, on 20th October.

On 31st December, 1930, Messrs Spiers and Pond Limited ceased to be the contractors for the catering on the Eastern and Western section of the Southern Railway, as the Frederick Hotels Limited, the refreshment contractors for the steamboats, secured the contract in open tender. The former firm became associated with the London, Chatham & Dover in the 'sixties, and retained the connection with that company until the formation of the Southern Railway. The connection with the London & South Western began in 1888, and with the South Eastern in 1899. They had no association with the London, Brighton & South Coast company. The lease of the South Western Hotel at Southampton remained undisturbed.

At the annual meeting on 26th February, 1931, the chairman mentioned that there had been an increase of 12,592,000 passengers carried by the electric trains' raising the receipts by £192,000. Outside the electrified area the number fell by 959,000 and the receipts therefrom by £544,000. Railway working expenditure was reduced by £246,000 to offset a decrease of £597,000 in the railway receipts.

On the subject of road transport, General Baring said:

We have slightly extended our activities during the past year, and at the present time have invested in these companies an amount of over £1,300,000. The dividends we have received, or shall receive, give us a return on the total amount invested of over 5½ per cent per annum. But, what is more, we have arrived at a means of co-ordination, which will inevitably lead to the benefit not only of the railway company, but the omnibus companies and the public. With each of these omnibus companies we have established a joint committee, whose duty it is to see that the interests of both parties are co-ordinated by the issue of combined tickets available by rail and omnibus, by the interavailability of tickets and by the correlation of fares and services wherever such is possible. We have now a financial interest in nearly all the large omnibus companies operating throughout our district outside the London Traffic Area.

In answer to a question, it was stated that the company had come to the end of their suburban electrification really, except for two or three small bits, viz., the line from Surbiton to Guildford via Woking, which included a part of the main line, and the Staines to Chertsey line. If these lines were electrified it meant rearranging the signalling, which was a very expensive thing.

Some magnificent new Pullman cars were introduced at the beginning of 1931 for the Ocean Liner Expresses between Waterloo and Southampton. On 5th July, 1931, the 'Bournemouth Belle', an all-Pullman express, began running. On the next day a very fine new station was opened at Hastings.

In reviewing the events of 1931, at the ninth annual general meeting, held on 29th February, 1932, Mr Loder, the deputy chairman, said:

Under the head of 'Railway Receipts', our passenger traffic shows a decline of £900,000. The number of passenger journeys, including journeys of season ticket holders, fell from 330 millions in 1930 to 324 millions in 1931, but this still leaves us with an increase of six million passenger journeys as compared with 1929. The decrease is less than two per cent, and can be accounted for by (1) the general trade depression, (2) intensive road competition, (3) the decline in Continental traffic as a result of the depreciation of the pound and the restrictions put upon foreign travel.

Traffic which had increased satisfactorily consisted of passengers to the Channel Islands, coal from the Kent collieries, and milk. Of the latter commodity, some was carried in large tanks specially built.

Sir Hilton Young and the Hon. Oliver Stanley resigned their seats on the Board on receiving appointments in the Government, and the Right Hon. L. S. Amery became a director. On 7th May, 1932, Brigadier-General the Hon. Everard Baring died. Mr G. W. E. Loder, afterwards Lord Wakehurst, was appointed to succeed him as chairman. Later, Mr Herbert William Corry was elected a director in the place of the Hon. Oliver Stanley.

In March the stations at Bricklayers' Arms (formerly S.E.R.) and Willow Walk (L.B.S.C.R.) were amalgamated, the former name being retained. On 30th April, the last surviving 'slip coach' made its last slip. This practice had been a feature of L.B.S.C.R. working for seventy-five years, but had been gradually discontinued for various reasons; principally the introduction of additional services. The L.C.D.R. had also used slip coaches a good deal: slips at

Beckenham, Swanley and Faversham continued for a year or two after grouping. On 16th May, a short line of 1¾ miles was opened, which had been authorised in 1929, and commenced in 1931, running from Middle Stoke Junction on the Hundred of Hoo, or Port Victoria, branch to a place in the Isle of Grain, called Allhallows-on-Sea, which was expected to develop into a seaside resort. Some justification for the optimistic view taken appeared from the fact that shortly after the original opening it was found necessary to provide a second line of rails on the branch on account of the volume of traffic. But the development was not successful in spite of through coaches being worked from London for a short time. In the same month a new and handsome station was opened at Dover, called the Priory station. There were originally four stations at Dover: Priory (L.C.D.R.), Town (S.E.R.,) Harbour (L.C.D.R.), and Pier; but with the conversion of the Pier into the Marine station, the Town and Harbour stations disappeared, leaving the Priory to serve the town, and the Marine mainly to act as a transfer station for Continental passengers.

On 17th July, 1932, the first section of the Brighton electrification scheme was opened, down to Three Bridges, 30 miles from Victoria. A central control station was erected at Three Bridges, and equipped to control the current at eighteen sub-stations. All sunlight is excluded from the building, and the artificial lighting of the interior is concealed, in order to avoid interference with the coloured lights on the switchboard. From the latter, every switch and circuit breaker on the Coulsdon to Brighton line of which there are about 350, can be opened or closed, its position being indicated by a coloured light. The board also contains instruments showing the amperage and voltage at each sub-station. The 30th December, 1932, saw the culmination of the great £2,700,000 electrification scheme linking Brighton & Worthing with London, when the Lord Mayor of the latter city travelled by special electric train to Worthing, and thence to Brighton. The work had taken two years to complete, and made the total electrified track of the Southern Railway up to 970 miles. New rolling stock built for the express services comprised 153 coaches, of which 38 were new Pullman cars.

Multiple unit trains were used for the fast services, consisting of six-coach units (of which twenty-three were provided), namely five corridor coaches and one Pullman. The Pullman cars were larger than any hitherto used in this country, being 68ft 8¾in long over the buffers, 12ft 5in from rail to top of roof and 8ft 11½in wide over the body. They were constructed all in steel, and designed with a view to maximum strength at vital points. Insulation against noise and change of temperature had special consideration. Fresh air was drawn from outside the car, and in cold weather passed through an electrical heating chamber.

Colour-light signalling was installed all the way from Coulsdon to Brighton. The signal-box at the latter place, which Sir Herbert Walker called 'a marvel of the engineering world' in his speech, replaced six others, and had 225 levers electrically interlocked.

It is worthy of notice that on 1st January, 1933, the 3 p.m. Exeter express was accelerated to run from Waterloo to Salisbury, 83.8 miles, in 87 minutes. This was the shortest time ever advertised between London and Salisbury, and the average speed – 57.8 miles an hour – the quickest run, start to stop, on the Southern Railway.

On 2nd January, 1933, the passenger trains between Brighton and Kemptown, and those on the Bishop's Waltham–Botley branch, were withdrawn.

The difficult economic conditions of the early 'thirties forced the closure of a number of branch lines. These are detailed in Appendix III, but there are one or two points worth mentioning. The Canterbury & Whitstable, which closed to passengers on 1st January, 1931, was the oldest constituent of the group, having been open for 96 years. The line up to the bleak terminus at the Dyke, near Brighton, was unusual in that it was closed for goods traffic in 1933, but passenger traffic continued until 1939. The Ruthern Bridge branch from Grogley Halt on the Bodmin & Wadebridge section was also of great antiquity, and has faced historians with a difficult problem in that it was officially closed on 30th December, 1933, six weeks after the passage of the last train.

The Lynton & Barnstaple Railway closing on 20th September, 1935, caused enthusiasts some distress, for this narrow-gauge line had many fanatical adherents, and it was hoped that resignalling and track-laying work only a few years earlier had guaranteed it a further span of life. The idea of preserving narrow-gauge lines as a tourist attraction had not at that time caught on, and no doubt if the branch had survived a few more years it would today be highly popular. As no use could be found for the rolling stock on the rest of the system, every item of equipment was sold by auction at the Pilton depot, the only locomotive to survive scrapping (*Lew*) being sent to South America. It should be noted, however, that three carriages were bought by local residents and two were left on short lengths of track near and at Snapper Halt; twenty-five years later one of these was purchased by the narrow-gauge Festiniog Railway in North Wales, and in a very modified condition will be running again after 64 years of existence during twenty-five of which it stood motionless and exposed to the elements.

There was only one other narrow-gauge passenger line in the Southern's area, that from Hythe to New Romney, and later extended to Dungeness. This was opened after the Grouping, and although its three main stations were also served by the Southern, the latter gave the R.H.D.R. no official cognisance, probably believing that its 15-in gauge made it a toy. However, the little line was successful in bringing about much holiday development along its piece of coast-line, and the Southern did later try to take advantage of some of the resulting traffic by opening stations at Dungeness-on-Sea and Greatstone-on-Sea parallel with the R.H.D.R. when the New Romney branch was re-routed.

At the annual general meeting held on 2nd March, 1933, the chairman again had to report fallings-off in traffic, but was able on the other hand to point to the very large saving on the expenditure account of £1,400,000; which was partly attributable to the changes in organisation rendered possible by the amalgamation. He was also able to comfort his hearers by saying that the Southern had not suffered from the trade depression so severely as the other three groups. He then made the following interesting reference to a new scheme of vast importance, namely a train ferry to the Continent.

Some four or five years ago we were approached by the French railway companies to consider the provision of a cross Channel train ferry service for goods traffic between a port on this side and a port in France. The proposal was under consideration when the question of the construction of the Channel Tunnel was again raised. This, you will remember, resulted in the setting up of a Committee by the Government in 1929 to consider the matter. After hearing the evidence of several witnesses . . . the Committee's Report resulted in the Government turning the proposal down.

He went on to say that as soon as the decision was known, the question of providing a train ferry was revived, with a result that it was decided to proceed with the matter, and the necessary powers were obtained from Parliament. The port chosen on the other side was Dunkerque; Dover, of course, being the one at this end.

The Committee referred to in the above speech had considered a number of schemes for cross-Channel communication, some of them of the 'wild-cat' order, but all more or less interesting. One was for a bridge – rejected owing to the interference with navigation. Others were for submerged tubes. There were two tunnel schemes, one, put forward by Mr William Collard, was to embrace a new electric line of 7-ft gauge all the way from London to Paris. The journey was to take $2\frac{3}{4}$ hours, and the cost to be nearly £200,000,000. This proposal the Committee did not approve of, but they reported in favour of the Channel Tunnel Company's scheme. However, the Govermnent would not have it.

On 1st July, 1933, a very fine new station was opened at Exeter, called 'Central', taking the place of the old Queen Street. Towards the end of the year, two new electrification schemes were decided upon, namely to Sevenoaks from Orpington and from Bickley Junction via Swanley, to be opened 1st January, 1935, adding another 23 miles to the electric tracks; and from Wivelsfield to Eastbourne and Hastings (60 miles, making a total of 1,146 of electrified track).

Speaking at the annual meeting in 1934, the chairman said that during the last six years gross receipts from Railway and Ancillary Businesses had fallen $16\frac{1}{2}$ per cent, and expenditure $17\frac{1}{2}$. To some extent the economies were the outcome of the expenditure on improvements and modernisation. As a striking example of what had been accomplished in that way, he mentioned the installation of modern signalling, which had enabled 200 boxes to be closed, and had saved £90,000 a year.

In 1933 there was an increase of £321,000 in passenger traffic, as compared with 1932; £150,000 of which was earned by the Brighton electric services; the number of passengers between London and Brighton alone increased by 520,000. During the Easter holidays of that year the number of people carried to Brighton alone was 150,000, which is more than the population of the town itself. The traffic was still improving, for, in January, 1934, 110,000 more passengers were conveyed in that area than in January, 1933.

On 23rd April, 1934, a completely vacuum-fitted goods train began running from London (Nine Elms) to Exmouth. It was timed to reach Salisbury (82 miles) in 106 minutes, at an average speed of $46\frac{1}{2}$ miles an hour. After a stop of 25 minutes at Salisbury, the 86 miles of heavily graded road thence to Exmouth Junction was covered in 140 minutes; the normal load being 49 wagons and a brake van.

On 1st May, the Sevenoaks electrification was completed as far as St Mary Cray, with most satisfactory results, the passenger traffic over that section increasing by over 73 per cent, as compared with May, 1933. The same day saw the inauguration of the Isle of Wight air service, mentioned in Chapter XIV.

The interim dividend announced on 26th July, 1934, contained the welcome announcement that for the half-year ending 30th June, the receipts from passengers had increased by £125,000 and, from goods, £155,000 as compared with the corresponding period of 1933.

Monday, 20th August, saw the introduction of a new regular air mail and passenger service all over the country, in which the railway companies co-operated. Those affecting the Southern Railway were from London to Southampton and Cowes. They were operated by Railway Air Services Limited.

A successful application was made to Parliament in 1934 for powers to build a loop line just over 4 miles long, from the main line near Folkestone to a junction with the same line 557 yards east of Abbots Cliff tunnel, to avoid the line being blocked by landslips.

During that year a modernised locomotive and carriage depot was built at Stewarts Lane, Battersea. Before the amalgamation, the Longhedge depot of the South Eastern & Chatham Railway was quite independent of the neighbouring depot of the Brighton and South Coast. Under the new scheme the latter was abandoned and the space rendered vacant was available for a lorry depot. Electrification having reduced the number of locomotives stabled at Battersea, it had been possible to accommodate them all in the modernised depot of the old South Eastern & Chatham Railway, which had been equipped with labour-saving appliances, including mechanical coaling and water softening plants. The former was capable of dealing with 300–400 tons of coal a day, and the latter with 10,000 gallons of water an hour.

Late in the year 1934 it was announced that two more short links were to be electrified, namely Lewisham–Nunhead, and Woodside–Sanderstead.

The seven years covered by this chapter were fairly fortunate ones with regard to accidents. A collision occurred at London Bridge on 9th July, 1928, whereby two passengers lost their lives. A light engine was waiting to go to the shed at New Cross, and, when a ground signal was put to 'clear' to allow it to draw forward to the next signal, the driver was misled by seeing a signal in advance of him at 'clear' and took it as his. The latter signal was, however, for an outgoing passenger train and the second signal was against the light engine. The driver overlooked the latter signal and allowed his engine to come into a broadside collision with the outgoing train.

The above accident arose from a most unusual cause, and was followed on 28th January, 1933, by a somewhat similar one, at Three Bridges, when, happily, there were no fatalities. The driver of an electric train took a clear signal as being his, whereas it was intended for a goods train in front of him, which he did not see in the dark.

On 25th May, 1933, an accident occurred at Raynes Park which caused the death of five out of the grand total of six passengers killed in train accidents on British railways during the year. A down passenger train became derailed owing to track repairing operations, which were considered to have been too extensive to have been undertaken in the time available; with the consequence that an up train came into collision with the derailed coaches.

The subject of Road Transport was touched upon in some remarks of General Baring's in 1931, which were quoted earlier in the chapter. Until 1928 the railway companies were not permitted to carry traffic entirely by road, but in that year Acts were passed, one of which was the Southern Railway (Road Transport) Act, 1928, which removed that disability.

For passenger traffic the Southern Railway has exercised these powers entirely by co-operation with the undermentioned existing road companies. In each case of working agreement was made between the existing operator and the company for the co-ordination of the two means of transport in a defined area. At the same time the company purchased from the existing owners not more than one half of the share capital of each of the road companies in question, the sum involved to the end of 1934 being £1,990,364.

The particular road companies collaborating with the Southern Railway were:

Aldershot and District Traction Co. Ltd.
East Kent Road Car Co. Ltd.
Hants and Dorset Motor Services Ltd.
Maidstone and District Motor Services Ltd.
Southdown Motor Services Ltd.
Devon General Omnibus and Touring Co. Ltd.
Southern National Omnibus Co. Ltd.
Southern Vectis Omnibus Co. Ltd.
Thames Valley Traction Co. Ltd.
Wilts and Dorset Motor Services Ltd.

They also acquired, jointly with the other three main line companies, the undertakings known as Carter Paterson & Co. Ltd., and Hays Wharf Cartage Co. Ltd., including Pickfords Ltd.

An event of importance to the railways' prestige was the opening on 4th October, of the Solent Flour Mills, the first large factory to be built upon the newly-reclaimed section of Southampton Docks (see Chapter XLI). In 1934 too, the Southern began seriously to apply the lessons of container traffic to the soft fruit trade, an important element of which was the strawberry harvest in Hampshire, particularly in the neighbourhood of Swanwick station, where special facilities were provided.

On 5th September, there was celebrated the Centenary of the

Bodmin & Wadebridge line. This was accorded full honours; the ex-B. & W. carriage which stood on the concourse at Waterloo was garlanded, and the special train on the branch had its engine (E216) decorated. There was an exhibition of relics at Wadebridge, including some of the original buildings and a portion of original track.

The last item that should be recorded in this chapter is the resignation of Lord Wakehurst at the end of 1934, who was succeeded in the chair by Mr Robert Holland-Martin, C.B.

XXXIV

The Southern from 1935 to 1939

WORK on the electrification of the Hastings line via Eastbourne was well advanced by the spring of 1935, and the formal opening of these services took place on 4th July (to the public 7th July). Besides the main line itself, the line from Haywards Heath to a junction with the East Grinstead line at Horsted Keynes was electrified, and also the Seaford branch. The main electrification was in fact carried through to Ore to enable train sheds to be set up there, and of the 16 sub-stations, eleven were controlled from Three Bridges and five from Ore. The fast trains comprised six-car sets, some with Pullmans, and the stopping services were worked at first by converted L.S.W.R. steam stock in two-car sets, and later by newly-built two car sets. An odd feature was that a steam pull-and-push set continued to operate some of the Seaford services as part of its duties on the non-electrified lines into Lewes. Careful thought was given to the provision of services, and usually the Horsted Keynes branch train ran through to Seaford, stopping behind the fast Eastbourne and Hastings train with which it connected at Haywards Heath. The fact that all Hastings trains ran into and out of Eastbourne (usually shedding half their coaches there) was not popular with passengers to points beyond Polegate.

The two small electrification projects mentioned in the last chapter were opened as follows: Nunhead–Lewisham 30th September, Woodside–Sanderstead on the same date. This latter line had been closed between Woodside and Selsdon Road from 15th March, 1915, and not all the halts and stations were reopened. The short length of line between Selsdon Road and South Croydon was not electrified, so Sanderstead was henceforth served by electric trains from Charing Cross and Cannon Street via Woodside, but by steam trains from Victoria and London Bridge via Croydon. Figures for passenger traffic on the electrified sections announced at the end of 1935 were very encouraging. On the Brighton line passengers had increased from 9,677,754 (to Brighton itself) in 1932 to 12,719,796 in 1934, and 1935 was likely to show a further million increase.

A large part of the Southern's resources were engaged in planning and effecting the electrification projects, and the ancilliary engineering works. The non-electrified services were not however forgotten, and the Bournemouth Belle Pullman train which had been introduced on 5th July, 1931, was made a daily working. New stock was built for the Bournemouth expresses, including an entirely new type of vestibule third with detachable tables, and apart from week-end reliefs all long distance trains were now formed from lavatory-fitted corridor stock throughout. At the same time the 14-coach sets of pre-grouping six-wheeled coaches which had for many years been used for Sunday excursion trains to the South Coast, picking up at suburban stations, finally disappeared. For shunting purposes the first three diesel-electric locomotives to run on the Southern were ordered from English Electric (assembled in S.R. workshops), and for freight trains a new series of bogie brake vans, similar to those converted from A.C. electric locomotives in 1934–5, was built.

The big event of the year, however, was the re-arrangement and resignalling of the lines into Waterloo station. The former arrangement had been (between Vauxhall and Wimbledon), south to north:

Down Local
Down Through
Up Through
Up Local

and between Waterloo and Vauxhall

Down Local
Down Through
Up Relief
Up Through
Up Local

Up electric trains approaching the south end of Waterloo had to cross the Up relief, Up Through, and Down Through, thus fouling all the main lines.

By putting in a fly-over near Durnsford Road, Wimbledon, and re-allocating the tracks, it was possible for electric trains to approach any platform without conflicting with other movements. The fly-over was finally opened on 17th May, 1936. The new arrangement was (south to north):

Down Local
Up Local
Down Through
Up Through
Up Relief

The three Windsor lines were unaffected.

At the same time a complete resignalling operation was carried out between Waterloo and Hampton Court Junction. The semaphore gantries, some of massive size, were replaced by four-aspect colour-light signals with route indicators. These indicators took the form of rows of white lights which could be presented at various angles to the vertical, thus giving the required information on the route to be followed. For instance, the Windsor line starter at Clapham Junction presented a row of lights corresponding approximately to the hour hand of a clock at 8, 9, and 10 o'clock respectively for the Kensington, Longhedge and Waterloo lines.

For some years the track requirements at the London termini had been changing, for electric working needed no engine release roads or coaling sidings, and a recognition of the changed circumstances occurred in August when the turntable at London Bridge (Central side) was removed. Thereafter such steam trains as were still worked were run in from New Cross Gate with the train engine at the rear already turned, and a pilot at the front. When a batch of evening trains worked by steam came close together, the first empty train would come in headed by the train engine for the second train, and the second by the third train's engine, and they would move to the head of their trains as soon as released by the departure of the previous one; finally the pilot from the last train to depart would clatter off to New Cross Gate running light. This gave the station an unhealthy empty look, and contrasted oddly with the times only three or four years earlier when a glorious jumble of locomotives from 'Remembrance' class down to 'E2' tanks could be found in the various engine roads of this station.

Another 'farewell appearance' occurred on 25th January, 1936, when for the last time the Southern played host to the crowned heads of Europe *en masse*. The occasion was the funeral of King George V, and on the 25th and the following day the Southern was called upon to supply seven special steamers, ten special trains, and thirteen special coaches on normal workings, to carry four Kings, one President, five Princes, and thirteen Delegations, to Victoria. Thanks to air travel and the decimation of the monarchy, the Southern would never again be asked to assume this role of the Royal Road to London, played so well by itself and its forebears since the 'forties, in quite so colourful a way. But it became realised that diplomatic greetings at London Airport are lacking in grandeur compared with the stately exit from Victoria Station in the shadow of Hudson's Furniture Repository, followed by the drive in a landau to the Palace, and there have been many occasions since when individual monarchs have trodden the red carpet on Platform 2 at Victoria.

Above: One of the three electric 'Brighton Belle', 5-BEL units, the only Pullman electric multiple unit in the world.

Below: Ex-L.B.S.C.R. 'J' class 4-6-2T No. 2325 with Maunsell cab.

'Lord Nelson' class 4-6-0 No. E859 on a Continental Express leaving Victoria (Eastern Section).

[*Locomotive Publishing Company*

Maunsell 'U1' class 2-6-0 No. A899 (Eastleigh 1931) at Waterloo. [*Locomotive Publishing Company*

Maunsell 'Schools' Class 4-4-0 No. E903, *Charterhouse*, at Charing Cross before the fitting of smoke deflectors.

6-PUL electric unit No. 3016 on a Hastings working near Lewes.   [*C. C. B. Herbert*

Above: A pre-opening publicity shot of two units of Portsmouth line express electric stock near Petersfield. The leading unit is 4-RES unit No. 3056 temporarily formed without restaurant accomodation.

[*British Railways*

Below: Interior of the buffet cars built for the Mid-Sussex electrification. [*British Railways*

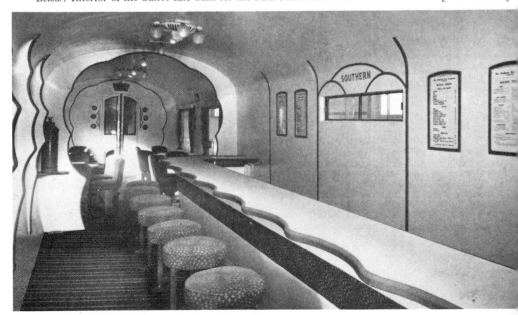

A development of great interest on the marine side was the construction east of the Lord Warden Hotel at Dover of a train ferry berth, from which on 13th October,* the Dover–Dunkerque train ferry service commenced to operate, the rolling stock being dark blue *Wagons-Lits* cars built specially by that company for through running between Victoria and Paris. The vessels are described in a later chapter: it is sufficient to say that the process of loose-coupling the sleeping cars, shunting them onto the various roads on the boat, and chaining them to the deck against rolling, was a lengthy and noisy process. In spite of this the new facility of going to bed at Victoria and waking up in Paris was much appreciated. Because of the great weight of these cars, the 'Night Ferry' as it was called, was double-headed through most of its steam-hauled days.

On the Newhaven service, a new type of Pullman buffet car, the *Myrtle*, rebuilt from a 1911 Brighton Pullman, was put into service.

Progress in one other sphere should be mentioned: the opening in 1936 at Waterloo Station of the first-ever public television theatre, taking a Baird transmission from Alexandra Palace during the Radio Show at Olympia.

An interesting innovation during 1937 was the laying of long-welded rails (180-ft lengths) in Merstham tunnel, for which operation special siding arrangements were made beside the avoiding line near Merstham station.

The further spread of electrification was the leading event of the year: this was the Mid-Sussex route to Portsmouth, and the services to Littlehampton and Bognor; also the cross line from Horsham to Three Bridges. Ancillary works included a new station at Horsham and a great many platform lengthenings, together with the replacement of the rolling bridge across the Arun at Ford by a fixed span. The plan called for 292 new vehicles, described in another chapter: some of the fast sets (4-car) incorporated a new kind of buffet with most modern decor, and unusual from the outside as there were almost no windows except at the ends. They contained a kitchen, bar and saloon, the latter being furnished with curved tables and revolving stools.

Apart from resignalling associated with the electrification projects there was a major scheme of signalling conversion at Victoria. In June a standard colour-light system took the place of the three-position electric semaphore system on the S.E.C.R. side, put in 1919, and of the more normal type put in on the Brighton side in 1911. It is of interest to note that at Victoria W. J. Sykes had in the

* Public service began on night of Oct 14/15th.

eighteen-eighties erected some pioneering electric shunt signals that lasted until the more modern system was inaugurated in 1919.

An odd event during this year was the appearance in April of a news item stating that 'The date of opening of Lullingstone station near Eynsford has been postponed'. In fact this new ferro-concrete station was never opened because the expected airport and housing development did not occur at that time. The war also changed the picture completely.

Matters were also coming to a head in regard to the Waterloo & City Tube railway, the equipment of which was all of 40 years old. Finally a 'Waterloo & City Protest Committee' waited upon the Chairman, who explained that as the line had opened so early (1898) it had not had the benefit of others' experience! He promised that the following steps would be taken:

(*a*) New rolling stock.
(*b*) Signalling system renewed.
(*c*) Rail joints welded.
(*d*) Collection of tickets at termini instead of on the train.

The new rolling stock did not however arrive until after the war had started.

It should be mentioned that in 1937 Sir Herbert Walker had retired from the position of General Manager, being succeeded by Mr G. S. Szlumper, Assistant General Manager since 1925. Next year, Mr H. Jones, the chief Electrical Engineer, retired, being succeeded by Mr A. Raworth.

The 1939 electrification project was also a major one: the extension on 2nd July, of electric working from existing termini to Maidstone East and West and Gillingham. Incidental work included abolishing restrictions on carriage width on the North Kent lines, the electrification of the last two steam-only platforms at Cannon Street, and a new station at Swanley Junction. The site of this station, built inside the Junction V with four separate platforms, was moved to the up side of the Junction and a new station of two island platforms built. At the old station it would have been impossible to divide electric trains in the platform, and it was foreseen that many trains would divide here, one half running down the main line to Gillingham, and the other either to Sevenoaks or via Otford Junction to Maidstone. Seventy-six two-car sets were built at Eastleigh for this new service.

XXXV

Southern Railway Locomotives

As the Chief Mechanical Engineer of the new Southern Railway, Mr R. E. L. Maunsell took over a very varied stud of locomotives, comprising examples of the work of fourteen different designers. Although he and his predecessor Wainwright on the Managing Committee had disposed of a great many of the former L.C.D.R. engines, he still had on his hands a number of 'B' and 'M' class tender engines, and 'A', 'R' and 'T' class tanks, none of which except for the 'R' class were very satisfactory for present traffic. On the senior line, the South Western, there was a large duplicate list, and on the Brighton line there was what amounted to a duplicate list, the older machines having been collected into the six hundreds. In other words, there was considerable scope for the axe.

This fell early on the remaining Chatham engines, and to make good the lack of locomotive power on this line Maunsell drafted from the South Western various 4-4-0 engines of the 'L11', 'D15', 'T9' and 'K10' classes. Then, to enable some of the earlier outside-cylinder 4-4-0 engines in the West of England to be withdrawn, the 'N' class 2-6-0 engines being built at Woolwich to smooth the run down of the Ordnance Factory were sent to work West of Exeter and proved very suitable for these fairly arduous lines.

The Brighton line suburban trains were somewhat short of suitable power: the 'I1' class 4-4-2T was underpowered, and the 'E1' class six-wheeled tanks were still handling some peak-hour commuters' trains. The decision was taken to rebuild the 'I1' class with larger boilers, and to bring in a number of Chatham 'R' class tanks to assist on the Central Section.

One of the classes for which no work could be found was the S.E.C.R. 'P' class. They were tried without success on the former Bodmin & Wadebridge line to Wenfordbridge, then being worked by old Beattie well-tanks (which in the event continued on this work until 1962), and no regular assignment was forthcoming. One 'P' was later employed on the construction of the Wimbledon–Sutton line, two were loaned at various times to the Kent & East Sussex Railway, another worked the declining Lee-on-the-Solent branch. The very clever rebuilding of the 'D' and 'E' class 4-4-0

engines on the former S.E.C.R. was discontinued, probably because Maunsell foresaw that when the Chatham line bridges were
strengthened there would be no call for a particularly light 4-4-0,
and the unrebuilt engines of this class continued in their existing
form, descending to lighter duties by the early 'thirties. Similarly,
the programme of rebuilding the 'C2' class 0-6-0 engines on the
Central section with larger high-pitched boilers was not continued;
although several appeared in their new form after the Grouping
the order had been placed earlier. This 'C2X' class however proved
a very useful investment, and examples were at work on empty
train duties in the London area as late as 1962.

The locomotive policy of Mr R. E. L. Maunsell was summed up
in an article by Mr J. Clayton, his Personal Assistant, in the *Southern
Railway Magazine*, of April, 1931, as follows:

(*a*) Engines to be well ahead of requirements in power, efficiency and ease
of maintenance, and suitable for operating on all sections of the railway.

(*b*) As few types as possible to cover the various services and these to be
looked upon as standard locomotives, in the construction of which standard
parts, such as boilers, cylinders, motion, tyres, axles, axle-boxes, fittings and
mountings to be interchangeable wherever possible.

(*c*) The Belpaire Boiler and Firebox with good grate area and heating surface.

(*d*) Long-lap piston valves requiring long-travel with its quicker valve events,
and in particular extended exhaust port openings so desirable to secure free
running.

(*e*) Simplicity of design with particular regard to get-at-ability, i.e. so constructed that parts can be got at readily.

(*f*) Foot-plate amenities – convenience and comfort of men studied and
provided for. For new designs full-size wooden models of the footplate embodying
the necessary fittings, handles, firing room, lookout, are provided for enginemen's
inspection, and suggestions invited in order to ensure the greatest convenience
in work, and thus avoid alterations after the engines are built.

(*g*) Lubrication of bearings, cylinders, etc., efficient but simple and accessible
without the necessity to leave the footplate for the purpose on the part of the
men when at work.

(*h*) Smoke-boxes and ashpans of good capacity and such as to ensure good
steaming properties.

These principles were embodied, as far as possible, in all designs
introduced after the amalgamation.

First, there were further engines of the S.E.C.R. 'N' class (2-6-0;
5ft 6in) A823–825, Ashford 1923; A826–875, Woolwich, 1924 and
1925. (Reference was made to these engines in Chapter XXX.) A
further set of fifteen 'N' class were turned out at Ashford in 1933:
Nos. 1400–1414.

In 1925 Armstrong, Whitworth and Co. completed nine 2-6-4
tanks of the 'K' (790) class, parts of which had been sent from
Ashford: Nos. A791–799. (One, No. A890, was built at Ashford

with three cylinders.) Another ten were built at Brighton in the following year: A800–809. All these were converted into tender engines called class 'U' (No. A890, 'U1'). While running as tanks, they bore the following names:

791	*River Adur*	798	*River Wey*	805	*River Camel*
792	,, *Arun*	799	,, *Test*	806	,, *Torridge*
793	,, *Ouse*	800	,, *Cray*	807	,, *Axe*
794	,, *Rother*	801	,, *Darenth*	808	,, *Char*
795	,, *Medway*	802	,, *Cuckmere*	809	,, *Dart*
796	,, *Stour*	803	,, *Itchen*	890	,, *Frome*
797	,, *Mole*	804	,, *Tamar*		

In 1926 fifteen additional 4-4-0 express engines on the lines of the 'L' class, called 'L1', were built by the North British Locomotive Co.: Nos. 753–759 and 782–789. They had smaller cylinders – 19½ by 26 – but higher pressure (180 lb as against 160) and had raised frames over driving wheels.

In 1928 further 2-6-0 engines appeared with 6-ft wheels, similar to the reconstructed tanks (class 'U'): Nos. A610–619 were built at Brighton, and A620–629 at Ashford; the latter works also supplying Nos. A630–639 in 1931. Many of these went to the Central and Western Sections.

The first of a new series of engines like the above, but with three cylinders 16 by 28in (Class 'U1') was completed at Eastleigh in 1931. There are twenty of them, Nos. A891–900 and 1901–1910, the latter batch coming out after the renumbering had commenced.

Five engines of the 'N1' class (2-6-0, with 5ft 6in wheels and three cylinders) were turned out at Ashford in 1931, Nos. A876–880.

In 1932 five 2-6-4 tanks, with 5ft 6in wheels and three cylinders 16½ by 28, called class 'W', were built at Eastleigh, Nos. 1911–1915, mainly for through goods between the S.R. and marshalling yards in North London.

There remain to be mentioned eight powerful 0-8-0 tanks with 4ft 8ins wheels and three 16in cylinders, known as class 'Z', which were built at Brighton in 1929, and numbered A950 to A957. These were later included in the Western section, retaining the same numbers (without the A).

No additions were made to the Brighton series of numbers, distinguished at first by the letter B, and in 1931 by being increased by 2000. The names bestowed on the Atlantics, and the large tanks when rebuilt, have been given in Chapter XXII.

Coming to the South Western series, these were at first differentiated by the letter E, which was dropped in 1931, the engines retaining their original numbers, except certain old ones, which, in accordance with South Western practice from the very first, having become duplicates, had had their numbers preceded by o. These had 3000 added.

In 1924 ten 4-6-0 engines, with 6-ft wheels, similar to Urie's 482 mixed traffic class ('H15'), were turned out at Eastleigh, Nos. 473–478 and 521–524. In the following year a series of ten 4-6-0 engines appeared, also from Eastleigh, Nos. 448–457, replacing some Drummond four-cylinder engines which were broken up and taking their distinctive inside-bearing tenders. They were the first of the celebrated 'King Arthur' class, the design being based on that of the large Urie engines, with certain improvements. The driving wheels were 6ft 7in, and cylinders 20½ by 28, as against 22 in the Uries. They had Maunsell superheaters, and 200 lb pressure. Weight in working order, with tender, 129 tons 1 cwt. The class, called 'N15', took in Urie's Nos. 736–755; thirty supplied by the North British Locomotive Company in 1925, Nos. 763–792; and fourteen built at Eastleigh in 1926 (the last in 1927), Nos. 793–806; seventy-four in all. The names were as follows:

448 *Sir Tristram*	753 *Melisande*	786 *Sir Lionel*
449 *Sir Torre*	754 *The Green Knight*	787 *Sir Menaduke*
450 *Sir Kay*	755 *The Red Knight*	788 *Sir Urre of the*
451 *Sir Lamorak*	763 *Sir Bors de Ganis*	*Mount*
452 *Sir Meliagrance*	764 *Sir Gawain*	789 *Sir Guy*
453 *King Arthur*	765 *Sir Gareth*	790 *Sir Villiars*
454 *Queen Guinevere*	766 *Sir Geraint*	791 *Sir Uwaine*
455 *Sir Launcelot*	767 *Sir Valence*	792 *Sir Hervis de Revel*
456 *Sir Galahad*	768 *Sir Balin*	793 *Sir Ontzlake*
457 *Sir Bedivere*	769 *Sir Balan*	794 *Sir Ector de Maris*
736 *Excalibur*	770 *Sir Prianius*	795 *Sir Dinadan*
737 *King Uther*	771 *Sir Sagramore*	796 *Sir Dodinas le*
738 *King Pellinore*	772 *Sir Percivale*	*Savage*
739 *King Leodegrance*	773 *Sir Lavaine*	797 *Sir Blamor de Ganis*
740 *Merlin*	774 *Sir Gaheris*	798 *Sir Hectimere*
741 *Joyous Gard*	775 *Sir Agravaine*	799 *Sir Ironside*
742 *Camelot*	776 *Sir Galagars*	800 *Sir Meleaus de Lile*
743 *Lyonnesse*	777 *Sir Lamiel*	801 *Sir Meliot de Logres*
744 *Maid of Astolat*	778 *Sir Pelleas*	802 *Sir Durnore*
745 *Tintagel*	779 *Sir Colgrevance*	803 *Sir Harry le Fise*
746 *Pendragon*	780 *Sir Persant*	*Lake*
747 *Elaine*	781 *Sir Aglovale*	804 *Sir Cador of Corn-*
748 *Vivien*	782 *Sir Brian*	*wall*
749 *Iseult*	783 *Sir Gillemere*	805 *Sir Constantine*
750 *Morgan le Fay*	784 *Sir Nerovens*	806 *Sir Galleron*
751 *Etarre*	785 *Sir Mador de la*	
752 *Linette*	*Porte*	

This perhaps the most famous 'Southern' class, was used at various times on every important express service, including the Continental

Express, Atlantic Coast Express and Southern Belle. On the Central and Eastern sections (except on the Continental Expresses) they ran with six-wheeled Maunsell tenders instead of the bogie Urie tenders.

Fifteen 4-6-0 goods engines with 5ft 7in wheels ('S15' class) were built at Eastleigh in 1927 (the last in 1928), Nos. 823–837.

In 1926 a magnificent new express engine appeared, named *Lord Nelson*, with 6ft 7in wheels and four cylinders 16½ by 26in. The inside cylinders, placed slightly in advance of the outside ones, drove the first coupled axle; the outside cylinders, the central one. The angles of the cranks were so arranged as to give eight separate impulses for each revolution of the wheels; which necessitated four separate (Walschaerts) valve gears. The weights of the revolving parts was kept extremely low by using 'Vibrac' high tensile steel; the boiler was 5ft 7in diameter, with the centre pitched at 9ft 2in above rail level, carried 220 lb of steam and was fitted with a Maunsell superheater. There were sixteen of them, not all precisely alike, all built at Eastleigh:

850	*Lord Nelson*	.	. 1926	858	*Lord Duncan*	.	. 1928
851	*Sir Francis Drake* .		. 1928	859	*Lord Hood* .	.	. 1929
852	*Sir Walter Raleigh*	.	,,	860	*Lord Hawke*	.	. ,,
853	*Sir Richard Grenville*	.	,,	861	*Lord Anson*	.	. ,,
854	*Howard of Effingham*	.	,,	862	*Lord Collingwood* .	.	,,
855	*Robert Blake*	.	. ,,	863	*Lord Rodney*	.	. ,,
856	*Lord St. Vincent*	.	. ,,	864	*Sir Martin Frobisher*	.	,,
857	*Lord Howe*	.	. ,,	865	*Sir John Hawkins*	.	. ,,

The following interesting description of the *Lord Nelson* appeared in an article by 'A Continental Engineer' in *The Engineer* of 25th May, 1928:

To cope in future with the hauling of trains weighing 500 tons, at an average speed of 55 m.p.h., the Southern Railway put on the rails in 1926 the first engine of the 'Nelson' class. It is a simple engine, but has four cylinders driving two different axles, coupled, the corresponding cranks being set at an angle of 135 deg. to obtain a more regular torque and an even draught, which makes the engine steam more freely. The steady pull that results from eight small blasts per revolution, instead of four stronger, increases, certainly, the regularity of the blast – the draught being irregular in the locomotive boiler, especially at low speed – and less unconsumed smoke and coal is drawn through the tubes.

The boiler of the 'Nelson' engines has a narrow fire-box of the Belpaire type. The tractive effort is 15 tons in round figures, more than that of many European 'Pacifics', but the grate area is only 33 sq. ft, the maximum possible with a narrow fire-box. This locomotive, weighing no more than 83 tons 10 cwt, and having a wheelbase of 29ft 6in, can develop the same tractive effort and the same power, and draw the same train as a 4-6-2 locomotive weighing at least 96 to 100 tons, and having a wheelbase of 36ft to 37ft. The adhesible weight is thus about 72 per cent of the total weight. This is a very interesting result, but the quality of the fuel must obviously be high.

To meet the necessity of obtaining a sufficiently large grate area, about the maximum possible when the wide fire-box is not resorted to, the water spaces are rather narrow but not exceptionally so. Boilers of this model ought to be washed out often, and with care. In this respect the wide fire-box would present advantages, but could not be applied to a 4-6-0 locomotive, and it would be the negation of the endeavours of the designer to avoid the use of a trailing uncoupled axle.

This fine locomotive presents some interesting details, and the balancing of reciprocating weights has been the object of a very complete investigation. Drawing a regular express from Waterloo to Salisbury, it has easily attained a speed of 83 m.p.h.

The *Lord Nelson* had a tractive effort which was greater than any other British engine and, for a time, put the Southern Railway in the position of having the most powerful locomotive in the country. Many experiments were tried with the engines in this class, which were seen on various duties on the Eastern and Western main lines in its 36 years of existence.

In 1930 a new departure was made by producing the most powerful 4-4-0 engine in Europe. It had 6ft 7in wheels, and three cylinders 16½ by 26in. Designated V, and popularly known as the 'Schools' class, all built at Eastleigh, as follows:

900 *Eton*	.	.	. 1930	915 *Brighton*	. . .	1933
901 *Winchester* .	.	.	,,	916 *Whitgift*	. . .	,,
902 *Wellington* .	.	.	,,	917 *Ardingly*	. . .	,,
903 *Charterhouse*.	.	.	,,	918 *Hurstpierpoint*	. .	,,
904 *Lancing*	.	.	,,	919 *Harrow*	. . .	,,
905 *Tonbridge* .	.	.	,,	920 *Rugby*	. . .	,,
906 *Sherborne* .	.	.	,,	921 *Shrewsbury*	. .	,,
907 *Dulwich* .	.	.	,,	922 *Marlborough*	. .	,,
908 *Westminster*	.	.	,,	923 *Uppingham* .	. .	,,
909 *St. Paul's* .	.	.	,,	924 *Haileybury* .	. .	1934
910 *Merchant Taylors* .	.	1932		925 *Cheltenham*	. .	,,
911 *Dover* .	.	.	,,	926 *Repton*	. . .	,,
912 *Downside* .	.	.	,,	927 *Clifton*	. . .	,,
913 *Christ's Hospital* .	.	,,		928 *Stowe*	. . .	,,
914 *Eastbourne* .	·	.	,,	929 *Malvern*	. . .	,,

(No. 923 was renamed *Bradfield*.)

In 1934 it was decided to have ten more:

930 *Radley*	933 *Kings-Canterbury*	937 *Epsom*
931 *Kings-Wimbledon*	934 *St. Lawrence*	938 *St. Olaves*
932 *Blundells*	935 *Sevenoaks*	939 *Leatherhead*
	936 *Cranleigh*	

The steam pressure was 220 lb per square inch. Round-topped fire-boxes had to be used instead of the usual Belpaire ones, from considerations of weight, which consisted of 21 tons on each coupled axle; only rendered possible by the beautiful balance and reduced 'hammer-blow' obtained by using three cylinders. Another advantage of the arrangement was that the latter being comparatively small, keep down the outside width, and enable the engines to work on sections of the line where the widest type could not run. The first examples appeared without smoke-deflectors, and went on to the South Eastern main line after first making a courtesy appearance at each school's home station.

In 1925 the Southern Railway added another engine to the Lynton & Barnstaple stud, from Manning Wardle: 188 *Lew*. The coupled wheels were 2ft 9in, and cylinders 10½ by 16.

In 1933 a tank of the 0-8-0 type, No. 949 *Hecate*, which had been built by Hawthorn, Leslie and Co. in 1904, was acquired from the Kent & East Sussex Railway. In exchange the latter took over No. 0335, one of the South Western saddle tanks built in 1876.

A Sentinel-Cammell light rail-car was supplied in 1933 for the branch line between Brighton and the Dyke. It has a 100 h.p. two-cylinder compound steam engine, with a vertical boiler working at 325 lb per square inch. The supplies of feed water and coal were both automatic, so the car could be controlled – from either end – by one man.

The car ran from the bodybuilders' in Birmingham to Brighton on 19th March, 1933, reaching 60 m.p.h. on occasion. The fuel consumption worked out at 4.88 lbs per mile. In service on the Dyke branch the car was subject to very heavy peak loadings, and possibly due to this it suffered a cracked frame. It was transferred on 2nd March, 1936, to the Westerham branch, where the workings required it to appear at Tonbridge shed daily for fuelling and so on. It worked in service back to Dunton Green (providing a connection between Tonbridge and the Sevenoaks electric service) and on this trip it was able again to show the mettlesome running apparent at its first main-line test run.

This was not the first Southern rail-car, as a Drewry four-wheel petrol-engined car had been purchased and worked between Ashford and New Romney and elsewhere, but was sold in 1934 to the Weston Clevedon & Portishead Light Railway.

In the early 'thirties some further inter-section transferences were made, including some L.B.S.C.R. 'D3' and 'E4' class to the Eastern Section for local passenger work; L.B.S.C.R. 'D1' and L.S.W.R. 'M7' class to the Eastern Section for motor-train duties; S.E.C.R. 'F1' 4-4-0's to the Western Section for the Reading lines. Meanwhile the 'D15' class 4-4-0 engines of L.S.W.R. origin had been sent to the Central Section for working the Worthing and Portsmouth lines, and after the Brighton electrification many of the 'King Arthurs' that had been allocated to the Central, and were running with six-wheeled tenders, began to handle the Folkestone trains out of Victoria and later Charing Cross and Cannon Street.

The Marsh 'Atlantics' had no job now on the line for which they were built. They were tried for a short while working fast trains on the Chatham line, but were returned to various duties on the Central section, along with the two 4-6-2T's. The 4-6-4T 'Remembrance' class engines had been converted to tender engines in 1934, with boiler pressure raised to 180 lbs, new cabs to enable them to run outside the Central Section, and 5,000-gallon Urie tenders. The vacuum brake was also substituted for the Westinghouse. Also in 1934, a 'Lord Nelson' class engine (No. 862) was fitted with a double-blast chimney of the KC design, similar to those used on the French 'Pacifics' of the Paris–Orleans line. The ex-S.E.C.R. 'L' class were now largely ousted from their former main line workings, and some of these appeared on the coast line west of Brighton.

In 1936 there appeared a further group of 'S15' mixed-traffic 4-6-0 engines (838–847), with eight-wheeled high-capacity tenders. These were frequently used at week-ends in the summer on excursion traffic out of Waterloo. After Mr Maunsell's retirement in 1937 his last class appeared, the 'Q' 0-6-0, a straightforward and powerful machine (Nos. 530–540) which proved to have a good turn of speed on passenger working. It had 19 by 26in cylinders and 5ft 1in wheels.

Mr O. V. Bulleid was the new C.M.E., and his first class appeared in 1941, called the 'Merchant Navy' Class (three 18 by 24in cylinders; 6ft 2in driving wheels). It made a complete break with tradition in a number of ways. It was the first 'Pacific' (4-6-2) tender engine on any of the S.R. lines: it was 'streamlined', having a casing like an upturned boat covering the entire engine; it had chain-driven radial valve gear to the designer's own pattern, patent disc wheels, and electric lighting at various points. Its numbering system too was new, and based on the Continental pattern. The first one was No. 21C1: that is 2 leading axles, 1 trailing axle, 3 (C) driving axles. The batch was numbered 21C1–21C20 and named after famous shipping lines.

Bulleid's second class, an extension of the 'Q' class 0-6-0, was also unconventional in that it had no running plate, the frame being completely exposed to facilitate maintenance. Nos. C1–C40 were built, and proved very powerful indeed for a six-wheeled engine. Dimensions of cylinders and wheels were the same as for the 'Q'. A light-weight version of the 'Merchant Navy' class also appeared, called the 'West Country' class being named after towns in the West. They were similar in almost all respects to the earlier class, except that the cylinders were $16\frac{3}{8}$ by 24, and the weight 86 tons against $92\frac{1}{2}$ tons: Nos. 21C101–21C145 were built under this class, and 21C146–21C170 under 'Battle of Britain' classification, being named after squadrons of fighters and personalities associated with the defence of Britain in 1940. The class was continued after nationalisation. Other additions to stock were 14 ex-U.S. army 0-6-0T engines (61–74: cylinders $16\frac{1}{2}$ by 24, wheels 4ft 6in) allocated to Southampton Docks, and two Co-Co electric locomotives(CC1–CC2) for mixed traffic work, built at Ashford in 1941 and 1945.

At the time of nationalisation, Bulleid had just built an even more revolutionary express engine, his 'Leader' class, with the boiler encased in an all-over body, resting on two six-wheel powered bogies: this was No. 36001 (the Continental notation having been abandoned) and ran a number of trials: Nos. 36002–3 were partially constructed, but after nationalisation the whole project was scrapped.

And so the twenty-four years of the Southern's locomotive history came to an end. Although power had increased very satisfactorily there was still, thanks to the six years of war during which there was no scrapping and very little building, a great multiplicity of classes, which owing to war-time expedients were dispersed somewhat haphazardly. For example, at this time no less than 24 classes of engine could be noted from time to time on the local service between Redhill and Tonbridge ('M7', 'R' 'H', 'D3' 0-4-4T; 'E4', 'E5' 0-6-2T; 'I3' 4-4-2T; 'C', 'C2X', 'Q', 'Q1' 0-6-0; 'B1', 'B4X', 'D', 'D1', 'E', 'E1', 'F1', 'L', 'L1' 4-4-0; 'N', 'U1', 'K' 2-6-0; 'S15' 4-6-0).

However, once peacetime requirements had been assessed, withdrawals began of some of the engines which, soldiering on regardless, had been giving visual evidence of their overhauls being overdue by leaking steam joints, dribbling tanks and frayed chimney rims.

It may be noted that after nationalisation a number of Bulleid 'Pacifics' were reconstructed with orthodox valve-gear and streamlining removed, for a further period of useful work, but once the process of electrification began again on the Eastern section the writing was on the wall for many fine express engines. The Southern classes had, however, earned an excellent reputation and are sure of an honoured place in railway history.

The names of the Bulleid Pacific locomotives built during the Southern regime were as follows:

Merchant Navy Class

21C1	*Channel Packet*	21C11	*General Steam Navigation*
21C2	*Union Castle*	21C12	*United States Line*
21C3	*Royal Mail*	21C13	*Blue Funnel*
21C4	*Cunard White Star*	21C14	*Nederlands Line*
21C5	*Canadian Pacific*	21C15	*Rotterdam Lloyd*
21C6	*Peninsular & Orient S.N. Co.*	21C16	*Elders & Fyffes*
21C7	*Aberdeen (Commonwealth)*	21C17	*Belgian Marine*
21C8	*Shaw Savill*	21C18	*British India Line*
21C9	*Orient Line*	21C19	*French Line C.G.T.*
21C10	*Blue Star*	21C20	*Bibby Line*

West Country Class

21C101	*Exeter*	21C125	*Whimple*
21C102	*Salisbury*	21C126	*Yes Tor*
21C103	*Plymouth*	21C127	*Taw Valley*
21C104	*Yeovil*	21C128	*Eddystone*
21C105	*Barnstaple*	21C129	*Lundy*
21C106	*Bude*	21C130	*Watersmeet*
21C107	*Wadebridge*	21C131	*Torrington*
21C108	*Padstow*	21C132	*Camelford*
21C109	*Lyme Regis*	21C133	*Chard*
21C110	*Sidmouth*	21C134	*Honiton*
21C111	*Tavistock*	21C135	*Shaftesbury*
21C112	*Launceston*	21C136	*Westward Ho!*
21C113	*Okehampton*	21C137	*Clovelly*
21C114	*Budleigh Salterton*	21C138	*Lynton*
21C115	*Exmouth*	21C139	*Boscastle*
21C116	*Bodmin*	21C140	*Crewkerne*
21C117	*Ilfracombe*	21C141	*Wilton*
21C118	*Axminster*	21C142	*Dorchester*
21C119	*Bideford*	21C143	*Coombe Martin*
21C120	*Seaton*	21C144	*Woolacombe*
21C121	*Dartmoor*	21C145	*Ottery St Mary*
21C122	*Exmoor*	21C146	*Braunton*
21C123	*Blackmore Vale*	21C147	*Callington*
21C124	*Tamar Valley*	21C148	*Crediton*

Battle of Britain Class

21C149	*Anti-Aircraft Command*	21C160	*75 Squadron*
21C150	*Royal Observer Corps*	21C161	*73 Squadron*
21C151	*Winston Churchill*	21C162	*17 Squadron*
21C152	*Lord Dowding*	21C163	*299 Squadron*
21C153	*Sir Keith Park*	21C164	*Fighter Command*
21C154	*Lord Beaverbrook*	21C165	*Hurricane*
21C155	*Fighter Pilot*	21C166	*Spitfire*
21C156	*Croydon*	21C167	*Tangmere*
21C157	*Biggin Hill*	21C168	*Kenley*
21C158	*Sir Frederick Pile*	21C169	*Hawkinge*
21C159	*Sir Archibald Sinclair*	21C170	*Manston*

Some brief notes on carriage stock developments may be of interest. At the time of the grouping amongst the Southern constituents only the L.S.W.R. had an appreciable number of corridor coaches. The S.E.C.R. had fitted out its Continental trains with new stock, but most trains to the coast were formed of permanently coupled sets of Wainwright coaches having internal corridors and lavatories only in the first and seconds. The L.B.S.C.R. had built a number of coaches known as 'Balloons' from their very high rounded roofs, but many of these were non-corridor, or vestibuled for working motor-trains, where the guard issued tickets. The L.S.W.R. carriage design therefore provided the springboard for new construction, and the first coaches built by the Southern were following on from L.S.W.R. tradition except for the bogies which were based upon Ashford practice.

Soon however, the Eastern section acquired a number of new trains (also made up in sets) somewhat similar to the 1921 Continental stock in many ways, but without the latter's inward-opening doors – there were doors only at each end – and peculiar blind brake-end with no corridor connection. They were constructed to narrow limits to enable them to work over the Tonbridge and Hastings line, where restrictions were in force; but they were also used on the London–Margate–Broadstairs–Ramsgate run where carriage stock had been very bad.

In 1929 there appeared an improved version of these carriages with the corridor windows carried up to roof level, giving a fine view of the passing countryside. These went onto the best trains on the Eastern and Western sections, the Central section being then due for electrification and receiving very little. These carriages were not built to Hastings line clearances.

Amongst the new stock were some first and third brake composites whose primary purpose was to cover off-peak workings on the Atlantic Coast Express, when only one vehicle might be required to run through to Torrington or Bude. In 1935 some vestibuled corridor thirds were built for the Bournemouth expresses, which were still in some cases being formed with non-corridor stock at peak times. There was now to be little change in design until the after-war years.

For the numerous push-pull services, two-coach sets adapted by the original companies were used: these included the rebuilt coach-portions of the S.E.C.R. and L.S.W.R. steam rail-cars. On the S.E.C.R. six-wheeled push-pull sets were used, (one being corridor-connected). As the original sets wore out, new ones were made up and equipped with control apparatus, using Wainwright bogie stock, and by 1946 some early Western section corridor coaches were being rebuilt for these duties.

For the carriage of passengers' luggage there were at the time of grouping a multiplicity of four and six-wheeled vans, many of considerable age, some being formed in with train sets. On the Western section train sets were operating comprising four bogie coaches and a six-wheeled van and on the Eastern section sets consisting of two L.C.D.R. bogies and a six-wheeled L.C.D.R. van. The former L.B.S.C.R. trains carried fewer vans, but there were some excellent bogie vans. As new carriage stock was built it incorporated enough luggage space to dispense with vans, but for certain trains such as Continental Expresses where the amount of luggage was considerable, Maunsell designed some long-wheelbase 'utility' vans, some of which were fitted with guards' compartments and periscopes; by 1935 it was becoming rare to see a van on long distance passenger trains except those which were particularly designated for mail traffic. Horse-boxes at the tail of a train were also a less common sight. A number of other specialised passenger-train vehicles disappeared during Southern days, such as 'aeroplane vans' (usually six-wheeled carriages with the insides stripped), 'bullion vans', and gas-cylinder vehicles; the last named were at one time seen attached to the rear of trains, but with the eclipse of gas-lighting they came to rest in various carriage sidings. The cylinders were usually mounted on a stripped carriage chassis; those on the Eastern and Western sections had most commonly a single cylinder, and on the Central two cylinders side by side.

Some rolling stock figures for the year 1934 may be of interest. The Southern Railway Company had in its steam-worked stock, 3,431 carriages of one uniform class, i.e. all first, all second, or all third-class, which altogether seated 19,866 first-class; 1,416 second-class – on the boat trains – and 161,529 third-class passengers. There were 1,466 composite carriages seating 23,891 first-class and 46,764 third; and 69 restaurant cars seating 1,071 first and 751 third-class passengers, the total seating capacity being therefore 255,288. Electrically-operated trains comprised 1,031 motor coaches and 964 trailers, seating 27,618 first class and 123,490 third; total 151,108 seats.

There were also 22 Post Office vans; 1,343 luggage, milk, fruit and brake vans, 178 carriage trucks, 443 horse-boxes, and 75 miscellaneous.

The Southern Railway also possessed, on 1st January, 1934,

24,469 open wagons, of which 24,375 were of a capacity of between 8 and 12 tons; 5,054 covered wagons, practically all of between 8 and 12 tons capacity; 851 mineral wagons; 2,770 wagons for special traffic, for cattle and for rails and timber, and 928 goods brakes. The total vehicles for freight traffic thus numbered 34,072. One further category consisted of 'Service Rolling Stock', of which there were 8 locomotives, 12 breakdown cranes, 55 travelling cranes, and 1,663 other vehicles.

XXXVI

Manufacturing and Repairing Works

THE Locomotive, Carriage and Wagon Works of the London & South Western Railway were originally at Nine Elms, but the Carriage and Wagon section was transferred to Eastleigh in 1890; the Locomotive Department following in 1909. On the formation of the Southern Railway in 1923, Eastleigh became the main centre for locomotive and carriage constructon.

The Locomotive Works were reorganised with a view to shortening the time required to repair the engines, and so reducing the number undergoing repair at one time; a result made possible by the introduction of a number of modern machine tools, a progressive repair system, and improved transport facilities between the various departments.

The construction of practically all new coaching stock for both steam and electric services was concentrated at Eastleigh, where the necessary accommodation has been provided by transferring carriage repairs to Lancing.

The closing of the Locomotive Works at Brighton, and the allocation of part of the Central Section engine stock to Eastleigh for repairs, materially increased the demand on the Locomotive Works, and well over a thousand engines were being maintained there in 1936, in addition to the construction of new ones.

The Works had, at this time, an area of 81 acres, 26 of which are covered by offices and shops. The Carriage Works were situated to the east of the London–Southampton line, and the Locomotive Works in the angle formed by the main and Portsmouth lines.

The Iron foundry consisted of two bays, each served by a 10-ton overhead travelling crane. There were also six 1-ton and one 2-ton hydraulic wall cranes. In one bay was a continuous casting plant, on which moulds were made on ten hydraulic moulding machines. The moulds were placed on a moving belt, and filled with molten metal as they passed the cupolas. They then passed on to the 'knockout grid', where they were broken open, and the castings placed on a conveyor for delivery to the 'fettling shop'. The three cupolas had an output of 90 tons per week.

The Boiler shop had two bays, each served by one 30 and one 20

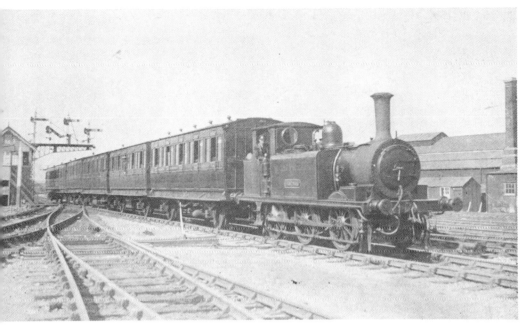

A1x class 0-6-0T No. W12 *Ventnor* on a train from Freshwater entering Newport I.O.W.; ex-L.C.D.R. 6-wheelers converted to 4-wheel. [*R. W. Kidner*

Folkestone train near Chelsfield with 'Schools' class 4-4-0 No. 902 *Wellington*, and early post-grouping Maunsell corridor stock. [*Locomotive Publishing Company*

Above: The last down train on the Lynton and Barnstable Railway near Blackmoor; 29th September, 1935. [*R. W. Kidner*

Below: The 'Night Ferry' double-headed, the train engine being an 'L' class 4-4-0 and the pilot a 'D1' class, No. 1487. The second vehicle is a special utility van built by the S.R. with centre "birdcage" roof lookout for working over the French railways. The first and third vehicles are French built specially for working on the S.R. [*Revd. D. Cawston*

Above: Two 'T14' 4-6-0 engines as rebuilt by Maunsell, in war-time livery at Nine Elms, 1944.

[*T. H. Watts*

Below: Maunsell's rebuild of the L.B.S.C.R. 4-4-2T 'I1' class, No. 2002 on Oxted line train **near** Hurst Green 1941.

[*S. Oborne*

Above : Post-war up 'Golden Arrow' at Sydenham with Bulleid 'Battle of Britain' class 4-6-2 No. 21C157.

[*E. R. Wethersett*

Below : 'N15X' class 4-6-0, rebuilt from L.B.S.C.R. 'L' class 4-6-4T, No. 2333 *Remembrance*, here seen in post war S.R. livery but with British Railways number.

[*A. N. Davenport*

ton overhead travelling crane. Here were shearing and punching machines; a 30-ft plate edge planing machine with hydraulic clamping rams; 12-ft vertical plate bending rolls; a 300-ton plate flanging press, served by a pyrometer-fitted oil furnace; a 75-ton hydraulic riveter, etc. Also two powerful air compressors and two hydraulic pumps.

In the Tube shop, boiler tubes were de-scaled, damaged ends cut off, the length restored by welding on a piece in a hydro-electric butt-welding machine; the output being about 1,500 per week.

The Machine shop was divided into five sections. One contained planers, slotters and shapers, and milling machines; the second, most of the centre lathes. The third was equipped with turret lathes for mass-production of bolts, screws, pins, etc. The fourth section contained a range of drilling machines. In an adjacent bay were the heavy machine tools: triple head frame slotter and driller, large planers and horizontal boring machines. There were also special turret lathes producing copper and steel stays from bar at the rate of 50 per hour each. All the larger machines had independent motor drives and, wherever necessary, air hoists were provided to serve them.

The Erecting shop occupied two bays, one for large engines and the other for small ones. The former was served by two 50-ton overhead travelling cranes, and the other by two 30-ton ones. The engines came in at one end, and were stripped. The parts removed were passed through a bath of boiling caustic soda large enough to take a complete engine bogie. The stripped frames were then moved up the shop while undergoing the various operations necessary. The reassembly of the engine then proceeded, and the complete engine was placed on a valve-setting machine. It was then taken to a weighbridge of 120 tons capacity, where the load on each wheel could be weighed separately.

There was a special equipment for bedding-on axle-boxes, a riveting fixture and rack for bogies, and a test bench for vacuum ejectors and lubricators. Part of a third bay was devoted to building new engines, and the end of the fourth bay to tender repairs.

Turning to the Carriage and Wagon Works, there was the Electrician's shop, which dealt with repairs to carriage train lighting, wiring, and dynamos; it also contained electro-plating baths for various fittings.

In the Saw-mill department the logs entered the Works under a 5-ton crane with 72-ft span, and were turned into planks by a horizontal band-saw, and cut to length by a cross-cut saw. The timber was then, after having been stored for a suitable time in the seasoning shed, passed to the saw-mill itself, where various machines cut it into the requisite shapes for coach parts; all the machines being so placed that it proceeded in correct sequence. Automatic machines sharpened the saws and cutters. All sawdust and chips were sucked away from each machine, and fed to the boiler furnaces.

In the Body shop, the coaches were erected in six stages:

Stage I. Underframe on wheels as received from Lancing Works, fitted with cell boxes, brake gear, steam heating pipes and dynamo gear.

Stage II. Bottom, sides and end bars, floor framing members and corrugated flooring bolted down.

Stage III. Sides, ends, corridor and compartment partitions erected and steel side panels screwed on. These details were previously assembled on jigs and put up as units.

Stage IV. Carlines, roof sticks and roofing boards fitted.

Stage V. Doors, etc., previously assembled on jigs, hung and fitted, and then passed for polishing.

Stage VI. Canvas covering to roof, cornices and water strips fitted. Corridor gangways placed in position.

Here the coach passed to (1) Finishing shop, (2) Polishing shop, and (3) Paint shop.

The original Brighton Works were opened in 1852. Some shops had been in existence prior to that date, but were not constructional works, being merely concerned with repairs to the locomotives, stationary engines, etc., and doing various metal work for other departments. The carriage and wagon work was at this time under a separate superintendent, and was carried out at various points; the shops at Brighton being separate from these works, and situated to the west of the main line. In August, 1852, Craven became 'Locomotive, Carriage and Wagon Superintendent', and in the next year we find him building carriages for the Crystal Palace line.

As the work grew, extensions had to be made to the Works, the addition of a new wheel shop being authorised in 1854 and further machinery in 1860. Constructional activities were of a very varied nature, and in 1855 they made two boilers for Maples' steamer *Paris*, signals for Norwood Junction, and cranes for Deptford wharf. A new carriage shop and further machinery came in 1861.

The physical difficulties involved in extending the shops were very great, and in 1866 serious consideration was given to the closing of the Works and concentration at New Cross, but the idea was not followed up. When Stroudley came on the scene in 1870, he asked for extensive additions to be made. In spite of the difficulties just mentioned, his plans were carried out. They involved the absorbing of a piece of ground at the north-east of the station on what was then known as the Prestonville Estate, together with serious encroachments on land originally intended for traffic purposes. The main objects of these changes were to concentrate the carriage and wagon workshops with the locomotive repairing shops on the east side of the railway and to remove the running sheds to a site previously occupied by the carriage shops, on the west side of the line; a new erecting shop was to be built, the existing one being turned into a smithy.

Further improvements followed in the form of an iron foundry; castings having previously been bought from outside; and a new carriage painting and cleaning shop; these being authorised in 1873 and 1878 respectively, the latter development costing some £25,000. Having thus acquired the means of turning out engines and carriages to his requirements, Stroudley embarked on his policy of standardisation of locomotives, carriages and wagons; attendant on which was the classification of engines and the formation of the coaches into 'set' trains for main line, branch or suburban work.

Owing to the development of the railway constructional work, it was decided in June, 1880, to build workshops for the steamers at Newhaven, and so relieve Brighton Works of this branch of work, but the control remained with Stroudley, who for some time past had been known as the Locomotive, Carriage, Wagon and Marine Superintendent. In 1881 a new coppersmith's shop was built; in the following year the works were called upon to repair the Langston–Brading goods ferry boat.

As time went on, the increase of work which was being handled led to the decision that it would be best to confine Brighton Works to locomotive construction and repairs, and to have separate carriage works elsewhere, and surveys were started in 1896 to obtain a suitable site, Lancing being eventually chosen, the works there remaining to be described later. In 1901 the transfer of nautical work to Newhaven was made complete, Billinton's concern with such matters thenceforward being merely in a consultative capacity.

The works at Ashford date from the early days of the South Eastern Railway, and are therefore over a hundred years old. The works were, on several occasions, extended and reorganised.

New wagon construction was concentrated at Ashford in S.R. days. Another noteworthy feature at Ashford was the chemical laboratory. It was opened by the South Eastern & Chatham in 1915, but in consequence of the amalgamation, an extension was necessary to deal with the extra work.

At Lancing Works, lying on a short spur from the coast line, the carriage shop was on the east side of the yard; the trimming and finishing shops being included therein. The paint and frame-building shops were on the west side. Both were 400ft long and 250ft wide, built in five bays running north and south, and with fifteen through roads. Between the two main buildings were smaller ones which served as a machine shop, a fitting shop, wheel, smiths', spring shops and the saw-mill; in an adjoining shop were built the goods brakes and 'utility vans'.

Further north was the timber yard and a natural drying shed. The works at Lancing asissted in the conversion of coaching stock so as to fit it for electrical operation. The conversion itself was made at Ashford and the coaches then went to Lancing for the electrical equipment to be put in the motor coaches, and for the vehicles, motor and trailer, to be painted.

All electrically-operated trains on the Southern Railway had the Westinghouse brake and a good deal of the equipment was put on at Lancing. *Per contra*, the steam-worked vehicles on the Central section had their Westinghouse brake equipment removed and replaced by the vacuum, as that brake, being used on the Western and Eastern sections, was made the standard for the Southern Railway.

A number of locomotive depots were modernised. These included Feltham, Exeter, Ashford, Hither Green* and Norwood.

The shed at the new Feltham depot was rectangular, and 475ft long by 125ft wide, and had a saw-tooth roof. There were six roads in the shed, each with an engine pit and each accommodating seven modern locomotives. The track was laid on ferro-concrete longitudinal bearings. Running the whole length of the shed there was a 50-ton electrically driven engine-hoist. The electrically-operated turntable of 65-ft diameter, with a working load of $162\frac{1}{2}$ tons, could be turned in 50 seconds.

There was also an electrically-operated coaling plant with a bunker capacity of 200 tons. The hoist would take a 20-ton wagon, and lift it 60 feet per minute, the wagon travelling along to the centre, and then being turned through an angle of 135 degrees. The average time for coaling an engine was $2\frac{1}{4}$ minutes. The stacking ground held 9,000 tons of coal. The ferro-concrete water tank had a capacity of 100,000 gallons.

The shed at Exeter – actually at Exmouth Junction – was a single-ended shed, with the entrance on the west side, 270ft long by 248ft 9in wide. It contained twelve shed roads and one lifting road –

* This in fact was an entirely new shed, opened in 1934, which was built on a former rubbish dump, within the triangle formed by the main line, the Dartford Loop, and the Lee-Hither Green (Goods) spur.

the last on the north side. Each road had a pit both inside and outside the shed, and a jib water column, at the outside pit, between each two roads.

There was a 65-ft electrically-operated turntable. Besides the mechanical coaling plants at Feltham and Exmouth Junction, there were three others – at Nine Elms, Ramsgate and Stewarts Lane.

The question of water softening was always a serious matter on the Southern Railway because of so much of it being in a chalky area. The plants were mostly of the vertical cylindrical type. One was supplied to the London, Brighton & South Coast company for London Bridge in 1914, and another in 1916 to Slades Green for the South Eastern & Chatham. The former had a capacity of 10,000 gallons per hour, and the latter 12,000 gallons per hour. The water supplied at Slades Green was from a deep well and had a hardness of about 30 deg. The water also had given great trouble from the fact of its causing a growth of algæ, so that two storage tanks into which it had been delivered were completely choked by a growth closely resembling seaweed. Besides depriving the water of its hardness, the algæ growth was completely stopped by the application of minute quantities of chlorine.

The plant supplied to Horsham in 1911 dealt with an entirely different problem. In that case the water was obtained from a deep well – clear and soft, showing not more than 1 to 2 degrees by the soap test. It was found, however, unsuitable for use in locomotive boilers from the fact that it caused the engines to prime and lose time. This action of the water was due to the presence in it of a large amount of bicarbonate of soda, but, by suitable chemical treatment, the latter was converted into other salts which have less tendency to cause priming.

Other plants were installed at Nine Elms, Hither Green, Stewarts Lane, Eastleigh, Dover and Ramsgate.

In 1913 the then London & South Western Railway, when Mr Jacomb-Hood was the chief engineer, established a concrete yard at Exmouth Junction. It occupied four acres of an area of about 28 acres, on the north side of the main line, which later also accommodated the Exeter engine shed, a marshalling yard, the Exeter division engineering shops, carriage and wagon repair shops, and a stores department for the West of England.

Among the items made at the depot were posts for fencing, gates, electrification cables, etc., pale fencing, mile and gradient-posts, standards for electric light, pedestals for point-rodding rollers, platform coping slabs, and brackets, etc. In addition to these general articles there may be noted, as then exceptional, the construction of buildings, in sections, for stores and of foot over-bridges. The weekly capacity of the works was about 4,500 articles.

The sleeper creosoting and chairing works, also a new switch and crossing shop, were at Redbridge, immediately west of Southampton. They not only had railway communication, but were on the river Test and, therefore, the untreated sleepers and timber could reach the depot by water. That facility, further, provided a tidal log-pond of an area of 5 acres, and a wharf frontage of 900ft. The area of land occupied was about 22 acres, and there were over 4 miles of sidings of standard gauge, and 500 yards of 2ft 6in gauge. The creosoting depot was founded in 1884 and was later modernised and enlarged. The switch and crossing shop and foundry was erected in 1924–25.

The standard rail latterly in use on the Southern Railway was adopted in 1923; being the 'British Standard Bull-head rail', 95 lb per yard; 60ft long. Fish-plates weighed 32 lb per pair; chairs 46 lb each. The keys were of teak.

The following are the approximate dates of introduction of various classes of rail:

L.S.W.R.	82 lb	30ft	Double headed			1882
,,	87 ,,	30,,	Bull	,,		1887
,,	90 ,,	30,,	,,	,,	(S.W.R. pattern)	1902
,,	90 ,,	45,,	,,	,,	,, ,,	1903
,,	90 ,,	45,,	,,	,,	(Brit. standard)	1908
S.E.R.	82 ,,	30,,	Double	,,		1882
,,	91¼ ,,	45,,	Bull	,,		1903
,,	95 ,,	45,,	,,	,,	(Brit. standard)	1908

Steel sleepers were used on a fairly extensive scale since the First World War, but they could not be used on the electrified lines, nor in track-circuited sections. In 1921 two thousand of the 'Sandberg' type were installed on the South Western section, and during 1929–34 about 125,000 of a similar, but heavier and improved type were laid down. They were made entirely of pressed steel, with loose sole-plates, and weighed 190 lb complete. Smaller numbers of two other types were also put in for purposes of trial.

Before the amalgamation the L.S.W.R. obtained nearly the whole of their track ballast from their quarry at Meldon, which is situated on the northern edge of Dartmoor at the foot of Yes Tor. The stone obtained here is an igneous rock, and the quarry is an interesting one from the geological aspect. In Southern days the demand for stone from the quarry steadily increased, and rendered necessary the installation of modern plant, both for winning the stone and afterwards crushing and screening it to the required size. After crushing, the stone was conveyed mechanically into long concrete bins from which it was discharged directly into 40-ton hopper wagons for dispatch to all parts of the system. These wagons were formed into trains of 10, carrying 400 tons of ballast, and in the busy season 8 or 9 trains left the quarry every week.

XXXVII

The Second World War

THE declaration of war meant that the Southern's further electrification plans must be shelved for the time being – in the event it was for 22 years – and that once again the constituent undertakings had to fashion their services into a weapon of war. From 1st September, the Minister of Transport took over the responsibility for all but a few minor railways. Crisis measures were adopted such as stationing armed guards on Charing Cross bridge and at other points, and removing Pullmans and restaurant cars from trains; the port of Dover was closed to civilian traffic; services were curtailed and rolling stock was re-rostered for evacuation trains. Order and counter-order followed each other rapidly: notice boards carried at the same time bills announcing 'Services Cut' and 'Services Restored', sometimes cancelling each other out. On 18th September, most of the electric Pullmans and restaurant cars were restored (to be finally removed for the duration more than two years later), and on 16th October, an emergency time-table of a permanent nature was announced. The service to Brighton for example was cut to 41 trains, while to the furthest-west point of Padstow there was only one train. A Railway Executive Committee was formed, with the Southern Railway General Manager, Mr G. S. Szlumper, as a member: he was shortly afterwards appointed Director of Transportation at the War Office, his place as General Manager being taken by Mr Eustace Missenden.

The 'phoney war' period proved more of a test of patience than of any new arrangements: however a tiresome event occurred on 28th November, when a large part of the track collapsed between the Abbotscliff and Shakespeare tunnels. The route was reopened on 7th January, 1940, but a further fall occurred nearby on 24th February. In June came the Dunkirk tragedy and the loss there or at Dieppe of five Southern vessels.

The change-over to a wartime footing proceeded steadily. The national requirements for locomotive power were somewhat differently distributed than in peacetime, and the Southern was in a position to dispose of power, since it was primarily a passenger line and most of its passengers were disappearing into the armed forces. The following loans of Southern locomotives were made to other companies:

Ten '*King Arthur*' class 4-6-0 engines to the L.N.E.R. for use in the North-East and Scotland (Nos. 739, 740, 742, 744, 747-51, 754).

Three 'Z' class 0-8-0T also to Scotland (Nos. 951, 955, 956). Five 'D1' 0-4-2T (Nos. 2699, 2229, 2284, 2358, 2605) and three 'H' class 0-4-4T (1177, 1184, 1259) to the L.M.S. for use in Perth, Ayr and other places.

One 'T9' 4-4-0 (304), whole of the 'S11' class 4-4-0, eight 'F1' 4-4-0 (1060, 1062, 1078, 1084, 1156, 1188, 1195, 1205); two 'B1' 4-4-0 (1441, 1446); four 'K10' 4-4-0 (137, 138, 388, 389) and six 'T1' 0-4-4-T (1-6) for the L.M.S. in the Midlands.

To the G.W.R. Nos. 2327-2332 (rebuilt '*Remembrance*' class) and Nos. 496-499 ('S15' 4-6-0).

'I2' Class 4-4-2T Nos. 2013-2019 went to the Longmoor Military Railway at Liss in Hampshire in April, 1942.

There were also some transferences within the system: the Marsh 'Atlantics' went first to Basingstoke and then in 1943 to the Charing Cross to Dover service (being shedded at Ashford) and back to their old Section in 1944. There were also innumerable cases of Southern engines working outside the system to facilitate inter-company transference of troop trains.

A certain amount of rebuilding work continued in spite of shortage of shed and coach staffs: by 1944 multiple blast chimneys were fitted to all the 'Lord Nelson' class, 19 'Schools', 6 'King Arthur', 1 'Q' class, and of course all 'Merchant Navy' and 'Q1' class engines.

The Headquarters of the Southern Railway were moved to Deepdene in Surrey, and a sad note was struck in 1940 by the announcement of the quashing of the Company's appeal against the decision of the Dorking Licensing Justices refusing to renew the licence for the Deepdene Hotel, which the Company had taken over. Sandbagged emergency centres were set up at 23 stations. A further precaution was the laying out of spare track assemblies complete with points and crossovers, for moving quickly to vital junctions which might be bombed.

Much thought was given to alternative routes to be used in case of lines being damaged by enemy action – and certainly the Southern was rich in alternative routes. One such embraced the Kent & East Sussex Light Railway, a private railway in which the Company was a debenture-holder; (the East Kent Light Railway from Shepherdswell to Wingham (Canterbury Road) and Richborough Port was in the same case). The K.E.S.R. had been laid with standard S.E.C.R. track from Headcorn to Rolvenden: but the portion from Rolvenden to Robertsbridge had been laid earlier by the

Rother Valley Railway, mostly in light flat-bottomed track. Sufficient relaying was carried out to enable standard freight trains to run by this route should the main lines be knocked out. Other strategic track alterations were made as follows:

An up loop connection from Winchester Junction to Worthy Down Platform (G.W.R.) open 5th May, 1943, to avoid fouling the S.R. main line.

The former L.C.D.R. bridge across the Medway at Rochester was restored for possible use, in November, 1942.

A curve at Dorking, completed on 3rd September, 1941, allowing trains to run from Horsham to Guildford and Reading.

A connection at Yeovil making it possible to run from Yeovil Junction to Pen Mill and Westbury without reversal at the Joint Station (13th October, 1943).

Reinstatement on 5th September, 1943, of the junction between the S.R. main line and the M.S.W.J.R. at Red Post Junction, Andover.

Reinstatement on 2nd March, 1941, of a Great War connection from Canterbury West to the East Line, the junction facing Chatham. This was mainly for strategic movements of rail-mounted heavy gun batteries.

A curve east of Crayford allowing through running between the Datrford loop and the North Kent and Bexleyheath lines without reversal at Dartford.

First class travel was abolished in the London area from 6th October, 1941: trains terminating within the London Transport area had 'firsts' demoted to 'third', and later of course suburban stock was built which was all third (or second as it became known after the war).

Two 'D1' class 0-4-2T engines were fitted experimentally with fire-fighting equipment. the necessary pumps being mounted behind the bunker: these were Nos. 2220 and 2252. Raids had begun in earnest, and on 15th October, 1940, a bomb struck the west chimney of Durnsford Road Power Station, putting half the station out of action. It was, however, back at full power 127 days later.

The Waterloo and City Line was closed from 25th October for a week, not as a result of enemy action, but to enable the new equipment to be installed. Each car had to be taken down singly by the lift beside the carriage sidings at Waterloo, and of course the replaced rolling stock had to be brought up (for many years this was stabled in a siding near Horley). The old stock had been of two forms: five 4-car sets supplied in 1897 by Jackson & Sharp of America, and single cars for midday use supplied by Dick Kerr of Preston. The former were replaced by entirely new stock finished in silver livery, capable of carrying 600 passengers in a five car train. The single cars remained for the time being to furnish the off-peak service.

A number of odd things happened during these years which

because of preoccupation with more important matters attracted little attention. One such was a proving run with a five-car Waterloo & City tube train to Brighton – enough in peace-time to make a train-spotter doubt his senses! Another was the escape and subsequent capture of a lion at Clapham Junction.

Progress was not entirely halted, and the arrival in service in 1941 of Mr Bulleid's first express engine, the 'Merchant Navy' Pacific, was the more interesting for its revolutionary character. This class and its successor the 'West Country' is described in Chapter XXXV: suffice it to say that the extra power of these machines was very soon put to the test in the country's interests. To provide more paths for military trains, it was decided to combine certain West of England trains: thus the 10.5 out of Waterloo became a sixteen-coach train with the following make-up: five for Ilfracombe, three for Plymouth, three for Padstow, one for Bude, two for Exeter, two for Salisbury. It was so long that it fouled the entrance to other platforms while standing. The record for these days seems to have been held by the 12.50 p.m. on 2nd December, 1941, when the new Pacific No. 21C10 hauled twenty coaches out of Waterloo. It should be emphasised that because of frequent reverse curves and consequent friction-resistance, the exit from Waterloo could find a 'King Arthur' labouring on ten coaches, and this feat of the Bulleid design deserves high praise.

In 1942 there appeared the first electric locomotive, No. CC1, carried on two 6-wheeled bogies and designed by Mr A. Raworth, the Chief Electrical Engineer: the first demonstration run took place on 17th January.

Damage from raids continued: in May, 1942, a fifteen-bomber attack smashed several electric trains in the sidings at Brighton and destroyed an arch of the London Road Viaduct. The 'D3' class engine 2365 got its own back later when, the boiler being punctured by a cannon-shell, the resulting rush of steam caused the hostile aircraft in question to crash.

Amongst jobs carried out in railway workshops was the conversion of six Western section dining-cars into hospital cars for the American Army, and the construction at Brighton of sixty-four L.M.S. type 2-8-0 locomotives in 1943-4.

The D-Day build up of course called for enormous efforts on the part of the railway. One quiet wayside station had fourteen miles of sidings laid to accommodate warlike material, and because any variety of weapon could be found there Micheldever was nicknamed 'Woolworths'. Men, vehicles and guns converged upon the south coast from all quarters: probably for the last time ever the Midland & South Western Junction route from Salisbury Plain to the south became a No. 1 priority with signal boxes manned around the clock: all day Maunsell's hard-working 'moguls' were working heavy 'foreign' trains forward by way of Kensington and Clapham Junction, *en route* to the transit camps behind the south coast embarkation points. With all station name boards removed to confuse enemy parachutists, the serviceman unversed in railway matters could be excused when, having started his journey at Cleethorpes and taken an unconscionable time creeping round the unfamiliar northern perimeter of London, on finally arriving at Eastleigh he enquired whether they were at Liverpool or Newcastle! It must also be recorded that when the day finally came, Southern boats, including the *Isle of Guernsey* and *Isle of Jersey* were off the Normandy beaches.

In 1944 the Chairman, Mr R. Holland-Martin retired, being succeeded by Col. Eric Gore-Brown. Meanwhile the flying bombs in Southern England were causing some havoc, diving on (amongst other railway centres) Bricklayers' Arms Junction, the skew bridge at Merstham, Camberwell overline bridge, Forest Hill station, West Croydon station, and Cow Lane Viaduct, Peckham. The last named was a very awkward event. The former L.C.D.R. viaduct collapsed on top of the former L.B.S.C.R. lines, causing a complete stoppage on both routes and requiring very heavy repair equipment to be mustered. Hungerford Bridge, which had earlier had an unexploded land-mine, was hit by a flying bomb: yet another near Southwark Park Road wrecked three running lines, which were left hanging like macaroni over a gaping hole in the brick embankment, in spite of which service was restored nine days later.

Nor must one forget that the shelling of Dover by long-range guns was continuous and five railwaymen died as a result of these attacks. The Southern helped to hit back, for long-range rail-mounted guns continuously on the move fired back a few rounds and then moved to a new firing point to confuse the enemy plotting units.

But soon the tide of war was receding: a useful morale-booster was the display at Waterloo Station of a Nazi flag hauled down from the St Malo headquarters of the Southern Railway by an ex-S.R. employee serving in the Royal Navy. Yet the end of actual hostilities saw little change in the Southern's role. The Channel ports were still restricted, and military traffic was heavy as the troops began to return, many of them being worked by special trains from Folkestone and Dover via Redhill to a large 'demob' centre at Guildford.

Now that it was all over, some facts and figures could be told. Many service chiefs and politicians paid tribute to the part played by the Southern's Southampton Docks. It was revealed that by the end of 1944 a million U.S. soldiers had sailed from this port, and between D-Day and VE-Day no less than 2,840,346 service and civilian personnel had been embarked or disembarked. Experience with the 'Ferry' vessels in transporting rolling stock to the battle zone had shown that if a specialised hinged bridge had existed much time would have been saved, and such a bridge was in existence at Southampton by the time the advancing tide of battle made it unnecessary.

It was also announced that one of the many 'specials' run during the war was a Pullman train leaving every night at 7.8 p.m. from the south end of Victoria station, adjacent to the B.O.A.C. building, for service personnel going to Hurn airport and the Poole flying boat base. Between 1941 and 1945 this train carried 30,000 passengers, many of them 'V.I.P.'s'.

XXXVIII

The End of the Southern

ONE of the first signs that peace – of a sort – really had returned was the gradual restoration of the Continental services. The *Isle of Jersey* went back on the Channel Islands service on 9th October, 1945, the old *Hantonia* having been restored some months earlier. The *Worthing* and *Isle of Guernsey* went onto the Dieppe route the same day. A special dispensation of the Ministry allowed a restaurant car to be restored to these services in view of the long sea passage.

On 22nd October the Ostend–Folkestone and London–Brussels services were restored, the latter running thrice weekly. The opening train was very fittingly hauled by the 'Pacific' locomotive No. 21C17 *Belgian Marine*. The 'Golden Arrow' train was restored on 15th April, 1946, with *Invicta* and the following day the Jersey–St Malo service was restored with the *Autocarrier*, a service from Jersey to Granville having been running since 15th January previously.

At this time Mr A. Raworth, the Chief Electrical Engineer, retired being succeeded by Mr C. M. Cock, an Australian. Due probably to staff shortages and general war exhaustion there were a great many minor accidents at about this time. For instance, on 21st August, 1944 two 'H' class tanks running light collided with a 'Schools' class on a train leaving Cannon Street and were both derailed, resulting in a spectacular scene but little real damage.

On 10th November, 1945, a West of England train ran into the rear of a Southampton train at Woking. Fortunately the front train was in motion, and although 30 people were injured, none were killed. On 19th March, 1946, at Mottingham an electric train ran into a stationary steam engine and the motorman was killed.

Now that demobilisation was proceeding apace, congestion on the London suburban lines was becoming serious. For the full services were not yet restored, but the passengers offering were rapidly resuming pre-war proportions. A Question in Parliament was asked in March, 1946, about the Dartford Loop Line, requesting the restoration of the Blackfriars service, but the Minister replied that this service could not be restored until the signal-box at Blackfriars, demolished by enemy action, could be rebuilt.

The position was, however, being improved by the construction of

35 new 4-car train sets and 116 trailers of a new type, seating 6-a-side, 420 per set, which were unusual in that the body sides were brought up to the central roof level. The trains had flat front ends with the word 'Southern' in large letters above the route indicator. New welding techniques played a large part in their construction. The odd trailer coaches were to be used to bring as many as possible of the old three-car suburban sets up to four cars. The former two-car trailer sets were being discarded, and for the present time a mixture of three-car and four-car sets was being operated, to the confusion of passengers.

The work of returning Pullman, pantry and restaurant cars back to the electric sets began in the Spring of 1946: one set (3030) had been running as a five-car set *with* a pantry car and had to be strengthened by adding a trailer. At the same time a number of 'West Country' class 4-6-2 engines were transferred to the Eastern Section, and went on the 'Golden Arrow' when it was reintroduced on 15th April, 1946.

Some six-coach steam sets for the Bournemouth line were built with wrap-over sides as in the new electric suburban stock: an innovation was the use of one 30-in brake cylinder in place of two 22in.

Early in 1947 a hundred locomotives were converted for oil-burning at Eastleigh and Ashford: the Fratton shed became almost entirely an oil-fuel depot. This was in anticipation of a coal shortage which turned out not so severe, and the switch back to coal-firing was made very soon.

On 20th June, 1947, the 'Devon Belle' Pullman train was instituted from Waterloo to Plymouth and Ilfracombe, splitting at Exeter. A feature of this train was a Pullman 1st and 3rd observation saloon at the rear of the train; converted from a former 59-ft Pullman car, it had a bar, pantry and 27 observation seats. It had of course to be turned as the observation section was only at one end, and the process of turning and remarshalling at Stewart's Lane depot made this train not a very popular one with the authorities. The car was designed by Mr R. Levin, who had earlier revamped a Pullman as the *Trianon Bar* for the 'Golden Arrow'.

On 15th December, 1947, the Dover–Dunkirk service was finally restored, the three Ferry vessels having been relieved of their wartime gear.

The Transport Act, requiring the nationalisation of all major railways, was passed on 6th August, 1947, and became effective on 1st January, 1948. The work of blotting out the Southern's identity began at once, and on 16th January the first engine in B.R. colours (temporary design with the number prefaced by the letter S) was sent to Waterloo for official inspection: this was the new 'West Country' No. 21C158.

A Railway Executive was set up to administer the nationalised railways, the Chairman of which was the former Southern General Manager, Sir Eustace Missenden: no fresh appointment was made for the final few months of the Southern's life. Mr C. M. Cock, the Chief Electrical Engineer, joined the Executive in the same capacity.

It may be asked how the Southern Railway differed, at the end of its 24 years life span, from its beginning. The answer must be qualified by saying that because of the war years much less progress had taken place than if the period had been one of undisturbed peace. The electrification programme had been pushed forward with remarkable zeal, and had successfully catered for the great up-surge in ·suburban building development which took place in the 'thirties. On most commuter lines twice as many trains were running as in 1923, with no more tracks into London – a tribute to the effect-iveness of the signalling system. Some – but not all – restrictions on weight and clearance had been abolished, and engineering works had overcome some previously endemic nuisances, such as the regular flooding of New Cross and Clock House stations and of a number of tunnels. Southampton Docks had been vastly improved, and traffic handling capacity at Dover much increased. There was very little passenger rolling stock of which anyone might be ashamed. But just as the Southern's earliest years were clouded by the debilitation resulting from the First World War, so its end took place in a measure of confusion resulting from the Second World War. Add to this that its middle years were spent under the shadow of the Great Depression, and you obtain a rather gloomy picture. But the Southern was never gloomy for long: its lines led to the Garden of England, the play-grounds of Sussex, and the splendid holiday beaches of the West. It never suffered the long rows of laid-up engines that made railways in the industrial parts of the country look so miserable in the slump years. It was after all the only British railway on which a French train ran daily, which had a whole section of its system separated from the mainland by several miles of water, and which turned for its non-passenger traffic more to flowers, fruit, and racehorses than to coal or steel.

XXXIX

The Southern Electrics

THE first electric stock completed under Southern auspices was of course the batch of twenty-one bogie motor cars for the Coulsdon North 'overhead electric'. But this was only an extension of L.B.S.C.R. practice, and in fact some of the trailer cars in this service appeared in L.B.S.C.R. livery even after the grouping. The motor-cars were built by Metropolitan-Cammell Carriage Wagon & Finance Co. Ltd., with four 250 h.p. G.E.C. motors in each: they measured 42ft in length and the trailers either 51ft 7in or 57ft 7in. The motors were numbered 10001–10021. After being withdrawn they were converted at Eastleigh in 1934 to 27-ton bogie goods brake vans.

As will appear later, most of the A.C. trailers found their way into D.C. electric stock. The two-car South London line trains were converted with little alteration, the dip in the roof-ends which had accommodated the current collectors being left. Two car sets were also run on the Wimbledon–West Croydon line when this was electrified and former A.C. trailers were converted for the purpose. These had a varied career. Originally first-class coaches on the three-car Crystal Palace line overhead electrics, they were removed because there were so few first-class passengers and ran on the steam commuter trains where they were nicknamed 'Ironclads' because of their girder frames. From this duty they were transfered for conversion to D.C. electrics.

It has previously been stated that when the L.S.W.R. carried out their electrification project in 1915, they constructed the electric train sets from former steam stock. This was also the pattern for the Eastern Section electrification in 1925, except that instead of accepting the short length of the old steam stock, the decision was taken to make the coaches sixty four feet in length, either by extending the short bogie-coach bodies or by mounting even shorter non-bogie bodies together on one frame. The result was a certain amount of lack of uniformity, some of the centre (trailer) coaches of the new three-car sets having a panelled-over gap in the middle. In the 1925–6 batch made up from former S.E.C.R. steam stock, all the motor coaches were third, and all the trailers had the formation 3 1 1 1 1 1 1 3. The motors were 275 h.p. two per motor coach;

457

sets numbered 1401–1495 and 1525–1534. At the same time 28 new steel-panelled three-car sets fitted with 300 h.p. motors were built for the Eastern Section (1496–1524) and 25 for the Western (1285–1310) the latter having more pointed front ends and round buffers. A further thirty sets made from S.E.C.R. steam stock (1601–1630) appeared in 1928 for Central Section use.

The principle of running two-car trailer sets between two three-car motor sets, established on the L.S.W.R., was followed on the Eastern Section: there were 70 loose-coupled sets made of L.B.S.C.R. nine-compartment 'third' steam stock (1051–1120) and forty-six sets made up from one short S.E.C.R. bogie coupled by a centre bar to a longer coach made from a nine-compartment L.S.W.R. third with two extra compartments built on. Later six similar sets (1188–94) were built, and twenty made up from ex-A.C. electric stock (1168–1187). Trailer sets were not used on the Caterham and Tadworth branches as these trains normally ran combined to Purley and split up there. For the later phases of suburban electrification the sets differed in having half the first class accommodation on one of the motors. The stock used to make these sets was of L.S.W.R., L.B.S.C.R. and A.C. electric origin, and numbers are given at the end of this chapter.

For country electrification it was believed that two-car sets would suffice and seventy-seven sets (1813–1890) were built in 1934 from L.S.W.R. steam stock for local service between Brighton and West Worthing, and later Hastings, and also for the riverside lines of the Western section. There was one motored bogie (one 275 h.p. motor). For the longer run out to Three Bridges and Reigate, new four-car sets were built, with one trailer coach a first and third composite lavatory (sets 1921–53, later 2921–2953). Motors were still 275 h.p.

Meanwhile the exciting business of designing sets for the fast run to Brighton had been undertaken, the choice being six-car sets with corridors between coaches but not between sets, with each end coach carrying two motor bogies each having two 225 h.p. motors (total weight of motor coach 59 tons). These were sets 2001–2020 (6-Pul) each with a new all-steel Pullman car 68 ft 8¾in overall incorporated; also sets 2041–2043 (6-City) with higher proportion of 'firsts'. For the electrified 'Brighton Belle' three five-car Pullman sets were built with a rather slimmer line than the others.

Public acclamation of the first-ever express multiple-unit sets was restrained. On the opening day of the 'Belle' a madrigal group in fancy dress had toured the train to demonstrate its smoothness and silence, but at speed the ladies were lurching somewhat, and the vestibuled end coaches of the six-car sets in particular soon acquired a bad reputation for bumping and shimmying. However, for the next stage of electrification to Eastbourne and Hastings, sets 2021–37 (6-Pan) were built, similar to the Brighton sets but with pantry car instead of Pullman. Several Pullman sets were transferred from the Brighton and Worthing service, being replaced by '6-Pan' sets so that the stock on both services became uniform. For the local services between Brighton and Hastings and Horsted Keynes and Seaford, two car corridor sets (2-Bil) were built to supplement the 2-Nol sets already in use. These were built to full clearances, thus presenting a large front surface, and as they had only one motor bogie, they sometimes experienced trouble with slipping when running along the Ouse Valley in the teeth of a southerly gale.

All the earlier trains had carried a letter on the front denoting the route. (An exception was the South London line two-coach trains, converted from A.C. stock which always carried the figure 2). Dot and dashes above the letter covered such route variations as Charing Cross or Cannon Street. Later it became necessary to try other variants, such as a V upside down for Sevenoaks via Main Line; but it was realised that for complex workings of the coast lines numbers would be required. From 1932 therefore new sets apart from a few late-built 3-Sub sets carried route indication numbers instead of letters illuminated at night. All short distance trains also carried boards on the sides of the motor coaches showing main destinations, and long-distance trains carried roof-boards.

For the electrification to Portsmouth a big change was made by extending the corridor through the ends of the set. This was necessary on a long run of this sort: to have part of a heavy load of Isle of Wight trippers unable to get to the restaurant car was unthinkable. The passage passed beside the driver's position and through the centre of the coach-end, the route indicator panel being offset. Sets Nos. 3054–3072 had restaurant cars, and No. 3101–3129 did not. Similarly of the sets built for the route via Horsham Nos. 3073–3085 had a buffet car in each, and Nos. 3130–3155 did not. As previously related, the buffet cars were very unusual both inside and out. All motor coaches of all these sets had one motor bogie with two 225-h.p. motors.

For the North Kent electrification in 1939, two-car sets only (2-Hal) were built, for this was really an outer-suburban project and such places as Maidstone and Chatham would still be served by steam-operated corridor trains on their way to the coast. The sets

(Nos. 2601–76) were somewhat different in appearance than previous two-car sets, and contained no side corridors or lavatories in the motor coach. A further sixteen sets were built in 1940; in that year four more 4-Lav sets were also built, similar to the original Three Bridges sets, but the coachwork and equipment similar to the 2-Hal type.

During the war the prototypes were produced of a new type of steel-bodied four-coach suburban set. The first few were in arrangement not unlike the 3-Sub of earlier years, and contained wide compartments intended for first-class. When it became clear that first-class would not be restored in the London area, the design was re-vamped and in later versions many of the coaches were saloons.

At the same time the remaining 3-Sub sets were strengthened by adding a further coach, either a new steel trailer or one cannibalised from another old set. The result of this was that one might find four entirely different types of carriage (and roof lines) in one set. Gradually things were tidied up, and a number of homogeneous sets of low-roofed ex-L.B.S.C.R. type or high-roofed ex-L.S.W.R. type coaches were marshalled together as four-car sets. Keen students could come across a number of interesting relics, such as ex-first class saloons embedded in lengthened ex-1915 stock, now incorporated with other coaches of different date; and by the end of the Southern era the occasional 1925 coach with its South Eastern Railway luggage rack brackets was something of an historical prize.

New suburban sets began arriving in considerable numbers, and in 1946 and 1947 there was a more-or-less permanent bonfire of electric train stock burning at Newhaven sidings, and scrapping was also carried out at Horsted Keynes and Gatwick. Some of the 1925 ex-L.B.S.C.R. trailer coaches were fitted with glycol tanks and run on the main lines on winter nights to cut down icing of the live rail. Some of the 1926 steel stock had its motors coupled in pairs and run as service trains. The allocation of stock became somewhat mixed; many 4-Sub sets were used as fast reliefs on the Brighton line.

After nationalisation one of the oddest of Southern projects came to fruition: two four-car double-decker trains. These were really half-decks, for the top passengers' feet were between the backs of the lower passengers. Owing to the difficulty in clearing top-deck passengers down the steps and out at busy stops, leading to lost time, the experiment was not followed up.

There was no break in construction of 4-Sub sets due to nationalisation; later sets, however, had more up-to-date equipment, and the driver's door was abolished, entry being from the guard's van.

Recently electric stock has been built for other regions of British Railways incorporating many 'Southern' features whose value was learned in the sometimes bitter battles from 1926 to 1947 to withstand the ever-strengthening tide of commuters.

S.R. Electric Sets

Set Numbers	Type	Original allocation & date		Body Origin
989–1000	2-car trailer	S.R. (R)	1937/8	L.B.S.C.R.
1001–1024	,, ,,	L.S.W.R.	1915	L.S.W.R.
1025–1037	,, ,,	S.R. (E)	1925	L.B.S.C.R.
1038–1050	,, ,,	S.R. (A)	1935	L.B.S.C.R., L.S.W.R.
1051–1120	,, ,,	S.R. (A)	1926	L.B.S.C.R.
1121–1167	,, ,,	S.R. (A)	1928/9	S.E.C.R., L.S.W.R.
1168–1187	,, ,,	S.R. (A)	1929/30	L.B.S.C.R.
1188–1194	,, ,,	S.R. (A)	1930/1	S.E.C.R., L.S.W.R.
1195–1198	,, ,,	S.R. (E)	1934	L.S.W.R.
1199–1200	,, ,,	S.R. (B)	1937	L.B.S.C.R.
1201–1284	3-Sub	L.S.W.R.	1915	L.S.W.R.
1285–1310	,,	S.R. (E)	1925	New
1401–1495	,,	S.R. (A)	1925	S.E.C.R.
1496–1524	,,	S.R. (A)	1925	New
1525–1534	,,	S.R. (A)	1926	S.E.C.R.
1579–1584	,,	S.R. (B)	1937	L.S.W.R.
1585–1599	,,	S.R. (B)	1934/5	L.S.W.R.
1600	,,	S.R. (B)	1933	L.B.S.C.R.
1601–1630	,,	S.R. (B)	1928	S.E.C.R.
1631–1657	,,	S.R. (B)	1928	L.B.S.C.R.
1658 1701	,,	S.R. (B)	1928	L.S.W.R.
1702–1759	,,	S.R. (B)	1928	L.B.S.C.R.
1760–1769	,,	S.R. (E)	1928/30	L.B.S.C.R.
1770–1772	,,	S.R. (B)	1930	L.B.S.C.R.
1773–1785	,,	S.R. (B)	1930	L.S.W.R.
1786–1796	,,	S.R. (B)	1931	L.S.W.R.
1797–1801	,,	S.R. (B)	1931/2	L.B.S.C.R.
1801–1812	2-Sub	(formerly 1901–1912)		
1813–1890	2-Nol	S.R. (B. & E.)	1934/6	L.S.W.R.
1891–1900	2-Bil	Hastings, etc.	1935	New
1901–1908	2-Sub	S. London	1929	A.C. elec.
1909–1912	,,	Croydon– Wim.	1930	A.C. elec.
1921–1953	4-Lav	Brighton	1931/2	New
2001–2020	6-Pul	Brighton	1932	New
2021–2039	6-Pan	Bognor, etc.	1935	New
2041–2043	6-City	Brighton	1932	New
2051–2053	5-Bel	S. Belle	1932	New
2011–2048	2-Bil	Portsmouth	1937	New
2047–2116	2-Bil	Mid-Sussex	1937	New
2117–2152	2-Bil	Reading, etc.	1938	New

Set Numbers	Type	Original allocation & date	Body Origin
2601–2676	2-Hal	North Kent 1939	New
2677–2692	2-Hal	,, ,, 1940	New
2921–2953	4-Lav	(formerly 1921–53)	New
2954–2955	4-Lav	Brighton 1940	New
3001–3039	6-Pul/Pan	(Formerly 2001–39)	New
3041–3043	6-City	(,, 2041–43)	New
3051–3053	5-Bel	(,, 2051–53)	New
3054–3072	4-Res	Portsmouth 1937	New
3073–3085	4-Buf	Bognor, etc. 1937	New
3101–3129	4-Cor	Portsmouth 1937/8	New
3130–3155	4-Cor	Bognor, etc. 1937/8	New
3156–3158	4-Cor	,, ,, 1946	New
4101–4102	4-Sub	General 1941	New
4103–4110	,,	,, 1945	New
4111–4120	,,	,, 1946	New
4121–4130	,,	,, 1946	New
4364–4376	,,	,, 1947	New

From 1942 onwards (and earlier for trailer sets) sets numbered below 1891 were subject to rebuilding and re-arrangement, all 3-Sub sets becoming four-car (unless scrapped) with numbers in the 4XXX range. No. 1600 was No. 1801 until 1934.

XL

Southern Railway Steamers

On its formation as from 1st January, 1923, the Southern Railway fleet comprised 21 vessels of over 250 net registered tonnage, as follows:

L.S.W.R.	10 (tonnage	4925)
S.E.C.R.	7 (,,	4977)
L.B.S.C.R.	4 (,,	2157)

The Brighton boats were in fact jointly owned with the French State Railways. There were also from the three companies 25 smaller boats totalling 4,115 tons.

The well-known sister ships, *Isle of Thanet* and *Maid of Kent* were placed in service after the constitution of the Southern Railway (on 24th July, 1925, and 6th November, 1925, respectively). They were built by Denny's. Their overall length was 342ft, with a breadth of 45ft, and the gross tonnage about 2,700. Twelve transverse watertight bulkheads, extending to the main deck, subdivided the hull, and there were watertight doors between the engine and boiler rooms. The doors were of the horizontal sliding type, operated by hand gear on the upper deck, and by hydraulic power from the bridge, where an electrical indicator repeats their position.

There is probably no steamship service where such demands are made on the boats as on the Dover–Calais and Folkestone–Boulogne. The passengers, for instance, were in Southern days mostly those accustomed to, and willing to pay for, what may be called luxury accommodation, while nearly all travelled with a considerable amount of luggage, most of which they desired to retain in their own immediate possession. As a result, the accommodation per head had to be much greater than that usually given. Another factor was that, in view of the comparatively short sea-passage, many prefered to remain on deck rather than go below. Plenty of promenade space was therefore necessary and, in that relation, the incidence of wet and 'dirty' weather had to be provided for. In addition to those difficulties there were the physical problems in the limitation of length and draught, added to which frequent heavy storms in the winter months have to be reckoned with.

The *Isle of Thanet* and *Maid of Kent* had accommodation for

1,000 first- and 400 second-class passengers, together with quarters for a crew of 63. On the boat deck were two *cabines-de-luxe* and eight private cabins. They were propelled by a twin set of single-reduction geared turbines of the Parsons type, and had five water-tube boilers of the Babcock-Wilcox pattern, working at 200 lb pressure, burning oil fuel.

In March, 1928, a new fast vessel, the *Canterbury*, was ordered from Messrs Denny for the Dover–Calais service in connection with the Pullman company's 'Golden Arrow' express. She was put into service on 15th May, 1929, and was generally similar to the last-mentioned boats, but had 2ft more beam, with a gross tonnage of 2,910. In addition to the deck, which carried the flying bridge, navigation room, captain's cabin and cabins for the chief officer and second officer respectively, there were the boat deck, the awning deck, the main deck and the lower deck. She was to start with first class only.

By the use, for the first time in these boats, of davits of the Welin over-frame type for the lifeboats, the boat deck was free of obstruction and a fine promenade was provided on that deck.

Steam was generated by four water-tube boilers of the Babcock-Wilcox type, working to a pressure of 225 lb per square inch, fired by oil fuel on the same firm's high-pressure sytem. Propulsion was by twin screws, the designed speed of the propellers, at full power, being 260 r.p.m. Each propeller shaft had a set of twin-geared turbines – one high-pressure and one low-pressure – each driving its own pinion through a flexible coupling.

The S.S. *Autocarrier*, built by D. and W. Henderson, was placed on the cross-Channel motor-car service in 1931, for the purpose of carrying cars and their owners between England and France. She carried about 35 cars and was licensed for 120 passengers.

Besides the above vessels, there were two fine turbine steamers on the Dover–Calais route belonging to the Société Anonyme de Gérance et d'Armament (S.A.G.A.); the *Côte d'Azur*, and the *Côte d'Argent*. They were of 3,009 tons, with 14,000 horse power, and had a speed of 23 knots.

On 1st May, 1932, the night service to Paris, etc., which had hitherto run in conjunction with the L.M.S.R. between Tilbury and Dunkerque, was transferred to Folkestone, whence the sea journey takes $4\frac{1}{4}$ hours, instead of $6\frac{1}{4}$ as before. The steamers used continued to be those of the Angleterre–Lorraine–Alsace company (A.L.A.), the *Alsacien*, *Picard* and *Flamand*, which were turbine steamers built by Denny. They originally belonged to the L.M.S.R., and were named *Duke of Argyll*, *Duke of Cumberland* and *Londonderry*.

Among the Southern cargo boats on the Dover and Folkestone services were the *Tonbridge* and *Minster* (1924); *Hythe* and *Whitstable* (1925); *Maidstone* (1926); the *Deal*, which, a sister ship to the *Hythe*, was of 685 gross tonnage, with triple expansion engines of 1,850 h.p., driving her at 15 knots. Like most of the cargo boats, except those on the Newhaven service, she was built by Henderson and Co.

Turning to the Newhaven fleet: on 4th March, 1928, the *Worthing* was launched by Denny, and on 5th September following was put into service between Newhaven and Dieppe, flying the flag of the Southern Railway and the French State Railways. Her gross registered tonnage was 2,294; i.h.p. 14,500; speed 25 knots; length 306ft; beam 38ft 8in. In general arrangement and appearance she was very similar to the latest Dover boats supplied by the same builders and already described. Steam was generated by four Yarrow water-tube boilers at 250 lb, and fired by oil fuel on the Thornycroft high-pressure system. There were twin screws, driven by geared turbines.

Yet another *Brighton* (the fifth), also built by Denny's, was placed in service in April, 1933. She sailed under the British flag, and was built on the lines of the *Worthing*, with all the latest improvements. The tonnage was 2,391, and h.p. 16,400. The vessel was fitted with triple-expansion geared turbines and Yarrow water-tube boilers burning oil fuel. Like the *Worthing*, at full speed she steamed 25 knots, which made her one of the world's fastest passenger steamships.

The main necessity for that high speed was to be found in the fact that the sea-passage is one of 64 nautical miles, as compared with the 21 miles between Dover and Calais, and the 28 miles between Folkestone and Boulogne. The rail journey between Dieppe and Paris is, however, about 30 miles shorter than between Boulogne and Paris, and about 60 miles less than between Calais and Paris. As a consequence, the higher speed on the sea-passage and the shorter rail journey combined put the Dieppe route in a very favourable position in regard to the overall length of the journey between London and Paris. There are, too, many who enjoy the sea trip and, still more numerous, those who find the conditions less trying in the wider channel journey than in the heaped-up waters of the Straits of Dover. Owing, further, to the shorter rail journey the through fares were less than by the other two routes. The Newhaven–Dieppe route was therefore, at that time, very popular.

The *Paris* (*IV*), *Versailles*, *Rouen* (*IV*) and *Newhaven* (*II*) which were mentioned in an earlier chapter, were improved and brought up to date. A cargo steamer, the *Rennes*, was added to the fleet in 1925.

The first two larger vessels in the Southampton fleet to be put into service by the combined southern railways were, in 1924, the sister ships *Dinard* and *St Briac*, built by Denny, and having a gross tonnage of 2,291. Their overall length was 325ft, and breadth, moulded, 41ft. Twelve transverse watertight bulkheads, extending to the main deck, subdivided the hull, and there were watertight doors between the engine-room and the boiler-room. What was an unusual feature in cross-Channel steamers, but which was a great addition of safety, was the provision of a double bottom over the whole length of the vessels.

They ran to St Malo, and were certified for carrying 1,340 passengers, sleeping accommodation being provided for 354, together with quarters for a crew of sixty. There were twin single-reduction geared turbines, each with a high- and a low-pressure unit; supplied with steam by two boilers, one single- and one double-ended, at a working pressure of 180 lb. They could be fired either by coal or oil. The *St Briac* was also used for 'cruises'.

In 1925 a service that had previously been given in the four summer months by the *Ardena* to Cherbourg was transferred so as to serve Caen and to displace one formerly run from Newhaven. It was, however, discontinued in 1931. Three fast cargo boats – the *Fratton*, *Ringwood* and *Haslemere* – for handling perishable traffic from French ports and the Channel Islands, were brought into use in 1925–6. They each had a tonnage of 760 and were built by D. and W. Henderson and Company.

At the end of the year 1928 it was decided to provide two new boats for the Channel Islands service, and orders for these – the *Isle of Jersey* and the *Isle of Guernsey* – were placed with Denny. The first named was launched on 22nd October following, and was put into commission on 12th March, 1930; the *Isle of Guernesy* followed a few weeks later. Both had a length, overall, of 306ft, a breadth, moulded, of 42ft, a depth, moulded, to the main deck of 16ft, and a gross tonnage of 2,143. The accommodation was for 800 first-class and 600 second-class passengers.

The *Isle of Sark* was launched on 12th November, 1931, and put in service in March, 1932. By the same builders, she was generally similar to the two just described, but had water-tube boilers and was very slightly larger, her tonnage being 2,211. All three ships were 5,400 i.h.p. The *Isle of Sark* had a 'Maierform' bow, which reduced the resistance to improve seagoing qualities in stormy weather.

On 2nd July, 1931, the Southampton–St Malo service was made a regular one, instead of tidal, thanks to the completion of a new harbour at the latter place, and on the following day a direct service was started from Southampton to Caen.

In June, 1932, a new service was commenced between Jersey and Granville and St Malo, run by the *Vera*, a twin-screw boat of 1,088 tons, built in 1898. In June, 1933, a new turbine ship, the *Brittany*, was put on, built by Denny's. She was of 1,445 tons, and carried about 850 passengers. She was the fourth of that name, No. 1 being a South Western boat of 1864, sold in the late 'eighties; No. 2 a Brighton company's boat, built in 1882; and No. 3 one of 1910 for the same company, which was renamed *Aldershot*.

Two other important Continental services must be mentioned, namely Dover Ostend and Gravesend–Rotterdam. The boats on the former belonged to the Belgian Goverment. There were five turbine steamers: *Princess Astrid, Prince Leopold, Prince Charles, Princess Joséphine Charlotte*, and *Princesse Marie-José*. In August, 1934, the fleet received a notable addition in the shape of the *Prince Badouin*, the first cross-Channel ship to be equipped with Diesel machinery. She had two sets of twelve-cylinder engines on the two-stroke cycle, capable of about 17,000 h.p., propelling her at $25\frac{1}{4}$ knots. All the boats were built by Cockerill of Seraign.

The Gravesend–Rotterdam service was being run by three steamers belonging to the Batavier line, (the oldest steamship line between England and Holland, having maintained a regular passenger service ever since 1830). The boats, which were renowned for their steadiness and smooth running were the *Batavier II, Batavier III* and *Batavier V*.

The Isle of Wight services remain to be dealt with. On the formation of the Southern Railway that company took over the jointly-owned steamers *Duchess of Albany* (1889), *Princess Margaret* (1893), *Duchess of Kent* (1889), *Duchess of Fife* (1899), and *Duchess of Norfolk* (1911), used in the Portsmouth–Southsea–Ryde service. In 1924 the company put on that route the *Shanklin*, built by Thornycroft and Co., and engined by D. and W. Henderson. The first two of the five, named above, were replaced in the summer of 1928 by the *Merstone* and *Portsdown*, constructed by the Caledon Shipbuilding and Engineering Co. They were 190ft in length, 25ft in breadth, accommodated 700 passengers, and had a speed of $13\frac{1}{2}$ knots.

Two new vessels built by the Fairfield Shipping and Engineering Co. – formerly John Elder and Co. – the *Southsea* and the *Whippingham*, were put on the Portsmouth–Ryde service in the summer of

1930. They were 50ft longer than the other vessels on the route and embodied various improvements. A later addition was the *Sandown*, (the first vessel on this route to have a 'cruiser' stern), built by Denny's to replace the *Duchess of Kent*, which had been running for 36 years in the service. All these boats were 'paddlers'.

There is also the service between the pier at the end of the Lymington branch and Yarmouth. In June, 1927, the *Freshwater* by White of Cowes, a paddle boat carrying 500 passengers, was placed into service on the route. This particular journey commences in the long, winding estuary of the River Lymington, down which the boats have to proceed before entering the Solent.

In July, 1927, a new departure was set up by the inauguration, between Portsmouth Harbour and Fishbourne in Wootton Creek in the Isle of Wight, of a ferry-boat service for the conveyance, in particular, of motor cars. The new services – which replaced transit by tow-boats – necessitated the construction of a slipway at Fishbourne, with a reinforced concrete road, 300 yards long. The *Fishbourne*, built by Denny and Brothers, was 125ft long overall, had a beam of 25ft, and was of the double-ended type. A hinged platform at each end let down on to concrete ramps, and cars passed off the boat at the opposite end to that by which they entered. The motive power was supplied by two sets of semi-Diesel engines, made by Norris, Henty and Gardner, which drove independent propellers and furnished a speed of 8 knots.

In July, 1928, Denny supplied a second motor-car boat, known as the *Wootton*. In design and equipment that vessel was generally similar to the *Fishbourne*. The loading and unloading platforms were, however, slightly longer and electrically operated. In 1930 a third motor ferry, the *Hilsea*, was put into service.

The year 1936 saw the inauguration of the Dover–Dunkerque Train Ferry. Three steamers were provided: the *Twickenham Ferry*, *Hampton Ferry*, and *Shepperton Ferry*. Each could carry a train of twelve sleeping-cars or 40 loaded goods wagons on four lines of rails which converged at the stern into two. There was a garage for 25 motor-cars and accommodation for many more.

The hulls were built by Swan, Hunter and Wigham Richardson; the turbines by the Parsons company, and the water-tube boilers by Yarrows. The latter were arranged to burn coal, with automatic stokers, owing to the facility with which they could be bunkered; the trucks running straight on board.

The *Shepperton Ferry* was transferred in 1936 to the *Société Anonyme de Navigation Angleterre–Lorraine–Alsace*. These three vessels were built by Swan Hunter with Parsons steam turbine propulsion: they were 360ft long with 60ft beam, and 12ft 6in draught. The cars were loose-coupled for shunting over the connecting ramps, and were chained to the deck against damage from rolling of the vessel. During the war these vessels were fitted with 84-ton derricks at the stern for transferring railway rolling stock on to open beaches, and the engines were converted to oil to cut turn-round time. They served with great distinction, following the Second Front battle eastwards from the Cherbourg peninsula.

In 1937 a further paddle-steamer for the Ryde service was added, the *Ryde*, by Denny, similar to the *Sandown* and carrying 1,050 passengers.

Also from Denny came in 1938 the *Lymington*, for the Yarmouth (I.O.W.) service. She was a car ferry with accommodation for 400 passengers as well as 16 cars, and her two 200-h.p. diesel engines, driving Voith-Sneider propellors, gave her 11 knots. The pitch of the propellors was controllable from the bridge and no rudders were fitted, the vessel being able by this control to move sideways from the constricted berth at Lymington and to manoeuvre in the narrow channel.

In 1939 a new vessel for the 'Golden Arrow' service, the *Invicta* was ready, but went almost at once into war service. She was of 4,178 tons, making $22\frac{1}{2}$ knots.

The record of the S.R. fleet during the Second World War was an illustrious one, but for that very reason no less than twelve of the vessels were lost. The two 'Maids' both went, the *Maid of Kent* being bombed at Dieppe on 21st May, 1940, and the *Maid of Orleans* sunk – probably by a mine – on 28th June, 1944 in the Channel. The *Normannia* and *Paris* were bombed at Dunkerque, the *Brighton* lost at Dieppe only four days after the *Maid of Kent*. Five days later still (29th May, 1940) the *Lorina* went down at Dunkerque. In 1941, whilst on Admiralty service, the *Portsdown*, *Southsea*, and *Tonbridge* were lost, the second-named somewhere off the East Coast. Finally, in the weeks after D-Day, the *Fratton* and *Minster* went down while on charter to the Ministry of War Transport.

It should also be mentioned that during the war a number of steamers from other waters were pressed into service at various times for cross-Channel transport for trooping leave and supply purposes.

The return of the vessels which survived, to their familiar and happier peace-time duties, has already been described.

In 1946 a new vessel built by the French came on to the Newhaven service: this was the *Arromanches*. In the same year three new boats for the Isle of Wight service were ordered from Denny's, to be powered by geared diesel engines. An interesting development, also for the Isle of Wight service, was the ordering from Denny's of a double-ended side-paddle vessel for the Lymington–Yarmouth service, with each paddle delivering 275 b.h.p. at 50 r.p.m., driven independently by D.C. motors from English Electric diesel engines.

By the end of the Southern days, the cross-Channel services had lost much of their glamour, the wealth, beauty and notables of post-war society mainly preferring the air. As Continental holidays became familiar to a wider cross-section of the population, however, the pressure on the services increased rather than diminished, becoming perhaps more seasonal, but calling still for that high degree of efficiency in operation which had been the hall-mark of the Channel steamers in the days when the 'ditch' was Britain's proud and unviolated barrier against the rest of the world.

XLI

Southern Railway Docks and Harbours

ONE of the most valuable possessions of the Southern Railway company was Southampton Docks. While their success had to a great extent been due to the London & South Western Railway, they also owed much to their position and surroundings. Southampton Water, on which the docks are situated, is greatly favoured by nature, being land-locked and sheltered throughout, and possessing two outlets to the sea, one to the east by Spithead, and the other westwards via the Needles.

There is also the remarkable peculiarity of a double high tide. The second high water occurs about two hours after the first, and between the two periods there is only a slight fall, which is often a great convenience for navigating officers.

In medieval times Southampton was of considerable importance, being the port of Winchester, and shipping great quantities of wool. In a letter to *The Times* on 20th February, 1930, Commander A. MacDermott, R.N., said that Southampton could claim to have had a dry dock as far back as 1434. The entrance was closed with a wall of mud, stone and brushwood as the tide receded.

During the reign of Henry VIII a decline set in, owing to various causes, such as the rise of London as a port, the loss of Winchester business owing to the suppression of the monastic institutions, and a prohibition of the export of wool.

Southampton Water is six miles long and one mile wide. The natural channel has been deepened by dredging and is not less than 600ft wide, and at low tide is at least 35ft deep, and in places 80ft deep. At high tide it is from 9 to 18ft deeper. The estuary is formed by the joining of the rivers Test and Itchen – really only small streams – and the docks are situated at the point where they unite; the Test enters at the head of Southampton Water, at a point north-west of Southampton, whilst the Itchen comes from the north-east and flows on the east side of the town. Though giving only a small supply of water, the two rivers effectively scour the channel between the docks and the Solent so that it is kept free of silt.

When the nineteenth century opened, the Southampton Corporation was charging certain dues, known as petty customs, on all imports and exports. The burgesses sought for the abolition of those charges, and desired that docks should be built. The Corporation was willing to surrender its rights on consideration of one-fifth of the harbour dues being paid over as compensation for the loss of the petty customs.

Powers in that behalf were given in 1803 and the Mayor, Recorder, Common Council, and ten other persons were appointed Harbour Commissioners. The one-fifth of the harbour dues payable to the Corporation remains to this day and is a source of considerable income to the town. The Town Quay and Royal Victoria Pier were opened by Princess, afterwards Queen, Victoria in 1831, and in 1836 the Southampton Dock Company was incorporated by an Act of Parliament and acquired 216 acres of ground, immediately adjoining the Town Quay, for £5,000. The plans were prepared by Francis Giles, then the engineer of the London & Southampton Railway, and to whom, and to his son Alfred, great credit is due for the preparation and execution of schemes that were bold in their conception and readily capable of extension. Giles realised that deep-water quays must be provided, so that ships could enter at any state of the tide and lie there to be unloaded, then be reloaded and sent away again, as quickly as possible. Other essentials were the provision of sheds, siding accommodation, communication with the main line, cranes, etc. All that those engineers did was laid out in such a way that the arrangements are practically on the same lines today, and give Southampton a reputation for quick dispatch.

The first work commenced by the Docks company after its incorporation in 1836 was what was then called the North East Open Dock – now known as the Outer Dock. The first stone was laid on 12th October, 1838, and the tide was admitted on 18th June, 1842, and, although not completed, the dock was used for the first time in the following August, when two of the Peninsular Oriental Steam Navigation Company's steamers entered it. One of those vessels landed passengers and luggage on the North Western Quay which were transferred to railway carriages and thus opened direct passenger communication between the dock side and London. On 1st July, 1843, the Outer Dock was publicly opened, and the P. and O. steamship *Pacha*, from Gibraltar, entered and discharged her cargo and, in due course, departed again. The Royal Mail Steam Packet Company also used that dock for its mail steamers to and from the West Indian and South American ports.

The quay wall of the Outer Dock was of the unusual height of 39ft. It was made 12ft thick at the base, tapering to 6½ft at the top,

Mixed traffic electric locomotive No. 20003, Ashford 1948.   [*Locomotive Publishing Company*

1941- type Waterloo & City 'tube' stock.   [*British Railways*

Above: Bulleid steel-bodied 1942- type 4-SUB electric unit No. 4105. [*British Railways*

Below: The Pullman observation car run at the rear of the 'Devon Belle.' [*British Railways*

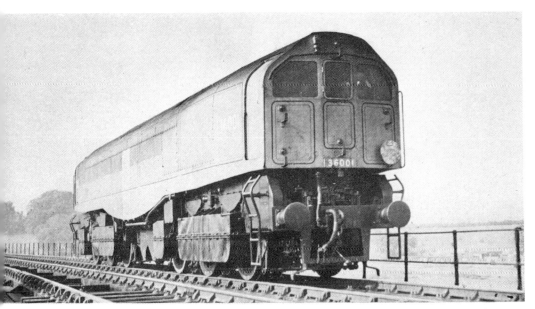

Bulleid's 'Leader' class 0-6-6-OT engine No. 36001 running smokebox end first near Lewes.

[*C. C. B. Herbert*

The *St. Briac*, built by Denny 1924 for the Southampton cross-channel services.   [*British Railways*

Above: The *Autocarrier,* built for cross-channel car traffic in 1931; the fore-runner of much larger ferry vessels, she carried only 35 cars. [*British Railways*

Below: The *Shanklin,* the first post-amalgamation vessel for the Portsmouth–Ryde service.

strengthened by counterforts, 5ft square, spaced 15ft apart centre to centre. It rested on a timber platform, 6in thick, constructed on the natural ground. The latter, for the most part, was of sandy clay, and sometimes of sand so fine that, when flooded with water, it soon became a quicksand. The wall itself was built of lime concrete, faced with brickwork up to low-water level and with granite above. Both before and after water was let into the dock the wall moved in places as soon as it was backed up. Eventually the movement was arrested by removing the filling at the back of the wall to a depth of about ten feet. It may be added here that, since 1910, various lengths of the wall have again shown signs of instability and expensive works have had to be carried out in order to stabilise them, such as sinking deep trenches immediately behind the wall, in which concrete buttresses have been built up.

The area of the Outer Dock was 16 acres. To meet the increasing requirements of traffic another, opening out of it, called the Inner Dock, was opened in 1851. In the meantime two dry docks had been constructed, followed by a third in 1854.

The Union Steamship Company – now part of the Union Castle Line – began to use Southampton in 1856, and for twenty years was accommodated in the Inner Dock. More facilities being required, the River Quay was constructed, and it was opened in 1876. No. 4 dry dock, between the River Quay and the entrance to the Outer Dock, was opened in 1877.

An event of note, immediately subsequent to the arrival of the Union Steamship Company, was that the North German Lloyd steamers commenced to embark and disembark passengers, by means of tenders, in Southampton Water in 1857 and the Hamburg American liners did the same in 1858.

A misfortune befell the port when, in 1873, the Peninsular & Oriental company – the first to use Southampton – began to withdraw its fleet therefrom and to centre it on London, finally leaving in January, 1882. Nevertheless, in spite of that drawback, the tonnage entering the port increased, and in 1877 exceeded for the first time 2,000,000 gross tons. The interest of the townspeople, as to the value of the property at their door, began to be be aroused, and in 1883 public meetings were held on the question of the Borough taking over the docks. Public ownership was not then the craze it has since become, and the Dock company, who admitted that their finances were giving them concern, approached the London & South Western Railway. As a result, Parliament, in 1886, sanctioned that company lending £250,000 to the Southampton Dock company on the security of a 4 per cent preference stock, specially created.

With the funds thus provided, it was decided by the Dock company in 1885 to construct the Empress Dock, which has a water area of 18½ acres – as compared with 16 acres for the Outer Dock and 10 acres for the Inner Dock. It was commenced in 1885 and opened by Queen Victoria on 26th July, 1890. At that time Southampton was the only port in Great Britain which ships of the deepest draught could enter or leave at any state of the tide.

Considerable trouble was experienced with the walls of the new dock. After the ground inside had been taken out, the north wall moved bodily forward two or three feet, and had to be rebuilt with deeper foundations. In order to steady the other walls, concrete blocks 20 by 15 by 12ft were sunk in front of the toes of the walls, set 30ft apart.

The opening of the Empress Dock did not afford the relief hoped for, and still further accommodation was required. The only source from which the necessary money could reasonably be obtained was the London & South Western Railway. In February, 1891, therefore, negotiations were entered into with a view of the railway company acquiring the property. The necessary Bill came before Parliament in 1892, and the result was that the South Western company purchased the docks as from 1st November, 1892.

Immediately the new owners entered upon their property, steps were taken to improve the equipment; e.g. an entirely new crane system was provided on all wharves and quays. On 4th March, 1893, the American Line steamer *New York* entered Southampton Docks, and that company began to use the port for its New York service via Cherbourg.

When the Prince of Wales Dock, as it was called, was opened, it was the largest in the world, being 745ft long and 91ft wide.

A new quay on the River Itchen was completed in 1895. Next came the South Quay and that on the River Test, which were completed in 1902. The stability of the wall of the latter was so great, that, later on, the ground in front of it was dredged away for an additional ten feet to accommodate larger vessels. In 1905 the old River Quay on the Itchen, which had been opened in 1876, was widened and deepened. A platform, 50ft wide, was built on reinforced concrete piles in front of the wall, and the berths dredged out to a depth of 30ft. The buildings were carried forward to the old wall, and the cranes and railway tracks removed to the new platform.

On 21st October, 1905 –the hundredth anniversary of the Battle of Trafalgar – the Trafalgar Dock was opened. Although, as it was then, the largest dry dock in the world, it had to be widened in 1912 to accommodate the *Olympic*.

In June, 1907, the White Star liner *Adriatic* sailed from Southampton to New York via Cherbourg, inaugurating a Wednesday service by that route, instead of from Liverpool via Queenstown. The inducements to forsake Liverpool were three: Continental traffic was acquired by going to Cherbourg; Southampton offered better facilities for passengers between boat and train; and it involved a rail journey to London a hundred miles shorter.

Special provision had to be made for the large White Star boats, and a new dock was made for them, opened in 1911. It was at first called the White Star Dock but, in view of its subsequent use by ships of other lines, was renamed the Ocean Dock. The Cunard came in 1920; the service commencing with the sailing of the *Mauretania* on 6th March. On the outbreak of the Great War, practically the whole of the docks were taken over and closed to civilian traffic, except a small part of the Outer Dock, from which the L.S.W.R. were allowed to run their cross-Channel services, but those were reduced very much, owing to the circumstances. The total number of personnel passing through the docks between 9th August, 1914, and 31st December, 1918, were 4,848,683 outwards, and 2,288,144 inwards; total 7,136,797. Stores were put on transports to the extent of 604,912 tons, while storeships took away 2,680,536 tons: a total of 3,285,448 tons. Sometimes between twenty-five and thirty vessels left in a single night.

An important post-war achievement was the provision of an immense floating dock, capable of lifting a ship of 60,000 tons. It was constructed by Sir W. G. Armstrong, Whitworth and Co., and opened by the Prince of Wales on 27th June, 1924. It was 960ft long with a clear width of entrance of 134ft; the draught of water over the keel-blocks being 38ft. The height from the bottom of the pontoon to the top deck of the side walls was over 70ft. When docking the *Majestic*, about 80,000 tons of water had to be pumped out to lift the ship; an operation that took about four hours.

Southampton continued to act as a magnet for liners. In July, 1925, after forty-four years' absence, the Peninsular & Oriental returned; the *Khyber* putting in on the 4th of that month to take in a cargo for the Far East. In the autumn of 1928 the North German Lloyd announced that when the *Bremen* and *Europa* were put into commission, the call at Plymouth on the way back from America would be abandoned, and all that company's steamers would call at

Southampton on their homeward journey, as they already did going outwards.

We now come to a bold stroke of policy by the Southern Railway. The bay between the Royal Pier and Millbrook Point, a distance of about two miles, which was a dreary expanse of mud and water, was reclaimed. The area so treated was 407 acres of mudland, and the river face on the reclaimed ground was, for the most part, formed by a quay wall, 7,400ft long, so designed as to admit of the berths outside of it being dredged, for a length of 3,500ft, to a depth of 45ft below low water, and of 40ft for the remainder, and to be approached by a deep-water channel having a depth of 35ft at low water. The scheme included eight sheds, each about 900ft long and 150ft wide, equipped with the most modern appliances for dealing expeditiously with passengers and cargo.

The scheme, further, was so designed as to permit of the provision of a jetty, about 4,500ft long and 400ft wide, distant about 600ft from the new quay. Vessels are able to berth on both sides of the jetty and, thus, the whole plan gives 15,500ft of quay and provides accommodation for twenty vessels of the largest size.

To the north of the cargo sheds is a large marshalling yard connected to the main line at Millbrook. The existing dock lines were joined to the new scheme by a connection with the Harbour Board's railway near the Royal Pier.

Included in the scheme was what was then the largest graving dock in the world.

The building of this dock – part of the £8,000,000 Docks Extension Scheme – was commenced in June, 1931. First an area of about half a square mile had to be reclaimed and pumped dry.

For ten days pumps were continually at work removing 50,000,000 gallons of water, and at the end of this period the sinking of the 43ft wide trenches for the walls of the dock was started.

With its floor of a thickness of 25ft of solid concrete, the dock was completed and filled by July, 1933.

Then followed the demolition of the seaward embankment and the dredging of the approaches and entrance to allow 35ft of water at low tide, not forgetting a swinging ground of the same depth at the entrance to allow the giant liners to turn into the dock.

On Wednesday, 26th July, 1933, His Majesty King George V, with Queen Mary and Their Royal Highnesses the Duke and Duchess of York, came up Southampton Water on the Royal Yacht *Victoria and Albert*, to visit and declare the new dock open under the name of 'The King George V Graving Dock'.

The dock is 1,200ft long, with a width of 165ft (135 at the entrance and between buttresses), with a height from the floor to cope of 59ft, the clear depth of water at high water neap tides being 45ft, and it could accommodate a ship of 100,000 tons. One and a quarter million cubic yards of earth had to be excavated. When full, it holds 58 million gallons of water. When a liner is inside, the water can be pumped out in four hours, by four 54in electrically operated centrifugal pumps, all under the control of one operator, who sits at a control desk, where a system of coloured lights tells him what pumps are running, and the position of every valve; the whole system being controlled by push buttons.

The gate is a steel caisson, 138ft 6in in length, 58ft 6in in depth, and 29ft thick, and was built on the River Tees, whence it was towed by sea to Southampton, the journey taking 8½ days.

Among the other harbours belonging to the Southern Railway, perhaps the most interesting historically is that of Newhaven. Prior to the year 1579 the River Ouse entered the sea at a point under Seaford Head, two and a half miles east of the present outlet. In that year a breach was made one mile to the west of the original outlet, and the latter has gradually filled up. The breach itself has also disappeared, as in 1620 a new outlet was made and the river took its present course. The town was then given the name of New Haven, having previously been known as Meeching.

In 1698 a Government survey was made of the port, and in 1730 the Harbour Board – the Trustees of Newhaven Harbour and of the Ouse Lower Navigation – was formed. On the advice of Smeaton the bed of the river was improved in 1767 and its course straightened; the embankments in the upper reaches of the river were also proceeded with. Four years later there was a depth of water on the bar of 11ft at high water and the bar itself was dry for 8ft at low water.

In 1788 two wooden piers, each 100ft in length, were built at the entrance to reclaim the depth of water, and in 1791 a new entrance was cut through to the eastward of what was then the east pier, but which is now the west pier. In 1793 that structure was made 360ft long; the entrance then was 110ft wide. In 1838 the then east pier was extended a further 130ft.

In 1847, in anticipation of the London, Brighton & South Coast Company obtaining powers to own and operate steamboats, the Newhaven Harbour Board obtained an Improvement Act. The reason for that step was that, at that time, steamers often had to wait outside for the tide in order that their passengers could be landed. The first vessel to run under the auspices of the Brighton company arrived on its station in July, 1852. It was soon appreciated that the traffic called for larger vessels, but before the *Lyons* and the *Orleans* of 1856 could be accommodated, the harbour had to be dredged at a cost of £10,000. Steam cranes were introduced on the docks in 1862. The following year the Harbour Board obtained powers to make further improvements, and under that authority the course of the river above the harbour was greatly changed. A reverse curve, 3,800ft in length, was taken out and in its place a straight cut 2,800ft long was made, and a timber drawbridge, erected in 1794, was replaced by a swing bridge.

In 1876 the London, Brighton & South Coast Company obtained powers to acquire the Harbour Board's property, but they were not exercised. Instead, the Newhaven Harbour Company was formed in 1878, which, further, was authorised to effect large extensions, and under section 18 of the Board's Act the railway company was empowered to advance money to it and to manage the property in perpetuity.

The present harbour is the result of these steps. A breakwater 28,00ft in length was erected, which runs from Burrow Point – westward of the harbour mouth and at the foot of Burrow Head – straight out to sea for 1,000ft, and then on a curve to the east for another 2,000ft; the extremity of the breakwater being at a point representing the present west pier extended in a straight line. A new east pier, 500 yards long, was built, and between the two piers was a width of 250ft, with a depth at low water of 12ft. Those improvements were completed in 1891.

In 1926 the Southern Railway obtained powers to absorb the Newhaven Harbour Company, which it did. One of the first things subsequently done was to replace the east pier, which was a timber structure, by one of reinforced concrete.

An important recent development at Dover is a new dock for the Train Ferry, which is to the north-west of the Admiralty Pier, and is built in concrete, 415 by 72ft. The maximum difference in the water level is 25ft. There is an electrically operated lifting bridge 60ft long, with two sets of rails to register with those on the steamers. Great difficulties have been experienced owing to the appearance of unexpected fissures in the chalk, through which huge quantities of fresh water percolate.

Folkestone harbour has some items of history that should be put upon record. When railway communication was given with that town in 1843 the harbour was choked up with an accumulation of sand and shingle, and its owners, owing to want of funds, were unable to improve matters. The South Eastern Railway Company thereupon purchased it and made it fit for service. Thus, the report for the half-year January–June, 1846, of the South Eastern and Continental Steam Packet Company, said:

The harbour at Folkestone has been improved so much by the works carried out there that the measure of the time at which steamers can leave it is no longer the depth of water in the harbour, but the depth of water over the rocks at its entrance, and those rocks are now being removed by divers.

Mention must also be made of some of the improvements effected in the harbour, pier and other facilities in the Isle of Wight after the railways there passed into the control of the Southern Railway. The timber pier-head at Ryde Pier was, for instance, replaced by one in reinforced concrete. The Medina Wharf at Cowes had its timber jetty superseded by a new quay, 738ft long, the wall of which is in mass concrete, reinforced by a mat of expanded steel, and giving a depth alongside at high tide of 20ft. Two 5-ton electrically driven coal transporters were amongst the modern machinery provided.

Besides those which have been already dealt with, the Southern Railway had docks, harbours or wharves at about twenty other places, also being one-third owner of the Chelsea dock of the West London Extension Railway.

On the Thames, for instance, there were the wharves at Battersea, Nine Elms, Blackfriars, Deptford, Angerstein's Wharf (Greenwich), and Gravesend. In the approach to the Thames there was the dock at Strood, the harbour at Whitstable, and the piers at Queenborough and Port Victoria.

There was a small harbour at Rye (the branch railway to which was closed in 1962); the wharf at Kingston-by-Sea near Shoreham, that at Littlehampton, and one at Langston. In Plymouth there was Stonehouse Pool, and in North Devon there were wharves at Barnstaple (including a wharf served by the narrow gauge Lynton branch), Bideford and Fremington. The latter, on the River Taw, was originally made by the North Devon Railway about 1855, and was improved to take three 1,000-ton steamers. There was a harbour at Padstow, which belonged to the Padstow Harbour Commission, but was operated by the Southern Railway.

The company was not a large canal owner, merely possessing the Gravesend and Higham Canal, 4 miles 38 chains in length, which has now been closed, and a third share in the Kensington Canal, which was only 33 chains, all told.

XLII

How the Southern Served the Public

THERE were certain directions in which the Southern came more into contact with the general public than any other railway. It had the densest surburban traffic, and the largest electrical service, together with the lion's share of the communication with the Continent.

With reference to the suburban traffic, taking the year 1934: between 7.0 a.m. and 10.0 a.m. no less than 558 trains arrived at Southern Railway stations in London with City workers, from which over 1,700 passengers alighted per minute. This statement is corroborated by the following table; the number of departures exceeds that of arrivals, because the former period is for four hours, whereas the latter is for three.

NUMBER OF PASSENGER TRAINS AND PASSENGERS
DEALT WITH AT LONDON STATIONS - 1934

Station	No. of trains arriving between 7.0 a.m. and 10.0 a.m.	No. of passengers arriving	No. of trains leaving between 4.0 p.m. and 8.0 p.m.	No. of passengers leaving
Ludgate Hill, St Paul's, Holborn . . .	54	20,558	57	17,545
Cannon Street	68	26,733	82	26,568
Charing Cross . .	59	29,141	75	33,015
Waterloo Junction . .	—	3,164	—	3,430
London Bridge (Eastern) .	15 (Low Level)	17,109*	19 (Low Level)	20,597*
London Bridge (Central) .	101	36,027	121	32,913
Victoria (Central) . .	80	27,313	106	32,823
Victoria (Eastern) . .	10	2,804	23	5,278
Waterloo . . .	124	38,628	161	43,114
Vauxhall . . .	—	2,639	—	2,977
City (Waterloo & City Rly.)	47	10,560	57	10,432
Totals . . .	558	214,676	701	228,692

* Includes passengers alighting from, or joining, Cannon Street and Charing Cross trains at London Bridge (High Level)

There was, in addition to the London Suburban, a very extensive residential traffic to and from coastal towns. Between 4.0 and 8.0 p.m. some 30 steam and 18 electric fast trains left the various London termini for these places (in 1934). The density of the steam traffic may be seen by the fact that during these hours 7 trains left for Hastings, 6 for Eastbourne, and 6 for Portsmouth; while the electric service in the same period included 12 trains to Brighton and 6 to Hove and Worthing. In all these cases, the traveller had a through coach to his destination, and there was a corresponding service of fast trains up each weekday morning.

The following cases give a good indication of the service provided. Among the electric expresses mentioned, seven of those to Brighton were non-stop, taking an hour on the journey; while those to Hove (52 miles) reached that point 67 minutes after departure, and Worthing (61 miles) 15 minutes later – the 5.4 p.m. from London Bridge improving on this time by 3 minutes, running to Preston Park (49¼ miles), with one intermediate stop, in 59 minutes. Steam business expresses which may be mentioned were the 5.52 p.m. Waterloo to Portsmouth, which reached Guildford (30½ miles) in 39 minutes, Haslemere (43 miles) in 65 minutes, and attained its destination, Portsmouth (73¾ miles) in 107 minutes after leaving London. There was also the 5.15 p.m. from Cannon Street to Margate and Ramsgate, which arrived at Whitstable Town (56 miles) the first stop, in 70 minutes, Herne Bay (59 miles) in 78 minutes, and Margate (71 miles) in 93 minutes.

There were also fine services to places which were at that time (1934) neither suburban nor seaside, such as Guildford, Tunbridge Wells, etc.

Holiday traffic was colossal. For example, on the Saturday before August Bank Holiday, 1934, the railway conveyed from Waterloo to various destinations about 70,000 people, of whom 23,000 had reserved their seats in advance; the other 47,000 being an unknown quantity, which had nevertheless to be coped with. From Victoria on that day 33,263 passengers went to Brighton, 44,929 to the Kent coast, and 10,358 to the Continent. The total number of passengers leaving the Southern Railway London terminal stations was 971,400 – in 2,538 trains. On the Portsmouth–Ryde service, 41,182 passengers and 553 motor cars were conveyed. On the Monday night 81,900 people left Brighton station.

The Southern Railway was very much concerned in the amusements of the people. There were, for instance, racecourses at Ascot, Aldershot, Ashey (Isle of Wight), Bournemouth, Brighton, Epsom,

Exeter, Folkestone, Fontwell Park, Gatwick, Goodwood, Hawthorn Hill, Hurst Park, Hambledon Hunt, Kempton Park, Lewes, Lingfield Park, Plumpton, Plymouth, Salisbury, Sandown Park, Windsor and Wye. For nearly all the meetings special trains were run. At Westenhanger, for the Folkestone meeting, there was a special racecourse platform, and the same provision existed at Gatwick, Kempton Park, and Sandown Park.

The international home matches of Rugby Football were of course played at Twickenham, where also the Oxford and Cambridge match was played. The accommodation at the station was enlarged so as satisfactorily to deal with the crowds that these matches drew. Nor must the pleasures to be found in the River Thames be forgotten. Practically all the popular resorts on that waterway were served by the Southern – Putney, Barnes, Kew, Richmond, Twickenham, Teddington, Kingston, Surbiton, Hampton Court, Molesey, Chertsey, Staines, Windsor, Eton, and on to Reading. For the Oxford and Cambridge boat race many special arrangements had to be made.

The Southern company provided many cross-country services. By the grouping of its own component companies, through trains were possible between, for instance, Brighton and Ilfracombe, and Brighton and Plymouth. Considerable convenience was also afforded to the public by through trains between Brighton and Margate (via Ashford and Canterbury) which gave communication at Ashford with Dover, Walmer, Deal and Sandwich.

Of cross-country services with which other companies were associated, mention first must be made of the 'Sunny South Special', which provided through communication, with restaurant cars, between Liverpool, Manchester, Birmingham, Leeds, etc., by the London, Midland & Scottish route, and Brighton, Eastbourne, etc., via Willesden Junction and Kensington (Addison Road). The train was worked by the Southern to and from Willesden, where the Chatham, Herne Bay and Margate and Ramsgate carriages were detached or attached.

The Great Western provided a train, with restaurant car, from Birkenhead to Deal, Brighton and Hastings via Reading, Guildford and Redhill. The Southern worked the trains from and to the Great Western station at Reading, and it was split at Redhill. For a time in the 'twenties through coaches from the former G.C.R. via Banbury were conveyed on these trains.

A useful through service that was established before grouping became effective was between Portsmouth and Bristol, also between

Portsmouth and Cardiff via Southampton and Salisbury. The latter was later a through train, with restaurant car, from and to Brighton, worked by the Southern Railway to Salisbury and back.

Portsmouth and the Great Western system were in through communication by a restaurant car train via Basingstoke. The train served Birkenhead and also Manchester, L.M.S., through carriages being provided from Portsmouth. Other services to the G.W.R. company include two from Portsmouth to Wolverhampton and one from Bournemouth to Reading. These services were considerably augmented on summer Saturdays to cater for the heavy week-end traffic which was handled.

Another similar train ran from Bournemouth via Basingstoke and Banbury to the London & North Eastern Railway. Through carriages were provided between Glasgow, Edinburgh, Newcastle, and Southampton Docks in connection with the cross-Channel steamers.

The oldest of all the cross-country services with which the Southern was associated was 'The Pines Express' between Liverpool, Manchester, Bradford, Nottingham, etc., on the London, Midland & Scottish Railway via Bath and the Somerset & Dorset Railway, jointly owned by that company and the Southern. In 1930 the S. & D.J. gave up its distinctive blue livery; the engines were painted in L.M.S. livery and the coaches in S.R. livery; The locomotives, which in addition to former S. & D.J. types, included M.R. 4-4-0 and 0-6-0 types, and later standard L.M.S. 4-6-0 engines, of course worked into the S.R. terminus in Bournemouth.

The Continental services must not be forgotten. There were nine routes (including that to the Channel Islands) owned by the Southern, and in each direction there were the following sailings:

Dover–Calais	Two services daily.
Folkestone–Boulogne	,, ,,
Folkestone–Dunkerque	Every week-night.
Newhaven–Dieppe	Two services daily.
Southampton–Havre ⎫	Every week-day in summer; alternate days
Southampton–Channel Islands ⎭	in winter.
Southampton–St Malo	Ranging once per week in winter to four times at the height of season.
Dover–Ostend	Three daily in summer, two in winter.
Gravesend–Rotterdam	One service each week-day.

From 6th October, 1936, the Night Ferry service replaced the former Folkestone–Dunkerque night service.

In addition to the above services there was a local service from Jersey to St Malo, mainly of an excursion character and generally operated by the steamer *Brittany*.

The Southern Railway filled a very important place in national affairs by its provision in peace-time for assisting the country's defence. There was quite a host of naval, military and air force centres on its system, and large and small detachments of ratings, troops and airmen were continually passing in connection with changing camps, summer camps, command training, manoeuvres, overseas transports, musketry practice, ceremonial occasions in London and elsewhere, etc.

This traffic moved from and to the following:

Naval Centres: Chatham, Sheerness, Dover, Portsmouth, Portland, Devonport.

Army Centres: Hounslow, Kingston, Windsor, Reading, Woking, Aldershot, Bordon, Brookwood, Farnborough, Winchester, Gosport, Portsmouth, Parkhurst, Chichester, Brighton, Wool, Portland, Salisbury Plain – Amesbury and Bulford stations, Porton, Exeter, Devonport and Plymouth, Bodmin, Gravesend, Chatham, Dover, Shorncliffe, Canterbury, Maidstone.

Air Force Centres: Manston (Margate), Kenley, Fawley, Salisbury Plain, Farnborough, Fort Brockhurst, Eastchurch, Folkestone, Chichester, Plymouth, Andover Junction, Kidbrooke.

There were numerous territorial encampments on the system. Among these were: Brighton, Worthing, Christchurch, Portsmouth, Lyndhurst Road, Aldershot, Shorncliffe, Canterbury, Falmer, Arundel, Wool, Netley, Salisbury Plain – Bulford and Amesbury stations – Bordon, Dover, Seaford, Crowborough, Weymouth, Brockenhurst, Sherborne, Martin Mill, Shoreham, Chichester, Gosport, Beaulieu Road, Okehampton, Manston. Huge volumes of traffic had to be dealt with in connection with Army Manoeuvres, Territorial training, and the arrival and departure of troops for overseas garrisons at Southampton.

The above was written as an 'Epilogue' by Dendy Marshall in 1934. By 1947 the line and its passengers had passed through another war, and the status of the railway as the main means of transport for work or leisure, portrayed above, had been eroded by increasing car ownership, the spread of rural bus services, and the replacement of many rural communities by London workers.

The Company had in its last years squarely faced the fact that all lines in the London orbit must be geared up to handle 'commuter' traffic in almost overwhelming quantities, but that traffic in hoppickers, race-goers, Glyndebourne opera visitors, Sussex ramblers, commercial travellers, soldiers on duty – the whole gamut of special passenger categories which had brought so much revenue in the past – was dying fast.

No one would wish to minimise the continuing importance of the Continental traffic, the Southampton Ocean Liner Expresses, the summer-time flood to the Devon and Cornwall coasts – but the answer to 'How the Southern Serves the Public' at the end of its life was a far shorter one than in 1934. It was responsible for making the best sense possible of the fundamental nonsense that so high a proportion of London workers were living a double life, and that their office and home spheres might be separated by anything up to seventy miles. It is time and not distance that matters to the commuter, and the ingenuity and experience of the Southern was to be dedicated to cutting down, minute by minute, the daily sojourn in its trains of the unwilling and often ungrateful commuter. Perhaps the measure of its success can only be fully appreciated by those who, like the present writer, once crept Londonwards in the steam trains of the 'twenties.

The Southern built up a system that has proved viable in conditions changed almost out of recognition in the twenty-five years of its life; its passenger services are probably the best-placed of the former 'Big Four' to face the even greater trials to come.

APPENDIX I

Chief Administrators and Officials

London & South Western Railway Company
(London & Southampton Railway Company until 1839)

CHAIRMEN

Sir Thomas Baring, Bart, M.P.	1832 to 1833
John Wright	1834 to 1836
John Easthope	1837 to 1840
Robert Garnett, M.P.	1841 to 1842
W. J. Chaplin	1843 to 1852
Hon. Francis Scott, M.P.	1853
Sir William Heathcote, Bart.	1854
W. J. Chaplin	1854 to 1858
Capt. Charles E. Mangles	1859 to 1872
C. Castleman	1873 to 1874
The Hon. Ralph H. Dutton	1875 to 1892
Wyndham S. Portal	1892 to 1899
Lieut.-Col. The Hon. H. W. Campbell	1899 to 1904
Sir Charles Scotter, Bart.	1904 to 1910
Sir Hugh Drummond, Bart.	1911 to 1922

GENERAL MANAGERS

C. Stovin (Traffic Manager)	1839
A. Scott (Traffic Manager)	1852
(General Manager)	1870
Sir Charles Scotter	1885
Sir Charles Owens	1898
Sir Herbert Walker	1912

SECRETARIES

E. L. Stephens	1832
W. Reed	1835
A. Morgan	1841
P. L. Campbell	1846
W. Harding	1849
C. J. Brydges	1852
A. Bulkley	1853
L. Crombie	1853
F. Clarke	1862
F. J. Macaulay	1880
G. Knight	1898

ENGINEERS

Francis Giles	1834
Joseph Locke	1837
Albino Martin	1840
John Bass	1849
John Strapp	1853
W. Jacomb	1870
E. Andrews	1887
J. W. Jacomb-Hood	1901
A. W. Szlumper	1914

LOCOMOTIVE SUPERINTENDENTS

Joseph Woods	1835
J. V. Gooch	1841
Joseph Beattie	1850
W. G. Beattie	1871
W. Adams	1878
D. Drummond	1895
R. W. Urie	1912

London, Brighton & South Coast Railway Company
(*London & Brighton Railway Company until 1846*)

CHAIRMEN

John Harman	1837 to 1843
J. M. Parsons	1843
Rowland Hill	1843 to 1846
C. P. Grenfell	1846 to 1848
Samuel Laing	1848 to 1855
Leo Schuster	1856 to 1866
P. N. Laurie	1866 to 1867
Col. W. B. Barttelot, M.P. . . .	1867
Samuel Laing	1867 to 1896
Lord Cottesloe	1896 to 1908
Earl of Bessborough	1908 to 1920
C. C. Macrae	1920 to 1922
G. W. E. Loder	1922

GENERAL MANAGERS

Peter Clarke (Manager) .	1846
G. Hawkins (Manager) .	1850
J. P. Knight	
(Traffic Manager) .	1869
(General Manager) .	1870
Sir Allen Sarle (Secretary and General Manager) .	1886
J. F. S. Gooday . .	1897
Sir William Forbes . .	1899

SECRETARIES

T. J. Buckton . . .	1846
F. Slight	1849
Sir Allen Sarle . .	1867
J. J. Brewer . . .	1898

ENGINEERS

R. Jacomb-Hood . .	1846
F. D. Banister . . .	1860
Sir Charles Morgan . .	1895
Sir James Ball . . .	1917
O. G. C. Drury . .	1920

LOCOMOTIVE SUPERINTENDENTS

—. Statham	?
John Gray . . .	1845
S. Kirtley . .	Feb. 1847
J. C. Craven . .	Dec. 1847
W. Stroudley . . .	1870
R. J. Billinton . .	1890
D. Earle Marsh . .	1905
L. B. Billinton . . .	1911

South Eastern Railway Company

CHAIRMEN

P. St. Leger Grenfell . . .	1836 to 1838
T. W. Tyndale	1838 to 1841
J. Baxendale	1841 to 1845
Sir John Kirkland . . .	1845
J. MacGregor	1845 to 1854
Sir John Campbell . . .	1854
Hon. James Byng . . .	1855 to 1866
Sir Edward Watkin . . .	1866 to 1894
Hon. James Byng . . .	1894
Sir Geo. Russell, Bart. . . .	1895 to 1898
H. Cosmo O. Bonsor . . .	1898 to 1922

GENERAL MANAGERS

Captain R. H. Barlow	.	1854
C. W. Eborall .	1855 to	1873
Sir Myles Fenton	. .	1880
W. R. Stevens		
(Chief Officer)	. .	1895
A. Wills .	. . .	1898

SECRETARIES

J. S. Yeats	. . .	1836
John Whitehead	. .	1841
Captain O'Brien	. .	1845
G. S. Herbert .	. .	1845
Samuel Smiles .	. .	1854
T. A. Chubb .	. .	1866
John Shaw	. . .	1868
W. R. Stevens .	. .	1887
C. Sheath		
(Deputy Secretary)	.	1895
(Secretary) .	. .	1898
C. Davis (Acting Secretary)		1922

ENGINEERS

William Cubitt	. .	1836
P. W. Barlow .	. .	1844
Thomas Drane	. .	1851
Peter Ashcroft	. .	1854
Francis Brady .	. .	1870
P. C. Tempest (Resident		
Engineer) .	. .	1897

LOCOMOTIVE SUPERINTENDENTS

Benjamin Cubitt	.	(?) 1842
J. I. Cudworth	. .	1845
A. M. Watkin .	. .	1876
R. C. Mansell .	. .	1877
James Stirling .	. .	1878

London, Chatham & Dover Railway Company
(*East Kent Railway Company 1852–1859*)

CHAIRMEN

Lord Sondes	. . . . .	1852 to 1866
Lord Harris.	. . . . .	1866 to 1867
G. Hodgkinson	. . . . .	1867 to 1873
J. Staats Forbes .	. . . .	1873 to 1904
Sir E. L. Pemberton	. . .	1904 to 1908
Sir Wm. Hart Dyke, Bart.	. . .	1908 to 1922

GENERAL MANAGER

J. Staats Forbes	1862 to	1904
Wm. Forbes		
(Traffic Manager)	1890 to	1899

SECRETARIES

G. F. Holroyd .	. .	1852
W. E. Johnson	. .	1863
G. W. Brooke .	. .	1867
John Morgan .	. .	1876
E. W. Livesey .	. .	1900
J. R. Dowdall .	. .	1916

ENGINEERS

John S. Valentine and		
William Mills	.	(?) 1852
Sir William and Joseph		
Cubitt .	. .	1853
William Mills .	. .	1858
G. B. Roche .	. .	1891

LOCOMOTIVE SUPERINTENDENTS

Sir W. Cubitt .	.	(?) 1853
W. Martley	. .	1860
W. Kirtley	. .	1874

South Eastern & Chatham Railway Companies' Managing Committee

CHAIRMAN
H. Cosmo O. Bonsor . . . . 1898 to 1922

GENERAL MANAGERS			ENGINEER		
A. Willis .	.	1898	P. C. Tempest .	.	1898
Vincent W. Hill	.	1900			
F. H. Dent	.	1911	LOCOMOTIVE SUPERINTENDENTS		
P. C. Tempest .	.	1920	H. S. Wainwright	.	1898
			R. E. L. Maunsell (Chief		
SECRETARIES			Mechanical Engineer) .	1913	
John Morgan ⎫					
C. Sheath ⎭ (Joint)	.	1898			
C. Davis (Acting)	.	1922			

Southern Railway

CHAIRMEN
Brigadier-General Sir Hugh Drummond, Bart.,
C.M.G. 1923
Brigadier-General The Hon. Everard Baring,
C.V.O., C.B.E. 1924
The Rt. Hon. Lord Wakehurst . . . 1932
Robert M. Holland-Martin, C.B. . . . 1935
Colonel Eric Gore-Brown, D.S.O. . . . 1944

GENERAL MANAGERS			CHIEF ENGINEERS		
Sir Herbert Ashcombe			A. W. Szlumper	.	1923
Walker, K.C.B. .	.	1923	G. Ellson .	.	1927
G. S. Szlumper, C.B.E.	.	1937	V. A. M. Robertson .	.	1944
Sir Eustace Missenden	.	1939			
John Elliot .	.	Oct. 1947	CHIEF ELECTRICAL ENGINEERS		
			H. Jones .	.	1923
			A. Raworth	.	1938
SECRETARIES			C. M. Cock	.	1945
John Jennings Brewer	.	1923			
Godfrey Knight	.	1923	CHIEF MECHANICAL ENGINEERS		
Francis Henry Willis	.	1930	R. E. L. Maunsell, C.B.E. .	1923	
Brigadier L. F. S. Dawes,			O. V. S. Bulleid, C.B.E.	.	1937
M.B.E. .	.	1936			
T. E. Brain (Acting)	.	1939			
S. E. Clark (Acting) .	.	1944			
Brigadier L. F. S. Dawes	.	1946			

APPENDIX II

Dates of Lines Opened

L S.W.R. Main Lines (geographical order)

Waterloo–Nine Elms	11 July, 1848
Nine Elms–Woking Common	19 May, 1838
Public opening	21 May, 1838
Woking Common–Shapley Heath (Winchfield) . . .	24 Sept., 1838
Shapley Heath–Basingstoke	10 June, 1839
Basingstoke–Andover	3 July, 1854
Andover–Salisbury	1 May, 1857
Salisbury–Gillingham (for passengers) . . .	2 May, 1859
,, ,, (for goods)	1 Sept., 1860
Gillingham–Sherborne (for passengers) . . .	7 May, 1860
,, ,, (for goods)	1 Sept., 1860
Sherborne–Yeovil (for passengers)	1 June, 1860
,, ,, (for goods)	1 Sept., 1860
Yeovil–Exeter (Queen Street) (for passengers) . . .	18 July, 1860
,, ,, ,, ,, (for goods)	1 Sept., 1860
Exeter (Queen Street)–Exeter (St. Davids)	1 Feb., 1862
Exeter–Crediton	12 May, 1851
(Broad gauge, and leased to the Bristol & Exeter Railway)	
Crediton–Fremington	1 Aug., 1854
(Completed by 12 July, 1854, but opening held pending the Board of Trade inspection for signalling. Operated by the Bristol & Exeter for the first year)	
Fremington–Bideford	2 Nov., 1855
Barnstaple–Ilfracombe	20 July, 1874
Barnstaple Junction–Barnstaple (Victoria Road) . . .	31 July, 1885
Bideford–Torrington	18 July, 1872
Coleford Junction–North Tawton	1 Nov., 1865
North Tawton–Okehampton Road (Belstone Corner) (4 miles from Okehampton)	8 Jan., 1867
Okehampton Road (Belstone Corner)–Okehampton . .	3 Oct., 1871
Okehampton–Lydford	12 Oct., 1874
Lydford–Devonport	1 June, 1890
(via Tavistock and Bere Alston)	
Plymouth (North Road)–Devonport	17 May, 1876
Meldon Junction–Holsworthy	20 Jan., 1879
Holsworthy–Bude	10 Aug., 1898
Halwill–Launceston	21 July, 1886
Launceston–Tresmeer	28 July, 1892
Tresmeer–Camelford	14 Aug., 1893

LINES OPENED—(*continued*)

Camelford–Delabole	18 Oct., 1893
Delabole–Wadebridge	1 June, 1895
Wadebridge–Padstow	27 Mar., 1899

Basingstoke–Winchester (throughout)	11 May, 1840
Winchester–Southampton	10 June, 1839
Northam curve–	1858
Southampton Junction–Blechynden (Southampton West) .	29 July, 1847
Blechynden–Brockenhurst	1 June, 1847
Brockenhurst–Christchurch $\left.\begin{array}{l}\text{Ceremonial}\end{array}\right.$.	5 Mar., 1888
Bournemouth (New)–Bournemouth West $\left.\begin{array}{l}\text{Public}\end{array}\right.$ . .	6 Mar., 1888
Christchurch–Bournemouth East (original station) . .	14 Mar., 1870
Bournemouth–Poole.	15 June, 1874
Branksome curve	1 June, 1893
Hamworthy Junction–Poole (Holes Bay curve) . . .	1 June, 1893
Alderbury Junction–West Moors	20 Dec., 1866
Hamworthy Junction–Dorchester	1 June, 1847
Dorchester–Weymouth (ex G.W.R.)	20 Jan., 1857

Woking–Guildford	5 May, 1845
Guildford–Godalming (Old station on site of present goods yard)	15 Oct., 1849
Godalming–Havant	1 Jan., 1859
Havant–Portsmouth.	14 June, 1847
Portsmouth Town–Portsmouth Harbour	2 Oct., 1876
(Joint with L.B.S.C.R.)	

L.S.W.R. Suburban lines, branches, spurs etc. (date order)

Bodmin–Wadebridge	4 July, 1834
Boscarne–Wenford Bridge	30 Sept., 1834
Grogley Halt–Ruthern Bridge	30 Sept., 1834
Bishopstoke–Gosport	29 Nov., 1841
Closed four days later and re-opened	7 Feb., 1842
Gosport Station–Clarence Victualling Yard. . . .	21 Sept., 1845
(Extension inside Yard, 1856)	
Battersea (Clapham Junction)–Richmond	27 July, 1846
Bishopstoke–Salisbury (Goods)	27 Jan., 1847
,, ,, (Passenger)	1 Mar., 1847
Brockenhurst–Dorchester	1 June, 1847
(via Ringwood and Wimborne)	
Weybridge–Chertsey	14 Feb., 1848
Farlington Junction and Portcreek Junction–Cosham (Goods)	26 July, 1848
Richmond–Datchet	22 Aug., 1848
Fareham–Cosham	1 Sept., 1848

Lines Opened—(*continued*)

Cosham–Portsmouth (for goods)	1 Sept., 1848
,, ,, (for passenger)	1 Oct., 1848
Southcote Junction–Basingstoke (ex G.W.R.) . . .	1 Nov., 1848
Hampton Court Junction–Hampton Court	1 Feb., 1849
Guildford–Ash Junction	20 Aug., 1849
Barnes–Smallberry Green (Isleworth).	22 Aug., 1849
Ash Junction–Farnham	8 Oct., 1849
Shalford Junction with S.E.R.	15 Oct., 1849
Datchet–Windsor	1 Dec., 1849
Loop Line–Feltham Junction	1 Feb., 1850
Smallberry Green–Hounslow	1 Feb., 1850
Farnham–Alton	28 July, 1852
Brookwood Cemetery Branch	Dec., 1854
Staines–Ascot	4 June, 1856
Ascot–Wokingham	9 July, 1856
Dorchester–Weymouth	20 Jan., 1857
Lymington Junction–Lymington	12 July, 1858
Epsom–Leatherhead	1 Feb., 1859
(Opened by L.S.W.R. Jointly worked with L.B.S.C.R.)	
Raynes Park (Wimbledon Junction)–Epsom . . .	4 April 1859
Havant–Cosham (via Farlington Junction) (for passengers) .	2 Jan., 1860
Exeter–Exmouth	1 May, 1861
Kew curve and Barnes curve	1 Feb., 1862
Ringwood–Christchurch	13 Nov., 1862
West London Extension	2 Mar., 1863
(Jointly with the L.B.S.C.R., L.N.W.R. and G.W.R.)	
Gosport–Stokes Bay	6 Apr., 1863
Chard Junction–Chard	8 May 1863
Botley–Bishops Waltham	1 June, 1863
Twickenham–Kingston	1 July , 1863
Petersfield–Midhurst	1 Sept., 1864
Strawberry Hill–Shepperton	1 Nov., 1864
Andover–Redbridge.	6 Mar., 1865
(Including the Kimbridge and Romsey connecting junction lines)	
Alton–Winchester	2 Oct., 1865
Weymouth–Portland (for goods)	16 Oct., 1865
,, ,, (for passengers)	1 Sept., 1889
Weymouth Harbour Tramway (for Goods) . . .	16 Oct., 1865
,, ,, ,, (for passengers) . . .	1 July, 1889
Longhedge Junction–Ludgate Junction	1866
Portwood (St. Denys)–Netley	5 Mar., 1866
Chertsey–Virginia Water	1 Oct., 1866
Midhurst extension	17 Dec., 1866
Colyton Junction (Seaton Junction)–Beer (Seaton) . .	16 Mar., 1868
Tulse Hill spur	1 Oct., 1868
Tooting, Merton and Wimbledon	1 Oct., 1868
(Transferred jointly to L.S.W. and L.B.S.C. in 1865)	
Malden–Kingston	1 Jan., 1869

Lines Opened—(*continued*)

Kensington (Addison Road)–Richmond	1 Jan., 1869
(via Turnham Green, Gunnersbury and Kew Gardens)	
Pirbright Junction (Brookwood)–Farnham	2 May, 1870
Callington–Calstock Quay	7 May, 1872
(East Cornwall Mineral Railway. Gauge 3ft 6in; later partly reconstructed as P.D. & S.W.J.L.R. and became part of S.R.)	
New Poole Junction–Poole	2 Dec., 1872
Sidmouth Junction–Sidmouth	6 July, 1874
Studland Road Junction (with M.D.R.)	1 June, 1877
Friary Junction–Friary Goods Depot.	1 Feb., 1878
Ascot–Sturt Lane Junction	18 Mar., 1878
Ash–Aldershot spur	1879
Frimley Junction–North Camp	2 June, 1879
Friary–North Quay	22 Oct., 1879
Twickenham fly-over	1882
Twickenham and Hounslow connecting curve	1 Jan., 1883
(Allowing for a circular service via Richmond or via Kew Bridge)	
Raynes Park 'flyunder'	16 Mar., 1884
Malden direct curve from Kingston loop to up line	25 Mar., 1884
Leatherhead–Effingham Junction	2 Feb., 1885
Hampton Ct. Junction–Guildford	2 Feb., 1885
(via Cobham)	
Wareham–Swanage	20 May, 1885
Hurstbourne–Fullerton	1 June, 1885
Fratton–Southsea	1 July, 1885
Staines curve	1 July, 1884
(Permitting direct running from Windsor to the Reading line)	
East Putney–Wimbledon	3 June, 1889
Spur to Point Pleasant	1 July, 1889
Netley–Fareham	2 Sept., 1889
Brookwood–Bisley	14 July, 1890
Winchester (Cheesehill)–Shawford (ex G.W.R.)	1 Oct., 1891
Plymstock branch	5 Sept., 1892
Ascot–Frimley Junction	11 June, 1893
Fort Brockhurst–Lee-on-the-Solent	12 May, 1894
(Lee-on-the-Solent Light Railway became part of S.R. in 1923)	
Wadebridge–Bodmin line joined to Main line	1 Nov., 1895
Tipton St. Johns–Budleigh Salterton	15 May, 1897
Yealmpton branch (later G.W.R.)	17 Jan., 1898
Lynton–Barnstaple (Town) Ceremonial 11 May 1898, Public	16 May, 1898
(Lynton & Barnstaple Railway, 1ft 11½in gauge, became part of S.R. in 1923)	
Waterloo & City Railway { Ceremonial	11 July, 1898
{ Public	8 Aug., 1898

Lines Opened—(*continued*)

Easton–Church Hope (for goods)	1 Oct., 1900
„ „ „ (for passenger)	1 Sept., 1902
Service through from Weymouth using Admiralty Tramway (opened 29 May 1874) between Portland and Church Hope	
Basingstoke–Alton	1 June, 1901
Newton Tony Junction–Amesbury	1 Oct., 1901
(Military traffic only)	
Public Traffic	2 June 1902
Byfleet Junction dive-under	1903
Alton–Fareham	1 June, 1903
Budleigh Salterton–Exmouth	1 June, 1903
Axminster–Lyme Regis	24 Aug., 1903
Amesbury Junction–Newton Tony Junction . . .	7 Aug., 1904
Fareham Tunnel avoiding (up) line (Meon Valley Line) .	2 Oct., 1904
(Down)	Sept., 1906
Bentley–Bordon	11 Dec., 1905
Amesbury–Bulford	1 June, 1906
Calstock–Bere Alston	2 Mar., 1908
(P.D. & S.W.J.L.R. reconstruction of East Cornwall Mineral: became part of S.R. in 1923)	
Hampton Court Junction dive-under	21 Oct., 1908
Hampton Court branch fly-over	July 1915
Dinton–Fovant (Military line)	15 Oct., 1915
Bisley–Deepcut (for goods)	25 July, 1917
Military Line only (for passengers)	1 Aug., 1917
Deepcut–Blackdown	Dec., 1917
Bovington Camp branch	9 Aug., 1919
(From Junction on the east side of Wool)	

Lines opened—S.R. (Western Section)

Totton–Fawley	20 July, 1925
Halwill Junction–Torrington	27 July, 1925
Wimbledon–South Merton	7 July, 1929
South Merton–Sutton	5 Jan., 1930
Motspur Park–Tolworth	29 May, 1938
Tolworth–Chessington South	28 May, 1939
Winchester Junction spur	5 May, 1943

Isle of Wight (date order)

Cowes–Newport	16 June, 1862
Ryde (St. Johns Road)–Shanklin	23 Aug., 1864
Brading–Brading Quay	23 Aug., 1864
Ryde Pier Tramway	28 Aug., 1864
(Extension Esplanade–St. Johns Road)	1 Aug., 1871

Lines Opened—*(continued)*

Shanklin–Ventnor	10 Sept., 1866
Sandown–Shide	1 Feb., 1875
Shide–Pan Lane	6 Oct., 1875
Smallbrook Junction–Newport	20 Dec., 1875
Pan Lane–Newport	1 June, 1879
Ryde Esplanade–Ryde St. Johns Road	5 Apr., 1880
(Railway replacing tramway)	
Ryde Pier Head–Ryde Esplanade	12 July, 1880
(Railway in addition to tramway)	
Brading–Bembridge	27 May, 1882
Newport–Freshwater (for goods)	10 Sept., 1888
,, ,, (for passenger)	20 July, 1889
Merstone–St. Lawrence	20 July, 1897
St. Lawrence–Ventnor	1 June, 1900

S. & D.J.R. (date order)

Somerset Central Railway (throughout)	28 Aug., 1854
Highbridge–Burnham-on-Sea	3 May, 1858
Glastonbury–Wells (for public)	15 Mar., 1859
Wimborne–Blandford (for public)	1 Nov., 1860
(The formal opening took place on 31 Oct. 1860)	
Cole–Templecombe	Nov., 1861
Evercreech–Glastonbury	3 Feb., 1862
Templecombe–Blandford	31 Aug., 1863
Templecombe, new spur connecting S. & D.J.R. with L.S.W.R. station, completed	Mar., 1870
New Poole Junction (Broadstone Junction)–Poole	2 Dec., 1872
Evercreech–Bath	20 July, 1874
Corfe Mullen Junction–Broadstone Junction curve	14 Dec., 1885
Edington Junction–Bridgwater	21 July, 1890

L.B.S.C.R. Main Lines (geographical order)

London Bridge Junction–Corbetts Lane Junction	14 Dec., 1836
(London and Greenwich)	
(For London and Croydon trains, 5 June 1839; for London and Brighton, 12 July 1841; for South Eastern Railway, 26 May, 1842)	
Corbetts Lane Junction–West Croydon	5 June, 1839
(Running powers over Greenwich Railway, London Bridge–Corbetts Lane)	
Croydon Junction (Norwood)–Haywards Heath	12 July, 1841
South Croydon–Stoats Nest	5 Nov., 1899
Stoats Nest–Earlswood (for goods)	5 Nov., 1899
,, ,, ,, (for passengers)	1 Apr., 1900
Haywards Heath–Brighton	21 Sept., 1841

LINES OPENED—*(continued)*

Brighton–Shoreham	12 May, 1840
Preston Park–Hove (spur)	1 July, 1879
Shoreham–Worthing	24 Nov., 1845
Worthing–Arundel and Littlehampton (at Lyminster)	16 Mar., 1846
Arundel and Littlehampton–Chichester	8 June, 1846
Ford–Littlehampton	17 Aug., 1863
Littlehampton direct line	1 Jan., 1887

(Giving direct access to Littlehampton from Worthing. Old West line closed and new West line opened)

Barnham–Bognor	1 June, 1864
Chichester–Havant	15 Mar., 1847
Havant–Langston	19 Jan., 1865
Langston–South Hayling (Hayling Island)	17 July, 1867
Havant–Portsmouth	14 June, 1847
Fratton–Southsea	1 July, 1885

(Joint with L.S.W.R.)

Portsmouth Town–Portsmouth Harbour	2 Oct., 1876

(Joint with L.S.W.R.)

Watering Island Jetty Line	15 Jan., 1878

Brighton–Lewes	8 June, 1846
Kemp Town Branch	2 Aug., 1869
Keymer Junction–Lewes	1 Oct., 1847
Southerham Junction–Newhaven Wharf	8 Dec., 1847
Newhaven Harbour–Seaford	1 June, 1864
Extension alongside Newhaven Quay	17 May, 1886
Lewes–St. Leonards (Bulverhythe)	27 June, 1846
Extended to St. Leonards near present West Marina	7 Nov., 1846
Polegate–Eastbourne	14 May, 1849
Stone Cross spur	1 Aug., 1871
New Junction (Polegate)	3 Oct., 1881

L.B.S.C.R. (Suburban lines, branches, spurs etc.) date order

West Croydon–Epsom Town	10 May, 1847
Three Bridges–Horsham	14 Feb., 1848
Polegate–Hailsham	14 May, 1849
Deptford Wharf Branch	2 July, 1849
Sydenham–Crystal Palace (L.L.) (for goods)	27 Mar., 1854
„ „ „ (for passenger)	10 June, 1854
Three Bridges–East Grinstead	9 July, 1855
Commercial Dock Branch	July, 1855
New Cross (Down side)–Lift Bridge Junction	Aug., 1855

(Connection from Deptford Wharf line)

West Croydon–Wimbledon	22 Oct., 1855

(Opened as joint with L.S.W., L.B.S.C.R. took lease in 1856 and ownership 1 Jan., 1866)

Lines Opened—(*continued*)

Crystal Palace (L.L.)–Wandsworth	1 Dec., 1856
Crystal Palace (L.L.)–Norwood Junction	1 Oct., 1857
New Wandsworth–Battersea Pier (Formal)	27 Mar., 1858
„ „ „ „ (Public)	29 Mar., 1858
Lewes (Uckfield Jc.)—Uckfield (Formal)	11 Oct., 1858
„ „ „ „ (Public)	18 Oct., 1858
Epsom–Leatherhead	1 Feb., 1859
(Opened by L.S.W.R.)	
L.B.S.C. traffic	8 Aug., 1859
Epsom Town–Epsom	8 Aug., 1859
Horsham–Petworth	10 Oct., 1859
Battersea Pier Junction–Victoria	1 Oct., 1860
Shoreham–Partridge Green	1 July, 1861
Partridge Green–Itchingfield Junction . . .	16 Sept., 1861
Battersea Wharf branch	30 Apr., 1862
Norwood Fork South–Windmill Bridge Junction . . .	1 May, 1862
Birkbeck–Norwood Junction spur	18 June, 1862
Windmill Bridge Junction–Balham	1 Dec., 1862
Norwood Fork–Selhurst	1 Dec., 1862
Clapham Junction–Kensington (W.L.E.)	2 Mar., 1863
Hardham Junction–Ford	3 Aug., 1863
Ford–Littlehampton	17 Aug., 1863
Barnham Junction–Bognor	1 June, 1864
Sutton–Epsom Downs	22 May, 1865
West Croydon–Selhurst fork	22 May, 1865
Cow Lane–Barrington Road	1 Aug., 1865
South Fork–Itchingfield Junction	2 Oct., 1865
West Horsham–Peasmarsh	2 Oct., 1865
Lavender Hill Junction–Factory Junction . . .	1 Mar., 1866
London Bridge–East Brixton	13 Aug., 1866
East Grinstead–Groombridge	1 Oct., 1866
Groombridge–Tunbridge Wells	1 Oct., 1866
Petworth–Midhurst	15 Oct., 1866
Midhurst (L.B.S.C.R.)–Midhurst (L.S.W.R.) . . .	17 Dec., 1866
Leatherhead (Old Joint Station)–Leatherhead (New L.B.S.C. Station)	4 Mar., 1867
Leatherhead–Dorking	11 Mar., 1867
Barrington Road Junction–Battersea Park . . .	1 May, 1867
Dorking–Horsham	1 May, 1867
Dorking Spur to S.E.R.	1 May, 1867
Battersea (High level line)	1 Dec., 1867
Central Croydon branch	1 Jan., 1868
Groombridge–Uckfield	3 Aug., 1868
Peckham Rye–Sutton	1 Oct., 1868
Balham spur–South London and Sutton	1 Oct., 1868
Tooting–Merton Park	1 Oct., 1868
(Joint with L.S.W.R.)	
Streatham–Wimbledon	1 Oct., 1868
Hamsey–Lewes (East)	1 Oct., 1868

Lines Opened—(*continued*)

Spur Deptford Wharf–Old Kent Road	15 May, 1869
New Cross (E.L.R.)–Wapping	7 Dec., 1869
Lower Norwood (West Norwood)–Tulse Hill . . .	1 Nov., 1870
South Bermondsey spur	1 Jan., 1871
Old Kent Road–Deptford Road Junction (E.L.R.) . .	13 Mar., 1871
Tulse Hill–Streatham Hill spur	1 Aug., 1871
Eastbourne spur	1 Aug., 1871
Spur Cambria Road to L.C.D.R.	1 July, 1872
Tunbridge Wells–Grove Junction (Goods) . . .	1867
,, ,, ,, ,, (Passenger) . . .	1 Feb., 1876
Hailsham–Heathfield	5 Apr., 1880
Heathfield–Redgate Mill Junction	1 Sept., 1880
Midhurst–Chichester	11 July, 1881
Polegate–Hailsham (New Junction)	3 Oct., 1881
East Grinstead–Culver Junction	1 Aug., 1882
Horsted Keynes–Haywards Heath	3 Sept., 1883
South Croydon East Grinstead (L.L.)	10 Mar., 1884
(Joint with S.E.R. South Croydon–Crowhurst Junction)	
East Grinstead (H.L.)–East Grinstead (L.L.) (spur) . .	10 Mar., 1884
Crowhurst Junction (S.E.R.) spur	10 Mar., 1884
,, ,, (To passenger trains)	1 Aug., 1884
New Cross (Up side)–Deptford Road Junction . . .	1 Oct., 1884
Woodside–Selsdon Road Junction	10 Aug., 1885
Streatham Common–Streatham spur	1 Jan., 1886
Dyke branch	1 Sept., 1887
Hurst Green Junction–Edenbridge	2 Jan., 1888
Edenbridge–Groombridge (Ashurst Junction) . . .	1 Oct., 1888
Eridge spur	1 Oct., 1888
Lewes new line (deviation)	17 June, 1889
Redgate Mill–Eridge	1 May, 1894
(Two single lines made one double)	

S.E.R. Main Lines (geographical order)

Charing Cross–London Bridge	11 Jan., 1864
Cannon Street extension	1 Sept., 1866
London Bridge–Corbetts Lane	14 Dec., 1836
(Running powers over the London & Greenwich)	
Corbetts Lane–Jolly Sailor (Norwood Junction) . . .	5 June, 1839
(Running powers over London & Croydon)	
Jolly Sailor (Norwood Junction)–Reigate Junction (Redhill) .	12 July, 1841
(Running powers over the London & Brighton Railway to Redhill until 19 July, 1842, when the S.E.R. purchased that section between a point just north of the present Coulsdon South station and Redhill. Running powers continued over the remainder)	
Reigate Junction–Tonbridge	26 May, 1842
Tonbridge–Headcorn	31 Aug., 1842

LINES OPENED—*(continued)*

Headcorn–Ashford (Private opening)	28 Nov., 1842
,, ,, (to public)	1 Dec., 1842
Ashford–Folkestone (west of viaduct)	28 June, 1843
Folkestone west of viaduct–Folkestone Junction . . .	18 Dec., 1843
Folkestone–Dover	7 Feb., 1844
Ashford–Canterbury	6 Feb., 1846
Canterbury–Ramsgate	13 Apr., 1846
Ramsgate Town–Margate Sands	1 Dec., 1846
Minster–Deal	1 July, 1847

North Kent East Junction–New Cross (St. John's) . .	30 July, 1849
New Cross (St. John's)–Chislehurst	1 July, 1865
Chislehurst–Tonbridge Junction (Goods)	3 Feb., 1868
Chislehurst–Sevenoaks (ceremonial)	2 Mar., 1868
,, ,, (public)	3 Mar., 1868
Sevenoaks–Tonbridge (local trains)	1 May, 1868
,, ,, (express trains)	1 June, 1868

Tonbridge–Tunbridge Wells	20 Sept., 1845
Tunbridge Wells–Robertsbridge	1 Sept., 1851
Robertsbridge–Battle	1 Jan., 1852
Battle–Bopeep Junction	1 Feb., 1852
Bopeep Junction–Hastings	13 Feb., 1851

S.E.R. Surburban Lines, branches, spurs etc. (date order)

Canterbury–Whitstable	3 May, 1830
Whitstable Harbour branch	19 Mar., 1832
London Bridge–Spa Road	14 Dec., 1836
Spa Road–Deptford	8 Feb., 1836
Deptford–Greenwich	24 Dec., 1838
Bricklayers Arms branch (S.E.)	1 May, 1844
Maidstone Road (Paddock Wood)–Maidstone . . .	25 Sept., 1844
Gravesend–Strood	23 Aug., 1847
(Double track on site of earlier single line which was opened on 10 Feb., 1845)	
Folkestone Harbour Branch (Goods)	1843
,, ,, ,, (Passengers)	1 Jan., 1849
Dorking–Redhill (Reigate Junction)	4 July, 1849
Reading–Farnborough	4 July, 1849
North Kent East Junction–Gravesend	30 July, 1849
(via Blackheath and Woolwich)	
Farnborough (Hants.)–Ash Junction	20 Aug., 1849
Dorking–Shalford	20 Aug., 1849

LINES OPENED—(*continued*)

(Guildford–Ash Junction L.S.W.R.)	20 Aug., 1849
Shalford–Guildford	15 Oct., 1849
(Running powers over L.S.W.R Shalford Jn.–Ash Jn.)	
North Kent West Junction–Surrey Canal Junction spur .	1 Sept., 1849
Hastings (Bopeep Junction)–Ashford	13 Feb., 1851
Angerstein Wharf branch	Oct., 1852
Rye–Rye Harbour	Mar., 1854
Strood–Maidstone	18 June, 1856
Purley (Godstone Road)–Caterham	5 Aug., 1856
(Caterham Railway became part of S.E.R. 1859)	
Lewisham Junction–Beckenham Junction	1 Jan., 1857
Tonbridge spur–allowing for direct running from Tonbridge to the Hastings line	1857
Reading (junction with G.W.R.)	1 Dec., 1858
St. Lawrence Loop	July, 1863
New Beckenham–Addiscombe Road	1 Apr., 1864
Dartford Loop Line	1 Sept., 1866
Parks Bridge Junction–Ladywell	Sept., 1866
Dorking spur (joining Guildford line with L.B.S.C.R. Horsham line)	1 May, 1867
Maze Hill–Charlton.	1 Jan., 1873
Sandling Junction–Sandgate (ceremonial)	9 Oct., 1874
,, ,, ,, (public)	10 Oct., 1874
Grove Park Junction–Bromley (Bromley North) . . .	1 Jan., 1878
Greenwich–Maze Hill	1 Feb., 1878
Blackfriars spur–connecting the L.C. & D. Herne Hill to Holborn line with the London Bridge to Charing Cross line .	1 June, 1878
Aldershot Junction–Aldershot Town	May, 1879
Dunton Green–Westerham	7 July, 1881
Buckland Junction–Deal (Joint S.E. and C. & D.) . .	15 June, 1881
Appledore–Lydd	7 Dec., 1881
Lydd–Dungeness (for goods)	7 Dec., 1881
,, ,, (for passengers)	1 Apr., 1883
Hoo Junction–Sharnal Street	1 Apr., 1882
Elmers End–Hayes	29 May, 1882
Kearsney Curve	1 July 1882
Sharnal Street–Port Victoria	11 Sept., 1882
Lydd–New Romney.	19 June, 1884
Selsdon–Woodside	10 Aug., 1885
(Jointly with L.B.S.C.R.)	
Cheriton Junction (Shorncliffe Camp)–Barham . . .	4 July, 1887
Barham–Harbledown Junction	1 July, 1889
Strood Junction–Rochester Common	20 July, 1891
Rochester Common–Chatham (Central)	1 Mar., 1892
Paddock Wood–Goudhurst (Hope Mill)	1 Oct., 1892
Goudhurst–Hawkhurst	4 Sept., 1893
Blackheath (near)–Slades Green (near)	1 May, 1895
(via Bexleyheath)	
Purley–Kingswood	2 Nov., 1897

LINES OPENED—(*continued*)

Lines opened—S.E. & C.R. (S.E. section)

Kingswood–Tadworth	1 July, 1900
Tadworth–Tattenham Corner	4 June, 1901
Crowhurst–Bexhill (now West)	1 June, 1902
Bickley–Orpington (down loop).	8 Sept., 1902
,, ,, (up loop)	14 Sept., 1902
Chislehurst–St. Mary Cray Junction (loops) . . .	19 June, 1904

Lines opened—S.R. (S.E. section)

Ramsgate loop (via St. Lawrence and Dumpton Park) .	2 July, 1926
Minster loop	7 July 1929
Lewisham loops (Nunhead–Lewisham) (for goods) . .	7 July, 1929
,, ,, (Lewisham–Hither Green) . . .	7 July, 1929
,, ,, (,, ,, ,, (electric trains) .	16 July, 1933
,, ,, (Nunhead–Lewisham) (for passengers). .	30 Sept., 1935
Stoke Junction–Allhallows-on-Sea	14 May, 1932
Greatstone Deviation, New Romney Branch . . .	4 July, 1937
Crayford Curve	11 Oct. 1942

L.C.D.R. Main Lines (geographical order)

Victoria–Battersea	3 Dec., 1860
(Running powers over the Victoria Station and Pimlico Railway)	
Stewarts Lane Junction–S. end of Victoria Bridge. . .	20 Dec., 1866
Stewarts Lane–Herne Hill	25 Aug., 1862
Herne Hill–Penge Junction (nr. present Kent House Station)	1 July, 1863
Bromley Junction–Bromley (Shortlands)	3 May, 1858
(W.E. & C.P.R. Farnborough Extension)	
Bromley (Shortlands)–Southborough Road (Bickley) . .	5 July, 1858
(Mid-Kent Railway Extension)	
Bickley–Rochester Bridge (Strood)	3 Dec., 1860
Rochester Bridge–Chatham	29 Mar., 1858
Chatham–Faversham	25 Jan., 1858
Faversham–Canterbury	9 July, 1860
Canterbury–Dover Town	22 July 1861
Dover Town–Dover Harbour	1 Nov., 1861
Admiralty Pier Branch	30 Aug., 1864
Faversham–Whitstable	1 Aug., 1860
Whitstable–Herne Bay	13 July, 1861
Herne Bay–Margate and to Ramsgate Harbour . . .	5 Oct., 1863

L.C.D.R. Suburban lines, branches, spurs etc. (date order)

Chatham–Strood	29 Mar., 1858
Faversham Creek branch	12 Apr., 1860
Sittingbourne–Sheerness	19 July, 1860
Sutton-at-Hone (Swanley)–Sevenoaks (Bat & Ball) . .	2 June, 1862

Lines Opened—(*continued*)

Herne Hill–Elephant & Castle	6 Oct.,	1862
Brixton–Loughborough Junction	1 May,	1863
Elephant & Castle–Blackfriars	1 June,	1864
Blackfriars–Ludgate Hill (East Street) (temporary station)	21 Dec.,	1864
Longhedge Junction–Factory Junction	1 July,	1865
Canterbury Road–Barrington Road	1 Aug.,	1865
Peckham Rye–Crystal Palace (H.L.)	1 Aug.,	1865
Stewarts Lane–Longhedge works	7 Oct.,	1865
Earls Street Junction (Ludgate Hill)–West Street Junction (Farringdon Street)	1 Jan.,	1866
Victoria Bridge–Prince of Wales Road	20 Dec.,	1866
Factory Junction–Shepperds Lane Brixton		1867
Tulse Hill–Herne Hill spur	1 Jan.,	1869
Sevenoaks (Bat & Ball)–Sevenoaks (Tubs Hill)	1 Aug.,	1869
Nunhead–Blackheath Hill	18 Sept.,	1871
Ludgate Hill–Holborn Viaduct	2 Mar.,	1874
Otford Junction–Maidstone	1 June,	1874
Queenborough Pier branch	15 May,	1876
Chatham Dockyard branch	16 Feb.,	1877
'Toomer' loop (re-opening)	2 Apr.,	1877
Buckland Junction–Deal	15 June	1881

      Jointly with the S.E.R.

Kearsney loop–Enabling L.C.D.R. trains to run direct to Deal without having to reverse at Dover Priory	1 July,	1882
Sheerness Town branch	1 June,	1883
Maidstone–Ashford	1 July,	1884
Fawkham–Gravesend	10 May,	1886
Blackheath Hill–Greenwich Park	1 Oct.,	1888
Ashford connecting line between L.C.D. and S.E. Stations	1 Nov.,	1891
Nunhead–Shortlands	1 July,	1892

      (Catford loop line)

Lines opened—*S.E. & C.R.* (L.C.D. section)

Queenborough–Leysdown	1 Aug.,	1901
Sheerness-on-Sea spur	2 Jan.,	1922

      Providing direct access to Sheerness-on-Sea from Sittingbourne without having to reverse at Sheerness Dockyard.

APPENDIX III

Dates of Lines Closed

Nine Elms Junction–Nine Elms (to passengers) . . .	11 July, 1848
Surrey Canal Junction–Bricklayers Arms (to passengers) .	Jan., 1852
Stewarts Lane Junction–Pimlico (to passengers) . . .	1 Oct., 1860
Itchingfield Junction South fork	1 Aug., 1867
Pouparts Junction–Battersea Pier Junction (to passengers) .	1 Dec., 1867
Hamsey–Uckfield Junction	1 Oct., 1868
Havant–Hayling Island	Jan., 1869
(Re-opened Aug., 1869)	
Central Croydon branch	1 Dec., 1871
(Re-opened 1 June, 1886)	
Hailsham (old junction)	3 Oct., 1881
Eastbourne (old junction)	3 Oct., 1881
Angmering–Ford Junction	1 Jan., 1887
(Original west-coast line)	
Lewes–Southerham Junction	3 Oct., 1889
(Deviation of line out of Lewes)	
Central Croydon branch (2nd closure)	1 Sept., 1890
Waterloo (S.E. & C.)–Waterloo (L. & S.W.) . . .	1911
Hamworthy Junction–Hamworthy (to passengers) . .	1 July, 1896
Strood–Chatham Central	1 Oct., 1911
Fratton–Southsea	Aug., 1914
Southampton Town–Royal Pier	Sept., 1914
Queenborough Pier Branch (to passengers) . . .	Nov., 1914
Gunnersbury—Chiswick Junction (to passengers) . .	22 Feb., 1915
,, ,, ,, (entirely) . . .	24 July, 1932
Forton Junction–Stokes Bay	1 Nov., 1915
(Purchased by the Admiralty in 1922)	
Snow Hill Junction–Holborn Viaduct L.L. . . .	2 Apr., 1916
Holborn Viaduct L.L.–Ludgate Hill	1 June, 1916
Woodside–Selsdon Road	1 Jan., 1917
(Until 30 Sept., 1935)	
Kensington (Addison Road)–Studland Road Junction . .	5 June, 1916
Basingstoke–Butts Junction	1 Jan., 1917
(Re-opened 18 Aug., 1924)	
Nunhead–Greenwich Park	1 Jan., 1917
(Partly re-opened later, but portion east of bridge over S.E.R. abandoned in 1929)	
Norwood Junction–Spur Junction (near present Birkbeck Station) (to passengers)	1 Jan., 1917

Lines Closed—*(continued)*

Nunhead–Crystal Palace (H.L.)

First closure	1 Jan., 1917
Re-opened	1 Mar., 1919
Closed again	22 May, 1944, until 4 Mar., 1946
Finally closed	20 Sept., 1954
Ramsgate Harbour branch	2 July, 1926
Ramsgate Town–Margate Sands	2 July, 1926
Tooting Junction–Merton Park	4 Mar., 1929
(via Merton Abbey)	
Canterbury–Whitstable (to passengers)	1 Jan., 1931
,, ,, (completely)	1 Dec., 1952
(Re-opened for a few weeks after the floods of 1953)	
Hythe–Sandgate	1 Apr., 1931
Hurstbourne Junction–Fullerton Junction	6 July, 1931
Closed to passengers. Junction near	
Hurstbourne removed	29 May, 1934
Track removed (to Longparish)	Oct., 1934
Fort Brockenhurst–Lee-on-the-Solent (to passengers)	1 Jan., 1931
,, ,, ,, (completely)	30 Sept., 1935
Basingstoke–Alton (to passengers)	12 Sept., 1932
,, ,, (completely)	1 June, 1936
Botley–Bishops Waltham (to passengers)	2 Jan., 1933
Dyke branch (to goods)	2 Jan., 1933
,, ,, (to passengers)	1 Jan., 1939
Kemp Town branch (to passengers)	2 Jan., 1933
Ruthern Bridge branch	30 Dec., 1933
Last train ran on 29 Nov., 1933	
Chichester–Midhurst (to passengers)	8 July, 1935
Lynton–Barnstaple (Town)	30 Sept., 1935
Ringwood–Christchurch	30 Sept., 1935
New Romney branch (Greatstone Deviation)–Dungeness	4 July, 1937
Ash Junction–Farnham (via Tongham)	4 July, 1937
Elham Valley line	
Passenger service, Canterbury–Lyminge	2 Dec., 1940
,, ,, Lyminge–Folkestone	3 May, 1943
,, ,, ,, ,, (restored)	7 Oct., 1946
,, ,, ,, ,, (suspended)	16 June, 1947

APPENDIX IV

Dates of Services Electrified

Date order

Victoria–London Bridge	*1 Dec., 1909
(via South London line)	
Battersea Park–Crystal Palace (Low Level) . . .	*12 May, 1911
(via Clapham Junction and Streatham Hill)	
Crystal Palace–Norwood Junction–Selhurst . . .	*1 June, 1912
Peckham Rye–West Norwood (official)	*1 June, 1912
(Trains actually commenced to run on 3 Mar., 1912)	
Waterloo–East Putney	25 Oct., 1915
Point Pleasant Junction–Shepperton	30 Jan., 1916
Clapham Junction–Wimbledon–Strawberry Hill . .	30 Jan., 1916
Hounslow Loop	12 Mar., 1916
Malden–Hampton Court	18 June, 1916
Hampton Court Junction–Claygate	20 Nov., 1916
Balham–Coulsdon North	*1 Apr., 1925
Sutton (via West Croydon)	*1 Apr. 1925
Victoria–Orpington (via Penge East)	12 July, 1925
Raynes Park–Dorking North	12 July, 1925
Nunhead–Crystal Palace (High Level) . . .	12 July, 1925
Leatherhead–Effingham Junction	12 July, 1925
Holborn Viaduct–Orpington (via Nunhead) . .	12 July, 1925
Claygate–Guildford (via Cobham)	12 July, 1925
Hayes–Elmers End	21 Sept., 1925

Charing Cross and Cannon Street	–Orpington	28 Feb., 1926
	–Bromley North . .	28 Feb., 1926
	–Addiscombe and Hayes .	28 Feb., 1926

Charing Cross and Cannon Street–Dartford (via Greenwich, Blackheath, Bexleyheath and Sidcup)	†19 July, 1926
London Bridge–Crystal Palace (Low Level) . . .	25 Mar., 1928
Charing Cross–Caterham and Tadworth	25 Mar., 1928
(Extended to Tattenham Corner)	
London Bridge–Victoria	17 June, 1928
(via South London Line. Replacing overhead system)	
Streatham Hill–London Bridge	17 June, 1928
(via Tulse Hill)	
London Bridge–Coulsdon North	17 June, 1928
(via Streatham and Streatham Common and via Norwood Junction)	

* Overhead system. † Restricted service 6 June 1926

LINES ELECTRIFIED—(*continued*)

London Bridge–London Bridge	17 June, 1928
(via Norwood Junction and Selhurst)	
London Bridge–Epsom Downs	17 June, 1928
(via Streatham and via Norwood Junction)	
London Bridge–Crystal Palace (Low Level) . . .	17 June, 1928
London Bridge–Dorking North and Effingham Junction .	3 Mar., 1929
(via Tulse Hill and Mitcham Junction)	
Victoria–Epsom (via Micham Junction)	3 Mar., 1929
Victoria–Beckenham Junction	3 Mar., 1929
(via Crystal Palace. Replacing overhead system between Victoria and Crystal Palace, Low Level)	
Victoria–Holborn Viaduct–Wimbledon	3 Mar., 1929
(via Tulse Hill and Haydons Road)	
Wimbledon–South Merton (new line)	7 July, 1929
Victoria–Coulsdon North and Sutton	22 Sept., 1929
(Replacement of overhead services)	
South Merton–Sutton (via St. Helier)	5 Jan., 1930
(New line)	
Whitton Junction and Hounslow Junction–Windsor . .	6 July, 1930
Dartford–Gravesend Central	6 July, 1930
Wimbledon–West Croydon (via Mitcham)	6 July, 1930
Purley–Three Bridges and Reigate	17 July, 1932
(via Redhill)	
Three Bridges–Brighton, Hove and Worthing . . .	1 Jan., 1933
Lewisham–Hither Green	16 July, 1933
†Bickley–St. Mary Cray	1 May 1934
Orpington–Sevenoaks (Tubs Hill)	6 Jan., 1935
Bickley and Chislehurst–Sevenoaks (Tubs Hill) . .	6 Jan., 1935
(via Swanley and Otford)	
Brighton and Haywards Heath–Eastbourne. . . .	7 July, 1935
Brighton etc.–Hastings and Ore.	7 July, 1935
Haywards Heath–Horsted Keynes	7 July, 1935
Brighton–Seaford	7 July, 1935
Nunhead–Lewisham	30 Sept., 1935
Woodside–Sanderstead	30 Sept., 1935
Hampton Court Junction–Chertsey and Staines . . .	3 Jan., 1937
†Hampton Court Junction–Guildford	3 Jan., 1937
Waterloo–Portsmouth	4 July, 1937
(via Woking and Haslemere)	
†Woking–Farnham	3 Jan., 1937
Woking–Alton	4 July, 1937
Motspur Park–Tolworth	29 May, 1938
Dorking North–Havant	3 July, 1938
(via Horsham and Arundel)	
Littlehampton branch	3 July, 1938
Barnham–Bognor Regis	3 July, 1938
Virginia Water–Ash Vale (via Ascot)	1 Jan., 1939
Ascot–Reading South	1 Jan., 1939

† Partial services.

Lines Electrified—(*continued*)

Tolworth–Chessington South (New line)	28 May, 1939
Frimley Junction–Sturt Lane Junction	1 Jan., 1939
Aldershot–Guildford	1 Jan., 1939
Otford–Maidstone East	2 July, 1939
Swanley–Gillingham (Kent)	2 July, 1939
Gravesend–Maidstone West and Rochester (via Strood)	2 July, 1939

APPENDIX V

Openings and Closings of Stations to 1948

STATIONS	OPENED	CLOSED
Abbey Wood	1850	
Addiscombe Road	1 Apr., 1864	
Addlestone	14 Feb., 1848	
Adisham	22 July 1861 [6]	
Admiralty Pier (see Dover)		
Albany Park	7 July, 1935	
Albert Road Bridge	1 July, 1904	8 Aug., 1914
Albert Road Halt	1 Oct., 1906	13 Jan., 1947
Aldershot	2 May, 1870	
Aldrington Halt (opened as 'Dyke Junction Halt')	15 Sept., 1905	
Allhallows-on-Sea (for special excursions 14 May, 1932)	16 May, 1932	
Alresford	2 Oct., 1865	
Alton	28 July, 1852	
Alverstone	1 Feb., 1875 [6]	
Amberley	3 Aug., 1863	
Amesbury	1 Oct., 1901	
Andover Junction	3 July, 1854 [6]	
Andover Town	6 Mar., 1865 [6]	
Anerley	5 June 1839	
Angerstein Wharf (goods) . . .	Oct., 1852	
Angmering	16 Mar., 1846	
Appledore	13 Feb., 1851	
Ardingly	3 Sept., 1883 [6]	
Arundel (opened as 'New Arundel') .	3 Aug., 1863	
Arundel and Littlehampton . . .	16 Mar., 1846	1 Sep., 1863
Ascot	4 June, 1856	
Ash (S.E.R.)	20 Aug., 1849	
Ashbury	10 Jan., 1879 [6]	
Ashey	20 Dec., 1875 [6]	
Ashford (L.C.D.R.)	1 July, 1884	1 Jan., 1899
Ashford (S.E.R.)	1 Dec., 1842	

Stations—(*continued*)	Opened	Closed
Ashford (Middlesex)	22 Aug., 1848	
Ash Green	8 Oct., 1849	4 July, 1937
Ashley Heath Halt . . .	1 Apr., 1927	
Ashtead	1 Feb., 1859[6]	
Ashurst	1 Oct., 1888	
Ash Vale (formerly 'North Camp & Ash Vale')	2 May, 1870	
Ashwater	21 July, 1886[6]	
Altantic Park Hostel Halt (opened for special arrangements only)	30 Oct., 1929	
Avon Lodge (private station) . .	. . 1862[7]	30 Sept., 1935
Axminster	18 July, 1860[6]	
Aylesford	18 June, 1856	
Aylesham Halt	1 July, 1928	
Bagshot	18 Mar., 1878	
Balcombe	12 July, 1841[6]	
Balham & Upper Tooting (formerly 'Balham')	1 Dec., 1856	
Bandon Halt	11 June, 1906	7 June, 1914
Bank (Ceremonial) . . .	11 July, 1898	
,, (Public)	8 Aug., 1898	
Banstead	22 May, 1865	
Barcombe (opened as 'New Barcombe') .	1 Aug., 1882[6]	
Barcombe Mills (opened as 'Barcombe') .	18 Oct., 1858[6]	
Barham	4 July, 1887	1 Dec., 1940
Barming	1 June, 1874	
Barnes	27 July, 1846	
Barnes Bridge	12 Mar., 1916	
Barnham	1 June, 1864	
Barnehurst.	1 May, 1895	
Barnstaple Junction . . .	1 Aug., 1854	
Barnstaple Town (formerly 'Barnstaple Quay')	20 July, 1874	
Re-sited	16 May, 1898	
Barnstaple Town Wharf (Lynton & Barnstaple Railway)	11 May, 1898	
Basingstoke	10 June, 1839	
Bat & Ball (opened as 'Sevenoaks (Bat & Ball'))	2 June, 1862	
Battersea (W.L.E.)	2 Mar., 1863	21 Oct. 1940
Battersea (L.B.S.C.R.) . . .	1 Oct., 1860	1 Nov., 1870
Battersea Park (L.B.S.C.) . . .	1 May, 1867	
Battersea Park Road (L.C.D.R.) . .	1 May, 1867	3 Apr., 1916
Battle	1 Jan., 1852	
Baynards	2 Oct., 1865	
Bearsted	1 July, 1884	
Beaulieu Road	1 June, 1847	Feb., 1860[1]
,, ,, ...	Nov., 1895[1]	
Beckenham Hill	1 July, 1892	

STATIONS—(*continued*)	OPENED	CLOSED
Beckenham Junction	1 Jan., 1857	
Beddington Lane Halt (opened as 'Beddington')	22 Oct., 1855	
Bedhampton Halt	1906	
Bekesbourne	22 July, 1861	
Bellingham	1 July, 1892	
Belmont (opened as 'California') . .	22 May, 1865	
Beltring & Branbridges Halt . .	1 Sept., 1909	
Beluncle Halt	July, 1906	
Belvedere	1859	
Bembridge	27 May, 1882	
Bentley	1854/5 [7]	
Bentworth & Lasham	1 June, 1901	1 Jan., 1917
,, ,, ...	18 Aug., 1924	12 Sept., 1932
Bere Alston	2 June, 1890	
Bere Ferrers	2 June, 1890	
Berrylands	16 Oct., 1933	
Berwick (Sussex)	27 June, 1846	
Betchworth	4 July, 1849	
Bexhill Central (opened as 'Bexhill') .	27 June, 1846 [6]	
Bexhill West (opened as 'Bexhill') .	1 June, 1902	
Bexley	1 Sept., 1866	
Bexleyheath	1 May, 1895	
Bickley (opened as 'Southborough Road')	5 July, 1858	
Bideford	2 Nov., 1855	
Re-sited	10 June, 1872	
Billingshurst	10 Oct., 1859	
Bingham Road	1 Sept., 1906	15 Mar., 1915
(Re-opened as 'Bingham Road Halt')	30 Sept., 1935	
Birchington-on-Sea	5 Oct., 1863	
Birkbeck	2 Mar., 1930	
Bishopsbourne	1 July, 1889	1 Dec., 1940
Bishopstone	26 Sept., 1938	
Bishopstone Halt	1 June, 1864	26 Sept., 1938
Re-opened as 'Bishopstone Beach Halt'	(Easter) 1939	1 Jan., 1942
Bishops Waltham	1 June, 1863	2 Jan., 1933
Bisley	14 July, 1890	
Bitterne (opened as 'Bitterne Road') .	5 Mar., 1866 [6]	
Blackfriars (S.E.R.)	11 Jan., 1864	1 Jan., 1869
Blackfriars Bridge (L.C.D.R.) . .	1 June, 1864	1 Oct., 1885
Blackheath	30 July, 1849	
Blackheath Hill	18 Sept., 1871	1 Jan., 1917
Blackmoor	11 May, 1898 [6]	30 Sept., 1935
Blackwater (I. of W.) . . .	1 Feb., 1875 [6]	
Blackwater (S.E.R.)	4 July, 1849	
Blean & Tyler Hill Halt . . .	Jan., 1908 [1]	1 Jan., 1931
Blechynden	1 June, 1847	5 Nov., 1892
(Replaced by Southampton West, now 'Central')		

STATIONS—(*continued*)	OPENED	CLOSED
Bodmin North (opened as 'Bodmin') .	1 Nov., 1895	
Bognor 1st Station (see Woodgate)		
2nd Station (terminus)	1 June 1864	
destroyed 1899 by fire; temporary buildings in use until 1902		
Bookham	2 Feb., 1885	
Bordon	11 Dec., 1905	
Borough Road	1 June, 1864	1 Apr., 1907
Boscombe	1 July, 1886	
Bosham	15 Mar., 1847	
Botley	29 Nov., 1841 [6]	
(Line was closed 3 Dec., 1841 and re-opened 7 Feb., 1842, see 'Lines Opened')		
Bournemouth (on site of present goods yard) subsequently renamed Bournemouth East.)	14 Mar., 1870	20 July, 1885
Bournemouth Central (replacing original East station)	20 July, 1885	
Bournemouth West	15 June., 1874	
Bow	1 Nov., 1865 [6]	
Boxhill & Westhumble (opened as 'West Humble')	11 Mar., 1867	
Bracknell	9 July, 1856	
Brading	23 Aug., 1864 [6]	
Bramber	1 July, 1861 [6]	
Brambledown Halt . . .	Mar., 1905	
Bramley & Wonersh . . .	2 Oct., 1865	
Bramshot Halt		
Branksome	1 June, 1893	
Brasted	7 July, 1881	
Bratton Fleming . . .	11 May, 1898	30 Sept., 1935
Braunton	20 July, 1874 [6]	
Breamore	20 Dec., 1866 [6]	
Brentford Central . . .	22 Aug., 1849	
Brentor	2 June, 1890	
Bricklayers Arms . . .	1 May, 1844	Jan., 1852
Bridestowe	12 Oct., 1874 [6]	
Bridge	1 July, 1889	1 Dec., 1940
Brighton	21 Sept., 1841*	
Brixton	25 Aug., 1862	
Broad Clyst		
Broadstairs	5 Oct., 1863	
Broadstone (formerly 'New Poole Junction')	1 June, 1847 [6]	
Brockenhurst	1 June, 1847	
Brockley	1871	

*open for Shoreham trains 12 May, 1840

STATIONS—(*continued*)	OPENED	CLOSED
Brockley Lane	June, 1872 [1]	1 Jan., 1917
Bromley North (opened as 'Bromley S.E.R.')	1 Jan., 1878	
Bromley South (opened as 'Bromley') .	22 Nov., 1858	
Brookland Halt	7 Dec., 1881	
Brookwood	1864	
Browndown Halt	12 May, 1894	1 May, 1930
Bude.	10 Aug., 1898 [6]	
Budleigh Salterton (opened as 'Salterton')	15 May, 1897 [6]	
Bulford	1 June, 1906	
Bulverhythe	27 July, 1846	7 Nov., 1846
Bungalow Town Halt (see 'Shoreham Airport')		
Burgess Hill	21 Sept., 1841	
Bursledon	2 Sept., 1889 [6]	
Buxted	3 Aug., 1868	
Byfleet & Woodham (see 'West Byfleet')		
Caffyns Halt	Dec., 1916 [1]	30 Sept., 1935
Calborne & Shalfleet	20 July, 1889 [6]	
California (see 'Belmont')		
Callington (opened as 'Callington Road')	2 Mar., 1908 [6]	
Calstock	2 Mar., 1908 [6]	
Camberley (formerly 'Camberley & York Town')	18 Mar., 1878	
Camberwell Gate (see 'Walworth Road')		
Camberwell New Road . . .	6 Oct., 1862	3 Apr., 1916
Camelford	14 Aug., 1893 [6]	
Camel's Head Halt	1 Nov., 1906	4 May, 1942
Cannon Street	1 Sept., 1866	
Canterbury (C. & W.) (Ceremonial) .	3 May, 1830	
,, ,, (Public) . .	4 May, 1830	6/7 Apr., 1846
Canterbury East (opened as 'Canterbury')	9 July, 1860	
Canterbury South (opened as 'South Canterbury')	1 July, 1889	1 Dec., 1940
	7 Oct., 1946	14 June, 1947
Canterbury West (opened as 'Canterbury')	6 Feb., 1846	
Carisbrooke	20 July, 1889 [6]	
Carshalton.	1 Oct., 1868 [6]	
Carshalton Beeches (formerly 'Beeches Halt')	1906	
Caterham	5 Aug., 1856	
Catford	1 July, 1892	
Catford Bridge	1 Jan., 1857	
Cattewater (Goods)	1888	
Central Croydon (see 'Croydon Central')		
Chandlers Ford	1 Mar., 1847	
Chapelton (opened as 'Chapeltown') .	1 Aug., 1854 [6]	Aug., 1860
,, ,, ,, ,, .	June, 1875	
Chard	8 May, 1863 [6]	

STATIONS—*(continued)*	OPENED	CLOSED
Chard Junction (opened as 'Chard Road')	18 July, 1860 [6]	
Charing	1 July, 1884	
Charing Cross	11 Jan., 1864	
Charlton	30 July, 1849	
Chartham	1859 [1]	
Chatham (L.C.D.R.) . . .	25 Jan., 1858	
Chatham Central (S.E.R.) . .	1 Mar., 1892	1 Oct., 1911
Chatham Dockyard (L.C.D.R.) .	16 Feb., 1877	
Cheam	10 May, 1847	
Chelfham	11 May, 1898 [6]	30 Sept., 1935
Chelsea (W.L.E.) . . .	2 Mar., 1863	21 Oct., 1940
Chelsfield	2 Mar., 1868	
Cheriton Halt	1 May, 1908	1 Dec., 1915
„ „	14 June, 1920	1 Feb., 1941
„ „	7 Oct., 1946	16 June, 1947
Chertsey	14 Feb., 1848	
Chessington North . . .	28 May, 1939	
Chessington South . . .	28 May, 1939	
Chestfield & Swalecliffe Halt .	6 July, 1930	
Chevening Halt	16 Apr., 1906	
Chichester	8 June, 1846	
Chilham	6 Feb., 1846	
Chilsworthy	1 June, 1909 [6]	
Chilworth & Albury . . .	20 Aug., 1849 [6]	
Chipstead (opened as 'Chipstead & Banstead Downs')	2 Nov., 1897	
Chislehurst (opened as 'Chislehurst & Bickley Park')	1 July, 1865	
Chislet Halt	1920	
Chiswick	22 Aug., 1849	
Christchurch	13 Nov., 1862	1 July, 1886
(Re-sited)	1 July, 1886	
Christ's Hospital	28 Apr., 1902	
Church Hope Cove . . .	1 Sept., 1902	
Church Manor Way . . .	1 Jan., 1917	1 Jan., 1920
Clandon	2 Feb., 1885	
Clapham (L.C.D.R.) (opened as 'Clapham & North Stockwell')	25 Aug., 1862	3 Apr. 1916
Clapham Common (opened as 'Wandsworth' and replaced by 'Clapham Junction')	21 May, 1838	2 Mar., 1863
Clapham Junction	2 Mar., 1863	
Clatford	6 Mar., 1865 [6]	
Claygate	2 Feb., 1885	
Cliddesden	1 June, 1901	1 Jan., 1917
„	18 Aug., 1924	12 Sept., 1932
Cliffe	31 Mar., 1882	
Clock House	1890	
Cliftonville (L.B.S.C.R.) . . .	1 Oct., 1865	

STATIONS—*(continued)*	OPENED	CLOSED
Clyst St. Mary & Digby Halt . .	1907/8	27 Sept., 1948
Cobham	2 Feb., 1885	
Cocking	11 July, 1881	8 July, 1935
Collington Halt (opened as 'Collington Wood Halt', closed and later re-opened as 'West Bexhill Halt' and finally renamed 'Collington Halt'	3 Sept., 1905	
Colyford	16 Mar., 1868 [6]	
Colyton (formerly 'Colyton Town') .	16 Mar., 1868 [6]	
Combpyne.	24 Aug., 1903	
Commercial Docks	July, 1856	1 Jan., 1867
Cooden Beach (formerly 'Cooden Halt')	*c* 1905	
Cooksbridge	1 Oct., 1847	
Coombe Road (opened as 'Combe Lane')	10 Aug., 1885	1 Jan., 1917
,, ,, ,, ,, ,, ,,	30 Sept., 1935	
Copplestone	1 Aug., 1854 [6]	
Corfe Castle	20 May, 1885	
Cosham	1 Sept., 1848	
Coulsdon North (opened as 'Stoats Nest', see entry)	5 Nov., 1899	
Coulsdon South (opened as 'Coulsdon').	1 Oct., 1889	
Cowden	1 Oct., 1888	
Cowes	16 June, 1862	
Cranbrook	4 Sept., 1893	
Cranleigh (opened as 'Cranley') . .	2 Oct., 1865	
Crawley	14 Feb., 1848	
Crayford	1 Sept., 1866	
Crediton	12 May, 1851 [6]	
Creekmoor Halt	19 June, 1933	
Crewkerne	18 July, 1860 [6]	
Crofton Park	1 July, 1892	
Crowborough & Jarvis Brook (opened as 'Rotherfield')	3 Aug., 1868	
Crowhurst	1 June, 1902	
Crowthorne (formerly 'Wellington College for Crowthorne')	1858/59	
Croydon Central (opened as 'Central Croydon')	1 Jan., 1868	1 Dec., 1871
	1 June, 1886	1 Sept., 1890
Crystal Palace (H.L.)	1 Aug., 1865	1 Jan., 1917
	1 Mar., 1919	22 May, 1944
,, ,, ,, Re-opened 4 March, 1946		
Crystal Palace (L.L.)	10 June, 1854	
Cuxton	18 June, 1856	
Daggons Road (opened as 'Daggens Road')	1876	
Dartford	30 July, 1849	
Datchet (opened as 'Datchett') . .	22 Aug., 1848	
Deal	1 July, 1847	
Dean	1 Mar., 1847 [6]	

Stations—(*continued*)	Opened	Closed
Deepdene (opened as 'Box Hill & Leather-head Road')	4 July, 1849 [6]	
Delabole	18 Oct., 1893 [6]	
Denmark Hill (L.B.S.C.R.) . . .	13 Aug., 1866 [6]	
Denmark Hill (L.C.D.R.) . . .	Dec., 1865 [1]	
Denton Halt	July, 1906	
Deptford	8 Feb., 1836	15 Mar., 1915
,,	19 July, 1926	
Devils Dyke	1 Sept., 1887	1 Jan., 1939
Devonport (Kings Road) . . .	17 May, 1876	
Dinton	2 May, 1859 [6]	
Doleham Halt	1 July, 1907	
Dorchester (terminus station, now 'South')	1 June, 1847	
Dorking North (opened as 'Dorking') .	11 Mar., 1867	
Dorking Town (opened as 'Dorking') .	4 July, 1849	
Dormans	10 Mar., 1884 [6]	
Dover, Admiralty Pier. . . .	1860	1919
Dover Harbour	1 Nov., 1861	10 July, 1927
Dover Marine (Military) . . .	2 Jan., 1915	
,, ,, (Public) . . .	18 Jan., 1919	
Dover Priory	22 July, 1861	
Dover Town (S.E.R.)	7 Feb., 1844	14 Oct., 1914
Downton	20 Dec., 1866	
Drayton	8 June, 1846	1 June, 1930
Droxford for Hambledon . . .	1 June, 1903	
Dumpton Park (Ceremonial) . .	2 July, 1926	
,, ,, (Public) . . .	19 July, 1926	
Dunbridge	1 Mar., 1847 [6]	
Dungeness (Goods)	7 Dec., 1881	
,, (Passenger) . . .	1 Apr., 1883	4 July, 1937
Dunmere Halt	3 Sept., 1888 [6]	
Dunsbear Halt	27 July, 1925	
Dunsland Cross	10 Jan., 1879 [6]	
Dunton Green (opened as 'Dunton Green & Riverhead')	2 Mar., 1868	
Durley Halt	Feb., 1910	2 Jan., 1933
Durrington-on-Sea	4 July, 1937	
Dyke, The	1 Sept., 1887	1 Jan., 1939
Earley	1863/4	
Earlsfield	1 Apr., 1884	
Earlswood	1868/9	
Eastbourne	14 May, 1849	1866
Resited	1866	
East Brixton (opened as 'Loughborough Park')	13 Aug., 1866	
East Budleigh	15 May, 1897 [6]	
East Croydon	12 July, 1841	
East Dulwich (formerly 'Champion Hill')	1 Oct., 1868	
East Farleigh	25 Sept., 1844	

STATIONS—*(continued)*	OPENED	CLOSED
East Grinstead	9 July, 1855	1 Oct., 1866
Resited	1 Oct., 1866	Oct., 1883
Resited	1 Aug., 1882	
Eastleigh (opened as 'Bishopstoke') .	10 June, 1839	
East Malling Halt	1913	
East Minster-on-Sea	1902	
Easton	9 Jan., 1902	
East Putney	3 June, 1889 [2]	
East Southsea (opened as 'Southsea') .	1 July, 1885	8 Aug., 1914
East Worthing Halt (see 'Ham Bridge Halt')		
Ebbsfleet & Cliffsend Halt . . .	May, 1908	1 Apr., 1933
Edenbridge	26 May, 1842	
Edenbridge Town (opened as 'Edenbridge')	2 Jan., 1888	
Eden Park	29 May, 1882	
Effingham Junction	2 July, 1888	
Eggesford	1 Aug., 1854 [8]	
Egham	4 June, 1856	
Egloskerry	28 July, 1892 [6]	
Elephant & Castle ('Temporary station)	6 Oct., 1862	
,, ,, (Present station) .	Feb., 1863	
Elham	4 July, 1887	1 Dec., 1940
Elmers End	1 Apr., 1864	
Elmore Halt	11 Apr., 1910	1 May, 1930
Elmstead Woods (opened as 'Elmstead')	1 July, 1904	
Elsted	1 Sept., 1864	
Eltham Park (opened as 'Shooters Hill & Eltham Park')	1 July, 1908	
Eltham (Well Hall) (opened as 'Well Hall')	1 May, 1895	
Emsworth	15 Mar., 1847	
Epsom	1 Feb., 1859	
Epsom Downs	22 May, 1865	
Epsom Town (formerly 'Epsom') . .	10 May, 1847	3 Mar., 1929
Eridge	3 Aug., 1868	
Erith	30 July, 1849	
Esher for Sandown Park (opened as 'Ditton Marsh')	21 May, 1838	
Etchingham	1 Sept., 1851	
Ewell East (formerly 'Ewell') . .	10 May, 1847	
Ewell West (formerly 'Ewell') . .	4 Apr., 1859	
Exeter Central (opened as 'Exeter Queen Street')	19 July, 1860	
Exeter St. Davids (opened to L.S.W.R. trains	1 Feb., 1862	
Exton (see 'Woodbury Road')		
Exmouth	1 May, 1861 [6]	
Eynsford	1 July, 1862	
Falconwood	1 Jan., 1936	

STATIONS—(*continued*)	OPENED	CLOSED
Falmer	8 June, 1846	1 Aug., 1865
Resited	1 Aug., 1865	
Fareham	29 Nov., 1841	3 Dec., 1841
(But see 'Lines Opened' section) .	7 Feb., 1842	
Faringdon Halt	1 June, 1903	
Farlington Halt	9 July, 1928	4 July, 1937
Farnborough	24 Sept., 1838 [6]	
Farnborough North (formerly 'Farnborough')	4 July, 1849	
Farncombe	1 May, 1897	
Farnham	8 Oct., 1849	
Farningham Road & Sutton-at-Hone .	3 Dec., 1860	
(opened as "Farningham & Sutton)"		
Faversham.	25 Jan., 1858	
Fawkham	June. 1872	
Fawley	20 July, 1925	
Faygate	14 Feb., 1848	
Feltham	22 Aug., 1848	
Fishbourne Halt	1 Apr., 1906	
Fishersgate Halt	15 Sept., 1905	
Fittleworth	2 Sept., 1889	
Fleet (formerly 'Fleetpond') . .	1847	
Folkestone (Temporary station) . .	28 June, 1843	18 Dec., 1843
Folkestone Central (Present station) .	1 Sept., 1884	
(opened as 'Cheriton Arch')		
Folkestone Harbour	1 Jan., 1849	1850
Resited	1850	
Folkestone Junction (opened as 'Folkestone')	18 Dec., 1843	
Folkestone Warren Halt (see 'Warren Halt')		
Ford (Devon) (opened as 'Ford') . .	2 June, 1890 [6]	
Ford (Sussex) (opened as 'Arundel') .	8 June, 1846	
Fordingbridge	20 Dec., 1866 [6]	
Forest Hill (opened as 'Dartmouth Arms')	5 June, 1839	
Forest Row	1 Oct., 1866	
Fort Brockhurst (formerly 'Brockhurst').	1865/6	
Fort Gomer Halt (formerly 'Privett') .	12 May, 1894	1 May, 1930
Fovant (Military traffic only) . .	15 Oct., 1915	
Frant	1 Sept., 1851	
Fratton	1 July, 1885	
Fremington	1 Aug., 1854	
Freshwater	20 July, 1889 [6]	
Friars Walk (see 'Lewes')		
Frimley	18 Mar., 1878	
Fullerton Junction (formerly 'Fullerton Bridge')	6 Mar., 1865 [6]	
Fulwell	1 Nov., 1864	
Gatwick	June, 1907 [1]	Nov., 1907 [1]
Gatwick Airport (opened as 'Tinsley Green')	30 Sept., 1935	

STATIONS—(*continued*)	OPENED	CLOSED
Gatwick Racecourse	1891	
Gillingham (Dorset) (opened as 'Gilling-ham')	2 May, 1859 [6]	
Gillingham (Kent) (opened as 'New Brompton')	1858	
Gipsy Hill	1 Dec., 1856 [7]	
Glynde	27 June, 1846	
Glyne Gap Halt	3 Sept., 1905	Sept., 1915 [1]
Godalming (Original station) . .	15 Oct., 1849	1 May, 1897
,, (Present station) . .	1 Jan., 1859	
Godshill	20 July, 1897 [6]	
Godstone	26 May, 1842	
Godstone Road (see 'Purley')		
Gomshall	20 Aug., 1849 [6]	
Goring-by-Sea (opened as 'Goring') .	16 Mar., 1846	
Gosport	29 Nov., 1841	3 Dec., 1841
,, ...	7 Feb., 1842	
Gosport Road & Alverstoke . .	Nov., 1866	1 Nov., 1915
Goudhurst (opened as 'Hope Mill for Goudhurst & Lamberhurst')	1 Oct., 1892	
Grain Crossing Halt	1906	
Grange Road	2 Apr., 1860	
Grateley	1 May, 1857 [6]	
Gravesend (Gravesend & Rochester Rly.)	10 Feb., 1845	13 Dec., 1846
,, ,, ,, (re-opened)	23 Aug., 1847	30 July, 1849
(Replaced by North Kent station) .	30 July, 1849	
Gravesend West Street . . .	10 May, 1886	
Greatstone-on-Sea	4 July, 1937	
Greenhithe	30 July, 1849	
Greenwich	24 Dec., 1838	
(Permanent station 1840, dismantled and rebuilt further back in 1878)		
Greenwich Park (opened as 'Greenwich')	1 Oct., 1888	1 Jan., 1917
Grogley Halt	4 July, 1834 [6]	
Groombridge	1 Oct., 1866	
Grosvenor Road (L.B.S.C.R.) . .	Nov., 1870 [1]	1 Apr., 1907
Grosvenor Road (L.C.D.R.) . .	1 Jan., 1867	1 Oct., 1911
Grove Ferry	13 Apr., 1846	
Grove Park	1 Nov., 1871	
Guildford	5 May, 1845	
Gunnersbury (opened as 'Brentford Road')	1 Jan., 1869	
Gunnislake	2 Mar., 1908	
Hackbridge	1 Oct., 1868	
Hailsham	14 May, 1849	
Halling	1890	
Halwill	10 Jan., 1879 [6]	
Hamble Halt	18 Nov., 1942	
Ham Bridge Halt (later 'East Worthing Halt')	May, 1906 [1]	

STATIONS—*(continued)*	OPENED	CLOSED
Hammersmith (Grove Road) . .	1 Jan., 1869	5 June, 1916
Hampden Park (opened as 'Willingdon')	1 Jan., 1888	
Hampton	1 Nov., 1864	
Hampton Court	1 Feb., 1849	
Hampton Wick	1 July, 1863	
Ham Street & Orlestone (formerly 'Ham Street')	13 Feb., 1851	
Hamworthy (opened as 'Poole') . .	1 June, 1847	1896
Hamworthy Junction	1 June, 1847 [6]	
Harrietsham	1 July, 1884	
Hartfield	1 Oct., 1866	
Hartington Road Halt . . .	1 Jan., 1906	1 June., 1911 [1]
Harty Road Halt	Mar., 1905	
Haslemere	1 Jan., 1859	
Hassocks (opened as 'Hassocks Gate') .	21 Sept., 1841	
Hastings	13 Feb., 1851	
Hatherleigh	27 July, 1925	
Havant	15 Mar., 1847	
Haven Street	20 Dec., 1875 [6]	
Hawkhurst	4 Sept., 1893	
Haydons Road (opened as 'Haydens Lane')	1 Oct., 1868	
Hayes	29 May 1882	
Hayling Island (formerly 'South Hayling')	17 July, 1867	
Haywards Heath	12 July, 1841	
Headcorn	31 Aug., 1842	
Heathfield & Cross-in-Hand . .	5 Apr., 1880	
Hellingly	5 Apr., 1880	
Henfield	1 July, 1861	
Hersham	28 Sept., 1936	
Herne Bay	13 July, 1861	
Herne Hill.	25 Aug., 1862	
Herriard	1 June, 1901	1 Jan., 1917
,, ...	18 Aug., 1924	12 Sept., 1932
Hever	1 Oct., 1888	
Higham	1845 [6]	
Higham (Re-opened)	23 Aug., 1847	
High Brooms (opened as 'Southborough')	1893	
High Halstow Halt	July, 1906	
High Rocks Halt	1 June, 1907	
Hildenborough	1 May, 1868	
Hilsea Halt	2 Nov., 1941	
Hinchley Wood	20 Oct., 1930	
Hinton Admiral (opened as 'Hinton') .	6 Mar., 1888 [6]	
Hither Green	1 June, 1895	
Holborn Viaduct	2 Mar., 1874	
Holborn Viaduct (L.L.) . . .	1 Aug., 1874	1 June, 1916
Hole	27 July, 1925	
Holland Road Halt . . .	15 Sept., 1905	

STATIONS—*(continued)*	OPENED	CLOSED
Hollingbourne	1 July, 1884	
Holmsley (opened as 'Christchurch Road')	1 June, 1847 [6]	
Holmwood	1 May, 1867	
Holsworthy	20 Jan., 1879 [6]	
Holton Heath	1 June, 1847	
Honiton	18 July, 1860	
Honor Oak	Dec., 1865	1 Jan., 1917
,, ,, ...	1 Mar., 1919	22 May, 1944
Re-opened 4 March, 1946		
Honor Oak Park	1 Apr., 1886	
Hook	2 July, 1883	
Horam (opened as 'Horeham Road for Waldron')	5 Apr., 1880	
Horley	12 July, 1841	1905
Re-sited further south . . .	1905	
Horringford	1 Feb., 1875 [6]	
Horsebridge	6 Mar., 1865 [6]	
Horsham	14 Feb., 1848	
Horsley (formerly 'Horsley & Ockham & Ripley')	2 Feb., 1885	
Horsmonden	1 Oct., 1892	
Horsted Keynes	1 Aug., 1882	
Hothfield Halt (opened as 'Hothfield') .	1 July, 1884	
Hounslow (present station) . . .	1 Feb., 1850	
Hove (original station) . . .	12 May, 1840	1 Mar., 1880
(Present station, opened as 'Cliftonville')	1 Oct., 1865	
Hurn (opened as 'Herne') . . .	13 Nov., 1862	30 Sept., 1935
Hurstbourne	1883	
Hurst Green (Halt)	1 June, 1907	
Hythe (Hants)	20 July, 1925	
Hythe (Kent)	9 Oct., 1874	3 May, 1943
Re-opened 1 Oct., 1945		
Idmiston Halt	3 Jan., 1943	
Ifield (opened as 'Lyons Crossing Halt') .	1 June, 1907	
Ilfracombe	20 July, 1874	
Instow	2 Nov., 1855	
Isfield	18 Oct., 1858	
Isleworth (opened as 'Hounslow') .	22 Aug., 1849	
(subsequently 'Smallberry Green')		
Itchen Abbas	2 Oct., 1865	
Jackwood Springs (Tunbridge Wells)	20 Sept., 1845	25 Nov., 1846
Jessie Road Bridge	1 July, 1904	8 Aug., 1914
Kearsney (opened as 'Ewell') . .	1 Aug., 1862	
Kempton Park (Race Traffic Only) .		
Kemp Town	2 Aug., 1869	2 Jan., 1933
Kemsing	1 June, 1874	
Kemsley Halt	1 Jan., 1927	
Kenley (opened as 'Coulsdon') . .	5 Aug., 1856	

Stations—(*continued*)	Opened	Closed
Kent House	1884	
Kew Bridge (opened as 'Kew') . .	22 Aug., 1849	
Kew Gardens	1 Jan., 1869	
Keymer Junction (on Lewes branch) .	1 Jan., 1862	1 Nov., 1883
Removed to North of junction on .	1 Aug., 1886	
and renamed 'Wivelsfield' 1 July, 1896		
Kidbrooke	1 May, 1895	
Kingscote	1 Aug., 1882 [6]	
Kings Ferry Bridge Halt . . .	Dec., 1922	
Kingsley Halt		
Kingston (original station at Surbiton) .	21 May, 1838	
Re-sited	1845	
Kingston (former terminal) . .	1 July, 1863	
Kingston (present station) . . .	1 Jan., 1869	
Kingston-on-Sea (opened as 'Kingston')	12 May, 1840	1 Apr., 1879 [1]
Kingswood & Burgh Heath . . .	2 Nov., 1897	
Knockholt (opened as 'Halstead for Knockholt')	1 May, 1876	
Knowle Halt (opened as 'Knowle Asylum Halt')	1 May, 1907	
Ladywell	1 Jan., 1857	
Lake Halt (Nr. Hamworthy) (used by shipyard employees)	Sept., 1918	
Lake Halt (I.O.W.) (conditional stop for cricket matches)	1904	
Lancing	24 Nov., 1845	
Langston	19 Jan., 1865	
Lapford	1 Aug., 1845 [6]	
Latchley	2 Mar., 1908 [6]	
Launceston	21 July, 1886 [6]	
Lavant	11 July, 1881	8 July, 1935
Leatherhead (original station, L.B.S.C.R./ L.S.W.R.)	1 Feb., 1859	4 Mar., 1867
Leatherhead (L.B.S.C.R. station)	4 Mar., 1867	
Leatherhead (separate L.S.W.R. station) All trains used L.B.S.C.R. station from 10 July, 1927	4 Mar., 1867	10 July, 1927
Lee (Kent) (opened as 'Lee') . .	1 Sept., 1866	
Lee-on-the-Solent	12 May, 1894	1 Jan., 1931
Lenham	1 July, 1884	
Lewes (Friars Walk station) . .	8 June, 1846	1 Nov., 1857
,, (second station) . . .	1 Nov., 1857	17 June, 1889
,, (present station) . . .	17 June, 1889	
Lewes Road	1 Sept., 1873	2 Jan., 1933
Lewisham (formerly 'Lewisham Junction')	30 July, 1849	
Lewisham Road	18 Sept., 1871	1 Jan., 1917
Leysdown	1 Aug., 1901	
Lingfield	10 Mar., 1884 [6]	
Lions Holt Halt	1907/8	

STATIONS—(continued)	OPENED	CLOSED
Liphook	1 Jan., 1859	
Liss	1 Jan., 1859	
Littleham	1 June, 1903 [6]	
Littlehampton		
Original station on main line . .	16 Mar., 1846	1 Sept., 1863
Present terminus on branch . .	17 Aug., 1863	
Littlehaven Halt (opened as 'Rusper Road Crossing Halt')	1 June, 1907	
London Bridge		
London & Greenwich Rly. . .	14 Dec., 1836	
London & Croydon Rly. . . .	5 June, 1839	
Through lines	11 Jan., 1864	
London Road (Brighton) . . .	1 Oct., 1877	
London Road (Guildford) . . .	2 Feb., 1885	
Longcross Halt	21 Sept., 1942	
Longfield Halt	1 July, 1913	
Longparish (opened as 'Long Parish') .	1 June, 1885 [6]	6 July, 1931
Lordship Lane	1 Sept., 1865 [1]	1 Jan., 1917
,, ,, ...	1 Mar., 1919	22 May, 1944
Re-opened 4 March, 1946		
Loughborough Junction Main Line .	1 Dec., 1872	
Platforms on the Cambria Road Spur	1 Dec., 1872	12 July, 1925
Platforms on the Brixton spur . .	1864	3 Apr., 1916
Lower Sydenham . . .	1 Jan., 1857	1906
Re-sited	1906	
Lucas Terrace Halt	Oct., 1905	
Luckett (opened as 'Stoke Climsland') .	2 Mar., 1908 [6]	
Ludgate Hill (temporary station) . .	21 Dec., 1864	1 June, 1865
,, ,, (permanent station) . .	1 June, 1865	3 Mar., 1929
Lydd-on-Sea for Dungeness	4 July, 1937	
Lydd Town (opened as 'Lydd') . .	7 Dec., 1881	
Lydford (formerly 'Lidford') . .	12 Oct., 1874 [6]	
Lyghe Halt (formerly 'Leigh Halt') .	1911	
Lyme Regis	24 Aug., 1903	
Lyminge	4 July, 1887	3 May, 1943
,, ...	7 Oct., 1946	16 June, 1947
Lymington (temporary terminus) . .	12 July, 1858	19 Sept., 1860
Lymington Pier	1 May, 1884	
Lymington Town	19 Sept., 1860	
Lyminster Halt	1 Aug., 1907	Sept., 1914 [1]
Lympstone		
Lyndhurst Road	1 June, 1847 [6]	
Lynton & Lynmouth (Lynton & Barnstaple Rly.) (Public)	11 May, 1898 / 16 May, 1898	30 Sept., 1935
Maddaford Moor Halt . . .	26 July, 1926	
Maidstone Barracks	1874	
Maidstone East (opened as 'Maidstone (C. & D.)')	1 June, 1874	
Maidstone West (opened as 'Maidstone')	25 Sept., 1844	

STATIONS—(*continued*)	OPENED	CLOSED
Malden (opened as 'Combe & Malden')	1846/7	
Malden Manor	29 May, 1938	
Malling (later 'West Malling') . .	1 June, 1874	
Marchwood	20 July, 1925	
Marden	31 Aug., 1842 [6]	
Margate (formerly 'Margate West (L.C.D.R.)')	5 Oct., 1863	
Margate Sands (opened as 'Margate (S.E.R.)')	1 Dec., 1846	2 July, 1926
Margate East	1870	
Martin Mill	15 June, 1881	
Mayfield	1 Sept., 1880	
Maze Hill	1 Jan., 1873	
Medstead & Four Marks (formerly 'Medstead')	1868/9 [7]	
Meeth Halt	27 July, 1925	
Melcombe Regis	1909	
Meopham	6 May, 1861	
Merstham	1 Dec., 1841	1843
„	4 Oct., 1844	
Merstone	1 Feb., 1875 [6]	
Merton Abbey	1 Oct., 1868 [6]	1 Jan., 1917
„ „	27 Aug., 1923	3 Mar., 1929
Merton Park (opened as Lower Merton)		
Merton Abbey line platforms . .	1 Oct., 1868	3 Mar., 1929
Mitcham Line platforms . . .	1 Nov., 1870	
Meyrick Park Halt	1 Mar., 1906	Oct., 1917 [1]
Micheldever (opened as 'Andover Road')	11 May, 1840	
Middle Stoke Halt	July, 1906	
Midhurst (L.B.S.C.)	15 Oct., 1866	11 July, 1881
Re-sited	11 July, 1881	
Midhurst (L.S.W.R.)	1 Sept., 1864	13 July, 1925
Milborne Port	7 May, 1860 [6]	
Milford	1 Jan., 1859	
Millbrook	*c.* 1860	
Mill Hill (I. of W.)	16 June, 1862 [6]	
Milton Range Halt	July, 1906	June, 1932 [1]
Milton Road Halt	July, 1906	1 May, 1915
Minster Junction	13 Apr., 1846 [1]	
Minster-on-Sea (opened as 'Minster (Sheppey)')	1 Aug., 1901	
Mitcham	22 Oct., 1855 [6]	
Mitcham Junction	1 Oct., 1868 [7]	
Monks Lane Halt	1 July, 1907	11 Sept., 1939
Morchard Road	1 Aug., 1854 [6]	
Morden Road Halt (opened as 'Morden Halt')	1857	
Morden South	5 Jan., 1930	
Moreton	1 June, 1847	

STATIONS—(*continued*)	OPENED	CLOSED
Mortehoe & Woolacombe (formerly 'Mortehoe (for Lee & Woolacombe)')	20 July, 1874 [6]	
Mortlake	27 July, 1846	
Motspur Park	12 July, 1925	
Mottingham (opened as 'Eltham') .	1 Sept., 1866	
Mottisfont	6 Mar., 1865 [6]	
Mountfield Halt	1923	
Mount Pleasant Road Halt . . .	1907/8	2 Jan., 1928
Nanstallon Halt	4 July, 1834 [6]	
Netley	5 Mar., 1866 [6]	
New Arundel (now 'Arundel') . .	3 Aug., 1863	
New Beckenham.	1 Apr., 1864	1866/7
Re-sited	1866/7	
New Brompton (see 'Gillingham (Kent)')		
Newchurch	1 Feb., 1875 [6]	
New Cross	1850	
New Cross Gate (opened as 'New Cross')	5 June, 1839	
New Croydon (now part of E. Croydon)	1 May, 1862	
New Eltham (opened as 'Pope Street') .	1 Apr., 1878	
Newhaven Harbour	17 May, 1886	
Newhaven Wharf	8 Dec., 1847 [6]	17 May 1886
Newhaven Town (opened as 'Newhaven')	8 Dec., 1847	
New Hythe	9 Dec., 1929	
Newick & Chailey	1 Aug., 1882	
Newington.	1 Aug., 1862	
New Milton	6 Mar., 1888 [6]	
Newport (I. of W.)	16 June, 1862	
,, (F.Y. & N.) . . .	14 July, 1913	1 Aug., 1923
,, Pan Lane (I. of W. Newport Junction)	6 Oct., 1875	1 June, 1879
New Romney & Littlestone-on-Sea .	19 June, 1884	
Newton Poppleford	15 May, 1897 [6]	
Newton St. Cyres	12 May, 1851 [6]	
Newton Tony	1 Oct., 1901 [6]	
New Wandsworth (replaced by 2nd Wandsworth Common)	29 Mar., 1858	1 Nov., 1869
Nine Elms	21 May, 1838	11 July, 1848
,, ,, (Queen Victoria's Private Station	1873	
Ningwood	20 July, 1889 [6]	
Norbiton	1 Jan., 1869	
Norbury	Jan., 1878	
Normans Bay Halt	11 Sept., 1905	
Northam	1 Dec., 1872	
North Camp (opened as 'North Camp, Aldershot')	1858	
North Dulwich	1 Oct., 1868	
Northfleet	1850 [7]	
North Hayling	17 July, 1867	

STATIONS—(*continued*)	OPENED	CLOSED
North Sheen	6 July, 1930	
North Tawton	1 Nov., 1865	
Norwood Junction (opened as 'Jolly Sailor' and re-sited)	5 June, 1839	
Nunhead	1 Sept., 1871	3 May, 1925
Re-sited	3 May, 1925	
Nursling	1883	
Nutbourne Halt	1 Apr., 1906	
Nutfield	1883	
Oakley	3 July, 1854 [6]	
Ockley	1 May, 1867	
Okehampton	3 Oct., 1871	
Old Kent Road & Hatcham (opened as 'Old Kent Road')	13 Aug., 1866	1 Jan., 1917
Ore	1 Jan., 1888	
Oreston	1 Jan., 1897	
Orpington	2 Mar., 1868	
Otford	1 Oct., 1882	
Otterham	14 Aug., 1893 [6]	
Ottery St. Mary	6 July, 1874 [6]	
Overton	3 July, 1854 [6]	
Oxshott & Fairmile	2 Feb., 1885	
Oxted	10 Mar., 1884	
Paddock Wood (opened as 'Maidstone Road')	31 Aug., 1842	
Padstow	27 Mar., 1899	
Pan Lane (I. of W. Newport Junction)	6 Oct., 1875 [6]	1 June, 1879
Parkstone	15 June, 1874	
Parracombe	May, 1903 [6]	30 Sept., 1935
Partridge Green	1 July, 1861	
Paulsgrove Halt (opened for race meetings only)	28 June, 1933	
Peckham Rye	1865 [3]	
,, ,,	13 Aug., 1866 [4]	
Penge East (opened as 'Penge Lane') .	1 July, 1863 [6]	
Penge West (opened as 'Penge') . .	5 June, 1839	*c* 1841
Re-opened 1 July, 1863		
Penshurst	26 May, 1842	
Petersfield	1 Jan., 1859	
Petrockstow	27 July, 1925	
Petts Wood	9 July, 1928	
Petworth	10 Oct., 1859	
Pevensey & Westham (opened as 'Westham & Pevensey')	27 June, 1846 [6]	
Pevensey Bay Halt	11 Sept., 1905	
Pimlico	29 Mar., 1858	1 Oct., 1860
Pinhoe	1872	
Plaistow (see 'Sundridge Park')		
Pluckley	1 Dec., 1842	

STATIONS—(*continued*)	OPENED	CLOSED
Plumpton	1863/4 [7]	
Plumstead	1859	
Plymouth Friary	1 July, 1891	
Plymouth North Road . . .	28 Mar., 1877	
Plymstock	5 Sept., 1892	
Pokesdown (opened as 'Boscombe') .	1 July, 1886	
Polegate	27 July, 1846	3 Oct., 1881
Re-sited about ½ mile east . .	3 Oct., 1881	
Polsloe Bridge Halt	1907/8	
Poole (later 'Hamworthy') . . .	1 June, 1847	
Poole	2 Dec., 1872	
Pope Street (see 'New Eltham') . .	1 Apr., 1878	
Porchester	1 Sept., 1848 [6]	
Port Isaac Road	1 June, 1895 [6]	
Portland	16 Oct., 1865 [6]	
Porton	1 May, 1857 [6]	
Portslade & West Hove . . .	12 May, 1840	July, 1847 [1]
(Original station opened as 'Portslade')	Oct., 1857	1881
Re-sited	1881	
Portsmouth & Southsea . . .	14 June, 1847	
Portsmouth Arms	1 Aug., 1854 [6]	
Portsmouth Harbour	2 Oct., 1876	
Portswood (see 'St. Denys')		
Port Victoria	11 Sept., 1882	
Preston Park (opened as 'Preston') .	1 Nov., 1869	
Privett	1 June, 1903	
Pulborough	10 Oct., 1859	
Purley (opened as 'Godstone Road') .	12 July, 1841	1 Oct., 1847
Re-opened as 'Caterham Junction'	5 Aug., 1856	
Purley Oaks	5 Nov., 1899	
Putney	27 July, 1846	
Queenborough	19 July, 1860	
Queenborough Pier	15 May, 1876	1 Mar., 1923
Queens Road (Battersea) . . .	1 Nov., 1877	
Queens Road (Peckham) (opened as 'Peckham')	13 Aug., 1866	
Radipole Halt	1904/5	
Rainham (opened as 'Rainham & Newington')	25 Jan., 1858	
Ramsgate Harbour (opened as 'Ramsgate (C. & D.)')	5 Oct., 1863	2 July, 1926
Ramsgate Town (opened as 'Ramsgate')	13 Apr., 1846	2 July, 1926
Re-sited	2 July, 1926	
Ravensbourne	1 July, 1892	
Ravenscourt Park (formerly 'Shaftesbury Road')	1 Apr., 1873	
Raynes Park	Oct., 1871	
Reading (S.E.R.)	4 July, 1849	
Redbridge	1 June, 1847	

STATIONS—(*continued*)	OPENED	CLOSED
Redhill (London & Brighton Railway) (opened as 'Reigate')	12 July, 1841	Apr./May 1844
Redhill (S.E.R.)	26 May, 1842	Apr./May 1844
Redhill (opened as 'Reigate' and on site of present station)	Apr./May, 1844	
Present station	1858	
Reedham (opened as 'Reedham Halt') .	1 Mar., 1911	
Reigate (present station) (opened as 'Reigate Town')	4 July, 1849	
Richborough Castle Halt . . .	19 June, 1933	11 Sept., 1939
Richmond	27 July, 1846	1848
Re-sited	1848	
Riddlesdown	5 June, 1927	
Ringwood	1 June, 1847 [6]	
Robertsbridge	1 Sept., 1851	
Rochester (Gravesend & Rochester Railway)	10 Feb., 1845	13 Dec., 1846
Re-opened as 'Strood' . . .	23 Aug., 1847	18 June, 1856
Re-sited	18 June, 1856	
Rochester L.C.D.R. (present site) .	1 Mar., 1892	
Rochester Bridge (L.C.D.R.) . .	Dec., 1860	1 Jan., 1917
Rochester Central (S.E.R.) (opened as 'Rochester') also known as Rochester Common	20 July, 1891	1 Oct., 1911
Rodwell		
Roffey Road Halt	1 June, 1907	3 Jan., 1937
Rogate for Harting	1 Sept., 1864	
Romsey	1 Mar., 1847	
Ropley	2 Oct., 1865	
Rosherville	10 May, 1886	16 July, 1933
Rotherfield & Mark Cross . . .	1 Sept., 1880	
Rowan Halt	18 Dec., 1933	1 Jan., 1939
Rowfant	9 July, 1855	
Rowlands Castle.	1 Jan., 1859	
Rudgwick	Nov., 1865	
Ryde Esplanade	5 Apr., 1880	
Ryde Pier Head	12 July, 1880	
Ryde St. Johns Road	23 Aug., 1864	
Rye	13 Feb., 1851	
Rye Harbour (freight only) . . .	Mar., 1854	
Ruthern Bridge	30 Sept., 1834	30 Dec., 1933
St. Budeaux (Victoria Road) (formerly 'St. Budeaux (for Saltash)')	2 June, 1890	
St. Denys (opened as 'Portswood') .	1 May, 1861	
St. Helens (I. of W.)	27 May, 1882	
St. Helier	5 Jan., 1930	
St. James Park Halt		
St. Johns	1 June, 1873	
St. Kew Highway	1 June, 1895 [6]	
St. Lawrence (I. of W.) . . .	20 July, 1897	

STATIONS—*(continued)*	OPENED	CLOSED
St. Lawrence (Pegwell Bay) . .	Oct., 1864	3 Apr., 1916
St. Leonards (Bulverhythe) . . .	27 June, 1846	7 Nov., 1846
St. Leonards (Warrior Square) . .	13 Feb., 1851	
St. Leonards (West Marina) . .	7 Nov., 1846	
St. Margarets	2 Oct., 1876	
St. Mary Cray	3 Dec., 1860	
St. Pauls (later Blackfriars) . . .	10 May, 1886	
Salfords (opened as 'Salford Halt') .	17 July, 1932	
Salisbury (present station) . . .	2 May, 1859	
Salisbury (Milford)	1 Mar., 1847	2 May, 1859
Sampford Courtenay (opened as 'Oke-hampton Road')	8 Jan., 1867	
Sanderstead	10 Mar., 1884	
Sandgate	9 Oct., 1874	1 Apr., 1931
Sandhurst Halt	1909	Dec., 1853
Sandling Junction	1 Jan., 1888	
Sandown (I. of W.)	23 Aug., 1864⁶	
Sandsfoot Castle Halt	1 Aug., 1932	
Sandwich	1 July, 1847	
Seaford	1 June, 1864	
Seaton	16 Mar., 1868	
Seaton Junction (opened as 'Colyton for Seaton')	18 July, 1860⁶	
Selham	1 July, 1872	
Selhurst	1 May, 1865	
Selling	3 Dec., 1860	
Selsdon (opened as 'Selsdon Road') .	1885	
Semley	2 May, 1859⁶	
Sevenoaks (Bat & Ball) . . .	2 June, 1862	
Sevenoaks (Tubs Hill) . . .	2 Mar., 1868	
Seven Stones Halt	June, 1910	1917
Shalford	20 Aug., 1849	
Shanklin (I. of W.)	23 Aug., 1864	
Sharnal Street	31 Mar., 1882	
Shawford & Twyford	1882	
Sheerness Dockyard (opened as 'Sheer-ness')	19 July, 1860	2 Jan., 1922
Sheerness East	1 Aug., 1901	
Sheerness-on-Sea	1 June, 1883	8 Nov., 1914
,, ...	2 Jan., 1922	
Sheffield Park (opened as 'Fletching & Sheffield Park')	1 Aug., 1882	
Shepherds Bush	May, 1874	5 June, 1916
Shepherds Well	22 July, 1861	
Shepperton	1 Nov., 1864	
Sherborne	7 May, 1860⁶	
Shide (I. of W.)	1 Feb., 1875⁶	
Sholing	5 Mar., 1866⁶	
Shooters Hill & Eltham Park . .	1 July, 1908	

STATIONS—(*continued*)	OPENED	CLOSED
Shoreham (Kent) (opened as 'Shoreham')	2 June, 1862	
Shoreham Airport	1 Oct., 1910	1 Jan., 1933
(opened as 'Bungalow Town Halt')	1 July, 1935	15 July, 1940
Shoreham-by-Sea (opened as 'Shoreham')	12 May, 1840	
Shorncliffe (opened as 'Shorncliffe Camp')	1 Nov., 1863 [1]	1 Feb., 1881
Re-sited	1 Feb., 1881	
Shortlands (opened as 'Bromley') . .	3 May, 1858	
Sidcup	Oct., 1866 [1]	
Sidley	1 June, 1902	
Sidmouth	6 July, 1874	
Sidmouth Junction (opened as 'Feniton')	18 July, 1860 [6]	
Singleton	11 July, 1881	8 July, 1935
Sittingbourne & Milton Regis (opened as 'Sittingbourne')	25 Jan., 1858	
Slades Green	1 July, 1900	
Slinfold	2 Oct., 1865	
Smeeth	1851/2 [7]	
Smitham	1 Jan., 1904	
Snailham Halt	1 July, 1907	
Snapper Halt	1903 [1]	30 Sept., 1935
Snodland	18 June, 1856	
Snowdown & Nonington Halt (opened as 'Snowdown Halt')	1914	
Snow Hill (later 'Holborn Viaduct Low Level')	1 Aug., 1874	1 June, 1916
Sole Street.	1 Feb., 1861	
Southampton Central (opened as 'Southampton West')	5 Nov., 1892	
Southampton (Royal Pier) . . .	Jan., 1891 [1]	Sept., 1914
Southampton Terminus . . .	10 June, 1839	
South Bermondsey (opened as 'Rotherhithe')	13 Aug., 1866	17 June, 1928
Re-sited	17 June, 1928	
Southborough (see 'High Brooms')		
Southbourne Halt	1 Apr., 1906	
South Croydon	1 Sept., 1865	
Southease & Rodmell Halt . . .	1 Sept., 1906	
Southfields.	3 June, 1889 [2]	
Southfleet	10 May, 1886	
South Merton	7 July, 1929	
South Molton Road	1 Aug., 1854 [6]	
Southsea (see East Southsea)		
South Street Halt	1911	1 Jan., 1931
Southwark Park	1 Oct., 1902	15 Mar., 1915
Southwater	16 Sept., 1861	
Southwick	12 May, 1840	
Spa Road	30 Oct., 1842	15 Mar., 1915
,, ,, (temporary terminus of London & Greenwich Railway)	8 Feb., 1836	14 Dec., 1836

STATIONS—*(continued)*	OPENED	CLOSED
Spencer Road Halt	1 Sept., 1906	15 Mar., 1915
Staines Central	22 Aug., 1848	
Staines High Street	1 July, 1884	1 Feb., 1916
Stamford Brook	1 Feb., 1912 [5]	
Staplehurst	31 Aug., 1842	
Stewarts Lane (L.B.S.C.R.) . . .	29 Mar., 1850	1 Dec., 1858
Stewarts Lane (L.C.D.R.) . . .	1 May, 1863	1 Jan., 1867
Steyning	1 July, 1861	
Stoats Nest (original station) . .	12 July, 1841	1 Dec., 1856
(Name transferred to Coulsdon North on opening of that station)		
Stockbridge	6 Mar., 1865 [6]	
Stoke Junction Halt	17 July, 1932	
Stokes Bay	6 Apr., 1863	1 Nov., 1915
Stone Cross Halt	1905	7 July, 1935
Stone Crossing Halt	2 Nov., 1908	
Stonegate (opened as 'Witherenden') .	1 Sept., 1851	
Stonehall & Lydden Halt . . .	1914	
Stonehouse Pool (Ocean Terminal) .	9 Apr., 1904	1911
Stoneleigh	17 July, 1932	
Strawberry Hill	1 Dec., 1873	
Streatham	1 Oct., 1868	
Streatham Common	1 Dec., 1862	
Streatham Hill (opened as 'Streatham') .	1 Dec., 1856 [7]	
Strood	23 Aug., 1847	
Sturry	1848	
Sunbury	1 Nov., 1864	
Sundridge Park (formerly 'Plaistow') .	1 Jan., 1878	
Sunningdale	4 June, 1856	
Sunnymeads	10 July, 1927	
Surbiton (opened as 'Kingston' and re-sited)	21 May, 1838	
Sutton	10 May, 1847	
Sutton Bingham	18 July, 1860 [6]	
Sutton Common	5 Jan., 1930	
Sutton West	5 Jan., 1930	
Swale Halt (opened as 'Kings Ferry Bridge Halt')	Dec., 1922	
Swanage	20 May, 1885	
Swanley (opened as 'Sevenoaks Junction')	1 July, 1862	16 Apr., 1939
Re-sited	16 Apr., 1939	
Swanscombe Halt	2 Nov., 1908	6 July, 1930
Re-sited	6 July, 1930	
Swanwick	2 Sept., 1889 [6]	
Sway	6 Mar., 1888 [6]	
Swaythling	1883	
Sydenham	5 June, 1839	
Sydenham Hill	Aug., 1863	
Syon Lane	5 July, 1931	

Stations—(*continued*)	Opened	Closed
Tadworth & Walton-on-the-Hill . .	1 July, 1900	
Tamerton Foliot (opened as 'Tamerton Foliott')	Jan., 1898	
Tankerton Halt	July, 1914[1]	1 Jan., 1931
Tattenham Corner	June, 1901	Sept., 1914
(Remained open for race traffic) .	25 Mar., 1928	
Tavistock	2 June, 1890	
Teddington (formerly 'Teddington Bushey Park')	1 July, 1863	
Templecombe (L.S.W.R.) . . .	7 May, 1860	
Teston Crossing Halt	1 Sept., 1909	
Teynham	25 Jan., 1858	
Thames Ditton	1851/2[7]	
Thornton Heath	1 Dec., 1862	
Three Bridges	12 July, 1841	
Three Oaks & Guestling Halt . .	1 July, 1907	
Tinsley Green (later 'Gatwick Airport').	30 Sept., 1935	
Tipton St. Johns (formerly 'Tipton') .	6 July, 1874[6]	
Tisbury	2 May, 1859[6]	
Tisted for Selborne	1 June, 1903	
Tivoli		
Tolworth	29 May, 1938	
Tonbridge (opened as 'Tunbridge') .	26 May, 1842	
Tongham	Oct., 1856	4 July, 1937
Tooting Junction	1 Oct., 1868	1 July, 1895
Re-sited	1 July, 1895	
Topsham	1 May, 1861[6]	
Torrington	18 July, 1872	
Totton (opened as 'Eling Junction') .	before Aug., 1868	
Tovil	1883/4	15 Mar., 1943
Tower Hill (Devon) . . .	21 July, 1886[6]	
Tresmeer	28 July, 1892[6]	
Tulse Hill	1 Oct., 1868	
Tunbridge Wells Central (opened as 'Tunbridge Wells')	20 Sept., 1845	25 Nov., 1846
Re-sited	25 Nov., 1846	
Tunbridge Wells West (opened as 'Tunbridge Wells')	1 Oct., 1866	
Turnchapel	1 Jan., 1897	
Turnham Green	1 Jan., 1869	
Twickenham	22 Aug., 1848	
Uckfield	18 Oct., 1858	
Umberleigh	1 Aug., 1854[6]	
Upper Halliford Halt (opened as 'Halliford Halt')	1 May, 1944	
Upper Sydenham	1 Aug., 1884	1 Jan., 1917
„ „	1 Mar., 1919	22 May, 1944
Re-opened 4 March, 1946		
Upper Warlingham	10 Mar., 1884	

STATIONS—(*continued*)	OPENED	CLOSED
Uralite Halt	July, 1906	
Vauxhall (opened as 'Vauxhall Bridge')	11 July, 1848	
Ventnor (I. of W.)	10 Sept., 1866	
Ventnor West (opened as 'Ventnor Town')	1 June, 1900	
Verwood	20 Dec., 1866	
Victoria (L.B.S.C.R.)	1 Oct., 1860	
Victoria (L.C.D.R.)	25 Aug., 1862	
Virginia Water	4 June, 1856	
Waddon	Feb., 1863	
Waddon Marsh Halt	6 July, 1930	
Wadebridge (opened to L.S.W.R. trains 1 June, 1895)	3 Sept., 1888	
Wadhurst	1 Sept., 1851	
Wallington (opened as 'Carshalton') .	10 May, 1847	
Walmer	15 June, 1881	
Walton-on-Thames (formerly 'Walton for Hersham')	21 May, 1838	
Walworth Road (opened as 'Camberwell Gate')	1 May, 1863	3 Apr., 1916
Wanborough	1 Sept., 1891	
Wandsworth (see Clapham Common)		
Wandsworth Common (original station)	1 Dec., 1856	1858
Wandsworth Common (2nd Station) (replacing New Wandsworth)	1 Nov., 1869	
Wandsworth Road	1 Mar., 1863	
Wandsworth Town (opened as 'Wandsworth')	27 July, 1846	
Warblington Halt	Nov., 1907 [1]	
Wareham	1 June, 1847	1886
Re-sited	1886	
Warlingham	5 Aug., 1856	
Warnham	1 May, 1867	
Warren Halt	1908	
Watchingwell Halt (Private Station)		
Watergate Halt	27 July, 1925	
Wateringbury	25 Sept., 1844	
Waterloo (opened as 'Waterloo Bridge').	11 July, 1848	
Waterloo Junction	1 Jan., 1869	
Well Hall	1 May, 1895	
Welling	1 May, 1895	
West Brompton (W.L.E.) . . .	1 Sept., 1866	21 Oct., 1940
West Byfleet (opened as Byfleet) . .	Dec., 1887	
Westcombe Park (formerly 'Coombe Farm Lane')	1879	
Westcott Range Halt		1928
West Croydon (opened as 'Croydon') .	5 June, 1839	
West Dulwich (opened as 'Dulwich') .	Oct., 1863 [7]	
Westenhanger (opened as 'Westenhanger & Hythe')	7 Feb., 1844	

STATIONS—(*continued*)	OPENED	CLOSED
Westerham	7 July, 1881	
Westgate-on-Sea	Apr., 1871	
West Grinstead	16 Sept., 1861	
Westham Halt	1908/9	
West Hoathly	1 Aug., 1882	
West Meon	1 June, 1903	
West Moors	1 Aug., 1867	
West Norwood (opened as 'Lower Norwood')	1 Dec., 1856 [7]	
Weston Mill Halt	1 Nov., 1906	Sept., 1921
West St. Leonards	1887	
West Sutton (see also 'Sutton West') .	5 Jan., 1930	
West Weybridge	10 July, 1927	
West Wickham	29 May, 1882	
West Worthing	4 Nov., 1889	
Weybridge.	21 May, 1838	
Weymouth	20 Jan., 1857	
Wherwell	1 June, 1885 [6]	6 July, 1931
Whimple	18 July, 1860 [6]	
Whippingham (I. of W.) . . .	20 Dec., 1875	
Whipton Bridge Halt	Mar., 1906 [1]	1 Jan., 1923
Whitchurch	3 July, 1854 [6]	
Whitstable (C. & W.) . . .	4 May, 1830	1 Jan., 1931
Whitstable Harbour (C. & W.) . .	19 Mar., 1832	Feb., 1894
Re-sited	Feb., 1894	1 Jan., 1931
Whitstable Town	1 Aug., 1860	
Whitstone & Bridgerule . . .	10 Aug., 1898 [6]	
Whitton	6 July, 1930	
Whitwell	20 July, 1897 [6]	
Whyteleafe	1 Jan., 1900	
Whyteleafe South (formerly 'Warlingham')	5 Aug., 1856 [6]	
Wickham	1 June, 1903	
Willingdon (now Hampden Park) .	1 Jan., 1888	
Wilton	2 May, 1859 [6]	
Wimbledon	21 May, 1838	
Wimbledon Chase	7 July, 1929	
Wimpledon Park	3 June, 1889 [2]	
Wimborne	1 June, 1847 [6]	
Winchelsea	13 Feb., 1851	
Winchester City (opened as 'Winchester')	10 June, 1839	
Winchfield (opened as 'Shapley Heath') .	24 Sept., 1838	
Windsor & Eton Riverside (opened as 'Windsor')	1 Dec., 1849	
Winnersh Halt	1910	
Withyham	1 Oct., 1866	
Witley	1 Jan., 1859	
Wivelsfield (opened as 'Keymer Junction')	1 Aug., 1886	
Woking	21 May, 1838	

STATIONS—(*continued*)	OPENED	CLOSED
Wokingham	4 July, 1849 [7]	
Woldingham (opened as 'Marden Park')	10 Mar., 1884	
Woodbury Road	1 May, 1861 [6]	
Woodgate for Bognor (opened as 'Bognor')	8 June, 1846	1 June, 1864
Woodmansterne	17 July, 1932	
Woodside	1871	
Woody Bay (formerly 'Wooda Bay') .	11 May, 1898	30 Sept., 1935
Wool	1 June, 1847	
Woolston	5 Mar., 1866 [6]	
Woolwich Arsenal	30 July, 1849	
Woolwich Dockyard	1850 [7]	
Wootton (I. of W.)	20 Dec., 1875 [6]	
Worcester Park (opened as 'Old Malden & Worcester Park')	4 Apr., 1859	
Worplesdon	1 Mar., 1883	
Worthing Central (opened as 'Worthing')	24 Nov., 1845	
Wrafton	20 July, 1874 [6]	
Wraysbury	22 Aug., 1848	
Wrotham & Borough Green (opened as 'Wrotham')	1 June, 1874	
Wroxall (I. of W.)	10 Sept., 1866 [6]	
Wye	6 Feb., 1846	
Wyke Regis Halt	1908/9	
Yalding	25 Sept., 1844	
Yapton	8 June, 1846	Oct., 1847 [1]
,, ...	June, 1849 [1]	1 June, 1864
Yarde Halt	27 July, 1925	
Yarmouth (I. of W.)	20 July, 1889 [6]	
Yeoford	1 Aug., 1854 [6]	
Yeovil Junction	1 June, 1860 [6]	
Yeovil Town	1 June, 1861	
York Road (see Battersea Park) . .		

Notes

[1] First or last appearance in timetable.
[2] To District line trains, opened to L.S.W.R. trains on 1 July, 1889.
[3] To L.C.&D.R. trains.
[4] To L.B.S.C.R. trains.
[5] To District line trains only on 1 Feb., 1912.
[6] Opening date of line.
[7] Date not confirmed.
Where a former station title is given, this is not necessarily the opening title.

Stations Renamed

Name	*Former Name*	*Until*
Addiscombe	Croydon (Addiscombe Road)	1 Apr., 1925
,,	Croydon (Addiscombe)	Mar., 1926
Aldrington Halt	Dyke Junction Halt	17 June, 1932
Andover Junction	Andover	6 Mar., 1865
Anerley	Anerley Bridge	*circa* 1840
Ash	Ash	July, 1855
,,	Ash & Aldershot	Sept., 1858
,,	Aldershot (Ash)	June, 1859
,,	Ash & Aldershot	June, 1863
,,	Ash Junction	Nov., 1926
Ash Vale	North Camp & Ash Vale	30 Mar., 1924
Ashford (Kent)	Ashford	9 July, 1923
Ashford (Middlesex)	Ashford	9 July, 1923
Balham & Upper Tooting	Balham	9 Mar., 1927
Bank	City	28 Oct., 1940
Banstead & Burgh Heath	Banstead	1 June, 1898
Banstead	Banstead & Burgh Heath	Aug., 1928
Barcombe	New Barcombe	1 Jan., 1885
Barcombe Mills	Barcombe	1 Jan., 1885
Bat & Ball	Sevenoaks	1 Aug., 1869
,, ,,	Sevenoaks (Bat & Ball)	5 June, 1950
Battersea Park (Old Station)	Battersea	1 July, 1862
Battersea Park	Battersea Park & York Road	1 June 1885
Battersea Park & York Road	York Road & Battersea Park	1 Jan., 1877
Bearsted & Thurnham	Bearsted	1 July, 1907
Beckenham Junction	Beckenham	1 Apr., 1864
Beddington Lane	Beddington	Jan., 1887
Belmont	California	1 Oct., 1875
Bexhill Central	Bexhill	9 July, 1923
Bexhill West	Bexhill-on-Sea	9 July, 1923
,, ,,	Bexhill (Eastern)	Nov., 1929*
Bickley	Southborough Road	1 Oct., 1860
Bishopstone Beach Halt	Bishopstone Halt	26 Sept., 1938
Renamed on re-opening at Easter 1939		
Bitterne	Bitterne Road	Nov., 1896*
Blackfriars	St. Pauls	1 Feb., 1937
Blackwater	Blackwater	Aug., 1851
,,	Blackwater & Sandhurst	June, 1852
,,	Blackwater	May, 1897

Name	*Former Name*	*Until*
Blackwater	Blackwater & York Town	1 June, 1913
,,	Blackwater & Camberley	9 July, 1923
Blackwater (I.o.W.)	Blackwater	9 July, 1923
Blean & Tyler Hill Halt	Tyler Hill Halt	May, 1912 to Dec., 1915*
Bognor Regis	Bognor	11 Sept., 1929
Bournemouth Central	Bournemouth East	1 May, 1899
Box Hill & Burford Bridge	West Humble	1 Nov., 1870
,, ,, ,,	Box Hill & Burford Bridge	May, 1896
,, ,, ,,	Box Hill	Dec., 1904*
Bramley & Wonersh	Bramley	1 June, 1888
Brentford Central	Brentford	5 June, 1950
Brighton	Brighton Central	30 Sept., 1935
Broadstone (Dorset)	Poole New Junction	Jan., 1875*
,, ,,	Poole Junction	July, 1883*
,, ,,	Poole Junction & Broadstone	Jan., 1887*
,, ,,	Broadstone & New Poole Junction	July, 1889*
,, ,,	Broadstone Junction	July, 1929*
Brockenhurst	Brokenhurst	Feb., 1849*
,,	Brockenhurst Junction	Jan., 1876
Bromley North	Bromley (S.E.R.)	June, 1899
Bromley South	Bromley (L.C.D.R.)	June, 1899
Budleigh Salterton	Salterton	June, 1898*
Burnham-on-Sea	Burnham	June, 1923
Callington for Stoke Climsland	Callington Road	1 Nov., 1909
Camberley	Camberley & York Town	9 July, 1923
Camberwell	Camberwell New Road	1 Oct., 1908
Canterbury East	Canterbury (L.C.D.R.)	July, 1899
Canterbury West	Canterbury (S.E.R.)	July, 1899
Carshalton Beeches	Beeches Halt	1 Apr., 1925
Caterham Junction (see 'Purley')		
Chard Central	Chard	Oct., 1879
,, ,,	Chard (Joint)	1 Feb., 1928
Chard Junction	Chard Road	Aug., 1872*
Chipstead	Chipstead & Banstead Downs	9 July, 1923
Chislehurst	Chislehurst & Bickley Park	1 Sept., 1866
Clapham	Clapham & North Stockwell	May, 1895*
,,	Clapham Road & North Stockwell	June, 1914*
,,	Clapham & North Stockwell	7 Oct., 1937
Clapham Common	Wandsworth	Aug., 1846*
Collington Halt	West Bexhill Halt	Dec., 1929
Colyton	Colyton Town	Sept., 1890*
Cooden Beach	Cooden Halt	7 July, 1935
Coulsdon North	Stoats Nest	1 June, 1911
,, ,,	Coulsdon & Smitham Downs	9 July, 1923
,, ,,	Coulsdon West	1 Aug., 1923
Coulsdon South	Coulsdon	Mar., 1896
,, ,,	Coulsdon & Cane Hill	9 July, 1923
,, ,,	Coulsdon East	1 Aug., 1923

Name	*Former Name*	*Until*
Cranleigh	Cranley	June, 1867*
Crowborough & Jarvis Brook	Rotherfield	1 Aug., 1880
,, ,, ,,	Crowborough	1 May, 1897
Crowthorne	Wellington College (for Crowthorne)	17 June, 1928
Croydon East Local	Croydon New	1 June, 1909
Crystal Palace (H.L.) & Upper Norwood	Crystal Palace	1 Nov., 1898
Datchet	Datchett	Sept., 1849
Deepdene	Box Hill & Leatherhead Road	Mar., 1851
,,	Box Hill	9 July, 1923
Denton Halt	Denton Road	(Nov., 1914 to Oct., 1919)*
Dorking North	Dorking	9 July, 1923
Dorking Town	Dorking	9 July, 1923
Dover Harbour	Dover Harbour	July, 1863
,, ,,	Dover Town & Harbour	June, 1899
Dover Marine	Dover (Admiralty Pier)	5 Dec., 1918
Dover Priory	Dover Town	July, 1863
Dumpton Park (for East Ramsgate)	Dumpton Park	12 Mar., 1927
Dunton Green	Dunton Green & Riverhead	1 July, 1873
Earlsfield & Summers Town	Earlsfield	1884
East Brixton	Loughborough Park	Jan., 1870
,, ,,	Loughborough Park & Brixton	1 Jan., 1894
East Croydon	East Croydon Main ⎱ East Croydon Local ⎰	July, 1924
East Croydon (Local)	New Croydon	1 June, 1909
East Dulwich	Champion Hill	1 June, 1888
Eastleigh	Bishopstoke	Dec., 1852*
,,	Bishopstoke Junction	July, 1889
,,	Eastleigh & Bishopstoke	July, 1923
Edenbridge Town	Edenbridge	1 May, 1896
Elmstead Woods	Elmstead	1 Oct., 1908
Eltham Park	Shooters Hill & Eltham Park	1 Oct., 1927
Eltham (Well Hall)	Well Hall	1 Oct., 1916
,, ,, ,,	Well Hall & North Eltham	1 Oct., 1927
†Epsom Town	Epsom	July, 1923
Ewell East	Ewell	9 July, 1923
Ewell West	Ewell	9 July, 1923
Exeter Central	Exeter Queen Street	1 July, 1933
Farringdon	Faringdon Platform (1 May, 1932 to 8 July, 1934)	
Farnborough North	Farnborough	9 July, 1923
Farningham Road & Sutton-at-Hone	Farningham & Sutton	Feb., 1862*
,, ,,	Farningham Road	Jan., 1872
Fleet	Fleetpond	1 July, 1869
Folkestone Central	Cheriton Arch	Sept., 1886
,, ,,	Radnor Park	1 June 1895

† Epsom until 1870 subsequently "TOWN" was dropped and revived July 1923.

Name	*Former Name*	*Until*
Folkestone Junction	Folkestone	July, 1849
,, ,,	Folkestone	Jan., 1852
,, ,,	Folkestone Junction	Sept., 1858
,, ,,	Folkestone Junction (Shorncliffe)	Nov., 1863
,, ,,	Folkestone Junction	Apr., 1884
,, ,,	Folkestone	June, 1897
Ford (Devon)	Ford	9 July, 1923
Ford (Sussex)	Ford for Arundel	Aug., 1863
,, ,,	Ford Junction	9 July, 1923
Fort Brockhurst	Brockhurst	May, 1894*
Fort Gomer Halt	Privett	Oct., 1909
Forest Hill	Dartmouth Arms	1845
,, ,,	Forest Hill for Lordship Lane	
Fratton	Fratton	4 July, 1905
Fratton & Southsea	Fratton & Southsea	1 Dec., 1921
Fullerton	Fullerton Bridge	Oct., 1871*
,,	Fullerton	May, 1889*
,,	Fullerton Junction	July, 1929*
Gatwick Airport	Tinsley Green (for Gatwick Airport)	1 June, 1936
Gillingham (Dorset)	Gillingham	9 July, 1923
Gillingham (Kent)	New Brompton	May, 1886*
,,	New Brompton & Gillingham	1 Oct., 1912
,,	Gillingham	9 July, 1923
Goring-by-Sea	Goring	6 July, 1908
Goudhurst	Hope Mill for Goudhurst and Lamberhurst	1 Jan., 1893
Gravesend Central	Gravesend (S.E.R.)	July, 1899
Gravesend West Street	Gravesend (C. & D.)	June, 1899*
Greenwich Park	Greenwich	1 July, 1900
Gunnersbury	Brentford Road	1 Nov., 1871
Hampden Park	Willingdon	1 July, 1903
Ham Street & Orlestone	Ham Street	1 Feb., 1897
Hamworthy	Poole	2 Dec., 1872
Hassocks	Hassocks Gate	1 Oct., 1881
Hamworthy Junction	Poole Junction	2 Dec., 1872
Haydons Road	Haydens Lane	1 Oct., 1889
Hayling Island	South Hayling	1 June, 1892
High Brooms	Southborough	21 Sept., 1925
Hinton Admiral	Hinton	1 May, 1888
Holborn Viaduct (L.L.)	Snow Hill	1 May, 1912
Holmesley	Christchurch Road	Feb., 1863*
Horam	Horeham Road for Waldron	Apr., 1891*
,,	Horeham Road & Waldron	1 Apr., 1900
,,	Waldron & Horeham Road	1 Jan., 1935
Horsley	Horsley and Ockham & Ripley	Dec., 1914*
Hothfield Halt	Hothfield	13 Aug., 1937
Hounslow	Hounslow	Oct., 1852*
,,	Hounslow & Whitton	6 July, 1930

Name	*Former Name*	*Until*
Hove	Cliftonville	1 July, 1879
,,	West Brighton	1 Oct., 1894
,,	Hove & West Brighton	1 July, 1895
Hurn	Herne	July, 1897*
Hythe	Hythe	21 Sept., 1925
,,	Hythe (Kent)	Nov., 1931
,,	Hythe for Sandgate	5 July, 1939
Ifield	Lyons Crossing Halt	6 July, 1907*
,,	Ifield Halt	6 July, 1930
Kearsney	Ewell	Mar., 1869
Kenley	Coulsdon	Dec., 1856
Kensington (Olympia)	Addison Road	19 Dec., 1945
Kew Bridge	Kew	Feb., 1869*
Kingston-on-Sea	Kingston	Dec., 1870*
Knockholt	Halstead for Knockholt	1 Oct., 1900
Knowle Platform	Knowle Asylum Halt	Aug., 1942
Littlehaven Halt	Rusper Road Crossing Halt	July, 1907*
,, ,,	Littlehaven Crossing Halt	Dec., 1907*
London Road, Brighton	London Road	9 July, 1923
London Road, Guildford	London Road	9 July, 1923
Longparish	Long Parish	1 July, 1890
Loughborough Junction	Loughborough Road	1 Dec., 1872*
Luckett	Stoke Climsland	1 Nov., 1909
Lydd Town	Lydd	4 July, 1937
Lyghe Halt	Leigh Halt	Apr., 1917
Lyminster	Littlehampton	Aug., 1863
Maidstone East	Maidstone (C. & D.)	July, 1899
Maidstone West	Maidstone (S.E.R.)	July, 1899
Malden	Combe & Malden	Nov., 1912
Margate Sands	Margate (S.E.R.)	June, 1899
Margate West	Margate (C. & D.)	June, 1899
Margate	Margate	Dec., 1880
,,	Margate & Cliftonville	June, 1899
,,	Margate West	11 July, 1926
Maze Hill for National Maritime Museum	Greenwich (Maze Hill)	Feb., 1878*
,, ,,	Maze Hill & East Greenwich	Feb., 1878*
,, ,,	Maze Hill & Greenwich Park	Jan., 1899*
,, ,,	Maze Hill & East Greenwich	27 July, 1937
Medstead & Four Marks	Medstead	1 Oct., 1937
Micheldever	Andover Road	Feb., 1856*
Minster-on-Sea	Minster (Sheppey)	June, 1907*
Mottingham	Eltham for Mottingham	1 Jan., 1892
,,	Eltham & Mottingham	Apr., 1916
,,	Eltham for Mottingham	Oct., 1922
,,	Eltham & Mottingham	1 Oct., 1927
New Cross Gate	New Cross	9 July, 1923
New Eltham	Pope Street	1 Jan., 1886
,, ,,	New Eltham & Pope Street	1 Oct., 1927

Name	*Former Name*	*Until*
Newhaven Harbour	Newhaven Wharf for Paris	Apr., 1884*
Newhaven Town	Newhaven	July, 1864*
North Camp	North Camp, Aldershot	June, 1863*
,, ,,	Aldershot Camp	May, 1879*
,, ,,	Aldershot	June, 1910
,, ,,	Aldershot (North Camp) & South Farnborough	9 July, 1923
,, ,,	Aldershot (North)	30 Mar., 1924
Norwood Junction	Jolly Sailor (Re-sited 1859)	Oct., 1846
Norwood Junction & South Norwood	Norwood Junction	1 Oct., 1910
Old Kent Road & Hatcham	Old Kent Road	1 Feb., 1870
Paddock Wood	Maidstone Road	24 Sept., 1844
Penge East	Penge Lane†	June, 1869
,, ,,	Penge	9 July, 1923
Penge West	Penge	(1863/1864)
,, ,,	Penge Bridges†	Aug., 1879*
,, ,,	Penge	9 July, 1923
Pevensey & Westham	Westham & Pevensey	Jan., 1851*
,, ,,	Pevensey & Westham	Nov., 1851*
,, ,,	Pevensey	Jan., 1890
Pokesdown	Boscombe	Oct., 1891
,,	Pokesdown (Boscombe)	1 May, 1897
Portslade & West Hove	Portslade	Apr., 1927
Preston Park	Preston	1 July, 1879
Purley	Godstone Road	1847
,,	Caterham Junction (from 1856 to 1 Oct., 1888)	
Queens Road Peckham	Peckham	1 Dec., 1866
Ramsgate Harbour	Ramsgate (C. & D.)	June, 1899
Ramsgate Town	Ramsgate (S.E.R.)	June, 1899
Redhill	Reigate	4 July, 1849
,,	Reigate Junction	Aug., 1858
,,	Redhill Junction	July, 1929
Reigate	Reigate Town	1 Nov., 1898
St. Denys	Portswood	1 Jan., 1876
St. James Park Halt	Lions Holt Halt	7 Oct., 1946
St. Leonards (West Marina)	Hastings & St. Leonards	13 Feb., 1851
,, ,, ,, ,,	St. Leonards	5 Dec., 1870
Salfords	Salfords Halt	1 Jan., 1935
Sampford Courtenay	Okehampton Road	3 Oct., 1871
,, ,,	Belstone Corner	1 Jan., 1872
Seaton Junction	Colyton for Seaton	16 Mar., 1868
,, ,,	Colyton Junction	1869*
Selsdon	Selsdon Road	30 Sept., 1935
Sevenoaks (Tubs Hill)	Seven Oaks	Apr., 1869
,,	Sevenoaks	(1871–3)
,,	Sevenoaks (Tubs Hill)	1 July, 1873

† Only Bradshaw **used** these suffixes 'Lane' and 'Bridges.' Company timetables always refer to 'Penge.'

Name	*Former Name*	*Until*
Sevenoaks (Tubs Hill)	Sevenoaks & Riverhead	June, 1875
,,	Sevenoaks (Tubs Hill) & Riverhead	(1877–80)
,,	Sevenoaks (Tubs Hill)	July, 1890
,,	Sevenoaks (Tubs Hill) & Riverhead	July, 1901
Sheerness Dockyard	Sheerness	1 June, 1883
Sheffield Park	Fletching & Sheffield Park	1 Jan., 1883*
Shoreham (Kent)	Shoreham	9 July, 1923
Shoreham-by-Sea	Shoreham	July, 1906
	Shoreham Harbour	Oct., 1906
Shorncliffe	Shorncliffe Camp	1 Dec., 1863
,,	Shorncliffe & Sandgate	1 Oct., 1874
,,	Shorncliffe Camp	20 Sept., 1926
Shortlands	Bromley	1 July, 1858
Sidmouth Junction	Feniton	July, 1861*
,, ,,	Ottery Road	Feb., 1868*
,, ,,	Ottery St. Mary	Apr., 1868*
,, ,,	Ottery Road	6 July, 1874
Sittingbourne & Milton Regis	Sittingbourne	1899
,, ,,	Sittingbourne & Milton	May, 1908
Southampton (West)	Blechynden	July, 1858
Southampton Central	Southampton West	7 July, 1935
Southampton Terminus (for Docks)	Southampton	July, 1858
,, ,,	Southampton Docks	Sept., 1896
,, ,,	Southampton Town & Docks	Nov., 1912
,, ,,	Southampton Town for Docks	9 July, 1923
South Bermondsey	Rotherhithe	Dec., 1869*
Staines Central	Staines	Jan., 1885
,, ,,	Staines	Sept., 1889
,, ,,	Staines Junction	Sept., 1923
Stonegate	Witherenden	Dec., 1851
,,	Ticehurst Road	16 June, 1947
Streatham Common	Streatham Common	1 Sept., 1868
,, ,,	Greyhound Lane	1 Jan., 1870
Streatham Hill	Streatham	1 Sept., 1868
,, ,,	Streatham & Brixton Hill	1 Jan., 1869
Strood	Rochester	July, 1849*
,,	Strood, Rochester & Chatham	June, 1852*
Sundridge Park	Plaistow	1 July, 1894
Surbiton	Kingston	Dec., 1852
,,	Kingston Junction	1 July, 1863
,,	Surbiton & Kingston	May, 1877*
Swale Halt	Kings Ferry Bridge Halt	1 July, 1929
Swanley	Sevenoaks Junction	1 Jan., 1871
,,	Swanley Junction	16 Apr., 1939
Tamerton Foliot	Tamerton Foliott	June, 1906*
Teddington	Teddington (Bushey Park)	July 1908
Teddington	Teddington & Bushey Park	Aug., 1911

Name	*Former Name*	*Until*
Tipton St. Johns	Tipton	Feb., 1881*
Tonbridge	Tunbridge	Jan., 1852
,,	Tunbridge Junction	May, 1893
,,	Tonbridge Junction	July, 1929
Tooting	Tooting Junction	1 Mar., 1938
Totton	Eling Junction	Apr., 1859*
Tunbridge Wells Central	Tunbridge Wells	9 July, 1923
Tunbridge Wells West	Tunbridge Wells	22 Aug., 1923
Upper Warlingham	Upper Warlingham	1 Jan., 1894
,, ,,	Upper Warlingham & Whyteleafe	1 Oct., 1900
Vauxhall	Vauxhall Bridge	1862/3
Ventnor West (I. of W.)	Ventnor Town	Sept., 1923*
Wallington	Carshalton	1 Sept., 1868
Walton-on-Thames	Walton for Hersham	30 Sept., 1935
Walworth Road	Camberwell Gate	Jan., 1865*
Wandsworth Town	Wandsworth	7 Oct., 1903
Waterloo (S.E.C.R.)	Waterloo Junction	7 July, 1935
West Byfleet	Byfleet & Woodham	May, 1914*
West Croydon	Croydon	Apr., 1851*
West Dulwich	Dulwich	20 Sept., 1926
Westenhanger	Westenhanger & Hythe	1874
West Norwood	Lower Norwood	1 Jan., 1886
Whitstable Town	(Became 'Whitstable-on-Sea' in July 1879)	
,, ,,	Whitstable (C. & D.)	June, 1899
Whitstable & Tankerton	Whitstable Town & Tankerton	1 Jan., 1936
Whitstable Harbour	Whitstable (S.E.)	June, 1899
Winchfield	Shapley Heath	
Windsor & Eton Riverside	Windsor	10 Dec., 1903
Winnersh Halt	Sindlesham & Hurst Halt	6 July, 1930
Witley	Witley for Chiddingfold	6 Oct., 1947
Wivelsfield	Keymer Junction	1 July, 1896
Woldingham	Marden Park	1 Jan., 1894
Woodgate for Bognor	Bognor	Nov., 1846
,, ,, ,,	Woodgate for Bognor	Oct., 1847
,, ,, ,,	Bognor	Jan., 1853*
Woodside (Surrey)	Woodside	1 Oct., 1908
,, ,,	Woodside & South Norwood	2 Oct., 1944
Worcester Park	Old Malden & Worcester Park	Feb., 1862*
Worthing Central	Worthing	5 July, 1936
York Road & Battersea Park	York Road	1 Nov., 1870

* Last appearance in timetable.

Dates in appendices refer, unless otherwise stated, to passenger traffic and do not necessarily apply to goods traffic.

The above Appendices II—VI were compiled by Mr. R. H. Clark

APPENDIX VII

Bibliography

(*a*) GENERAL

The Railways of Great Britain and Ireland. Francis Whishaw, 1840 (quoted below as W.).

The Railways of the United Kingdom, statistically considered. H. Scrivenor, 1849.

A History of the English Railway, 1820–1845. John Francis, 1851.

The Railways of England. W. M. Acworth, 1889 (3rd edition).

Express Trains, English and Foreign. E. Foxwell and T. E. Farrer, 1889.

Our Railways. John Pendleton, 1896.

The Railways of Great Britain. Lord Monkswell, 1913; 2nd edition, 1926.

British Railways and the Great War. Edwin A. Pratt, 1921.

Railway Amalgamation in Great Britain. W. E. Simnett, 1923.

Early British Railways. Henry Grote Lewin, 1925 (quoted below as L.).

Railway Accidents, Legislation and Statistics. H. Raynar Wilson, 1925.

The British Steam Locomotive, 1825–1925. E. L. Ahrons, 1927.

A Hundred Years of Inland Transport. C. E. R. Sherrington, 1934.

Britain's Railway Liveries. E. Carter, 1949.

19th Century Railway Carriages. Hamilton Ellis. *Modern Transport.*

War on the Line, Southern Railway. 1947.

Southern Electric. G. T. Moody. (Third edition, 1960).

A Regional History of the Railways of Great Britain:

    1. The West Country, D. St. John Thomas 1962.

    2. Southern England, H. P. White 1962.

(*b*) SURREY IRON RAILWAY

The Grand Surrey Iron Railway. F. G. Bing, 1931.

Also an article by W. B. Paley, *The Engineer*, 5th January, 1900.

Manning and Bray's 'History of Surrey' (1814) just mentions the Acts of Parliament.

There is no entry on the subject in the index to the Victoria County History of Surrey (1914), but a description appears in Vol. II, pp. 256–8.

It is ignored by the Surrey Archaeological Collections.

For foreign references, see Chapter I.

(*c*) CANTERBURY & WHITSTABLE RAILWAY

History of the Canterbury & Whitstable Railway. The Rev. R. B. Fellows, 1930; W.

(*d*) BODMIN & WADEBRIDGE RAILWAY

W.; L. Also articles: 'The Bodmin and Wadebridge Railway', by John Bosham, *Railway Magazine*, August 1900; and 'Communications in Cornwall, Past and Present', by J. B. Collins, *Railway Magazine*, September–November 1911.

(*e*) LONDON & GREENWICH RAILWAY
The First Railway in London. A. R. Bennett, 1912.
W.; L. Also articles: 'The London and Greenwich Railway', by Herbert Rake, *Railway Magazine*, January, 1903.

(*f*) LONDON & CROYDON RAILWAY
W.; L. Also 'The Locomotives of the London, Brighton and South Coast Railway, 1839–1903'.
The information on the subject of atmospheric railways is derived from various books and documents in the Samuda Collection.

(*g*) LONDON & SOUTH WESTERN RAILWAY
A Royal Road, Sam Fay, 1883.
The L. & S.W.R. G. A. Sekon, 1896.
Also:
History of a Railway (Salisbury and Yeovil). Louis H. Ruegg, 1878.
The Railways of the Isle of Wight. P. C. Allen, 1928.
Articles: 'The History of the London and South Western Railway Locomotives', *The Locomotive*, 1903–8, etc.
L. & S.W.R. Locomotives. F. Burt.
Waterloo Station Centenary, Southern Railway, 1948.
The Isle of Wight Railways. R. Michael Robbins. (Second edition 1963).
The Somerset & Dorset Railway. Barrie & Clinker (1948).

(*h*) LONDON, BRIGHTON & SOUTH COAST RAILWAY
No book has been published dealing with the history of this line. The information has had to be gathered from reports, pamphlets, and works of a general nature. On the other hand, the locomotives have been exhaustively described in 'The Locomotives of the L.B. & S.C.R., 1839–1903', by F. Burtt, 1903; and one with a similar title, but '1903–1923', by J. N. Maskelyne, 1928.
Articles: 'Early Locomotives of the L.B. & S.C.R.', by A. R. Bennett, *The Locomotive*, 1908–1910.

(*i*) SOUTH EASTERN RAILWAY
General Statement of the Position and Projects of the Company, 1845–6. (Issued by the Board).
Industrial Guide to the London & Dover Railway, Mead: 1845.
The History of the South Eastern Railway. By G. A. Sekon, 1895.
Articles on 'The Early Locomotives of the S.E.R.', *Railway Magazine*, vol. XX, p. 473; XXI, pp. 52, 150, 256.
'Stirling's Engines on the S.E.R.', *Locomotive*, vols. VIII, IX.
The S.E. & C.R. Locomotive List. N. Wakeman (1953).
The South Eastern & Chatham Railway. R. Kidner. (Second edition, 1963).
The Caterham Railway, J. Spence (1952).

(*j*) LONDON, CHATHAM & DOVER RAILWAY
Articles in *The Railway and Travel Monthly*, vols. XIX to XXI. By G. A. Sekon.
'Locomotive History of the L.C. and D.R.', *Locomotive*, vols, VI–XI, by W. V. Cauchis.

(*k*) STEAMBOATS
Cross-Channel and Coastal Paddle Steamers. By Frank Burtt, 1934.
Articles in *The Engineer* during 1901.
English Channel Packet Boats, Graseman & McLachlan.

Index

A

Abbot's Cliff tunnel, 284
Accidents, 36, 64, 121, 134, 154, 204, 213, 226, 236, 239, 245, 247, 292, 304, 313, 315, 336, 345, 348, 357, 363, 368, 407, 419, 454
Acton Wells Jn., 116
Adams, Wm., 126, 132, 171
Addiscombe Rd., 296
Addison Rd., 126
Admiralty Pier (Dover), 296, 331
Air services, 190, 419
Akerman, J. Y., 31
Akers-Douglas, 355
Aldershot (see also North Camp), 126
Alderson, Capt. R., 195 *et seq.*
Allhallows-on-Sea, 415
Alton, 87, 109, 139
——, Alresford & Winchester Ry., 109
Amalgamation Tribunal, 503 *et seq.*
Ambulance trains, 151, 246, 365
Amesbury, 138, 155
Andover, 75, 90, 96, 98, 110, 128
—— & Redbridge Canal, 83, 110, 135
—— —— Railway, 99 *seq.*
Andrews, E., 137
Anerley, 39
Angerstein Wharf, 364
Appledore, 312
Armoured truck, 236
Army Railway Council, 147
Arun bridge, 219
Arundel, 203
Ascot, 126, 135
Ash Jn., 289
Ashcroft, Peter, 362
Ashford, 292, 340, 357
—— Works, 443
Atmospheric railways, 43 *seq.*, 209
Axminster, 139

B

Babington Smith, Sir Henry, 391
Balcombe, 201, 248
Balham, 216
Ball, J. B., 245
Banister, F. D., 213
Banstead & Epsom Downs Ry., 219
Barham, 312
Baring, Brig.-Gen. The Hon. Everard, 393
Barlow, P. W., 289, 292
——, Capt. R. H., 295
——, W. H., 292

Barnes, 81, 127
Barnstaple, 77, 90, 479
—— & Ilfracombe Ry., 119, 135
Barrington Rd. Jn., 220
Barttelot, Col. W. B., 222
Basingstoke, 53 *seq.*, 61, 91, 97
—— & Alton Lt. Ry., 137
—— & Didcot Jn. Ry., 69
—— Canal, 58
—— & Newbury, 67
Bath, 119, 125
Battersea, 328
—— Bridge, 211
—— Park, 220
—— Wharf, 210
Battle, 290
Baxendale, J., 291
Beattie, Joseph, 117, 163 *seq.*
——, W. G., 117, 126
Beaulieu Rd., 103
Beckenham, 296, 327, 406
—— Lewes & Brighton Ry., 217
——, New, 296
Belstone Corner, 115
Bembridge, 186
Bentley, 140
Bere Alston, 118, 131, 140
Bessborough, Earl of, 243
Bexhill, 356
Bexleyheath Ry., 314, 366
Bickley, 327, 362
Bidder, G. P., 215
Bideford & Westward Ho! Ry., 138
—— Extension Ry., 90, 103, 118
Billinton, L. B., 244, 394
——, R. J., 235, 240, 265, 269
Birmingham, Bristol & Thames Jn. Ry., 108
Bishopstoke, 72, 100
Bishop's Waltham Ry., 107
Bisley, 131
Blackfriars, 328, 332
—— (S.E.R.) 298
Blackheath Hill, 337
Blandford, 102
Blechynden, 74
Board of Trade Conference, 141
Bodmer's engines, 60, 250, 421
Bodmin & Wadebridge Ry., Chap. III, also 111, 115, 127, 421
Bognor, 218
Bonsor, Sir H. Cosmo, 314, 355, 393
Bo-Peep tunnel, 294
Bordon, 140

547

Boscarne, 27, 28, 127
Botley, 107, 416
Bournemouth, 106, 117, 119, 130, 135
'Bournemouth Belle', 414
Brading, 186
Brady, Francis, 362
Braithwaite & Milner, 34
Branksome, 133
Brassey & Co., 167
——, Thos., 58, 62, 96, 99
Brent sidings, 116
Brentford & Richmond Ry., 88
Brewer, J. J., 238
Bricklayer's Arms, 32, 41 *seq.*, 209, 286, 414
Bridgwater Ry., 131
Brighton, 195, 201, 218, 234
—— & Chichester Ry., 81, 203
—— & Dyke Ry., 235, 392
——, Lewes & Hastings Ry., 204, 294
——, Uckfield & Tunbridge Wells Ry., 222
—— Works, 236, 246, 442
'Brighton Belle', 243, 458
Bristol & Exeter Ry., 74, 77, 114, 124
Brixton, 220
Broadstone Jn., 118, 128
Brockenhurst, 98, 103
Bromley Direct Ry., 310
Brookwood, 118, 131
Brunel, I. K., 45, 46, 54
Bruton, 102
Buckton, T. J., 208
Bude, 111, 133
Budleigh Salterton Ry., 133
Bulford, 138
Buller, J. W., 78
Buriton tunnel, 100
Burnham-on-Sea, 98, 103, 125
Bushill, T. H., 106
Byng, The Hon. J., 314

C

Cab signals, 64
Callington, 118
Calstock, 118, 140
Camelford, 133
Campbell, Lt.-Col. H. W., 133, 139
Canals:
 Andover & Redbridge, 83, 110, 135
 Basingstoke, 58
 Croydon, 11, 38
 Exeter, 29
 Gravesend & Higham, 479
 Kensington, 479
 Thames & Medway, 287
Cannon St., 105, 296, 363, 400
—— Bridge, 298, 363
Canterbury (see C. & W. Ry.), 287, 289, 326
—— & Whitstable Ry., Chap. II, also 289, 416
Cardew, Major P., 240

Carriages:
 L. & Greenwich, 35
 L.B. & S.C.R., 241
 L.C.D.R., 339
 L.S.W.R., 72, 86, 137
 S.E. & C.R., 356
 S.E.R., 323
 S.R., 437, 455
Castleman, Chas., 69, 126
Caterham, 296, 315
—— Ry., 296, 315
Cattewater, 120
Central Cornwall Ry. (see also Launceston Bodmin & Wadebridge Ry.), 112
Central Kent Ry., 324
Channel Ferry, 417, 425
—— Tunnel, 303, 312, 398, 417
Chaplin, W. J., 55, 91, 99, 207
Chard Ry., 107
Charing Cross, 296, 357, 400, 411
—— bridge, 362, 404
—— Ry., 105, 296
Charlton, 303
Chatham, 326, 338
Chelsea, 108
——Dock, 479
Chertsey, 80, 111
Chichester, 81, 203, 232
—— & Midhurst Ry., 223, 232
Chipstead Valley Ry., 315
Chislehurst, 299, 356
Chobham, 92, 97
Christchurch, 106, 117
Church Hope, 110
City & S. London Ry., 395
Clapham Jn., 60, 75, 107, 125, 127, 135, 217, 336
Clarence Pier (Portsmouth), 120
Clarke, Peter, 208
Clayton tunnel, 201
Clegg & Samuda, 43
Cliftonville curve, 226
'Club Train', 344
Cock, C. M., 456
Cole, 125
Coleford Jn., 111, 115
Colesbrook Viaduct, 287
Colours of engines, 171, 174, 257, 265, 269
Colyton Jn., 116
Commercial Dock, 356
Compound engines, 173
'Consolidation Act' 1854, 93 *seq.*
'Continental Agreement', 338, 343
Copplestone, 142
Corbett's Lane, 38, 233, 290
Corfe Mullen Jn., 128
'Corkscrew line', 69, 126
Cornwall Ry., 27
Cosham, 82
Cottesloe, Lord, 238, 243
Coulsdon, 237
Courthope, Sir G. L., 393
Cowes, 183, 479

Cowes & Newport Ry., 183 *seq.*
Cow Lane Jn., 220
Cowley Bridge, 77, 103
Cox, E. C., 394
Crampton engines, 250
——, T. R., 325
Cranbrook & Paddock Wood Ry., 313
Craven, J. C., 250, 257
Credition, 76, 96, 135
Crowborough tunnel, 223
Crowhurst, 356
—— Jn., 226, 234
Croydon, 5, 11, 207, 216,
         see also L. & C. Ry.
- —— Canal, 11, 38
—— Central, 223
——, Merstham & Godstone Ry., 13
——, New, 216
——, Oxted & E. Grinstead Ry., 225, 234
Crystal Palace, 209, 240, 241
—— —— (H.L.), 332
Cubitt, Benjamin, 316
——, Sir Wm., 45, 46, 73, 283
Cudworth, J. I., 309, 316
Culver Jn., 232
Cundy, N. W., 194

D

Dalhousie, Earl, 69
Dartford, 299
Dartmouth Arms, 39
Dachet, 75, 81
Dawson, Sir Philip, 241
Deal, 287, 331, 339, 340
Deepdene, 449
Delabole, 133
Dent, Sir F. H., 360, 362
Denton, 287
Deptford, 30, 207
Devon & Cornwall Central Ry., 28, 124
—— & Dorset Ry., 91
Devonport, 124
Didcot, 72, 98
Dieppe, 233, 245
Direct L. & Portsmouth Ry. (atmospheric),
    73 *seq.*
Direct Portsmouth Ry. (Brassey's), 99, 135
Ditton Marsh, see Esher
Dixon, John, 19
Dorchester, 74, 91, 97
Dorking, 82, 223
——, Brighton & Arundel Ry., 46
Dorset Central Ry., 102, 125
Dottin, A. R., 31, 53
Dover, 285, 326, 331, 339, 357, 361, 365,
    396, 415, 425
—— & Deal Ry., 340
—— Harbour, 359, 478
Dowdall, J. R., 489
Downton, 135
Drane, Thos., 293
Drummond, Dugald, 132, 144, 175

Drummond, Brig. Gen. Sir Hugh, 393
Drury, O. G. C., 245, 394
Dungeness, 312, 417
Dunton Green, 312
Durnsford Rd. Power House, 146
Dutton, The Hon. R. H., 127, 132
Dyke Branch, 235
Dyke, Sir W. Hart, 360

E

Earlsfield, 207
Earlswood, 237
East Cornwall Mineral Ry., 118, 140
East Grinstead, 232
—— —— Groombridge & Tunbridge
         Wells Ry., 222
—— —— Ry., 212
East Kent Lt. Ry., 402, 449
—— Ry., 295, 325
—— London Ry., 225, 308, 360, 398
Eastbourne, 207
Eastleigh (see also Bishopstoke), 141
—— Works, 141, 151, 440
Eastern, 110
Eborall, C. W., 295, 303
Edenbridge, 221, 235
Eddy, E. M. G., 314
Edington Jn., 131
Effingham Jn., 127
Egham, 80
Electric lighting, 232
—— telegraphs, 62, 287
—— rolling stock, Chap. XXXIX, also 241
Electrification:
    L.B.S.C.R., 241, *seq.*
    L.S.W.R., 143
    S.E.C.R., 369
    S.R., 399, 409, 411, 415, 418, 419, 422,
        425
Elham Valley Ry., 312
Ellson, G., 394, 407
Epsom, 4, 102, 207, 213
—— & Leatherhead Ry., 109, 213
—— & S.W.R., 44
—— Downs, 219
Eridge, 226
Errington, J. E., 93
Esher, 60
Evercreech, 119
Exeter, 77 *seq.*, 87 *seq.*, 103, 418
—— & Credition Ry., 77, 87, 107
—— & Exmouth Ry., 103
——, Yeovil & Dorchester Ry., 102
Exmouth, 103, 139, 155, 444

F

Factory Jn., 110, 217
Fareham, 111, 130, 139
Farlington Jn., 81
Farmer, J. S., 215

Farnham, Hants., 61, 118, 155
Farringdon St., 328
Faversham, 326, 330
—— Creek, 326
Fawkham, Gravesend Ry., 341
Fay, Sir Sam, 133, 138
Feltham, 152, 444
Fenton, Sir Myles, 311, 314
First class (abolition in London), 450
Fletcher & Jennings, 29
Folkestone, 285, 413, 419
—— Harbour, 286, 289, 306, 308, 413, 478
Forbes, J. Staats, 238, 331, 336, 338
——, Sir Wm., 338, 393
Ford Jn., 203, 218, 235
Forest Hill, 38, 39
Forrester & Co., 4
Fort Brockhurst, 133
Fossick & Hackworth, 317
Fowler, Sir J., 211
Foxcote, 134
Fratton & Southsea line, 127, 234
Fremington, 78, 90, 479
Freshwater, Yarmouth & Newport Ry., 187
Fullerton Jn., 128

G

Gibbs, Joseph, 187 *et seq.*
Giles, Francis, 54, 185
Gillingham, 102
Glastonbury, 96, 102
—— canal, 96
Godalming, 73, 82, 100
'Golden Arrow' express, 412, 454
Gooch, J. Viret, 160, 163
Gooday, J. F. S., 238, 245
Gore-Brown, Major E., 452
Gosport, 61, 62, 99, 106, 111
Goudhurst, 304
Graham, Sir J., 92
Grateley, 138, 155
Gravesend, 287
—— & Rochester Ry., 287
Gray, John, 250
G.N.R., 309, 332, 338, 339, 359
G.W.R., 67 *et seq.*, 70, 74, 360, 365, 482
Greenwich (see L. & G. Ry.), also 311
—— & Gravesend Ry., see N. Kent Ry.
—— Observatory, 287, 303
—— Park, 220, 337, 366
Greenwood, David, 243
Gregory, Sir C. H., 215
Grenfell, C. P., 208
Groombridge, 221, 223, 227, 235
Grove Park, 310
Guildford, 87, 127, 289
—— Extension Ry., 73, 82
—— Junction Ry., 66
——, Kingston & London Ry., 127
Gunnersbury, 116

H

Hackbridge, 14
Hackworth & Co., 250
Hailsham, 207, 221, 226
'Hall *v.* L.B.S.C.R.', 233
Halwill, 128
Hampton Court, 83, 146
—— Wick, 88
Hamworthy (see also Poole), 106, 118, 133
Hardham Jn., 218
Hardinge, Lord, 91
Harman, John, 202
Harrison, Sir F., 361, 367
——, Wm., 95
Haslemere, 100
Hastings, 204, 290, 294
Havant, 82, 99, 102, 223
Hawkhurst, 304, 313
Hawkins, Geo., 209, 229
Hawkshaw, John, 297, 298
Hayes, 312
Hayle Ry., 111
Hayling Ry., 223
Haywards Heath, 201, 232
Headcorn, 284
Heathcote, Sir Wm., 92
Heathfield, 226
Henfield, 216
Herbert, Sidney, 92
Herne Bay & Faversham Ry., 330
Herne Hill, 328
Highbridge, 96
Hill, Rowland, 202
——, Vincent, 360, 361
Hither Green, 299, 406
Holborn Viaduct, 337
'Hole-in-the-wall' box, 229
Holes Bay curve, 133
Holland-Martin, R., 452
Holmes, H., 138, 146
Holmsley, 104
Holsworthy, 111, 115, 127, 133
Horringford, 185
Horsham, 207, 223
—— & Guildford Direct Ry., 219 *et seq.*
——, Dorking & Leatherhead Ry., 223
——, West, 219
Horsted Keynes, 232
Houghton, R. H., 394
——, E. J., 241
Hounslow, 81, 127
Hove, 226
Hundred of Hoo Ry., 311
Hurst Green Jn., 235
Hurstbourne, 128
Hythe & Sandgate Ry., 303

I

Ilfracombe Ry., 120
Interlocking, 135, 229, 302, 346
Isle of Wight, 98, 107, 119

Isle of Wight Central Ry., 184
—— Ry., 184
Itchingfield Jn., 216

J

Jacomb, Wm., 129
Jacomb-Hood, J. W., 137, 145
——, R., 137, 208, 213, 215, 237
James, Wm., 18 *et seq.*, 193
'Jenny Lind' engines, 250, 252
Jessop, Wm., 12, 13, 16
Joint Locomotive Committee, 48 *et seq.*
Jolly Sailor, 39, 200
Jones, A. D., 394
—— & Potts, 159
——, Herbert, 145
Joy, David, 250

K

Kearsney loop, 340
Kemptown, 217
Kendall's brake, 346
Kensington, 88
Kent & E. Sussex Ry., 358, 449
Kentish Ry., 281
Kew, 88
Keymer branch, 207
Kimbridge, 99
Kingston & London Ry., 129
Kingston-on-Thames, 60, 64, 107, 116
Kingswood, 315
Kirtley, S., 250
——, W., 339
Knight, Godfrey, 133
——, J. P., 224, 235
Knowle Jn., 139

L

Laffan, Capt., 76
Laing, Samuel, 208, 222, 237
Laira Bridge, 120
Lancing Works, 240, 444
Langdon, W. E., 117
Langstone, 223
Lardner, Dr., 100
Launceston, 131
—— & S. Devon Ry., 111, 124
——, Bodmin & Wadebridge Jn. Ry., 111 *et seq.*
Laurie, P. N., 222
Lavender Hill, 110
Leatherhead, 127, 213, 223
Lee-on-the-Solent Ry., 133
Lenham & Faversham line, 340
Lennox, Lord Geo., 195
Lewes, 204, 234
—— & E. Grinstead Ry., 234
—— & Uckfield Ry., 212
Lewisham, 295, 406
Leysdown, 356

Litchfield tunnel, 61
Littlehampton, 218, 219, 235, 246
Locke, Joseph, 19, 45, 57, 92
Locomotives:
Bodmin & Wadebridge, 28
Canterbury & Whitstable, 23
Isle of Wight, 183 *et seq.*
L. & Brighton, 49
L. & Croydon, 47
L. & Greenwich, 34
L. & Southampton, 159
L.B.S.C.R., Chaps. XX-XXII
L.C.D.R., Chap. XXIX
L.S.W.R., Chaps. XII, XIII
S.E.C.R., Chap. XXXI
S.E.R., 60, Chap. XXVI
S.R., Chap. XXXV
Loder, G. W. E. (Lord Wakehurst), 393 414, 421
L. & Brighton Ry., 40, 41
L. & Croydon Ry., 31, 40, Chap. V
L. & Greenwich Ry., Chap. IV
L. & Southampton Ry., Chap. VI
London Bridge, 31, 39, 41, 42, 75, 230, 290, 405, 424
L.B.S.C.R., Chap. XVI *et seq.*
—— steamers, Chap. XXII
L.C.D.R., Chaps. XXVII, XXVIII, also 299, 311, 312
L.S.W.R., Chap. VII *et seq.*
L.C.D.R. steamers, 311
L., Lewes & Brighton Ry., 221
Longhedge Jn., 108
—— Works, 360
Longparish, 128
Louis Philippe, 85
Ludgate Hill, 110, 328
Lydd Ry., 312
Lydford, 111, 124
Lyme Regis, 139
Lymington, 98
—— Ry., 96
Lynton & Barnstaple Ry., 156, 416

M

Macaulay, F. J., 133
Macrae, C. C., 245
Maidstone, 286, 330
—— & Ashford Ry., 340, 341
—— Road, 286
Malden, 107, 127
Manchester & Southampton Ry., 83
Mangles, Capt. C. E., 105
Mann, 339
Mansell, R. C., 301, 320
Margate, 287, 330, 402
Marsh, D. E., 240, 244, 269
—— Mills, 120
Marshall & Co., 35
Martello tunnel, 284, 309
Martley, William, 339
Maunsell, R. E. L., 178, 361, 394

Maze Hill, 303, 309
Medhurst, Geo., 43
Medina Wharf, 183, 479
Medway Bridges, 406, 450
Meldon Jn., 111, 127
—— Quarry, 447
—— Viaduct, 136
Meon Valley line, 139
Merstham, Chap. I, 196, 201, 237, 425
Merstone, 187
Metropolitan District Ry., 116, 126, 127, 129, 144, 225, 395, 398
—— Extension, L.S.W.R., 110
—— ——, L.C.D.R., 333
—— Ry., 309, 328, 336, 398
Mid Kent Ry., 296, 327
Mid Sussex Ry., 109, 213, 218, 223
Mid-Hants Ry., 109
Midhurst, 109, 284
Midland & S.W.J.R., 143
—— Ry., 102, 119, 125, 338, 339, 359
Miles of track:
  L.B.S.C.R., 248
  L.S.W.R., 152
  S.E.C.R., 368
  S.R., 506
Milford, 97
Military traffic, 147 *et seq.*, 245
Millbay, 124
Millbrook Foundry, 159
Minster, 287
Missenden, E., 448, 456
Mitcham, 224
Moorgate, 336
Morden, 395
Morgan, A., 201
——, Sir C. L., 237, 245,
——, John, 355
Morris, 325
Motor omnibuses, 139
—— trains, 242, 437

N

Nationalisation, 455
Netley, 111, 130
Nevill, Lord Henry, 393
New Cross, 38, 202, 225, 286, 363
—— Croydon, 216
—— Poole Jn., 119
—— Romsey, 312
Newark brake trials, 230
Newbury, 68 *et seq.*
Newhaven, 207, 246, 402, 443
—— Harbour, 260, 402, 477
Newmarket Arch, 213
Newport, I. of W., 185
——, Godshill & St. L. Ry., 187
'Night Ferry' 425, 483
Nine Elms, 58, 64, 76, 93
—— —— Works, 141, 440
N.S.W.J.R., 88, 116
North Camp, 126

North Devon & Cornwall Jn. Ry., 398
—— —— Ry., 96, 126, 166 (see also Taw Vale Ry.)
—— Kent E. Jn., 288
—— —— Ry., 25, 287
—— Road (Plymouth), 124
—— Tawton, 115
Northam Jn., 98
Norwood, 199, 211, 241, 248
——, West, 241
Nunhead, 344

O

Oakley, Sir Henry, 233, 236
'Ocean Specials', 140, 142
Oil fuel, 269, 455
Okehampton Ry., 111, 124
Old Kent Road, 220, 309
Orpington, 356
Otford, 331, 346
Ouse Valley line, 218, 229
—— —— Viaduct, 201, 221
Owens, Sir C. J., 132, 139, 142, 144
Oxford, 71
Oxted & Groombridge Ry., 235
Oxted tunnel, 234

P

Paddock Wood, 287, 304, 313
Padstow, 133, 479
Palmer, H. R., 195 *et seq.*
Palmerston, Lord, 91
Pan Lane, 185
Panter, W., 140
'Parliamentary trains', 72
Parsons, J. M., 202
Partridge Green, 216
Patcham tunnel, 201
Peasmarsh, 101, 219
Peckham Rye, 220, 241
Pemberton, Sir E. L., 360
Penge, 327
—— tunnel, 328, 347
Petersfield Ry., 109
Petworth, 213, 223
'Pines Express', 483
Pirbright Jn., 118, 156
Plym Bridge, 120
Plymouth, 124, 131
—— & Dartmoor Ry., 120, 124 *et seq.*
——, Devonport & S.W.R., 118, 140, 156
Point Pleasant Jn., 130
Polhill tunnel, 299
Poole, 106, 118, 119
Popham Tunnel, 61
Portal, Sir W. S., 132, 133, 138, 393
Portcreek Jn., 82, 102
Portland, 109
Portsmouth, 73, 99, 101, 119
—— Harbour, 119, 225
Portswood, 111
Port Victoria, 311

Pouparts Jn., 217
Pratt, E. A., 488
Preece, Sir Wm., 117, 229
Preston Park, 226
Prince Consort, 85
Princetown Ry., 120
Prosser's patent railway, 66
Pullman cars, 130, 232, 235, 339, 360, 363, 414, 415, 425, 455, 458
Putney, 77, 129

Q

'Quadruple Treaty', 113, 118
Queen Victoria, 81, 85, 122
Queenborough, 311, 330, 339, 356

R

Race-courses, 482
Rail motors, 139, 188, 269
Rails:
   Bodmin & Wadebridge, 27
   Canterbury & Whitstable, 22
   L. & Croydon, 39
   L.C.D.R., 337
   L.S.W.R., 446
   S.E.R., 293, 292, 446
   Surrey Iron Ry., 13
Railway Executive Committee, 148
Railways Act 1921, 391
Ramsgate, 287, 330, 402
Rastrick, J. U., 200 *et seq.*
Raworth, A., 394
Raynes Park, 102
Reading, 71, 97
—— Guildford & Reigate Ry., 82, 97, 100, 289, 295
Redbridge, 83, 135
Redhill, 233, 237, 284
Reigate, 284
Rennie, Sir John, 193, 195, 324
Richborough, 150, 366
Richmond, 116, 126
—— & W. End Ry., 75
Riddlesdown, 407
Ringwood, 104, 106
——, Christchurch & Bournemouth Ry., 106, 117
Road transport, 420
Robertsbridge, 290
Robinson superheater, 178
Rochester, 360
—— & Chatham Extension line, 313
Rockley, Lord, 138
Romney, Hythe & Dymchurch Railway, 417
Romsey, 83, 110
Rudgwick, 219
Ruthern Bridge, 26, 27, 111
Ryde, 107, 183
—— & Newport Ry., 185
—— Pier, 186, 479
Rye, 207, 289, 479

S

St. Denys, 111
St. Helens, I. of W., 186
St. Leonards, 204, 224
St. Mary Cray, 327
St. Paul's, 341
Salisbury, 72, 90, 93
—— & Dorset, Ry., 111
—— & Yeovil Ry., 98, 126
—— Market House Ry., 98 *et seq.*
Salomons, Sir David, 393
Samuda Bros., 73
Sandown, I. of W., 185
Sarle, Sir Allen, 235, 238, 240
Saxby, John, 215, 229
—— & Farmer, 301
Scanes, E. A., 394
Schmidt superheater, 178
Schuster, Leo, 222
Scott, Archibald, 87, 105, 125, 127, 138
——, F. Finlay, 243, 394
——, The Hon. Francis, 91
Scotter, Sir Chas., 127, 133, 139, 143
Seaford, 219, 247
Seaton & Beer Ry., 116
—— Jn. (see Colyton Jn.)
Second class, 146, 396
Selhurst, 241
Selsdon Rd., 235
Sentinel-Cammell car, 433
Sevenoaks, 299, 330
——, Maidstone & Tonbridge Ry., 331, 347 *et seq.*
Shakespeare Tunnel, 284, 367
Shalford, 82, 100, 289
Shanklin, 183
Shapley (Basingstoke), 61
Sharnal St., 311
Sharp, Roberts & Co., 48 *et seq.*
Shawford, 131
Sheath, Chas., 314, 355
Sheerness, 330, 341
Shepperton, 109
Sheppey Lt. Ry., 356
Sherborne, 102
Shide, 185
Shoreham, 201, 216
Shorncliffe, 312, 343
Shortlands, 327, 344
—— & Nunhead Ry., 344
Sidmouth Ry., 114, 179
Signals:
   Canterbury & Whitstable Ry., 24
   L. & Brighton Ry., 36
   L. & Croydon Ry., 36, 50
   L. & Greenwich Ry., 36
   L.B.S.C.R., 229
   L.C.D.R., 229, 346
   L.S.W.R., 84, 128, 136
   S.R., 404, 423, 425
   S.E.R., 42, 300, 306
   Waterloo & City Ry., 134
Simmons, Capt., 76, 80

Sittingbourne, 330
—— & Sheerness Ry., 330
Slades Green, 315
Sleeping car, 140
Slight, F., 208
Slip carriages, 414
Smith, Sir Fredk., 62, 64
Smith's vacuum brake, 302
Snow Hill, 337
Solent tunnel, 189
Somerset & Dorset Ry., 96, 102, 119, 483
—— Central Ry., 98, 102, 125
Sondes, Lord, 325
S. Devon Ry., 103, 114
S.E.C.R., Chap. XXX
S.E.R., Chaps. XXIII-XXVI, 47, 195 *et seq.* 232 *et seq.*
S. London line, 220, 240
S.W. & I. of W.J.R., 189
Southampton, Chap. VI, 98, 130, 149, 156, 453, (see also L. & S. Ry.,)
—— & Dorchester Ry., 74, 106
—— Docks, 131, 148, 379, 420, 471 *et seq.*
—— engines, 174
—— West, 74
'Southern Belle', 235
S.R., Chaps. XXXIII-XXXVIII
—— Docks and Harbour, Chap. XLI
—— officials, Appendix I
—— steamers, Chap. XL
Southsea, 127
Southwark Park, 356
Spa Road, 30
Staines, 75, 80, 110, 129
——, Wokingham & Woking Ry., 96, 111
Steamers:
    L.B.S.C.R., Chap. XXII
    L.C.D.R., Chap. XXXI
    L.S.W.R., Chap. XIII
    S.E.C.R., Chap. XXXI
    S.E.R., 331
    S.R., Chap. XL
Stephenson, Geo., 19
——, Robt., 35, 45, 74, 194, 380
Stevens, W. R., 314
Stewarts Lane, 419
Stirling, James, 320
Stoke, Kent, 311
Stokes Bay Ry., 106
Stone Cross, 224
Stonehouse Pool, 124
Strapp, John, 117
Strawberry Hill, 109
Streatham, 224
Strood, 296, 326, 340
Stroudley, Wm., 235, 258, Chap. XXI
Studland Rd. Jn., 116, 126, 144
Sturt Lane Jn., 126
'Sunny South Special', 240, 482
Surbition, 107, 127
Surrey & Sussex Jn. Ry., 220, 234
—— Iron Ry., 11 *et seq.*

Surrey, Sussex, Hants, Wilts & Somerset Ry., 193
Sutton, Surrey, 207
—— Harbour (Plymouth), 80, 120, 131
Swale bridge, 330, 363
Swanage, 128
Swanley, 330
Sway, 130
Sydenham, 209, 289
Sykes interlocking bar, 128
——, W. R., 346
Szlumper, A. W., 145, 394, 407
——, G. S., 148, 394, 407, 448

T

Tadworth, 315
Tattenham Corner, 315, 356
Tavistock, 131
—— & S. Devon Ry., 120
Taw Vale Ry., 78 *et seq.*
Tayleur & Co., 34, 159
Teddington, 88
Tempest, Sir P. C., 362, 393
Templecombe, 102, 119
Thames & Medway Canal, 287
—— Valley Ry., 109, 135
Three Bridges, 212, 415
Tipton St. John's, 133
Tonbridge, 284, 329
'Toomer loop', 340
Tooting, Merton & Wimbledon Ry., 117, 224, 226
Topsham, 103
Torrington, 111, 118, 398
Totton, Hythe & Fawley Ry., 398
Track circuiting, 128
Train communication, 123, 230,
—— ferries, 150, 425
Tresmeer, 131, 133
Truro, 111 *et seq.*
Tulse Hill, 336
Tunbridge Wells, 220, 222, 232, 287
—— —— & Eastbourne Ry., 226
Tunnel Jn., 98
Turbine steamers, 386, 387
Turnbull, Sir R., 245
Turn Chapel, 121
Turnham Green, 116, 144
Twickenham, 107, 127
Tyer, Edw., 134
Tyler, Sir H., 302

U

Uckfield, 212, 223, 232
Umberleigh, 142
Urie, R. W., 145, 394

V

Vacuum brake, 135, 230
Vallance, John, 43

Vauxhall, 128, 131
Ventnor, 183
Verrinder, E. W., 120, 132
Victoria Station, 108, 210, 238, 241, 396, 424
—— & Pimlico Ry., 210, 327
Vignoles, Chas., 32, 194
'Vignoles' line', 288
Virginia Water, 111

W

Waddon, 14
Wadebridge, 115, 127, 133, 155
Wainwright, H. S., 314, 361
——, W., 314
Waldron, 226
Walker, C. V., 300
——, Sir H. A., 144, 393
Waller's Ash tunnel, 61
Wandsworth, 60, 210
—— Road, 110, 220, 336
War damage, 452, 469
Wareham, 128
Warner, Surrey, 140, 394
Warren Cutting, 292
—— Halt, 362
Waterloo, 76, 105, 120, 126 *et seq.*, 128, 131, 141, 143, 152, 423
—— & City Ry., 133 *et seq.*, 140, 426, 450
—— & Whitehall Ry., 116
—— Jn., 115, 143, 298
Watkin, A. M., 309
——, Sir Edw., 299, 303, 308, 314, 355
Weald of Kent Ry., 303
Wells, 102
Wenford Bridge, 26
West, G. F., 146, 394
W. Cornwall Ry., 112
W. Croydon, 38
W. End & C. Palace Ry., 211, 327
W. London Extension, 106, 217, 331
W. Norwood, 241
W. Wickham & Hayes Ry., 312

West Wickham, 312
Westbury, 97
Westerham Valley Ry., 312
Westinghouse brake, 215
Weybridge, 60, 111
Weymouth & Portland Ry., 109
White, G. T., 132
Williams, Sir Robt., 393
——, W. J., 235
——, W. M., 119 *et seq.*
Willis, A., 355
——, F. H., 394
Willow Walk, 209, 291, 414
Wilts., Som. & Weymouth Ry., 90, 97, 98
Wimbledon, 60, 118 412
—— & Sutton Ry., 395 413
—— & W. Metro. Jn. Ry., 130
Wimborne, 102, 104
Winchester, 61, 109, 131
Windmill Bridge Jn., 216
Windsor, 81 *et seq.*
——, Staines & S.W. Ry., 75, 80
Withyham, 235
Witley, 100
Wivelsfield, 207
Woking, 60, 141
Wokingham, 96
Woods, Joseph, 158
Woodside & S. Croydon Ry., 235
Woolwich, 288
—— Arsenal, 299
Workmen's tickets, 224, 299
—— trains, 333
Worthing, 203
Worting Jn., 140
Wrotham, 347

Y

Yarmouth, I. of W., 187
Yeoford, 111, 124
Yeovil, 93, 102, 103
—— & Exeter Ry., 80
Yorke, Sir A., 360